interpersonal communication

fourth canadian edition

relating to others

Steven A. Beebe
Southwest Texas State University

Susan J. Beebe
Southwest Texas State University

Mark V. Redmond
Iowa State University

Terri M. Geerinck
Sir Sandford Fleming College

PEARSON

Toronto

Dedicated to our families

Mark and Matthew Beebe
Peggy, Nicholas, and Eric Redmond, and Beth Maroney
Skyler, Adelaide, and Rod Manley

Library and Archives Canada Cataloguing in Publication

Interpersonal communication: relating to others / Steven A. Beebe ... [et al.]. — 4th Canadian ed.

Includes index.
ISBN 0-205-45992-7

     1. Interpersonal communication—Textbooks.
I. Beebe, Steven A., 1950–
BF637.C45I68 2007   153.6   C2005-907086-2

ISBN 0-205-45992-7

Vice President, Editorial Director: Michael J. Young
Executive Editor: Dave Ward
Sponsoring Editor: Carolin Sweig
Marketing Manager: Leigh-Anne Graham
Associate Editor: Jon Maxfield
Production Editor: Kevin Leung
Copy Editor: Martin Townsend
Proofreader: Bonnie DiMalta
Production Coordinator: Janis Raisen
Composition: Christine Velakis
Photo Research: Amanda McCormick
Art Director: Julia Hall
Cover and Interior Design: Anthony Leung
Cover Image: Alberto Ruggieri/GettyImages

Statistics Canada information is used with the permission of the Minister of Industry, as Minister responsible for Statistics Canada. Information on the availability of the wide range of data from Statistics Canada can be obtained from Statistics Canada's Regional Offices, its World Wide Web site at http://www.statcan.ca, and its toll-free access number 1-800-263-1136.

    4 5   11 10 09 08 07

Printed and bound in the USA.

Contents

List of Features

Preface

The secret to effective interpersonal relationships is not really a secret. It's a fundamental principle that transcends both culture and time. Distilled to its three-word essence, the centuries-old "secret" is: be other-oriented. By being other-oriented, we don't mean that you are not self-reflexively aware of who you are or that you abandon any sensitivity to your own thoughts and behaviour. We do suggest, however, that being other-oriented involves the mindful process of considering the thoughts, needs, and values of others, rather than an egocentric focus on self. We didn't invent this principle of being other-oriented; it is the foundation of every major faith movement, religion, and human value system in the world. It was also the foundation of the first three Canadian editions of *Interpersonal Communication: Relating to Others*, and it continues as the central theme of the fourth Canadian edition.

This book was written to be the primary text for courses in interpersonal communication. We've written this book for college and university students ages 18 to 80 who are seeking research-based principles and skills to enhance their interpersonal relationships. We emphasize *research-based* because this is not merely a book of "how to" techniques to "win friends and influence people." Our ideas are based on decades of communication research and reflect the latest thinking about how human beings relate to each other. Our balance of principles and skills is designed to help students enhance their own command of communication skills, as well as to give them insights into why people communicate as they do in interpersonal situations.

This approach is designed to help students enhance their own repertoires of communication skills, as well as give them insights into the hows and whys of human relationships. We continue to emphasize the importance of relationship development and present skills to help maintain quality interpersonal relationships.

Our Approach to Interpersonal Communication

An Emphasis on Others

Although becoming other-oriented is challenging, we believe it is worth the effort; mastering this ability will result in lifelong relationship rewards. Considering the thoughts and feelings of others is a prerequisite for understanding and improving interpersonal communication. Our other-oriented approach gently but consistently reminds students about the importance of seeing the world as others see it. At the heart of understanding and developing relationships with others is the process of considering how others are affected by our communication.

Becoming other-oriented is not a single skill but rather a composite of principles and skills. Foremost among them are self-awareness and self-knowledge; we suggest that true empathy and sensitivity are possible only when we feel secure about our own identity. In addition, becoming other-oriented includes all of the classic skills and principles typically taught in interpersonal communication courses, such as listening, giving feedback, conflict management skills, and verbal and non-verbal skills, and places additional emphasis on the importance of the perceptions, thoughts, attitudes, beliefs, values, and emotions of others.

Toward the end of each chapter, we include a feature called "Becoming Other-Oriented," in which we identify a principle or skill to help you become more aware of others. We also use a margin icon, like the one in the margin here, to highlight other-oriented ideas and strategies throughout the book.

An Emphasis on Diversity

It's impossible to be other-oriented without being willing to acknowledge diversity. Inherent in our other-oriented approach is the theme that people differ in significant ways. It is because of those diverse differences that we need skills and principles that allow us to develop common links so we can establish meaningful interpersonal relationships with others. The body of research about gender- and culture-based differences in communication behaviour has continued to grow; the last decade saw a significant leap in our understanding of the role that differences in culture, gender, religion, political perspectives, and other points of view have on people's ability to connect to others. In this book, we do more, however, than just point to differences between human beings. Using a competency-based approach, we present practical, research-based strategies for increasing understanding when interacting with those who are different from us.

Communication occurs when people find commonalities in meaning that transcend their differences. In Chapter 8, "Interpersonal Communication and Cultural Diversity," we not only identify barriers to competent intercultural communication but also present strategies to bridge the chasm of differences that too often divide rather than unite people. In addition, we distill research conclusions and communication strategies for understanding differences in the "Understanding Diversity" features in every chapter. But our discussion of diversity is not merely window dressing; through examples, illustrations, and research conclusions liberally woven throughout the book, we identify ways to become other-oriented despite differences we encounter in people of the other gender or of other cultures or ideologies.

An Emphasis on Relationships

Relationships are the ongoing connections we make with others through interpersonal communication. As the book's subtitle, *Relating to Others,* suggests, we highlight the importance of cultivating relationships by developing an increased awareness of and sensitivity to our relationships with others. We discuss how relationships work and how to improve them. We link communication skills with principles that help explain and predict how relationships begin, develop, and sometimes decline. Our emphasis on relationships is reflected in the broad range of relationship types we consider in our discussions, including relationships with friends, lovers, family, and co-workers, and even relationships formed and developed over the Internet. Communication researchers have contributed significant insights to relationship development and maintenance. We rely on the latest communication research to give students the benefit of state-of-the-art thinking about how relationships can be improved.

An Emphasis on the Internet and Interpersonal Relationships

Contemporary technology has a profound influence on how we relate to others, not just online but in person as well. In every chapter, we discuss research findings about how our electronic connections affect our face-to-face relationships. We continue to offer "Weblinks" at the end of each chapter, which enrich and enliven chapter content with supplemental readings and activities (they all worked at the time of writing). Although our primary focus remains on live, face-to-face communication, we believe we cannot and should not ignore the ever-increasing role of technology in interpersonal communication.

An Emphasis on Canadian Content

Interpersonal Communication continues to supply Canadian contexts to provide "at home" relevance to all the topics covered in the book and to facilitate personal identification with these lessons by Canadian students. These objectives are achieved through the following features:

- Special "In Canada. . ." boxes, several which are new, and many more updated to reflect new information and research
- Excerpts from reports of noted Canadian research institutions
- Presentation of relevant Canadian statistics
- Quotations and anecdotes from prominent Canadians
- Photographic images that are identifiably Canadian (e.g., Canadian personalities, sports teams, locations, etc.)
- Links to related Canadian websites

Throughout the book, we emphasize that there are no surefire prescriptions for achieving satisfying relationships or peak communication experiences. But we do believe that, armed with a solid grasp of principles, students can adapt research-based strategies to their own purposes and become more skilled at initiating and managing interactions with others.

New Features of the Fourth Canadian Edition

The features that made our first three editions successful have been retained in the fourth Canadian edition. Our other-oriented approach, emphasis on diversity, focus on relationships, and expanded coverage of technology, combined with our balanced discussion of principles and skills, are the key reasons both students and instructors praise the book.

Because new research about interpersonal communication continues to unfold, and because we wish to continuously refine our approach to presenting both classic and contemporary research, we've made several changes to make this book the best possible resource for learning about interpersonal communication. Here's a summary of some of the key revisions we've made to the fourth edition:

- An expansion of the final two chapters from the previous edition into three chapters, to capture the relevant aspects of new interpersonal communication research
- Updated research conclusions about interpersonal communication in every chapter
- New examples, illustrations, and cartoons to help students see connections between research conclusions and their own lives
- A new margin icon to highlight other-oriented material
- A new feature, included in every chapter, called "Applying Theory and Research," in which we select a theory or recent research article and apply the information to students' lives in an interesting and meaningful way
- Another new feature, also in every chapter, called "Becoming Other-Oriented," in which we spotlight principles and strategies based on our signature concept, to help students focus on the interests and needs of others
- More weblinks to lead students to supplemental information about interpersonal communication
- Movement of relevant material from the former Chapter 5, on emotions, to more logical areas of the text in other chapters. For example, recognizing emotions is now part of Chapter 6 on non-verbal communication, and the material on anger has now been moved to Chapter 7 as part of the topic of managing emotions during a conflict.

In addition we made the following additions and changes to individual chapters.

Chapter 1:
- New information about social learning theory added to the discussion of interpersonal communication competence

Chapter 2:
- Enriched discussion of symbolic interaction theory
- New information about understanding cultural differences in self-disclosure

Chapter 3:
- New information about diversity and perception
- New information about the fundamental attribution error and self-serving bias
- Additional discussion and applications of politeness theory

Chapter 4:
- New information about shifting attention as a barrier to interpersonal listening
- New information about listener apprehension
- Information about confirmation and disconfirmation moved from Chapter 5 to Chapter 4's expanded discussion of responding skills
- A streamlined and fine-tuned discussion of critical listening skills

Chapter 5:
- A stronger discussion of developing supportive communication skills

Chapter 6:
- A stress on the importance of using supportive non-verbal behaviour with others
- Description of the characteristics of people who are skilled in interpreting non-verbal communication

Chapter 7:
- An improved definition of interpersonal conflict
- New material about cultural differences and preferred conflict management style
- A revised discussion of conflict management styles, identifying five rather than three styles
- New information about negotiation skills

Chapter 8:
- Updated information about the importance of diversity in our lives
- Expanded discussion of how to be interculturally competent

Chapter 9:
- In the discussion of the nature of interpersonal relationships, a new focus on intimacy, attraction, and power
- New information on the principles of power in relationships and the negotiation of relational power

Chapter 10:
- Additional information about male and female initiation of date requests
- Reorganization of the discussion of skills and strategies used in initiating, escalating, and maintaining interpersonal relationships

Chapter 11:
- Rearrangement and update of the content of this chapter, with enhanced emphasis on interpersonal relationships and the Internet
- Additional material on family relations, including gay and lesbian families
- Description of the role and impact of family rituals on interpersonal communication
- New information on workplace romances

With respect to structure, the fourth Canadian edition continues to feature three parts containing 11 chapters. While the emotions chapter had been a good addition to the text, it lacked connection with the focus of the book's approach. Thus, the three parts have been re-arranged with the final three chapters focusing on interpersonal communication relationships.

The result is a better-structured text with the addition of new and relevant material.

Part I: Foundations of Interpersonal Communication focuses on the prerequisites of interpersonal communication. Chapter 1 traces the evolution of interpersonal communication theory, defines key concepts, and begins exploring the link between interpersonal communication and relationships. Chapter 2 encourages students to examine their own self-concept and self-esteem as they study theoretical frameworks and constructs. Chapter 3 examines the perception process, emphasizing tendencies that interfere with relational development and suggesting ways to combat them.

Part II: Interpersonal Communication Skills focuses on the basic skills and competencies required for effective interpersonal relationships. Chapter 4 focuses on listening and responding with accuracy and empathy. Chapters on understanding the power of language and verbal messages (Chapter 5) and perceiving and interpreting non-verbal cues (Chapter 6) continue to develop students' understanding of interpersonal skills. Chapter 7 examines conflict and suggests ways to manage conflict and solve problems as essential interpersonal skills. "Interpersonal Communication and Cultural Diversity" (Chapter 8) gives students an opportunity to understand relationships in a diverse population; a better understanding of the impact of cultural differences on communication will help students achieve positive interactions within this diverse milieu.

Part III: Interpersonal Communication in Relationships, significantly revised, examines more deeply the nature of relationships that we experience in life. "Understanding Interpersonal Relationships" (Chapter 9) presents the way relationships develop and unfold, and discusses how trust, intimacy, and power affect relationship development. "Developing, Maintaining, and Ending Interpersonal Relationships" (Chapter 10) explores how relationships escalate and end, and offers strategies for developing and maintaining relationships. Finally, in Chapter 11, we look more closely at relationships at home, on the Internet, and at work.

Our Partnership with Instructors

As important as we think a textbook is, it is only one tool that facilitates student learning. In the fourth edition of *Interpersonal Communication: Relating to Others,* we continue our tradition of offering a wide variety of instructional resources to help instructors teach and students learn principles and skills of interpersonal communication.

Built into the book is a vast array of pedagogical features:

● A chapter-opening quotation to provide an initial captivating focal point for the chapter
● A list of chapter learning objectives
● A comprehensive chapter-opening outline of key content
● "Understanding Diversity" features that highlight applications of interpersonal communication in a diverse world
● "Building Your Skills" features that help students see the connection between knowing and doing
● New "Becoming Other-Oriented" features that help students understand the signature theme of the book
● A new other-oriented icon appearing in the margin to highlight material that focuses on the needs and concerns of others
● Liberal use of "Recap" features to help students distill the essence of key concepts and terms
● A margin glossary of all boldface terms in the text
● Chapter-end questions that focus on critical thinking and ethics to spark thought and class discussion
● Chapter-end "For Your Journal" questions and activities to prompt reflection and application
● "Learning with Others," chapter-end collaborative learning activities and exercises
● New end-of-chapter "Weblinks" to supplemental resources and activities

Instructor Supplements

● *Instructor's Manual* (ISBN 0-205-48994-X) includes teaching suggestions, suggested course syllabi, and guidelines for using the complete teaching-learning package.
● *Test Item File* is presented in hard copy (ISBN 0-205-48996-6) or computerized format (ISBN 0-205-48993-1) in TestGen 7.2 for Windows® and Macintosh®.
● *PowerPoint® Presentations* (ISBN 0-205-48992-3) can be used to enhance lectures and tutorial instruction. These slides are also posted on the Companion Website (www.pearsoned.ca/beebe).
● *Instructor's Resource CD-ROM* (ISBN 0-205-48995-8). This interactive CD contains all of the supplements available for instructors.

Student Supplements

● *Interactive Companion Website* (www.pearsoned.ca/beebe) includes learning objectives, practice tests, interactive exercises, and additional weblinks for every chapter.

Acknowledgments

The authors are grateful to those colleagues who acted as reviewers for this Canadian edition, including Sherry Ferguson, University of Ottawa; Jenepher Lennox Terrion, University of Ottawa; Stan Chung, Okanagan University College; Marcel Paul Carpenter, SAIT; Kathryn A. Levine, University of Manitoba; Patricia Campbell, Red Deer College; as well as a couple of people who wished to remain anonymous. Also, thanks to all of the people at Pearson Education Canada who managed to keep this book on track and on schedule.

Part One

1

"Group Chat," © Diana Ong/Superstock

Foundations of Interpersonal Communication

The first three chapters present fundamental concepts that frame our study of interpersonal communication. In Chapter 1, you will learn answers to these questions: What is interpersonal communication? What is the connection between interpersonal communication and interpersonal relationships? Why is it important to study relationships? What can I do to improve my relationships with others? Chapter 2 offers concepts and skills to help you understand more about who you are and how your self-concept and sense of self-worth influence your relationships. In Chapter 3, you will learn that perception plays a key role in effective interpersonal communication. By recognizing the factors that influence your perceptions and by actively analyzing the meaning of perceptual information, you can become more adept at sharing your sense of the world with others.

1

Introduction to Interpersonal Communication

After you study this chapter

you should be able to ...

1. Compare and contrast definitions of communication, human communication, and interpersonal communication.

2. Explain why it is useful to study interpersonal communication.

3. Compare and contrast communication as action, interaction, and transaction.

4. Describe the key components of the communication process.

5. Discuss five principles of interpersonal communication.

6. Describe four interpersonal communication myths.

7. Identify strategies that can improve your communication effectiveness.

- What Is Interpersonal Communication?

- The Importance of Interpersonal Communication to Our Lives

- An Evolving Model for Human and Interpersonal Communication

- Mediated Interpersonal Communication: A New Frontier

- Principles of Interpersonal Communication

- Interpersonal Communication Myths

- How to Improve Your Own Interpersonal Communication Effectiveness

Communication is to a relationship what breathing is to maintaining life.

VIRGINIA SATIR

nterpersonal communication is like breathing; it is a requirement for life, and, like breathing, it is inescapable. Unless you live in isolation, you communicate interpersonally every day. Listening to your roommate, talking to a teacher, meeting for lunch with a friend, and talking to your parents or your spouse are all examples of interpersonal communication.

It is impossible *not* to communicate with others. Even before we are born, we respond to movement and sound. With our first cry, we announce to others that we are here. Once we make contact with others, we communicate, and we continue to do so until our last breath. Even though many of our messages are not verbalized, we nonetheless intentionally, and sometimes unintentionally, send messages to others. Without interpersonal communication, a special form of human communication that occurs as we manage our relationships, people suffer and even die. Recluses, hermits, and people isolated in solitary confinement dream and hallucinate about talking with others face to face.

Interpersonal communication is at the core of our existence. Think of the number of times you communicate with someone each day, as you work, eat, study, shop, or go about your other daily activities. Most people spend between 80 and 90 percent of their waking hours engaging in some form of interpersonal communication.[1] It is through these exchanges that we develop interpersonal relationships with others.[2]

Because these relationships are so important in our lives, later chapters will focus on the communication skills and principles that explain and predict how we develop, sustain, and sometimes end them. We'll explore such questions as: Why do we like some people and not others? How can we interpret other people's unspoken messages with greater accuracy? Why do some relationships blossom and others deteriorate? How can we better manage disagreements with others? How can we better understand our relationships with our family, friends, and co-workers?

This chapter charts the course ahead, addressing key questions about what interpersonal communication is and why it is important. We will begin by seeing how our understanding of the interpersonal communication process has evolved. We will conclude by examining how we initiate and sustain relationships through interpersonal communication.

In face-to-face encounters, we simultaneously exchange both verbal and non-verbal messages that result in shared meanings. Through this kind of interrelation, we build relationships with others. (Robert Brenner/Photo Edit)

communication. The process of acting upon information.

human communication. The process of making sense out of the world and attempting to share that sense with others by creating meaning through the use of verbal and non-verbal messages.

interpersonal communication. The process of interacting simultaneously with another person and mutually influencing each other, usually for the purpose of managing relationships.

impersonal communication. Communication that occurs when we treat people as objects, or when we respond to their roles rather than to who they are as unique persons.

What Is Interpersonal Communication?

To understand interpersonal communication, we must begin by understanding how it relates to two broader categories: communication in general and human communication. Scholars have attempted to arrive at a general definition of communication for decades, yet experts cannot agree on a single one. One research team counted more than 126 published definitions;[3] however, in the broadest sense, **communication** is the process of acting on information.[4] For instance, one person does or says something, and someone else thinks or does something in response to the first person's actions or words, as he or she understands them.

Communication is not unique to humans. It is possible, for example, for you to act on information from your dog. She barks; you feed her. This definition also suggests that your dog can act on information from you. You head for the cupboard to feed her; she wags her tail and jumps up in the air, anticipating her dinner. Researchers do study communication between species as well as communication systems within single animal species, but these fields of study are beyond the scope of this book. The focus of our study is on a form of human communication: people communicating with other people.[5]

To refine our broad definition, we can say that **human communication** is the process of making sense out of the world and sharing that sense with others by creating meaning through the use of verbal and non-verbal messages.[6] We learn about the world by listening, observing, tasting, touching, and smelling; then we share our conclusions with others. Human communication encompasses many media, including speeches, songs, radio and television broadcasts, e-mail, letters, books, articles, poems, and advertisements.

Interpersonal communication is a special form of human communication that occurs when we interact simultaneously with another person and mutually influence each other, usually for the purpose of managing relationships. Three essential elements of this definition determine the unique nature of interpersonal communication apart from other forms of human communication.[7]

Interpersonal Communication Is a Distinctive Form of Communication

For years, many scholars defined interpersonal communication simply as communication that occurs when two people interact face to face. This limited definition suggests that if two people are interacting, then they are interpersonally communicating. Today, interpersonal communication is defined not just by the number of people who communicate but also by the quality of the communication. Interpersonal communication occurs not when you simply interact with someone, but when you treat the other as a unique human being.

Think of all human communication as ranging on a continuum from impersonal to interpersonal communication. **Impersonal communication** occurs when you treat people as objects, or when you respond to their roles rather than to who they are as unique people. Philosopher Martin Buber influenced our thinking about human communication when he presented the concept of true dialogue as the essence of true, authentic communication.[8] He described communication as consisting of two different qualities of relationships. He discussed an "I–It" relationship as an impersonal one; the other person is viewed as an "It" rather than as an authentic, genuine person. When you buy a pair of socks at a clothing store, you have a two-person, face-to-face, relatively brief interaction with someone. You communicate. Yet that interchange could hardly be described as intimate or personal. When you ask a server in a restaurant for a glass of water, you are interacting with the role, not necessarily with the individual. You know nothing personal about him (or her), and he knows nothing personal about you (unless he eavesdrops by your table).

 Recap

COMPARING KEY DEFINITIONS

Term	Definition
Communication	The process of acting on information
Human communication	The process of making sense out of the world and sharing that sense with others
Interpersonal communication	The process of two people interacting with each other and mutually influencing each other, usually for the purpose of managing relationships

Interpersonal communication occurs when you interact with another person as a unique, authentic individual rather than as object or "It." Buber calls this kind of relationship an "I–Thou" relationship. An "I–Thou" relationship involves true dialogue. It is not self-centred. The communicators have developed an attitude toward each other that is honest, open, spontaneous, non-judgmental, and based on equality rather than superiority.[9] Exchanges such as those with the sock-seller or the server have the potential to become true interpersonal communication dialogue if you begin to interact with these people as unique individuals. If, for example, during your conversation with the server, you discover you were born in the same town and develop other personal links, the impersonal, role-oriented communication becomes more personal, and the quality of the communication moves toward the intimate end of the continuum.

We're not suggesting that the goal of every communication exchange is to develop a personal, intimate dialogue. Often, such as when you are buying socks or asking for a glass of water at a restaurant, it may not be appropriate to develop personal relationships with others just because you are talking with them.

Although interpersonal communication is more intimate and reveals more about the people involved than does impersonal communication, not all interpersonal communication involves sharing closely guarded personal information. As we discuss later in the book, there are degrees of intimacy when interacting with others. Table 1.1 compares and contrasts interpersonal communication with impersonal communication.

Interpersonal Communication Involves Mutual Influence between Individuals

Mutual influence means that all partners are affected by the interactions, not just one person. Interpersonal communication may or may not involve words. The interaction may be fleeting or enduring. While you are talking and your mother is listening, you are also simultaneously observing your mother's non-verbal expressions. Just

Table 1.1

The Continuum between Interpersonal Communication
and Impersonal Communication

Interpersonal Communication	Impersonal Communication
• People are treated as unique individuals.	• People are treated as objects.
• People communicate in an "I–Thou" relationship. You are special.	• People communicate in an "I–It" relationship. You have a role to perform.
• There is true dialogue and honest sharing of self with others.	• There is mechanical, stilted interaction; no honest sharing of feelings.
• Interpersonal communication often involves communicating with someone you care about, such as a good friend or cherished family member.	• Impersonal communication involves communicating with people such as sales clerks and waitpersons—you have no history with them and you expect no future with them.

because she is not speaking does not mean she is not communicating. She not only hears what you have to say, but also observes how you say it.

The degree of mutual influence varies a great deal from interaction to interaction. You probably would not be affected a great deal by a brief smile that you receive from a travelling companion on a bus but would be greatly affected by your lover telling you he or she is leaving you. Every interpersonal communication interaction influences us. Sometimes it changes our lives dramatically, sometimes in small ways. Long-lasting interpersonal relationships are sustained not by one person giving and another taking but by a spirit of mutual equality. Both you and your partner listen and respond with respect for each other. There is no attempt to manipulate others. True dialogue, says researcher Daniel Yankelovich, involves a collaborative climate. It's not about winning and losing an argument. It's about being understood and accepted.[10]

Buber asserts that the quality of being fully "present" when communicating with another person is an essential part of an "I–Thou" relationship.[11] To be present is to give your full attention to the other person. The quality of interpersonal communication is enhanced when both you and your communication partner are simultaneously present and focused on each other.

Interpersonal Communication Is the Fundamental Means We Use to Manage Our Relationships

relationship. An ongoing connection made with another person through interpersonal communication.

An interpersonal **relationship** is the ongoing connection you make with another person through interpersonal communication. Relationships go through a series of developmental stages. The initial stages of relationships often involve sharing less intimate or personal information. Later stages evolve to include more intimate conversations and behaviours.

You initiate and form relationships by communicating with others whom you find attractive in some way. You seek to increase your interactions with people with whom you wish to develop relationships, and you continually interpersonally communicate to maintain the relationship. You also use interpersonal communication to end relationships that you have decided are no longer viable.

In this book, we define interpersonal communication as a unique form of human communication. There are other forms of communication, as well. **Mass communication** occurs when someone communicates the same message to many people at once, but the creator of the message is usually not physically present, and listeners have virtually no opportunity to respond immediately to the speaker. Messages communicated via radio and TV are examples of mass communication. **Public communication** occurs when a speaker addresses a large audience in person. **Small-group communication** occurs when a group of from three to fifteen people meet to interact with a common purpose and mutually influence one another. The purpose of the gathering could be to solve a problem, make a decision, learn, or just have fun. While communicating with others in a small group, it is also possible to communicate with others interpersonally—to communicate to manage a relationship with one or more individuals in the group. Finally, **intrapersonal communication** is communication with oneself. Thinking is perhaps the best example of intrapersonal communication. In our discussion of self and communication in Chapter 2, we discuss the relationships between one's thoughts and one's interpersonal communication with others.

mass communication. Type of communication that occurs when one person issues the same message to many people at once; the creator of the message is usually not present and there is virtually no opportunity for listeners to respond to the speaker.

public communication. Type of communication that occurs when a speaker addresses a large audience in person.

small-group communication. Type of communication that occurs when a group of from three to fifteen people meet to interact with a common purpose and mutually influence one another.

intrapersonal communication. Communication with oneself; thinking.

The Importance of Interpersonal Communication to Our Lives

Why study interpersonal communication? Because it touches every aspect of your life. Developing quality interpersonal relationships with others is not only pleasant or desirable; it is vital for your well-being. Learning how to understand and improve interpersonal communication can improve relationships with family, loved ones, friends, and colleagues and can enhance the quality of physical and emotional health.

Improve Relationships with Family

Relating to family members can be a challenge. The divorce statistics in Canada document the difficulties that can occur when people live in relationships with each other: about half of all marriages end in divorce. We don't claim that you will avoid all family conflicts or that your family relationships will always be harmonious if you learn principles and skills of interpersonal communication. You can, however, develop more options for how to respond when family communication challenges come your way. You will be more likely to develop creative, constructive solutions to family conflict if you understand what's happening and can promote true dialogue with your spouse, parent, brother, or sister. Furthermore, family relationships play a major role in determining how you interact with others. Family communication author Virginia Satir calls family communication "the largest single factor determining the kinds of relationships [people make] with others."[12]

Effective interpersonal skills are essential to the development of meaningful, caring relationships.
(Lori Adamski Peek/Tony Stone Images)

Improve Relationships with Friends and Lovers

We cannot choose our biological families, but we do choose our friends. Friends are people we choose to be with because we like them and, usually, they like us. We expect friends to be honest, open, and affectionate; to confide in us, respect us, and constructively work through disagreements.[13] We depend on them to fill many roles. According to one researcher, friends provide useful information (about job vacancies, where to shop, the best places to eat, etc.); needed services (help us when we need it); companionship; emotional support; and even financial assistance.[14] Friends also develop and share unique meanings, private jokes, and other coded messages that only they can understand.[15] Why do we choose some people as friends and develop a reciprocal mistrust of others? The quality of our relationships with others hinges on the quality of our communication. Therefore, learning communication patterns, principles, and prescriptions can help answer this question and improve our relationships with the friends we have.

For unmarried people, developing friendships and falling in love are the top-rated sources of satisfaction and happiness in life.[16] Conversely, losing a relationship is among life's most stressful events.[17] Most individuals between the ages of 19 and 24 report that they have had from five to six romantic relationships and have been "in love" once or twice.[18] Studying interpersonal communication may not unravel *all* of the mysteries of romantic love and friendship, but it can offer insight into our behaviour. Without companions and close friends, opportunities for intimacy and stress-minimizing interpersonal communication are diminished. Although being involved in intimate interpersonal relationships can lead to conflict and feelings of anger and frustration, researchers suggest that when all is said and done, having close relationships with others is a major source of personal happiness.[19] Studying how to enhance the quality of your communication with others can make life more enjoyable and enhance your overall well-being.

Improve Relationships with Colleagues

In many ways, our colleagues at work are like family members. Although we choose our friends and lovers, we don't always have the same flexibility in choosing whom we work with or for. Understanding how relationships develop on the job can help us avoid conflict and stress and increase our sense of satisfaction. In addition, our success or failure in a job often hinges on how well we get along with our supervisor and our peers. Most job performance reviews give the boss a chance to make comments about how well we work with others. Moreover, recent studies have shown that training workers to relate and communicate as a team improves quality and productivity in many occupations, so more and more workplaces are adopting teamwork as a management strategy. Many Canadian companies rely on teams for increased productivity; among the notable team-based companies are Imperial Oil, Amex Canada, Honeywell, IBM Canada, and Pratt and Whitney, to name just a few. In fact, few companies rely solely on the individual efforts of employees. The Conference Board of Canada and its partners (including business organizations and

In Canada...

WHAT SKILLS WILL I NEED FOR EMPLOYMENT?

If your job search is going to be successful, from the beginning you need to know not just your own goals, but what employers are looking for. Courses that teach interpersonal communication skills can help you improve your own skills and become a more attractive candidate. The Conference Board of Canada has published a brochure that outlines an Employability Skills Profile based on information gathered from hundreds of Canadian employers. This brochure can assist you in developing various skills.

The brochure summarizes the skills that are in demand under three headings: Academic Skills, Personal Management Skills, and Teamwork Skills. Under the heading of Personal Management Skills, the brochure notes that employers need a person who has self-esteem and confidence, who recognizes and respects people's diversity and individual differences, who has a positive attitude toward learning, growth, and personal health, and who has the ability to identify and suggest new ideas to get the job done in a creative way. Within the area of Teamwork Skills, the brochure discusses many aspects, including respecting the thoughts and opinions of others in the group,

using conflict management strategies to facilitate "give and take" and thereby achieve group results, and planning and making decisions with others and supporting those outcomes.

Although many may view these as "soft skills," there is no doubt that in an economic climate where getting a job can be "hard," these skills may be the ones that may set you apart from other candidates.

Throughout the text, these "In Canada..." boxes highlight Canadian research and issues with Canadian sources. In Chapter 11, you will find the Employability Skills presented in full.

Source: ED399484 95 Employability Skills Profile: What Are Employers Looking For? Author: Mary Ann McLaughlin.

---

training/education partners) have identified teamwork skills as one of the three main areas of essential employability skills.[20] Chapter 11 includes this chart in its entirety.

Improve Your Physical and Emotional Health

Intimate interpersonal relationships are vital to your health. Research has shown that the lack or loss of a relationship can lead to ill health and even death. Physicians have long observed that patients who are widowed or divorced experience more medical problems such as heart disease, cancer, pneumonia, and diabetes than do married people.[21] Grief-stricken spouses are more likely than others to die prematurely,[22] especially around the time of the departed spouse's birthday or near their wedding anniversary.[23] One Canadian study found that married retired couples reported happier relationships than older couples where one was retired and the other was still working.[24] Being childless also can shorten your life. One research team found that middle-aged, childless wives were almost two and one-half times more likely to die in a given year than those who had at least one child.[25] Terminally ill patients with a limited number of friends or no social support die sooner than those with stronger ties.[26] Loneliness can kill.

Research findings are similar for mental illness: widowed and divorced individuals are more likely to experience mental illness, especially depression, than those in ongoing relationships.[27] In fact, **depression** is the most commonly diagnosed mental illness. The Canadian Mental Health Association has estimated that 15 percent of the population will have a major depressive episode at some point in their lives.[28]

depression. A widespread emotional disorder in which the person has problems with sadness, changes in appetite, difficulty sleeping, and a decrease in activities, interests, and energy.

On the positive side, however, establishing a quality social support system can be a major factor in improving and maintaining your health. One study suggests that the more attached we are to at least one other person, the longer we live.[29]

All of these findings show that the stress of loneliness can make us sick, but if we have support from people who care about us, we can adjust to life's tumbles and challenges. By learning more about effective communication, you are paving the way for closer, more satisfying relationships and a longer life.

An Evolving Model for Human and Interpersonal Communication

Today, we know that interpersonal communication is more than simply transferring or exchanging messages with others; it is a complex process of creating meaning. To understand this process, it is useful to see how our perspective on the human communication process has evolved over the past half-century.[30] We will begin with the simplest and oldest model of the human communication process and then discuss more contemporary models.

Human Communication As Action: Message Transfer

"Did you get my message?" This simple sentence summarizes the communication-as-action approach to human communication. Communication takes place when a message is sent and received, period. It is a way of transferring meaning from sender to receiver.

Figure 1.1 shows a basic model that depicts communication as a linear input–output process. Today, although they view the process differently, researchers still define most of the key components in this model in basically the same way.

Source

The transmitter (now called the **source**), the originator of that thought or emotion, puts the thought or emotion into a code that can be understood by a receiver. Translating ideas, feelings, and thoughts into a code is called **encoding**. Vocalizing a word, gesturing, or establishing eye contact are signals that we use to encode our thoughts into a message that can be decoded by the receiver. **Decoding** is the opposite of encoding. The words or unspoken signals are interpreted by the receiver.

source. The originator of a thought or emotion who puts the thought or emotion into a code that can be understood by a receiver.

encoding. The translation of ideas, feelings, and thoughts into a code.

decoding. The interpretation of ideas, feelings, and thoughts that have been translated into a code.

Figure 1.1
A Simple Model of Human Communication As Action

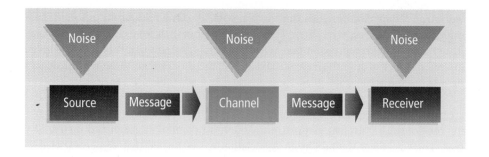

🌑 Receiver

The **receiver** is the person who decodes and attempts to make sense out of what the source encoded. Think of a radio station with a source broadcasting to a receiver that picks up the station's signal. In human communication, however, there is something between the source and the receiver: we filter messages through past experiences, attitudes, beliefs, values, prejudices, and biases.

🌑 Message

The **message** comprises the written, spoken, and unspoken elements of communication to which we assign meaning. You can send a message intentionally (talking to a professor before class) or unintentionally (falling asleep during class), verbally ("Hi. How are you?"), non-verbally (a smile and a handshake), or in written form (this book).

🌑 Channel

A message is communicated from sender to receiver via some pathway called a **channel**. Channels correspond to your senses. When you call your mother on the telephone, the channel is an auditory one. When you talk with your mother face to face, the channels are many. You see her: the visual channel. You hear her: the auditory channel. You may smell her perfume: the olfactory channel. You may hug her: the tactile channel.

🌑 Noise

Noise is anything that interferes with a message and keeps if from being understood and achieving its intended effect. Without noise, all of our messages would be communicated with sublime accuracy. However, noise is always present. It may be literal, such as the obnoxious roar of a gas-powered lawn mower. Or it may be psychological; for instance, instead of concentrating on your teacher's lecture, you may start thinking about the chores you need to finish before the end of the day. Whichever kind it is, noise gets in the way of the message and may even distort it. Communicating accurate messages involves minimizing both external and psychological noise.

Although the action approach is simple and straightforward, it has a key flaw: human communication rarely, if ever, is as simple and efficient as "what we put in is what we get out." Others cannot automatically know what you mean just because you think you know what you mean. In the early 1940s, when the action approach was formulated, communication scholars had already begun identifying an array of key elements in the communication process, the complexity of which the action approach overlooked.

Human Communication As Interaction: Message Exchange

The next big leap in our understanding of human communication came in the late 1940s and early 1950s. The communication-as-interaction perspective used the same elements as the action models but added two new ones: feedback and context.

Think of a table tennis game. Messages, like the ball, bounce back and forth. We talk; someone listens and responds. We respond to their response, and so forth. This perspective can be summarized using a physical principle: for every action there is a reaction.

receiver. The person who decodes a message and attempts to make sense out of what the source has encoded.

message. The written, spoken, and unspoken elements of communication to which people assign meaning.

channel. The pathway by which messages are sent.

noise. Information, either literal or psychological, that interferes with the accurate reception of the communication of the message.

Feedback is the response to the message. Without feedback, communication is rarely effective. When you order a black olive pizza, your server encodes the message internally and says, "That's a black olive pizza, right?" The server must provide feedback to ensure that he or she has understood the message correctly.

Feedback is really a response message. Like other messages, it can be intentional (your mother hugs you when you announce that you are on the dean's list) or unintentional (a yawn as your professor drones on about models of communication); verbal ("That's a black olive pizza, right?") or non-verbal (blushing after being asked to dance).

A second component recognized by the interaction perspective is **context**—the physical and psychological communication environment. All communication takes place in some context. As the cliché goes, "Everyone has to be somewhere." A conversation with a good friend on the beach would likely differ from one the two of you might have in a funeral home. Context encompasses not only the physical environment but also the number of people present and their relationship with the communicators, the communication goal, and the culture in which the communicators are steeped.

This approach, as shown in Figure 1.2, is more realistic, but it still has limitations. Although it emphasizes feedback and context, it does not quite capture the complexity of the process if the communication takes place simultaneously. In interpersonal situations, both the source and the receiver send and receive messages at the same time.

Human Communication As Transaction: Message Creation

The communication-as-transaction perspective, developed in the 1960s, acknowledges that when we talk to each other, we are constantly reacting to what our partner is saying. The majority of scholars today view it as the most realistic model for interpersonal communication. It uses the same components to describe communication, such as action and interaction. However, in this model, all of the interaction is simultaneous. As Figure 1.3 indicates, we send and receive messages

Figure 1.2
A Model for Communication As Interaction
Interaction models of communication include feedback as a response to a message sent by the communication source and context as the environment for communication.

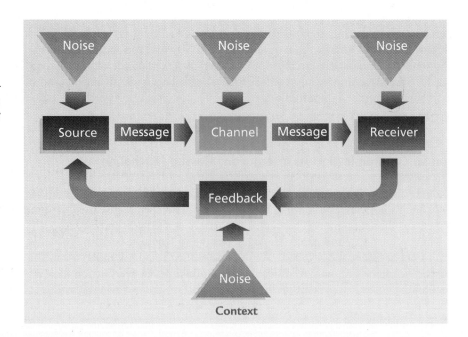

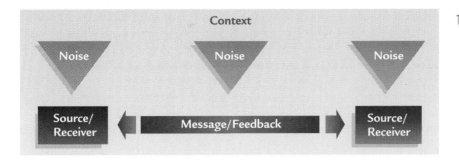

Figure 1.3
A Model for Communication As Mutual Transaction
In this model, the source and the receiver of a message experience communication simultaneously.

concurrently. Even as we talk, we are also interpreting our partner's non-verbal and verbal responses.

Transactional communication also occurs within a context defined more broadly than by action or interaction. Transactional communication suggests that communication is influenced by a force that may not be immediately evident to the communication partners. The past experiences and cultures of the people involved in the communication, the setting of the communication, and the thoughts and emotions of the communicators all influence how messages are interpreted. Whereas communication as action or interaction views communication as linear—there are specific causes and effects that can explain how messages are interpreted—communication as transaction is much more complicated. An understanding of the relationships that you and your conversation partner establish changes from moment to moment as the conversation unfolds and as your thoughts influence how you respond to the message. A transactional approach to communication suggests that no single cause explains why you interpret messages the way you do. In fact, it is inappropriate to point to a single factor to explain how you are making sense of the messages of others; communication is messier than that. The meaning of messages in interpersonal relationships evolves from the past, is influenced by the present, and is affected by visions of the future.

One researcher has said that interpersonal communication is "the coordinated management of meaning" through **episodes**, during which the message of one person influences the message of another.[31] Technically, only the sender and receiver of those messages can determine where one episode ends and another begins.

episodes. A sequence of interaction between individuals during which the message of one person influences the message of another.

▶ **Recap**

COMPONENTS OF THE HUMAN COMMUNICATION PROCESS

Term	Definition
Source	Human being who has an idea or emotion.
Receiver	Person or group toward whom the source directs messages, intentionally or unintentionally.
Message	Written, spoken, and unspoken elements of communication to which we assign meaning.
Channel	Pathway through which messages pass between source and receiver.
Noise	Anything, either literal or psychological, that interferes with the clear reception and interpretation of a message.
Encoding	Translation of ideas, feelings, and thoughts into a code.
Decoding	Interpretation of ideas, feelings, and thoughts that have been translated into a code.
Context	Physical and psychological communication environment.
Feedback	Verbal and non-verbal responses to messages.

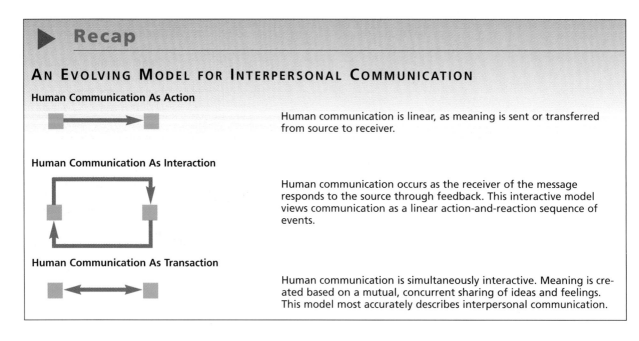

▶ **Recap**

AN EVOLVING MODEL FOR INTERPERSONAL COMMUNICATION

Human Communication As Action

Human communication is linear, as meaning is sent or transferred from source to receiver.

Human Communication As Interaction

Human communication occurs as the receiver of the message responds to the source through feedback. This interactive model views communication as a linear action-and-reaction sequence of events.

Human Communication As Transaction

Human communication is simultaneously interactive. Meaning is created based on a mutual, concurrent sharing of ideas and feelings. This model most accurately describes interpersonal communication.

Mediated Interpersonal Communication: A New Frontier

Today's technology allows us to expand our definition of interpersonal communication. Instead of having to rely on face-to-face contact for our interpersonal exchanges, we can now use various types of media to carry our interpersonal messages. Telephones, faxes, e-mail, and electronic chat rooms are among the sometimes bewildering assortment of devices through which we can interact, exercise mutual influence, and develop interpersonal relationships. When we use one of these media to carry the message, we are using **mediated interpersonal communication**.

At present, the most effective interpersonal communication still occurs when there are no media filters to interfere with the clarity of the message or to delay feedback from the receiver of the message. For this reason, our key focus in this book will be on unmediated interaction between people.

However, we will also begin to explore the new frontier in interpersonal communication. Can you communicate interpersonally with someone on the Internet? Can relationships be developed without an in-person meeting? Research suggests that some long-distance relationships can be as satisfying as face-to-face relationships.[32] College freshmen and their parents report that e-mail reduces homesickness as well as the sadness parents often feel as their son or daughter leaves home. The past few years have seen an increase in the number of people who meet in a chat room on the Internet and eventually develop a face-to-face relationship. Canadians are among the world's most enthusiastic users of the Internet, according to a 2004-2005 survey, with 78 percent reporting having used the Internet in the past three months.[33] The past few years have seen an increase in the number of conventional relationships that began in chat rooms on the Internet. In 2002, more than 35 million Americans

mediated interpersonal communication.
Communication with others established or maintained by using media (such as e-mail, telephone, or fax) rather than a face-to-face encounter.

visited online dating sites each month. By 2003, that number had swelled to 45 million, with the numbers continuing to skyrocket.[34] Although these are American statistics, given the popularity of Internet usage in Canada, we can probably extrapolate that Canadians are also visiting dating sites in relatively high numbers.

People have even developed new ways to communicate the feelings, emotions, and other responses that make it possible to communicate non-verbally. You are probably familiar with emoticons (keyboard symbols like :-O). You can also communicate emotions via e-mail by "screaming:" typing in all capital letters to shout the message. In still other situations, you might respond to someone by verbally describing non-verbal behaviours: "I am frowning right now as I read your message."

Of course, just as not all face-to-face communication is interpersonal communication, not all mediated communication results in unique relationships with others. One of the key differences in these mediated communication situations is the reduced level of non-verbal cues. Even if you use emoticons, when you can't see the other person's facial expression, amount of eye contact, or whether he or she seems interested in what you are saying, accurately communicating your meaning, especially your feelings and emotions, can be challenging.

A growing body of research, however, suggests that when you interact with people using computer-mediated communication, you can compensate for the lack of non-verbal cues. If you've been interacting with someone over a period of several weeks or months, you begin to pick up cues about his or her emotions and feelings just from the words he or she uses and from what you have learned about that person and his or her behaviour.

Communication researcher Joseph Walther and his colleagues have developed a **social information-processing theory** that explains how you can develop quality relationships with others via e-mail and other electronic means.[35] According to this theory, a key difference between face-to-face and computer-mediated communication is the rate at which information reaches you. During live, in-person communication, you process a lot of information quickly; you process the words you hear as well as the myriad of non-verbal cues you see (facial expression and body posture) and hear (tone of voice and use of pauses). During e-mail interactions, there is less information to process, so it takes a bit longer for the relationship to develop—but it does develop as you learn more about your e-mail partner's likes, dislikes, and feelings. Also, if you expect to communicate with your electronic communication partner again, there is evidence that you will pay more attention to the relationship cues that develop. In one study, Joseph Walther and Judee Burgoon found that the development of relationships between people who met face to face differed little from those between people who had computer-mediated interactions.[36] In fact, they found the computer-mediated group actually developed *more* socially rich relationships than the face-to-face group.

A study by Lisa Tidwell and Joseph Walther investigated how computer-mediated communication affects how much and how quickly people reveal information about themselves and the overall impressions people form of one another.[37] In comparing computer-mediated exchanges with face-to-face conversations, Tidwell and Walther found that people in computer-mediated "conversations" asked more direct

social information-processing theory. Explains how people use information they receive from others via electronic media such as e-mail to develop relationships.

questions, which resulted in people's revealing *more* information about themselves, not less, when online. The pattern of differences between computer-mediated communication and face-to-face communication is still being discovered as computer-mediated communication becomes an even more significant part of modern life.

Because of technology, some electronic interpersonal exchanges may not be simultaneous. Nonetheless, there is mutual understanding, and the communication can be truly personal rather than impersonal. We suggest that these electronic communication exchanges, even though not as rich in non-verbal and relational information, can mirror characteristics of face-to-face interpersonal communication in the sense that you are developing or maintaining a unique relationship with someone. In addition, electronically mediated relationships can involve mutual influence, and e-mailing someone that you'd like to marry—or divorce—that person, or just get together for a cup of coffee, illustrates how e-messages can alter both lives and relationships. Clearly, not all e-mail correspondence is interpersonal communication; today's technology, however, sometimes makes it possible to emulate in cyberspace the characteristics of interpersonal transactions.

 ## Applying Theory and Research

DOES YOUR LEVEL OF COMMUNICATION APPREHENSION PREDICT THE TYPE OF RELATIONSHIPS YOU HAVE WITH OTHERS ONLINE?

Do people "meet" others online to overcome some of the apprehension they may feel when they communicate with people face to face? Michelle Mazur and Ryan Burns wanted to know whether Internet relationships that blossomed online can be explained in part because communicating in cyberspace arouses less communication apprehension, especially for people who are shy or introverted. They administered a survey via the Internet to people who had met their romantic partners online and who used the Internet to maintain their relationships. Participants completed measures to assess their general level

of communication apprehension (how anxious or nervous they are when communicating with others), their level of introversion (shyness), and their relational interdependence (how connected or close they are with their partners).

The researchers found out that people who are generally more apprehensive about communicating with other people in face-to-face situations reported that their relationship with their online romantic partner was interdependent or close. Stated another way, people who are highly apprehensive about communicating with others report their online relationships as important to them. On the other hand, the researchers found that people who scored high as introverts (because they communicate less than others in face-to-face situations) reported lower levels of connectedness in their online relationships.

APPLYING THE RESEARCH TO YOUR LIFE

What do the results of this study mean? If you are apprehensive about communicating with other people in live, face-to-face situations, you may be more comfortable communicating with people via the Internet. People who are highly anxious and apprehensive about communicating with others face to face can nonetheless satisfy their need to connect with others by relating to others online. This study also suggests that if you are introverted (shy about establishing relationships with others), you will be more likely to "keep to yourself" online; you will perceive your relationship with others as more independent, which suggests more separateness than closeness in a relationship. There's a difference between wanting to keep to yourself (introversion) and just being apprehensive about communicating with others. If you are communication

Continued

apprehensive, you become *nervous* when you have to talk to others. If you're an introvert, you generally are *shy* and more reluctant to connect to others. Communication apprehension is more specifically a description of how much anxiety you experience when talking with others. Cyberspace can be liberating for you if you're apprehensive about communicating with others; you may be less anxious about sharing informa-

tion about yourself if you don't have to look at the other person while you're communicating with him or her. If you're simply introverted or shy, you may reach out to others online but still prefer relationships in which you and your partner are less interlinked or interdependent. Researchers don't yet have all the answers about similarities and differences between communicating online and communicating face to

face. They do have evidence, however, that if you are apprehensive about communicating in person, you will likely be more comfortable communicating via the Internet.

We'll be revisiting the subject of communication apprehension in Chapter 2.

Source: Michelle A. Mazur and Ryan J. Burns, "Perceptions of Relational Interdependence in Online Relationships: The Effects of Communication Apprehension and Introversion," Communication Research Reports, 17(4), (2000): 397–406.

One research team suggests that the richness of a communication channel can be measured by four criteria: (1) the amount of feedback that the communicators can receive; (2) the number of cues that the channel can convey and that can be interpreted by a receiver; (3) the variety of language that communicators use; and (4) the potential for expressing emotions and feelings.[38] Using these four criteria, researchers have developed a continuum (communication-rich to communication-lean) of communication channels. The model presented in Figure 1.4 illustrates this continuum.

There is some evidence that when an individual has a negative message to communicate, such as the intention of breaking off a relationship, he or she may select a less-rich communication message—that is, he or she may be more likely to send a letter or an e-mail rather than share the bad news face to face.[39] By the same reasoning, a person may prefer to share good news in person, so that positive reaction to the message can be directly enjoyed.

In summary, we believe this new frontier of electronic communication makes it possible for people to develop interpersonal relationships with others who are miles away. We agree with Joseph Walther and Lisa Tidwell that:

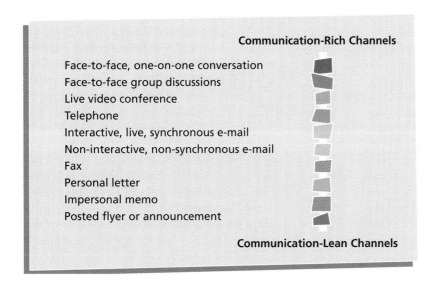

Figure 1.4
A Continuum of Communication-Rich and Communication-Lean Channels of Communication

Adapted from L. K. Trevino, R. L. Draft, and R. H. Lengel, "Understanding Managers' Media Choices: A Symbolic Interactionist Perspective." In *Organizations and Communication Technology,* edited by J. Fulk and C. Steinfield (Newbury Park, CA: Sage, 1990), 71–94.

"I'm afraid you misunderstood...
I said I'd like a mango."

The "Information Superhighway" is clearly not just a road for moving data from one place to another but a roadside where people pass each other, occasionally meet, and decide to travel together. You can't see very much of other drivers at first, unless you do travel together for some time. There are highway bandits, to be sure, who are not as they appear to be—one must drive defensively—and there are conflicts and disagreements online as there are off-road, too.[40]

Principles of Interpersonal Communication

As we introduce the study of interpersonal communication in this chapter, it is useful to present fundamental principles that help explain the nature of this phenomenon. Underlying our current understanding of interpersonal communication are five principles: interpersonal communication connects us to others, is irreversible, is complicated, is governed by rules, and involves both content and relationship dimensions.

Interpersonal Communication Connects Us to Others

Unless you live in a cave or have become a cloistered monk, you interact with others every day. Even if you work at home in front of a glowing computer screen, you encounter other people in the course of living your life. The opportunities for interpersonal communication are ubiquitous—they are everywhere. It is through inescapable interpersonal communication with others that we affect and are affected by other human beings.

We agree with author H. D. Duncan, who said, "We do not relate and then talk, but relate in talk." Fundamental to an understanding of interpersonal communication is the assumption that the quality of interpersonal relationships stems from the quality of communication with others. It's been said that people can't *not* communicate. Even though this perspective is debated among communication scholars because people often don't intend to express ideas or feelings, without question interpersonal communication is inescapable in the 21st century. Try to think of a time when you are *not* communicating. Hard to do, isn't it? How about when you're asleep? If you fall asleep while reading this book, others who see you may draw conclusions about you; perhaps they will think you attended a great party last night when, in reality, you stayed up late studying for a biology exam. In your interpersonal conversations with others, people may similarly draw an unintended conclusion about your interest in them if you inadvertently yawn while a friend of yours is telling you about the record-size fish he caught on his recent trip to British Columbia. You didn't intend to offend him; you were just exhausted. Our point is that even when you may not be conscious of what you're doing, you are connecting to others through the ever-present process of communication.

The inescapable nature of interpersonal communication doesn't mean others will *accurately* decode your message; it does mean that others are drawing inferences about you and your behaviour—they may be right or they may be wrong. Even as you silently stand in a crowded elevator, your lack of eye contact with others communicates your unwillingness to interact with fellow passengers. Your unspoken messages, even when you are asleep, provide cues that others interpret. Remember that *people often judge you by your behaviour, not your intent.* Your interpersonal communication is how you develop connections to others. Even in well-established interpersonal relationships, you may be evoking an unintended response to your behaviour.

Interpersonal Communication Is Irreversible

"Disregard that last statement made by the witness," instructs the judge. Yet, the clever lawyer knows that, once her client has stated that her husband gave her a black eye during an argument, the jury cannot really "disregard" the statement. This principle applies to all forms of oral communication. We may try to modify the meaning of a spoken message by saying something like, "Oh, I really didn't mean it." But, in most cases, the damage has been done. Once created, communication has a reality about it that is comparable to the physical property of matter; it can't be uncreated. As the helical model in Figure 1.5 suggests, once interpersonal communication begins, it never loops back on itself. Instead, it continues to be shaped by the events, experiences, and thoughts of the communication partners. A Russian proverb nicely summarizes the point: "Once a word goes out of your mouth, you can never swallow it again."

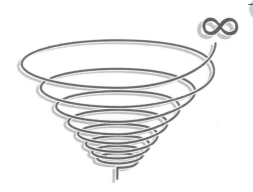

Figure 1.5 Interpersonal Communication Is Irreversible
This helical model shows that interpersonal communication never loops back on itself. It expands as the communication partners contribute their thoughts and experiences to the exchange.

Source: Copyright © F. E. X. Dance in *Human Communication Theory* (Holt, Rinehart and Winston, 1967), 294. Reprinted with permission.

Interpersonal Communication Is Complicated

No form of communication is simple. If any were, we would know how to reduce the number of misunderstandings and conflicts in our world. Because of the number of variables involved in interpersonal exchanges, even simple requests are extremely complex. Communication theorists have noted that whenever you communicate with another person, there are really at least six "people" involved: (1) who you think you are; (2) who you think the other person is; (3) who you think the other person thinks you are; (4) who the other person thinks he or she is; (5) who the other person thinks you are; and (6) who the other person thinks you think he or she is.[41] Whew, and when you add more people to the interaction, it becomes even more involved.

Moreover, when humans communicate, they interpret information from others as symbols. A **symbol** is merely a representation of something else, and it can have various meanings and interpretations. Language is a system of symbols. In English,

symbol. A representation of something else.

symbols do not resemble the words they represent. The word (symbol) for *cow* does not look at all like a cow; someone, somewhere decided that "cow" should mean a beast that chews a cud and gives milk. The reliance on symbols to communicate poses a communication challenge; we are often misinterpreted. Sometimes we don't know the code. Only if you are conversant with *Canadian* English will you know that "riding" refers to an electoral district; "allophone" refers to a Quebecker whose first language is neither French nor English; and "poutine" is french fries with cheese curds and gravy.

Messages are not always interpreted as we intend them. Osmo Wiio, a Finnish communication scholar, points out the messiness of communicating with others when he suggests the following maxims:

> If communication can fail, it will.
>
> If a message can be understood in different ways, it will be understood in just that way which does the most harm.
>
> There is always somebody who knows better than you what you meant by your message.
>
> The more communication there is, the more difficult it is for communication to succeed.[42]

Although we are not as pessimistic as Professor Wiio, we do suggest that the task of understanding each other is challenging.

Interpersonal Communication Is Governed by Rules

When you play the board game Monopoly, you know that there are explicit rules about how to get out of jail, buy Boardwalk, or pass "Go" and get 200 dollars. The rules are written down. When you play a game with others, there may even be some unwritten rules, such as when you play Monopoly with Grandpa, always let him buy Boardwalk. He gets grumpy as a bear before breakfast if he doesn't get to buy it. Similar rules govern how you communicate with others. Most of these rules are embedded in your culture or discussed verbally rather than in a written rulebook.

rule. A prescription for behaviour that indicates what is obligated, preferred, or prohibited in certain communication situations or contexts.

According to communication researcher Susan Shimanoff, a **rule** is a "followable prescription that indicates what behaviour is obligated, preferred, or prohibited in certain contexts."[43] The rules that help define appropriate and inappropriate communication in any given situation may be *explicit* or *implicit*. For your interpersonal communication class, explicit rules are probably spelled out in your syllabus, but your instructor has other rules that are more implicit. They are not written or verbalized because you learned them long ago: only one person speaks at a time, you raise your hand to be called on, you do not talk on your cellphone during class.

Interpersonal communication rules are developed by the people involved in the interaction and by the culture in which the individuals are communicating. Many times we learn communication rules from experience, by observing and interacting with others.

British researcher Michael Argyle and his colleagues asked people to identify general rules for relationship development and maintenance and then rate their importance. Here are the most important rules:[44]

Partners should respect the other's privacy.

Partners should not reveal each other's secrets.

Partners should look the other person in the eye during conversation.

Partners should not criticize the other person publicly.

Although we may modify rules to achieve the goals of our relationships, these general rules remain fairly constant. In interpersonal relationships, the rules of a relationship are mutually defined and agreed on. Most of us don't like to be told what to do or how to behave all the time. The expectations and rules are continually renegotiated as the relationship unfolds. Few of us learn relationship rules by copying them from a book. Most of us learn these rules from experience, through observing and interacting with family members and friends. Individuals who grow up in environments in which these rules are not observed may not know how to behave in close relationships.

For many of us, friendships are vital to our personal well-being. By improving our interpersonal communication skills, we can learn how to improve our friendships.
(Ian Shaw/Tony Stone Images)

Interpersonal Communication Involves Both Content and Relationship Dimensions

What you say (your words) and how you say it (your tone of voice, amount of eye contact, facial expression, and posture) can reveal much about the true meaning of your message. If one of your roommates loudly and abruptly bellows, "HEY, DORK! CLEAN THIS ROOM!" and another roommate sends the same verbal message but more gently and playfully—"Hey, dork. Clean this room."—both are communicating a message seeking the same outcome. However, the two messages have different relationship cues. The first, shouted message suggests that your roommate may be frustrated that the room still has echoes of last night's pizza party, whereas roommate number two's teasing request suggests he or she may be fondly amused by your untidiness.

The **content** of a communication message consists of the new information, ideas, or suggested actions that the speaker wishes to share. The **relationship dimension** of a communication message is usually more implied; it offers cues about the emotions, attitudes, and amount of power and control the speaker feels toward the other.[45]

Another way of distinguishing between the content and relationship dimensions of communication is to consider that the content of a message refers to *what* is said. Relationship cues refer to *how* it is communicated. This distinction explains why reading a transcript of what someone says can reveal a quite different meaning from actually hearing the person say the message.

content.   New information, ideas, or suggested actions that a speaker wishes to share.

relationship dimension. The implied aspect of a communication message, which conveys information about emotions, attitudes, power, and control.

Interpersonal Communication Myths

Several common misconceptions about interpersonal communication can under-mine the quality of your interpersonal relationships with others. As we embark on our study of interpersonal communication, it's just as important to unlearn some commonly-held misconceptions as it is to learn research conclusions and time-tested principles of interpersonal communication. Don't believe the following myths.

Myth #1: "More Words Will Make the Meaning Clearer"

More is not necessarily better. Just as there is a time to talk, there is a time to be silent. Piling on more words when your interpersonal communication partner is already baffled by what you are talking about can make matters worse. If someone is confused, hurt, or angry, continuing to add verbiage may hurt, not help. Maybe you just need to stop and listen rather than talk. Or ask a question and then just silently wait for an answer. Or perhaps, rather than words, your friend needs a non-verbal message of reassurance, a hug, a smile, or a nod of your head in agreement. Just as a picture can be worth a thousand words, demonstrating to someone what you mean can be more powerful than continuing to pile on the words. To keep going and going like the Energizer Bunny may only make matters worse. When you communicate feelings and attitudes, your non-verbal, unspoken expressions are where the action is.

Are we suggesting that more communication is always bad? No. Just don't fall into the trap of believing that more words will solve all problems, enhance the quality of inter-personal relationships, and make the meaning clearer. There is a time to stop talking and listen.

Myth #2: "Meanings Are in Words"

In and of itself, a word has no meaning, whether it's spoken or written. It's just a sound, marks on paper, or characters on a computer screen. Meaning resides in people, not words. Other people provide the meaning to connect the dots between the word you've spoken and the meaning you have intended to create. However, sometimes people connect the dots in a way you have not intended. Words are symbols we use to communi-cate with others. Because a symbol is something that represents something else, a symbol, by its very nature, can have different meanings for different people. Even the best wordsmith or professional speech writer can use words that result in missed meaning and uncertainty. Differences in culture, back-ground, education, and experience often explain why words create different mean-ings for different people. When you greet your aunt by enthusiastically demanding, "What's up?" she may find your greeting too informal and think you're being rude. However, to your best buddy, offering a slurred "What's up?" is just a normal way of

Instead of focusing entirely on the message we want to con-vey, we can sometimes com-municate even more effectively when we take the time to be other-oriented—to listen to what others are saying. (Masterfile/Masterfile)

saying "Hello." You intend no disrespect to your aunt, but she may take your collo-quial welcome the wrong way. Our point: just because you've spoken it, don't assume others will always catch what you throw to them. Meanings are in people, not in words.

Myth #3: "Information Equals Communication"

"How many times do I have to tell you not to use the copy machine?" "Can't you read? It's in the syllabus." "It's in the policy and procedure manual." "Are you deaf? I've told you that I love you several times." Each of these exasperated communica-tors seems to have thought erroneously that information is the same thing as com-munication. However, information is not communication. This simple yet powerful principle helps combat the myth that if you say it or write it, then communication has taken place.

Earlier in the chapter, we defined communication at the most basic level as act-ing on information. If you say your message but no one hears it (like the proverbial tree that falls silently in the forest), does that mean there has been communication? The message you thought you sent is not really communication just because you've put your thoughts into a code. Encoding does not always ensure decoding and as we have already discussed, even if someone has decoded the message, it could be differ-ent from the one you intended. Information is not communication.

Myth #4: "Interpersonal Relationship Problems Are Always Communication Problems"

"You don't understand me!" shouts Paul to his exasperated partner Pat, "We just can't communicate anymore!" Paul seems to think the problem he and Pat are having is a communication problem, but Paul and Pat may understand each other perfectly; they may simply disagree. Although it's certainly true that conflict and discord in interpersonal relationships can occur because of misunderstandings, not *all* conflicts and bumpy relationships stem from misunderstandings. There could be several explanations for why a relationship is experiencing turbulence. Perhaps the communication partners are very clear when communicating, but they are so self-centred or self-absorbed that the quality of the relationship suffers. Or, perhaps the communication partners just don't like each other; or, if they do like and understand each other, they just disagree. The message has been understood but rejected. Although missed meaning may be a contributing factor in interpersonal conflict, it's a myth to assume that all relational discord stems from misunderstanding.

Even though one purpose of this course is to help you enhance the quality of your relationships by becoming a better communicator, we don't claim that *all* interper-sonal conflict stems from misunderstanding one another. Nor are we claiming that learning principles and skills of interpersonal communication will solve all your interpersonal relationship problems. One of this text's authors was approached by a potential client who said, "I understand you are a communication consultant. I need help with my communication skills. *Do something to me* to make me a better com-municator." However, communication skill development does not work like Harry Potter's magic wand; there's not something that can be "done to" someone to enhance communication ability. Even if there were a wizard's wand to make all your commu-nication perfectly understood by others, and theirs by you, your interpersonal rela-tionships would undoubtedly still experience stress and conflict.

How to Improve Your Own Interpersonal Communication Effectiveness

Now that we have previewed the study of interpersonal communication, you may be saying to yourself, "Well, that's all well and good, but is it possible to improve my own interpersonal communication? Aren't some people just born to have better interpersonal skills than others?" Just as some people have more musical talent or greater skill at passing a puck, evidence suggests that some people may have an inborn, biological talent for communicating with others.[46] You probably know people who have never had a course in communication but who develop sensitive, caring interpersonal relationships with others.

A growing body of research called the **communibiological approach** to communication suggests that some people inherit certain traits that affect the way they communicate with others. There may be a genetic basis for why people communicate as they do. For example, you or people you know may have been born to have more stage fright or anxiety when communicating with others.[47] Additionally, some people may not be as comfortable interacting in interpersonal situations as others are.

So what are the implications of the communibiological approach to communication? Does this mean you can't improve your interpersonal communication? *Absolutely not!* Some researchers and teachers believe, however, that the communibiological approach gives too much weight to biology and not enough to how we can learn to compensate for what nature did not give us.[48] The underlying premise of our study of interpersonal communication is that you can learn ways to enhance the quality of your interpersonal relationships with others.

Social learning theory suggests that we can learn how to adapt and adjust our behaviour toward others; how we behave is not solely dependent on our genetic makeup. By observing and interacting with others (hence the name *social* learning), we discover that we can adapt and adjust our behaviour. Although biology unquestionably plays a key role in how we behave, we can't blame biology for all aspects of our behaviour. We believe that people can learn how to enhance their communication competence.

To be competent in communication is to communicate in ways that are perceived to be both *effective* and *appropriate*.[49] You communicate effectively when your message is understood by others and achieves its intended effect. For example, if you want your roommate to stop using your hair dryer, and after you talk to your roommate he stops using your hair dryer, your message has been effective.

Competent communication should also be appropriate. By *appropriate*, we mean that the communicator should consider the time, place, and overall context of the message and should be sensitive to the feelings and attitudes of the listener. If you got your roommate to stop using your hair dryer by saying, "If you don't stop using my hair dryer, I'm going to throw your underwear out in the street!" your high-handed tactics would not be perceived as appropriate. Your message might be effective—your roommate might understand you and stop using your hair dryer—but not appropriate; thus, you would not get an award for being a competent communicator. A calm conversation with your roommate that is understood, achieves the intended effect, is appropriate to the time and place, and considers both your needs and the needs of your roommate would be labelled competent. Note that we suggested that your needs as a communicator should be considered when you

communibiological approach. Theoretical perspective that suggests a person's communication behaviour can be predicted based on personal traits that result from his or her genetic background.

social learning theory. Theory of human behaviour that suggests we can learn how to adapt and adjust our behaviour toward others; how we behave is not solely dependent on our genetic or biological makeup.

communicate appropriately with others. Being appropriate does not mean that you abandon your self-respect and always bend to please others.

Although competence may seem like a straightforward concept, there is an important underlying issue: who determines what is appropriate? Communication scholar Mary Jane Collier suggests that competence is a concept based on privilege; to label someone as competent means that another person has made a judgment as to what is appropriate or inappropriate behaviour. Collier asks the following questions: "... competence and acceptance for whom? Who decides the criteria? Who doesn't? Competent or acceptable on the basis of what social and historical context?"[50] What Collier points out is that we have to be careful not to insist on one approach (our own approach) to interpersonal communication competence. *There is no single best way to communicate with others.* There are, however, avenues that can help you become both more effective and more appropriate when communicating with others. We suggest the following six-part strategy for becoming a more effective communicator.

Become Knowledgeable

By reading this chapter, you have already begun to improve your communication skills. Competent communicators are knowledgeable. They know how communication works. They understand the components, principles, and rules of the communication process. As you read on in this book, you will learn theories, principles, concepts, and rules that will permit you to explain and predict how humans communicate.

Understanding these things is a necessary prerequisite for enhancing your interpersonal effectiveness, but this kind of knowledge alone does not make you competent. You would not let someone fix your car's carburetor if he or she had only read a book on the subject. Knowledge must be coupled with skill, and we acquire skill through practice.

Become Skilled

Effective communicators know how to translate knowledge into action. You can memorize the characteristics of a good listener but still not listen well. To develop skill requires practice and helpful feedback from others who can confirm the appropriateness of your actions.

Learning a social skill is not that different from learning how to drive a car or operate a computer.[51] To learn any skill, you must break it down into subskills that you can learn and practise. "Hear it, see it, do it, correct it" is the formula that seems to work best for learning any new behaviours.[52] In this book, we will examine the elements of complex skills such as listening, offer activities that will let you practise the skill, and provide opportunities for you to receive feedback and correct your application of the skill.

Become Motivated

Practising skills requires work. You need to be motivated to use your information and skill. You must want to improve, and you must have a genuine desire to connect with others if you wish to become a competent communicator. You may know people who understand how to drive a car and have the skill to drive, yet are reluctant to get behind the wheel. Or, maybe you know someone who took a course in public speaking but is still too frightened to stand in front of a crowd. Similarly, you may pass a test about interpersonal communication principles with flying colours, but, unless you are motivated to use your new-found skills, your interactions with others may not improve.

Become Flexible

In this book, we do not identify tidy lists of strategies that you can use to "win friends and influence people," as Dale Carnegie has. The same set of skills is not effective in every situation, so competent communicators do not assume that "one size fits all." Rather, they assess each unique situation and adapt their behaviour to achieve the desired outcome. They examine the context, the situation, and the needs, goals, and messages of others to establish and maintain relationships.

Become Ethical

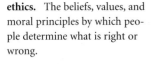

Ethics are the beliefs, values, and moral principles by which we determine what is right or wrong. Ethics and ethical behaviour have long been a critical component of human behaviour. Effective interpersonal communicators are ethical. To be an ethical communicator means to be sensitive to the needs of others, to give people choices rather than forcing them to act a certain way. Unethical communicators believe that they know what other people need, even without asking them for their preferences. As we discuss in Chapter 6, being manipulative and forcing opinions on others usually results in a climate of defensiveness. Effective communicators seek to establish trust and reduce interpersonal barriers, rather than erect them. Ethical communicators keep confidences; they keep private information that others wish to be kept private. They also do not intentionally decrease others' feelings of self-worth. Another key element in being an ethical communicator is honesty. If you intentionally lie or distort the truth, then you are not communicating ethically or effectively. At the end of each chapter, we offer a section called "Focus on Ethics" in which we pose ethical questions to help you explore the ethics of interpersonal relationships.

ethics. The beliefs, values, and moral principles by which people determine what is right or wrong.

other-oriented communicator. One who considers the thoughts, feelings, and perspectives of communication partners while maintaining his or her own integrity.

Become Other-Oriented

The signature concept for our study of interpersonal communication is the goal of becoming other-oriented in relationships. To be an **other-oriented communicator** is to consider the thoughts, needs, experiences, personality, feelings, motives, desires, culture, and goals of our communication partners, while still maintaining our own integrity. The choices we make in forming our messages, in deciding how to best express those messages, and in deciding when and where to deliver those messages will be more effective when we consider the other person's thoughts and feelings. *To emphasize the importance of being an other-oriented communicator, throughout this book, we'll use this margin icon to highlight discussions of being other-oriented.*

Being other-oriented involves a conscious effort to consider the world from the point of view of those with whom you interact. This effort occurs almost automatically when you are communicating with those you like or who are similar to you. Thinking about the thoughts and feelings of those you dislike or who are different from you is more difficult and requires more effort and commitment.

Think about a person you dislike. Do you truly understand the factors in his or her life that have had an impact on the way he or she behaves? Do you appreciate the emotions he or she feels? If you're not confident you can accurately understand the thoughts and feelings of a person you dislike, it probably signals the need to work on your ability to be other-oriented.

Sometimes we are **egocentric communicators**; we create messages without giving much thought to the person who is listening. To be egocentric is to be self-focused and self-absorbed. Scholars of evolution might argue that our tendency to look out for Number One ensures the continuation of the human species and is therefore a good thing. Yet, it is difficult to communicate effectively when we focus exclusively on ourselves. If we fail to adapt our message to our listener, we may not be successful in achieving our intended communication goal. Other people can often perceive whether we're self-focused or other-oriented (especially if the person we're talking with is a sensitive, other-oriented communicator).

Ethical communicators are sensitive to the needs of others.

egocentric communicators. A person who creates messages without giving much thought to the person who is listening; a person who is self-focused and self-absorbed.

When we have a need to purge ourselves emotionally or to confirm our sense of self-importance, we may find ourselves speaking without considering the thoughts and feelings of our listener. However, doing so usually undermines our relationships with others. A self-focused communicator often alienates others. Fortunately, research suggests that, almost by necessity, we adapt to our partner in order to carry on a conversation.[53] This adaptation includes such things as simply asking questions in response to our partner's disclosures, finding topics of mutual interest to discuss, selecting words and examples that are meaningful to our partner, and avoiding topics that we don't feel comfortable discussing with another person.

Adapting messages to others does *not* mean that we tell them only what they want to hear; that would be unethical. Nor does being considerate of others mean abandoning all concern for our own interests; that would be unwise. Other-oriented communicators maintain their own personal integrity while simultaneously being aware of the thoughts and feelings of others. Being other-oriented is more than just being "nice."[54] It involves being principled enough to be considerate of others but making mindful choices about how and when to adapt interpersonal messages to others.

How do you become other-oriented? Being other-oriented is really a collection of skills rather than a single skill. We devote considerable discussion throughout the book to developing this collection of essential communication skills.[55]

Focusing on others begins with an accurate understanding of your self-concept and self-esteem; we discuss these foundation principles in the next chapter. As you will learn in Chapter 3, developing an accurate perception of both yourself and others is an important element of effectively relating to others.

Being other-oriented is more than just having a set of skills or behaviours. It also includes developing positive, healthy attitudes about others. In 1951, Carl Rogers wrote a pioneering book called *Client-Centered Therapy,* which transformed the field of psychotherapy. In it, Rogers explains how genuine positive regard for another

Figure 1.6
Other-Orientation
This figure represents an other-oriented perspective and will be used throughout the textbook.

person and an open and supportive communication climate lay the foundation for trusting relationships. Rogers emphasizes the importance of listening in connection to another human being, which we explore in depth in Chapter 4.

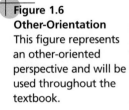 **Becoming Other-Oriented**

CONSIDER OTHERS' NEEDS AND PERSPECTIVES WITHOUT ABANDONING YOUR OWN INTEGRITY

At the heart of our study of interpersonal communication is the principle of becoming other-oriented. To be other-oriented means that you become aware of others' thoughts, feelings, goals, and needs and respond appropriately in ways that offer personal support. It does not mean that you abandon your own needs and interests or that you diminish your self-respect. To have integrity is to behave in a thoughtful, integrated way toward others while being true to your core beliefs and values. To be other-oriented is to have integrity; you don't just agree with others or give in to the demands of others in encounters with them.

Do you know a sycophant? A *sycophant* is a person who praises others only to manipulate emotions so that his or her needs are met. Sycophants may look as though they are focused on others, but their behaviour is merely self-serving. A sycophant is not other-oriented. A person who is truly other-oriented is aware of the thoughts, feelings, and needs of others and then mindfully and honestly chooses to respond to those needs. To enhance your other-oriented awareness and skill takes practice. Throughout the book, we will offer both principles and opportunities to practise the skill and mindset of being other-oriented.

To develop an awareness of other-orientation with a communication partner, role-play the following interpersonal situations in two ways. First, role-play the scene as a communicator who is not other-oriented but rather self-focused. Then re-enact the same scene as a communicator who is other-oriented—someone who considers the thoughts and feelings of the other person while maintaining his or her own integrity.

Suggested situations:

- Return a broken DVD player to a department store salesperson.
- Correct a grocery store cashier who has scanned an item at the wrong price.
- Meet with a teacher who has given your son or daughter a failing grade.
- Ask your professor for a one-day extension on a paper that is due tomorrow.
- Ask someone for a donation to a worthy cause.
- Ask a professor for permission to get into a class that has reached its maximum enrolment.
- Accept an unappealing compact disc as a gift from a friend.
- Remind your son or daughter that he or she needs to practise the cello.

People gain insight into others' feelings by being sensitive to non-verbal messages as well as to the explicit verbal statements they make. We discuss verbal communication skills in Chapter 5 and non-verbal communication skills in Chapter 6. The skills and principles of managing conflict presented in Chapter 7 provide tools and ideas for understanding others when you disagree.

Becoming other-oriented also involves adapting to those who may be considerably different from you. Your communication partner may have a different cultural background, be of the opposite sex, or be older or younger than you. In Chapter 8, we explore some of these differences, especially cultural differences that can sometimes challenge effective and appropriate communication with others; we also suggest specific strategies to help you adapt to others who differ from yourself. Throughout the text, we include "Understanding Diversity" boxes like the one that appears in this section to help you develop your sensitivity to important issues related to cultural diversity.

 Understanding Diversity

CULTURAL DIFFERENCES CAN LEAD TO MISINTERPRETATION

In a culturally diverse society, we can make mistakes without meaning to offend or confuse the other person. Our goal is not to be insulting or misunderstood; it's just that cultures differ and sometimes the differences can lead to unintended errors.

The following true story of an international communication misunderstanding demonstrates the importance of making sure that the message being conveyed is the message intended. Not long ago, a delegation of Canadian business people visited Japan to promote international trade. As a spontaneous gesture of goodwill toward their Japanese hosts, one of the Canadian delegates decided to sport a decorative shirt that bore some Japanese characters on an ornate background. Only toward the end of a dinner reception was the Canadian delegate informed by a Japanese journalist that the characters were an advertisement message equivalent to "Eat at Joe's Diner." Surely some of the Japanese business hosts must have interpreted the Canadian's "goodwill" gesture as an inappropriate form of cheap advertising.

The same kinds of misunderstandings can happen in interpersonal exchanges between people with different first languages. Meanings are fragile. Consider the following exchanges between two good friends, Paula (an anglophone) and Marie-Joseph (a francophone):

Paula: It was just the way my boss *looked* at me during my presentation. He says it went well, but I'm not so sure.

Marie-Joseph: Paula, maybe you are being a bit too sensible.

Paula: I sure wish I could find a copy of Peter C. Newman's latest book to buy for my father's birthday.

Marie-Joseph: Have you tried the library on Broadview Street?

Only if Paula knows French would she realize that *sensible* is the French word for *sensitive*, which is the message Marie-Joseph wished to convey in the first dialogue. *Librairie* is the French word for *bookstore*, which is what Marie-Joseph was actually referring to in the second dialogue. It's always wise to question your communication partners to make sure they share your understanding of a word or symbol.

Chapters 9, 10, and 11 build on the principles of interpersonal relationships introduced in this chapter to help you understand how relationships evolve, are maintained, and sometimes end. The final chapter applies our discussion of other-oriented interpersonal communication to various contexts such as families, friends, and colleagues. Our goal is to help you to better understand how you relate to others and to develop enhanced interpersonal skills.

▶ Recap

HOW CAN YOU IMPROVE YOUR COMMUNICATION EFFECTIVENESS?

Become Knowledgeable	Learn principles, concepts, and ideas.
Become Skilled	Translate knowledge into action.
Become Motivated	Resolve to use your knowledge and skill.
Become Flexible	Select the right behaviour; one size does not fit all.
Become Ethical	Offer choices, establish trust, and reduce barriers to interpersonal communication.
Become Other-Oriented	Focus on others rather than only on your needs.

Summary

At the most basic level, communication is the process of acting on information. Human communication is the process of making sense out of the world and sharing that sense with others. Interpersonal communication is the process of developing a unique relationship with another person by interacting and sharing mutual influence. Early models viewed human communication as a simple message-transfer process. Later models evolved to view communication as interaction and then as transaction. Contemporary approaches to interpersonal communication emphasize the simultaneous nature of influencing others. They identify seven key components in the interpersonal communication process: source, receiver, message, channel, noise, context, and feedback. Electronic media may encourage further evolution of our models for interpersonal communication.

The goal of this book is to help you improve your interpersonal skills and relationships. Interpersonal relationships range from impersonal to intimate, are complementary or symmetrical, are governed by rules, and involve both content and relationship dimensions. The most effective interpersonal communicators are not swayed by common myths about communication. Rather, they are knowledgeable, skilled, motivated, flexible, ethical, and other-oriented. Learning to connect with others is the key to establishing satisfying relationships.

For Discussion and Review

🖤 Focus on Critical Thinking

1. Analyze a recent interpersonal exchange with someone that did not go well. Write down some of the dialogue. Did the other person understand you? Did your communication have the intended effect? Was your message ethical?

2. Make a relationship scale on a piece of paper and label it "impersonal" at one end and "intimate" at the other. Place your family members and closest friends on the scale; then compare and discuss your entries with your classmates.

3. What rules govern your relationship with your mother? Your father? Your communication teacher? Your roommate or spouse?

Focus on Ethics

4. Think about your primary goal for this course. Is it to develop strategies to achieve your own personal goals? Is it to develop sensitivity to the needs of others? What is behind your desire to achieve your goal? Is your purpose ethical?

5. Your parents want you to visit them for the holidays. You would rather spend the time with a friend. You don't want to hurt your parents' feelings, so you tell them that you have an important project that you are working on; you won't be able to come home for the holidays. Your message is understood. It achieves the intended effect; you don't go home. Explain why you think your message is ethical or unethical.

For Your Journal

1. Try to identify at least three personal goals for improving your interpersonal relationships. Write several specific objectives that you hope to accomplish by the end of this course.

2. Briefly, describe a recent communication exchange that was not effective. Perhaps you or your communication partner did not understand the message, or the message may not have achieved its intended goal, or it may have been unethical. Analyze the communication exchange, applying the components of communication discussed in this chapter. For example, what was the communication context? What were sources of internal and external noise? Did you have problems encoding and decoding? Were there problems with the communication channel?

3. Keep a one-day log of your electronically mediated interactions (e.g., phone calls, e-mail messages, fax messages). Describe each one, noting whether there was a greater emphasis on the content or emotional elements of the messages you exchanged during the interaction.

Learning with Others

1. Working with a group of your classmates, develop a five-minute lesson to teach one of the following concepts to your class:

   a. How interpersonal relationships range from impersonal to intimate

   b. Human communication as action

   c. Human communication as interaction

   d. Human communication as transaction

   e. How interpersonal relationships are governed by rules

   f. How to improve communication effectiveness

2. Working with a small group of one to two classmates, log onto your Research Navigator. Your task is to find at least one article that offers some suggestions for improving your interpersonal skills. Briefly summarize the article and decide which of the six strategies it best fits. For example, does it offer specific skills, is it a research article that will expand your knowledge base, or does it combine more than one strategy area? Share your findings with the class. This is a fun way to introduce the class and to have some lively discussion about what you need to learn to become a more effective communicator.

Weblinks

www.cmha.ca/bins/content_page.asp?cid=4-42-214   From the Canadian Mental Health Association: Ten tips for mental health.

www.cpa-apc.org   This is the home page for the Canadian Psychiatric Association.

www.newconversations.net   This site provides self-help information, encouragement, and teaching materials for better communication at work, with family and friends, and in the community. It also offers free books, essays, and exercises to help you improve your interpersonal skills.

www.queendom.com/tests/index.html   Take the social anxiety test to assess how comfortable you are when interacting with other people. Then test your own level of interpersonal communication skills with the Communication Skills Test.

www.communicationarena.com/links_assoc.asp   This is the Communication Arena, with weblinks to many associations including communication associations.

www.natcom.org   The National Communication Association is the largest association of communication scholars and professionals in the world. This site provides a wealth of information about the study of human communication.

2 Interpersonal Communication and Self

After you study this chapter

you should be able to . . .

1. Define, compare, and contrast the meanings of "self-concept" and "self-esteem."

2. Identify factors that shape the development of your self-concept.

3. List and describe strategies for improving your self-esteem.

4. Describe how your self-concept affects your relationships with others.

5. Describe the process of appropriate self-disclosure, including two models of self-disclosure.

• Self-Concept: Who Are You?

• Self-Esteem: Your Self-Worth

• Improving Your Self-Esteem

• How Self-Concept and Self-Esteem Affect Interpersonal Communication and Relationships

• Self-disclosure: Connecting Self to Others Through Talk

• Characteristics of Self-Disclosure

*There's only one corner of the universe
you can be certain of improving, and
that's your own self.*

ALDOUS HUXLEY

Philosophers suggest that there are three basic questions to which we all seek answers: (1) Who am I? (2) Why am I here? and (3) Who are all these others? In this chapter, we will focus on these essential questions. We view them as progressive. Grappling with the question of who you are and seeking to define a purpose for your life are fundamental to understanding others and becoming other-oriented in your interpersonal communication and your relationships.

Fundamentally, all of your communication starts or ends with you. When you are the communicator, you intentionally or unintentionally code your thoughts and emotions to be interpreted by another. When you receive a message, you interpret the information through your own frame of reference. Your self-image and self-worth, as well as your needs, values, beliefs, and attitudes, serve as filters for your communication with others. As you develop and establish relationships, you may become more aware of these filters, and, perhaps, you will have the desire to alter them. A close relationship often provides the impetus for change.

To better understand the role that self-concept plays in interpersonal communication, we will explore the first two basic questions, "Who am I?" and "Why am I here?" by trying to discover the meaning of self. We will examine the multi-faceted dimensions of our self-concept, learn how it develops, and compare self-concept with self-esteem. Then we will move to the third basic question, "Who are all these others?" What you choose to tell and not tell others about yourself reveals important clues about who you are, what you value, and how you relate to another person. We will explore the process of self-disclosure—purposefully revealing information about yourself—later in this chapter.

Self-Concept: Who Are You?

You can begin your journey of self-discovery by trying the exercise in the Building Your Skills box "Who Are You?"

Building Your Skills

WHO ARE YOU?

Consider this question: Who are you? More specifically, ask yourself this question 10 times. Write your responses in the spaces provided here or on a separate piece of paper. It may be challenging to identify 10 aspects of yourself; the Spanish writer Cervantes said, "... to know thyself... is the most difficult lesson in the world." Your answers will help you begin to explore your self-concept and self-esteem in this chapter.

I am _____   I am _____

I am _____   I am _____

I am _____   I am _____

I am _____   I am _____

I am _____   I am _____

---

self. The sum total of who a person is; a person's central inner force.

self-concept. A person's subjective description of who the person thinks he or she is.

attitude. Learned predisposition to respond to a person, object, or idea in a favourable or unfavourable way.

How did you answer the question, "Who are you?" Perhaps your self-descriptions identify activities in which you participate. Or they may list groups and organizations to which you belong or some of the roles you assume, such as student, child, or parent. All of these things are, indeed, parts of your **self**, the sum total of who you are. Karen Horney defines "self" as "that central inner force, common to all human beings and yet unique in each, which is the deep source of growth."[1]

Your answers are also part of your **self-concept**. Your self-concept is your subjective description of who you *think* you are—it is filtered through your own perceptions. For example, you may have great musical talent, but you may not believe in it enough to think of yourself as a musician. We can view self-concept as the labels we consistently use to describe ourselves to others.

Who you are is also reflected in the attitudes, beliefs, and values that you hold. These are learned constructs that shape your behaviour and self-image. An **attitude** is a learned predisposition to respond to a person, object, or idea in a favourable or unfavourable way. Attitudes reflect what you like and what you don't like. If you like school, butter pecan ice cream, and your mother, you hold positive attitudes toward these things. You were not born with a fondness for butter pecan ice cream; you learned to like it, just as some people learn to enjoy the taste of snails, raw fish, or puréed turnips.

Beliefs are the ways in which you structure your understanding of reality—what is true and what is false. Most of your beliefs are based on previous experience. You trust that the sun will rise in the morning and that you will get burned if you put your hand on a hot stove.

How are attitudes and beliefs related? They often function quite independently of one another. You may have a favourable attitude toward something and still believe negative things about it. You may believe, for example, that your college hockey team will not win the provincial championship this year, though you may be a big fan. Or you may believe that a God exists, yet not always like what that God does. Beliefs have to do with what is true or not true; attitudes reflect likes and dislikes.

Values are enduring concepts of good and bad, right and wrong. Your values are more resistant to change than either your attitudes or your beliefs. They are also more difficult for most people to identify. Values are so central to who you are that it is difficult to isolate them. For example, when you go to the supermarket, you may spend a few minutes deciding which cookies to buy, but you probably do not spend much time deciding whether you will steal the cookies or pay for them. Our values are instilled in us by our earliest interpersonal relationships; for almost all of us, our parents shape our values. The chart in Figure 2.1 shows that values are central to our behaviour and concept of self, and that what we believe to be true or false stems from our values. Attitudes are at the outer edge of the circle because they are the most likely to change. You may like your co-worker today but not tomorrow, even though you *believe* the person will come to work every day and you still *value* the concept of friendship.

beliefs.   The ways in which you structure your understanding of reality—what is true and what is false.

values.   Enduring concepts of good and bad, right and wrong.

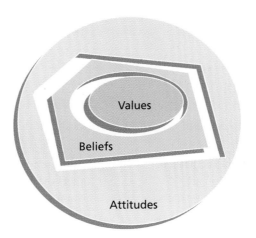

Figure 2.1
Values, Beliefs, and Attitudes in Relation to Self

► **Recap**

WHO YOU ARE IS REFLECTED IN YOUR ATTITUDES, BELIEFS, AND VALUES

	Definition	Dimensions	Example
Attitudes	Learned predispositions to respond favourably or unfavourably toward something.	Likes–Dislikes	You like ice cream, incense, and cats.
Beliefs	The ways in which we structure reality.	True–False	You believe your parents love you.
Values	Enduring concepts of what is right and wrong.	Good–Bad	You value honesty and truth.

One Or Many Selves?

Shakespeare's famous line, "To thine own self be true," suggests that you have a single self to which you can be true. Do you have just one self? Or is there a more real "you" buried somewhere within? "I'm just not myself this morning," sighs Sandy, as she drags herself out the front door to head for her office. If she is not herself, then *who is she?* Most scholars conclude that we have a core set of behaviours, attitudes, beliefs, and values that constitute our self—the sum total of who we are. However, our *concept* of self can and does change, depending on circumstances and influences.

In addition, our self-concepts are often different from the way others see us. We almost always behave differently in public than we do in private. Sociologist Erving Goffman suggests that, like actors and actresses, we have "on stage" behaviours when others are watching and "backstage" behaviours when they are not.

Perhaps the most enduring and widely-accepted framework for describing who you are was developed by the philosopher William James. He identified three components of the self: the material self, the social self, and the spiritual self. We will continue our exploration by examining these components.

Building Your Skills

DIMENSIONS OF YOUR SELF

Take another look at your responses to the question, "Who are you?" Divide your list according to James's three components of the self. If nothing on your original list relates to one of these "selves," make a new entry here so that you have a response for each of them.

Material Self

References to the physical elements that reflect who you are.

Example:

I collect antiques.

_____

_____

_____

_____

Social Self

References to interactions with others that reflect who you are.

Example:

I am a member of the Chess Club.

_____

_____

_____

_____

Spiritual Self

References to your reflections about values, morals, and beliefs.

Example:

I believe in a higher spiritual being.

_____

_____

_____

_____

The Material Self

Perhaps you've heard the statement, "You are what you eat." The **material self** goes a step further by suggesting, "You are what you have." The material self is a total of all of the tangible things you own: your possessions, your home, your body. As you examine your list of responses to the question, "Who are you?" note whether any of your statements refers to one of your physical attributes or something you own.

One element of the material self gets considerable attention in our culture: the body. Do you like the way you look? Most of us, if we're honest, would like to change something about our appearance. When there is a discrepancy between our desired material self and our self-concept, we may respond to eliminate the discrepancy. We may try to lose weight, change the shape of our nose, or acquire more hair. The multi-billion-dollar diet industry is just one of many that profit from our collective desire to change our appearance. We also attempt to keep up with the proverbial Joneses by wanting more expensive clothes, cars, and homes. By extension, what we own becomes who we are. The bigger, better, and more luxurious our possessions, we may subconsciously conclude, the better *we* are.

The Social Self

Look at your "Who are you?" list once more. How many of your responses relate to your **social self**, the part of you that interacts with others? William James believed that you have many social selves— that depending on the friend, family member, colleague, or acquaintance with whom you are interacting, you change the way you are. A person has, said James, as many social selves as there are people who recognize him or her.

For example, when you talk to your best friend, you are willing to "let down your hair" and reveal more thoughts and feelings than you would in a conversation with your communication professor, or even your parents. Each relationship that you have with another person is unique because you bring to it a unique social self.

material self.   Your concept of self as reflected in a total of all the tangible things you own.

social self.   Your concept of self as developed through your personal, social interactions with others.

spiritual self.   Your concept of self based on your thoughts and introspections about your values and moral standards.

Peter Blake sought to explore his self-dimensions by painting his self-portrait. What qualities does this self-portrait reveal about the artist?
(Tate Gallery, London/Art Resources)

The Spiritual Self

Your **spiritual self** consists of all your internal thoughts and introspections about your values and moral standards. It is not dependent on what you own or with whom you talk; it is the essence of who you *think* you are, and of your *feelings* about yourself, apart from external evaluations. It is an amalgam of your religious beliefs and your sense of who you are in relation to other forces in the universe. Your spiritual self is the part of you that answers the question, "Why am I here?"

▶ **Recap**

WILLIAM JAMES'S DIMENSIONS OF SELF

	Definition	Examples
Material Self	All of the physical elements that reflect who you are.	Possessions, car, home, body, clothes.
Social Self	The self as reflected through your interactions with others; actually, a variety of selves that respond to changes in situations and roles.	Your informal self interacting with your best friend; your formal self inter acting with your professors.
Spiritual Self	Introspections about values, morals, and beliefs.	Religious belief or disbelief; regard for life in all its forms.

How Your Self-Concept Develops

James's three elements define the dimensions of the self, but they do not tell us where our "Who am I?" responses come from. In truth, we can only speculate about their origins. Some psychologists and sociologists have advanced theories that suggest we learn who we are through four basic means: (1) our interactions with other individuals, (2) our association with groups, (3) roles we assume, and (4) our own labels. Like James's framework, this one does not cover every base in our study of self, but its constructs can provide some clues about how our own self-concepts develop.

Interaction with Individuals

looking-glass. Concept that suggests you learn who you are based on your interactions with others, which are reflected back to you.

reflected appraisal. Another term for the looking-glass self. You learn who you are based on how others treat you.

In 1902, Charles Horton Cooley first advanced the notion that we form our self-concepts by seeing ourselves in a kind of figurative **looking glass**: we learn who we are by interacting with others, much as we look into a mirror and see our reflection. This is also referred to as **reflected appraisal**. In other words, we develop self concepts that often match or correspond to the ways in which we believe others see us. Like Cooley, George Herbert Mead also believed that our behaviour and our sense of who we are, are a consequence of our relationship with others. Harry Stack Sullivan theorized that from birth to death, our self changes primarily because of how people respond to us. One sage noted, "We are not only our brother's keeper; we are our brother's maker."

The process begins at birth. Our names, one of the primary ways we identify ourselves, are given to us by someone else. During the early years of our lives, our parents are the key individuals who shape who we are. If our parents encouraged us to play the piano, we probably play now. As we become less dependent on our parents, our friends become highly influential in shaping our attitudes, beliefs, and values. Friends continue to provide feedback on how well we perform certain tasks. This, in turn, helps us shape our sense of identity as adults—we must acknowledge our talents in math, language, or art in our own minds before we can say that we are mathematicians, linguists, or artists.

Fortunately, not *every* comment affects our sense of who we think we are or our own self-worth. We are likely to incorporate the comments of others into our self-concept under three conditions:

- First, we are more likely to believe another's statement if he or she repeats something we have heard several times. If one person casually tells us we have a talent for singing, we are not likely to launch a search for an agent and a recording contract. However, if several individuals tell us on many different occasions that we have a talent for singing, we may decide to do something about it.

- Second, we are more likely to value another's statements if he or she has already earned our confidence. If we believe the individual is competent, trustworthy, and qualified to make a judgment about us, then we are more likely to believe it. You would be more likely to think you were a talented singer if you heard it from singing star Céline Dion rather than your Aunt Sally. Again, while we are very young, our parents are the dominant voices of credibility and authority. If they tell us repeatedly that we are spoiled and sloppy, then we will probably come to view ourselves that way. If they tell us we are loving, gifted, and charming, we are likely to believe it.

- Third, we are likely to incorporate another's comments into our own concept of self if the comments are consistent with other comments and our own experience. If your boss tells you that you work too slowly, but for years people have been urging you to slow down, then your previous experience will probably encourage you to challenge your boss's evaluation.

Others also influence our beliefs about who we are through **social comparison**, assessing ourselves in relations to others' skills, abilities, traits, and behaviours. We use social comparison to further understand ourselves in relation to others. We compare ourselves against **reference groups**. Obviously, the groups that we choose to measure ourselves against have a major impact on our self-concept. For example, if you wish to find out if you are smarter than other students in a particular course, you ask others how they did on a recent test. If you scored higher than everyone else, you may label yourself "smart," and if you scored lower than everyone else, you may label yourself "dumb." This type of social comparison is about deciding whether we are *superior* or *inferior* to others. We also use social comparison to gauge how much we are like (the same as) others or how much we differ from others. For example, if you enjoy classical music and peers at school belittle you for this musical preference, you may decide that you have strange taste in music.

Obviously, the outcome of these social comparisons depends very much on the people or groups we use for measurement. Unfortunately, some of us compare ourselves to inappropriate reference groups. Several research studies have illustrated the power of reference groups in developing poor self-concepts and self-esteem (read more on social comparison and self-esteem in the next section). Recent research on body image has illustrated the "quest for thin" and how many people try vainly to reach target weights that are unrealistic or even dangerous to their health. A recent Canadian study demonstrates the power of wanting to be thin in young people: 27 percent of girls aged 12 to 18 years had disordered attitudes and behaviours, including thinking they were fat, binge eating, self-induced vomiting, and current dieting.[2]

Association with Groups

I'm a Liberal. I'm a Girl Guide Leader. I'm a Hindu. I'm a coach. I'm a member of the Lakeshore Dirt Riders. Each of these self-descriptive statements has something in common. They answer the "Who are you?" question by providing identification with a group or organization. Reflect once more on your responses to the "Who are you?" question. How many responses associate you with a group? Religious groups, political groups, ethnic groups, social groups, study groups, and occupational and professional groups play important roles in determining our self-concept. Some of

social comparison. A process whereby we assess our traits, skills, beliefs, and so on by comparing ourselves with selected others.

reference groups. Groups selected by an individual to compare his or her abilities, characteristics, or some other aspect of personality.

these groups we are born into; others we choose on our own. Either way, these group associations are significant parts of our identities. In the *In Canada* box, you will find the compelling true story of Ian Stewart, a Canadian journalist, who describes being shot while on the job. Still seeing himself as a writer and a journalist, he felt the need to document the tragic events and his slow recovery.

In Canada...

A LONG JOURNEY HOME

These are a few excerpts from the story of Ian Stewart, a Canadian journalist who was shot on January 9, 1999, while covering a civil war in Africa. His award-winning story from November 24, 1999, is the account of his courageous struggle back toward health after being shot in the head.

I floated in a grey fog illuminated by the flickering of fluorescent lights. Someone was calling my name over and over, but the voice sounded far away. Blurry faces hovered over me. Shadows, then gone . . .

Wavering on that boundary between sleep and awareness, I couldn't lift my head from the pillow... Something was awfully wrong. Why couldn't I feel my leg?

Weeks drifted by. The mist that had enshrouded my brain began to lift. Destruction and death haunted my hospital dreams. Silhouettes of palm trees swayed against a cobalt sky streaked red and yellow by tracer bullets. Waking hours were no better. Lying on rubber sheets, I struggled to stop the walls as they spun by.

Adding to the torment, I have never been able to remember what happened when we were shot. With no recollection of the most cataclysmic moment of my life, each day is a battle against the incomprehensible.

Of course, I have been told how it happened. Our station wagon turned a corner and came upon five armed men in American-style jeans and flip-flops. Oddly, one was wearing a bowler hat. He raised his automatic rifle and fired a burst. Our escort returned fire, killing the shooter and another rebel. It was over in seconds. David had been cut by flying glass. I had been shot in the head. Myles had been killed instantly, the 24th AP journalist to die in the line of duty in the organization's 151 years...

Over the next several hours, David and AP Abidjan correspondent Tim Sullivan (now bureau chief) saved my life, pleading and cajoling my way onto a succession of airplanes that would hop across Africa and on to England and modern medical care. It was late Monday night by the time I was carried into London's Hospital for Neurology and Neurosurgery. With the dirty field dressing still around my head, I was wheeled past a shocked couple who had just rushed from Toronto...

I can't say when I began to realize the gravity of my wound. Because of the very nature of a brain injury, patients often find it hard to understand and almost impossible to accept. The consequences of my injury were almost entirely physical. My left arm and hand were paralysed, my left leg impaired...

But there were other complications. For days, I struggled just to understand where I was... My brain was a crystal goblet shattered into a million slivers of fading dreams and dashed hopes. I have been piecing it back together, one sliver at a time... Ten weeks after the shooting, I returned to my parents' home on Toronto's Lake Ontario waterfront.

For months I have struggled to adjust to life with a disability. I don't ever want to forget even the smallest detail of this experience. Two months after returning to Toronto, I have improved enough to walk with a cane. On June 3, a Thursday, I walk into a medical supply centre to return my wheelchair.

Once I was an athlete, a football player. Now I shuffle a few yards, stop to catch my breath, sit for a spell. As a wire service reporter, I used to whip out several stories a day. Now I spend months on this one, pecking at the keys with my one good hand. My therapist says that in time, my left arm will regain some function. How much is impossible to say...

Myles, David and I were naive to hope our reporting could make people care about a little war in Africa. In fact, Freetown might never have made your daily newspaper had it not been for the death of one western journalist and wounding of another.

Will I continue to work as a journalist when I am well enough to work? Yes, and most likely I'll go back overseas.

Will I risk my life for a story again? No. Not even if the world cares next time.

Source: Ian Stewart, "A Long Journey Home." November 24, 1999, **www. apme.com/writing_awards/stewart_ story.html.** *Used with permission of The Canadian Press.*

As we have already noted, peer pressure is a powerful force in shaping attitudes and behaviour, and adolescents are particularly susceptible to it. However, adolescents are not alone in allowing the attitudes, beliefs, and values of others to shape their expectations and behaviour. To varying degrees, most adults ask themselves, "What will the neighbours think?" and "What will my family think?" when they are making choices.

Associating with groups is especially important for people who are not part of the dominant culture. Some gays and lesbians, for example, may find the support provided by associating with other gays and lesbians to be beneficial to their well-being. The groups you associate with provide not only information about your identity but also needed social support.

Roles We Assume

Look again at your answers to the "Who are you?" question. Perhaps you see words or phrases that signify a role you often assume. Father, aunt, sister, uncle, manager, salesperson, teacher, and student are labels that imply certain expectations for behaviour, and they are important in shaping self-concept. Couples who live together before they marry often report that marriage alters their relationship. Before, they may have shared domestic duties, such as doing dishes and laundry. However, when they assume the labels of "husband" and "wife," they may slip into traditional roles. Husbands don't do laundry. Wives don't mow the grass. These stereotypical role expectations that they learned long ago may require extensive discussion and negotiation. Couples who report the highest satisfaction with marriage agree on their expectations regarding roles ("We agree that I'll do laundry and you'll mow the grass").[3]

One reason we assume traditional roles automatically is that our gender group asserts a powerful influence from birth on. As soon as parents know the sex of their child, many begin placing their children in the group by following cultural rules. They may paint the nursery pink for a girl, blue for a boy. Boys may get a catcher's mitt, a train set, or a hockey stick for their birthdays; girls may get dolls, frilly dresses, and tea sets. These cultural conventions and expectations play a major role in shaping our self-concept and our behaviour. We describe male babies as strong, solid, and independent; female babies are cute, cuddly, and sweet.[4] Recent research suggests that, until the age of three, children themselves are not acutely aware of sex roles. Between the ages of three and five, however, masculine and feminine roles begin to emerge,[5] and they are usually solidified between the ages of five and seven.

In North American culture, it is often accepted, or even encouraged, for boys to exhibit rough-and-tumble, aggressive behaviour when they interact with one another.
(Tony Freeman/ PhotoEdit)

androgynous role. A gender role that includes both masculine and feminine qualities.

symbolic interaction theory. The theory that people make sense of the world on the basis of their interactions with other people.

Although it is changing, North American culture is still male-dominated. What we consider appropriate and inappropriate behaviour is often different for males and females. In group and team meetings, for example, task-oriented, male-dominated roles are valued more than feminine, relationship-building roles.[6] We often applaud fathers who work 60 hours a week as "diligent and hard-working" but criticize mothers who do the same as "neglectful and selfish." Although this kind of example is becoming outdated as society slowly changes, it can still be observed in many workplaces.

Although our culture defines certain roles as masculine or feminine, we still exercise individual choices about our gender roles. One researcher developed an inventory designed to assess whether you play traditional masculine, feminine, or androgynous roles.[7] Because an **androgynous role** is both masculine and feminine, this role encompasses a greater repertoire of actions and behaviours.

Applying Theory and Research

SYMBOLIC INTERACTION THEORY

We defined human communication as the way we make sense of the world and share that sense with others by creating meaning through verbal and non-verbal messages. **Symbolic interaction theory** is based on the assumption that we each make sense of the world based on our interactions with others. We interpret what a word, symbol, or experience means based, in part, on how other people react to our use of words and symbols. Even our own understanding of who we think we are (our self-concept) is influenced by who others tell us we are. Central to understanding ourselves is understanding the importance of other people in shaping our self-understanding. Symbolic interaction theory has had a major influence on communication theory because of the pervasive way our communication with others influences our attitudes, beliefs, values, and self-concept.

George Herbert Mead is credited with the development of symbolic interaction theory, although Mead did not write extensively about his theory.[8] One of Mead's students, Herbert Blumer, actually coined the term "symbolic interaction" to describe the process through which our interactions with others influence our thoughts about others, our life experiences, and ourselves. Mead believed that we cannot have a concept of our own self-identity without interactions with other people.

APPLYING THE RESEARCH TO YOUR LIFE

Symbolic interaction theory suggests that you make sense out of your world and your life experiences based on the influence of your family, friends, and other people with whom you communicate. Because of the far-reaching influence of others on your life, it's sometimes hard to be consciously aware of how other people shape your thoughts about yourself and others. Consider the following questions to explore how other people have shaped your understanding of your self-concept and attitudes you hold.

1. How have other people helped shape your own sense of your skills and talents? Identify specific people and recall things they have said to you that have either reinforced or contradicted your understanding of your own abilities and skills.

2. How do you and your friends and family members talk about your attitudes toward the college or university you now attend? How do other people, especially your family and friends, describe your school, either positively or negatively? How do their comments influence your own attitudes about your school?

3. Has your own concept of who you are undergone dramatic changes? What role did the comments and expressed attitudes of your family, friends, and co-workers have on how you changed your self-concept?

Source: George Herbert Mead, Mind, Self, and Society (Chicago: University of Chicago Press, 1934).

Self-Labels

Although our self-concept is deeply affected by others, we are not blank slates for them to write on. The labels we use to describe our own attitudes, beliefs, values, and actions also play a role in shaping our self-concept.

Where do we acquire our labels? One way that we label ourselves is through a process of self-reflexiveness. We interpret what we experience; we are self-reflexive. **Self-reflexiveness** is the human ability to think about what we are doing while we are doing it. We talk to ourselves about ourselves. We are both participants and observers in all that we do. This dual role encourages us to use labels to describe who we are.

When you were younger, perhaps you dreamed of becoming an NHL hockey player or a movie star. Your coach or your teacher may have told you that you were a great player or a terrific actor, but as you matured, you probably began observing yourself more critically. You scored no goals; you did not get the starring role in local theatre productions. So you self-reflexively decided that you were not, deep down, a hockey player or an actor, even though others may have labelled you as "talented." However, sometimes, through this self-observation, we discover strengths that encourage us to assume new labels. A woman we know never thought of herself as "heroic" until she went through 72 hours of labour before giving birth and then nursed her baby right after delivery.

Your Personality

The concept of personality is central to **psychology**, the study of how our thinking influences how we behave. According to psychologist Lester Lefton, your **personality** consists of a set of enduring internal predispositions and behavioural characteristics that, together, describe how you react to your environment.[9] Understanding the forces that shape your personality is central to increasing your awareness of your self-concept and how you relate to others. Your personality influences whether you are outgoing or shy, humorous or serious, mellow or nervous, and a host of other descriptions that could be used to describe general traits or characteristics about you. There remains a considerable debate as to how much of your personality is influenced by genetics— traits you inherit from your ancestors—and how much is learned behaviour. Does nature or nurture play the predominant role in your personality? As we noted in Chapter 1, the communibiological approach to communication suggests that a major factor affecting how people communicate with others is genetic makeup.[10] Others argue that although it's true that communication behaviour is influenced by genes, we should not forget that humans can learn to adjust and adapt.[11]

One personality characteristic that communication researchers have spent considerable time studying is comfort or discomfort with interactions with other people. Some people just don't like talking with others.[12] In interpersonal communication situations, we may say someone is shy. **Shyness** is the behavioural tendency not to talk with others. One study found that about 40 percent of adults reported they were shy.[13] In public-speaking situations, we say a person has stage fright; a better term to describe this feeling is "communication apprehension." **Communication apprehension**, according to communication experts James McCroskey and Virginia Richmond, is "the fear or anxiety associated with either real or anticipated communication with another person or persons."[14] One study found that up to 80 percent of the population experiences some degree of nervousness or apprehension when they speak in public.[15] Another study found that about 20 percent of people are considerably anxious when they give a speech.[16] What makes some people apprehensive about communicating with others? Again, we get back to

self-reflexiveness. The human ability to think about what we are doing while we are doing it.

psychology. Study of how thinking influences behaviour.

personality. Set of enduring internal predispositions and behavioural characteristics that, as a whole, describes how people react to their environment.

shyness. Tendency not to talk or interact with other people. A discomfort or inhibition in interpersonal situations that interferes with the pursuit of goals.

communication apprehension. Fear or anxiety associated with either real or anticipated communication with other people.

willingness to communicate.
General characteristic that describes an individual's tendency to be shy or apprehensive about communicating with others.

the nature–nurture issue. Heredity plays an important role in whether you are going to feel nervous or anxious when communicating with someone else. However, so does whether you were reinforced for talking with others as a child, as well as other experiences that are part of your culture and learning.

Your overall **willingness to communicate** with others is a general way of summarizing the shyness or apprehension that you feel when talking with others in a variety of situations, including interpersonal conversations. If you are unwilling to communicate with others, you will be less comfortable in a career that forces you to interact with others. To assess your willingness to communicate, take the self-test developed by McCroskey and Richmond in the Building Your Skills box below. The test will give you an overall score as well as a score in specific communication situations such as meetings, interpersonal conversations, communicating with strangers, and communicating with friends.

Understanding the factors that influence your self-concept—such as your interactions with individuals and groups, the roles you assume, your self-labels, and your personality, including your overall comfort level in communicating with others—can help you understand who you are and why you interact (or don't interact) with others. However, it's not only who you are that influences your communication; your overall sense of self-esteem or self-worth also affects how you express yourself and respond to others.

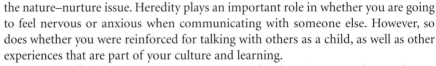

Building Your Skills

Assessing Your Willingness to Communicate

Willingness-to-Communicate (WTC) Scale

Directions: In the following 20 situations, a person might choose to communicate or not to communicate. Presume you have *completely free choice.* Determine the percentage of times you would *choose to initiate communication* in each type of situation. Indicate in the space at the left what percentage of the time you would choose to communicate. Choose any numbers between 0 and 100.

_____ 1. Talk with a service station attendant.
_____ 2. Talk with a physician.
_____ 3. Present a talk to a group of strangers.
_____ 4. Talk with an acquaintance while standing in line.
_____ 5. Talk with a salesperson in a store.
_____ 6. Talk in a large meeting of friends.
_____ 7. Talk with a police officer.
_____ 8. Talk in a small group of strangers.
_____ 9. Talk with a friend while standing in line.
_____ 10. Talk with a server in a restaurant.
_____ 11. Talk in a large meeting of acquaintances.
_____ 12. Talk with a stranger while standing in line.
_____ 13. Talk with an office assistant.
_____ 14. Present a talk to a group of friends.
_____ 15. Talk in a small group of acquaintances.
_____ 16. Talk with a garbage collector.
_____ 17. Talk in a large meeting of strangers.
_____ 18. Talk with a spouse (or girlfriend or boyfriend).
_____ 19. Talk in a small group of friends.
_____ 20. Present a talk to a group of acquaintances.

Source: James C. McCloskey and Virginia P. Richmond, Fundamentals of Human Communication: An Interpersonal Perspective (Prospect Heights, IL: Waveland Press, 1996), 53.

Continued

COMPUTING SCORES ON THE WILLINGNESS-TO-COMMUNICATE SCALE

Scoring: The WTC permits computation of one total score and seven subscores. The range for all scores is 0–100. Follow the procedures outlined below.

1. Group discussion—Add scores for items 8, 15, and 19; divide sum by 3.
   Scores 89 = high WTC, scores below 57 = low WTC in this context.
2. Meetings—Add scores for items 6, 11, and 17; divide sum by 3.
   Scores 80 = high WTC, scores below 39 = low WTC in this context.
3. Interpersonal—Add scores for items 4, 9, and 12; divide sum by 3.
   Scores 94 = high WTC, scores below 64 = low WTC in this context.
4. Public speaking—Add scores for items 3, 14, and 20; divide sum by 3.
   Scores 78 = high WTC, scores below 33 = low WTC in this context.
5. Stranger—Add scores for items 3, 8, 12, and 17; divide sum by 4.
   Scores 63 = high WTC, scores below 18 = low WTC with these receivers.
6. Acquaintance—Add scores for items 4, 11, 15, and 20; divide sum by 4.
   Scores 92 = high WTC, scores below 57 = low WTC with these receivers.
7. Friends—Add scores for items 6, 9, 14, and 19; divide sum by 4.
   Scores 99 = high WTC, scores below 71 = low WTC with these receivers.

To compute the total score for the WTC, add the totals for stranger, friend, and acquaintance; then divide by 3. Scores above 82 = high WTC, below 52 = low WTC.

Self-Esteem: Your Self-Worth

Your self-esteem is closely related to your self-concept. Through your self-concept, you *describe* who you are. Through your **self-esteem (self-worth)**, you *evaluate* who you are. The term "self-worth" is often used interchangeably with "self-esteem." We derive our sense of self-worth from comparing ourselves with others: "I'm good at playing soccer" (because I beat others); "I can't cook" (because others cook better than I do); "I'm not good at meeting people" (most people I know seem to be more comfortable interacting with others); "I can't fix a broken toilet" (but my brothers and my mom and dad can). Each of these statements implies a judgment about how well or badly you can perform certain tasks, with implied references to how well others perform the same tasks. A belief that you cannot fix a broken toilet or cook like a chef may not in itself lower your self-esteem. However, if there are *several* things you cannot do well, or *many* important tasks that you cannot seem to master, these shortcomings may begin to colour your overall sense of worth.

Psychologist Eric Berne developed the concept of a **life position** to describe our overall sense of our own worth and that of others.[17] He identified four life positions: (1) "I'm OK, you're OK," or positive regard for self and others; (2) "I'm OK, you're not OK," or positive regard for self and low regard for others; (3) "I'm not OK, you're OK," or low self-regard and positive regard for others; and (4) "I'm not OK, you're

self-esteem (self-worth). Your evaluation of your worth or value as reflected in your perception of such things as your skills, abilities, talents, and appearance.

life position. Your feeling of being either "OK" or "not OK" as reflected in your sense of worth and self-esteem.

face. A person's positive perception of himself or herself in interactions with others.

facework. Using communication to maintain your own positive self-perception (self-face) or to support, reinforce, or challenge someone else's self-perception (other-face).

not OK," or low regard for both self and others. Your life position is a driving force in your relationships with others. People in the "I'm OK, you're OK" position have the best chance for healthy relationships because they have discovered their own talents and also recognize that others have been given talents different from their own.

Another way communication researchers talk about being "OK" is by referring to what is called "face." **Face** is a person's positive perception of himself or herself in interactions with others.[18] **Facework** is the use of communication to maintain one's own positive self-perception (self-face) or to support, reinforce, or even challenge someone else's self-perception (other-face).[19] You are involved in facework, for example, when you announce to your parents that you made the dean's list during your most recent semester in college. By telling them the good news about your academic success, you're using communication to maintain your parents' positive image of you and thus reinforce your own positive self-image. The effort you expend to save face (protect your positive image) reflects the kind of perception you want others to have of you. You may also engage in facework to maintain the esteem of others. When your roommate's mother calls and you tell her that your roommate is studying in the library when she's actually at a party, you're also engaging in facework.

©2000 Thaves. Reprinted with permission. Newspaper dist. by NEA, Inc.

In Canada...

CAMPUS DRINKING: AN ATTEMPT TO IMPROVE LOW SELF-ESTEEM?

How many students start college or university unsure of themselves? Perhaps everything is new and unfamiliar—living in residence or an apartment, in a new city or town, with no friends on the new campus. Many colleges start the new semester with orientation activities so that students can meet each other and get to know the campus. How many of these activities involve alcohol, and do students have a drink or two to relax or feel better about themselves so that they can meet others more easily?

While we cannot answer those questions, recent research points out that drinking and drug use among many students (and not just university students) continues to be a problem. The Centre for Addiction and Mental Health's *Ontario Student Drug Use Survey* is the longest ongoing school survey of adolescents up to grade 12 in Canada.[i] The same agency's *Canadian Campus Survey* is done every two years. The school survey describes drug use in 2003 and changes since 1977. It includes several drugs such as tobacco, cannabis, and alcohol. The latest results, from the spring of 2003, show that the use of alcohol among students is still a significant cause for concern. Alcohol remains the most widely used drug. In 2003, about two-thirds (66 percent) of students reported drinking during the past year. Males were more likely to drink than females. About one-quarter

Continued

(26 percent) of students reported binge drinking (five or more drinks on one occasion) at least once during the month before the survey. About one-fifth (19 percent) of students reported drinking at hazardous levels. This number represents some 186 700 students. Alcohol and binge drinking have continued in a stable but elevated pattern, as have inhalant, cannabis, ecstasy, and hallucinogen use. An interesting finding that may tie in with self-esteem is that about eight percent (8/100 students) reported both hazardous drinking and elevated psychological distress (symptoms of anxiety and depression). This pattern may continue as students enter higher education.

On college and university campuses, now as in the past, is drinking something to be concerned about? A campus survey does indicate that drinking can become a problem for many students.[ii] In 2003, alcohol use is the highest among first-year students and those living in residence. The most recent results indicate that 63 percent of students reported drinking five or more drinks on a single occasion and 34 percent reported consuming more than eight drinks in one sitting at least once a month. When drinking to get drunk, students drank the most (8.9 drinks). Reasons given for this behaviour included celebrating or being at a party (5.7 drinks), forgetting worries (5.5 drinks), and to feel good (5.4 drinks). Among the alcohol-related problems reported by students were missed classes due to hangovers, memory loss, and actions they regretted. The lead researcher, Louis Gliksman, states that heavy drinking for this age group could result in a number of problems. Among the list of problems he identifies are broken relationships, academic difficulties, accidents, and legal and administrative problems, all of which could affect students' futures. Obviously, high alcohol consumption and alcohol abuse are an ongoing campus problem.

Sources: i. Edward M. Adlaf and Angela Paglia, Drug Use Among Ontario Students 1977–2003, OSDUS Highlights, CAMH Research Document Series, No. 14, Centre for Addiction and Mental Health, 2003; The 2003 OSDS Drug Report: Executive Summary, Centre for Addiction and Mental Health.
ii. "First National Study of Drug Use Among University Students Released by the Centre for Addiction and Mental Health Shows 'Heavy' Drinking to Be a Significant Concern," *Centre for Addiction and Mental Health, News Release,* March 29, 2000.

Improving Your Self-Esteem

We have already seen how low self-esteem can affect our own communication and interactions. In recent years, teachers, psychologists, ministers, rabbis, social workers, and even politicians have suggested that many of our societal problems stem from our collective feelings of low self-esteem. Our feelings of low self-worth may contribute to our choosing the wrong partners; to becoming dependent on drugs, alcohol, or other substances; and to experiencing problems with eating and other vital activities. So we owe it to society, as well as to ourselves, to maintain or develop a healthy sense of self-esteem.

Although no simple list of tricks can easily transform low self-esteem into feelings of being valued and appreciated, you can make improvements in the ways you think about yourself and interact with others. We'll explore seven proven techniques that have helped others.

Practise Positive Self-Talk

Cycling champion Lance Armstrong is also a cancer survivor. When he got sick, he told a friend, "Cancer picked the wrong guy. When it looked around for a body to

Positive self-talk can help us focus on our own goals and improve our performance levels even when the goals seem insurmountable. (Canadian Cancer Society)

intrapersonal communication. Communication within one's own mind, including self-talk.

visualization. A technique of imagining that you are performing a particular task in a certain way. Positive visualization can enhance your self-esteem.

hang out in, it made a big mistake when it chose mine. Big mistake."[20] The positive self-talk reflected in his words undoubtedly helped Armstrong to overcome the challenge of cancer and go on to win the Tour de France several times. Every Canadian knows only too well the story of Terry Fox and his battle with the cancer that ended his young life. Through it all, he remained upbeat, and his positive attitude enabled him to run an equivalent to a marathon every day for 143 days. He has been described as Canada's true hero.[21]

Intrapersonal communication is communication within one's own mind—self-talk. Realistic, positive self-talk can have a reassuring effect on your level of self-worth and on your interactions with others. Conversely, repeating negative messages about your lack of skill and ability can keep you from trying and achieving. Sports psychologist Karlene Sugarman claims, "Positive self-talk will help your performance, negative self-talk will make matters worse. Positive self-talk helps you to develop secure attitudes toward your performance and validates your capabilities.[22]

For example, imagine that you have an algebra test coming up. If you are not optimistic about your performance on the test, you may be tempted to let your self-fulfilling prophecy come true by not studying. However, by reminding yourself (talking to yourself) about the importance of study and effort, you may be able to change your defeatist outlook. If you tell yourself, "I don't have to fail if I study," or "If I seek help from the teacher and spend more time on algebra, I can master these formulas," you may motivate yourself to improve your performance. Improved performance can enhance your confidence and self-worth. Of course, blind faith without hard work won't succeed. Self-talk is not a substitute for effort; it can, however, keep you on track and help you, ultimately, to achieve your goal.

Visualize a Positive Image of Yourself

Visualization takes the notion of self-talk one step further. Besides just telling yourself that you can achieve your goal, you can actually try to "see" yourself conversing effectively with others, performing well on a project, or emphasizing some other desirable behaviour. Recent research suggests that an apprehensive public speaker can manage his or her fears not only by developing skill in public speaking but also by visualizing positive results when speaking to an audience.[23] If you are one of the many people who fears speaking in public, try visualizing yourself walking to the lectern, taking out your well-prepared notes, and delivering an interesting, well-received speech. This visualization of positive results enhances confidence and speaking skill. The same technique can be used to boost your sense of self-worth about other tasks or skills. Of course, your visualization should be realistic and coupled with a plan to achieve your goal.

Avoid Comparing Yourself with Others

Even before we are born, we are compared with others. The latest medical technology lets us see sonograms of fetuses still in the womb, so parents may begin comparing children with their siblings or other babies before birth. For the rest of our lives we are compared with others, and, rather than celebrating our uniqueness, comparisons usually point up who is bigger, brighter, and more beautiful. Most of us have had the experience of being chosen last to play on a sports team, being passed over for promotion, or standing unasked against the wall at a dance.

In North American culture, we may be tempted to judge our self-worth by our material possessions and personal appearance. If we know someone who has a newer car (or simply a car, if we rely on public transportation), a smaller waistline, or a higher grade point average, we may feel diminished. Comparisons such as, "He has more money than I have," or "She looks better than I look," are likely to deflate our self-worth. One-hundred-and-one-year-old Sadie and 103-year-old Bessie Delaney, sisters who have endured racial prejudice, have inspired many by their refusal to let what they did not have deter their sense of personal accomplishment. In their best-selling book, *Having Our Say*, these two family matriarchs write of the value of emphasizing what we have, rather than comparing our lack of resources with others who have more.

BALLARD STREET copyright © Van Amarongen. Reprinted with permission of Creators Syndicate.

Michael continually measures himself against others.

Rather than focusing on others who seemingly are better off, focus on the unique attributes that make you who you are. Avoid judging your own value in comparison with that of others. A healthy, positive self-concept is fuelled not by judgments of others but by a genuine sense of worth that we recognize in ourselves.

Reframe Appropriately

Reframing is the process of redefining events and experiences from a different point of view. Just as reframing a work of art can give the painting a whole new look, reframing events that cause us to devalue our self-worth can change our perspective. Research suggests that in times of family stress, individuals who are able to engage in self-talk and describe the event from someone else's perspective manage stress more successfully. If, for example, you get a report from your supervisor that says you should improve one area of your performance, instead of listening to the self-talk that says you're bad at your job, reframe the event within a larger context: tell yourself that one negative comment does not mean you are hopeless as a worker.

reframing. The process of redefining events and experiences from a different point of view.

Of course, all negative experiences should not be lightly tossed off and left unexamined because you can learn and profit from your mistakes. However, it is important to remember that our worth as human beings is not contingent on a single letter grade, a single response from a prospective employer, or a single play in a football game. Looking at the big picture—what effect this small event will have on your whole life, on society, on history—places negative experiences that we all have in a realistic context.

Develop Honest Relationships

Having at least one other person who can help you objectively and honestly reflect on your virtues and vices can be extremely beneficial in fostering a healthy, positive self-image. As we noted earlier, other people play a major role in shaping our self-concept and self-esteem. The more credible the source of information, the more likely we are to believe it. Having a trusted friend, family member, colleague, or counsellor who can listen without judging you and give you the straight scoop about yourself can help you avoid "pity parties." Prolonged periods of self-pity left unchecked and unconfirmed can lead to feelings of inferiority. Later in this chapter, we will discuss how honest relationships are developed through the process of self-disclosure.

Let Go of the Past

Your self-concept is not a fixed construct. Nor was it implanted at birth to remain constant for the rest of your life. Things change. You change. Others change. Individuals with low self-esteem may be locking on to events and experiences that happened years ago and tenaciously refusing to let go of them. Someone wrote, "The lightning bug is brilliant, but it hasn't much of a mind; it blunders through existence with its headlight on behind." Looking back at what we can't change only reinforces a sense of helplessness. Constantly replaying negative experiences in our mental DVD player only serves to make our sense of worth more difficult to change. Becoming aware of the changes that have occurred, and can occur, in your life can assist you in developing a more realistic assessment of your value. If you were over-weight as a child, you may have a difficult time accepting that your worth does not hinge on the pounds you carried years ago. Being open and receptive to change in self-worth is important to developing a healthy self-concept. Longfellow's advice to let go of the past remains wise today: "Look not mournfully into the past. It comes not back again. Wisely improve the Present. It is thine. Go forth to meet the shadowy future, without fear..."

Seek Support

Some of your self-image problems may be so ingrained that you need professional help. A trained counsellor, religious leader, or therapist can help you sort through them. Therapists usually take a psychoanalytic approach, inviting you to search for experiences in your past that may help you first to understand your feelings and then to change them. Other counsellors use different techniques. If you are not sure to whom to turn for a referral, you can start with your school counselling services. Or, if you are near a medical school teaching hospital, you can contact the counselling or psychotherapy office there for a referral.

Because you have spent your whole lifetime developing your self-esteem, it is not easy to make big changes. However, as we have seen, talking through our problems can make a difference. As communication researchers Frank E. Dance and Carl Larson see it, "Speech communication empowers each of us to share in the development of our own self-concept and the fulfillment of that self-concept."[24]

> ▶ **Recap**

STRATEGIES FOR IMPROVING YOUR SELF-ESTEEM

Engage in Positive Self-Talk	If you're having a bad hair day, tell yourself that you have beautiful eyes and lots of friends who like you anyway.
Visualize	If you feel nervous before a meeting, visualize everyone in the room congratulating you on your great ideas.
Avoid Comparisons	Focus on what you can do to enhance your own talents and abilities.
Reframe Appropriately	If you experience one failure, keep the larger picture in mind rather than focusing on that isolated incident.
Develop Honest Relationships	Cultivate friends in whom you can confide and who will give you honest feedback for improving your skills and abilities.
Let Go of the Past	Try not to dwell on negative experiences in your past; instead focus on ways to enhance your abilities in the future.
Seek Support	Talk with professional counsellors who can help you identify your gifts and talents.

How Self-Concept and Self-Esteem Affect Interpersonal Communication and Relationships

Your self-concept and self-esteem act as filters in every interaction with others. They determine how you approach, respond to, and interpret messages. Specifically, your self-concept and self-esteem affect your ability to be sensitive to others, your overall expectations for yourself (through self-fulfilling prophecy), your interpretation of messages, and your typical communication style.

Self and Others

We have suggested the importance of becoming other-oriented—being sensitive to the thoughts and feelings of others—as a requisite for developing quality interpersonal relationships with others. The process of becoming other-oriented begins with **social decentring**—consciously thinking about another person's thoughts and feelings. However, before you begin to decentre—to try to understand another person from another perspective—it is important for you to feel centred—to know yourself and to understand how others see you.

Becoming other-oriented involves recognizing that your self is different from that of others. As the Peanuts cartoon shown on page 56 reminds us, the world does not

social decentring. Cognitive process in which you take into account another person's thoughts, feelings, values, background, and perspective.

PEANUTS

PEANUTS reprinted by permission of UFS Inc.

revole around our solitary selves. Others influence our actions and our self-image. George Herbert Mead suggests that we develop an "I," which is based on our own perspective of ourselves, and a "Me," which is an image of ourselves based upon the collective responses we receive and interpret from others. Being aware of how your concept of self ("I") differs from the perceptions others have of you ("Me") is an important first step in developing an other-orientation.

When we begin the social-decentring process, we often interpret our observations of others by using our own selves as a frame of reference, especially if we do not know the other person well.[25] For example, if you are nervous and frightened when you have to take a test, you might assume that your friend feels the same way. You may need to remind yourself that the other person is separate from you and has a different set of responses.

specific-other perspective. The process of relying on observed or imagined information about another person that is used to predict that person's behaviour.

When you use a **specific-other perspective**, you rely on information that you have observed or that you can imagine about a particular person to predict his or her reactions. If, for example, you know first-hand that your sister hates it when someone eats off her plate during dinner, you may use that experience to conclude that she would dislike sharing a bag of popcorn at the movies.

generalized-other perspective. The process of relying on observed or imagined information about many people or people in general to predict a person's behaviour.

Sometimes a **generalized-other perspective** will be more useful. When you decentre, you can apply knowledge and personal theories that you have about people in general or about specific subgroups to the person with whom you are interacting. For example, you might think that your economics professor, who holds a Ph.D., would prefer to be addressed as *Professor* rather than as *Mister* because almost all of your other professors with doctorates prefer to be called *Professor*.

self-fulfilling prophecy. The notion that predictions about your future actions are likely to come true because you believe that they will come true.

Your ability to predict how others will respond to you is based on your ability to understand how your sense of the world is similar to, and different from, theirs. First you must know yourself well. Then you can know and understand others. The best way to improve your ability to decentre is to notice how others respond when you act on the predictions and assumptions you have made about them. You may discover that you have not moved out of your own frame of reference enough to make an accurate prediction about another person.

Self-Fulfilling Prophecy

What people believe about themselves often comes true because they expect it to come true. Their expectations become a **self-fulfilling prophecy**. If you think you will fail the math quiz because you have labelled yourself inept at math, then you must overcome not only your math deficiency but your low expectations of yourself. The theme of George Bernard Shaw's *Pygmalion* (the source for the Broadway musical *My Fair Lady*) is, "If you treat a girl like a flower girl, that's all she will ever be. If you treat her like a princess, she may be one." Your attitudes, beliefs, and general expectations about your performance have a powerful and profound effect on your behaviour.

The medical profession is learning the power that attitudes and expectations have over healing. Physician Howard Brody's research suggests that in many instances, just giving patients a placebo—a pill with no medicine in it—or telling patients that they have been operated on when they haven't had an operation can yield positive medical results. In his book, *The Placebo Response,* Dr. Brody tells of a woman with debilitating Parkinson's disease who made a miraculous recovery; her only treatment was the doctors' telling her that they had completed a medical procedure.[26] They hadn't. Yet before the "treatment," she could barely walk; after it, she could easily pace around the room. There is a clear link, suggests Dr. Brody, between mental state and physical health. Patients who believe they will improve are more likely to improve.

Self and Interpretation of Messages

Do you remember Eeyore, the donkey from the stories about Winnie-the-Pooh and his friends? Eeyore lived in the gloomiest part of the Hundred Acre Wood and had a self-image to match. In one story, which used to be a favourite of the son of one of your authors, all of the animals congregated on a stormy night to check on Eeyore:

As Professor Henry Higgins said about Eliza Doolittle, "If you treat a girl like a flower girl, that's all she will ever be. If you treat her like a princess she may be one."
(Shooting Star)

> . . . they all came to the part of the forest known as Eeyore's gloomy place. On this stormy night it was terribly gloomy indeed—or it would have been were it not for Christopher Robin. He was there with a big umbrella.
>
> "I've invited Eeyore to come and stay with me until the storm is over," said Christopher Robin.
>
> "If it ever is," said Eeyore, "which doesn't seem likely. Not that anybody asked me, you understand. But then, they hardly ever do."[27]

Perhaps you know, or have known, an Eeyore—someone whose low self-esteem colours how he or she interprets messages and interacts with others. According to research, such people are more likely to have the following traits:[28]

- They are more sensitive to criticism and negative feedback from others.
- They are more critical of others.
- They believe they are not popular or respected by others.
- They expect to be rejected by others.
- They dislike being observed when performing.
- They feel threatened by people who they feel are superior.
- They expect to lose when competing with others.
- They are overly responsive to praise and compliments.
- They evaluate their overall behaviour as inferior to that of others.

The Pooh stories offer an antidote to Eeyore's gloom in the character of the optimistic Tigger, who assumes that everyone shares his exuberance for life:

> . . . when Owl reached Piglet's house, Tigger was there. He was bouncing on his tail, as Tiggers do, and shouting to Piglet. "Come on," he cried. "You can do it! It's fun!"[29]

If, like Tigger, your sense of self-worth is high, research suggests that:

- You will have higher expectations for solving problems.
- You will think more highly of others.
- You will be more likely to accept praise and accolades from others without feeling embarrassed.
- You will be more comfortable having others observe you when you perform.
- You will be more likely to admit you have both strengths and weaknesses.
- You will be more comfortable when you interact with others who view themselves as highly competent.
- You will expect other people to accept you for who you are.
- You will be more likely to seek opportunities to improve skills that need improving.
- You will evaluate your overall behaviour more positively than would people with lower self-esteem.[30]

selective exposure. A principle that suggests we tend to place ourselves in situations that are consistent with our self-concept and self-esteem.

Reflecting the assumption that our self-concept influences our behaviour is the principle of **selective exposure**, which suggests that we tend to place ourselves in situations consistent with the person we think we are. Whom do you usually find at an Anglican church on Sunday morning? Anglicans. Who are the attendees at a Liberal convention? Liberals. If you view yourself as a good student who wants an A in the class, where are you likely to be during class time? We behave in ways that reinforce our perception of self, both in our interpretation of messages and in our behaviour.

Self and Interpersonal Needs

need for inclusion. Interpersonal need to be included and to include others in social activities.

According to social psychologist Will Schutz, our concept of who we are, coupled with our need to interact with others, profoundly influences how we communicate with others. Schutz identifies three primary social needs that affect the degree of communication we have with others: the need for inclusion, the need for control, and the need for affection.[31] The **need for inclusion** suggests that each of us has a need to be included in the activities of others. We all need human contact and fellowship. We need to be invited to join others, and perhaps we need to invite others to join us. Of course, the level and intensity of this need differs from person to person, but even loners desire some social contact. Our need to include others and be included in activities may stem, in part, from our concept of ourselves as either a "party person" or a loner.

need for control. Interpersonal need for some degree of domination in our relationships as well as the need to be controlled.

The second need, the **need for control**, suggests that we also need some degree of influence over the relationships we establish with others. We may also have a need to be controlled because we desire some level of stability and comfort in our interactions with others. If we view ourselves as people who are comfortable being in charge, we are more likely to give orders to others rather than take orders from them.

need for affection. Interpersonal need to give and receive love, personal support, warmth, and intimacy.

And finally, we each have a **need for affection**. We need to give and receive love, support, warmth, and intimacy, although the amounts we need vary enormously from person to person. If we have a high need for affection, we will more likely place ourselves in situations where that need can be met. The greater our inclusion, control, and affection needs are, the more likely it is that we will actively seek others as friends and initiate communication with them.

Self and Communication Style

Our self-concept and self-esteem affect not only the way we feel about ourselves, the way we interpret messages, and our personal performance; they also influence the way we *deliver* messages and treat other people. Each of us has a **communication style** (or **social style**) that is identifiable by the habitual ways in which we behave toward others. The style we adopt helps others interpret our messages. As they get to know you, other people begin to expect you to behave in a certain way, based upon previous associations with you.

How do we develop our communication style? Many communication researchers, sociologists, and psychologists believe that we have certain underlying traits or personality characteristics that influence how we interact with others. Some scholars believe these traits stem from genetics—we are born with certain personality characteristics. We are who we are because that's the way we are made.[32] Others emphasize the **social learning approach**—we communicate with others as we do because of our interactions with others such as our parents and friends. The truth is that we cannot yet explain exactly how we come to communicate as we do.

Even though we don't know the precise role of nature or nurture in determining how we communicate, most inventories of personality or communication style focus on two primary dimensions that underlie how we interact with others—assertiveness and responsiveness.[33] **Assertiveness** is the tendency to make requests, ask for information, and generally pursue our own rights and best interests. An assertive style is sometimes called a "masculine" style. By masculine, we don't mean that only males can be assertive, but in many cultures, being assertive is synonymous with being masculine. You are assertive when you seek information if you are confused, or direct others to help you get what you need.

Responsiveness is the tendency to be sensitive to the needs of others. Being other-oriented and sympathetic to the pain of others and placing the feelings of others above your own feelings are examples of being responsive. Researchers sometimes label responsiveness a "feminine" quality. Again, this does not mean that only women are or should be responsive but only that many cultures stereotype being responsive as a traditional behaviour of females.

What is your communication style? To assess your style of communication on the assertiveness and responsiveness dimensions, take the "Sociocommunicative Orientation" test by James McCroskey and Virginia Richmond in the *Building Your Skills* box on page 60. You may discover that you test higher on one dimension than on the others. It's also possible to be high on both or low on both. Assertiveness and responsiveness are two different dimensions; you need not have just one or the other.

What many of you will want to know is, "What is the best communication style? Should I be assertive or responsive?" The truth is, there is no one best style for every situation. It depends. Sometimes the appropriate thing to do is to assert yourself—to ask or even demand that you receive what you need and have a right to receive. In other situations, it may be more appropriate to be less confrontational. Maintaining the quality of the relationship by simply listening and being thoughtfully responsive to others may be best. The appropriateness of your communication style involves issues we will discuss in future chapters, such as how you adapt to culture and gender differences, your needs, the needs and rights of others, and the goal of your communication.

communication style (social style). Your consistent way of relating to others based upon your personality, self-concept and self-esteem.

social learning approach. Theoretical perspective that suggests the origins of our communication styles lie in what we learn, directly and indirectly, from other people.

assertiveness. Tendency to make requests, ask for information, and generally pursue your own rights and best interests.

responsiveness. Tendency to be sensitive to the needs of others, including being sympathetic to the pain of others and placing the feelings of others above your own feelings.

Building Your Skills

SOCIOCOMMUNICATIVE ORIENTATION

Directions: The following questionnaire lists 20 personality characteristics. Please indicate the degree to which you believe each of these characteristics applies to you, as you normally communicate with others, by marking whether you (5) strongly agree that it applies, (4) agree that it applies, (3) are undecided, (2) disagree that it applies, or (1) strongly disagree that it applies. There are no right or wrong answers. Work quickly; record your first impression.

_____   1. Helpful

_____   2. Defends own beliefs

_____   3. Independent

_____   4. Responsive to others

_____   5. Forceful

_____   6. Has strong personality

_____   7. Sympathetic

_____   8. Compassionate

_____   9. Assertive

_____   10. Sensitive to the needs of others

_____   11. Dominant

_____   12. Sincere

_____   13. Gentle

_____   14. Willing to take a stand

_____   15. Warm

_____   16. Tender

_____   17. Friendly

_____   18. Acts as a leader

_____   19. Aggressive

_____   20. Competitive

Scoring: Items 2, 3, 5, 6, 9, 11, 14, 18, 19, and 20 measure assertiveness. Add the scores on these items to get your assertiveness score. Items 1, 4, 7, 8, 10, 12, 13, 15, 16, and 17 measure responsiveness. Add the scores on these items to get your responsiveness score. Scores range from 50 to 10. The higher your score, the higher your orientation as assertive and responsive.

Source: James C. McCroskey and Virginia P. Richmond, Fundamentals of Human Communication: An Interpersonal Perspective (Prospect Heights, IL: Waveland Press, 1996), 91.

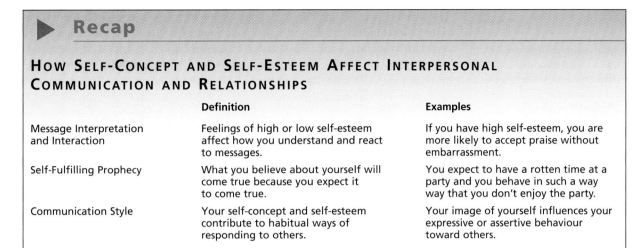

> ▶ **Recap**
>
> ## How Self-Concept and Self-Esteem Affect Interpersonal Communication and Relationships
>
> | | Definition | Examples |
> |---|---|---|
> | Message Interpretation and Interaction | Feelings of high or low self-esteem affect how you understand and react to messages. | If you have high self-esteem, you are more likely to accept praise without embarrassment. |
> | Self-Fulfilling Prophecy | What you believe about yourself will come true because you expect it to come true. | You expect to have a rotten time at a party and you behave in such a way that you don't enjoy the party. |
> | Communication Style | Your self-concept and self-esteem contribute to habitual ways of responding to others. | Your image of yourself influences your expressive or assertive behaviour toward others. |

Self-Disclosure: Connecting Self to Others Through Talk

One important way people develop and revise their self-concept is by receiving other people's reactions to their self-disclosure. **Self-disclosure** occurs when you purpose-fully provide information to others about yourself that they would not learn if you did not tell them. People can learn your approximate age, height, and weight by just observing you, but they can't learn your *exact* age, height, or weight unless you tell them. Self-disclosure ranges from revealing innocuous information about who you are to admitting your deepest fears and most private fantasies. Disclosing personal information not only provides a basis for another person to understand you better, it conveys your level of trust and acceptance of the other person. Because others self-disclose, you are able to learn information about them and deepen your interpersonal relationships with them.[34] To help explore the relationships among self-concept, self-esteem, and self-disclosure, we will describe how self-disclosure occurs, note how people become aware of who they are through self-disclosure, and identify general characteristics of self-disclosure.

Interpersonal relationships cannot achieve intimacy without self-disclosure. Without true self-disclosure, you form only superficial relationships. You can confirm another person's self-concept, and have your self-concept confirmed, only if both you and your partner have revealed yourselves to each other.

self-disclosure. Purposefully providing information to others that they would not learn if you did not tell them.

Understanding the Depth and Breadth of Self-Disclosure: The Social Penetration Model of Self-Disclosure

What makes your best friend your best friend? Undoubtedly, one characteristic is that you have shared your most personal information with him or her. You share more personal information over a broader range of topics with people you know well and who know you, than you do with people you know only superficially.

social penetration model.
Model of self-disclosure and relational development that reflects both depth and breadth of shared information.

Researchers Irwin Altman and Dalmas Taylor developed a model called **social penetration model** that illustrates how much and what kinds of information people reveal in various stages of a relationship.[35] Their model starts with a circle that represents all the potential information about yourself that you could disclose to someone (see Figure 2.2, circle A). This circle is divided into many pieces, like a pie, with each piece representing a particular aspect of self. For instance, some pieces in your pie might relate to athletic activities, religious beliefs, family, school, recreational activities, political interests, and fears. These pieces of pie represent the breadth of topics or information available about you.

In addition, the concentric circles in the pie represent the depth of information you could disclose. By depth, we mean how personal or intimate the information is; telling your friend about your fear of elevators is more intimate than telling someone that your favourite ice cream is homemade vanilla. The smallest circle represents the most personal information. Each of your relationships represents a degree of social penetration, or the extent to which the other person has penetrated your concentric circles (depth) and shared pieces of your pie (breadth). For example, the shading on circle B shows a relationship that involves a high degree of penetration but of only one aspect of self. Perhaps you have a good friend with whom you study and go to the library, but you don't spend much time socializing with your friend; it's all work and no play with this friend. You might have disclosed some personal or intimate information to your friend about your study skills and weaknesses but little about your family, hobbies, political views, or other aspects of who you are.

Understanding Diversity

CULTURAL DIFFERENCES IN SELF-DISCLOSURE

The social penetration model of self-disclosure, as described above, suggests that self-disclosure can be described by both breadth—the number of topics we discuss—and depth—the level of intimacy we establish with others. Do cultural differences affect how much we disclose to one another? Several researchers suggest that the answer is yes. People's cultural backgrounds affect both the kinds of things they reveal and the intimacy of the information about themselves they share with others. Intercultural communication scholar William Gudykunst found that North Americans are

more likely than Japanese to reveal more personal and intimate information about themselves with people whom they consider to be close friends.[36] North Americans were more likely than the Japanese to talk about their sex lives, dating patterns, and love interests and to reveal their emotions. A researcher investigating Korean communication patterns found that North Americans tend to disclose more than Koreans about their marital status, sexual morality, and use of birth control.[37] However, Koreans were more likely than North Americans to talk about issues related to education and family rules. What are the larger implications of these studies? Simply this: the amount of self-disclosure that is considered appropriate is learned;

the level of self-disclosure with which we are comfortable varies from culture to culture. Cultural norms influence how much we reveal about our selves.

Your relationships with your instructors probably look a little like circle B, with its limited breadth. In circle C, more pieces of the pie are shaded, but the information is all fairly safe, superficial information about yourself, such as where you went to school, your hometown, or your major. These would be the kind of disclosures associated with a new friendship. Circle D represents almost complete social penetration, the kind achieved in an intimate, well-developed relationship in which a large amount of self-disclosure has occurred.

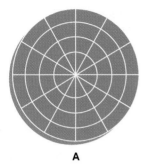

A

Your self " with all its various dimensions. The pies represent the breadth of your "self," and the rings represent depth.

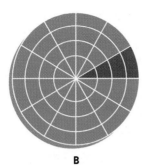

B

A limited relationship in which one dimension of your "self" has been disclosed to another person.

C

A relationship with greater breadth than B but with no intimacy.

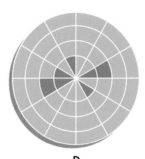

D

A highly intimate, close relationship in which there has been extensive breadth and depth of disclosure.

Figure 2.2
Social Penetration Models

Understanding How We Learn about Ourselves from Others: The Johari Window Model of Self-Disclosure

To disclose information to others, you must first be aware of who you are. Your **self-awareness** is your understanding of who you are. In addition to just thinking about who you are, asking others for information about yourself and then listening to what they tell you can enhance your self-awareness. There are a variety of personality tests, such as the Myers-Briggs personality inventory, that may give you additional insight into your interests, style, and ways of relating to others. Most colleges and universities have a career services office where you can take vocational aptitude tests to help you identify careers that fit who you are.

The **Johari Window model** nicely summarizes how your awareness of who you are is influenced by your own level of disclosure, as well as by how much others share information *about* you *with* you. (The name "Johari Window" sounds somewhat mystical and exotic, but "Johari" is simply a combination of the first names of the creators of the model, Joseph Luft and Harry Ingham.[38]) As Figure 2.3 on page 64 shows, the model looks like a window. Like the circles in the social penetration model, the window represents the self. Your self includes everything about you, including things even you don't yet see or realize. One axis is divided into what you have come to know about yourself and what you don't yet know about who you are. The other axis represents what someone else may know about you and not know about you. The intersection of these categories creates a four-panel, or four-quadrant, window.

self-awareness. A person's conscious understanding of who he or she is.

Johari Window model. Model of self-disclosure that reflects the movement of information about yourself from Blind and Unknown quadrants to Hidden and Open ones.

Figure 2.3
The Johari Window

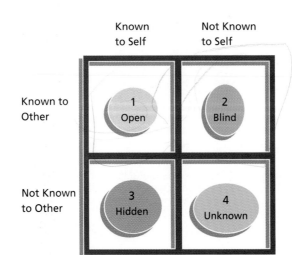

Quadrant 1 is an *open area*. The open area contains information that others know about you and that you are also aware of—such as your age, your occupation, and other things you might mention about yourself. At first glance, all four quadrants in the window appear to be the same size, but that may not be the case (in fact, it probably isn't). In the case of quadrant 1, the more information that you reveal about yourself, the larger this quadrant will be. Put another way, the more you open up to others, the larger the open area will be.

Quadrant 2 is a *blind area*. This part of the window contains information that other people know about you but that you do not know. Perhaps when you were in grade school, someone put a sign on your back that said, "Kick me." Everyone was aware of the sign but you. The blind area of the Johari Window represents much the same situation. For example, you may see yourself as generous, but others may see you as a tightwad. As you learn how others see you, the blind area of the Johari Window gets smaller. Generally, the more accurately you know yourself and perceive how others see you, the better your chances of establishing open and honest relationships with others.

Quadrant 3 is a *hidden area*. This area contains information that you know about yourself but that others do not know about you. You can probably think of many facts, thoughts, feelings, and fantasies that you would not want anyone else to know. They may be feelings you have about another person or something you've done privately in the past that you'd be embarrassed to share with others. The point here is not to suggest you should share all information in the hidden area with others. It is useful to know, however, that part of who you are is known by some people but remains hidden from others.

Quadrant 4 in an *unknown area*. This area contains information that is unknown to both you and others. These are things you do not know about yourself *yet*. Perhaps you do not know how you will react under certain stressful situations. Maybe you are not sure what stand you will take on a certain issue next year or even next week. Other people may also not be aware of how you would respond or behave under certain conditions. Your personal potential, your untapped physical and mental resources, are unknown. You can assume that this area exists because eventually some (though not necessarily all) of these things become known to you, to others, or to both you and others. Because you can never know yourself completely, the unknown quadrant will always exist; you can only guess at its current size because the information it contains is unavailable to you.

As we did with the social penetration model, we can draw Johari Windows to represent each of our relationships (see Figure 2.4). Window A shows a new or restricted relationship for someone who knows himself or herself very well. The open and blind quadrants are small, but the unknown quadrant is also small. Window B shows a very intimate relationship, in which both individuals are open and disclosing.

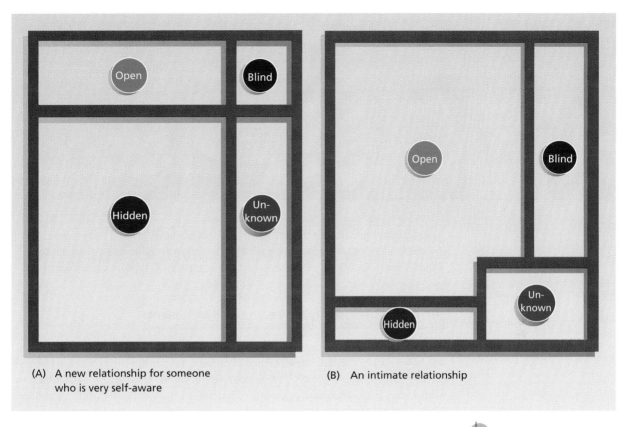

(A)   A new relationship for someone who is very self-aware

(B)   An intimate relationship

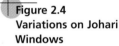

Figure 2.4
Variations on Johari Windows

We've discussed what self-disclosure is and described two models that explain how self-disclosure works and affects your understanding of who you think you are. Next we will describe characteristics of self-disclosure and discuss how disclosure, both appropriate and inappropriate, can affect our interpersonal relationships with others.

Characteristics of Self-Disclosure

Mike was sitting alone at the counter at his neighbourhood diner enjoying his favourite meatloaf sandwich. Just as he was reaching for the ketchup bottle, a young woman on the stool next to him struck up a conversation with him. Within 10 minutes, Mike not only learned where this woman was from but also whom she dated, how much money she made last year, and how embarrassed she was when her parents found her in a compromising position with her boyfriend on the front porch (which she described in vivid detail, complete with sound effects). Have you had the experience of meeting someone who told you more than you wanted to know about himself or herself? Although self-disclosure is a means of establishing relationships with others, revealing too much too soon or making the disclosure only a one-way stream of revelatory information violates self-disclosure norms for most North Americans. It is by revealing who we are in the normal course of conversations that others come to know us and (we often hope) grow to like us.[39]

Researchers have found that we self-disclose in predictable ways. For example, there is some evidence that women are slightly more likely to self-disclose than are men.[40] The following discussion describes other characteristics of appropriate self-disclosure.

Self-Disclosure Usually Moves in Small Increments

What made Mike so uncomfortable during his meeting with his dining neighbour was how much information he learned about his companion in such a short period of time. Most people usually reveal information about themselves a little bit at a time, rather than delivering a condensed version of their autobiography all at once. Most North Americans would share Mike's discomfort at learning too much too soon. Monitor your own self-disclosure. Are you revealing information at a greater depth sooner than you should? If you do, others may find your disclosure disquieting. Appropriate self-disclosure should be well timed to suit the occasion and the expectations of the individuals involved.

Self-Disclosure Moves from Less Personal to More Personal Information

As the social penetration model illustrates, we can describe the depth of our self-disclosure by the intimacy level of the information we share. If we move too quickly to more intimate information before we've developed a history with someone, we violate social norms or expectations our partner may have. John Powell, author of the book, *Why Am I Afraid to Tell You Who I Am?*, notes that the information we reveal about ourselves often progresses through the following predictable levels:[41]

Level 5: *Cliché communication.* We first establish verbal contact with others by saying something that lets the other person know we acknowledge his or her presence. Standard phrases such as "Hello" or "Hi, how are you?" or the more contemporary "What's up?" signal the desire to initiate a relationship, even if it is a brief, superficial one.

Level 4: *Facts and biographical information.* After using cliché phrases and responses to establish contact, we typically next reveal non-threatening information about ourselves, such as our names, hometowns, or majors.

Level 3: *Attitudes and personal ideas.* After noting our name and other basic information, we often begin sharing more personal information such as our attitudes about work or school, or other relatively safe topics. At this level, the information is not too threatening or revealing, but we do begin to talk about our likes and dislikes or about what we assume are non-controversial topics.

Level 2: *Personal feelings.* At this level, we discuss topics and issues that are exceedingly more personal. After we've developed rapport with someone, we then share more intimate fears, secrets, and attitudes. Increasingly, we take risks when we share this information. It requires trust to share these personal feelings.

Level 1: *Peak communication.* Powell calls this the ultimate level of self-disclosure that is seldom reached; his other name for level 1 communication is "gut level" communication. Only with our most intimate friends do we reveal such personal information, and it's possible, says Powell, that we may not reach this level of intimacy with our life partners, parents, or children. Peak communication is rare because of the risk and trust involved in being so open and revealing.

Self-Disclosure Is Reciprocal

In mainstream North American culture, when people share information about themselves, they expect their communication partners to share similar information about themselves. If you introduce yourself by name to someone, you expect that person to respond by telling you his or her name. This cultural rule allows people to use disclosure as a strategy for gaining information and reducing uncertainty. The reciprocal nature of self-disclosure is called the **dyadic effect**: you disclose to me, and I'll disclose to you.

dyadic effect. The reciprocal nature of self-disclosure: you disclose to me, and I'll disclose to you.

Self-Disclosure Involves Risk

Although self-disclosure is a building block for establishing intimacy with others, it can be risky. Once you disclose something to someone, that person can now share the information with others; that person has additional power if the information is something you'd rather not have others know.

There is also the risk of rejection when you tell someone something that is personal. As Powell comments, "If I tell you who I am, and you do not like who I am, that is all that I have."[42] Once you reveal what you believe is your true nature or personal feeling and you are rejected or rebuffed, you can't explain your rejection away by saying, "Oh, they don't know the real me." If you've revealed what you honestly believe is "the real you," experiencing disapproval from your partner can hurt worse than if your partner did not know "the real you."

There is evidence that people are likelier to disclose more personal information about themselves when they communicate online than they would when communicating with others face to face. Communication researchers Lisa Tidwell and Joseph Walther wanted to know whether there are differences between face-to-face conversations and e-mail conversations in amount of self-disclosure, perceptions of confidence, and effectiveness of communication. They found that when people communicate via e-mail, they exchange information more directly with each other and perceive themselves and others to be more "conversationally effective" because they are more direct. E-mail conversation partners also reported that they were more confident when communicating online than they were in their face-to-face encounters.[43] Although researchers still have much to learn about communicating via e-mail and the Internet, the more structured nature of this context of communication is helping them learn more about the nature of self-disclosure and interpersonal communication patterns.

Self-Disclosure Involves Trust

As we have already noted, to know something personal about someone is to have power over that person. If someone has shared information with you, you have the power to reveal that information to others. To reveal personal information about someone that was shared with you in confidence is unethical. If you've made a promise not to reveal something, you should keep it. Using personal information against others to manipulate and control is a misuse of the trust that was placed in you.[44] According to British social psychologists Michael Argyle, Monica Henderson, and Adrian Furnham, one of the most fundamental expectations people have of their friends is that they will not reveal confidences. When you say, "Oh, I won't tell anyone. Your secret's safe with me," mean it.

Perhaps the most intimate secrets are known by family members; our parents and siblings know quite a few things about us that we'd rather others not know. Interpersonal communication researchers Anita Vangelisti, John Caughlin, and Lindsay Timmerman found several factors that may help predict whether we do or don't disclose family secrets. For example, we would be *more* likely to share a family secret under certain conditions:

- During an intimate conversation with another person, we found out that this person had a similar problem, or we thought revealing the secret would help the other person.
- We thought the secret would eventually come to light even if we didn't reveal the secret.
- There was some urgency or importance in revealing the secret; if we didn't reveal the secret, the concealment would create more problems than revealing the secret would cause.
- We thought the family member wouldn't mind if the secret were told; the family member would still accept us.
- It seemed like a normal and natural thing to reveal, given the topic of conversation; if the topic came up, we might disclose the secret.[45]

You might read this list and become worried that your family members might tell things they know about you that you'd rather others not know. Not to worry (too much). The researchers also found that there were some secrets that people would never disclose.

Self-Disclosure over Time: Enhancing Intimacy

Self-disclosure is often associated with relationship development because it is through the process of revealing information about yourself that it becomes possible for relationships to become more intimate. However, simply disclosing information about yourself is no guarantee that your relationship will become intimate.[46]

(Note that when we talk about intimacy and self-disclosure, we're not just talking about sex; rather, we're talking about both greater depth and breadth of self-disclosure.) In an intimate friendship, we become aware of things about our friend that few if any other people may know. Intimacy occurs through the process of self-disclosure.

As relationships move toward intimacy, they typically include periods of high self-disclosure early in the relationship. However, the *amount* of information that is disclosed decreases as the relationship becomes more and more intimate. In other words, there is generally more self-disclosing activity earlier in a relationship than later. As a relationship proceeds, we begin sharing low-risk information fairly rapidly, move on to sharing higher-risk information, and then finally, share our most personal disclosures. The more intimate the relationship becomes, the more intimate the information that is disclosed. The sculpture in the photo represents the way we reveal ourselves when we are with close friends; with our best friends, we may reveal what is behind our "masks." Holding back from sharing intimate information signals a reluctance to escalate the relationship. The amount of information that we have to share about ourselves is finite, so we slow down as we have less left to disclose.

Graph A in Figure 2.5 on page 70 illustrates a typical disclosure pattern over the course of a long and intimate relationship. The peaks and valleys represent periods of variable disclosure. Note that most of the disclosure takes place in the beginning of the relationship. Not all relationships progress this way, however. The relationship in graph B represents two individuals who started to get to know each other but were interrupted before they became close friends. They might have stopped because of some conflict, indecisiveness about pursuing the relationship, or external circumstances that limited opportunities for interacting. When the disclosure resumed, it became more intense. Graph C represents two individuals who probably knew each other as acquaintances for some time but never really had the opportunity or inclination to self-disclose. Once they did begin to escalate the relationship, however, there was a steep rise in self-disclosure. This graph might represent two co-workers who eventually start dating, or two students who have shared a class or two together before striking up a friendship.

Generally, a dramatic increase or decrease in self-disclosure reflects some significant change in the relationship. Even long-term relationships have significant increases and decreases in disclosure that signify changes. Before the birth of a first child, for example, both parents might disclose their fears and expectations about child rearing, and the information might have a profound effect on the relationship.

Interpersonal relationships cannot achieve intimacy without self-disclosure. Without true self-disclosure, we form only superficial relationships. You can confirm another person's self-concept and have your self-concept confirmed only if both you and your partner have revealed yourselves to each other.

Future chapters will discuss the essential other-oriented skills of perceiving others accurately, using and understanding verbal and non-verbal messages, and listening empathetically.

As we develop a relationship, we reveal more of ourselves, removing the masks that we routinely use with strangers. (Sandra Rice)

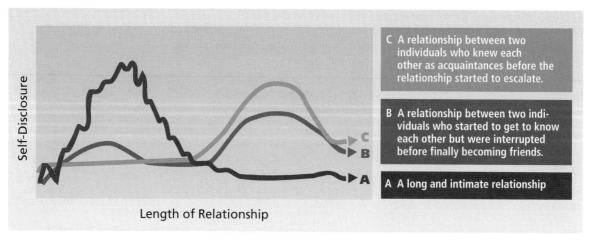

Figure 2.5
Self-Disclosure and Relational Development

Building Your Skills

SELF-DISCLOSURE PATTERNS

Think about two of your current relationships and draw a graph like those in Figure 2.5 to show how the self-disclosure has progressed in each of them. How do the patterns compare? What do the differences or similarities reflect about the two relationships? What caused the peaks and valleys? Were there times when one person tried to increase the rate of self-disclosure, and the other person rejected that attempt? What happened?

Becoming Other-Oriented

A WORLD VIEW

It is sometimes a challenge to avoid becoming self absorbed— focusing exclusively on yourself and not others. There is evidence that the challenge of becoming other-oriented rather than self-absorbed is not new. Most world religions emphasize a common spiritual theme, known in Christianity as the Golden Rule: Do unto others as you would have others do unto you. This "rule" is the basis for most ethical codes throughout the world and has been the foundation of ideas about how we should treat others for centuries. The following excerpts from various religious traditions emphasize the importance of becoming other-oriented.

Hinduism	This is the sum of duty: do nothing to others that would cause pain if done to you.
Buddhism	One should seek for others the happiness one desires for oneself.
Taoism	Regard your neighbour's gain as your own gain, and your neighbour's loss as your loss.
Confucianism	Is there one principle that ought to be acted on throughout one's whole life? Surely it is the principle of loving-kindness: do not unto others what you would not have them do unto you.
Zoroastrianism	The nature alone is good that refrains from doing unto another whatsoever is not good for itself.
Judaism	What is hateful to you, do not do to others. That is the entire law: all the rest is but commentary.
Islam	No one of you is a believer until he desires for his brother that which he desires for himself.
Christianity	Do unto others what you would have others do unto you.

Source: Adapted from Wayne Ham, Man's Living Religions (Independence, MO: Herald Publishing House, 1966), 39–40.

▶ Recap

CHARACTERISTICS OF APPROPRIATE SELF-DISCLOSURE

Self-disclosure usually moves in small increments.	Don't be in a hurry to tell someone too much about yourself too quickly.
Self-disclosure moves from less personal to more personal information.	Revealing personal feelings and intimate information without establishing a foundation of sharing less personal information is likely to make your communication partner feel uncomfortable.
Self-disclosure is reciprocal.	Appropriate self-disclosure involves dyadic interaction; it should not be a one-way monologue.
Self-disclosure involves risk.	"But if I tell you who I am, you may not like who I am, and that is all that I have." You run the risk of being rejected by others when you disclose to them.
Self-disclosure involves trust.	Disclosing to others means you trust them not to reveal your secrets to others or use the personal information against you. When others self-disclose, you have an ethical responsibility to keep confidential what you've learned.
Self-disclosure has the potential to enhance the quality of our interpersonal relationships.	Revealing information about yourself makes it possible for relationships to become more intimate.

Summary

We all seek answers to three questions: "Who am I?" "Why am I here?" "Who are all these others?" William James answered the first question by dividing the self into three parts. The material self includes our bodies and those tangible possessions that give us identity. The social self is the part that engages in interactions with others. The spiritual self consists of thoughts and assumptions about values and moral standards and beliefs about forces that influence our lives. Other theorists conclude that our self-concept develops through interaction with other people. The groups we belong to also give us identity. Our roles as sisters, brothers, students, and parents are important in how we view who we are; the roles we assume provide labels for who we are. We also make our own observations about ourselves apart from others, and about groups or roles we assume. Our gender plays a key part in affecting our view of who we are in relationship to others.

Given the importance of developing a positive sense of self-esteem, we have identified strategies that can enhance your self-worth. Those strategies include engaging in positive self-talk, using positive visualization, avoiding comparisons with others, reframing, developing honest relationships, letting go of the past, and seeking support when needed.

Our sense of self relates to self-disclosure. Self-disclosure occurs when we purposefully provide information to others that they would not learn if we did not tell them. The social penetration model of self-disclosure describes how the depth and breadth of our disclosure can affect our relationships. The Johari Window model of self-disclosure provides an explanation of the relationship between our self-awareness and self-disclosure. The four quadrants in the Johari Window (Open, Hidden, Unknown, and Blind) reflect how much information we and others know about ourselves. As we develop relationships, the sizes of these windows change relative to one another. Appropriate self-disclosure: (1) moves in small increments, (2) moves from less to more personal information, (3) is reciprocal, (4) involves risk, and (5) involves trust.

Finally, self-disclosure has the potential to enhance the quality of our interpersonal relationships. The amount of information we disclose decreases as a relationship becomes more intimate. We first are likely to share low-risk information; as the relationship matures, we typically disclose more personal, high-risk information.

For Discussion and Review

🌑 Focus on Critical Thinking

1. Joel, who is 30 years old, married, and has two children suffers from feelings of low self-esteem. Although he has many friends and a wife who loves him, he feels that others perform much better than he does at work. What strategies would help Joel enhance his self-esteem?

2. Using the online Research Navigator, access the following article: J. J. Jones, S. Bennett, M. P. Olmsted, M. L. Lawson, and G. Rodin. "Disordered Eating Attitudes and Behaviours in Teenaged Girls: A School-Based Study." *Canadian Medical Association Journal,* 165(5), (2001): 547–553. Or you may find another article about eating disorders and self-concept using Research Navigator. In what ways does this study tie in with the theories of self-concept and self-esteem? After reading this chapter, what advice would you give a young teenage girl about weight preoccupation?

3. Provide an original example of how visualization might help you enhance your self-esteem. Describe the positive scene in detail.

4. Provide an example from your own experiences that illustrates the Johari Window model of self-disclosure.

🌑 Focus on Ethics

5. Discuss the ethical implications of using untrue flattery to enhance a friend's self-esteem.

6. There are many self-help books on the market that claim to enrich your social life by providing surefire techniques for enhancing self-esteem. Do you think these claims are ethical? Why or why not?

7. Aelish has long planned to attend a top-notch graduate program in psychology. Her grades, however, are only in the C and B range. Her SAT scores are average. Should she try to reframe this factual information or deal with her problem in another way?

8. Susan would like to become better friends with Kaled. She decides to disclose some personal information to Kaled, hoping that this self-disclosure will increase feelings of intimacy between them. Is it ethical to self-disclose to others as a strategy to enhance intimacy in a relationship?

For Your Journal

1. Record goals for your self-talk and note your self-talk messages day by day. You might want to organize your journal around specific topics such as academic achievement, personal appearance, shyness, or social skills. Under Academic Achievement, you could write: "I will monitor my self-talk messages to keep myself on track while I study for two hours each day." Your Personal Appearance self-talk goal may be to tell yourself something positive about your appearance instead of thinking about only what you don't like.

2. Write in your journal the 10 responses you wrote for the Building Your Skills: Who Are You? questionnaire on page 38. Put a marker in your journal at this page for viewing at the end of the course. At the end of the course, again write 10 responses to the "Who are you?" question without looking at your earlier responses. What are the differences in your responses? How do you explain them?

3. If someone were to walk into one of your favourite rooms in your place of residence, what conclusions might he or she draw about your social style? Are you neat and well-organized? Or does your room have the characteristics of an expressive personality? Write a brief description of who you are from a social style perspective based on the clues in your room.

Learning with Others

1. Place the following list of values in order from 1 to 14. In a group with other students, compare your answers. Discuss how your personal ranking of these values influences your interaction with others.

_____ Honesty		_____ Justice	
_____ Salvation		_____ Wealth	
_____ A comfortable life		_____ Beauty	
_____ Good health		_____ Equality	
_____ Human rights		_____ Freedom	
_____ Peace _____		_____ Personal happiness	
_____ Fulfilling work		_____ A personal code of ethics	

2. You are going to create a a coat of arms (in the shape of a shield) that represents your life. Draw a large outline of a shield that fills an entire sheet of paper. Divide your coat of arms into four equal sections. In the upper right-hand section, draw or symbolize something at which you have skill or talent. In the upper left-hand section, draw or symbolize something you are trying to improve or a new skill you are learning. In the lower right-hand section, draw or symbolize your most prized material possession. Finally, in the lower left-hand section, write three words that you hope someone would use to describe you.

Share your coat of arms with other students. Tell your classmates why you drew what you did. Discuss how your coat of arms reflects your attitudes, beliefs, and values.

3. Go through your personal music library of tapes or CDs and identify a selection that best symbolizes you. Your selection may be based on either the lyrics or the music. Bring your selection to class and play it for your classmates. (Your instructor will bring a tape or CD player.) Tell why this music symbolizes you. Discuss with classmates how today's music provides a glimpse of our culture and a vehicle for self-expression.

Weblinks

www.social-anxiety.com   This is an excellent site by the Berent Associates. It contains a great deal of information about shyness and social phobias and includes case studies.

www.shyness.com   This site, sponsored by The Shyness Institute, has a host of resources on shyness including, symptoms, causes, consequences, and treatment.

www.queendom.com   This site is devoted to tests including personality tests. Some of the tests are for fun while others have good reliability and validity.

www.abacon.com/commstudies/interpersonal/indisclosure.html   Want to learn more about the Johari Window? This site about self-disclosure helps explain this concept and gives you an opportunity to complete an interactive activity and take a short quiz to test your understanding of it.

http://paceinc.gospelcom.net//html/comtic8.htm   A more detailed site on self-disclosure that also includes the Johari Window.

Interpersonal Communication and Perception

After you study this chapter

you should be able to ...

1. Define "perception" and "interpersonal perception."

2. Identify and explain the three stages of interpersonal perception.

3. Describe the relationship between interpersonal communication and interpersonal perception.

4. Explain how we form impressions of others, describe others, and interpret others' behaviour.

5. Identify the eight factors that distort the accuracy of our interpersonal perceptions.

6. Offer six suggestions for improving your interpersonal perceptions.

- Understanding the Interpersonal Perception Process

- Perception and Interpersonal Communication

- Perceiving Others

- Identifying Barriers to Accurate Perceptions

- Improving Your Perceptual Skills

What you see and what you hear depends a good deal on where you are standing. It also depends on what sort of person you are.

C. S. LEWIS

Look at the painting in Figure 3.1 on page 78. What is happening and what has happened? What is the relationship among the individuals in the painting? You probably have deduced that the boy was running away from home, the police officer found him, and then the officer took the boy into the local coffee shop for ice cream or some other treat. Perhaps you think that the server is wistfully recalling his own days of running away as a child. What are your feelings about the police officer? Do you see him as a friendly and caring person who has a good understanding of kids?

In Chapter 1, we defined human communication as the process of making sense of the world and sharing that sense with others by creating meaning through the use of verbal and non-verbal messages. In this chapter, we discuss the first half of that definition: the process of making sense of our world. How we make sense out of what we experience is the starting point for what we share with others. As human beings, we interpret and attribute meaning to what we observe or experience, particularly if what we are observing is other people. We tend to make inferences about their motives, personalities, and other traits based on their physical qualities and behaviours. Those who are skilled at making observations and interpretations have a head start in developing effective interpersonal relationships.

Most of the time, we are unaware of our own perception process. For example, you may not have realized that you were drawing conclusions about the painting until you read the questions above. However, we may become aware of the process when differences in perception cause a conflict or disagreement. In truth, no two individuals ever perceive the same thing in exactly the same way. Fortunately, communication tools, such as conversation, allow us to create shared meanings despite the differences in our perceptions.

Our perceptions are influenced by who we are, including the accumulation of our experiences. If you have had several bad experiences with the police, for example, you may not view the police officer in the painting in Figure 3.1 as a friendly person. Or if you know something about the life and work of Norman Rockwell, the illustrator who painted the picture, you may view all his works as representations of an idyllic American culture and society that existed only in his mind. As we noted in Chapter 2, everything we perceive is filtered through our self-concept.[1] It is important to recognize and examine factors that might distort the accuracy of our interpretations. We can also reduce inaccuracies by applying an other-oriented approach as we interact with people. By focusing on how others perceive the world, we can reduce the amount of distortion that our own self-concepts impose on our perceptions.

Figure 3.1
***The Runaway*. Original oil painting for a *Saturday Evening Post* cover, September 20, 1958. Old Corner House Collection, Stockbridge, Massachusetts.**

Source: Printed by permission of the Rockwell Family Trust. Copyright © *The Runaway*, the Norman Rockwell Family Trust.

 Before we turn to the role that perception plays in interpersonal communication, let's first take a closer look at the interpersonal perception process itself.

Building Your Skills

PERCEPTUAL DIFFERENCES

Think of two instances in which you and a friend had a very similar perception of something—perhaps the food in a restaurant, a scene in a movie, or some behaviour you observed in some other person. How did you know that you and your friend had similar perceptions? What factors in your backgrounds influenced the way you each perceived the experience?

Now think of two instances in which you and a friend had differ-ent perceptions of the same thing. How did you discover that you and your friend had different percep-tions? To what factors in each of your backgrounds do you attribute these different perceptions? What effects did the differences in percep-tion have on your interactions?

Understanding the Interpersonal Perception Process

perception. Experiencing the world and making sense out of what is experienced.

What is perception? We collect information about our world through our five senses. We make sense of the world through perception. **Perception** is the process of under-standing or making sense of sensory experiences. For example, a sound travels through the air, vibrates on your eardrum, activates the nerves, and sends a signal to the brain. Perception allows you to define what that sound means. A similar sequence of events takes place when you see, smell, feel, or taste something. The process of perception also includes organizing and interpreting information provided by the senses. You come out of a building and see wet pavement and puddles of water, hear thunder, smell a distinct odour caused by ions, and observe drops of falling water. You integrate all those bits of information and conclude that it is raining and has been for a while.

Our perceptions of other people, however, include analysis and interpretation that go beyond simple interpretation of sensory information. **Interpersonal perception** is the process by which we decide what people are like and give meaning to their actions. It includes making judgments about personality and drawing inferences from what we have observed.[2] When you meet someone new, you *select* certain information to attend to (you note whether the person is male or female, has an accent, smiles, uses a friendly tone of voice), as well as particular personal information (the person is from Lunenburg, Nova Scotia). You then *organize* the information under some category that is recognizable to you, such as "a friendly Maritimer." Then you *interpret* the organized perceptions: this person is trustworthy, honest, hardworking, and likeable.

In our discussion, we will focus on this kind of interpersonal perception, which relates to understanding our observations of other people. We will begin by examining the three stages of the interpersonal perception process that we described above: selecting, organizing, and interpreting what we observe.

interpersonal perception. The process of selecting, organizing, and interpreting one's observations of other people.

selective perception. Directing one's attention to specific stimuli and consequently ignoring other stimuli.

Stage One: Selecting

Sit for a minute after you read this passage and try to tune into all the sensory input you are receiving: consider the feel of your socks against your feet, the pressure of the floor on your heels, the pressure of the piece of furniture against your body as you sit, the buzzing sounds from various sources around you—this "white noise" might come from a refrigerator, a personal computer, fluorescent lights, water in pipes, voices, passing traffic, or your own heartbeat, or churning stomach. What do you smell? What do you see? Without moving your eyes, turn your awareness to the images you see in the corner of your vision. What colours do you see? What shapes? What taste is in your mouth? How do the pages of this book feel against your fingertips? Now stop reading and consider all these sensations. Try to focus on all of them at the same time. You can't. The number of sensations we can attend to at any given time is limited. We are, therefore, selective about which sensations make it through to the level of awareness. Perhaps you close your eyes or sit in the dark as you listen to music. This allows you to select more auditory sensations because you are eliminating visual ones.

During the selection stage, you attempt to simplify the stimuli that flood in through your senses, using various techniques. You use perceptual filters to screen out constant sensations that you have learned are unimportant, such as the sensations of your clothes against your skin and the surrounding white noise and smells. However, you do attend to the sensation of the elastic in your slacks if it pulls too tight because a threshold of arousal is crossed, forcing the brain to attend to that stimulus. Each of your senses has such a threshold.

Directing our attention to specific stimuli and consequently ignoring others is called **selective perception**. Your eye and your brain do not work like a camera, which records everything in the picture. Basically, photographs capture what your camera "sees" through its viewfinder. In contrast, your brain doesn't necessarily process *everything* you see through your "viewfinders," your eyes. Similarly, your sense of hearing is not a microphone that picks up every audible sound. Your brain selects sounds that are significant or important to you in some way and brings them to your conscious attention.

In a court of law, eyewitness testimony often determines whether someone is found innocent or guilty of a crime. Recent research suggests, however, that a witness's powers of observation are not flawless. In fact, scientists have discovered several perceptual errors in eyewitness testimony. Many innocent people have been convicted because of what a witness thought he or she saw or heard.[3] As this evidence documents, the eye is not a camera; the ear is not a microphone.

Stage Two: Organizing

Look at the four items in Figure 3.2. What does each of them mean to you? If you are like most people, you will perceive item A as the word *interpersonal*, item B as a circle, C as a rabbit, and D as a telephone number. Strictly speaking, none of those perceptions is correct. We'll discuss why after we explore the second stage of perception: organization.

After we select which stimuli we are going to attend to and process, we start to organize them into convenient, understandable, and efficient patterns that allow us to make sense of what we have observed. Organizing makes it easier for us to process complex information because it allows us to impose the familiar onto the unfamiliar and because we can easily store and recall simple patterns. For example, when you look at item C in Figure 3.2, you see the pattern of dots, which you then identify as a rabbit because *rabbit* is a concept you know and to which you attach various meanings. The set of dots does not have meaning for you in and of itself; nor would it be meaningful for you to attend to each particular dot or to the dots' relationship to one another. It would be possible to create a mathematical model of the dots indicating their placement on an X–Y grid, but such a model would be extremely complex and difficult to observe and remember. It's much easier to organize the dots in a way that refers to something stored in your memory: a rabbit. For similar reasons, we organize patterns of stars in the sky into various animals and familiar shapes like the bear, the crab, and the Big and Little Dippers. As we do for the pattern of dots making up the rabbit, we search for and apply patterns to our perceptions of people.

Figure 3.2
What Do You See?

A. **N T R P R S N L**

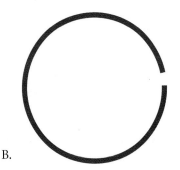

B.

C.

D. **5 5 5   4 4 3 3**

The way we organize information depends partly on the way we punctuate it. **Punctuation** is the process of making sense out of stimuli by grouping, dividing, organizing, separating, and categorizing information when communicating with others.[4] Just as the punctuation marks on this page help you make sense of each sentence, punctuation in the perception process makes it possible for you to see patterns in information. Item D in Figure 3.2 looks like a telephone number because it has three numbers followed by four numbers. You might also remember that 555 is the prefix you use for calling long-distance information. However, the digits could just as easily represent two totally independent numbers: 555 followed by the number 4433. How we interpret the numbers depends on how we punctuate or separate them. When we record information, we use commas, periods, dashes, and colons to signal meanings and interpretations. In our minds, sometimes we impose punctuation marks where we believe they should be. We may, for example, have mentally inserted a hyphen between 555 and 4433, even though no hyphen actually appears there.

When it comes to punctuating relational events and behaviours, we each develop our own separate set of standards. You will sometimes experience difficulties and disagreements because of differences in how you and your partner choose to punctuate a conversational exchange or shared sequence of events.[5] Suppose you and a friend have been talking about her recent school problems. After a few moments of silence, you assume that your conversation on that topic has ended, so you start talking about your recent job interview. Later on, you find out that you offended your friend because she had not punctuated the conversation the same way. She believed that her problems should still have been the focus of the conversation.

In addition to punctuating, you also **superimpose**, or place a familiar structure on information you select. Looking again at Figure 3.2, you can see that our inclination to *superimpose*, or place a familiar structure on information we select, also leads us to create a familiar word from the meaningless assemblage of letters in item A, and to label the figure in item B a circle, even though circles are continuous lines without gaps on the right side. We apply the same principles and search for and apply patterns in our perception of people. When we have an incomplete picture of another human being, we impose a pattern or structure, classify the person on the basis of the information we do have, and fill in the gaps. Filling in these gaps is known as **closure**. We apply these principles to our interaction with other people. We fill in the gaps in our knowledge based on how people dress, how they speak, the manner in which they speak, and other bits and pieces of incomplete information.

Stage Three: Interpreting

You see your best friend across a crowded room at a party. Your friend waves to you, and you say to yourself, "He wants to talk with me." Or you nervously wait as your British literature teacher hands back the results of the last exam. When the professor calls your name, she frowns ever so slightly; your heart sinks. You think, "I must have bombed on the test." Or, while you were out, your administrative assistant left you a note saying that your sister has called. You're worried. You reflect, "My tightwad sister never uses her daytime cellphone minutes to call during the day. There must be something wrong." In each of these situations, you're trying to make sense out of the information you hear or see. You're attempting to interpret the meaning of the verbal and non-verbal cues you experience.

punctuation. Making sense out of stimuli by grouping, dividing, organizing, separating, and categorizing information.

superimpose. To place a familiar structure on information you select.

closure. The filling in of missing information.

Once we have selected and organized stimuli into familiar patterns, we are ready to interpret what they mean. We attach meaning to all that we observe, hear, taste, smell, and touch. Our interpretations may not be accurate, but we make them nonetheless. We learn through socialization and our own recurring experiences to attribute particular meaning to particular stimuli. In some cases, the meanings are fairly standard, as with language, for example. You read the word "computer," and you have some sense of what that word means, but other instances are much more personal.

If you shake someone's hand and it feels like a wet, dead fish, what is your reaction and interpretation? If you notice someone you don't know winking at you from across a room, what do you think? If a toddler is crying in a room full of people and a woman comes over and picks the child up, what do you assume about the woman? If you see a student glance over at another student's exam paper and then record an answer, what do you think the student has done? All of these are examples that show we impose meaning on what we observe to complete the perceptual process.

Building Your Skills

PERCEPTUAL INTERPRETATIONS

Find a place where you can sit and watch people for a while. Write down as many points as you can that you are able to observe about the people who pass by or who are seated nearby. Try to make some interpreta-tions based on your observations, just as Sherlock Holmes might have done. What do you notice about their clothing, their shoes, the man-ner in which they walk? What are they carrying with them? Do they seem to be in a hurry? Can you tell which are students, teachers, or members of other professions? If you are watching other students, can you tell what their majors are?

If you get the chance, you might approach some of these people and see how accurate your observations are. People are generally open to hearing positive perceptions about themselves. You may want to hold back on sharing negative percep-tions.

Recap

THE INTERPERSONAL PERCEPTION PROCESS

Term	Explanation	Examples
Selection	The first stage in the perceptual process, in which we select and simplify sensations for our awareness.	Sitting in your apartment, where you hear lots of traffic sounds and car horns, you attend to a particular rhythmic car honking that seems to be right outside your door.
Organization	The second stage in the perceptual process, in which we assemble stimuli into convenient and efficient patterns or categories.	You put together the honking horn and your anticipation of a friend arriving to pick you up to drive to a movie that starts in five minutes.
Interpretation	The final stage in perception, in which we assign meaning to what we have observed.	You decide the honking horn must be your friend's signal to you to come out to the car quickly because she is running late.

Perception and Interpersonal Communication

In the midst of interpersonal communication, interpersonal perception is a two-way street. Our perceptions of others affect the ways in which we communicate with them, and their perceptions of us affect the way they communicate with us.

We continually modify the topics, the language, and the manner in which we communicate according to the perceptions we have of others. For example, if you observe a woman dressed in a track suit running in a park, you might conclude that she is a physical fitness fanatic. Then, if you strike up a conversation with her, you might bring up topics such as physical fitness, sports, and diet. However, if she informs you that she knows nothing about those things and has just started jogging to offset the time she spends watching videos and eating potato chips, then you would probably shift your focus according to a revised perception. You might start talking about movies or the relative merits of rippled versus plain potato chips. Similarly, if you were talking to a child, you would probably use simple language. If you were talking to a person who is hearing impaired, you might slow down your speech and enunciate more clearly. The way that others talk and behave also tells us a great deal about how they perceive us. Maybe you can remember the first time someone younger than you called you "sir" or "madam" (if it hasn't happened yet, it will). It probably surprised you to realize that someone perceived you as "old," or as someone with authority. We also analyze others' reactions to us for clues about their conception of who we are. As an example, suppose your new college friends go out to play basketball, your favourite sport, but do not invite you. When you later ask them why, they say they think of you as the unathletic, studious type. Sometimes others' perceptions of us are surprising. If we never ask, we may never discover that they are inaccurate. The degree to which others have a conception of us that is different from our own is often a measure of the quality of the relationship. The stronger the interpersonal relationship, the closer our self-perceptions are to the perceptions others have of us.[6]

How much we notice about another person's communication behaviour relates to our level of interest and need. Perception can be either a passive or an active process. **Passive perception** occurs simply because our senses are in operation. We see, hear, smell, taste, and feel things around us without any conscious attempt to do so. **Active perception** is the process of seeking out specific information by intentionally observing and questioning; we make a conscious effort to figure out what we are experiencing. We've all heard noises that startle us and make us wonder, "What was that?" We then try to recall the sound and identify it, or we might investigate—seek out additional information.

If you can gain information and reduce your uncertainty about others, then you can predict their reactions and behaviours, adapt your behaviours and strategies, and therefore maximize the likelihood of fulfilling your social needs.[7] Although this might sound calculating, it really isn't. If you enjoy outdoor activities, such as camping and hiking, one of your goals in establishing social relationships is probably to find others who share your interest. So observing, questioning, and processing information to determine a potential friend's interests can help you assess whether the relationship will meet your goals. In Chapter 4, we discuss ways to improve your ability to gain information through more effective listening.

passive perception. Perception that occurs because your senses are in operation.

active perception. Perception that occurs because you seek out specific information through intentional observation and questioning.

Perceiving Others

impressions. A collection of perceptions about others that you maintain and use to interpret their behaviours.

impression formation theory. Theory that explains how you develop perceptions about people and how you maintain and use those perceptions to interpret their behaviours.

primacy effect. Placing heavy emphasis on the first pieces of information that we observe about another to form an impression.

recency effect. Placing heavy emphasis on the most recent information we have observed about another to form or modify our impression.

As we collect information about others, we organize and interpret that information in various ways. Interpersonal perception involves three processes: forming impressions of others; applying implicit personality theories and the use of mental constructs, which we use to organize information about people; and finally, developing attribution theories, which help us explain why people behave the way they do.

How We Form Impressions of Others

Impressions are collections of perceptions about others that we maintain and use to interpret their behaviours. Impressions tend to be very general: "She seemed nice," "He was very friendly," or "What a nerd!" According to **impression formation theory**, we form these impressions through perceptions of physical qualities and behaviour, information people disclose about themselves, and information that third parties tell us. We select, organize, and interpret all of these perceptions to create a general impression. In the *In Canada* box, you will find a brief history and some facts about Buzz Hargrove. What is your current impression of this CAW leader? After reading the feature, did your impression change at all? We tend to form these impressions readily and part with them reluctantly. When we first meet someone, we form a first impression without having much information, and we often hold on to this impression throughout the relationship.

In one study conducted by Solomon Asch, individuals were asked to provide an evaluation of two people based on two lists of adjectives.[8] The list for the first person gave the following characteristics: *intelligent, industrious, impulsive, critical, stubborn,* and *envious.* The list for the other person had the same adjectives but in reverse order. Although the content was identical, respondents gave the first person a more positive evaluation than the second. One explanation for this is that the first words in each list created a first impression that respondents used to interpret the remaining adjectives. In a similar manner, the first impressions we form about someone often affect our interpretation of subsequent perceptions of them.

This effect of attending to the first pieces of information that we observe is called the **primacy effect**. We also tend to put a lot of stock in the last thing we observed, which is called the **recency effect**.[9] For example, if you thought for years that your friend is honest, but today, you discover that she lied to you about something important, that lie will likely have a greater impact on your impression of her than the honest behaviour she has displayed for years.

We also attempt to manage the impressions others form of us. We make guesses about how other people will interpret our own physical displays and behaviours; as a result, we attempt to manipulate those displays and behaviours to our advantage. Think about the first day of classes this semester. Did you think about what clothes

When we're not sure about the meaning intended by another's message, it is wise to actively check out the meaning by asking what he or she meant by the words.
(Bob Daemmrich/Stock Boston)

you were going to wear to class? Did you give some thought to how your hair looked or how your breath smelled? Most of us choose clothes that we think will create a positive statement and reflect who we are. In this way, we attempt to manage the impressions others form of us. Our ability to manage such impressions effectively depends on our ability to socially decentre (as discussed in the next chapter) by looking at ourselves from other people's perspectives. The more accurate you are at determining how others will react to appearances and behaviours, the more potential you have for adapting the way you look and behave.

In Canada...

BUZZ HARGROVE: WHAT'S YOUR IMPRESSION?

What is your impression of Buzz Hargrove, leader of the Canadian Auto Workers Union?
(CP Photo/Frank Gunn)

According to one source, you either love him or hate him. Or maybe some people just love to hate him. He has been called a lot of things, from showman to bully to bluffer. Whatever your perceptions are of Buzz Hargrove, he is one of the most influential and powerful public figures in Canada today. As the leader of the Canadian Auto Workers (CAW) since 1992, he has fought many battles including re-election to several three-year terms.

He was born Basil Eldon Hargrove in 1944 in Bath, New Brunswick, and was the sixth of 10 children. His father, Percy, was a carpenter who worked at logging camps during the winter. The family was poor and his mother, Eileen, grew potatoes to pay for the children's clothes. His mother left the family by 1958, leaving him and his siblings with their difficult father. At 16, Hargrove dropped out of school after finishing grade 10 and drifted from job to job. Finally, in 1964, he landed in the Windsor Chrysler plant in Ontario while visiting his older brother. Ken Gerrard, the plant chairman for the union local, helped him get a job on the line making seat cushions.

In 1965, the same year the Canada–US Auto Pact was rectified, Hargrove was elected as shop steward. That's when he met union leader Bob White. Hargrove was at White's side during the rebellion against the American UAW leaders, which eventually led to the creation of a new union, the CAW. Until White left the CAW for the presidency of the Canadian Labour Congress, the two worked closely together, and in 1992 Hargrove took over the helm. Since then, he has made friends and enemies in management and union alike.[i] Also, it should be noted that he is a member of the New Democratic Party and is quite vocal in his views on what he thinks the party should and should not do. Here are just a few of the events in the history of Hargrove's leadership of the CAW. Consult your local newspaper's business section and you will continue to find him in the news.

- In 1995, according to one source, the NDP convinced themselves that it was Hargrove and the public-sector unions that were responsible for the decline in the NDP vote from 39 percent to 21 percent. By 1999, the vote had collapsed to 12 percent. Blame it on Buzz?[ii]

- In 1996, after finishing the last round of negotiations with the "Big Three" car companies (Chrysler, General Motors, and Ford), Hargrove announced the final deal with Ford with a box of Pablum and a baby spoon in hand. He was quoted as saying that the company would take to his demands "like babies to their first solid foods: they spit it out at first but learn to like it."[iii]

- Shortly after signing a new collective agreement in October 1998, the Canadian National

Continued

Railway Co. announced that it was eliminating 3000 jobs from its current payroll of 6000 employees. Labour leaders, including Hargrove, expressed their outrage. Hargrove in particular was vocal as investors rewarded the company by driving up its share price in the face of such "fiscal responsibility." This was not the first time that company shares had appreciated in the wake of major layoffs or plant closures. According to Hargrove, the corporations and the government are to blame: "What corporations have achieved is nothing less than the systematic dismantling of the socio-economic system that Canadians have built over the last four decades."[iv]

● In December 2000, Hargrove and Ken Georgetti were feuding over shop-floor raiding. Georgetti is the chief of the Canadian Labour Congress (CLC), an umbrella organization to which the CAW belongs. The CLC was not pleased with how the CAW had been drawing new memberships from two other unions (the Service Employees International Union and the Public Service Alliance of Canada). Such "poaching" is prohibited by the CLC constitution. Hargrove's position is that all working people should have a say as to what union they belong to. According to one article, Hargrove was right, as unions provide a service for which customers pay (through union dues).[v]

● In February 2003, he urged Ontario doctors from the Ontario Medical Association to mobilize around fees for service and declare their independence from the Ontario government. "The one thing that has to be absolutely clear is the independence of the bargaining agent from the employer," Hargrove told a conference held by the Coalition of Family Physicians in Toronto. At the conference he also criticized the provincial government on a number of other issues, including tax cuts.[vi]

Sources: i. Deirdre McMurdy and Luke Fisher, "Big Bad Buzz," *Maclean's*, December 16, 1996, 22–24; CBC TV's *Life and Times* biographies, "Buzz Hargrove: Labour of Love," www.tv.cbc.ca/lifeandtimes/bio2000/hargrove.htm.
ii. Geoff Bickerton, "Buzz, Battles and Bombs," *Canadian Dimension*, Fall 1999, Vol. 33 (4/5), 16.
iii. Canadian Press, "Big Three Talks End with Ford Deal," *Canadian News Digest*, Wednesday, November 6, 1996, www.canoe.ca/NewsArchiveNov96/candigest_nov6.html.
iv. Deirdre McMurdy, "Passionate, but Wrong," *Maclean's*, November 30, 1998, 64.
v. Derek DeCloet, "Brother Against Brother," *Canadian Business*, June 12, 2000, 103.
vi. Canadian Press, "Buzz Hargrove Tells Ontario Doctors to Mobilize," Saturday, February 22, 2003, www.ctv.ca/servlet/ArticleNews/story/CTVNews/1045966934878_80.

How We Describe Others

Do you like to "people watch?" When we have time on our hands while waiting for a friend, we often start looking at people and making guesses about what these strangers do for a living, or whether they are friendly or grumpy, peaceful or petulant, kind or mean. We make assumptions about their personality. Even with people we know well, we don't know everything about them. When attempting to understand others, we rely on these guesses or assumptions to describe their characteristics and personalities.

These hunches help us to develop an **implicit personality theory**, a pattern of associated qualities that we attribute to people, which allows us to understand them—whether we met them 10 minutes ago or 10 years ago. We make guesses about who other people are, based on the information we have about them. Implicit personality theory provides a way of organizing the vast array of information we have about people's personalities.[10] Implicit personality theories are essentially stereotypes that we apply to people in general. We accomplish perceptual closure through the use of implicit personality theory; that is, we are able to fill in the blanks

implicit personality theory. Our own set of beliefs and hypotheses about what people are like.

about a person's personality without actually having to observe additional qualities. Once you have determined that someone is a "warm" person, you automatically associate other related terms. Your implicit personality theory may be similar to that held by others in your culture, but each person forms his or her own individual theory. There is more consistency between the personality frameworks you use to judge two strangers than there is between the personality frameworks that you and another person use to describe the same stranger.

Implicit personality theories allow us to manage a lot of information effectively, but they can also lead us to incorrect conclusions about other people. How accurately does "happy" describe a "warm" person? No doubt some warm people are very unhappy. In assuming a connection between these two concepts, you might have reached an erroneous conclusion about the other person. When you assume the warm person is happy, you might not perceive the person's need for support and nurturing. As a result, your responses will be inappropriate and lead to ineffective interpersonal communication. Therefore, while implicit personality theories may fill in some of the blanks about a person, the danger is that we will operate under the theory without attempting to gather more information or to check out what may be incorrect perceptions.

One feature common to most of our implicit personality theories is the tendency to put people into two categories: those we like and those we don't like. When we observe people we like, there is often a **halo effect**; we attribute a variety of positive qualities to them because we like them. If you like me, then you will assume I have nothing except angelic qualities: I am nice to other people, warm and caring, fun to be with, and have a great sense of humour. On the other hand, if you don't like me, you may think of me as a devil, attributing to me a variety of negative qualities. This is called the **horn effect**. Research suggests that during periods of conflict in our relationships, we are more likely to attribute negative behaviours to the other person than we are to ourselves.[11]

In support of the premise underlying the horn effect, researchers Dominic Infante and Andrew Rancer observed that some people have a tendency to see the worst in others, which causes them to lash out and be verbally aggressive.[12] There is also evidence that some people interpret any negative feedback they receive as a personal attack, no matter how carefully the feedback is worded.[13] For many people, there is no such thing as "constructive criticism." Like those afflicted with severe sunburn, such people perceive even a mild suggestion presented with a light touch as a stinging rebuke.

Although implicit personality theory describes how we organize and interpret our perceptions of people's personalities in general, we develop categories for people, called **constructs**, that help us explain our perceptions of a specific person. When constructs are used to categorize people, they are referred to as **personal constructs**. Constructs are bipolar in their dimensions. Personal constructs represent qualities that allow us to categorize people into one of two groups of polar

halo effect.   Attributing a variety of positive qualities to those we like.

horn effect.   Attributing a variety of negative qualities to those we dislike.

constructs.   Bipolar qualities that you associate with people as you conceptualize them.

personal constructs.   Specific qualities or attributes we associate with each person we know.

To help us understand the people we know, we develop a set of personal constructs for each person. A highly perceptive person may see a whole array of constructs for this woman: whimsical, warm, dependable, friendly, generous, and kind. A person with a less developed set of constructs may see only the whimsical side of her.
(Brigid Allig/Tony Stone Images)

opposites: friendly or unfriendly, intelligent or unintelligent, graceful or clumsy, extrovert or introvert, funny or serious, conservative or liberal, overachiever or underachiever, playful or studious and so on.

How We Interpret the Behaviour of Others

"I know why Alice didn't come to our meeting. She just doesn't like me," says Cathy. "She also just wants people to think she's too busy to be bothered with our little group." Cathy not only seems to have formed a negative impression of Alice, but she also harbours a hunch as to why Alice didn't come to the meeting. Cathy is attributing meaning to Alice's behaviour. Even though Alice could have just forgotten about the meeting, Cathy thinks Alice's absence is caused by feelings of superiority and contempt. Cathy's assumptions about Alice can be explained by attribution theory.

Attribution theory explains how we ascribe specific motives and causes to the behaviours of others. It helps us interpret what people do and why they are doing it. Suppose a student sitting next to you in class gets up in the middle of the lecture and walks out. Why did the student leave? Did the student become angry at something the instructor said? No, the lecturer was simply describing types of cloud formations. Was the student sick? You remember noticing that the student looked a little flushed and occasionally winced. Maybe the student had an upset stomach. Or maybe the student is a bit of a rebel and often does things like leave in the middle of a class.

Social psychologist Fritz Heider said that we are "naive psychologists"[14] because we all seek to explain the motives people have for their actions. These explanations are naive because we do not create them in a systematic or scientific manner but rather by applying common sense to our observations. Developing the most credible explanation for the behaviour of others is the goal of the **attribution** process.

Causal attribution theory identifies three potential causes for any person's action: circumstance, a stimulus, or the person her- or himself.[15] Attributing to *circumstance* means that you believe a person acts in a certain way because the situation leaves no choice. This way of thinking places responsibility for the action outside the person. You would be attributing to circumstance if you believed the student quickly left the classroom because of an upset stomach. Concluding that the student left because the instructor said something inappropriate would be attributing the student's action to the *stimulus* (the instructor). However, if you knew the instructor hadn't said anything out of line and that the student was perfectly healthy, you might place the responsibility for the action on the student. Attributing to the *person* means that you believe there is some quality about the person that caused the observed behaviour.

attribution theory. Theory that explains how you generate explanations for people's behaviours.

attribution. The reasons we develop to explain the behaviours of others.

causal attribution theory. One theory of attribution, based on determining whether a person's actions are caused by circumstance, a stimulus, or the person.

To explore how attributions to a person affect us, interpersonal communication researchers Anita Vangelisti and Stacy Young wanted to know whether intentionally hurtful words inflict more pain than unintentionally hurtful comments.[16] As you might suspect, if we think someone intends to hurt us, spiteful words have more sting and bite than if we believe someone does not intend to hurt our feelings. Our attributions are factors in our impressions.

Standpoint theory is yet another framework that seeks to explain how we interpret the behaviour of others. The theory is relatively simple: we each see the world differently because we're each viewing it from a different position. Some people have positions of power and others do not; the resources we have to help us make our way through life provide a lens through which we view the world and the people in it. The quotation from C. S. Lewis that opens this chapter points to the power of perspective: where you stand makes a difference in what you see.

standpoint theory. The theory that a person's social position, power, or cultural background influences how the person perceives the behaviour of others; where you stand makes a difference in what you see.

Standpoint theory explains why people with differing cultural backgrounds have different perceptions of others' behaviour. In the early 19th century, German philosopher Georg Hegel noted this simple but powerful explanation of why people see and experience the world differently.[17] Hegel was especially interested in how one's standpoint was determined in part by one's power and influence. For example, people who have greater power and more influence in a particular culture may not be aware of their power and influence and how this power affects their perceptions of others. People with less power (which in many cultures includes women and people of colour) may be acutely aware of the power they don't have.

A number of factors affect the accuracy of our attributions: our ability to make effective and complete observations; the degree to which we are able to observe directly the cause and the effect; the completeness of our information; our position or standpoint; and our ability to rule out other causes. It is also helpful to know how unique a person's response is to the particular stimulus, to compare the person's response to how other people typically respond, and to know whether the person usually responds to the stimulus in the same way each time. Even with the most complete information, however, we can never completely understand another person's action because we cannot become the other person. Fortunately, we can improve our level of understanding by becoming more sensitive to the assumptions or theories we use to make attributions.

Understanding Diversity

THE POWER OF PERSPECTIVE

As noted in our discussion of standpoint theory, where you stand makes a difference in what you see and how you interpret human behaviour. Since the recent nationwide debate about the rights of gays and lesbians to marry, discussion about perceptions of the power and influence of different cultural groups has become more common. Religious leaders, political leaders, and most Canadians in general are becoming much more sensitive to how deeply these beliefs about what is right, wrong, moral, immoral, just, and unjust are held across different groups.

Men and women, blacks and whites, Jews and Christians, Muslims and Hindus, Hispanics and Asians, Aboriginals and non-Aboriginals, English-Canadians and French-Canadians, gay people and straight people, all experience life from their own cultural standpoint, which means they all have perceptions about their influence on others. To become more other-oriented is to become aware of your own perceived place in society and to be more sensitive to how that position of power or lack of power affects how you perceive others with a different standpoint.

To explore applications of standpoint theory in your life, consider the following questions:

1. How would you describe your standpoint in terms of power and influence in your school, at work, or in your family? Have you ever experienced rejection, alienation, or discrimination based on how others perceived you?

2. How would other people in your life (parents, siblings, children, co-workers, employers, or friends) describe your power and influence on them?

3. How does your standpoint influence your relationship with others? Identify a specific relationship with a teacher, co-worker, or family member in which different standpoints influence the quality of the relationship in either positive or negative ways.

4. What can you do to become more aware of how your standpoint influences your interactions with others? How can your increased awareness enhance the quality of your interpersonal communication with others?

 ## Recap

HOW WE ORGANIZE AND INTERPRET INTERPERSONAL PERCEPTIONS TO PERCEIVE OTHERS

Theory	Definition	Examples
Impression Formation	We form general perspectives we have of others based on general physical qualities, behaviours, and disclosed information.	Categorizing people as nice, friendly, shy, or handsome.
Implicit Personality	We form our own personal general theory about the way people think and behave.	"If she is intelligent, then she must be caring, too."
Attribution Theory	We develop reasons to explain the behaviours of others. We attribute others' actions to the circumstance, to a stimulus, or to the person.	"I guess she didn't return my call because she doesn't like me." "He's just letting off steam because he had a bad week of exams."
Causal Attribution Theory	We ascribe a person's actions to circumstance, a stimulus, or the person himself or herself.	"He didn't go to class because his alarm didn't go off." "He didn't go to class because it was a makeup session." "He didn't go to class because he is bored by it."
Standpoint Theory	We interpret the behaviour of others through the lens of our own social position, power, or cultural background.	"He won't join the fraternity because he doesn't understand how important that network can be to his professional career."

Identifying Barriers to Accurate Perceptions

Think about the most recent interaction you have had with a stranger. Do you remember the person's age, sex, race, or body size? Did the person have any distinguishing features such as a beard, tattoos, or a loud voice? The qualities you recall will most likely serve as the basis for attributions you make about that person's behaviour. However, these attributions, based on your first impressions, might be highly inaccurate. We each see the world from our own unique perspective. This perspective is clouded by a number of distortions and barriers that contribute to inaccurate interpersonal perception. We'll examine these barriers next.

Ignoring Information

Sometimes we overlook important information because we give too much weight to information that is obvious and superficial.[18] Why do we ignore important information that may be staring us in the face? The answer lies in what we learned about attribution theory. We tend to explain the motives for a person's actions on the basis of the most obvious information rather than on any in-depth information we might have. When meeting someone new, we perceive his or her physical qualities first: colour of skin, body size and shape, age, sex, and other obvious physical characteristics. We overattribute to these qualities because they are so vivid and available. We have all been victims of these kinds of attributions, some of us more than others. Often, we are unaware that others are making biased attributions because they do not express them openly. However, sometimes we can tell by the way others react to us and treat us.

One female student described a job interview in which the male interviewer talked at her for 15 minutes and then abruptly dismissed her without asking a single question. A male friend of hers with less distinguished academic qualifications and work experience spent 40 minutes fielding questions from this same interviewer. Did the interviewer have a sex bias? Probably. Looking only at the female student's gender, he attributed qualities to her that he decided would make her unsuitable for the job. Instead of looking at the more specific information her résumé provided, he simply disregarded it. As discussed earlier, this tendency reflects our desire to simplify stimuli, but it can be dangerous and unfair.

Overgeneralizing

We treat small amounts of information as if they were highly representative.[19] This tendency also leads us to draw inaccurate, prejudicial conclusions.[20] Your authors, for example, may talk to two students from your school, and then we may generalize the impression we have of those two students to the entire student population. In a similar way, we tend to assume that the small sampling we have of another person's behaviour is a valid representation of who that person is. As we saw in Figure 3.2, we create a rabbit even when we have only a few dots on which to base our perception.

Oversimplifying

We prefer simple explanations to complex ones. When Terry picks you up late to go to a movie, she says, "Sorry, I lost track of the time." The next day, Christine also picks you up late to go to a movie. She says, "Sorry. You wouldn't believe how busy I've been. I ran out of hot water when I was showering and my hair dryer must be busted. It kept shutting off. Then I stopped to get something to eat and it took forever to get my order. Then it turned out they had it all messed up and had to redo it." Who's explanation can you accept more easily—Terry's or Christine's?

Usually, we prefer simple explanations; they tend to be more believable and easier to use in making sense of another's actions. In reality, our behaviours are affected by a multitude of factors, as Christine's explanation indicates. Unfortunately, it takes a lot of effort to understand what makes another person do what he or she does—more effort than we are typically willing to give.

Stereotyping

stereotype   Set of qualities that you attribute to a person because of the person's membership in some category.

Preconceived notions about what they expect to find may keep people from seeing what's before their eyes and ears. We see what we want to see, hear what we want to hear. We stereotype others. To **stereotype** someone is to place the person in a rigid category and then interpret all the person's behaviour from the framework of that category. The word "stereotype" was originally a printing term, referring to a metal plate that was cast from type set by a printer. The plate would print the same page of type over and over again. When we stereotype people, we place them into inflexible, all-compassing categories. We "print" the same judgments on anyone placed into a given category. We may even choose to ignore contradictory information that we receive directly from the other person. Instead of adjusting our conception of that person, we adjust our perception. The halo and horn effects discussed earlier are reflections of this tendency. For example, if an instructor gets an excellent paper from a student who she has concluded is not particularly bright or motivated, she may tend to find errors and shortcomings that are not really there, or she may even accuse the student of plagiarism.

Stereotyping others is apparently widespread. It's not limited to one cultural group. In a study investigating whether people from a variety of cultural backgrounds make stereotypical judgments of others, researchers found that stereotyping is rampant in many cultures.[21] In this study, participants from Australia, Botswana, Canada, Kenya, Nigeria, South Africa, Zambia, Zimbabwe, and the United States all consistently formed stereotypes of others.

Categorizing individuals is not an inherently bad thing to do, but it is harmful to hang on to an inflexible image of another person in the face of contradictory information. For example, not all mothers are responsible or loving, but because North American culture reveres motherhood, we may not easily process our perceptions of a mother who is abusive or negligent.

Imposing Consistency

We overestimate the consistency and constancy of others' behaviours. When we organize our perceptions, we also tend to ignore fluctuation in people's behaviours and see them as consistent. We believe that if someone acted a certain way one day, he or she will continue to act that way in the future. Perhaps you have embarrassed yourself in front of a new acquaintance by acting in a foolish and silly manner. At another encounter with this new acquaintance, you realize that the person is continuing to see your behaviour as foolish, even though you don't intend it to be seen that way. The other person is imposing consistency on your inconsistent behaviour.

In fact, everyone's behaviour varies from day to day. Some days we are in a bad mood, and our behaviour on those days does not represent what we are generally like. As intimacy develops in relationships, we interact with our partners in a variety of activities that provide a more complete picture of our true nature.

Focusing on the Negative

We give more weight to negative information than to positive information.[22] Job interviewers often ask interviewees to describe their strengths and weaknesses. If you describe five great strengths and one weakness, it is likely that the interviewer will attend more to the one weakness you mention than to the strengths. We seem to recognize this bias and compensate for it when we first meet someone by sharing only positive information about ourselves.

Stereotypes can help us make sense out of the wide range of stimuli we encounter every day. However, we also need to be sure that we don't overuse stereotypes and fail to see people as individuals.
(Bill Bachmann/The Image Works)

Building Your Skills

PRECONCEIVED EXPLANATIONS

Think about your own preconceptions about cause–effect relationships. For each of the following, think about what your first explanation of the cause would be:

- A person not calling back after a first date
- A server giving you lousy service
- Your car not being repaired after you have paid a high service fee
- A teacher being late for class
- A child who beats up other kids
- A student who copies test answers from the student next to him
- A mother who refuses to let her teenage son drive the car on Friday nights

Now go back and generate as many alternative explanations for each behaviour as you can. How can you be sure which explanation is correct?

In another of the Solomon Asch experiments on impression formation, participants heard one of the following two lists of terms describing a person: (1) intelligent, skillful, industrious, warm, determined, practical, cautious; or (2) intelligent, skillful, industrious, cold, determined, practical, cautious.[23] The only difference in these two lists is the use of "warm" in the first list and "cold" in the second. Despite the presence of six other terms, those with the "cold" list had a much more negative impression of the person than those with the "warm" list. One piece of negative information can have a disproportionate effect on our impressions and negate the effect of several positive pieces of information.

Making a Fundamental Attribution Error

People are more likely to believe that others are to blame when things go wrong than to believe that the problem was beyond their control. Your parents were looking forward to celebrating their 25th wedding anniversary. They planned a quiet family celebration at a restaurant. You set your personal digital assistant to remind you one week before the anniversary dinner to buy them a present to give to them at the dinner. You hadn't anticipated, however, that you'd lose your Palm Pilot. When the phone rang and your mom asked, "Where are you?" it all came jarringly back to you: today was their anniversary, and you'd forgotten it. Not only did you forget to buy them a present, but you forgot to attend the dinner. Your parents were hurt. Your mother's quivering, "How could you forget?" still sears your conscience. Your parents' hurt feelings evolved into anger. They think you just didn't care enough about them to remember such an important day. Rather than thinking that there might be an explanation for why you forgot their important day, they blame you for your thoughtlessness. Although they certainly have a right to be upset, their assuming that you don't care about them is an example of what researchers call a fundamental attribution error.

A **fundamental attribution error** occurs when a person believes that the cause of a problem is something personally controllable (such as forgetting an important date because you don't care about your parents) rather than something uncontrollable (losing your personal digital assistant and having no back-up system to remind you of the event).[24] As summarized by communication researcher Kory Floyd, fundamental attribution error "predicts that, all other things being equal, people are more likely to attribute others' behavior to internal, controllable causes than to external, uncontrollable causes."[25] For example, fundamental attribution error would predict that you're more likely to assume that the person who cuts you off in traffic is a jerk rather than that he's trying to get out of the way of the truck that's tailgating him. If you assume another person made a conscious choice to hurt you instead of considering that there may be other reasons for the person's behaviour that are beyond the person's control, you've made a fundamental attribution error.

Exhibiting Self-Serving Bias

People are more likely to save face by believing that they are not the cause of a problem. In other words, people assume that other people or events are more than likely the source of problems or events that may put them in an unfavourable light. In one classic episode of *The Simpsons,* Bart Simpson creates a popular catch phrase by saying, "I didn't do it" when he clearly was the cause of a calamity. Whether he is lighting Lisa's hair on fire, calling Moe's tavern asking for Al Coholic, or putting baby Maggie on the roof, Bart defends himself from judgment simply by saying, "I didn't do it." We chuckle at Bart's antics and would never stoop to such juvenile pranks. Yet there is evidence that when we do cause a problem or make a mistake, we are more likely to blame someone else rather than ourselves. Bart's "I didn't do it" approach to life represents self-serving bias.

Self-serving bias is the tendency to perceive our own behaviour as more positive than others' behaviour. Sociologist Erving Goffman was one of the first to note this tendency when he wrote his classic book, *The Presentation of Self in Everyday Life.*[26] We are likely, for example, to attribute our own personal success to our hard work and effort rather than to external, uncontrollable causes. You get an A on your

fundamental attribution error. Attributing another person's behaviour to internal, controllable causes rather than to external, uncontrollable causes.

self-serving bias. The tendency to perceive our own behaviour as more positive than others' behaviour.

anthropology paper because, you think, "I'm smart." When you get an F on your history paper, it's because your neighbour's loud party kept you up all night and you couldn't study. Self-serving bias is the tendency to take credit for the good things that happen to you and to say, "I didn't do it" or "It's not my fault" when bad things happen to you.[27] Research has consistently found that we try to make sense out of the world by first protecting our own sense of positive self-regard.[28] The self-serving bias in the way we attribute meaning to what others do and the events that occur in our lives is one of the obstacles to becoming other-oriented. Blaming others and blaming external causes rather than owning up to our own foibles can keep us from taking an honest look at ourselves. Of course, there are many times when, in fact, you "didn't do it." The challenge lies in sorting out when you are at fault and when you're not. Self-serving bias makes it difficult to make that decision objectively. However, simply being aware of your self-serving bias may help you become more objective and accurate in identifying the causes of calamities in your life.

Recap

BARRIERS TO ACCURATE PERCEPTIONS

Ignoring Information	We give too much weight to information that is obvious and superficial.
Overgeneralizing	We treat small amounts of information as if they were highly representative.
Oversimplifying	We prefer simple explanations to complex ones.
Stereotyping	We allow our pre-existing rigid expectations about others to influence our perceptions.
Imposing consistency	We overestimate the consistency and constancy of others' behaviour.
Focusing on the negative	We give more weight to negative information than to positive information.
Making a fundamental than to attribution error	We are more likely to believe that others are to blame when things go wrong assume that the cause of the problem was beyond their control.
Exhibiting self-serving bias	We save face by believing that other people, not ourselves, are the cause of problems; when things go right, it's because of our own skills and abilities rather than help from others.

 ## Applying Theory and Research

POLITENESS THEORY

Social psychologists Penelope Brown and Stephen Levinson suggest that people from all cultures have a universal need to be treated with politeness.[29] Politeness theory predicts that we will have a positive perception of people who treat us politely and respectfully. Although people from different cultures have varying levels of need to be treated politely, what seems clear is that everyone needs to be valued and appreciated.

A concept related to politeness theory is the need to project a positive image or to have a positive face. Sociologist Erving Goffman suggests that saving face is important for most people.[30] As we discussed in Chapter 2, by "face" we mean more than just our physical face; we're talking about an overall projection of a positive image to other people. Because of our need to be treated politely, our perceptions of others are affected when people violate our expectations and do or say things that are impolite or cause us to lose face. It is polite to help others save face and protect their positive self-image. We behave in ways to help us present the best possible image of ourselves to others.

To have a positive face is to be approved of and liked by others. When people treat us with politeness, they help contribute to a positive face. Providing compliments, behaving respectfully, and showing concern for others are all ways of using positive politeness to help others project a positive face. All would be well and good if we could always provide positive, confirming comments to others, but that simply is not realistic or possible. We engage in face-threatening acts when we communicate in a way that undermines someone's positive face. According to politeness theory, people can communicate in a variety of ways that are face-threatening. The following list is arranged from most to least face-threatening.

1. Bluntly communicating a negative message ("Your office is a mess.")

2. Delivering the negative message but also communicating a posi-tive face-saving message ("Your office is a mess, but perhaps messy is the look you want.")

3. Delivering the negative message but offering a counter-explana-tion to help the person save face ("Your office is a mess, but that's understandable given how much work you do around here.")

4. Communicating the negative message but doing so "off the record" or in such an indirect way that the other person saves face. ("I'm not supposed to tell you this, but even though your office is a mess, the boss is impressed with how well you seem to find everything.")

5. Not communicating any mes-sage that would cause someone to lose face

APPLYING THE RESEARCH TO YOUR LIFE

How is politeness theory of value to you? By being aware of people's need for politeness to help them save face, you can try to be more aware of how you communicate negative messages to others. You can help others main-tain a positive face by consciously trying to be more indirect or to offer a counter-explanation when you deliver a negative message.

Consider the following questions as you apply politeness theory to your own relationships:

1. If you have a face-threatening message for a friend or loved one, what would be a way of express-ing yourself while also letting the other person save face?

2. How are your perceptions of others influenced by the man-ner in which they help you save face? Provide an example of when someone helped you save face and that effort had a posi-tive effect on how you perceived the person.

3. Is being polite and trying to help someone save face merely a way to manipulate others so that they perceive you in a favourable way?

Source: P. Brown and S. Levinson, Politeness: Some Universals in Language Usage (Cambridge, UK: Cambridge University Press, 1987).

Improving Your Perceptual Skills

With so many barriers to perceiving and interpreting other people's behaviour accu-rately, what can you do to improve your perceptual skills? Increasing your awareness of the factors that lead to inaccuracy will help initially, and you will find further suggestions in this section. Ultimately, your improvement will depend on your will-ingness to do three things: (1) to grow as you expand your experiences, (2) to communicate about your perceptions with others, and (3) to seek out and consider others' perceptions of you. Realize that you have had a lifetime to develop these barriers and that it will take time, commitment, and effort to overcome their effects.

Just by reading this chapter, you've gained a greater understanding of how the perception process affects your relationship with others. Use your knowledge of the perceptual process to sharpen your own perceptions and conclusions. Here are additional strategies to help you become a more accurate perceiver.

Link Details with the Big Picture

Any skilled detective knows how to take a small piece of information or evidence and use it to reach a broader conclusion. Skilled perceivers keep the big picture in mind as they look for clues about a person. In this chapter, we have encouraged you to become more sensitive to details when observing others. However, be cautious of taking one scrap of evidence and spinning out inaccurate conclusions about a person. Just because someone may dress differently from you or have a pronounced accent, don't rush to judgment about the person's competence based on such few snatches of information. Look and listen for other cues about your new acquaintance that can help you to develop a more accurate understanding of who that person is. As we noted in this chapter, what we see first (primacy) or last (recency) may have the most powerful effect on our overall conclusion. Try not to use the early information to cast a quick or rigid judgment that may be inaccurate. Look at all the details you've gathered.

Become Aware of Others' Perceptions of You

The best athletes don't avoid hearing criticisms and observations from their coaches. Instead, they seek out as much feedback as they can about what they are doing right and wrong. Olympic training often involves the use of videotaped replays and computer analysis so that athletes can see themselves as others see them and use that perspective to improve their performance. It is difficult to be objective about our own behaviour, so feedback from others can help us with our self-perceptions. The strongest relationships are those in which the partners are willing to share and to be receptive to the perceptions of the other.

Increase Your Awareness

Your senses are constantly bombarding you with information, much of which you ignore. You can increase the amount of information that you process from your senses by consciously attending to the input. When you interact with others, try to identify one new thing to focus on and observe each time. Watch their gestures, their eyes, the wrinkles around their eyes, their foot movements; listen to their tone of voice. Each observation will provide information that potentially can improve the quality of your interactions. You may create additional problems, however, if you focus so narrowly on one element that you miss others or overestimate the meaning of irrelevant information. Try to notice as much detail as possible, but keep the entire picture in view.

Become Other-Oriented

Effective interpersonal perception depends on the ability to understand where others are coming from, to get inside their heads, to see things from their perspectives.

Becoming other-oriented involves a two-step process: social decentring (consciously *thinking* about another's thoughts and feelings) and empathizing (*responding emotionally* to another's feelings).[31] What does your boss think and feel when you arrive late for work? What would your spouse think and feel if you brought a dog home as a surprise gift? Throughout this book, we offer suggestions for becoming other-oriented, for reminding yourself that the world does not revolve around you. Being other-oriented enables you to increase your understanding of others and improve your ability to predict and adapt to what others do and say.

To improve your ability to socially decentre and to empathize, strive for two key goals: (1) gather as much information as possible about the circumstances that are affecting the other person; and (2) gather as much information as possible about the other person. In the next chapter, we expand on these ideas as we discuss in more detail how to adapt to others by decentring and empathizing. As we've emphasized before, being other-oriented is not a single skill but a family of related communication skills (such as socially decentring, empathizing, listening, responding, interpreting verbal and non-verbal messages, appropriately adapting to others, and managing conflict).

Ten Questions That Can Help You Become Other-Oriented

1. What factors or circumstances are affecting the person?
2. How can I determine whether there are factors I don't know about or don't fully understand?
3. What do I know about this person that explains his or her behaviour and feelings?
4. What is going through the other person's mind at this time?
5. What are the other person's feelings at this time?
6. What other explanations could there be for the person's actions?
7. What would I think if I were in the same situation?
8. How would I feel if I were in the same situation?
9. What would other people think if they were in that situation?
10. What would other people feel if they were in that situation?

Use Perception Checking

When we observe others' behaviour and make attributions about why they are doing what they are doing, we can be inaccurate and make mistakes. These mistakes can affect your relationships with others and lead to serious miscommunication. You can check out the accuracy of your perceptions and attributions indirectly and directly. Checking out your perceptions also displays your other-orientation and allows you to more fully understand the motives and causes of others' behaviours. By checking your perceptions, you reduce uncertainty and clarify that your perceptions are accurate. **Indirect perception checking** involves seeking additional information through

indirect perception checking. Seeking additional information to confirm or refute interpretations you are making through passive perception.

passive perception to either confirm or refute your interpretations. If you suspect someone is angry with you but is not admitting it, for example, you could look for more cues in his or her tone of voice, eye contact, and body movements to find more cues to confirm your suspicion. You could also ask questions or listen more intently to the person's words and language.

Direct perception checking involves asking straight out if your interpretations of a perception are correct. This often is not easy to do for several reasons: we don't like to admit uncertainty or suspicions to others; we might not trust that they will respond honestly; and if our interpretations are wrong, we might suffer embarrassment or anger. However, asking someone to confirm a perception shows that you are committed to understanding his or her behaviour. If your friend's voice sounds weary and her posture is sagging, you may assume that she is depressed or upset. If you ask, "I get the feeling from your tone of voice and the way you're acting that you are kind of down and depressed; what's wrong?" Your friend can then either provide another interpretation, such as "I'm just tired; I had a busy week," or expand on your interpretation: "Yeah, things haven't been going very well..." Your observation might also be a revelation: "Really? I didn't realize I was acting that way. I guess I am a little down." The *Building Your Skills* box on page 93 outlines a straightforward method of perception checking. The real key is to be honest and direct with the other person while using tact, diplomacy, and empathy.

direct perception checking. Asking for confirmation or refutation from the observed person of an interpretation of a perception about him or her.

Be Sensitive to Cultural Differences

Although Chapter 8 deals with diversity and cultural differences in greater detail, it is appropriate to touch on the subject here. Cultures can influence perception in many ways. For example, in some Asian cultures, eye contact is seen as disrespectful, especially to those in authority. Yet in North America, if no eye contact is given, many people feel the person is lying or hiding something. By simply realizing that cultures differ in what is acceptable or unacceptable behaviours, you will be less likely to make perceptual errors. The potential for interpersonal communication problems will diminish if you keep these simple ideas with you when interpreting a person's behaviour if he or she is from a culture different from your own.

Summary

Interpersonal perception is a fundamental element of interpersonal communication. Our communication and interpersonal relationships are affected by the way we perceive those with whom we interact. Interpersonal perception is more than just the arousal of the senses; it also involves selecting, organizing, and interpreting what we observe to decide what people are like and to give meaning to their actions.

Our perceptions of others affect how we communicate, and how others perceive us affects how they communicate with us. Interpersonal perception can be a passive or active process. It is passive when only our senses are in operation; it is active when we feel a need for information and intentionally seek it. We are motivated to seek information in situations that have high amounts of uncertainty. Perception of information helps reduce uncertainty and provides us with more control of the situation.

Interpersonal perception affects and is affected by the development of impressions, our own implicit personality theories, and attributions. Our general impressions of individuals are often affected by primacy and recency effects; we pay particular attention to the first things we notice and the most recent things we notice about others. In our interactions with others, we all seem to operate as "naive psychologists," developing and applying our own implicit personality theories. These implicit personality theories represent the general way we believe people behave. We develop specific personal constructs that represent the qualities we associate with specific people we know. Finally, we try to explain the actions and behaviours of others through the process of attribution. According to attribution theorists, we seek to find out the intent and cause of a person's action; we see a person's action as a response to a given circumstance, a particular stimulus, or the person's own personality. To make rational and accurate attributions, we must overcome perceptual barriers. We can identify nine specific tendencies that distort the accuracy of our attributions, such as focusing on obvious or negative information.

The following suggestions will help you to improve your interpersonal perception: (1) link details with the big picture; (2) become aware of others' perceptions of you; (3) increase your awareness; (4) become other-oriented; (5) use perception checking; and (6) be sensitive to cultural differences.

For Discussion and Review

Focus on Critical Thinking

1. Think about some of your recent interpersonal conflicts. How would you describe your perception of the problem? How do you think the others would describe their perceptions of it? What role did perception play in contributing to or resolving the conflict?

2. What do you think contributes to the development of the tendencies that cause us to perceive people inaccurately? How might the effects of those factors be minimized or eliminated?

Focus on Ethics

3. Do you have a right in an intimate relationship to expect your partner to share his or her perceptions of you, whether those perceptions are positive or negative? Explain your reasoning.

4. If you are aware of how you are distorting your own perceptions and attributions, should you try to change them? Is it a moral obligation? Explain your reasoning.

For Your Journal

1. As you interact with a friend, try to assess your awareness level of the cues that are being communicated. Ask your friend to confirm your interpretation of the cues that you have observed. How effective and accurate were you at picking up information?

2. Use the list of barriers to accurate perception to do a self-analysis. Which barriers influence your perceptions the most? What problems do those distortions create in your interactions with others?

3. Choose one of the suggestions for improving your perceptions. Develop a plan for what you will do in your next interaction to apply that suggestion. Try the suggestion; then write an evaluation of how well you applied the suggestion, how well the suggestion worked, and how you might modify your plan to apply the suggestion in the future.

Learning with Others

1. Choose an advertisement, magazine illustration, photograph, or painting that shows a group of people and bring it to class. In groups of four or five, pass around the pictures. For each picture, write down a few words to describe your perceptions about what you see in the picture. What are the people doing? What is their relationship to one another? What is each one like? How is each one feeling? Why are they doing what they are doing? After you have finished, share with one another what you have written down. Try to determine why there are differences. What factors influenced your initial perceptions?

2. Pair up with someone in class whom you do not know and have not interacted with before. Without saying anything to each other, write down the words from the following list that you think apply to the other person. Now converse for five minutes. In a separate section of your paper, write down any additional words that you believe apply to the person. You can go back and put a line through any of the words in the first list that you now think are inaccurate. Share with your partner what words you put down before and during the conversation, and what words you changed. Have your partner share his or her perceptions of you. Discuss, as best you can, the reasons you chose each word.

intelligent	athletic	artistic	studious
nice	funny	conceited	friendly
introverted	extroverted	hard-working	shy
talented	popular	inquisitive	moody
emotional	happy	brave	responsible
leader	follower	uncertain	confused

3. An interesting area of research that was lightly touched on in this chapter, in the section on the process of perception (Stage 1: Selecting) is the area of eyewitness testimony and the accuracy of such testimony. Research has pointed out the fallibility of memory under a number of conditions. Two of these conditions are the presence of alcohol and the presence of emotions.

   In small groups or teams, choose one of the following Canadian studies or find another related study using your research navigator.

- J. C. Yuille and P. A. Tollestrup, Some Effects of Alcohol on Eyewitness Memory, *Journal of Applied Psychology,* 75 (3), 1990, 268–273.

- S. Porter, L. Spencer and A. R. Birt, Blinded by Emotion? Effect of Emotionality of a Scene on Susceptibility to False Memories, *Canadian Journal of Behavioural Science,* 35 (2), 165–175.

Using these studies, discuss the following questions.

a.   Based on the research, how accurate is memory?

b.   Can courts rely exclusively on eyewitness testimony?

c.   What suggestions would you make to improve such testimony?

Weblinks

www.macleans.ca   Read the most current issue of *Maclean's* or search the magazine's archives.

www.selfgrowth.com/index.html   This is a site devoted to personal growth, self-improvement, and self-help. You can sign up to receive a free newsletter.

http://novaonline.nv.cc.va.us/eli/spd110td/interper/index.html   Learn more about the perception process at this site; explore how the way you make sense out of the world affects the way you communicate with others.

http://ase.tufts.edu/psychology/ambady   Visit the Tufts Interpersonal Communication Lab, with great links to research and articles about social relations topics including interpersonal perception.

Part Two

2

Interpersonal Communication Skills

People judge you by your behaviour, not by your intentions. The following five chapters focus on research-based communication skills that will help you monitor and shape your behaviour to improve the quality of your relationships. Chapter 4 offers tips and strategies for listening to others and confirming your understanding of what you hear. Chapter 5 explores how the words we use, and misuse, affect our relationships with others. Meanings, as we'll learn, are in people, not in words themselves. Becoming other-oriented involves both listening to the words and reading the behaviour cues of others. Chapter 6 focuses on the scope and importance of unspoken messages. We will explore the implications of the adage, "Actions speak louder than words." Chapter 7 then discusses conflict and teaches some basic strategies to manage conflict and disagreements with others. Do cultural differences have an impact on our understanding of our relationships with others? The final chapter in this section looks at the impact of cultural diversity on interpersonal communication.

4 Listening and Responding

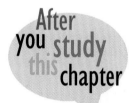

After you study this chapter

you should be able to . . .

1. Describe five elements of the listening process.

2. Identify characteristics of four listening styles.

3. Understand why we listen and name several important barriers to effective listening.

4. Identify ways to improve other-orientation and listening skills.

5. Identify responding skills and understand strategies for improving them.

- Listening Defined

- Listening Styles

- Listening Barriers

- Improving Your Listening, Comprehension, and Responding Skills

- Improving Critical Listening and Responding Skills

- Responding to Confirm or Disconfirm Others

- Improving Empathic Listening and Responding Skills

- Improving Your Responding Skills

I never learned anything while I was talking.

LARRY KING

Think about your best friend. What are some of the qualities you most admire in your friend? Many people would respond that one of the most valued qualities in a friend is his or her just being there—supporting, comforting, and listening. As theologian Henri Nouwen so eloquently put it:

> Listening is much more than allowing another to talk while waiting for a chance to respond. Listening is paying full attention to others and welcoming them into our very beings. . . . Listening is a form of spiritual hospitality by which you invite strangers to become friends, to get to know their inner selves more fully, and even dare to be silent with you.[1]

Simply stated, friends listen. They listen even if we sometimes say foolish things. Again, Nouwen describes it well: "True listeners no longer have an inner need to make their presence known. They are free to receive, to welcome, to accept."[2] As we consider the essential skills of interpersonal communication, the skill of listening to others would be at or near the top of the list in terms of importance.[3] Skilled communicators do more than impassively listen—they appropriately respond to what we say. They confirm that they understand and care for us by providing both verbal and non-verbal feedback. In this chapter, we explore the interpersonal communication skills of listening and responding.

You spend more time listening than participating in any other communication activity. In fact, you spend more time listening to others than doing almost anything else. Typical North Americans spend more than 80 percent of an average day communicating with other people, and as the pie chart in Figure 4.1 shows, they spend 45 percent of that communication time listening to others.[4] It is interesting to note that the focus of most people's formal communication training, writing, is actually the activity to which they devote the least amount of communication time. Chances are that until now you have had no formal training in listening. In this chapter, we focus on this often neglected, yet absolutely essential, skill for developing quality interpersonal relationships. Listening is the process by which people learn the most about others. In addition, we explore ways to respond appropriately to others.

**Figure 4.1
What You Do with Your Communication Time**

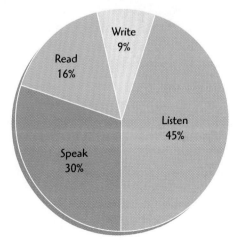

Listening Defined

listening. The process of selecting, attending, understanding, remembering, and responding to sounds and messages.

hearing. The physiological process of decoding sounds.

selecting. The process of sorting through various sounds competing for your attention.

attending. The process of focusing on a particular sound or message.

"Did you hear what I said?" demands a father who has been lecturing his teenage son on the importance of hanging up his clothes. In fact, the boy has *heard* him, but he may not have been *listening*. **Listening** is a complex process we use to make sense out of what we hear. **Hearing** is the physiological process of decoding sounds. You hear when the sound vibrations reach your eardrum and buzz the middle-ear bones: the hammer, anvil, and stirrup. Eventually, the sound vibrations are translated into electrical impulses that reach the brain. To listen to something, you must first select that sound from competing sounds. To truly listen involves four activities—selecting, attending, understanding, and remembering. Then we confirm that listening has occurred by responding.

Selecting

Selecting a sound means focusing on it as you sort through the various sounds competing for your attention. As you listen to another in an interpersonal context, you focus on the words and non-verbal messages of your partner. Even now, as you are reading this book, there are undoubtedly countless noises within earshot. Stop reading for a moment and sort through the various sounds around you. Do you hear music? Is there noise from outside? How about the murmur of voices, the tick of a clock, the hum of a computer, the whoosh of an air conditioner or a furnace? To listen, you must select which of these sounds will receive your attention.

Healthy family relations result when parents and children are able to develop people-oriented listening styles. (Michael Newman/PhotoEdit)

Attending

After selecting a sound, you then focus on it—**attending** to it. Attention can be fleeting. You may attend to the sound for a moment and then move on or return to other thoughts or other sounds. Typically, you attend to those sounds and messages that meet your needs or are consistent with what you think you should be focusing on. If you are hungry, you may select and then attend to a commercial for a sizzling burger or a crispy-crust pizza. Information that is novel, humorous, or intense, or that somehow relates to you, also may capture your attention. Over 30 years later, many Canadians still recall Prime Minister Trudeau's "fuddle-duddle" episode. Trudeau had been accused of violating parliamentary rules by mouthing a particular four-letter word, while making a matching hand gesture, in the House of Commons. Trudeau's quick response to his accusers ("I may have just mouthed 'fuddle-duddle'") became a shared joke among the Canadian media and public alike, even sparking a boom in "fuddle-duddle" T-shirts. The collective attention of the nation had been temporarily drawn away from more pressing issues of the time, which, by now, are forgotten by most.

In general, conflict, humour, new ideas, and real or concrete things command your attention more easily than abstract theories that do not relate to your interests or needs.

Understanding

Whereas hearing is a physiological phenomenon, **understanding** is the process of assigning meaning to the sounds you select and to which you attend. There are several theories about how you assign meaning to words you hear, but there is no universally accepted notion of how this process works. We know that people understand best if they can relate what they are hearing to something they already know. For this reason, the use of analogy and comparison is effective when explaining complex material or abstract ideas.

A second basic principle about how people understand others is that the greater the similarity between individuals, the greater the likelihood for more accurate understanding. Individuals from different cultures who have substantially different religions, family lifestyles, values, and attitudes often have difficulty understanding each other, particularly in the early phases of a relationship.

You understand best that which you also experience. Perhaps you have heard the Montessori school philosophy: I hear, I forget; I see, I remember; I experience, I understand. Hearing alone does not provide us with understanding. We hear over one billion words each year, but we understand only a fraction of that number. In Chapter 3, we discussed the processes involved in perception and observed that different people can reach dramatically different conclusions about the same events and messages, based on their previous experiences. A key to establishing relationships with others is trying to understand those differences in experience to arrive at a common meaning for the messages we exchange.

understanding. Assigning meaning to messages.

remembering. Recalling information that has been communicated.

Remembering

Remembering is recalling information. Some researchers theorize that you store every detail you have ever heard or witnessed; your mind operates like a video camera, but you cannot retrieve or remember all of the tapes. Sometimes you are present, yet you have no recollection of what occurred.

Our brains have both short-term and long-term memory storage systems. Short-term memory is where you store almost all the information you hear. You look up a phone number in the telephone book, mumble the number to yourself, and then dial

Do you remember where you were when you heard about the tsunami on December 26, 2004?
(AP Photo/Choo Younkong, Pool)

the number only to discover that the line is busy. Three minutes later you have to look up the number again because it did not get stored in your long-term memory. Our short-term storage area is very limited. Just as airports have only a few short-term parking spaces, but many spaces for long-term parking, our brains can accommodate only a few things of fleeting significance but acres of important information. We forget hundreds of snippets and bits of insignificant information that pass through our brains each day.

The information we store in long-term memory includes events, conversations, and other data that are significant for us. We tend to remember dramatic and vital information, as well as seemingly inconsequential details connected with such information. Many of us can recall in poignant detail how Wayne Gretzky tearfully announced his trade from the Edmonton Oilers to the Los Angeles Kings (OK, those of us over the age of 20). Do you remember what you were doing when you heard about the most devastating tsunami of recent history on December 26, 2004?

Memories of those first home videos from the great tsunami became indelible images in the collective memory of Canadians, and we responded with the largest donations the Canadian Red Cross has ever received to aid in a single disaster. Information makes it to long-term memory because of its significance to us. The more recent events will also be well remembered by most of us. On March 3, 2005, four RCMP officers were shot during a raid on a farm in Alberta. It was the first time in Canada that so many police officers had been shot and killed in one incident. You are more likely to recall the details of this tragedy if you work in law enforcement or have close friends or loved ones who do.

Responding

responding. Confirming your understanding of a message.

Interpersonal communication is interactive; it involves both talking and **responding**. You respond to people to let them know you understand their messages. Responses can be non-verbal; direct eye contact and head nods let your partner know you're tuned in. Or, you can respond verbally by asking questions to confirm the content of the message ("Are you saying you don't want us to spend as much time together as we once did?") or by making statements that reflect the feelings of the speaker ("So you are frustrated that you have to wait for someone to drive you where you want to go"). We will discuss responding skills in more detail later in the chapter.

▶ **Recap**

WHAT IS LISTENING?

Selecting	Sorting through various sounds that compete for your attention.
Attending	Focusing on a particular sound or message.
Understanding	Assigning meaning to messages.
Remembering	Recalling information that has been communicated.
Responding	Confirming your understanding of a message.

Listening Styles

What's your listening style? Do you focus more on the content of the message than on the feelings being expressed by the speaker? Or do you prefer brief sound bites of information? Your **listening style** is your preferred way of making sense out of the spoken messages you hear. Listening researchers Kitty Watson, Larry Barker, and James Weaver found that listeners tend to fall into one of four listening styles: people-oriented, action-oriented, content-oriented, or time-oriented.[5]

People-Oriented Listeners

As you might suspect from the label, **people-oriented listeners** tend to be comfortable with and skilled at listening to people's feelings and emotions. They are likely to empathize and search for common areas of interest. People-oriented listeners embody many of the attributes of being other-oriented that we've discussed throughout the book—they seek strong interpersonal connections when listening to others. Preliminary evidence suggests that people-oriented listeners may be less apprehensive when interacting with others in small-group and interpersonal interactions.[6]

Action-Oriented Listeners

An **action-oriented listener** prefers information that is well-organized, brief, and error-free. An action-oriented listener doesn't like the speaker to tell lengthy stories and digress. The action-oriented listener may think, "Get to the point" or "What am I supposed to do with this information?" when hearing a message filled with too many anecdotes or rambling, disorganized bits of information. Whereas a people-oriented listener would be more likely to focus on the feelings of the person telling the story, the action-oriented listener wants to know the point or the punch line. There is new evidence to suggest that action-oriented listeners are more likely to be more skeptical when listening to information. Researchers call this skepticism **second-guessing**—questioning the ideas and assumptions underlying a message. Rather than taking the information they hear at face value, action-oriented listeners are more likely to reinterpret or evaluate the literal message to determine whether it is true or false—they make another guess (hence the term *second-guessing*) as to whether the information they are listening to is accurate.[7]

Content-Oriented Listeners

If you are a **content-oriented listener**, you are more comfortable listening to complex, detailed information than are people with other listening styles. A content-oriented listener hones in on the facts, details, and evidence in a message. In fact, if a message does not have ample supporting evidence and specific details, the content-oriented listener is more likely to reject the message. Like the action-oriented listener, content-oriented listeners are likely to make second guesses about the messages they hear. Content-oriented listeners are also less apprehensive when communicating with others in group and interpersonal situations.[8] Content-oriented listeners would make good judges or lawyers; they focus on issues and arguments and listen to see whether a conclusion that a speaker reaches is accurate or credible.

Time-Oriented Listeners

time-oriented listener. Listener who likes messages delivered succinctly.

You're a **time-oriented listener** if you like your messages delivered succinctly. Time-oriented listeners are keenly aware of how much time they have for listening. Their to-do lists and in-baskets are often overflowing, so they want messages delivered quickly and briefly. Whereas a people-oriented listener might enjoy spending time over a cup of coffee catching up on the day's activities, a time-oriented listener is more like a drive-by listener. He or she may think, "Just give me what I need so I can keep on moving to my next task or hear my next message," or "Stop rambling and just get to the point quickly."

Knowing your listening style can help you understand how to adapt better to various listening situations. If, for example, you know that you are a time-oriented or action-oriented listener and your friend or companion is a people-oriented listener, you and your friend will need to adjust both your speaking and listening styles. When speaking to an action-oriented listener, give the listener a brief preview of what you will be talking about. You could say, "Phil, there are three things I'd like to share with you." Stick to that structure. When speaking to a people-oriented listener, realize that he or she will feel rushed or hurried if you skip information about feelings or relationships. A people-oriented listener prefers to spend more time talking about emotions than do those with other listening styles. A time-oriented listener would like information summarized like a crisply written business memo, punctuated with bullets and lists of essential information.

What is the best listening style? It depends on the listening situation and the communication context and objectives. In a high-pressure, fast-paced job such as stock trading, you don't have time to listen to stories about clients' families or the latest TV show; you need information delivered quickly and efficiently. A father, listening to a daughter talk about what a rotten day at school she had, would find a people-oriented listening style the most effective approach as his daughter pours her heart out about life's challenges and frustrations. Being aware of your own preferred listening style and the needs of your communication partner can help you adopt a listening style that best suits the situation.

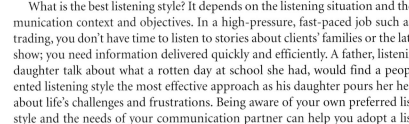

Listening Barriers

Even though we spend so much of our communication time listening, most of us don't listen as well as we should. Twenty-four hours after we hear a speech, a class lecture, or a sermon, we forget more than half of what was said, and it gets worse. Within another 24 hours, we forget half of what we remembered, so we really remember only a quarter of the lecture.

Our interpersonal listening skills are not much better. If anything, they may be worse. When you listen to a speech or lecture, you have a clearly defined listening role; one person talks and you are expected to listen. However, in interpersonal situations, you may have to alternate quickly between speaking and listening. This

takes considerable skill and concentration. Often, you are thinking of what you want to say next rather than listening.

One surprising study found that we sometimes pay more attention to strangers than to intimate friends or partners.[9] Married couples in the study tended to interrupt each other more often and were generally less polite to one another than were strangers involved in a decision-making task. Apparently, we take listening shortcuts when communicating with others in close relationships, and as the *Understanding Diversity* box below suggests, often the problem is gender-related.

Most interpersonal listening problems can be traced to a single source: ourselves. While listening to others, we also "talk" to ourselves. Our internal thoughts are like a play-by-play sportscast. We mentally comment on the words and sights that we select and to which we attend. If we keep those comments focused on the message, they may be useful, but we often attend to our own internal dialogues instead of to others' messages. Then our listening effectiveness plummets.

Inattentive listening is a bit like channel surfing when we watch TV—pushing the remote control button to switch from channel to channel, avoiding commercials, and focusing for brief periods on attention-grabbing program "bites." When we listen to others, we may fleetingly tune in to the conversation for a moment, decide that the content is uninteresting, and then focus on a personal thought. These thoughts are barriers to communication, and they come in a variety of forms, addressed in the following sections.

 Understanding Diversity

WHO LISTENS BETTER: MEN OR WOMEN?

Research provides no definitive answer to this question. There is evidence that men and women listen differently and have different expectations about the role of listening and talking. Deborah Tannen suggests that one of the most common complaints wives have about their husbands is, "He doesn't listen to me anymore," along with, "He doesn't talk to me anymore." Another scholar noted that complaints about lack of communication are usually at the top of women's lists of reasons for divorce but are mentioned much less often by men. Since both men and women are participating in the same conversation, why are women often more dissatisfied with the listening and talking process than men? Tannen's explanation: women and men expect different things from conversations.

One researcher suggests that men and women may have different

Continued

attention styles. When men listen, they may be looking for a new structure or organizational pattern, or to separate bits of information they hear. They continually shape, form, observe, inquire, and direct energy toward a chosen goal. Men's attention style is reported to be more emotionally controlled than women's attention style. Women are described as more subjective, empathic, and emotionally involved as they listen. They are more likely to search for relationships among parts of a pattern and to rely on more intuitive perceptions of feelings. They are also more easily distracted by competing details. Females may hear more of the message because they reject less of it. These differences in attention styles and the way men and women process information, the researcher suggests, can potentially affect listening, even though we have no direct evidence linking attention style to listening skill.

Another researcher suggests that when men listen, they listen to solve a problem; men are more task-oriented. Women listen to seek new information to enhance understanding. There is additional evidence that men may be more goal-oriented when they listen. What are the implications of these research studies? It may mean that men and women focus on different parts of messages and have different listening objectives. These differences can affect relationship development. Males may need to recognize that while they are attending to a message and looking for new structure to solve a problem or achieve a goal, they may hear less of the message and therefore listen less effectively. And even though many females may hear more of the message, they may need to make connections between the parts of the information they hear to look for major ideas, rather than just focus on the details. In any case, gender-based differences in attention style and information processing may account for some of the relational problems that husbands and wives, lovers, siblings, and other male–female pairs experience.[10]

Being Self-Absorbed

You're in your local grocery store during "rush hour." It appears that most of your community has decided to forage for food at the same time. As you are trying to get in and out of the store quickly, it seems that many of the harried shoppers are oblivious to those around them. They stop in the aisle, blocking the path for others (including you). They elbow their way into crowded checkout stands, and the "express lane" that limits customers to 10 items or fewer is backed up because more than one shopper has difficulty counting to 10. You find yourself becoming tense—not just because you are hungry and need sustenance, but it seems that the grocery store is filled with people who are self-absorbed. They are focused on getting their needs met but ignoring the needs of others.

Self-absorbed listeners are focused on their needs rather than those of their communication partner; to them, the message is about *them,* not the other person. During conversations with a self-absorbed communicator, it is difficult sustaining communication about anything except the self-absorbed partner's ideas, experiences, and stories. This problem is also called **conversational narcissism**. To be narcissistic is to be in love with oneself, like the mythical Greek character Narcissus, who became enamoured with his reflection in a pool of water.[11]

The self-absorbed listener is actively involved in doing several things other than listening. The self-absorbed person is much more likely to interrupt others in mid-sentence, often just in search of ways to focus the attention on him- or herself.

The self-absorbed listener is also not focusing on his or her partner's message but is instead thinking about what he or she is going to say next. This focus on an internal message can keep a listener from selecting and attending to the other person's message. If you are supposed to be listening to Aunt Mae tell about her recent trip to the Elmira Fall Fair but are eager to hit her up for a loan, your personal agenda will

conversational narcissism. Overly focusing on personal agendas and being self-absorbed rather than focusing on the needs and ideas communicated by others.

serve as a barrier to your listening ability. Or you may simply decide that Aunt Mae's monologue is boring and unimportant and give yourself permission to tune out as she drones on. Like humorist James Thurber's famous daydreamer, Walter Mitty, you may eventually find yourself unable to respond cogently, lost in your own world.[12]

How do you short-circuit this listening problem? First, diagnose it. Note consciously when you find yourself drifting off, thinking about your agenda rather than concentrating on the speaker. Second, throttle up your powers of concentration when you find your internal messages are distracting you from listening well. If you notice that you are "telling" yourself that Aunt Mae's anecdote is boring, you can also mentally remind yourself to listen with greater energy and focus.

Unchecked Emotions

Words are powerful symbols that affect our attitudes, our behaviour, and even our blood pressure. Words arouse us emotionally. **Emotional noise** occurs when our emotional arousal interferes with communication effectiveness. If you grew up in a home in which R-rated language was never used, then four-letter words may be distracting to you. Words that insult your religious or ethnic heritage can also be fighting words. Most of us respond to certain trigger words like a bull to a waving cape; we want to charge in to correct the speaker or, perhaps, even do battle with him or her.

emotional noise.
Communication interfered with by emotional arousal causes emotional noise.

Building Your Skills

IDENTIFYING EMOTIONAL "HOT BUTTONS"

Following are some listening situations and phrases that may cause you to become emotional. Check those that are "hot buttons" for you as a listener, and add others that strongly affect you, positively or negatively.

_____ "You never/always..."
_____ Know-it-all attitudes
_____ Individuals who smoke cigarettes or cigars while talking to you
_____ "Shut up!"
_____ Being ignored
_____ Bad grammar
_____ "You never listen."
_____ Obscene language
_____ Whining
_____ "What you should do is..."

_____ Being interrupted

Others:
_____
_____
_____

Knowing what your emotional hot buttons are can help prevent your overreacting when they are pushed.

Source: Adapted from Diane Bone, The Business of Listening (Los Altos, CA: Crisp Publications, 1995), 52.

Sometimes it is not specific words but rather concepts or ideas that cause an emotional eruption. Some talk-radio hosts try to boost their ratings by purposely using demagogic language that elicits passionate responses. Although listening to such conflict can be interesting and entertaining, when your own emotions become aroused, you may lose your ability to converse effectively. Strong emotions can interfere with focusing on the message of another.

The emotional state of the speaker may also affect your ability to understand and evaluate what you hear. One researcher found that if you are listening to someone who is emotionally distraught, you will be more likely to focus on his or her emotions than on the content of the message.[13] Another researcher advises that when you are communicating with someone who is emotionally excited, you should remain calm and focused, and try simply to communicate your interest in the other person.[14]

Your listening challenge is to avoid emotional sidetracks and to keep your attention focused on the message. When your internal dialogue is kicked into high gear by objectionable words or concepts, or by an emotional speaker, make an effort to quiet it down and steer back to the subject at hand.

Criticizing the Speaker

The late Mother Teresa once said, "If you judge people, you have no time to love them." Being critical of the speaker may distract us from focusing on the message. As we learned in Chapter 3, most people are especially distracted by appearances, forming impressions of others based solely on non-verbal information. Superficial factors such as clothing, body size and shape, age, and ethnicity all affect our interpretation of a message.

It is important to monitor your internal dialogue to make sure you are focusing on the message rather than criticizing the messenger. Good listeners say to themselves, "While it may be distracting, I am simply not going to let the appearance of this speaker keep my attention from the message."

Speech Rate vs Thought Rate

Your ability to think faster than people speak is another listening pitfall. The average person speaks at a rate of 125 words a minute. Some folks talk a bit faster, others more slowly. You, on the other hand, have the ability to process up to 600 or 800 words a minute. The difference between your mental ability to handle words and the speed at which they arrive at your cortical centres can cause you to daydream and tune the speaker in and out, while giving you the illusion that you are concentrating more attentively than you actually are.[15]

You can turn your listening speed into an advantage if you use the extra time instead to summarize what a speaker is saying. By periodically sprinkling in mental summaries during a conversation, you can dramatically increase your listening ability and make the speech-rate/thought-rate difference work to your advantage.

Shifting Attention

Some people can do two things at once, and some people can't. The ability to multitask—to work on several tasks simultaneously—is a valued skill for administrative assistants, but some people have more difficulty multi-tasking than others. When it comes to listening to more than one message at a time, research suggests that men are more likely to have difficulty attending to multiple messages; when they are focused on a message, they may have more difficulty than women in carrying on a conversation with another person.[16] Men have a tendency to lock on to a message, while women seem more adept at shifting between two or more simultaneous messages. When many men watch a TV program, they may seem lost in their video world—oblivious to other voices around them. Women, on the other hand, are more likely to be carrying on a conversation with one person and also focusing on a message they may hear nearby. No, this difference doesn't mean that women are more likely to eavesdrop intentionally—simply that some women have greater potential to listen to two things at once.

What are the implications of this research? It may be especially important for women to stop and focus on the message of others, rather than on either internal or external competing messages. Men may need to be sensitive to others who may want to speak to them, rather than becoming oblivious to their surroundings and fixated on their own internal message or on a single external message such as sports, news, opera, or a movie on TV. Being able to stop competing thoughts and focus on a single message can enhance comprehension of the message on which you are focused.[17] It's useful, however, to make sure this message is the most important one to which you should be attending.

Information Overload

We live in an information-rich age. We are all constantly bombarded with sight and sound images, and experts suggest that the volume of information competing for our attention is likely to become even greater in the future. Incoming messages and information on computers, fax machines, car phones, and other technological devices can interrupt conversations and distract us from listening to others.

Be on the alert for these information interruptions when you are talking with others. Don't assume that because you are ready to talk, the other person is ready to listen. If your message is particularly sensitive or important, you may want to ask your listening partner, "Is this a good time to talk?" Even if he or she says yes, look for eye contact and a responsive facial expression to make sure the positive response is genuine.

Information overload can prevent us from being able to communicate effectively with people around us.

External Noise

As you will recall, all of the communication models we saw in Chapter 1 include the element of noise—distractions that take your focus away from the message. Many households seem to be addicted to noise. Often there is a TV on (sometimes more than one), a computer game beeping, and music emanating from another room. These, and other sounds, compete with your attention when you are listening to others.

Besides literal noise, there are other potential sources of distraction. A headline in the evening paper about the latest details in a lurid sex scandal may "shout" for your attention, just when your son wants to talk with you about his latest science-fiction story. A desire to listen to your new CD may drown out your partner's overtures to a heart-to-heart about budget problems. Music, TV, books, and video games can all lure you away from more important listening tasks.

Distractions make it difficult to sustain attention to a message. You have a choice to make. You can attempt to listen through the labyrinth of competing distractions, or you can modify the environment to reduce them. Turning off the stereo, setting down the paper, and establishing eye contact with the speaker can help to minimize the noise barrier.

 In Canada...

ARE CELL PHONES A DANGEROUS LISTENING DISTRACTION?

Many things can distract us when we are trying to listen and respond to others. One modern distraction—the use of cell phones—may be dangerously distracting to drivers, though whether it is actually dangerous or not remains controversial. In Canada, Newfoundland and Labrador is the only province so far to ban the use of a cell phone while driving.[i] We appear to be behind several other countries, including the United States, Australia, Great Britain, and Spain.[ii] In the United States, 11 states and the District of Columbia have laws restricting cell phones while driving. New Hampshire has an interesting twist: the state outlaws any distracting activity while driving including eating, drinking, fussing with makeup or hair, or talking on a cell phone.[iii] There drivers can pay up to $1000 if police find that any distracting activity caused an accident. Can drivers pay attention to

the road while listening and talking to others on their cell phones? Should Canada have a law that states drivers must pull over if talking on a cell phone? As you may recall from our discussion of perception in Chapter 3, people must selectively attend to stimuli, and we cannot pay attention to all incoming sensations.

So what do you think? Can you listen and respond appropriately and drive carefully (paying close attention to other cars, staying on your side of the road, and so on)? Two researchers who surveyed people who had been in collisions have some hard data that may change your mind if you are one of those who think that you can drive safely while on a cell phone.[iv] In their research, they found that drivers were four times more likely to have a collision when using a cell phone than when not using one. Of interest, the collision statistics did not change according to the time of day (dark or light), the season, or whether the driver was making or receiving a call. Being engaged on a cell phone was much riskier than listening to the radio, talking to passengers, and other activities that commonly occur while driving.

The study was carried out only with drivers who had experienced a collision that did not cause personal injury, so the researchers had no data on accidents that actually caused injuries or fatalities. However, their study did demonstrate that the risk of collision increased greatly at higher speeds. Also, the people in the study all agreed on at least one thing: they regretted the use of their phones after the crash. So before making that call or receiving one while driving, you may want to ask yourself one question: is it worth the risk?

Sources: i. *Canadian Press, "Other Provinces Eye Newfoundland Cell Phone Ban," retrieved from CTV.ca, www.ctv.ca/servlet/ArticleNews/ story/CTVNews/1072061630532_2?s_name= &no_ads=.*
ii. *Ford and Harrison LLP Management Update, "A Risky Call: Employer Limitation of Employee Cell Phone Use." December 1999, www.fordharrison.com/fordharrison/publica-tions/publications/MgmtUpdt?MU1299, retrieved 3/30/2005.*
iii. *Eric Kelderman, "State Laws Vary on Driving Distractions," Stateline.org, March 22, 2005, www.stateline.org/live/ViewPage.action? siteNodeId=137&languageId=1&contentId*
iv. *Donald A. Redelmeier and Robert J. Tibshirani, "Car Phones and Car Crashes: Some Popular Misconceptions," Canadian Medical Association Journal, 164 (11), (2001), 1581–1582.*

Listener Apprehension

Not only do some people become nervous and apprehensive about speaking to others, but some are anxious about listening to others. Listener apprehension is the fear of misunderstanding or misinterpreting, or of not being able to adjust psychologically to messages spoken by others.[18] Because some people are nervous or worried about missing the message, they *do* misunderstand the message; their fear and apprehension keep them from absorbing it. If you are one of those people who are nervous when listening, you may experience difficulty understanding all you hear.

If you're an apprehensive listener, you will have to work harder when you listen to others. When listening to a public speech, it may be acceptable to use a tape or digital recorder or to start taking notes; it's not appropriate or even always possible to make a recording or take notes during interpersonal conversations. If you're on the phone, you can take notes when you listen to help you remember the message content, but taping phone conversations without the other speaker's consent is unethical. Whether you're face-to-face with the speaker or on the phone, what you can do is try to mentally summarize the message as you're listening to it. Concentrating on the message by mentally summarizing what you hear can help take your mind off your anxiety and help you focus on the message.

 ▶ **Recap**

OVERCOMING BARRIERS TO LISTENING

Listening Barriers	To Overcome the Barrier
Being Self-Absorbed	Consciously become aware of the self-focus and shift attention.
Unchecked Emotions	Use self-talk to manage emotions.
Criticizing the Speaker	Focus on the message, not the messenger.
Speech Rate vs Thought Rate	Use the difference between speech rate and thought rate to mentally summarize the message.
Shifting Attention	Focus on the most important message vying for your attention.
Information Overload	Realize when you are—or when your partner is—tired or distracted and not ready to listen.
External Noise	Take charge of the listening environment by eliminating the distraction.
Listener Apprehension	Concentrate on the message as you mentally summarize what you hear.

Improving Your Listening, Comprehension, and Responding Skills

Many of the listening problems we have identified stem from focusing on ourselves rather than on the messages of others. Dale Carnegie, in his classic book *How to Win Friends and Influence People,* offered this tip to enhance interpersonal relationships: "Focus first on being interested, not interesting."[19] In essence, he was affirming the importance of being other-oriented when listening to others.

You can begin improving your listening skills by following three steps you probably first encountered in elementary school: (1) stop, (2) look, and (3) listen, and then two more: (4) ask questions and (5) reflect content by paraphrasing. Simple as they may seem, these steps can provide the necessary structure to help you refocus your mental energies and improve your listening power. Let's consider each step separately.

Stop

To select and attend to the messages of others, we must tap into our internal dialogue and stop our own running commentary about issues and ideas that are self-focused rather than other-focused. As we learned in Chapter 1, "decentring" is the term that describes the process of stepping away from our own concerns to think about the thoughts and feelings of our partner. If we treat decentring as a skill, we can learn to shift our internal dialogue to focus on others, although at first it will require conscious effort.

A model of how we learn any skill, attributed by many to Abraham Maslow, suggests that we operate at one of four skill levels:

- Unconscious incompetence
- Conscious incompetence
- Conscious competence
- Unconscious competence

The first level—*unconscious incompetence*—means that we are unaware of our own incompetence. We don't know that we don't know. For example, before you read this chapter, you may simply not have been aware that you are distracted by your internal dialogue when you interact with others.

The second level is *conscious incompetence*. Here, we become aware or conscious that we are not competent; we know that we don't know. You may now be aware that you are an easily distracted listener, but you do not know how to solve the problem.

Level three is *conscious competence*; we have become aware that we know something, but it has not yet become an integrated habit. You might have to work at decentring when you first begin using it as you listen.

The final level of skill attainment is *unconscious competence*. At this level, your skills have become second nature to you. After the age of six, most people who were raised in Canada are unconsciously competent at tying their shoes; it is automatic. In the same way, you may become so skilled in the decentring process that you do it as the rule rather than as an exception. At this level, you will also probably have the capacity to empathize, or "feel," with others as you listen.

Two researchers studied how to enhance the performance of "professional listeners" who work in call centres—places where customers call to order products, make product suggestions, or even offer complaints.[20] They found that customers preferred listeners who were focused and communicated that they were devoting their full attention to the caller. Specially trained listeners who avoided distractions, honed in on the essence of a caller's message, and stopped to focus on what the callers were telling them increased customers' confidence and satisfaction in the speaker–listener relationship. The researchers also concluded that the ability to stop and focus on the comments of others can be taught. People who learn how to stop mental distractions can improve their listening comprehension.

Look

Non-verbal messages are powerful. As the primary ways in which we communicate feelings, emotions, and attitudes, they play a major role in the total communication process, particularly in the development of relationships. Facial expressions and vocal cues, as well as eye contact, posture, and use of gestures and movement can dramatically colour the meaning of a message. When the non-verbal message contradicts the verbal message, we almost always believe the non-verbal message In listening to others, it is vital that you focus not only on the words but also on the non-verbal messages. Listen with your eyes as well as your ears.

Another reason to look at someone is to establish eye contact, which signals that you are focusing your interest and attention on him or her. If your eyes are glancing over your partner's head, looking for someone else, or if you are constantly peeking at your watch, your partner will rightfully get the message that you're not really listening. One researcher found that we telegraph our desire to change roles from listener to speaker by increasing our eye contact, using gestures such as a raised finger, and shifting our posture.[21] So it is important to maintain eye contact and monitor your partner's non-verbal signals when you are speaking as well as listening.

It is also important, however, not to be distracted by non-verbal cues that may prevent us from interpreting the message correctly. A research team asked one group of college students to listen to a counsellor and another group to both view and listen.[22] The students then rated the counsellor's effectiveness. Students who both saw and heard the counsellor perceived him as *less* effective because his distracting non-verbal behaviours affected their evaluations. We will provide more information about how to enhance your skill in interpreting the non-verbal messages of others in Chapter 6.

Other non-verbal distractions can include characteristics of a person's voice, including his or her accent. As the *In Canada* feature illustrates, in such a diverse nation, encountering accents frequently is likelier, with so many people speaking English or French as a second or even third or fourth language.

 ## In Canada...

LISTENING TO OTHERS IN A CULTURALLY DIVERSE NATION

English and French are the two predominant tongues in Canada. According to the 2001 Census, approximately 88 percent of the Canadian population speak one or the other at home.[i] Anglophones speak English as a first language, francophones speak French as a first language, and allophones (as they are most commonly known in Quebec) speak any other language as their first language. Large urban centres tend to be the most linguistically diverse, as 80 percent of allophones live in these cities.[ii]

In the 2001 census, for the first time, languages spoken at work were investigated. English was the most common with French and Chinese in second and third place respectively.[iii] For many people in the workplace who do not normally speak English, the language can be a formidable barrier, particularly if English is not spoken at home.

With such a diversity of languages, we need to pay special attention when listening to others who may be struggling with a new language. Listening can be a challenge when we are faced with accents, missed or misplaced words, wrong phrasing, or the silence of non-comprehension. Use the suggestions in this text to improve listening to those who are trying to speak your native tongue.

Linguistic diversity is just one of the many challenges and strengths of a multicultural nation.

i. *Canada Census, 2001 Table Data, "Language Most Often Spoken at Home on a Regular Basis," www.statcan.ca/english/census01/products/standards/themes/RetrieveProductTable.*
ii. *"Canadian Issues: Languages in Canada," 1996, www.nais.ccm.emr.ca/school net/issues/html/langøø1.html. iii. Canada Census, 2001 Table Data, "Frequency of Language at Work, by provinces and territories." www.statcan.ca/english/Pgdb/demo44A.htm.*

Listen

After making a concerted effort to stop distracting internal dialogue and to look for non-verbal cues, you will then be in a better position to understand the verbal messages of others. To listen is to do more than focus on facts; it is to search for the essence of the speaker's thoughts. We recommend the following strategies to help you improve your listening skill.

1. *Determine your listening goal.* You listen to other people for several reasons—to learn, to enjoy yourself, to evaluate, or to provide empathic support. With so many potential listening goals and options, it is useful to decide consciously what your listening objective is.

    If you are listening to someone give you directions to the city park, then your mental summaries should focus on the details of when to turn left and how many streets past the stoplight you go before you turn right. The details are crucial to achieving your objective. If, in contrast, your neighbour is telling you about her father's triple bypass operation, then your goal is to empathize. It is probably not important that you be able to recall when her father checked into the hospital or other details. Your job is to listen patiently and to provide emotional support. Clarifying your listening objective in your own mind can help you use appropriate skills to maximize your listening effectiveness.

2. *Transform listening barriers into listening goals.* If you can transform the listening barriers you read about earlier into listening goals, you will be well on your way to improving your listening skill. Make it a goal not to focus on your personal agenda. Make it a goal to use self-talk to manage emotional noise. Set a goal not to criticize the speaker. Remind yourself before each conversation to do mental summaries that capitalize on the differences between your information processing rate and the speaker's verbal delivery rate. In addition, make it your business to choose a communication environment that is free of distraction from other incoming information or noise.

3. *When your listening goal is to remember a message, mentally summarize the details of the message.* This suggestion may seem to contradict the suggestion to avoid focusing only on facts, but it is important to have a grasp of the details your partner provides. As we noted earlier, you can process words much more quickly than a person speaks. So, periodically, summarize the names, dates, and locations in the message. Organize the speaker's factual information into appropriate categories or try to place events in chronological order. Without a full understanding of the details, you will likely miss the speaker's major point.

4. *Mentally weave these summaries into a focused major point or series of major ideas.* Facts usually make the most sense when we can use them to help support an idea or major point. So, as you summarize, try to link the facts you have organized in your mind with key ideas and principles. Use the facts to enhance your critical thinking as you analyze, synthesize, evaluate, and finally summarize the key points or ideas your listening partner is making.[23]

5. *Practise listening to challenging material.* To improve or even maintain any skill, you need to practise it. Listening experts suggest that listening skills deteriorate if people do not practise what they know. Listening to difficult, challenging material can sharpen listening skills, so good listeners practise by listening to documentaries, debates, and other challenging material rather than mindless sitcoms and other material that entertains but does not engage them mentally.

Ask Questions

Sometimes when others share a momentous occurrence, the story may tumble out in a rambling, disorganized way. You can help sort through the story if you ask questions to identify the sequence of events. "What happened first?" and "Then what happened?" can help both you and your partner clarify what happened.

If your partner is using words or phrases that you don't understand, ask for definitions. "He's just so lackadaisical!" moans Meghan. "What do you mean by *lackadaisical*? Could you give me an example?" asks Mikhail. Sometimes asking for an example helps the speaker sort through the events as well.

Of course, if you are trying to understand another's feelings, you can ask how he or she is feeling or how the event or situation made him or her feel. Often, however, nonverbal cues are more revealing than a verbal disclosure about feelings and emotions.

Reflect Content by Paraphrasing

After you try to imagine how you would feel under similar circumstances and to make sure you have an accurate understanding of the events that occurred, you need to check your understanding of the facts. Respond with a statement such as:

"Are you saying ... ?"

"You seem to be describing ..."

"So, the point you are making seems to be ..."

"Here is what I understand you to mean ..."

"So, here is what seemed to happen ..."

Then, summarize the events, details, or key points you think the speaker is trying to convey. This is not a word-for-word repetition of what the speaker has said; nor do you need to summarize the content of *each* phrase or minor detail. Rather, you are **paraphrasing**: offering a verbal summary of your partner's message to check the accuracy of your understanding. Here is an example:

paraphrasing.   Checking the accuracy of your understanding by offering a verbal summary of your partner's message.

Jamal: This week I've got so much extra work to do. I'm sorry I'm not keeping the place clean. I know it's my turn to do the dishes tonight, but I have to get back to work. Could you do the dishes tonight?

Brigid: So you want me to do the dishes tonight and for the rest of the week. Right?

Jamal: Well, I'd like you to help with the dishes tonight. I think I can handle it for the rest of the week.

Brigid: OK. I'll do them tonight and you do them tomorrow.

Jamal: Thanks for helping me out here.

Research conducted in clinical counselling settings found that when a listener paraphrases the content and feelings of a speaker, the speaker is more likely to trust and value the listener.[24] Paraphrasing to check understanding is also a vital skill to use when you are trying to reconcile a difference of opinion. Chapter 7 will show you how to use it in that context.

Becoming Other-Oriented

IDENTIFYING MESSAGE DETAILS AND MAJOR IDEAS

How skilled are you at noting both the details of a message and its major ideas? To become a skilled listener, it's important to know how to identify both of these aspects of what someone is telling you. Here's a chance to practise your skill in identifying and remembering bits of information, as well as the main meaning of a message.

Read each of the following statements. After you have read each statement, cover it with your hand or a piece of paper. First, list as many of the details as you can recall from the message. Second, summarize your understanding of the major idea or key point of the message. As a variation on this activity, rather than reading the statement,

have someone read the statement to you and then identify the details and major idea.

Statement 1: "I'm very confused. I reserved our conference room for 1:00 p.m. today for an important meeting. We all know that conference space is tight. I reserved the room last week with the administrative assistant. Now I learn that you are planning to use the conference room at noon for a two-hour meeting. It's now 11:00 a.m. We need to solve this problem soon. I have no other option for holding my meeting, and if I don't hold my meeting today, the boss is going to be upset."

Statement 2: "Hello, Marcia? I'm calling on my cell phone. Where are you? I thought you were supposed to meet me at the circle drive 45 minutes ago. You know I can't be late for my seminar this evening.

What do you mean, you're waiting at the circle drive? I don't see you. No, I'm at Switzler Hall circle drive. You're where? No, that's not the circle drive I meant. I thought you'd know where I meant. Don't you ever listen? If you hurry, I can just make it to the seminar."

Statement 3: "Oh, Mary, I just don't know what to do. My daughter announced that when she turns 18 next week she's going get a large tattoo and put a ring in her nose and belly button. She said it's something she's always wanted to do and now she can do it without my permission. She's always been such a sweet, compliant girl, but she seems to have turned wacky. I've tried talking with her, and her father isn't much help. He thinks it may look 'cool.' I just don't want her to look like a freak when she has her senior picture taken next month."

Recap

HOW TO IMPROVE YOUR LISTENING SKILLS

Listening Skills	Definition	Action
Stop	Tune out distracting, competing messages.	Become conscious of being distracted; use self-talk to remain focused.
Look	Become aware of the speaker's non-verbal cues; monitor your own non-verbal cues to communicate your interest in the speaker.	Establish eye contact; avoid fidgeting or performing other tasks when someone is speaking to you. Listen with your eyes.
Listen	Create meaning from your partner's verbal and non-verbal messages.	Mentally summarize details; link these details with main ideas.
Ask questions	Clarify words, events, and feelings by questioning the speaker.	Ask for definitions and examples; clarify sequence of events.
Reflect content by paraphrasing when appropriate	Briefly state the essence of what the speaker has said to ensure the accuracy of your understanding.	Summarize the key events, details, or points of what the speaker has said.

Improving Empathic Listening and Responding Skills

When your friends have "one of those days," perhaps they seek you out to talk about it. They may not have any real problems to solve—perhaps it was just a day filled with miscommunication and squabbles with their partners or co-workers, but they want to tell you the details. Your friends are seeking a listener who focuses attention on them and understands what they are saying. At the heart of being other-oriented is cultivating **empathy**—feeling what someone else is feeling. The word "empathy" comes from a Greek word for *passion* and is related to the German word "Einfuhling," which means *to feel with.*

Developing empathy is not a single skill but a collection of skills that help you predict how others will respond. Daniel Goleman's book, *Emotional Intelligence,* is an outstanding resource that discusses the role and importance of our emotions in developing empathy with others.[25] Goleman has found evidence that people who are emotionally intelligent—sensitive to others, empathic, and other-oriented—have better interpersonal relationships. Goleman summarizes the centrality of emotions in developing empathy by quoting Antoine de Saint-Exupéry: "It is with the heart that one sees rightly; what is essential is invisible to the eye."[26]

Good listening, especially listening to empathize with another, is active, not passive. To listen passively is to avoid displaying any behaviour that lets the speaker know we are listening.[27] Passive listeners sit with a blank stare or a frozen facial expression. Their thoughts and feelings could be anywhere, for all the speaker knows. Those who engage in **active listening**, in contrast, respond mentally, verbally, and non-verbally to a speaker's message. This serves several specific functions. First, it can be a measure of how accurately you have understood the message. If you burst out laughing as your friend tells you about losing his house in a flood, he'll know you misunderstood what he was saying. Second, your responses indicate whether you agree or disagree with the comments others make. If you tell your friend that you do not approve of her comments on abortion, she'll know your position on the information she shared. Finally, your responses tell speakers how they are affecting others. Like radar that guides high-tech weapons, your feedback provides information to help others decide whether or not to correct the course of their messages.

Of course, listening to empathize is only one of the possible listening goals you may have. We are not suggesting that ferreting out someone's emotions is the goal of every listening encounter. This would be tedious for both you and your listening partners, but when you do want to listen empathically and respond, you must shift the focus to your partner and try to understand the message from his or her perspective.[28]

The quiz in the *Building Your Skills* box, "Test Your Empathy Ability," on page 126 can help you determine how effectively you empathize with others. We then discuss strategies that you can use to enhance your empathic skills.

empathy. Feeling what others are feeling, rather than just acknowledging that they are feeling a certain way.

active listening. Interactive process of responding mentally, verbally, and non-verbally to a speaker's message.

Building Your Skills

TEST YOUR EMPATHY ABILITY

Empathy is an emotional capability that often grows out of a conscious decentring process. It is the ability to move away from yourself enough to "feel for" another person. However, it does not mean abandoning your own self. On the contrary, empathic people often have a strong self-concept and high self-esteem, which enable them to be generous with others. Take this short test to assess your empathy. Respond to each statement by indicating the degree to which the statement is true regarding the way you typically communicate with others. When you think of how you communicate, is the statement always false (answer 1), usually false (answer 2), sometimes false and sometimes true (answer 3), usually true (answer 4), or always true (answer 5)?

_____ 1. I try to understand others' experiences from their perspectives.

_____ 2. I follow the Golden Rule ("Do unto others as you would have them do unto you") when communicating with others.

_____ 3. I can "tune in" to emotions others are experiencing when we communicate.

_____ 4. When trying to understand how others feel, I imagine how I would feel in their situation.

_____ 5. I am able to tell what others are feeling without being told.

_____ 6. Others experience the same feelings I do in any given situation.

_____ 7. When others are having problems, I can imagine how they feel.

_____ 8. I find it hard to understand the emotions others experience.

_____ 9. I try to see others as they want me to.

_____ 10. I never seem to know what others are thinking when we communicate.

To find your score, first reverse the responses for the even-numbered items (if you wrote 1, make it 5; if you wrote 2, make it 4; if you wrote 3, leave it as 3; if you wrote 4, make it 2; if you wrote 5, make it 1). Next, add the numbers next to each statement. Scores range from 10 to 50. The higher your score, the more you are able to empathize.

Source: William Gudykunst, Bridging Differences, 3rd ed. (Thousand Oaks, CA: Sage, 1998), 234.

Understand Your Partner's Feelings: Imagine How You Would Feel

If your goal is to empathize or "feel" with your partner, you might begin by imagining how you would feel under the same circumstances. If your partner comes home dejected from being hassled at work, try to recall how you felt when that happened to you. If a friend calls to tell you his or her mother died, try to imagine how you would feel if the situation were reversed. Of course, your reaction to these events might be different from your partner's or your friend's. You may need to decentre and remember how your partner felt in other similar situations to understand how he or she is feeling now.

Paraphrase Emotions

The bottom line in empathic responding is to make certain that you accurately understand how the other person is feeling. Again, you can paraphrase, beginning with such phrases as:

"So, you are feeling..."

"You must feel..."

"So, now you feel..."

"Emotionally, you must be feeling..."

In the following example of empathic responding, the listener asks questions, summarizes content, and summarizes feelings.

David: I think I'm in over my head. My boss gave me a job to do and I just don't know how to do it. I'm afraid I've bitten off more than I can chew.

José: *[thinks how he would feel if he were given an important task at work but did not know how to complete it, then he asks for more information]:* What job did she ask you to do?

David: I'm supposed to do an inventory of all of the items in the warehouse on the VAX computer system and have it finished by the end of the week. I don't have the foggiest notion of how to start. I've never even used that system.

José: *[summarizing feelings]* So, you feel panicked because you may not have enough time to learn the system *and* do the inventory.

David: Well, I'm not only panicked, I'm afraid I may be fired.

José :   *[summarizing feelings]* So, your fear that you might lose your job is getting in the way of just focusing on the task and seeing what you can get done. It's making you feel like you made a mistake in taking this job.

David: That's exactly how I feel.

Note that toward the end of the dialogue, José has to make a couple of tries to summarize David's feelings accurately. Also note that José does a good job of just listening and responding without giving advice. Just by being an active listener, you can help your partner clarify a problem.

You can better understand a partner's feelings—empathize with him or her—if you listen and try to recall how you might have felt in similar situations. (Gerard Loucel/Tony Stone Images)

sympathize.   Acknowledge that someone may be feeling bad.

Building Your Skills

SYMPATHY VERSUS EMPATHY

Most card shops have a sympathy card section. Such cards let people know you realize they are feeling bad about the death of someone close to them. To **sympathize** is to say you are sorry—that you want to offer your support and acknowledge that someone is feeling bad. Empathy goes one step further than sympathy. Empathy means that you try to perceive the world from another's perspective; you attempt to feel what someone else feels.

Respond to the following sample situations with sympathy and with empathy.

1. A good friend of yours just phoned to tell you that her dog, a well-loved 14-year-old pet, has just died.

    Respond with sympathy:

    _____

    _____

    _____

Respond with empathy:

_____

_____

_____

2. Your older brother comes to visit you and tells you that he and his wife are getting a divorce after 20 years of marriage.

    Respond with sympathy:

    _____

    _____

    _____

    Respond with sympathy:

    _____

    _____

    _____

3. A friend tells you that she just got fired from her job.

    Respond with sympathy:

    _____

    _____

    _____

    Respond with empathy:

    _____

    _____

    _____

    Source: From William Gudykunst, Bridging Differences, 2nd ed. (Thousand Oaks, CA: Sage Publications, 1994). Reprinted by permission of Sage Publications, Inc.

Researcher John Gottman summarizes several specific ways to make listening active rather than passive:[29]

- Start by asking questions.
- Ask questions about people's goals and visions of the future.
- Look for commonalities.
- Tune in with all your attention.
- Respond with an occasional brief nod or sound.
- From time to time, paraphrase what the speaker says.
- Maintain the right amount of eye contact.
- Let go of your own agenda.

We have discussed responding and the active listening process from a tidy step-by-step textbook approach. In practice, you may have to back up and clarify content, ask more questions, and rethink how you would feel before you attempt to summarize how someone else feels. Conversely, you may be able to summarize feelings *without* asking questions or summarizing content if the message is clear and it relates to a situation with which you are very familiar. Overusing this skill can slow down a conversation and make the other person uncomfortable or irritated. However, if you use it judiciously, paraphrasing can help both you and your partner keep focused on the issues and ideas at hand.

Reflecting content or feeling through paraphrasing can be especially useful in the following situations:

- Before you take an important action
- Before you argue or criticize
- When your partner has strong feelings or wants to talk over a problem
- When your partner is speaking "in code" or using unclear abbreviations
- When your partner wants to understand *your* feelings and thoughts
- When you are "talking to yourself" to clarify an issue in your own mind
- When you encounter new ideas[30]

Sometimes, however, you truly don't understand how another person really feels. At times like this, be cautious of telling others, "I know just how you feel." It may be more important simply to let others know that you care about them than to grill them about their feelings.

If you do decide to use paraphrasing skills, keep the following guidelines in mind:

- Use your own words.
- Don't go beyond the information communicated by the speaker.
- Be concise.
- Be specific.
- Be accurate.

Do *not* use paraphrasing skills if you aren't able to be open and accepting; if you do not trust the other person to find his or her own solution; if you are using these skills as a way of hiding yourself from another; or if you feel pressured, hassled, or tired. Also, as we have already discussed, overuse of paraphrasing can be distracting and unnatural.

Don't be discouraged if your initial attempts to use these skills seem awkward and uncomfortable. Any new skill takes time to learn and use well. The instructions and samples you have seen here should serve as a guide, rather than as hard-and-fast prescriptions to follow during each conversation.

Building Your Skills

LISTENING AND PARAPHRASING CONTENT AND EMOTION

Working in groups of three, ask person A to briefly identify a problem or conflict that he or she is having (or has had) with another person (co-worker, supervisor, partner, or family member). Person B should use questioning, content paraphrasing, and emotion paraphrasing skills to explore the problem. Person C should observe the discussion and evaluate person B's listening and reflecting skills, using the Observer Checklist. Make a check mark next to all of the skills that person B uses effectively.

Continued

OBSERVER CHECKLIST

Non-Verbal Skills:

_____ Direct eye contact

_____ Open, relaxed body posture

_____ Uncrossed arms

_____ Uncrossed legs

_____ Appropriate hand gestures

_____ Reinforcing nods

_____ Responsive facial expression

_____ Appropriate tone of voice

_____ Appropriate volume

Verbal Skills:

_____ Effective and appropriate questions

_____ Accurate paraphrasing of content

_____ Accurate paraphrasing of emotion

_____ Timely paraphrasing

_____ Didn't interrupt the speaker

▶▶▶ Applying Theory and Research

LISTENING TO OTHERS' STORIES AS CO-STORYTELLER

A study conducted by communication researchers Janet Bavelas, Linda Coates, and Trudy Johnson sought to investigate what kinds of responses listeners make when listening to a personal story and how those responses affect the speaker. To investigate the effect of listeners' responses to a storyteller, they had one person listen and another person tell a story about a time when she or he had experienced a close call—such as narrowly missing being hurt or injured. In one condition, the listener was just to listen and make no comments. In the second condition, the listener was to listen and summarize the gist of what the speaker was saying in a sentence or two. The third condition had the listener actively paraphrase what the speaker was saying. For the fourth condition, the listeners were to listen while mentally counting how many days it was until Christmas. Although this last condition sounds like a bizarre task, the purpose was to explore the effects of having a listener supposedly listening but not paying attention to what the speaker was saying. The researchers wanted to know whether how a listener responded to what a speaker was saying had an impact on how the speaker told the story.

APPLYING THE RESEARCH TO YOUR LIFE

The researchers found that when the listener made no responses to the speaker, the speaker told the story less effectively. When speakers had a listener who made specific responses and responded in meaningful ways, the speakers were better at telling their story. The researchers also discovered that listeners are more likely to make specific rather than general comments later in the narrative. This observation makes sense; more specific comments are more likely to occur later in a story because the listener has had time to learn about the major elements in the story he or she is listening to. The results suggest that an effective listener is really a "co-narrator," or active participant in the communication process, rather than merely a passive listener. It's not that specific comments are better than general comments; what's important is that the responses the listener makes should be appropriate. Comments that fit the story can actually help the speaker gauge how effectively he or she is telling the story. Without any responses, the speaker may think the listener isn't really interested in the story. The kinds of responses a listener makes during

Continued

an effective conversation are different from those a listener makes if a speaker is delivering a monologue. Because communication is a transaction, a dynamic process in which meaning is created between speaker and listener, the kinds of responses a listener makes should be authentic, not "canned" or stilted.

What do these results mean to you? If, while your friend is pouring her heart out about the exasperating experience of having a flat tire in the rain, you respond with a vacant look and periodically grunt, "Uh-uh," or "OK," or " Ah," your mumbles may lead your friend to believe you aren't really listening all that closely. In addition, if your friend thinks you aren't interested or listening to her story, she may either cut the story short or try to throttle up the drama of the story to get your attention. On the other hand, if you appropriately paraphrase the worst parts of her experience, or provide well-timed responses that fit with what she is saying, she's more likely to believe that you are really listening and that you care about her ordeal.

Empathic listeners respond at appropriate times, with appropriate words and phrases; they don't just mumble responses here and there. Responding to a speaker is, in some respects, like being a co-storyteller or co-narrator of the story; your listening and responding help shape the story. So if you're listening to someone tell a boring story, it may be partially your fault. A good listener can help bring out the best in a speaker.

Source: J. B. Bavelas, L. Coates, and T. Johnson, "Listeners as Co-Narrators," Journal of Personality and Social Psychology, 79, 6 (2000): 941–952.

LISTEN

When I ask you to listen to me and you start giving advice, you have not done what I asked.

When I ask you to listen to me and you begin to tell me why I shouldn't feel that way, you are trampling on my feelings.

When I ask you to listen to me and you feel you have to do something to solve my problems, you have failed me, strange as that may seem.

Listen! All I asked, was that you listen. Not talk or do—just hear me.

Advice is cheap: 50 cents will get you both Dear Abby and Billy Graham in the same newspaper.

And I can do for myself; I'm not helpless. Maybe discouraged and faltering, but not helpless.

When you do something for me that I can and need to do for myself, you contribute to my fear and weakness.

But when you accept as a simple fact that I do feel what I feel, no matter how irrational, then I quit trying to convince you and can get about the business of understanding what's behind this irrational feeling.

And when that's clear, the answers are obvious and I don't need advice.

Irrational feelings make sense when we understand what's behind them.

Perhaps that's why prayer works, sometimes, for some people—because God is mute, and doesn't give advice or try to fix things.

God just listens and lets you work it out for yourself.

So, please listen and just hear me, and, if you want to talk, wait a minute for your turn, and I'll listen to you.

                                                                              Anonymous

Responding to Confirm or Disconfirm Others

Couple A:

Wife to husband: "I just don't feel appreciated anymore."
Husband to wife: "Margaret, I'm so very sorry. I love you. You're the most important person in the world to me."

Couple B:

Wife to husband: "I just don't feel appreciated anymore."
Husband to wife: "Well, what about my feelings? Don't my feelings count? You'll have to do what you have to do. What's for dinner?"

confirming response.
Statement that causes another person to value himself or herself more.

disconfirming response.
Statement that causes another person to value himself or herself less.

It doesn't take an expert in interpersonal communication to know that Couple B's relationship is not warm and confirming. Researchers have studied the specific kinds of responses people offer to others.[31] Some responses are confirming; other responses are disconfirming. A **confirming response** is an other-oriented statement that causes others to value themselves more; wife A is likely to value herself more after her husband's confirming response. A **disconfirming response** is a statement that causes others to value themselves less. Wife B knows first-hand what it's like to have her feelings ignored and disconfirmed. Are you aware of whether your responses to others confirm them or disconfirm them? To help you be more aware of the kinds of responses you make to others, we'll review the results of studies that identify both confirming and disconfirming responses.[32]

Provide Confirming Responses

The adage "People judge us by our words and behaviour rather than by our intent" summarizes the underlying principle of confirming responses. Those who receive your messages determine whether they have the effect you intended. Formulating confirming responses requires careful listening and attention to the other person. Does it really matter whether we confirm others? Marriage researcher John Gottman used video cameras and microphones to observe couples interacting in an apartment over an extended period of time. He found that a significant predictor of divorce was neglecting to confirm or affirm one's marriage partner during typical, everyday conversation—even though couples who were less likely to divorce spent only a few seconds more confirming their partner than couples who eventually did divorce. His research conclusion has a powerful implication: long-lasting relationships are characterized by supportive, confirming messages.[33] We will describe several kinds of confirming responses in this section.

Direct Acknowledgment

When you respond directly to something another person says to you, you are acknowledging not only the statement but also that the person is worth responding to.

Joan: It's a great day for a canoe trip.

Mariko: Yes, Joan, it's wonderful to be outside.

Agreement about Judgments

When you confirm someone's evaluation of something, you are also affirming that person's sense of taste and judgment.

Nancy: I think the steel guitar player's riff was fantastic.

Victor: Yes, I think it was the best part of the performance.

Supportive Response

When you express reassurance and understanding, you are confirming a person's right to his or her feelings.

Pierre: I'm disappointed that I only scored 60 on my interpersonal communication test.

Sarah: I'm sorry to see you so frustrated, Pierre. I know that test was important to you.

Clarifying Response

When you seek greater understanding of another person's message, you are confirming that he or she is worth your time and trouble. Clarifying responses also encourage the other person to talk in order to explore his or her feelings.

Larry: I'm not feeling very good about my family situation these days.

Tyrone: Is it tough with you and Margo working different shifts?

Expression of Positive Feeling

We feel confirmed or valued when someone else agrees with our expression of joy or excitement.

Lorraine: I'm so excited! I just got accepted into law school.

Dorette: Congrats! I'm so proud of you! You deserve it.

Compliment

When you tell people that you like what they have done or said, what they are wearing, or how they look, you are confirming their sense of worth.

Jean-Christophe: Did you get the invitation to my party?

Manny: Yes! It looked so professional. I didn't know you could do graphics like that on the computer. You're talented!

In each of these examples, note how the responder provides comments that confirm the worth or value of the other person, but keep in mind that confirming responses should be sincere. Offering false praise is manipulative, and your communication partner will probably sniff out your phoniness.

Avoid Disconfirming Responses

Some statements and responses can undermine another person's self-worth. We offer these categories so that you can avoid using them and also recognize them when someone uses them to chip away at your self-image and self-esteem.

Impervious Response

When a person fails to acknowledge your statement or attempt to communicate, even though you know he or she heard you, you may feel a sense of awkwardness or embarrassment.

Rosa: I loved your speech, Harvey.

Harvey: [No response, verbal or non-verbal.]

Interrupting Response

When people interrupt you, they are implying that what they have to say is more important than what you have to say. In effect, they could also be implying that they are more important than you are.

Anna: I just heard on the news that—

Omar: Oh yes, the stock market just went down 100 points.

Irrelevant Response

An irrelevant response is one that has nothing at all to do with what you were saying. Chances are your partner is not listening to you at all.

Arnold: First we're flying next Tuesday to Vancouver, and then taking the cruise up to Alaska. I can hardly wait.

Peter: They're predicting freezing rain here tonight.

The real message Peter is sending is, "I have more important things on my mind."

Tangential Response

A tangential response is one that acknowledges you but that is only minimally related to what you are talking about. Again, it indicates that the other person isn't really attending to your message.

Richard: This new program will help us stay within our budget.

Samantha: Yeah. I think I'll save some bucks and send this letter by regular mail.

Impersonal Response

By intellectualizing and using the third person, this type of response distances the speaker from the other person. It also has the effect of trivializing what the other person has said.

Diana: Hey, Bill. I'd like to talk with you for a minute about getting your permission to take my vacation in July.

Bill: One tends to become interested in recreational pursuits about this time of year, doesn't one?

🌑 Incoherent Response

When a speaker mumbles, rambles, or makes some unintelligible effort to respond, you may end up wondering if what you said was of any value or use to the listener.

Paolo: George, here's my suggestion for the merger deal with Techstar. Let's make them an offer of 48 dollars a share and see how they respond.

George: Huh? Well... so... well... hmmm... I'm not sure.

🌑 Incongruous Response

When a verbal message is inconsistent with non-verbal behaviour, people usually believe the non-verbal message, but they usually feel confused as well. An incongruous response is like a malfunctioning traffic light with red and green lights flashing simultaneously—you're just not sure whether the speaker wants you to go or stay.

Sue: Honey, do you want me to go grocery shopping with you?

Steve [shouting]: OF COURSE I DO! WHY ARE YOU ASKING?

Although it may be impossible to eliminate all disconfirming responses from your repertoire, becoming aware of the power of your words and monitoring your conversation for offensive phrases may help you avoid unexpected and perhaps devastating consequences.

▶ ## Recap

HOW TO RESPOND WITH EMPATHY

Responding with Empathy	Action
Understand Your Partner's Feelings	Ask yourself how you would feel if you had experienced a similar situation, or recall how you did feel under similar circumstances. Or recall how your partner felt under similar circumstances.
Paraphrase Emotions	When appropriate, try to summarize what you think your partner may be feeling.
Provide Confirming Responses	Acknowledge what others say to you, confirm others' judgments, offer supportive responses, seek to clarify others' messages, affirm others' positive feelings, and pay sincere compliments.
Avoid Disconfirming Responses	Provide some acknowledgment of others' attempts to communicate; do not interrupt; avoid irrelevant, tangential, impersonal, incoherent, or incongruous responses.

Improving Critical Listening and Responding Skills

After putting it off for several months and being heckled by all of your friends about getting into the 21st century, you've decided to buy a cell phone. As you begin to talk to your friends, you're surprised to find a bewildering number of factors to consider: What type of air plan do you need? What company should you go with? Do you want a phone that can take pictures or do text messaging? How many weekend minutes, evening minutes, or daily minutes of calling time do you need? You decide to head to a store to see if a salesperson can help you sort through the maze of options. The salesperson is friendly enough, but you become even more overwhelmed with the number of options, bells, and whistles to consider. As you try to make this decision, your listening goal is not to empathize with those who extol the virtues of cell phones. Nor are you preparing to take a multiple-choice test on the subject. To sort through the information, you need to listen critically.

critical listening. Listening in which the goal is to evaluate and assess the quality, appropriateness, value, or importance of information.

information triage. Ability to sort good information from less useful or valid information.

Critical listening involves listening to evaluate the quality, appropriateness, value, or importance of the information you hear. *The goal of a critical listener is to use information to make a choice.* Whether you're selecting a new phone, deciding whom to vote for, choosing a potential date, or evaluating a new business plan, you will be faced with many opportunities to use your critical listening skills in interpersonal situations.

Identify Useful and Flawed Information

A critical listener is not necessarily one who offers negative comments. A critical listener seeks to identify both good information and information that is flawed or less helpful. We call this process **information triage**. "Triage" is a term borrowed from French to describe the process used by emergency medical personnel to determine which of several patients is the most severely ill or injured and needs immediate medical attention. Information triage is a process of evaluating and sorting out issues. An effective critical listener performs information triage; he or she is able to distinguish useful and accurate information and conclusions from information that is less useful, as well as conclusions that are inaccurate or invalid.

How do you develop the skill of information triage? Initially, critical listening involves the same strategies as listening to comprehend that we discussed earlier. Before you evaluate information, it's vital that you first *understand* the information. To listen critically, you then examine the logic or reasoning used in the message. However, while you are doing this, you must also be mindful of whether you are basing your evaluation on observed or verifiable *fact* or *inference*—a conclusion based on partial information. Although courses in logic, argumentation, and public speaking often present skills to help you evaluate information, it's also important to listen critically during interpersonal conversations.

Avoid Jumping to Conclusions

Imagine that you are a detective investigating a death. You are given the following information: (1) Leo and Moshia are found lying together on the floor; (2) Leo and Moshia are both dead; (3) Leo and Moshia are surrounded by water and broken glass; (4) on the sofa near Leo and Moshia is a cat with its back arched, apparently ready to defend itself.

Given these sketchy details, do you, the detective assigned to the case, have any theories about the cause of Leo and Moshia's demise? Perhaps they slipped on the water, crashed into a table, broke a vase, and died (that would explain the water and broken glass). Or maybe their attacker recently left the scene, and the cat is still distressed by the commotion. Clearly, you could make several inferences (conclusions based on partial information) as to the probable cause of death. Oh yes, there is one detail we forgot to mention: Leo and Moshia are fish. Does that help?

People often spin grand explanations and hypotheses based on sketchy details. Acting on inferences, people may act as though the "facts" clearly point to a specific conclusion. Determining the difference between a fact and an inference can help you more accurately use language to reach valid conclusions about what you see and experience.

Effective critical listening skills are crucial in a business environment.

What makes a fact a fact? Most students, when asked this question, respond by saying, "A fact is something that has been proven true." If that is the case, *how* has something been proven true? In a court of law, a **fact** is something that has been observed or witnessed. Anything else is speculation or inference.

> "Did you see my client in your house, taking your jewellery?" asks the wise attorney.
>
> "No," says the plaintiff.
>
> "Then you do not know for a fact that my client is a thief."
>
> "I guess not," the plaintiff admits.

Problems occur when we respond to something as if it were a fact (something observed), when in reality, it is an **inference** (a conclusion based on speculation):

> "It's a fact that your mother doesn't like me."
>
> "It's a fact that you will be poor all of your life."
>
> "It's a fact that you will fail this course."

Each of these statements, although it might very well be true, misuses the term "fact." If you cannot recognize when you are making an inference instead of stating a fact, you may give your judgments more credibility than they deserve. Being sensitive to the differences between facts and inferences can improve both critical listening and responding skills.

fact. Something that has been directly observed to be true and thus has been proven to be true.

inference. Conclusion based on speculation.

Improving Your Responding Skills

We've offered several strategies for responding to others when your goal is to comprehend information, empathize with others, or evaluate messages. Regardless of your communication goal, we'll now present several additional strategies to enhance your skill in responding to others. The timing of the response, usefulness of the information, amount of detail, and descriptiveness of the response are useful strategies to consider when responding to others.

When you are teaching someone a new skill, the timing of your feedback is just as important as what you say. When should this grown-up tell the child he is helping how to improve his bicycle riding?
(Marc Romanelli/The Image Bank/Getty)

Provide Well-Timed Responses

Feedback is usually most effective when you offer it at the earliest opportunity, particularly if your objective is to teach someone a skill. For example, if you are teaching someone how to make your famous egg rolls, you provide a step-by-step commentary as you watch your pupil. If he or she makes a mistake, you don't wait until the egg rolls are finished to say that he or she left out the cabbage. Your pupil needs immediate feedback to finish the rest of the sequence successfully.

Sometimes, however, if a person is already sensitive and upset about something, delaying feedback can be wise. Use your critical thinking skills to analyze when feedback will do the most good. Rather than automatically offering immediate correction, use the just-in-time (JIT) approach and provide feedback just before the person might make another mistake. If, for example, your daughter typically rushes through math tests and fails to check her work, remind her right before her next test to double-check her answers, not immediately after the test she just failed. To provide feedback about a relationship, select a mutually agreeable place and time when both of you are rested and relaxed; avoid hurling feedback at someone "for his or her own good" immediately after he or she offends you.

Provide Usable Information

Perhaps you've heard this advice: "Never try to teach a pig to sing. It wastes your time. It doesn't sound pretty, and it annoys the pig." When you provide information to someone, be certain that it is useful and relevant. How can you make sure your partner can use the information you share? Be other-oriented; put yourself in your partner's mindset. Ask yourself, "If I were this person, how would I respond to this information? Is it information I can act on? Or is it information that may make matters worse?" Under the guise of effective feedback, we may be tempted to reveal to others our complete range of feelings and emotions. However, research suggests that selective feedback is best. In one study, married couples who practised selective self-disclosure were more satisfied than couples who told everything they knew or were feeling.[34] Immersing your partner in information that is irrelevant or that may be damaging to the relationship may be cathartic, but it may not enhance the quality of your relationship or improve understanding.

Avoid Unnecessary Details

When you are selecting meaningful information, try to cut down on the volume of information. Don't overwhelm your listener with details that obscure the key point of your feedback. Give only the highlights that will benefit the listener. Be brief.

Be Descriptive Rather Than Evaluative

"You're an awful driver!" shouts Doris at her husband, Frank. Although Doris may feel she has provided simple feedback to her spouse about his skills, Frank will probably not respond warmly, or even listen closely, to her feedback. If Doris tries to be more descriptive and less evaluative, then he might be inclined to listen. Less offensive comments might include, "Frank, you are travelling 70 kilometres per hour in a 50 kilometre zone," or "Frank, I get very nervous when you zigzag so fast through the highway traffic." They describe Frank's behaviour rather than render judgments about him that are likely to trigger a defensive, passive listening reaction.

Building Your Skills

PRACTISING YOUR RESPONDING SKILLS

The purpose of this exercise is to help you practise your responding skills. Read each of the following situations and then write each of the four types of responses, just as if you were talking to someone:

1. *Ask questions:* Probe for more information.

2. *Paraphrase content:* What is the essence of the message?

3. *Provide a decentring response:* What is the other person thinking?

4. *Provide an empathic response:* What is the other person feeling?

Now pair up with another person and compare your responses. If necessary, revise one or more of your responses to make sure it is appropriate.

Situation 1: "I'm not sure what to do. My life seems consumed with work. I'm trying to go to school, I work more than 20 hours a week, and when I get home I have the kids to take care of. I'm exhausted. But I can't quit my job; I need the money. And if I drop out of school, it just means I'll be stuck with a minimum-wage job longer. I have to take care of my kids—I can't just stop meeting their needs. But what about me? I'm exhausted, and I know I can't keep going on like this."

Situation 2: "I'm really struggling with what to do about my religion. When I was growing up, my family and I would always attend a very liberal church; there were few rules and no list of dos and don'ts. As I've grown older, my beliefs have changed because I find I need more structure in my life. I've started worshipping with another group that holds more conservative views toward religion. The problem is that my parents, family, and even many of my friends believe I'm betraying them and my own heritage; my change in church affiliation is affecting my relationship with them. I just don't feel comfortable at the church I used to attend, but I also don't want to create conflict with my family and friends."

Situation 3: "I'm really not sure what to do about my relationship with Ben. We've been together for about a year now. I moved in with him a couple of months ago. But lately we've had more friction between us; we seem to disagree about more things. It seems to me that we want different things out of our relationship. I'm comfortable with just keeping things as they are, but Ben would like to make a more serious commitment. The increased conflict we're having makes me question whether our relationship will work out in the long term."

Source: Adapted from David W. Johnson, Reaching Out: Interpersonal Effectiveness and Self-Actualization (Boston: Allyn & Bacon, 2000), 234.

▶ Recap

SUGGESTIONS FOR IMPROVING RESPONDING SKILLS

Provide Well-Timed Responses	Sometimes immediate feedback is best; at other times provide a just-in-time (JIT) response when it will do the most good.
Provide Meaningful Information	Select information that your partner can act on rather than making vague comments or suggestions that are beyond his or her capabilities.
Avoid Unnecessary Details	Avoid information overload; don't bombard the listener with too much information; keep your comments focused on major points.
Be Descriptive	Don't evaluate your listening partner; focus on behaviour rather than personality.

Summary

Listening effectively to others is the most essential skill required for establishing other-oriented relationships. Listening, the process of making sense out of what we hear, includes selecting, attending, understanding, remembering, and responding to others. Preferred listening styles vary from person to person and include people-oriented, action-oriented, content-oriented, and time-oriented listening.

Most of us don't listen effectively because we are self-oriented instead of other-oriented. Barriers to effective listening include being self-focused, being distracted by emotional noise, criticizing the speaker, wasting the difference between speech and thought rates, shifting attention, being distracted by information overload and external noise, and experiencing listener apprehension.

To become better listeners, we can pursue three seemingly simple steps: stop, look, and listen. To stop means to avoid tuning in to our own distracting messages and to become mindful of what others are saying. To look is to observe and interpret unspoken messages—non-verbal communication skills and principles will be discussed in greater detail in Chapter 6. After stopping and looking, we can then listen more effectively to others by focusing on details and the speaker's key ideas. Being other-oriented does not mean that you should abandon your own convictions or values, but rather that you should make a conscious effort to pay attention to the needs and concerns of others. After we complete these three steps, we should ask questions and reflect content by paraphrasing.

We can further improve our ability to listen and respond empathically by seeking to understand our partner's feelings, paraphrasing his or her emotions, and providing confirming responses. We can further improve our ability to listen and respond critically by looking for faulty logic and being consciously competent at distinguishing facts from inferences. Also, we can improve our skills at responding, regardless of the communication objective, by providing well-timed responses; providing usable information; avoiding unnecessary details; and being descriptive rather than evaluative.

For Discussion and Review

Focus on Critical Thinking

1. Identify two situations during the past 24 hours in which you were an effective or ineffective listener. What factors contributed to the listening skill (or lack of skill) you demonstrated?

2. Miranda and Salvador often disagree about who should handle some of the child-rearing tasks in their home. When they have discussions on these issues, what are some effective listening skills and strategies that they could use to make sure they understand one another?

3. Jason and Ahmed are roommates. They both work hard each day and come home exhausted. What suggestions would you offer to help them listen effectively even when they are tired?

Focus on Ethics

4. Is it possible for paraphrasing and active listening to become a way to manipulate others? Support your answer.

5. Your friend asks you how you like her new dress. You really feel it is a bit too revealing, but it is time for the two of you to leave for your evening activities. Should you respond honestly, even though it may mean that you and your friend will be late for an important event?

6. Your roommate wants to tell you about his day. You are tired and really don't want to hear all of the details. Should you fake attention so that you won't hurt his feelings or should you simply tell your roommate that you are tired and would rather not hear about the details right now?

For Your Journal

1. Keep this checklist (first published in the *International Listening Association Newsletter*) with you one full day to monitor your listening problems.

A Checklist for Listeners

Today I. . .
Interrupted other people _____ times.
Misunderstood other people _____ times.
Lost track of a conversation _____ times.
Stopped making eye contact with a speaker _____ times.
Asked someone to repeat himself/herself _____ times.
Let my mind wander while listening to someone _____ times.
Changed the subject in the middle of a conversation _____ times.
Jumped to a conclusion about what someone was going to say _____ times.

Reacted emotionally to what someone was saying before they finished
_____ times.

When the 24 hours have passed, review your personal listening statistics. What
changes would you like to make in your listening behaviour?

2. Monitor and then jot down notes about your own self-talk during a conversation with another person. What competing thoughts and ideas occurred to
you while you were conversing with your partner? What did you do to refocus
on the message?

Learning with Others

1. Charting Your Listening Cycle

Are you a morning person or an evening person? Use the chart shown here to plot
your listening energy cycle. Draw a line starting at 6:00 a.m. showing the highs and
lows of your potential listening effectiveness. If, for example, you are usually still
asleep at 6:00 a.m., your line will be at 0 and start upward when you awake. If you
are a morning person, your line will peak in the morning. Or, perhaps your line
will indicate that you listen best in the evening.

After you have charted your typical daily listening cycle, gather in small
groups with your classmates to compare. Identify listening strategies that can help
you capitalize on your listening "up" periods. Also, based upon this chapter and
your own experiences, identify ways to enhance your listening when you traditionally have low listening energy.

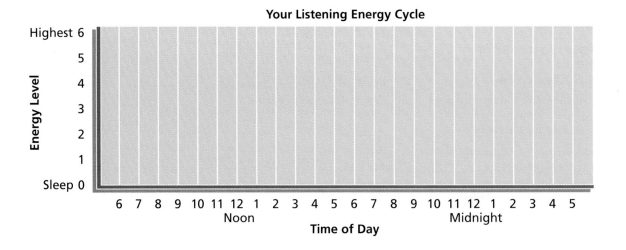

2. Assign one student from your group to speak very slowly on a difficult subject. The other members of the group should write down short summaries during pauses in the speech. Compare summaries with others in the group.

3. Log on to Research Navigator. Find an article to share about improving listening skills. (*Hint:* Use psychology as your database and "listening skill" as your keyword.) There are many great articles in this area. Share the findings of your article with your group or class. Compare the suggestions made for improvement with the suggestions in this chapter.

Weblinks

http://facstaff.bloomu.edu/jtomlins/stress.htm   Stress affects your ability to listen and concentrate. Take a stress test provided by *Newsweek* magazine.

www.selfgrowth.com/test.html   Visit this site and choose from the various tests.

www.ihhp.com/sasqtest.htm   This is another site that provides a short quiz to assess your skill in being sensitive to your own and others' emotions.

www-ai.ijs.si/eliza/eliza.html   Can computers listen and respond to human communication? At this site, you'll meet "Eliza," who "listens" and then responds to you. Ask Eliza questions, and she will answer.

5

Verbal Communication Skills

After you study this chapter

you should be able to . . .

1. Describe the relationship between words and meaning.

2. Explain how words influence us and our culture.

3. Identify word barriers and know how to manage them.

4. Discuss how the words we use affect our relationships with others.

5. Understand supportive approaches to relating to others.

● Understanding How Words Work

● Recognizing the Power of Words

● Avoiding Word Barriers

● Using Words to Establish Supportive Relationships

● Using Words to Be Appropriately Assertive

ords are powerful. Those who use them skilfully can exert great influence with just a few of them. Consider these notable achievements:

Shakespeare expressed the quintessence of the human condition in Hamlet's famous "To be or not to be" soliloquy—just under 300 words long.

Several of our religions adhere to a comprehensive moral code expressed in even fewer words: the Ten Commandments.

Words have great power in our private lives as well. In this chapter, we will examine ways to use words more effectively in interpersonal relationships. We'll investigate how to harness the power that words have to affect our emotions, thoughts, and actions, and we'll describe links between language and culture. We will also identify communication barriers that may keep you from using words effectively and note strategies and skills for managing those barriers. Finally, we will examine the role of speech in establishing supportive relationships with others.

According to one study, a person's ability to use words—more specifically, to participate in conversation with others—is one of the best predictors of communication competence.[1] People who simply didn't talk much were perceived as being less interpersonally skilled than people who spent an appropriate amount of time engaged in conversation with others. This chapter is designed to help you better understand the power of words and to use them with greater skill and confidence.

Understanding How Words Work

As you read the printed words on this page, how are you able to make sense out of these black marks? When you hear words spoken by others, how are you able to interpret those sounds? Although there are several theories that attempt to explain how we learn language and ascribe meaning to both printed and uttered words, there is no single, universally held view that neatly clarifies the mystery.

Here's one thing that *is* known about words and meaning: *meanings are in people, not in words.* As we noted in Chapter 1, one of the myths about communication is that words contain meaning. They don't. Meaning is created because words, which are arbitrary symbols, are used within a specific context and interpreted within a cultural framework to yield both denotative and connotative meaning. It's inaccurate to assume that a word means the same thing to everyone. The transactional nature of interpersonal communication suggests that meaning is co-created through the process of using and making sense out of words. People construct their reality based on how they use words to make sense of the world. Words don't mean anything until someone interprets them and creates meaning. Now let's unpack that last sentence to gain a fuller appreciation of the transactional nature of words and meaning.

Words Are Symbols

symbols. A word, sound, or visual device that represents a thought, concept, or object.

referents. The things that a symbol represents.

thoughts. The mental process of creating a category, idea, or image triggered by a referent or symbol.

As we noted in Chapter 1, words are **symbols** that represent something else. A printed word triggers an image, sound, concept, or experience. Take the word "cat" for instance. The word may conjure up in your mind's eye a hissing creature with bared claws and fangs. Or, perhaps you envision a cherished pet curled up by a fireplace.

The classic model in Figure 5.1 was developed by one pair of researchers to explain how we use words as symbols, noting relationships between *symbols* (words), *referents*, and *thoughts*.[2] **Referents** are the things the symbols (words) represent. **Thought** is the mental process of creating a category, idea, or image triggered by the referent or the symbol. So, these three elements: words, referents, and thoughts become inextricably linked. Although some scholars find this model too simplistic to explain how we link all words to a meaning, it does illustrate the process for most concepts, people, and tangible things.

Figure 5.1
Triangle of Meaning

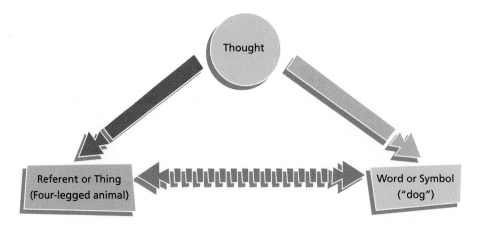

Words Are Arbitrary

Charles Hockett, a linguist (a person who studies the origin and nature of language), suggested that words are, for the most part, arbitrary.[3] There's not an obvious reason why many words represent what they refer to. In English, as in all languages, words arbitrarily represent something else. The word "dog," for example, does not *sound* like a dog or *look* at all like a dog. Yet there is a clear connection in your mind between your pet pooch and the symbol "dog." The words we use have agreed-upon general meanings, but there is not typically a logical connection between a word and what it represents. Yes, some words, such as "buzz," "hum," "snort," and "giggle," do re-create the sounds they represent, and many words can trace their origin to other languages. However, most of the time words have an arbitrary meaning. A linguistic group, such as all the people who speak the English language, has agreed that the word "tree," for example, will represent the thing with bark, branches, and leaves that is growing in your yard or a nearby park. The arbitrary nature of most words means that there is no inherent meaning in a word. Therefore, unless we develop a common meaning for a word, misunderstanding and miscommunication may occur.

Words Are Context Bound

Your English or speech communication teacher has, undoubtedly, cautioned you that taking something out of context changes its meaning. Symbols derive their meaning from the situation in which they are used. The term "old man" could refer to a male over the age of 70, your father, your teacher, your principal, or your boss. We would need to know the context of the two symbols "old" and "man" to decipher their specific meaning. The transactional nature of communication emphasizes how meaning is created through discussion.

Words Are Culturally Bound

Culture consists of the rules, norms, values, and mores of a group of people, which have been learned and shaped from one generation to the next. The meaning of a symbol such as a word can change from culture to culture. Some years ago, General Motors sold a car called a Nova. In English, "nova" means *bright star*—an appropriate name for a car. In Spanish, however, it sounds like the words "no va," which translate as, *It does not go.* As you can imagine, this name was not a great sales tool for the Spanish-speaking market.

One way to measure how words reflect culture is to consider the new words that become new entries in dictionaries. Here are some of the recent additions to *Webster's New World College Dictionary,* published at the start of the 21st century.

Bubba: A slang term that means *brother*

Pumped: Enthusiastic, confident

Viewbook: Richly illustrated booklet produced by a college or university for prospective students

Slamming: Switching someone's long-distance phone service without a person's knowledge

Megaplex: Many movie screens in a single place, which show different features

Racial profiling: Alleged to be a policy of police who stop vehicles that are driven by people from a particular racial or ethnic group

Face time: Time spent in the presence of someone

Hat hair: Hair that becomes matted after wearing a hat

Of course, new phrases can also become common. What about "double-double," for all of the coffee drinkers? This phrase is widely understood in Canada, but one author used it recently in the United States and was rewarded with a blank stare.

The study of words and meaning is called *semantics*. One important body of semantic theory, known as **symbolic interaction**, suggests that as a society we are bound together because of our common use of symbols. Originally developed by sociologists as a way of making sense out of how societies and groups are linked together,[4] the theory of symbolic interaction also illuminates how we use our common understanding of symbols to form interpersonal relationships. Common symbols foster links in understanding and, therefore, lead to satisfying relationships. Of course, even within a given culture, we misunderstand each other's messages. However, the more similar the cultures of the communication partners, the greater the chance for a meeting of meanings.

Some researchers, such as linguist Deborah Tannen, suggest that gender plays a major role in how we interpret certain verbal messages.[5] Women tend to interpret messages based on how personally supportive they perceive the message to be. Men, according to Tannen, are more likely to interpret messages based on issues related to dominance and power. Research confirms that psychological gender is a better predictor than biological sex of the general framework we use to interpret messages.[6] Clearly, our life experiences help us interpret the words we hear.

symbolic interaction. A theory that suggests societies are bound together through the common use of symbols.

denotative meaning. The restrictive or literal meaning of a word.

Words Communicate Denotative and Connotative Meaning

Language is the vehicle through which we share our sense of the world with others. Through language we transfer our experience into symbols and then use the symbols to share our experience. However, as we learned in Chapter 1, the process of symbol sharing through language is not just a simple process of uttering a word and having its meaning clearly understood by another. Messages convey both content and feelings. So, our language conveys meaning on two levels: the denotative and the connotative.

The **denotative meaning** of a word creates content. The denotation of a word is its restrictive or literal meaning. For example, here is one dictionary definition for the word "school":

> An institution for the instruction of children; an institution for instruction in a skill or business; a college or a university.[7]

This definition is the literal or denotative definition of the word; it describes what "school" means in North American culture.

The **connotative meaning** of a word conveys feelings. Words also have personal and subjective meanings for us. The word "school" to you might mean a wonderful, exciting place where you meet your friends, have a good time, and occasionally take tests and perform other tasks that keep you from enjoying fellowship with your chums. To others, "school" could be a restrictive, burdensome obligation that stands in the way of making money and getting on with life. The connotative meaning of a word is more specialized. The denotative or objective meaning of the word "school" can be found in your *Oxford, Gage,* or *Webster's* dictionary; your connotative, subjective response to the word probably does not appear there.

Most of us can agree on the denotative meaning for the word "school," but the connotative meaning will be different for everybody.
(Ellen Senisi/The Image Works)

connotative meaning. The personal and subjective meaning of a word.

Words Communicate Concrete Or Abstract Meaning

Words can be placed along a continuum from abstract to concrete. We call a word *concrete* if we can experience its referent with one of our senses; if we can see it, touch it, smell it, taste it, or hear it, then it's concrete. If we cannot do these things with the referent, then the word is abstract. We can visualize the progression from abstract to concrete as a ladder:

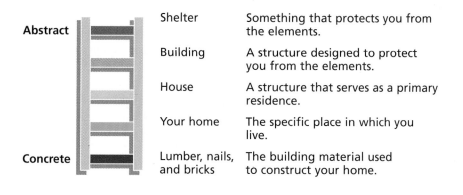

Abstract	Shelter	Something that protects you from the elements.
	Building	A structure designed to protect you from the elements.
	House	A structure that serves as a primary residence.
	Your home	The specific place in which you live.
Concrete	Lumber, nails, and bricks	The building material used to construct your home.

In general, the more concrete the language, the easier it is for others to understand.

Recognizing the Power of Words

Sticks and stones may break my bones,
But words can never hurt me.

This old schoolyard chant may provide a ready retort for the desperate victim of name-calling, but it is hardly convincing. With more insight, the poet Robert Browning wrote, "Words break no bones; hearts though sometimes;" and in his book, *Science and Sanity*, mathematician and engineer Alfred Korzybski argued that the words we use (and misuse) have tremendous effects on our thoughts and actions.[8] Browning and Korzybski were right. As we said at the beginning of this chapter, words have power.

Words Have Power to Create

"To name is to call into existence—to call out of nothingness,"[9] wrote French philosopher Georges Gusdorff. Words give us a tool to create our world by naming and labelling what we experience. Undoubtedly, you learned in your elementary science class that Sir Isaac Newton discovered gravity. Perhaps it would be more accurate to say that he *labelled* rather than discovered it. His use of the word "gravity" gave us a cognitive category; we now converse about the force of the earth that keeps us from flying into space. Words give us the symbolic vehicles to communicate our creations and discoveries to others.

When you label something as "good" or "bad," you are using language to create your own vision of how you experience the world. If you tell a friend that the movie you saw last night was vulgar and obscene, you are not only providing your friend with a critique of the movie, you are also communicating your sense of what is appropriate and inappropriate.

As we noted in Chapter 2, you create your self-worth largely with self-talk and with the labels you apply to yourself. One theorist believes that you also create your moods and emotional state with the words you use to label your feelings.[10] If you get fired from a job, you might say that you feel angry and helpless, or you might declare that you feel liberated and excited. The first response might lead to depression, and the second to happiness. One fascinating study conducted over a 35-year period found that people who described the world in pessimistic terms when they were younger were in poorer health during middle age than those who had been optimistic.[11] Your words and corresponding outlook have the power to affect your health.

Words Have Power to Affect Thoughts and Actions

How about some horse meat for supper tonight? Most of us find such a question quite strange. Why? Horse meat is not something we typically eat. One theorist argues that horse meat is not a featured delicacy at the local supermarket simply because we have no other word for it. Your butcher does not advertise pig meat or cow meat; labelling the meat as pork chops, ham, and sausage, or as steak and ribs makes it sound more appetizing. Advertisers have long known that the way a product is labelled affects our propensity to purchase it.

Words can distort how we view and evaluate others. When we label someone as good, bad, shabby, or chic, it distorts our perception of the other person. Read the *In Canada* feature for research findings on the use of labels to signify a cultural group and how these labels may affect our perceptions of a group.

In Canada...

LABELS ARE WORDS THAT AFFECT OUR EVALUATION OF OTHERS

The words that we use to label people of other cultures and groups affect how we evaluate them. A study examined labels and their effects on people's attitudes toward Canada's native peoples. In the past, Native Canadians were often just labelled "Indians" with no thought about the impact of this labelling. More recently, a variety of labels have been used to refer to Canada's indigenous peoples. The labels of Aboriginal Peoples, Native Peoples, Native Indians, First Nations People, and Native Canadians were used in the study to assess attitudes, stereotypes, and emotions towards several target groups including Native Canadians. The results indicate that how groups are labelled affects our perceptions in both positive and negative ways.[i] These labels affect whether or not a group or a person with a particular label will be evaluated more positively or negatively. Once we have evaluated another group, our behaviour may be based on that label and evaluation. Of interest, the labels Native Canadians and First Nations People elicited the least favourable evaluations compared with the other three labels in this study.[i]

Although this study was done in the late 1990s, it still serves as a reminder of how words that we use to label groups or people are powerful influences. Although attitudes cannot always predict behaviour, there is little doubt that attitudes often do influence behaviour in positive and negative ways.[ii] To learn more about the attitude–behaviour relationship, you may want to examine some texts in social psychology, such as the one listed here.

Sources: i. *Darrell W. Donakowski and Victoria M. Esses, "Native Canadians, First Nations, or Aboriginals: The Effect of Labels on Attitudes Toward Native Peoples," Canadian Journal of Behavioural Science, 28(2), (1996): 86–91. Copyright 1996 Canadian Psychological Association. Reprinted with permission.* ii. *Also J. E. Alcock, D. W. Carment, and S. W. Sadava, A Textbook of Social Psychology (Scarborough, ON: Prentice-Hall Canada, 1998).*

Words also have the power to affect policies and procedures by painting powerful pictures that garner support for or against everything from government funding to legalizing or illegalizing behaviours. Consider words used today in political debates: "terrorist" versus "freedom fighter," for instance, or "marijuana user" versus "drug addict." A quick examination of any Canadian newspaper illustrates the use of words like these to influence attitudes and behaviour.

Words Have Power to Affect and Reflect Culture

In the early part of the 20th century, anthropologist Edward Sapir and his student Benjamin Whorf worked simultaneously to refine a theory called **linguistic determinism**.[12] The essence of linguistic determinism is that language shapes the way we think. Our words also reflect our thoughts and our culture. A related principle, called **linguistic relativity**, states that each language has unique elements embedded within it. Together these two principles form the underlying elements in the **Sapir-Whorf hypothesis**, which suggests that language shapes our culture and culture shapes our language.

To prove the theory, Benjamin Whorf studied the languages of several cultures, particularly that of Hopi Native Americans. He discovered that in Hopi, one word (the word *masa'ytaka*) is used for every creature that flies, except for birds. While this

linguistic determinism. A theory that describes how use of language determines or influences thoughts and perceptions.

linguistic relativity. The theory that each language includes some unique features that are not found in other languages.

Sapir-Whorf hypothesis. Based on the principles of linguistic determinism and linguistic relativity, the hypothesis that language shapes our thoughts and culture, and our culture and thoughts affect the language we use to describe our world.

seems odd to an English-speaker, because the English language has many different words for different flying creatures (and things such as airplanes, balloons, and rockets), for the Hopi, flying creatures (or objects) constitute a single category. Whorf saw this as proof of his hypothesis that the words we use reflect our culture and our culture influences our words.

Similarly, today's highly-developed technological culture has given rise to many new words that reflect the importance we place on technology; terms such as "PC," "hard drive," and "gigabytes" weren't part of your grandparents' language. Also, the fact that a certain type of behaviour is now labelled Attention-Deficit/Hyperactivity Disorder (ADHD) is an example of how words can create a reality in a culture. Grandpa might argue that there weren't any ADHD kids in his day—some kids were just "rowdy."[13]

Although today most linguists don't support the Sapir-Whorf hypothesis in its most extreme interpretation, there is evidence nonetheless to suggest that the words we use do, to some extent, reflect our culture; they reflect our thoughts and how we view the world. To understand your culture as well as your thoughts, the Sapir-Whorf hypothesis suggests that you study the words you use to gain insight about yourself and your culture.

If an impartial investigator from another culture were to study a transcript of all of your spoken utterances last week, what would he or she learn about you and the culture in which you live? If you frequently used words like "MP3" and "download," the investigator would know that these things are important to you, but the investigator might not know what they mean if they were not also part of his or her culture.

world view. A culturally acquired perspective for interpreting experiences.

Words not only reflect your culture; there is evidence that they mould it. Perhaps you've heard that Eskimos have 23 different words for snow. Even though they really don't have quite that many, the Inuit do have more words for snow than most residents of Florida do, for example.[14] In Canada, we are quite familiar with our bilingual food containers such as cereal boxes. When your Canadian author had friends visiting from the United States, the children were fascinated by this "oddity" and spent some time in the pantry looking at all the cans and boxes. French-English bilingualism is so pervasive in Canadian culture that most of us don't give this kind of labelling a second thought. We just automatically turn to the side that we can read most easily.

These examples also show that the words we use and listen to affect our **world view**—how we interpret what we experience. If you were to don someone else's prescription glasses, the world would literally look different to you, and the glasses would either enhance or inhibit your ability to see the world around you. In a sense, your world view is your own set of prescription glasses, which you formulate over time, based on your experiences, attitudes, beliefs, values, and needs. The words you use to describe your view of the world reflect and further shape your perspective, and you, in turn, help to shape your culture's collective world view through your use of language.

The "tech-speak" spoken here may help create the special culture these individuals share. (Mark Richards/PhotoEdit)

Avoiding Word Barriers

According to theologian and educator Ruel Howe, a communication barrier is "something that keeps meaning from meeting."[15] Words have the power to create monumental misunderstandings as well as deep connections. Although it is true that meanings are in people, not in words, sometimes assumptions or inaccurate use of words hinder understanding. Let's identify some of the specific barriers to understanding that we can create through language.

Bypassing: One Word, Two Thoughts

A student pilot was on his first solo flight. When he called the tower for flight instructions, the control tower said, "Would you please give us your altitude and position?" The pilot said, "I'm 180 cm tall, and I'm sitting up front."

Bypassing occurs when the same words mean different things to different people. Meaning is fragile, and the English language is imprecise in many areas. One researcher estimated that the 500 words we use most often in our daily conversations with others have over 14 000 different dictionary definitions, and this number does not take into account personal connotations. So, it is no wonder that bypassing is a common communication problem.

We all know that Pavlov's dog salivated when he heard the bell that he had learned to associate with food. Sometimes we respond to symbols the way Pavlov's dog did to the bell, forgetting that symbols (words) can have more than one meaning.

bypassing.   Miscommunicating because of different understandings of the same words.

Building Your Skills

THE TALKAHOLIC SCALE

Are you a "talkaholic," or do you know someone who is? The simple description of a talkaholic is someone who talks more than most people. Being other-oriented not only means being a good listener as we discussed in Chapter 4, but it also means being sensitive to how much you talk. Talkaholics often oververbalize. They are sometimes insensitive to others' need for information. No, we're not suggesting that you refrain from contributing to conversation and at times, it is appropriate and expected that you'll talk and others listen but consider whether you may be a conversation dominator. Take the following test developed by communication researchers James McCroskey and Virginia Richmond to determine your talkaholic quotient. The higher your score, the higher your tendency to be a talkaholic when relating to others.

Directions: The questionnaire on page 154 includes 16 statements about talking behaviour. Please indicate the degree to which you believe each of them applies to you by marking, on the line before each item, whether you (5) strongly agree that it applies, (4) agree that it applies, (3) are undecided, (2) disagree that it applies, or (1) strongly disagree that it applies. There are no right or wrong answers. Work quickly; record your first impression.

Continued

_____   1. Often I keep quiet when I know I should talk.

_____   2. I talk more than I should sometimes.

_____   3. Often I talk when I know I should keep quiet.

_____   4. Sometimes I keep quiet when I know it would be to my advantage to talk.

_____   5. I am a talkaholic.

_____   6. Sometimes I feel compelled to keep quiet.

_____   7. In general, I talk more than I should.

_____   8. I am a compulsive talker.

_____   9. I am not a talker; rarely do I talk in communication situations.

_____   10. Quite a few people have said I talk too much.

_____   11. I just can't stop talking too much.

_____   12. In general, I talk less than I should.

_____   13. I am *not* a talkaholic.

_____   14. Sometimes I talk when I know it would be to my advantage to keep quiet.

_____   15. I talk less than I should sometimes.

_____   16. I am *not* a compulsive talker.

Scoring: To determine your score on this scale, complete the following steps:

Step 1.   Add the scores for items 2, 3, 5, 7, 8, 10, 11, and 14.

Step 2.   Add the scores for items 13 and 16.

Step 3.   Complete the following formula: Talkaholic score = 12 + total from step 1 − total from step 2.

A score of 40 or above suggests that you are a talkaholic.

Source: James C. McCroskey and Virginia P. Richmond, Fundamentals of Human Communication: An Interpersonal Perspective (Prospect Heights, IL: Waveland Press, 1996), 66.

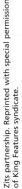

Lack of Precision: Uncertain Meaning

Alice Roosevelt Longworth writes about the investigation of a merchant sailor. "Do you," asked the interrogator, "have any pornographic literature?"

"Pornographic literature!" the sailor burst out indignantly. "I don't even have a pornograph!"

At a ceremony in a university chapel, a woman in her 90s buttonholed an usher and commanded, "Be sure you get me a seat up front, young man. I understand they've always had trouble with the agnostics in the chapel!"

Each of these examples, along with the Far Side cartoon, illustrates a **malapropism**—a confusion of one word or phrase for another that sounds similar to it. You have probably heard people confuse such word pairs as "construction" and "instruction," and "subscription" and "prescription." Although this confusion may at times be humorous, it can also result in failure to communicate clearly. So, too, can using words out of context, using inappropriate grammar, or putting words in the wrong order. Confusion is the inevitable result, as these sentences taken from a letter to a welfare department illustrate:

> I want my money as quickly as I can get it. I've been in bed with the doctor for two weeks, and it didn't do me any good. If things don't improve, I will have to send for another doctor.

And the following statements appeared in church bulletins:

> The eighth-graders will be presenting Shakespeare's *Hamlet* in the church basement on Friday at 7:00 p.m. The congregation is invited to attend this tragedy.

> This afternoon there will be meetings in the North and South ends of the church—children will be baptized at both ends.

These are funny examples, but in fact, unclear language can launch a war or sink a ship. It is vital to remember that *meanings are in people, not in words.* We give symbols meaning; we do not receive inherent meaning *from* symbols. If you are other-oriented, you will assess how someone else will respond to your message and you will try to select those symbols that he or she is most likely to interpret as you intend.

For most communication, the object is to be as specific and concrete as possible. Vague language creates confusion and frustration. Consider this example:

Sasha: Where's the aluminum foil?

Pam: In the drawer.

Sasha: What drawer?

Pam: In the kitchen.

Sasha: But where in the kitchen?

Pam: By the fridge.

Ha ha ha, Biff. Guess what? After we go to the drugstore and the post office, I'm going to the vet's to get tutored.

malapropism.   Confusion of one word or phrase for another that sounds similar to it.

Sasha: But which one? There are five drawers.

Pam: Oh, the second one from the top.

Sasha: Why didn't you say so in the first place?

Is it possible to be too precise? It is if you use a **restricted code** that has a meaning your listener does not know. A restricted code involves the use of words that have a particular meaning to a subgroup or culture. For example, most children grow up learning their own family's secret words. Sometimes, we develop abbreviations or specialized terms that make sense and save time when we speak to others in our group. Musicians, for example, use special terms that relate to reading and performing music. Most computer hackers know that a "screamer" is someone whose messages in cyberspace are all in CAPITAL LETTERS. Ham radio operators use codes to communicate over the airwaves. Yet, in each instance, this shorthand language would make little sense to an outsider. In fact, groups that rely on restricted codes may have greater cohesiveness because of this shared "secret" language or **jargon**. Whatever your line of work, guard against lapsing into phrases that can be interpreted only by a few.

When people have known one another for a long time, they also may use restricted codes for their exchanges. The Blondie cartoon is an example of how married couples can communicate using a code that no outsider could ever interpret.

restricted code. A vocabulary of words that have a particular meaning to a person, group, or culture.

jargon. Another name for restricted code; specialized terms or abbreviations the meanings of which are known only to members of a specific group.

allness. The tendency to use language to make unqualified, often untrue generalizations.

BLONDIE

Allness: The Language of Generalization

The tendency to use language to make unqualified, often untrue generalizations is called **allness**. Allness statements deny individual differences or variations. Statements such as, "All women are poor drivers" and "People from the American South love iced tea" are generalizations that imply the person making the pronouncement has examined all the information and has reached a definitive conclusion. Although our world would be much simpler if we *could* make such statements without straining reality, reality rarely, if ever, provides evidence to support sweeping generalizations. For example, although research conclusions document differences between the way men and women communicate, it is inaccurate to say that all women are more emotional and that all men are task-oriented. Empathic, other-oriented speakers avoid making judgments of others based only upon conventional wisdom or traditionally-held attitudes and beliefs. If you respond to others (of a different gender, sexual orientation, or ethnicity) based on stereotypical concepts, you will diminish your understanding and the quality of the relationship.

One way to avoid untrue generalizations is to remind yourself that your use and interpretation of a word is unique. Saying the words "to me" either to yourself or out loud before you offer an opinion or make a pronouncement can help communicate to others (and remind yourself) that your view is uniquely yours. Rather than announcing, "Curfews for teenagers are ridiculous," you could say, "To me, curfews for teenagers are ridiculous."

Indexing your comments and remarks is another way to help you avoid generalizing. To index is to acknowledge that each individual is unique. Rather than announcing that all doctors are abrupt, you could say, "My child's pediatrician spends a lot of time with me, but my internist never answers my questions." This helps you remember that doctors are not all the same.

indexing. A way of avoiding allness statements by separating one situation, person, or example from others.

static evaluation. Pronouncing judgment on something without taking changes into consideration.

Static Evaluation: The Language of Rigidity

You change. Your world changes. An ancient Greek philosopher said it best: "You can never step in the same river twice." A **static evaluation** is a statement that fails to recognize change. Labels, in particular, have a tendency to freeze-frame our awareness. Ruth, known as the class nerd in high school, is today a successful and polished businessperson; the old label does not fit.

In addition, some of us suffer from hardening of the categories. Our world view is so rigid that we can never change or expand our perspective. However, the world is a technicolour moving target. Just about the time we think we have things neatly figured out and categorized, something moves. Our labels may not reflect the buzzing, booming, zipping process of change. It is important to acknowledge that perception is a process and to avoid trying to nail things down permanently into all-inclusive categories.

General semanticists use the metaphorical expression "the map is not the territory" to illustrate the concept of static evaluation. Like a word, a map symbolizes or represents reality. Yet, our road system is constantly changing. New roads are built, old ones are closed. If you were to use a 1949 map to guide you from St. Andrews, New Brunswick to Winnipeg, Manitoba, the current highway system would not even be on it, and you would probably lose your way. Similarly, if we use old labels and do not adjust our thinking to accommodate change, we will be semantically lost.

Perhaps you have a parent who still uses "old maps." When you come home to visit, your parent expects that you will be there for dinner each night and will still eat four helpings at every meal. Your parent may not understand that you have changed, and his or her old map does not function well in your new territory. You may have to help construct a new one.

To avoid static evaluation yourself, try dating your observations and indicate to others the time period from which you are drawing your conclusion. If your second cousin comes to town for a visit, say, "When I last saw you, you loved to listen to Céline Dion." This allows for the possibility that your cousin's tastes may have changed since you saw her last, but most importantly, try to observe and acknowledge changes in others. If you are practising what you know about becoming other-oriented, you are unlikely to erect this barrier.

Polarization: The Language of Extremes

polarization. Describing and evaluating what we observe in extremes, such as good or bad, old or new, beautiful or ugly.

Describing and evaluating what we observe in terms of extremes, such as good or bad, old or new, beautiful or ugly, brilliant or stupid, is known as **polarization**. General semanticists remind us that the world in which we live comes not in black and white but in a variety of colours, hues, and shades. If you describe things in extremes, leaving out the middle ground, then your language does not accurately reflect reality, and because of the power of words to create, you may believe your own pronouncements.

"You either love me or you don't love me," says Kamal.

"You're *always* trying to control me," replies Lise.

Both people are overstating the case, using language to polarize their perceptions of the experience.

Family counsellors who listen to family feuds find that the tendency to see things from an either–or point of view is a classic symptom of a troubled relationship. Placing the entire blame on your partner for a problem in your relationship is an example of polarizing. Few relational difficulties are exclusively one-sided.

Biased Language: Insensitivity Toward Others

Using words that reflect your biases toward people of other cultures or ethnic groups, the other gender, or of a different sexual orientation—or people who are simply different from you—can create a word barrier for your listeners. Because words, including the words used to describe people, have power to create and affect thoughts and behaviour, they can affect the quality of relationships with others. Although media commentators often debate the merits of "political correctness," it is also clear that biased or stereotyping language can offend others. Three types of language missteps, in particular, reflect poorly on the speaker and can affect interpersonal relationships with others: sexist language, ethnic or racially biased language, and elitist language—language that assumes superiority.

Avoid Sexist Language

Sexist language is the use of words that reflect stereotypical attitudes or that describe roles in exclusively male or female terms.

Words such as "alder*man*," "mail*man*," and *man*kind" ignore the fact that women are part of the workforce and the human race. Contrast these with "city councillor," "letter carrier," and "humankind," which are gender neutral and allow for the inclusion of both men and women. Or, rather than eliminating the word "man" from your vocabulary, try to use appropriate labels when you know the gender of the subject. A male police officer is a *policeman*; a female police officer is a *policewoman*. Rather than salesperson, you could say *salesman* or *saleswoman*, depending on the gender of the seller.

Scholar H. S. O'Donnell found that even dictionaries fall into patterns of describing men and women with discriminatory language.[16] Included in the *Oxford English Dictionary* definition for "woman" are: (1) an adult female being, (2) a female servant, (3) a lady-love or mistress, and (4) a wife. Men are described in more positive and distinguished terms: (1) a human being, (2) the human creation regarded abstractly, (3) an adult male endowed with many qualities, and (4) a person of importance of position. Though dictionaries like the *Oxford* aim to describe language as it is and was really spoken, rather than prescribe how it should be spoken in an ideal world, definitions such as these reflect clear historical prejudices in our society.

Many of our social conventions also diminish or ignore the importance of women:

Sexist	Unbiased
I'd like you to meet Dr. and Mrs. John Chao.	I'd like you to meet Dr. Susan Ho and Dr. John Chao. They are husband and wife. or I'd like you to meet John Chao and Susan Ho. They're both doctors at the Hôtel Dieu.
Let me introduce Beverly and Tom Bertolone.	Let me introduce Mr. Tom Bertolone and his wife Beverly.

We have, however, made more substantial progress in reflecting changes and changed attitudes toward women in the professional arena. Compare the terms we now use to describe workers with those used in the 1950s:

Terms Used Today	Terms Used in 1950s
Flight attendant	Stewardess
Firefighter	Fireman
Police officer	Policeman
Physician	Female doctor
Office workers	Girls at work
Ms	Miss/Mrs.
People/humans/humankind	Mankind

Consciously remembering to use non-sexist language will result in several benefits.[17] First, non-sexist language reflects non-sexist attitudes. Your attitudes are reflected in your speech and your speech affects your attitudes. Monitoring your speech for sexist remarks can help you monitor your attitudes about sexist assumptions. Second, using non-sexist language will help you become more other-oriented.

Monitoring your language for sexist remarks will reflect your sensitivity to others. Third, non-sexist language will make your speech more contemporary and unambiguous. By substituting the word "humankind" for "mankind," for example, you can communicate that you are including all people, not just men, in your observation or statement. Finally, your non-sexist language will empower others. By eliminating sexist bias from your speech, you will help confirm the value of all the individuals with whom you interact.

In addition to the debate over language that reflects gender, there is considerable and controversial discussion about the language used to describe minority sexual orientations. Regardless of your personal views, the principle of being other-oriented suggests that you can be sensitive in your choice of words when you speak or write on this subject. Your attitude toward another person's sexual orientation should not undermine your goal of being an effective communicator. Labelling someone a *fag*, *queer*, or *dyke* is not only likely to be offensive and hurtful to the person being labelled; it will also reflect poorly on the sensitivity of the person doing the labelling. In most circles, the preferred terms for people who are homosexual are "gay" for men and "lesbian" for women. We're not suggesting that certain words be expunged from dictionaries or never be uttered; we are suggesting that when describing others, people should be sensitive to how they wish to be addressed and discussed.

Avoid Ethnic Or Racially Biased Language

In addition to monitoring your language for sexual stereotypes, avoid racial and ethnic stereotypes. Monitor your speech so you are not, even unconsciously, using phrases that depict a racial or ethnic group in a negative or stereotypical fashion. How do you feel about being called a Canuck? A student writer of an American university paper who used the term "Canucks" to refer to the large number of Canadians moving into the entertainment field in the United States was fired for it. He was later rehired after a large number of Canadians expressed that they did not find the term offensive.[18] Phrases such as "There are too many Indians and not enough chiefs," or "I jewed him down" (to negotiate a good price) demonstrate an insensitivity to members of other cultural groups. The underlying principle in avoiding biased language is to be other-oriented and to imagine how the listener might react to your words. As illustrated in the *In Canada* feature earlier in the chapter, how we label others can affect our perceptions. A sensitive, other-oriented communicator keeps abreast of changes in preferred labels and adopts the designations currently preferred by members of the ethnic groups themselves.

Avoid Language That Demeans a Person's Age, Ability, Or Social Class

Language barriers are created not only when someone uses sexist or racially biased language but also when someone disparages a person's age, mental or physical ability, or social standing. Calling someone a "geezer," "retard," or "trailer trash" may seem harmless or humorous to some, but others may perceive these labels as insensitive or insulting.[19]

Discriminating against someone because of age is a growing problem in the workplace. In some occupations, as a worker moves into his or her 50s, it may be difficult to change jobs or find work. Despite laws designed to guard against age discrimination, it clearly exists. As we have noted, the language that people use has power to affect attitudes and behaviour. This is why using negative terms to describe the elderly can be a subtle—or sometimes not-so-subtle—way of expressing disrespect toward an older generation.

Similarly, the way a person describes people with disabilities can negatively affect how that person is perceived. A study by researcher John Seiter and his colleagues found that when individuals referred to people with disabilities by demeaning or disparaging names, those individuals were perceived as less trustworthy, competent, persuasive, and sociable than when they described the same people in more positive or heroic terms.[20] At the end of their study, the authors note, "communicators who want to be effective should avoid using derogatory language." Guard against calling attention to someone as a "cripple," "retarded," "dim-witted," or "mental;" these terms are offensive. As one common expression puts it: much truth's spoken when you're just jokin'. Even though it may seem innocent to use such words to label others, it can alter your perceptions of others as well as reflect poorly on you. Although there clearly are differences in ability among people, because of a variety of factors, be sensitive to your use of language. As suggested by communication researcher Dawn Braithwaite, the preferred terms are "disabled people" or "people with disabilities."[21]

Also monitor the way you talk about someone's social class. Although some societies and cultures make considerable distinctions among classes, it is nonetheless offensive today to use words that are intended to demean someone's social class. Terms such as "welfare recipients," "manual labourers," and "blue-collar workers" are often used derogatorily. Avoid labelling someone in a way that shows disrespect toward the person's social standing, education, or socioeconomic status.

▶ ## Recap

WORD BARRIERS

Barrier	Definition	Examples
Bypassing	Confusion caused by the fact that the same word may evoke different meanings for different people	W.C. " might mean *wayside chapel* to a Swiss and *water closet* (toilet) to someone from England.
Lack of clarity	Using words inappropriately or in imprecise ways	Sign in an Acapulco hotel: "The manager has personally passed all the water served here."
Allness	Lumping things or people into all-encompassing categories	All women like flowers on their birthday.
Static evaluation	Labelling people, objects, and events without considering change	You still call your 28-year-old nephew a juvenile delinquent because he spray-painted your fence when he was 11.
Polarization	Using either–or terms—good or bad, right or wrong	You're either for me or against me.
Biased language	Using language that reflects gender, racial, ethnic, age, ability, or class biases	My mom is a mailman.

Using Words to Establish Supportive Relationships

"I'm going to win this argument."

"You're wrong and I'm right. It's as simple as that."

"You're going to do it my way or else!"

"Listen, you're a woman, so how would you know?"

None of these statements is likely to result in a positive communication climate. All four are likely to result in debate rather than true dialogue. The words you hear and use are central to your establishing a quality or positive relationship with others. Author and researcher Daniel Yankelovich suggests that the goal of conversations with others should be to establish a genuine dialogue rather than to verbally arm-wrestle a partner in order to win the argument.[22] A true dialogue involves establishing a climate of equality, listening with empathy, and trying to bring assumptions into the open. Expressing equality, empathy, and openness and avoiding biases are more likely to occur if you approach conversations as dialogue rather than debate. As shown in Table 5.1, in true dialogue, people look for common ground rather than using a war of words to defend a position.

For more than three decades, Jack Gibb's observational research has been used as a framework for both describing and prescribing verbal behaviours that contribute to feelings of either supportiveness or defensiveness.[23] Gibb spent several years listening to and observing groups of individuals in meetings and conversations, noting that some exchanges seemed to create a supportive climate, whereas others created a defensive one. Words and actions, he concluded, are tools we use to let someone know whether we support them or not. Now let's consider how you can use words to create a supportive climate rather than an antagonistic or defensive one.

Table 5.1
Debate and Dialogue Compared

Debate	Dialogue
There is one right answer, and you have it.	Many people have pieces of the answer; together you can find the best solution.
The goal is to win.	The goal is to seek common ground and agreement.
The focus is on combat; prove that you are right and the other person is wrong.	The focus is on collaboration; seek common understanding.
Search for weakness and errors in others' positions.	Search for strengths and value the truth in what others say.
Defend your views.	Use the contributions of others to improve your thinking.

Source: Adapted from Daniel Yankelovich, The Magic of Dialogue: Transforming Conflict into Cooperation (New York: Simon & Schuster, 1999), 39–40.

Describe Your Own Feelings Instead of Evaluating the Behaviour of Others

Most of us don't like to be judged or evaluated. Criticizing and name-calling, obviously, can create relational problems but so can our attempts to diagnose others' problems or win their affection with insincere praise. In fact, any form of evaluation creates a climate of defensiveness. As Winston Churchill declared, "I am always ready to learn, although I do not always like being taught." Correcting others, even when we are doing it "for their own good," can raise their hackles.

One way to avoid evaluating others is to eliminate the accusatory "you" from your language. Statements such as, "You always come in late for supper," or "You need to pick up the dirty clothes in your room," attack a person's sense of self-worth and usually result in a defensive reaction.

Instead, use the word "I" to describe your own feelings and thoughts about a situation or event: "I find it hard to keep your supper warm when you're late," or "I don't enjoy the extra work of picking up your dirty clothes." When you describe your own feelings instead of berating the receiver of the message, you are in essence taking ownership of the problem. This approach leads to greater openness and trust because your listener does not feel rejected or that you are trying to control him or her. Also, when you express your emotions, make sure you choose the right words to communicate your feelings. The *Building Your Skills* box below will help you practise expressing your feelings accurately with "I" language.

Building Your Skills

PRACTISE USING "I" LANGUAGE

An essential skill in being supportive rather than defensive is describing what you want with "I" language rather than "you" language. Rephrase the following "you" statements into "I" statements.

"You" Language	"I" Language
1. You are messy when you cook.	_____
2. Your driving is terrible.	_____
3. You never listen to me.	_____
4. You just lie on the couch and never offer to help me.	_____
5. You always decide what movie we see.	_____

Solve Problems Instead of Trying to Control Others

When you were younger, your parents gave you rules to keep you safe. Even though you may have resented their control, you needed to know what was too hot to touch, when not to cross the street, and not to stick your finger in a light socket. Now that you are an adult, when people treat you like a child, it often means they are trying to control your behaviour, to take away your options. In truth, we have little or no control over someone else's behaviour.

Most of us don't like to be controlled. Someone who presumes to tell us what's good for us, instead of helping us puzzle through issues and problems, is likely to engender defensiveness. Open-ended questions such as, "What seems to be the problem?" or "How can we deal with the issue?" create a more supportive climate than critical comments such as, "Here's where you are wrong," or commands such as, "Don't do that!"

Be Genuine Rather Than Manipulative

To be genuine means that you honestly seek to be yourself rather than someone you are not. It also means taking an honest interest in others and considering the uniqueness of each individual and situation, avoiding generalizations or strategies that focus only on your own needs and desires. A manipulative person has hidden agendas; a genuine person uses words to discuss issues and problems openly and honestly.

Carl Rogers, the founder of person-centred counselling, suggests that true understanding and dialogue occur when people adopt a genuine or honest positive regard for others.[24] If your goal is to look out only for your own interests, your language will reflect your self-focus. At the heart of being genuine is being other-oriented—being sincerely interested in those with whom you communicate. Although it's unrealistic to assume you will become best friends with everyone you meet, you can, suggests Rogers, work to develop an unselfish interest, or what he called an unconditional positive regard for others. It may be hard to do, but the effort will be rewarded with a more positive communication climate.

Empathize Instead of Remaining Detached from Others

Empathy is one of the hallmarks of supportive relationships. As we learned earlier, empathy is the ability to understand the feelings of others and to predict the emotional responses they will have to different situations.

Being empathic is the essence of being other-oriented. The opposite of empathy is neutrality. To be neutral is to be indifferent or apathetic toward another. Even when you express anger or irritation toward another, you are investing some energy in the relationship.

After an unsuccessful attempt to persuade his family to take a trip to Banff National Park, Preston declared, "I don't care what you think, that's where we're going." His proclamation reflects a disregard for the feelings of others in his family. This insensitivity is self-defeating. The defensive climate Preston creates with his words will probably prevent the whole family from enjoying the vacation.

An essential skill in being supportive rather than defensive is describing what you want with "I" language rather than "you" language. Could the use of "I" language help this couple?
(Chip Henderson/ Tony Stone Images)

Building Your Skills

SUPPORTIVE-DEFENSIVE COMMUNICATION ROLE-PLAY

Divide into groups of two to four people. Each team or group should prepare a short play depicting one of the supportive or defensive communication responses described in this chapter. Perform your play for the class or another team to see if they can identify the type of supportive or defensive communication behaviour your team is portraying. Consider one of the following situations or develop one of your own:

- Speaking with a professor about a grade
- Returning a broken item to a store
- Talking with your child about his or her marks
- Responding to a telemarketing salesperson who calls you during dinner
- Talking with one of your employees who made a work-related mistake
- Rebooking a flight because your flight was cancelled by the airline
- Taking an order from a customer at a fast-food restaurant
- Receiving a complaint from a customer about poor service
- Talking with someone who has knocked on your door inviting you to his or her church
- Asking someone to turn down the stereo or TV while you are trying to study

Variation: Instead of illustrating supportive and defensive communication, role-play an example of one of the confirming or disconfirming communication behaviours discussed in Chapter 4.

Be Flexible Rather Than Rigid Toward Others

Most people don't like someone who always seems certain that he or she is right. A "you're wrong, I'm right" attitude creates a defensive climate. This does not mean that you should have no opinions and go through life blithely agreeing to everything. Also, it doesn't mean that there is *never* one answer that is right and others that are wrong. However, instead of making rigid pronouncements, you can use phrases such as, "I may be wrong, but it seems to me..." or "Here's one way to look at this problem." This manner of speaking gives your opinions a softer edge that allows room for others to express a point of view.

 Applying Theory and Research

THE POWER OF A KIND WORD

Comforting messages are those intended to help reduce the amount of stress people feel during times of turbulence, personal change, and anxiety. Researcher Amy Bippus wanted to find out what types of comforting messages people consider truly helpful. She also wanted to analyze the general categories of messages of comfort and to consider whether the skill with which a comfort message was presented influenced how the receiver felt about being comforted.

She first interviewed people about their experiences of talking with a friend about something that

Continued

"stressed out" the friend. People who had offered messages of comfort thought that talking with a friend who was under stress helped improve the friend's mood, helped the friend adopt a positive attitude, and helped distract the friend from the problem.

Bippus then conducted another study in which people completed a questionnaire about their experiences of having a friend offer comfort and try to reduce stress. She wanted to know whether there were general categories or types of comments that were helpful when providing comfort to someone. The analysis of the data identified five categories of skilled comforting behaviour. The most important category was Other-Orientation, followed by Problem Solving, Relating, Refraining from General Negativity, and Different Perspective. The positive outcomes that resulted from the comforting messages were Positive Mood, Empowerment, and Stopped Rumination.

APPLYING THE RESEARCH TO YOUR LIFE

The results of this study provide the good news that talking to people who offer comfort and support can help you manage stress and anxiety. One of the most important things you can do to offer helpful and comforting comments echoes a theme we have stressed throughout this book: be other-oriented. When providing comfort to someone else, don't focus on your own problems and concerns; focus on the concerns and needs of the other person. Helping to sort through the problem and relating and listening positively to the other person are also valuable kinds of supportive behaviour. Finally, avoiding being negative—emphasizing the positive instead—and simply helping the other person to gain a new perspective are also especially helpful types of comforting behaviour.

Providing comforting messages helps enhance a person's mood, empowers the person so he or she feels renewed or energized, and also helps the other person to stop wallowing in the problem and reframe the situation in a new, positive way. Although people sometimes need professional counsellors during times of stress and change, this study suggests that finding a good listener who offers positive, comforting messages can also help during times of anxiety and stress.

Source: Amy M. Bippus, "Recipients' Criteria for Evaluating the Skillfulness of Comforting Communication and the Outcomes of Comforting Interactions," Communication Monographs, 68, 3 (September 2001): 301–313.

Present Yourself As Equal Rather Than Superior

elaborated code. Using many words and various ways of describing an idea or concept to communicate its meaning.

You can antagonize others by letting them know that you view yourself as better or brighter than they are. You may be gifted and intelligent, but it's not necessary to announce it, and although some people have the responsibility and authority to manage others, "pulling rank" does not usually produce a cooperative climate. With phrases such as, "Let's work on this together," or "We each have a valid perspective," you can avoid erecting walls of resentment and suspicion.

Also, avoid using abstract language to impress others. Keep your messages short and clear, and use informal language. When you communicate with someone from another culture, you may need to use an **elaborated code** to get your message across. This means that your messages will have to be more explicit, but they should not be condescending. Two of your authors remember vividly trying to explain to a French exchange student what a fire ant is. First, we had to translate *ant* into French, and then we had to provide scientific, descriptive, and narrative evidence to help the student understand how these tiny, biting insects terrorize people in the southern part of the United States.

Building Your Skills

EXPRESSING YOUR EMOTIONS

Communication is enhanced if you can clearly express the emotions you are feeling. One way to communicate your emotions is to describe how you are feeling with a well-chosen word or phrase. The following list gives you several options for expressing your feelings in positive, neutral, or negative terms. Categorizing these terms as positive, neutral, or negative doesn't mean that you should only use positive or neutral terms and avoid negative terms. What's important is that you select a word that accurately helps you communicate your emotions to others.

Positive		Neutral	Negative	
calm	hopeful	amazed	afraid	helpless
cheerful	hysterical	ambivalent	alone	horrible
comfortable	interested	apathetic	angry	humiliated
confident	joyful	bashful	annoyed	intimidated
content	loving	bored	bitter	listless
delighted	optimistic	detached	confused	mad
ecstatic	passionate	hurried	defeated	mean
elated	peaceful	lukewarm	defensive	miserable
enthusiastic	playful	numb	depressed	paranoid
excited	pleased	possessive	devastated	rebellious
flattered	refreshed	sentimental	disappointed	regretful
free	romantic	vulnerable	disgusted	resentful
friendly	sexy		disturbed	restless
glad	tender		empty	sad
grateful	warm		exhausted	shocked
happy	willing		fearful	suspicious
high	wonderful		frustrated	terrified
			furious	ugly
			guilty	

To practise expressing your emotions, imagine yourself in each of the following situations, and use some of the words listed here to write a response for each situation. Describe your response using either a single word or a short phrase, such as "I feel angry," or express your feelings in terms of what you'd like to do, such as "I'd be so embarrassed I would sink through the floor" or "I would feel like leaving and never coming back to this house."

- You have several thousand dollars charged to your credit cards, and you have just been fired from your job.
- Your best friend, with whom you spend a lot of time, is moving to another country.
- You have just learned that your adored aunt has died and left you a $35 000 inheritance.
- Even though you do your best to keep your room clean, your roommate is complaining again that you are a slob.
- You have brought your two-year-old son to a worship service, but he talks and runs around during the service and will not sit still. Other worshippers are looking at you with disapproval.
- You arrive at your vacation hotel only to discover that they do not have a reservation for you, and you do not have your room confirmation number.

Building Your Skills

USING WORD PICTURES TO EXPRESS YOUR FEELINGS

A **word picture** is a short statement or story that dramatizes an emotion you experience. Using a visual image can add extra power in expressing your feelings when a simple descriptive word may not suffice. Word pictures can be used to clarify how you feel, to offer praise or correction, and to create greater intimacy. Communicating your feelings and emotions is a key goal of word pictures. An effective way to express your emotions through a word picture is to use a simile. As you may remember from your English class,

a simile is a comparison that uses the word "like" or "as" to clarify the image you want to communicate. "When you forgot my birthday, I felt like crumbs swept from the table," exclaimed Marge to her forgetful husband. Or, after a hard day's work, Jeff told his family, "I feel like a worn-out punching bag—I've been pounded time and time again, and now I feel torn and scuffed. I need a few minutes of peace and quiet before I join in the family conversation." His visual image helped communicate how exhausted he really felt. The best word pictures use an experience or image to which the listener can relate. To practise your skill, try to develop word pic-

tures to express in a powerful and memorable way the feelings you might have in the following situations.

- You have just learned that a cherished family pet has died.
- You want to tell your friends how happy you are when you learn you received an A in a difficult course.
- You've asked your sister not to leave empty milk cartons in the refrigerator, but you discover another empty carton in the fridge.
- Your family is planning a vacation but didn't ask you to be involved in the planning.

---

word picture. Short statement or story that illustrates or describes an emotion; word pictures often use a simile (a comparison using the word *like* or *as*) to clarify the image.

Underlying the goal of creating a supportive rather than a defensive communication climate is the importance of providing emotional support when communicating with others. A basic principle of all healthy interpersonal relationships is the importance of communicating positive, supportive messages that communicate liking or affection.[25] Several researchers have documented that providing verbal messages of comfort and support, not surprisingly, enhances the quality of a relationship.[26] As a relationship develops over time and the communication partners gain more credibility and influence, messages of comfort play an even more important role in maintaining the quality of the interpersonal relationship.[27] We use not only words of comfort but, as you will learn in Chapter 6, non-verbal expressions of comfort as well.[28]

Communication researchers have documented the power of humour in helping to turn a tense, potentially conflict-producing confrontation into a more supportive, positive conversation. A study by communication researcher Amy Bippus found that most people report using humour as a way of providing comfort to others.[29] Humour also was perceived as a productive way to help a distressed person better cope with problems and stress.

> ► **Recap**
>
> ## USING SUPPORTIVE COMMUNICATION AND AVOIDING DEFENSIVE COMMUNICATION
>
> **Supportive Communication Is . . .**
>
> **Descriptive:** Use "I" language that describes your own feelings and ideas.
>
> **Problem-Oriented:** Aim communication at solving problems and generating multiple options.
>
> **Spontaneously Genuine:** Develop a here-and-now orientation. Be honest and authentic rather than fake and phony.
>
> **Empathic:** Be emotionally involved in the conversation; attempt to understand what your partner is thinking and feeling.
>
> **Provisionally Flexible:** Be open to receiving new information; demonstrate flexibility in the positions you take.
>
> **Equal:** Adopt a communication style based on mutual respect and assume each person has a right to express ideas and share information.
>
> **Defensive Communication Is . . .**
>
> **Evaluative:** Avoid using "you" language that attacks the worth of another person.
>
> **Controlling:** Don't attempt to get others to do *only* what you want them to do in order to control the outcome.
>
> **Strategically Manipulative:** Avoid planning your conversation in advance to get what you want. Don't develop a script to manipulate and accomplish your goal.
>
> **Neutrally Detached:** Avoid being emotionally indifferent or creating the impression that you don't care how another person is feeling.
>
> **Certain and Rigid:** Don't take a dogmatic, entrenched, or rigid position on issues; be willing to listen to others.
>
> **Superior:** Avoid assuming an attitude or mindset that you and your ideas are better than others.

Using Words to Be Appropriately Assertive

Sometimes the people we encounter aren't other-oriented. As discussed in this chapter, some people may communicate in a way that creates a defensive climate, which may increase feelings of mistrust and even anger. At times you run across people who are verbally aggressive, obnoxious, or worse—they may try to coerce or intimidate you into doing things you'd rather not do. Should the other-oriented person just politely accept obnoxious verbal assaults? No, being other-oriented doesn't mean you should ignore such boorish behaviour. Nor do you have to respond in the same way you have been treated. Rather than return mean-spirited aggressiveness with an equally inappropriate stream of aggressive words or rude behaviour, consider using your verbal skills to be appropriately assertive. To be **assertive** is to make requests, ask for information, stand up for your rights, and generally pursue your own best interests without denying your communication partner's rights.

assertive. Able to pursue one's own best interests without denying the rights of one's communication partner.

Each individual has rights. You have the right to refuse a request someone makes of you, the right to express your feelings as long as you don't trample on the feelings of others, and the right to have your personal needs met if this doesn't infringe on the rights of others. Assertive people let their communication partners know when a message or behaviour is infringing on their rights.

Your human rights such as the right to express your feelings and to be free from aggressive behaviour (including sexual harassment) extend to the world of work. In the workplace, you have the right to be assertive and to not tolerate any kind of harassment. Your college or university must have policies and procedures to protect your rights and a procedure to report harassment or aggression. These rights are part of the Canadian Human Rights Act and the Canada Labour Code, as well as provincial and territorial human rights codes.

Some people confuse the terms "assertive" and "aggressive." Being **aggressive** means pursuing your interests by denying the rights of others. Assertiveness is other-oriented; aggressiveness is exclusively self-oriented. Aggressive people blame, judge, and evaluate to get what they want. Aggressive communicators use defensive communication tactics, including such intimidating non-verbal cues as steely stares, a bombastic voice, and flailing gestures. Assertive people can ask for what they want without judging or evaluating their partners.

aggressive. Expressing one's interests while denying the rights of others by blaming, judging, and evaluating other people.

When presenting the dos and don'ts of appropriate verbal communication in this chapter, we've often emphasized strategies for initiating communication with others. Sometimes what's most challenging is to respond appropriately when another person (who has not taken a course in interpersonal communication) comes at you with an inappropriately aggressive, argumentative, or defensive message, especially if the inappropriate message that's hurled at you takes you by surprise. You do not have to be passive when you are on the receiving end of such messages. We suggest instead that an effective communicator is appropriately assertive.

One approach to responding to aggressive or other inappropriate communication that we've already discussed is to use "I" messages to express your thoughts and feelings rather than "you" messages. "You creep! You ate the last breakfast taco" is an aggressive, defensive "you" statement. In contrast, "I haven't had breakfast yet. I asked you to save a taco for me; now I won't have anything to eat for breakfast" is an assertive statement of your rights and describes the consequences of violating them.

 Recap

ASSERTIVENESS VERSUS AGGRESSIVENESS

Assertiveness	Aggressiveness
Expresses your interests without denying the rights of others	Expresses your interests and denies the rights of others
Is other-oriented	Is self-oriented
Describes what you want	Evaluates the other person
Discloses your needs using "I" messages	Discloses your needs using "you" messages

Behaving Assertively: Five Steps

Many people have a tendency to withdraw in the face of controversy, even when their rights are being violated or denied. However, you can develop skill in asserting yourself by practising five key suggestions.[30]

● Describe

Describe how you view the situation. To assert your position, you first need to describe how you view the situation. You need to be assertive because the other person has not been other-oriented. For example, Doug is growing increasingly frustrated with Maria's tardiness for weekly staff meetings. He approaches the problem by first describing his observation: "I have noticed that you are usually 15 minutes late to our weekly staff meetings." A key to communicating your assertive message is to monitor your non-verbal message, especially your voice. Avoid sarcasm or excessive vocal intensity. Calmly yet confidently describe the problem.

● Disclose

Disclose your feelings. After describing the situation from your perspective, let the other person know how you feel.[31] Disclosing your feelings will help build empathy and avoid lengthy harangues about the other person's unjust treatment. "I feel you don't take our weekly meetings seriously," continues Doug as he asserts his desire for Maria to be on time to the meeting. Note that Doug does not talk about how others are feeling ("Every member of our group is tired of your coming in late"); he describes how *he* feels.

● Identify Effects

Next, you can *identify the effects* of the other person's behaviour on you or others. "When you are late, it disrupts our meeting," says Doug.

● Be Silent

Wait. After taking the first three steps, simply wait for a response. Some people find this step hard. Again, be sure to monitor your non-verbal cues. Make sure your facial expression does not contradict your verbal message. Delivering an assertive message with a broad grin might create a double bind for your listener, who may not be sure what the primary message is—the verbal one or the non-verbal one.

Becoming Other-Oriented

BUMPER STICKER SLOGANS

The key to shared understanding is to focus on the needs, goals, and mindset of your communication partner. Throughout this chapter, we have emphasized how to develop an other-oriented approach when communicating verbally. To help you remember some of the essential principles of being other-oriented, consider the following "bumper sticker" slogans:

Meanings are in people, not in words.

Words are arbitrary, contextually, and culturally bound symbols that can have denotative and connotative, concrete or abstract meaning. Focus on what the words may mean to your partner.

Think before you speak.

Words have tremendous power in our lives. They create and affect people's emotions and actions, as well as affecting and reflecting culture. Before you speak, consider the impact your words will have on others. Remember that words can hurt—and once spoken, words cannot be taken back.

SAY WHAT YOU MEAN; MEAN WHAT YOU SAY

Choose your words with care. Be mindful of the potential for miscommunication and misunderstanding. The spoken word belongs half to the person who speaks and half to the person who understands.

Speak to others as you think they'd like to be spoken to.

Words can engender a supportive communication climate or create defensiveness, which can lead to misunderstandings. Try to put yourself in your partner's place when you're conversing with others.

Paraphrase

Paraphrase content and feelings. After the other person responds, paraphrase both the content and the feelings of the message. Suppose Maria says, "Oh, I'm sorry. I didn't realize I was creating a problem. I have another meeting that usually goes overtime. It's difficult for me to arrive at the start of our meeting on time." Doug could respond, "So the key problem is a time conflict with another meeting. It must make you feel frustrated to try to do two things at once."

If the other person is evasive, unresponsive, or aggressive, you'll need to cycle through the steps again. Clearly describe what the other person is doing that is not acceptable; disclose how you feel; identify the effects; wait; then paraphrase and clarify as needed. A key goal of an assertive response is to seek an empathic connection between you and your partner. Paraphrasing feelings is a way of ensuring that both parties are connecting.

If you tend to withdraw from conflict, how can you become assertive? Visualizing can help. Think of a past situation in which you wished you had been more assertive and then mentally replay the situation, imagining what you might have said. Also practise verbalizing assertive statements. When you are able to be appropriately assertive, consciously congratulate yourself for sticking up for your rights. To sharpen your assertiveness skills, try Building Your Skills: How to Assert Yourself.

Building Your Skills

HOW TO ASSERT YOURSELF

Working with a partner, describe a situation in which you could have been more assertive. Ask your partner to assume the role of the person toward whom you should have been more assertive. Now replay the situation, using the following skills:

1. *Describe:* Tell the other person that what he or she is doing bothers you. Describe rather than evaluate.

2. *Disclose:* Then tell the other person how you feel. For example, "I feel *X* when you do *Y*."

3. *Identify effects:* Tell the other person the effects of his or her behaviour on you or your group. Be as clear and descriptive as you can.

4. *Wait:* After you have described, disclosed, and identified the effects, wait for a response.

5. *Paraphrase:* Use reflective listening skills, such as questioning, paraphrasing content, and paraphrasing feelings.

OBSERVATION OF ASSERTIVENESS SKILLS

Ask your classmates to observe your role play and provide feedback, using the following checklist. When you have finished asserting your point of view, reverse roles.

_____ Clearly describes what the problem was

_____ Effectively discloses how he or she felt

_____ Clearly describes the effects of the behaviour

_____ Pauses or waits after describing the effects

_____ Uses effective questions to promote understanding

_____ Accurately paraphrases content

_____ Accurately paraphrases feelings

_____ Has good eye contact

_____ Leans forward while speaking

_____ Has an open body posture

_____ Has appropriate voice tone and quality

▶ Recap

HOW TO ASSERT YOURSELF

Step	Example
1. Describe.	"I see you haven't completed the report yet."
2. Disclose.	"I feel the work I ask you to do is not a priority with you."
3. Identify effects.	"Without that report, our team will not achieve our goal."
4. Be silent.	Wait for a response.
5. Use reflective listening:	
Question.	"Do you understand how I feel?"
Paraphrase content.	"So you were not aware the report was late."
Paraphrase feelings.	"Perhaps you feel embarrassed."

Summary

The words we use have great power to affect our self-image and to influence the relationships we establish with others. English words are symbols that refer to objects, events, people, and ideas. They are arbitrary. We interpret their meaning through the context and culture to which they belong. Communication is complex because most words have both denotative (literal) meanings and connotative (subjective) meanings and because words range from concrete to abstract.

The power of words stems from their ability to create images and to influence our thoughts, feelings, and actions. There is also an important link between the words we use and our culture. Language shapes culture and culture shapes language. Our view of the world is influenced by our vocabulary and the categories we have created with words.

Several word barriers can contribute to misunderstanding in interpersonal communications. Bypassing occurs when a word means one thing to one person and another thing to someone else. Our verbal expressions may lack clarity either because we make language errors or because the meaning we want to convey is not clear to us. Allness statements can mislead and alienate listeners because the speaker falsely implies that he or she knows all there is to know about something. Another barrier, static evaluation, fails to take changes into account and uses outdated labels and categories. Polarization is the language of extremes; when someone thinks in black and white, many shades of meaning disappear. Finally, biased language that is insensitive to others creates noise that interferes with the meaning of a message.

The words you use can enhance or detract from the quality of relationships you establish with others. People who use supportive communication avoid using language that in any way labels or demeans others. Supportive communication is descriptive rather than evaluative, problem-oriented rather than control-oriented, genuine rather than contrived or manipulative, empathic rather than neutral, flexible rather than rigid, and equal rather than superior.

When you become the target of inappropriate, non–other-oriented verbal attacks or intimidating behaviour, we suggest that you respond assertively. To be assertive involves five steps: describe, disclose, identify effects, silently wait, and then paraphrase what your communication partner has said. Being a competent communicator involves listening and then appropriately responding to enhance, rather than detract from, the quality of interpersonal communication.

For Discussion and Review

🔘 Focus on Critical Thinking

1. Yasmina and Paul are having an argument. Paul shouts, "You're constantly criticizing me! You don't let me make any important decisions!" How could Paul communicate how he feels in a more supportive way?

2. Allan asked Jessie to pick him up after work at the circle drive at 5:30 p.m. Jessie waited patiently at the circle drive on the other side of campus and finally went home at 6:30 p.m., having seen no sign of Allan. Allan was waiting at the circle drive behind his office rather than at the one on the other side of the campus. What word barriers do you think led to this misunderstanding?

3. Rephrase the following statements to use less biased language:
    a. I'd like to introduce Mr. Russell Goldberg and his wife Muriel.
    b. In an office memo: "Several gals have been leaving their purses at their desks."

4. Rephrase the following statements, using the skill of indexing.
    a. All politicians want power and control over others.
    b. All daycare workers are underpaid.
    c. All Vancouverites like to brag about how great their city is.

Focus on Ethics

5. If you really don't want to listen to your co-worker go into details about her latest holiday trip or the recent escapades of her children or grandchildren, is it appropriate to tell her that you'd rather not hear her "news?" Support your response.

6. Is it ethical to correct someone when he or she uses sexist language or makes a stereotypical remark about someone's ethnicity, gender, or sexual orientation? What if that person is your boss or your teacher? Explain your answer.

7. Is it ethical to mask your true feelings of anger and irritation with someone by using supportive statements or confirming statements when what you really want to do is tell him or her "the truth" in no uncertain terms?

For Your Journal

1. Keep a log of examples of word barriers you experience or encounter. Note examples of bypassing, lack of precision in language, and other uses of words that inhibit communication. The examples could come from your own verbal exchanges or those that you observe in the conversations of others.

2. Make a list of words that are in your vocabulary today that were not in your vocabulary five years ago. Include new words that you may have learned in school as well as words that were not generally used or that have been coined in the last half-decade (e.g., "googled" or "podcasting").

3. Record a sample dialogue between you and another person that would illustrate the steps for being assertive.

Learning with Others

1. Think of a bypass miscommunication that you've experienced. Share your recollection with a small group and compare your feelings and responses with those of others.

2. In your group, choose one person to play a recently divorced person whose ex-spouse is not abiding by a child custody agreement and insists on seeing the children at odd hours. Another person should play the role of a trusted friend who only listens and responds. Ask the trusted friend to use the skills he or she learned in this chapter along with the effective listening skills presented in Chapter 4. Then, do a group evaluation of his or her response.

3. Using Research Navigator, find one article about human rights in Canada. This can be an article that promotes human rights such as one from an organization that is working to protect the rights of a minority or cultural group, or it could be an article about the violation of such rights. Share your article with the class.

Weblinks

www.statcan.ca   This is the site for Statistics Canada. There are statistics on everything the Canadian government collects, such as demographics, exercise frequency, family size, and so on. Also, there is access from this site to a number of other links including research and other Canadian sites.

www.vandruff.com/art_converse.html   Conversational Terrorism: How NOT to Talk: This site offers several types and examples of "conversational terrorism" that are both informative and humorous.

www.ethics.ubc.ca/resources   This is a site from the University of British Columbia about ethics and has several links to other such sites.

http://familyfun.go.com/parenting/child/skills/feature/dony108scwords   In the article, "Words That Hurt: What You Should Never Say to Your Kids" by Charles E. Schaefer, you will discover how words can indeed wound children more deeply than a physical blow.

http://www.cwu.edu/~cwuchci   This site gives a biography of Washoe, a chimpanzee who was the first non-human to acquire a human language: American Sign Language.

www.pcwebopaedia.com   Uncertain of the meaning of a word that you find on the Internet? Look it up on the "Webopaedia." This site will help you interpret words you don't understand.

http://linguistlist.org/~ask-ling   Ask-a-Linguist is a service provided by The Linguist List, an Internet network for professional linguists. This site is designed to allow anyone interested in language or linguistics to ask a question and get a response from a panel of professional linguists.

6

Non-Verbal Communication Skills

After you study this chapter

you should be able to ...

1. Explain why non-verbal communication is an important and challenging area of study.

2. Describe the functions of non-verbal communication in inter-personal relationships.

3. Summarize research findings that describe codes of non-verbal communication behaviour.

4. Describe three dimensions for interpreting non-verbal behaviour.

5. Formulate a strategy for improving your ability to interpret non-verbal messages accurately.

- Why Learn about Non-Verbal Communication?

- The Challenge of Interpreting Non-Verbal Messages

- Non-Verbal Communication Codes

- Interpreting Non-Verbal Communication

- Improving Your Ability to Interpret Non-Verbal Messages

> *What you are speaks so loudly that I cannot hear what you say.*
>
> RALPH WALDO EMERSON

Pierre: Lisa, will you get the telephone?

Lisa: Get it yourself!

Pierre: Hey! Why so testy? All I asked you to do was answer the phone!

f we could view a video recording of Pierre and Lisa's interaction, we could more clearly see the source of the conflict between them. Pierre's tone of voice and his scowling facial expression made his simple request seem more like an order.

As we noted in Chapter 1, communication has both content and emotional dimensions. Our tone of voice, eye contact, facial expressions, posture, movement, vocal cues, appearance, use of personal space, manipulation of the communication environment, and other non-verbal cues reveal how we feel toward others. We can define **non-verbal communication** as behaviour other than written or spoken language that creates meaning for someone. In this chapter, we will focus on how non-verbal communication affects the quality of our interpersonal relationships. As we identify the functions and codes of non-verbal cues, we will also explore ways to improve our skill in interpreting the non-verbal messages of others.

> **non-verbal communication.** Behaviour other than written or spoken language that creates meaning for someone.

Why Learn about Non-Verbal Communication?

When you are sitting in a public place, such as a shopping mall, airport, or bus stop, do you make assumptions about what other people might be like as you observe their non-verbal behaviour? Most of us are people watchers, and we rely on non-verbal communication cues to predict how others may feel about and react to us. Non-verbal communication plays a major role in relationship development because it is also the main channel we use to communicate our feelings and attitudes toward others. However, because much of our non-verbal communication behaviour is unconscious, most of us have limited awareness or understanding of it. We begin examining non-verbal communication by looking at the ways we use it.

Non-Verbal Messages Communicate Our Feelings and Attitudes

Amin knew that he was in trouble the moment he walked into the room. His wife Sandra gave him a steely stare. Her brow was furrowed and her arms were crossed. On the table was a dish of cold lobster Newburg, candles burnt to nubs, and dirty dishes at all but one place setting: his. Amin was in the doghouse for forgetting the dinner party his wife had planned, and he needed no words from her to sense the depth of her displeasure.

Albert Mehrabian concluded that as little as seven percent of the emotional meaning of a message is communicated through explicit verbal channels.[1] The most significant source of emotional communication is our face. According to Mehrabian's study, it channels as much as 55 percent of our meaning. Vocal cues such as volume, pitch, and intensity communicate another 38 percent of our emotional meaning. In all, we communicate approximately 93 percent of the emotional meaning of our messages non-verbally. Although these percentages do not apply to every communication situation, the results of Mehrabian's investigation do illustrate the potential power of non-verbal cues in communicating emotion.[2] Researchers are continuing to find new ways to measure the impact and power of non-verbal messages in the communication of emotions.[3]

When we interact with others, we base our feelings and emotional responses not on what our partner says but, rather, on what he or she does. We also alter our non-verbal communication to suit different relationships. With good friends, you let down your guard; you may slouch, scratch, and take off your shoes to show you trust them. However, if you were interviewing for a job or meeting your future in-laws for the first time, your posture would probably be stiffer and your smiles more carefully controlled as you try to convey the impression that you are mature, competent, and respectable.

Non-Verbal Messages Are More Believable

"Honey, do you love me?" asks Brenda.

"OF COURSE I LOVE YOU! HAVEN'T I ALWAYS TOLD YOU THAT I LOVE YOU? I LOVE YOU!" shouts Jim, keeping his eyes glued to his morning newspaper.

Brenda will probably feel less than reassured by Jim's pledge of affection. The contradiction between his spoken message of love and his non-verbal message of irritation and lack of interest will leave her wondering about his true feelings.

Actions speak louder than words. This cliché became a cliché because non-verbal communication is more believable than verbal communication. Non-verbal messages are more difficult to fake. One research team concluded that we use the following cues, listed in order of most to least important, to help us discern when a person is lying:[4]

- Greater time lag in response to a question
- Reduced eye contact
- Increased shifts in posture
- Unfilled pauses
- Less smiling
- Slower speech
- Higher pitch in voice

- More deliberate pronunciation and articulation of words

It is difficult to manipulate an array of non-verbal cues, so a skilled other-oriented observer can see when our true feelings leak out. One research team has identified the face, hands, and feet as key sources of non-verbal leakage cues.[5] Are you aware of what your fingers and toes are doing as you are reading this book? Even if we become experts at masking and manipulating our faces, we may first signal lack of interest or boredom with another person by finger wiggling or toe wagging. Or, we may twiddle a pen or pencil. When we become emotionally aroused, the pupils of our eyes dilate, and we may blush, sweat, or change our breathing patterns.[6] Lie detectors rely on these unconscious cues. A polygraph measures a person's heart and breathing rate, as well as the electrical resistance of the skin (called galvanic skin response), to determine whether he or she is giving truthful verbal responses.

Non-Verbal Messages Work with Verbal Messages to Create Meaning

Portrait artists pay close attention to non-verbal cues such as posture, facial expression, and gesture to capture their subjects' personalities. What do the non-verbal cues reveal about this Spanish dancer? (John Singer Sargent, *Belle Epoque*. Erich Lessing/Art Resource)

Although we rely heavily on non-verbal messages, they do not operate independently of spoken messages in our relationships. Instead, verbal and non-verbal cues work together in two primary ways to help us make sense of others' messages.

1. *Non-verbal cues substitute for, repeat, contradict, or regulate verbal messages.* An extended thumb signals that a hitchhiker would like a ride. A circle formed by the thumb and index finger can either signal that everything is A-OK or convey an obscene message. When someone asks, "Which way did he go?" you can silently point to the back door. In these instances, you are substituting non-verbal cues for a verbal message.

    You can also use non-verbal cues to repeat or reinforce your words. "Where is the personnel department?" asks a job applicant. "Three flights up. Take the elevator," says the security guard, pointing to the elevator. The guard's pointing gesture repeats her verbal instruction and clarifies the message.

    "Sure, this is a good time to talk about the Henrikson merger," says the business executive, nervously looking at her watch, stuffing papers into her attaché case, and avoiding eye contact with her co-worker. In this instance, the non-verbal cues contradict the verbal ones, and as you learned earlier, the non-verbal message is almost always the one we believe.

    We also use non-verbal cues to regulate our participation in verbal exchanges. In most informal meetings, it is not appropriate or necessary to signal your desire to speak by raising your hand. Yet somehow you are able to signal to others when you'd like to speak and when you'd rather not talk. How does this happen? You use eye contact, raised eyebrows, an open mouth, or perhaps a single raised index finger to signal that you would like to make a point. If your colleagues do not see these signals, especially the eye contact, they may think you are not interested in talking.[7]

2. *Non-verbal cues accent and complement verbal messages.* "Unless you vote for me as your university student president, we will continue to see increased tuition," yells James. While delivering his impassioned plea to the school board, James also loudly slaps the lectern to accent his message and reinforce its intensity. A

scolding mother's wagging finger and an angry supervisor's raised voice are other non-verbal cues that accent verbal messages.

Simtultaneous and complementary verbal and non-verbal messages can also help colour the emotion we are expressing or the attitude we are conveying.

The length of a hug while you tell your son you are proud of him provides additional information about the intensity of your pride. The firmness of your handshake when you greet a job interviewer can confirm your verbal claim that you are eager for employment.

People Respond and Adapt to Others Through Non-Verbal Messages

interaction adaptation theory. Theory suggesting that people interact with others by adapting to what others are doing.

interactional synchrony. The mirroring of each other's non-verbal behaviour by communication partners.

Even though we discuss verbal messages and non-verbal messages in separate chapters in this book, verbal and non-verbal cues often work together to create meaning. Also keep in mind that interpersonal communication, especially the expression of non-verbal messages, is a transactional process. Meaning is created simultaneously between those communicating. **Interaction adaptation theory** describes the transactive process of how people adapt to the communication behaviour of others.

Based on interaction adaptation theory, researcher Judee Burgoon and her colleagues have concluded that non-verbal cues play a key role in how people adapt to others.[8] If, for example, your friend leans forward to tell a story, you may lean forward to listen. Or if during a meeting you sit with folded arms, unconvinced of what you are hearing, you may look around the conference table and find others with similarly folded arms. As if we are part of an intricate dance, when we communicate, we relate to others by responding to their movements, eye contact, gestures, and other non-verbal cues.

Sometimes we relate by mirroring the posture or behaviour of others. Or we may find ourselves gesturing in sync with someone's vocal pattern. At times, you are conscious of such mirroring of behaviour, which is called **interactional synchrony**. At other times, you may not be aware that when your friend folds her arms while talking with you, you also fold your arms across your chest in a similar way. One researcher found that people evaluate such synchrony as positive; somewhat synchronized behaviour (but not so synchronized that it feels as though someone is purposefully imitating you) communicates partners' mutual interest and positive regard.[9]

Non-Verbal Communication Plays a Major Role in Interpersonal Relationships

As we learned in Chapter 1, communication is inescapable; one researcher suggests that as much as 65 percent of the social meaning in our messages is based on non-verbal communication.[10] Of course, the meaning that others interpret from your behaviour may not be the one you intended, and the inferences they draw based on non-verbal information may be right or wrong.

We learned in Chapter 3 that we begin making judgments about strangers just a fraction of a second after meeting them, based on non-verbal information. Within the first four minutes of interaction, we scope the other out and draw conclusions about him or her.[11] Another research team found that you may decide whether a date is going to be pleasant or dull during the first 30 seconds of meeting your partner, before your partner has had time to utter much more than, "Hello."[12] Non-verbal cues are the ones that form first impressions, accurate or not.

Non-verbal expressions of support are important when providing comforting messages to others during times of stress and anxiety. Communication researchers Susanne Jones and Laura Guerrero found that being non-verbally expressive and supportive is important in helping people cope with stress.[13] Providing empathic, supportive facial expressions and vocal cues, hugs, and positive touch helps reduce stress and enhance a person's overall well-being.

Non-verbal cues are important not only when people initiate relationships but also as they maintain and develop mature relationships with others. In fact, the more intimate the relationship, the more people use and understand the non-verbal cues of their partners. Communication researchers Ascan Koerner and Mary Anne Fitzpatrick have found that a spouse's ability to interpret non-verbal cues accurately significantly enhances marital satisfaction on the part of the other spouse.[14] It seems that if you can accurately identify your partner's moods and emotions, your partner is more satisfied with the quality of the relationship.

Long-married couples spend less time verbalizing their feelings and emotions to each other than they did when they were first dating; each learns how to interpret the other's subtle non-verbal cues. If your spouse is silent during dinner, you may know that the day was a tough one and you should give her a wide berth and if when you put on your new lime green pants, your boyfriend grimaces as he asks, "New pants?" you may understand that he does not love them. In fact, all of us are more likely to use non-verbal cues to convey negative messages than to announce explicitly our dislike of something or someone. People also use non-verbal cues to signal changes in the level of satisfaction with a relationship. When we want to cool things off, we may start using a less vibrant tone of voice and cut back on eye contact and physical contact with our partner.

 Applying Theory and Research

ADAPTING TO INTIMACY

Interaction adaptation theory, discussed on page 182, suggests that we adapt to the behaviour of people around us. Researchers in one study wanted to find out how different levels of intimacy affect how one partner will adapt or respond to the other. There were four different levels of intimacy in this study: very low intimacy, low intimacy, high intimacy, and very high intimacy. There was also a control group in which there was no expression of intimacy between the two partners.

First, the experimenters had two people interact in a small apartment. After the couple's short conversation, the researchers asked one person to come into another room to fill out a questionnaire while the other person, the target of the study, stayed in the first room to complete a questionnaire. The person who left the room was then instructed to be either intimate or highly intimate, or to exhibit a low or a very low level of intimacy with the other person when they had a second conversation. In the high or very high intimacy group, the second member of

the couple was told to increase his or her non-verbal intimacy toward the partner by "moving somewhat closer to [the] partner, smiling more, using more eye contact and perhaps touching the partner." The subjects were also told to be "warmer and more flirtatious with their partner." Those in the very high intimacy condition were given the same instructions but were told to be dramatically intimate. People who had the low intimacy conversation were told to "act colder and more disinterested" toward their partner. In the very low intimacy condition, the

Continued

subjects were told to move far away from their partners, smile much less, use much less eye contact, and act extremely bored.

What the researchers were really looking at was how the target person adapted to the person who came back in the room. Targets in the two intimacy treatments (intimate and highly intimate) responded by also being *more* intimate—smiling, moving closer to their partners, and being more pleasant and engaging. Targets in the two low intimacy conditions also mirrored what their partners were doing and became *less* non-verbally pleasant—defined in part by having less eye contact and not smiling—as well as becoming more verbally hostile. The

researchers reported that the targets also used "verbal repair strategies," meaning that they asked what was wrong and attempted to understand why the other person was acting less intimate. In summary, people adapted by mirroring the behaviour of the other person; in the low intimacy condition, the target used conversation to try to understand what was happening.

APPLYING THE RESEARCH TO YOUR LIFE

This study suggests that people are likely to adapt their non-verbal behaviour to mirror what their partner does. If a friend or another person you know increases non-verbal intimacy, there is the likelihood that

you will also increase your non-verbal intimacy. If an acquaintance is not intimate or is standoffish, you're also likely to be less open and responsive to that person. When people disconfirm you in obvious ways, such as by saying negative things about you or not looking at you or frowning at you when talking to you, you're likely not only to reciprocate but also to compensate for such disconfirming behaviour.

Source: Laura K. Guerrero, Susanne M. Jones, and Judee K. Burgoon, "Responses to Nonverbal Intimacy Change in Romantic Dyads: Effects of Behavioral Valence and Degree of Behavioral Change on Nonverbal and Verbal Reactions," Communication Monographs, 67 (December 2000): 325–46.

▶ Recap

REASONS TO STUDY NON-VERBAL COMMUNICATION

1.   Non-verbal messages communicate our feelings and attitudes.
2.   Non-verbal messages are usually more believable than verbal messages.
3   Non-verbal messages work with verbal messages to create meaning.
      ■ Non-verbal cues substitute for, repeat, contradict, or regulate verbal messages.
      ■ Non-verbal cues accent and complement emotional messages.
4.   People respond and adapt to others through non-verbal messages.
5.   Non-verbal messages play a major role in initiating, maintaining, and developing interpersonal relationships.

The Challenge of Interpreting Non-Verbal Messages

Even though we have made great claims for the value of studying non-verbal behaviours, it is not always easy to decipher unspoken messages.[15] We have dictionaries to help us interpret words, but we have no handy reference book to help us decode non-verbal cues. Although the phrase "body language" is often used in casual conversation, there are no universal or agreed-on interpretations of specific body movements or gestures. To help you with the decoding process, we are going to classify some common types of non-verbal behaviours, but first, you should be aware of some of the difficulties inherent in attempting a classification.

Non-Verbal Messages Are Often Ambiguous

Most words carry a meaning that everyone who speaks the same language can recognize. However, the meaning of non-verbal messages may be known only to the person displaying them. Perhaps even more importantly, that person may not intend for the behaviour to have any meaning at all, and some people have difficulty expressing their emotions non-verbally. They may have a frozen facial expression or a monotone voice. Or they may be teasing you, but their deadpan expressions lead you to believe that their negative comments are heartfelt. Often, it is tough to draw meaningful conclusions about another person's behaviour, even if we know him or her quite well.

Non-Verbal Messages Are Continuous

Words are discrete entities; they have a beginning and an end. You can point to the first word in this sentence and underline the last one. Our non-verbal behaviours are not as easily dissected. Like the sweep of a second hand on a clock, non-verbal behaviours are continuous. Some, such as a slap or a hand clap, have definite beginnings and endings, but more often than not, your non-verbal behaviour unfolds without clearly defined starting and stopping points. Gestures, facial expressions, and even eye contact can flow from one situation to the next with seamless ease. Researchers have difficulty studying non-verbal cues because of this continuous stream, so trying to categorize and interpret them will be challenging for us as well.

Non-Verbal Cues Are Multi-Channelled

Have you ever tried to watch two or more TV programs at once? Some televisions let you see as many as eight programs simultaneously so that you can keep up with three ball games and two soap operas and view commercials on the three other channels. Like the multi-channel TV, non-verbal cues come simultaneously to our perception centre from a variety of sources. Just as you can really watch only one channel at a time on your multi-channel television—although you can move from program to

program very rapidly—so, too, can you actually attend to only one non-verbal cue at a time.[16] One researcher suspects that negative non-verbal messages (frowns, grimaces, lack of eye contact) command attention before positive messages when the two compete.[17] Moreover, if the non-verbal message contradicts the verbal message, then we may have trouble interpreting either one correctly.[18]

Non-Verbal Interpretation Is Culture Based

There is some evidence that humans from every culture smile when they are happy and frown when they are unhappy.[19] We also all raise or flash our eyebrows when meeting or greeting others, and young children in many cultures wave to signal they want their mothers, raise their arms to be picked up, and suck their thumbs for comfort.[20] All this suggests that there is some underlying basis for expressing emotion and that there are some universal non-verbal emotional expressions. Yet, each culture also develops unique rules for displaying and interpreting these gestures and expressions.

Understanding Diversity

CULTURAL DIFFERENCES IN INTERPRETING NON-VERBAL MESSAGES

Research investigating non-verbal communication in a variety of cultures confirms that individuals interpret non-verbal messages from their unique cultural perspective. Note the following conclusions:[21]

FACIAL EXPRESSIONS

One research team found that facial expressions conveying happiness, sadness, anger, disgust, and surprise were the same in 68 to 92 percent of the cultures examined. All humans probably share the same neurophysiological basis for expressing emotions, but we learn different rules for sending and interpreting the expressions. For example, the Japanese culture does not reinforce the show of negative emotions; it is important for Japanese to "save face" and to help others save face as well.

EYE CONTACT

There seems to be more eye contact in interpersonal interactions between Arabs, South Americans, and Greeks than between people from other cultures. There is evidence that some black Americans look at others less often than white Americans do when sending and receiving messages. One of the most universal expressions among cultures appears to be the eyebrow flash (the sudden raising of the eyebrows when meeting someone or interacting with others).

GESTURES

Hand and body gestures with the most shared meaning among Africans, North Americans, and South Americans include pointing, shrugging, head nodding, clapping, thumbs down, waving hello, and beckoning. There are, however, regional variations within cultures; it is not wise to assume that all people in a given culture share the same meaning for certain gestures. The OK gesture made by forming a circle with the thumb and finger has sexual connotations in some South American and Caribbean countries. In France, the OK sign means worthless.

SPACE

Arabs, Latin Americans, and southern Europeans seem to stand closer to others than people from east and south Asia and northern Europe. If you have been to Britain, you know that people queue or wait for buses in orderly straight lines. In France, however, queuing is less orderly and individuals are more likely to push forward to be the next customer or get the next seat on the bus. As with gestures, however, there are regional variations in spatial preferences.

There is no common cross-cultural dictionary of non-verbal meaning. There are well-established norms for non-verbal behaviour for each culture, however, and conscientious travellers will make an effort to learn these norms for the culture they are visiting. How accurate is the advice given in the *In Canada* box on page 187 for visitors to Canada? Given Canada's rapidly changing immigrant population (discussed in Chapter 8), how long can these norms be expected to remain valid?

In Canada...

RULES FOR NON-VERBAL COMMUNICATION IN CANADA

What are the rules for non-verbal communication in Canada? In one "bible" of protocol for doing business in 60 different countries, readers are provided the following advice on non-verbal rules of behaviour with Canadians (note that this is not the complete list). This book was written in 1994. Do you see any changes in these rules or are they still the same now? Do you think the distinctions between French Canadians and British Canadians are fair reflections given the country's diversity today?

- In Canada, the standard greeting is a smile, often accompanied by a nod, wave, and/or verbal greeting.
- In business situations, a handshake is used upon greeting or introduction.
- Canadian business people expect a firm handshake (web-to-web contact), direct eye contact, and an open, friendly manner. A weak handshake may be taken as a sign of weakness.
- Older men usually wait for women to offer their hand before shaking.
- French Canadians also have a fairly firm handshake, and they shake hands more often: upon greetings, introductions, and departures, even if the person has been greeted earlier that day.
- Good friends and family members sometimes embrace, especially among the French. A kissing of both cheeks may also occur, especially among the French.
- The standard distance between you and your conversation partner should be 60 cm. British Canadians are uncomfortable standing any closer to another person. French Canadians may stand slightly closer.
- Canadians, especially those of British descent, do not tend toward frequent or expansive gesturing.
- The backslap is a sign of close friendship among British Canadians. It is rarely used among the French Canadians.
- Direct eye contact shows that you are sincere, although it should not be too intense. Some minorities look away to show respect.
- When sitting, Canadians often look very relaxed. Men may sit with the ankle of one leg on the knee of the other or prop their feet up on chairs or desks.
- In business situations, maintain good posture and a less casual pose.
- In most of Canada, to call the waiter or waitress over, briefly wave to get his or her attention. To call for the cheque, make a writing gesture. In Quebec, it is only necessary to nod the head backwards or to make a discreet wave of the hand.

Source: From T. Morrison, W. A. Conaway, and G. A. Borden, Kiss, Bow, or Shake Hands: How to Do Business in Sixty Different Countries (Holbrook, Mass.: Bob Adams, Inc., 1994).

Non-Verbal Communication Codes

Keeping all of these challenges to our understanding in mind, we can begin looking at the categories of non-verbal information that researchers have studied: movement and gestures, eye contact, facial expressions, use of space and territory, touch, and personal appearance. Although we will concentrate on the codes that fall within these categories in mainstream Western culture, we will also try to look at codes for other cultures and subcultures.

Body Movement, Posture, and Gestures

In 1771, when British explorer Captain Cook arrived in the South Pacific islands of New Hebrides (today the nation of Vanuatu), he didn't speak the language of the natives. His only way of communicating was sign language. Through gestures, pointing, and hand waving, he established contact with the natives. There is evidence that people have used gestures to communicate since ancient times—especially to bridge cultural and language differences. The first record of using sign language to communicate is found in Xenophon's *The March Up Country*, in which unspoken gestures were used to help the Greeks cross Asia Minor in about 400 BC. Even when we do speak the same language as others, we use gestures to help us make our point.[22]

kinesics.   The study of human movement and gestures.

Kinesics is the study of human movement and gestures. It was Francis Bacon who noted, "As the tongue speaketh to the ear, so the hand speaketh to the eye." We have long recognized that the movement and gestures we exhibit provide valuable information to others. Various scholars and researchers have proposed paradigms for analyzing and coding these movements and gestures, just as we do for spoken or written language.[23]

One paradigm identifies four stages of "quasi-courtship behaviour."[24] The first stage is *courtship readiness*. When we are attracted to someone, we may suck in our stomach, tense our muscles, and stand up straight. The second stage, includes *preening behaviours*: we manipulate our appearance by combing our hair, applying makeup, straightening our tie, pulling up our socks, and double-checking our appearance in the mirror. In the third stage, we demonstrate *positional cues*, using our posture and body orientation to be seen and noticed by others. Here, the classic Norman Rockwell painting shows teenagers illustrating typical preening and positional cues.

One researcher recently found 52 gestures and non-verbal behaviours that women use to signal an interest in men. Among the most common unspoken flirting cues were: smiling and surveying a crowded room with the eyes, and moving closer to the object of affection.[25] These cues intensify in the fourth stage of quasi-courtship behaviour, *appeals to invitation*, using close proximity, exposed skin, open body positions, and eye contact to signal availability and interest. Subjects in one study reported that they were aware of using all these techniques to promote an intimate relationship. In fact, we use these quasi-courtship behaviours to some extent in almost any situation in which we are trying to gain favourable attention from another.

Can you identify the quasi-courtship behaviour in this painting?
(Printed by permission of the Norman Rockwell Family Trust. Copyright © *Soda Jerk*, The Norman Rockwell Family Trust)

Another team of researchers focused on non-verbal behaviours that make us label a person warm and friendly or cold and distant.[26] They found that "warm" people face their communication partners directly, smile more, make more direct eye contact, fidget less, and generally make fewer unnecessary hand movements. "Cold" people make less eye contact, smile less, fidget more, and turn away from their partners.

Posture and body orientation reveal important information. Open body posture (uncrossed arms and legs) communicates that we are receptive and responsive listeners. When we are trying to decrease our contact with someone, say at a party or family gathering, we are likely to turn away from the individual we want to avoid.

Your body orientation and posture provide important cues to your interest and willingness to continue or end communication with someone.

Albert Mehrabian has identified the non-verbal cues that contribute to perceptions of liking.[27] He found that an open body and arm position, a forward lean, and a more relaxed posture communicate liking. When we are attempting to persuade someone, we typically have more eye contact and a more direct body orientation; we are more likely to lean forward and closer to others.

Another team of researchers tried to classify movement and gestures according to their function. They identified five categories: emblems, illustrators, affect displays, regulators, and adaptors.[28]

Building Your Skills

COMMUNICATING INTEREST

Non-verbally play the roles of both a good listener and a poor listener. First, imagine that you are listening to someone talk. As a good listener, how would you communicate your interest in what the person is saying without uttering a word? Note your posture, eye contact, presence or lack of hand movement. Are your arms and legs crossed?

Now role-play a poor listener—someone who appears to be bored or even irritated by what a speaker is saying. What are the differences in the cues you use?

🔹 Emblems

Non-verbal cues that have specific, generally understood meanings in a given culture and may actually substitute for a word or phrase are called **emblems**. When you are busy typing a report that is due the next day and your young son rushes in to ask for permission to buy a new computer game, you turn from your computer and hold up an open palm to indicate your desire for uninterrupted quiet. To communicate your enthusiastic enjoyment of a violin soloist at a concert, you applaud wildly. You want your children to stop talking in the library, so you put an index finger up to your pursed lips.

🔹 Illustrators

We frequently accompany a verbal message with **illustrators** that either contradict, accent, or complement the message. Slamming a book closed while announcing, "I don't want to read this anymore," or pounding a lectern while proclaiming, "This point is important!" are two examples of non-verbal behaviours that accent the verbal message. Typically, we use non-verbal illustrators at the beginning of clauses or phrases.[29] TV newscasters, for example, turn a page to signal that they are moving to a new story or topic. Most of us use illustrators to help us communicate information about the size, shape, and spatial relationships of objects. You probably even use them when you talk on the phone, though probably not as many as you use in face-to-face conversation.[30]

🔹 Affect Displays

Non-verbal movements and postures used to communicate emotion are called **affect displays**, which as we saw in the last chapter are used to display how we feel. As early as 1872, when Charles Darwin systematically studied the expression of emotion in

emblems.   Non-verbal cues that have specific, generally understood meanings in a given culture and that may substitute for a word or phrase.

illustrators.   Non-verbal behaviour that accompanies a verbal message and either contradicts, accents, or complements it.

affect displays.   Non-verbal behaviour that communicates emotions.

both humans and animals,[31] people recognized that non-verbal cues are the primary ways to communicate emotion. Our facial expressions, vocal cues, posture, and gestures convey the intensity of our emotions.[32] If you are happy, for example, your face will telegraph your joy to others, but the movement of your hands, the openness of your posture, and the speed with which you move will tell others *how* happy you are. Similarly, if you are feeling depressed, your face will probably reveal your sadness or dejection, while your slumped shoulders and lowered head will indicate the intensity of your despair. When we are feeling friendly, we use a soft tone of voice, an open smile, and a relaxed posture.[33] When we feel neutral about an issue, we signal that feeling by putting little expression on our face or in our voice. When we feel hostile, we use a harsh voice, frown with our teeth showing, and keep our posture tense and rigid.

Regulators

regulators. Non-verbal messages that help control the interaction or level of communication among people.

We use **regulators** to control the interaction or flow of communication between ourselves and another person. When we are eager to respond to a message, we make eye contact, raise our eyebrows, open our mouth, raise an index finger, and lean forward slightly. When we do not want to be part of the conversation, we do the opposite: we avert our eyes, close our mouth, cross our arms, and lean back in our seats or away from the verbal action.

Adaptors

adaptors. Non-verbal behaviours that help satisfy a personal need and help a person adapt or respond to the immediate situation.

When we are cold, we reach for a sweater or wrap our arms around our chests to keep warm. When the temperature is 36° C in the shade and there is no breeze, we reach for a fan to make our own breeze. These behaviours are examples of **adaptors**—non-verbal behaviours that help us to satisfy a personal need and adapt to the immediate situation. When you adjust your glasses, scratch a mosquito bite, or comb your hair, you are using movement to help you manage your personal needs.

The Five Categories and Interpersonal Communication

How will understanding these five categories of non-verbal behaviour help you understand others and your own interpersonal communication? They give you a new and more precise way to think about your own behaviour. By noting how often you use emblems instead of words to communicate a message, you can recognize how important emblems are in your relationships with others. The more you rely on emblems that have unique meanings for you and your partner, the more intimate the interpersonal relationship. Also, start to notice whether your non-verbal behaviour contradicts what you say. Monitoring your use of illustrators can help you determine whether you are sending mixed signals to others. Be aware of how you display affect. Knowing that your face and voice communicate emotion, and that posture and gesture indicate the intensity of your feelings, can help you understand how others make inferences about your feelings and attitudes. If other people have difficulty interpreting your emotional state, you may not be projecting your feelings non-verbally. Finally, notice how you use adaptors. Individuals who do not learn the cultural norms of displaying adaptors can have a difficult time socially. For example, if you were never taught not to comb your hair or belch at the table, you may find you receive few dinner invitations.

Since non-verbal cues are ambiguous, it's not a good idea to use them to achieve a specific objective. However, as you have seen, people are more likely to respond in predictable ways if you use behaviours they can recognize and interpret easily.

▶ **Recap**

CATEGORIES OF MOVEMENT AND GESTURES

Category	Definition	Examples
Emblems	Behaviours that have specific, generally understood meaning	Raising a thumb to hitchhike a ride
Illustrators	Cues that accompany verbal messages and provide meaning for the message	Pounding the podium to emphasize a point
Affect Displays	Expressions of emotion	Hugging someone to express love
Regulators	Cues that control and manage the flow of communication between others	Looking at someone when you wish to speak
Adaptors	Behaviours that help you adapt to your environment	Scratching, combing your hair

🔵 Eye Contact

Whether you choose to look at someone or avert your gaze has an enormous impact on your relationship with that person.[34] Researchers have identified four functions for eye contact in interpersonal interactions.[35]

First, eye contact serves a *cognitive* function because it gives you information about another person's thought processes. For example, if your communication partner breaks eye contact after you ask him or her a question, you will know that he or she is probably thinking of something to say.

Second, we use eye contact to *monitor* the behaviour of others. We receive a major portion of the information we obtain through our eyes. We look at others to determine whether they are receptive to our messages. In fact, this search for feedback is implicit in the word for the centre part of the eye, "pupil," which comes from the Latin word *pupilla* or "little doll." When you look into someone's eyes, you can see a miniature reflection of yourself.[36]

Third, eye contact is one of the most powerful *regulatory* cues we use to signal when we want to talk and when we don't want to communicate. Your authors have noticed that when they ask questions such as, "Who can tell me the four functions of eye contact?" students quickly, yet unobtrusively, avert their eyes to signal, "Don't call on me." When we do want to communicate with others, for example when we're standing in line at the bakery, we fix our eyes on the sales clerk to signal, "My turn next. Please wait on me."

Finally, the area around our eyes serves an *expressive* function. The eyes have been called the "mirror of the soul" because they reveal our emotions to others. We may cry, blink, and widen or narrow our gaze to express our feelings.

Researchers Mark Knapp and Judith Hall have summarized conclusions on nonverbal communication that predict when you are most and least likely to have eye contact with someone, as shown in Table 6.1.[37]

When we do establish eye contact with others, it may seem that our gaze is constant. Yet, research suggests that we actually spend the majority of our time looking at something other than the person's eyes. One research team found that we focus on something else, including our partner's mouth, 57 percent of the time.[38] Not surprisingly then, facial expressions are another rich source of information in our communication with others.

Table 6.1
When Are You More and Less Likely to Have Eye Contact with Someone?

You Are More Likely to Have Eye Contact When You	You Are Less Likely to Have Eye Contact When You
Like or love your communication partner	Do not like your communication partner
Are physically distant from him or her	Are physically close to him or her
Are discussing easy, impersonal topics	Are discussing difficult, intimate topics
Have nothing else to look at	Have other things to look at
Are interested in your partner's reactions	Are not interested in your partner's reactions
Are trying to dominate or persuade your partner	Are not trying to dominate or persuade your partner
Are from a culture that emphasizes eye contact	Are from a culture that de-emphasizes eye contact
Are an extrovert	Are an introvert
Have a high need to affiliate or to be included	Have a low need to affiliate or do not need to be included
Are dependent on your partner (and your partner is not responsive)	Are more independent of your partner (and your partner is responsive to you)
Are listening rather than talking	Are talking rather than listening
Are female	Are male

Source: Adapted from Mark L. Knapp and Judith A. Hall, Nonverbal Communication in Human Interaction (Fort Worth, Texas: Harcourt Brace, 1997), 390–391.

▶ **Recap**

FUNCTIONS OF EYE CONTACT

Cognitive	Provides cues about our thinking and thought processes
Monitoring	Provides information about how others are responding to us; we monitor to seek feedback
Regulatory	Manages the flow of communication; we use eye contact to signal when we do and do not want to interact with another person
Expressive	Provides information about feelings, emotions, and attitude

Facial Expressions

You tell your parents that you will not be able to spend the holidays with them because you have decided to take your children skiing. You present your partner with a new abstract art painting that you would like to hang in your bedroom. As the personnel director reviews your résumé, you sit in silence across the desk from her or him. In each of these situations, you would be eagerly awaiting some reaction from the other person, and what you would be scanning is his or her face. The face is the exhibit gallery for our emotional displays, and although we often try to manipulate our facial cues to project a premeditated feeling, our faces may still betray our true emotions to others.[39]

To interpret our communication partner's facial expressions accurately, we need to put our other-orientation skills to work, focusing on what the other person may be thinking or feeling. It helps if we know the person well, can see his or her whole face, have plenty of time to watch it, and understand the situation that prompted the emotion.[40] However, it is also helpful to know the cues for "reading" facial expressions.

Your face is versatile. According to one research team, it is capable of producing over 250 000 different expressions.[41] Research suggests that women have greater variety in their emotional expressions and spend more time smiling than men,[42] but all of our expressions can be grouped under six primary emotional categories; the following list describes the changes that occur on our faces for each one.[43]

Surprise: Wide-open eyes; raised and wrinkled brow; open mouth.

Fear: Open mouth; tense skin under the eyes; wrinkles in the centre of the forehead.

Disgust: Raised or curled upper lip; wrinkled nose; raised cheeks; lowered brow; lowered upper eyelid.

Anger: Tensed lower eyelid; either pursed lips or open mouth; lowered and wrinkled brow; staring eyes.

Happiness: Smiling; mouth may be open or closed; raised cheeks; wrinkles around lower eyelids.

Sadness: Lip may tremble; corners of the lips turn downward; corners of the upper eyelid may be raised.

The face is an exhibit gallery for our emotions. The messages we convey through thousands of different expressions are usually more powerful and direct than verbal ones. (Bob Daemmrich/Stock Boston)

How accurately do we interpret emotions expressed on the face? Several studies have attempted to measure subjects' skill in identifying emotional expressions of others. They have found that reading facial expression is a tricky business. According to one research team, even though our faces provide a great deal of information about emotions, we have learned how to control our facial expressions.[44] In addition, facial expressions seem to be contagious. A study from the United States illustrated this "contagion effect." A researcher who showed his subjects video clips of former US president Ronald Reagan giving speeches discovered that they were likely to smile when Reagan smiled and frown when Reagan appeared angry or threatening.[45] Another study found that people were better able to judge the accuracy of facial expressions when the expressions were more complex.[46] The distinctiveness of a facial expression with compound meanings may be what makes it easier to interpret. It is also probable that people have more practice interpreting facial expressions with compound meanings than they do those that communicate a single emotion such as sadness or happiness.

At the opposite end of the spectrum from complex facial expressions are what psychologist Paul Ekman calls "microexpressions," fleeting facial expressions that may last only 0.05 of a second. Most of Ekman's test groups, including policemen and judges, have difficulty detecting microexpressions. On the other hand, Buddhists, whom Ekman calls "gymnasts of the mind," may be surprisingly sensitive to microexpressions.[47]

Building Your Skills

FACIAL EXPRESSION QUIZ

Divide the class into teams of two people. Person A should select one of the six primary emotions communicated by the face and attempt to display the emotion to person B by using the phrase, "May I help you?" The six primary emotions are happiness, sadness, surprise, dis-

gust, anger, and fear. Communicate all six emotions in random order while verbalizing this phrase. Some will be easier to identify and do than others!

Person B should attempt to identify the emotions expressed by person A and list them in order.

When person A has communicated all six emotions, he or she can reverse roles with person B.

1. _____

2. _____

3. _____

4. _____

5. _____

6. _____

Vocal Cues

A Spanish electronics engineer recently devoted four years to studying the cries of his baby son and approximately 100 other infants. His work resulted in the production of a calculator-size translator called WhyCry. Its inventor claims that the machine can translate a baby's cry into one of five icons ("hungry," "sleepy," "uncomfortable," "stressed," or "bored") with 87 percent accuracy, a figure that rises to 98 percent when parents use a "symptom table" of body language.[48]

Whether you are an infant or an adult, your voice is a primary tool for communicating information about the nature of relationships between you and others.[49] We use our voices to present one message on the surface (with words) and usually a more accurate expression of our feelings with our vocal quality. Say the following sentence out loud: "This looks great." Now say it sarcastically; you really don't think it looks great: "This looks great." Clearly, your vocal cues provide the real meaning.

Some vocal expressions of emotion are easier to identify than others. Expressions of joy and anger are obvious ones, whereas shame and love are the most difficult emotions to identify based on vocal cues alone.[50] We are also likely to confuse fear with nervousness, love with sadness, and pride with satisfaction.

Our voices also provide information about our self-confidence and our knowledge of the subject matter in our messages. Most of us would conclude that a speaker who mumbles, speaks slowly, consistently mispronounces words, and uses "uhs" and "ums" is less credible and persuasive than one who speaks clearly, rapidly, and fluently.[51] Even though mispronunciations and vocalized pauses ("ums" and "ahs") seem to have a negative effect on credibility, they do not seem to be a major impediment to attitude change. People may, for example, think that you are less knowledgeable if you stammer, but you may still be able to get your persuasive message across.

In addition to providing information about emotions, self-confidence, and knowledge, vocal cues, known as **backchannel cues**, also serve a regulatory function in interpersonal situations, signalling when we want to talk and when we don't. When we are finished talking, we may lower the pitch of our final word. When we want to talk, we may start by interjecting sounds such as "I... I... I..." or "Ah... Ah... Ah..." to interrupt the speaker and grab the verbal ball. We also may use more cues such as, "Sure," "I understand," "Uh-huh," or "OK" to signal that we understand the message of the other person and now we want to talk or end the conversation. These backchannel cues are particularly useful in telephone conversations when we have no other non-verbal cues to help us signal that we would like to get off the phone.

Not only "ums" and "ahs" but also speaking rate influences our perception of others. One team of researchers found that North Americans evaluated speakers with a moderate to slightly faster speaking rate as more "socially attractive" than speakers who had a slow rate of speech.[52] North American listeners also seem to prefer a speaking rate that is equal to or slightly faster than their own speaking rate.

Sometimes it is not what we say, or even how we say it, that communicates our feelings. Being silent may communicate volumes. One researcher, in commenting about the importance of silence in speech, said: "Silence is to speech as white paper is to this print. ... The entire system of spoken language would fail without [people's] ability to both tolerate and create sign sequences of silence-sound-silence units."[53]

Would you be comfortable just sitting silently with a good friend? Sidney Baker's theory of silence suggests that the more at ease we are when we share a silence with a close friend, the more comfortable we are with just being together and enjoying each other's companionship. People feel a need to talk until there is nothing left to say and all uncertainty between partners has been managed. In most long-term relationships, partners may not feel a need to fill the air with sound. Just being together to enjoy each other's company may be most fulfilling. Psychologist S. J. Baker calls such moments "positive silence."[54] While watching a sunset with a close friend, for example, there may be no need to narrate what you are seeing—it's enough just to experience it.

Personal Space

Imagine that you are sitting alone in a booth at your local pizza parlour. As you sit munching your thin-and-crispy pepperoni pizza, you are startled when a complete stranger sits down in your booth directly across from you. With several empty tables and booths in the restaurant, you feel very uncomfortable that this unknown individual has invaded "your" area.

Normally, we do not think much about the rules we observe regarding personal space, but in fact, every culture has fairly rigid ways of regulating space in social interactions. Violations of these rules can be alarming and, as in the preceding scenario, even threatening. How close we are willing to get to others relates to how well we know them and to considerations of power and status.

One of the pioneers in helping us understand the silent language of personal space was Edward T. Hall. His study of **proxemics** investigated how close or how far

backchannel cues. Non-verbal cues, typically vocal cues, that signal your wish to begin or end a conversation.

proxemics. The study of how close to or far away from people and objects we position ourselves.

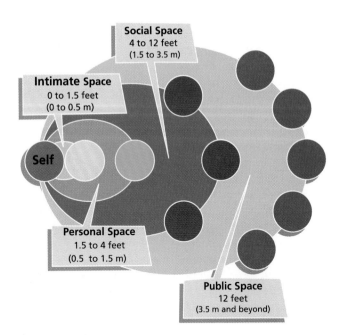

Intimate Space
0 to 1.5 feet
(0 to 0.5 m)

Social Space
4 to 12 feet
(1.5 to 3.5 m)

Self

Personal Space
1.5 to 4 feet
(0.5 to 1.5 m)

Public Space
12 feet
(3.5 m and beyond)

**Figure 6.1
Edwin T. Hall's Four
Zones of Space**

intimate space.   Zone One—
space most often used for very
personal or intimate communication, ranging from zero to one
and one half feet (0–0.5 m,
approximately).

personal space.   Zone Two—
space most often used for conversation with family and
friends, ranging from one and
one half to four feet (approximately 0.5–1.5 m).

social space.   Zone Three—
space most often used for group
discussion, ranging from four to
12 feet (about 1.5–3.5 m).

public space.   Zone Four—
space most often used by public
speakers or one speaking to
many people, ranging from 12
feet (about 3.5 m) and beyond.

territoriality.   The study of how
animals and humans use space
and objects to communicate
occupancy or ownership of space.

away we arrange ourselves around people and
things.[55] Hall identified four spatial zones that we
unconsciously define for ourselves, as shown in
Figure 6.1. When we are between zero and one and
one half feet (up to about 0.5 m) from someone, we
are occupying **intimate space**. This is the zone in
which the most intimate interpersonal communication occurs. It is open only to those with whom we
are well-acquainted, unless we are forced to stand in
an elevator, a fast-food line, or some other crowded
space.

The second zone, which ranges from one and
one half to four feet (about 0.5–1.5 m), is called
personal space. Most of our conversations with
family and friends occur in this zone. If someone
we don't know well invades this space on purpose,
we may feel uncomfortable.

Zone Three, called **social space**, ranges from
four to 12 feet (about 1.5–3.5 m). Most group interaction, as well as many of our professional relationships, take place in this zone. The interaction tends
to be more formal than that in the first two zones.

Public space, the fourth zone, begins at 12 feet (about 3.5 m). Interpersonal communication does not usually occur in this zone, and many public speakers and
teachers position themselves even farther from their audience.

The specific space that you and others choose depends on several variables.[56] The
more you like someone, the closer to them you will stand. We allow individuals with
high status to surround themselves with more space than we allow for people with
lower status. Large people also usually have more space around them than smaller
people, and women stand closer to others than do men.[57] All of us tend to stand
closer to others in a large room than we do in a small room.

In a group, who's in charge, who's important, and who talks to whom are reflected
by the spatial arrangement we self-select. The more dominant group members tend
to select seats at the head of a table, while the shyer individuals often select a corner
seat at a rectangular table.[58]

Territory

Territoriality is the study of how humans and animals use space and objects to communicate occupancy or ownership of space. You assumed "ownership" of the booth
in the pizza parlour and the accompanying "right" to determine who sat with you
because you and your pizza were occupying the booth. In addition to invading your
personal space, the intrusive stranger broke the rules that govern territoriality.

We announce our ownership of space with territorial markers—things that signify that the area has been claimed—much as explorers once planted a flag claiming
uncharted land for their monarch. When you are studying at the library, for example, and need to get up and check a reference at the computerized card catalogue,
you might leave behind a notebook or a pencil. At seaside resorts, people save beach
and poolside chairs by placing towels on them to "claim" the chairs for the day. In
rural areas, landowners post signs at the borders of their property to keep hunters

> ## Recap
>
> ### EDWARD T. HALL'S CLASSIFICATION OF SPATIAL ZONES
>
> | | Definition | Examples |
> |---|---|---|
> | Zone One | Intimate space | Zero to one and one half feet (0–0.5 m) |
> | Zone Two | Personal space | One and one half to four feet (about 0.5–1.5 m) |
> | Zone Three | Social space | Four to 12 feet (about 1.5–3.5 m) |
> | Zone Four | Public space | Twelve feet (3.5 m) and beyond |

off their territory. Signs, locks, electronic security systems, and other devices secure our home and office territories.

We also use markers to indicate where our space stops and someone else's starts. "Good fences make good neighbours," wrote the poet Robert Frost. When someone sits too close, we may try to erect a physical barrier, such as a stack of books or a napkin holder, or we might use our body as a shield by turning away. If the intruder does not get the hint that "this land is our land," we ultimately resort to words to announce that the space is occupied.

Touch

Standing elbow to elbow in a crowded elevator, you may find yourself in physical contact with total strangers. As you stiffen your body and avert your eyes, a baffling sense of shame floods over you. If you are sitting at a conference table and you accidentally brush the toe of your shoe against your colleague's ankle, you may jerk away and may even blush or apologize. Why do we react this way to unpremeditated touching? Normally, we touch to express intimacy. When intimacy is not our intended message, we instinctively react to modify the impression.

Countless studies have shown that intimate touching is vital to our personal development and well-being.[59] Infants and children need it to confirm that they are valued and loved. Many hospitals invite volunteers in to hold and rock newborns whose mothers cannot do it themselves. Advocates of breastfeeding argue that the intimate touching it entails strengthens the bond between mother and child.[60]

The amount of touch we need, tolerate, receive, and initiate depends on many factors. The amount and kind of touching you receive in your family is one big influence. If your mother or father greets you with hugs, caresses, and kisses, then you probably do this to others. If your family is less demonstrative, you may be restrained

Appearance Counts. What role do you think appearance plays in the selection of television hosts? (CBC)

yourself. Studies show that most of us are more likely to touch people when we are feeling friendly, happy, or under other specific circumstances:[61]

- When we ask someone to do something for us
- When we share rather than ask for information
- When we try to persuade someone to do something
- When we are talking about intimate topics
- When we are in social settings that we choose rather than in professional settings that are part of our job
- When we are excited to share good news
- When we listen to a troubled or worried friend

Appearance

In all of our interactions with others, appearance counts. Our culture places a high value on our weight, our hairstyle, and our clothes; these things are particularly important in the early stages of relationship development. Attractive females have an easier time persuading others than do those who are perceived as less attractive. In general, we think attractive people are more credible, happier, more popular, more sociable, and even more prosperous than less attractive people.[62] A recent Canadian study continues to illustrate the importance that we put on appearance, especially weight, often with the result of unhealthy and even disordered eating behaviours.[63]

There is also evidence that if you believe that others think a person is attractive, you'll be more likely to evaluate that person as attractive as well.[64] To test this self-fulfilling prophecy effect, researchers had subjects conduct interviews with people. Some subjects were told they were meeting a person others had rated as attractive. Other subjects interviewed a person they were led to believe had been evaluated as less attractive by others. If they thought they were interviewing someone whom others evaluated as attractive, then research subjects, too, were more likely to evaluate the person as attractive. Similarly, if they thought they were interviewing someone rated less attractive by others, then the interviewers evaluated the person they were interviewing as less attractive. Rather than supporting the adage "What you see is what you get," the study found that "What you expect to see is what you think you got."

It was in Chapter 2 that we discussed the link between our self-concept and personal appearance. The shape and size of your body also affects how others perceive you. Heavier and rounder individuals are often perceived to be older, more old-fashioned, less good-looking, more talkative, and more good-natured than thin people,

Clothes Affect Perceptions. How is the superior status of senior-ranking RCMP officers conveyed through their orders of full dress? (© RCMP/1995-041 (G))

who are perceived to be more ambitious, more suspicious of others, more uptight and tense, more negative, and less talkative. Muscular and athletically fit individuals are seen as better looking, taller, and more adventurous. These perceptions are, in fact, so common that they have become easily recognizable stereotypes, on which casting directors for movies, TV shows, and plays rely when selecting actors.

Aside from keeping us warm and within the legal bounds of decency, our clothes also affect how others perceive us. In institutional settings, an individual's rank is typically denoted by his or her uniform, as with the orders of dress for the Royal Canadian Mounted Police. On a less formal level, "social" rank is also inferred from the clothes we wear. For example, one study found that a man who jaywalked while dressed in nice clothes attracted more fellow violators than he did when he was shabbily attired.[65] Studies have attempted to identify a "power" look and magazines are constantly giving us prescriptions for ways to be attractive and stylish; however, outside of uniformed institutions, there really is no formula for dressing for success.[66] Styles and expectations about appearances change. We have only to look at the clothing norms of the 1960s, 1970s, or 1980s to note how they are different from those of today.

▶ **Recap**

CODES OF NON-VERBAL COMMUNICATION

Movements and Gestures	Communicate information, status, warmth, credibility, interest in others, attitudes, liking
Eye Contact	Serves cognitive, monitoring, regulatory, and expressive functions
Facial Expressions	Express emotions
Vocal Cues	Communicate emotion through pitch, rate, volume, and quality, and modify the meaning of messages
Personal Space	Provides information about status, power, and intimacy
Territory	Provides cues to use, ownership, or occupancy of space
Touch	Communicates intimacy, affection, or rejection
Appearance	Influences perceptions of credibility and attraction

---

Interpreting Non-Verbal Communication

So what does it all mean? How do we make sense out of the postures, movements, gestures, eye contact, facial expressions, uses of space and territory, touch, and appearance of others? Albert Mehrabian has found that we synthesize and interpret non-verbal cues along three primary dimensions: *immediacy, arousal,* and *dominance.*[67]

Immediacy

Sometimes, we are not able to put our finger on the precise reason we find a person likeable or unlikeable. Mehrabian believes that immediacy cues are a likely explanation. **Immediacy** cues are behaviours that communicate liking and engender feelings of pleasure. The principle underlying immediacy is simple: we move toward persons and things we like and avoid or move away from those we dislike. Immediacy cues physically increase our sensory awareness of others.

immediacy. The feelings of liking, pleasure, and closeness communicated by such non-verbal cues as eye contact, forward lean, touch, and open body orientation.

Our use of space and territory is not the only cue that contributes to positive or negative feelings. Mehrabian has noted several other non-verbal cues that increase immediacy. One of the most powerful is touch; others include a forward lean, increased eye contact, and an open body orientation. The meaning of these behaviours is usually implied rather than explicitly spelled out in words.

Not surprisingly, communication researcher Lois Hinkle found that spouses who reported high feelings of affection for their mates reported that their mates responded by expressing more immediacy cues toward them.[68] There is also evidence that when someone expresses immediate or pleasant non-verbal messages toward us, we reciprocate by responding in a pleasant manner. Researchers Judee Burgoon and Beth Le Poire found that people adapt their non-verbal messages to others.[69] When people express immediacy or liking toward you, you are more likely to reciprocate and express a similar sentiment toward them. Immediacy is contagious. Yet another research study found that expressions of non-verbal immediacy on the part of someone trying to offer support and comfort to another person, such as closer personal distance, touching, and forward lean, helped reduce the other person's stress and tension.[70]

In brief, to communicate that we like someone, we use these cues:[71]

Proximity:	Close, forward lean
Body Orientation:	Direct, but could be side by side
Eye Contact:	Eye contact and mutual eye contact
Facial Expression:	Smiling
Gestures:	Head nods, movement
Posture:	Open, arms oriented toward others
Touch:	Cultural- and context-appropriate touch
Voice:	Higher pitch, upward pitch

Arousal

The face, voice, and movement are primary indicators of **arousal**. If we see arousal cues, we conclude that another person is responsive to and interested in us. If the person acts passive or dull, we conclude that he or she is uninterested.

When you approach someone and ask whether he or she has a minute or two to talk, that person may signal interest with a change in facial expression and more animated vocal cues. People who are aroused and interested in you show animation in their face, voice, and gestures. A forward lean, a flash of the eyebrows, and a nod of the head are other cues that implicitly communicate arousal. Someone who says, "Sure, I have time to talk with you," in a monotone and with a flat, expressionless face is communicating the opposite. Think of arousal as an on–off switch. Sleeping is the ultimate switched-off state.

arousal. The feelings of interest and excitement communicated by such non-verbal cues as vocal expression, facial expressions, and gestures.

Dominance

The third dimension of Mehrabian's framework for implicit cues communicates the balance of power in a relationship. **Dominance** cues communicate status, position, and importance.[72] A person of high status tends to have a relaxed body posture when interacting with a person of lower status.[73] When you talk to a professor, he may lean back in his chair, put his feet on the desk, and fold his hands behind his head during the conversation. However, unless your professor is a colleague or a friend, you will maintain a relatively formal posture during your interaction in his office.

Another dominance cue is the use of space. High-status individuals usually have more space around them; they have bigger offices and more "barriers" protecting them. A receptionist in an office is usually easily accessible, but to reach the president of the company, you may have to navigate through several corridors, and past several administrative assistants and an executive assistant who are "guarding" the door.

Other power cues that communicate feelings of dominance include the use of furniture, clothing, and locations. You study at a table in the library; the college president has a large private desk. You may wear jeans and a T-shirt to class; the head of the university wears a business suit. Your residence room is tiny and closely surrounded by many others; the president's house is large, surrounded by a lush, landscaped garden in a prestigious neighbourhood. We use space, territory, posture, and artifacts such as clothing and furniture to signal feelings of dominance or submissiveness in the presence of others.

Psychologist Michael Argyle summarizes the non-verbal cues that communicate dominance:[74]

dominance.   The feelings of power, status, and control communicated by such non-verbal cues as a relaxed posture, greater personal space, and protected personal space.

Use of Space:	Height (on a platform or standing)
	Facing a group
	More space
Eye Contact:	Less with lower status
	More when talking
	More when initially establishing dominance
	More when staring to establish power
Face:	No smile, frown, mature adult features
Touch:	Initiating touch
Voice:	Loud, low pitch, greater pitch range
	Slow, more interruptions, more talk
	Slight hesitation before speaking
Gesture:	Pointing at the other or at his or her property
Posture:	Standing, hands on hips, expanded chest, more relaxed

Understanding Diversity

GENDER DIFFERENCES AND NON-VERBAL COMMUNICATION

There is evidence that men and women display and interpret non-verbal cues differently.[75]

EYE CONTACT

Women usually have a more prolonged gaze with others than do men. Women, however, are less likely to just stare at someone; they break eye contact more frequently than men. In general, women receive more eye contact from others than do men.

SPACE

Men tend to have more space around them than do women. Women both approach and are approached more closely than men, and when conversing with others, women seem to prefer side-by-side interactions.

FACIAL EXPRESSION

Research suggests that women smile more than men. It is also reported that women tend to be more emotionally expressive with their faces than men; this is, perhaps, related to the conclusion that women are more skilled at both sending and interpreting facial expressions.

GESTURE AND POSTURE

Overall, women appear to use fewer and less expansive gestures than men. Women are more likely, for example, to rest their hands on the arms of a chair while seated; men are more likely to use gestures. Men and women position their legs differently: women cross their legs at the knees or ankles while men are more likely to sit with the ankle of one leg on the knee of the other or with their legs apart.

TOUCH

Men are more likely to initiate touch with others than are women. Women are touched more than men. Men and women also attribute dif- ferent meaning to touch; women are more likely to associate touch with warmth and expressiveness than are men. (We should add a note of caution here. It is wise to take care about whom and when we touch. Touch may be unwelcome and can easily be misinterpreted as harassment. It may be appropriate to hug a friend who has just received a promotion, but it may not be appropriate to hug a co-worker who conveys similar news.)

VOCAL CUES

Vocal patterns may be more related to biological differences in the vocal register than other non-verbal behaviours. Women speak in both higher and softer tones than do men. Women also use their voice to communicate a greater range of emotions than do men. Women are also more likely to raise their pitch when making statements; some people interpret the rising pattern (as in asking a question) as an indication of greater uncertainty.

 ## Recap

DIMENSIONS FOR INTERPRETING NON-VERBAL BEHAVIOUR

Dimension	Definition	Non-Verbal Cues
Immediacy	Cues that communicate liking and pleasure	Eye contact, touch, forward lean, close distances
Arousal	Cues that communicate active interest and emotional involvement	Eye contact, varied vocal cues, animated facial expressions, forward lean, movement
Dominance	Cues that communicate status and power	Protected space, relaxed posture, status symbols

Improving Your Ability to Interpret Non-Verbal Messages

As we have already cautioned, there are no universal dictionaries to which you can turn for help in interpreting specific non-verbal behaviours. People interpret messages of others based on their own experiences and cultural perspective.

One theory that helps explain how to interpret non-verbal messages is called **Expectancy Violation Theory**. Developed by Burgoon and several of her colleagues, this theory suggests that each of us enters a relationship with certain preconceived expectations as to how we expect others to behave.[76] For example, when meeting a business colleague for the first time, most Canadians would expect someone to smile, extend his or her hand, and say, "Hello, I'm Steve Beebe" (or whatever the person's name is). If, instead, the person clasps two hands together and bows demurely without uttering a word, the non-verbal behaviour (or verbal behaviour for that matter) is not what we expected. This violation of our expectation would result in us thinking about what the "violator" of our expectations might mean when bowing instead of offering to shake our hand. When our expectations are violated, we may feel uncomfortable.

Research by communication researchers Beth Le Poire and Stephen Yoshimura found that we tend to adapt to the behaviour of others, even when their behaviour is not what we expected.[77] If someone behaves in a pleasant way to us by smiling, establishing eye contact, and maintaining an open body posture, we are more likely to reciprocate by displaying equally pleasant non-verbal messages. We interpret the messages of others by considering how we *expect* others to treat us and by adapting to others.

Some people are simply better at interpreting non-verbal cues than others. The ability to interpret non-verbal cues is *not* related to a person's ethnicity, amount of education, or intelligence, but it *is* related to certain personality traits. Research offers some clues as to who is the most skilled at encoding non-verbal messages:[78]

1. People who are better at accurately expressing their feelings and emotions are also better able to interpret non-verbal expressions from others.

2. People who are skilled in interpreting one channel of information (for example, facial expression or vocal cues) are likely to be more accurate at interpreting non-verbal messages from other channels (such as posture or use of space).

3. People with certain personality characteristics have been found to interpret non-verbal messages more accurately. For instance, people who are extroverted, have high self-esteem, are non-dogmatic, are not shy, and are expressive typically do a better job of interpreting non-verbal messages than do people who do not have these personality characteristics.

4. People who select such people-oriented jobs as teacher, salesperson, and nurse often have better-than-average skill in interpreting non-verbal messages.

Even if you don't have a natural talent for interpreting non-verbal cues, with training and practice, you can enhance your sensitivity and accuracy in interpreting them. Several principles and key skills can help you to interpret others' non-verbal messages.

Expectancy Violation Theory. Theory that you interpret the messages of others based on how you expect others to behave.

Consider Non-Verbal Cues in Context

Just as quoting an expert out of context can change the meaning of a statement, try-ing to draw conclusions from an isolated snatch of behaviour or a single cue can lead to misinterpretations. Beware of looking at someone's folded arms and concluding that he or she does not like you or is not interested in what you are saying. It could be that the air conditioner is set too low and the person is just trying to keep warm.

Look for Clusters of Non-Verbal Cues

Instead of focusing on a specific cue, look for corroborating cues that can lead to a more accurate conclusion about the meaning of a behaviour. Is the person making eye contact? Is he or she facing you? How far away is he or she standing from you?

Always consider non-verbal behaviours in conjunction with other non-verbal cues, the environment, and the person's verbal message.

Consider Past Experiences When Interpreting Non-Verbal Cues

Familiarity may breed contempt, but it also increases our ability to interpret another's non-verbal behaviour. You may have learned, for example, that when your mother started crying when you played the piano, it meant she was proud of you, not melancholy. Family members can probably interpret one another's non-verbal cues more accurately than can those from outside the family. However, after know-ing someone over a period of time, you begin to increase your sensitivity to certain glances, silences, movements, and vocal cues that might be overlooked or misunder-stood by others.

Check Your Perceptions with Others

You judge others by their behaviour, not by their intent. The only way to know what people intend is to ask them whether you have interpreted their behaviour correctly. However, before you blurt out a hunch, first consider the context and confirming cues; think about this person's previous behaviour. Then, if you are still confused or uncertain about the meaning of a behaviour, ask for clarification. For example, if you receive a tremendous job offer that requires you to move to a new province, and your partner greets your enthusiastic announcement with silence, you could ask, "Does your silence mean that you're opposed to the move, or are you speechless with excitement?" Then wait for a response.

Or suppose you work in the kitchen all day to make a turkey dinner for your friend from Japan. After her first bite, you see her eyes open wide and her lips purse up. So you ask, "Does the expression that I see on your face mean that you don't care for the taste?"

This key skill is called **perception checking**. As we saw in Chapter 3, you can follow four steps to check someone's perception. First, observe and describe the non-verbal cues, making a point to note such variables as amount of eye contact, posture, use of gestures, facial expression, and tone of voice. Second, try to interpret what the individual is expressing through his or her non-verbal behaviour. Next, check your perception by asking him or her if it is accurate. End by using some sort of closure

perception checking.
The skill of asking someone whether your interpretation of his or her non-verbal behaviour is accurate.

that indicates you understand the behaviour, as in the example below. Of course, we are not suggesting that you need to go through life constantly checking everyone's non-verbal cues. Overusing this skill would be irritating to most people. We are suggesting, however, that when you are uncertain of how someone feels, and it is important to know, a perception check may be in order. Consider this example:

Dana: Hi, Mum. I'm sorry Erik and I missed the family reunion last week. It's been a hectic week. The kids had something going on every night and we just needed to rest.

Muriel: *[frowns, has little eye contact, folds her arms, and uses a flat voice.]:* Oh, don't worry about it.

Dana: I know you said don't worry about it, Mum, but it looks like you are still upset. I know that look of yours. I also hear in your voice that you are not really pleased. Is it really OK, or are you still a little miffed?

Muriel: Well, yes, to be honest, Dad and I were really looking forward to getting all of the kids together.

Dana: I'm sorry, Mum. We will make an effort to be at the next one. Thanks for sharing with me how you really felt.

Addressing your question to a specific non-verbal cue will help you interpret your partner's behaviour in future interactions as well. As we noted earlier, evidence suggests that the longer couples are together, the more they rely on non-verbal behaviour to communicate. One study claims that most couples spend less than 11 minutes a week in sustained conversation.[79] Even after 50 years, however, conversation is still required occasionally to clarify non-verbal responses.

▶ **Recap**

HOW TO CHECK YOUR PERCEPTIONS OF OTHERS' NON-VERBAL CUES

Steps	Consider
1. Observe their non-verbal behaviour.	Are they frowning? Do they have eye contact? Are their arms crossed? What is their tone of voice? What is their posture?
2. Form a mental impression of what you think they mean.	Are they happy, sad, angry? Is the non-verbal message contradicting the verbal message?
3. Ask to check whether your perception is accurate.	"Are you upset? You look angry." "Your expression and your voice suggest you don't believe me. Do you think I'm lying?" "The look on your face tells me you really like it. Do you?"

Be Aware That the Non-Verbal Expression of Emotion Is Contagious

Have you ever noticed that when you watch a funny movie, you are more likely to laugh out loud if other people around you are laughing? Or when you are around people who are sad or remorseful, you are more likely to feel and express sadness? There's a reason why this happens. Non-verbal emotional expressions are contagious. People often display the same emotions that a communication partner is displaying. **Emotional contagion theory** suggests that people tend to "catch" the emotions of others.[80] Interpersonal interactions can affect your non-verbal expression of emotions.[81] The ancient Roman orator Cicero knew this when he gave advice to public speakers. He said if you want your audience to experience joy, you must be a joyful speaker. Or, if you want to communicate fear, then you should express fear when you speak. Knowing that you tend to catch or imitate the emotions of others can help you interpret your own non-verbal messages and those of others; you may be imitating the emotional expression of others around you.

emotional contagion theory.
Theory that emotional expression is contagious; people can "catch" emotions just by observing each other's emotional expressions.

Becoming Other-Oriented

CHECKING PERCEPTIONS

We have identified several strategies to improve your skill at interpreting the non-verbal messages of others, including being able to check your perceptions of others. Accurately perceiving others gets to the heart of becoming other-oriented.

Look at the photographs. First, note the non-verbal behaviour of the target person in the picture. Next, form a mental impression of what you think the other person is thinking and feeling. Finally, compose a perception-checking question that the other person in the photo could ask to confirm the target person's thoughts and feelings.

PHOTO 1

A. Describe the student's non-verbal behaviour.

B. What do you think the student is thinking and feeling?

C. What is a perception-checking question the teacher could ask her student?

PHOTO 2

A. Describe the customer's non-verbal behaviour.

B. What do you think the customer is thinking and feeling?

C. What is a perception-checking question the salesman could ask the customer?

Summary

Unspoken messages have a major effect on interpersonal relationships. The primary way in which you communicate feelings, emotions, and attitudes is through non-verbal cues. When there is a contradiction between your verbal and non-verbal messages, others almost always believe the non-verbal one. However, non-verbal messages usually work with verbal messages to create meaning. It is primarily through non-verbal messages that people respond and adapt to others and initiate, maintain, and develop interpersonal relationships. Important as they are, non-verbal messages can also be challenging. They are usually more ambiguous than verbal messages. Although some non-verbal messages have a definite beginning and ending, most are part of a seamless flow of movement, gestures, glances, and inflections. Also, there are culture-based differences in the way we learn and interpret unspoken messages.

Non-verbal cues can be categorized and studied to reveal the codes to our unspoken communication. Movement, posture, and gestures communicate both content and expressive information when we use them as emblems, illustrators, affect displays, regulators, and adaptors. Eye contact is an important code for regulating interaction in interpersonal exchanges. Facial expressions and vocal cues provide a wealth of information about our emotions. Our use of personal space and territory communicates a variety of messages relating to power, status, and other relational concerns. Touch is one of the most powerful cues to communicate liking; and our appearance telegraphs to others how we wish to be treated and how we perceive our role in relation to them.

One of the prime fascinations with non-verbal messages is the potential to understand hidden meaning communicated through unspoken codes. It is more difficult to read non-verbal cues than the words on this page, but there is a general framework that can help you assess the non-verbal messages of others, as well as your own non-verbal expressions. Researchers have identified three primary dimensions for interpreting non-verbal messages: immediacy cues provide information about liking and disliking; arousal cues alert others to our interest and level of engagement with them; and position, power, and status are communicated through dominance cues.

To enhance your skill in interpreting non-verbal messages, always consider the context in which you observed the cues and look for clusters of non-verbal behaviours. The longer you have known someone, the easier it is to interpret his or her unspoken messages, but, to verify whether you understand someone's non-verbal behaviour, you should ask whether your interpretation is accurate.

For Discussion and Review

Focus on Critical Thinking

1. Gabriella has had difficulty getting hired as a manager. One of her best friends suggested that she pay more attention to her non-verbal behaviour when she is interviewed for a job. What advice would you give Gabriella to ensure that she monitors her non-verbal interview behaviour?

2. Greg has been told that he sometimes comes across as cold, aloof, and stand-offish. What could Greg do to communicate his sincere desire to be interpersonally warm and approachable?

Focus on Ethics

3. Achmed really wants to be hired as a salesperson. He hires a fashion consultant to recommend what he should wear and determine how he should look when he interviews for a job. In general, is it ethical to manipulate your appearance to impress others?

4. Is it appropriate to draw definitive conclusions about another's personality and attitudes based only on a "reading" of his or her other non-verbal cues? Support your answer.

5. Is it ethical for salespersons, politicians, and others who wish to make favourable impressions to alter their non-verbal messages to get you to like them, vote for them, or buy their products? Explain your answer.

For Your Journal

1. With a VCR or digital video recorder, record 15 minutes of a TV drama or situation comedy. View the program with the sound turned off. Using the four principles of interpreting non-verbal messages, describe the meaning of the non-verbal messages you watch. After you have made written observations in your journal, view the program with full sound and determine how accurate your interpretations were.

2. Mehrabian has suggested that we convey 55 percent of our emotional meaning through facial expressions, 38 percent through vocal cues, and only seven percent through verbal statements. Spend 30 minutes observing four or five people in a public place, such as a mall, airport, or student centre, and attempt to prove or disprove Mehrabian's conclusions. Before you begin your people watching, design a method for recording your observations in your journal.

Learning with Others

1. Go on a non-verbal communication scavenger hunt. Your instructor will ask you to observe your family members and friends to find one or more of the following sets of non-verbal communicators:

   a.   Examples of emblems, illustrators, affect displays, regulators, adaptors.

   b.   Examples of how people use the four zones of personal space.

   c.   Examples of immediacy, arousal, and dominance.

   d.   Examples of the cognitive, monitoring, regulatory, and expressive functions of eye contact.

   e.   Examples of clothing that reveal intentions or personality traits.

2. Spend some time observing people in a public place, such as a restaurant, airport terminal, student centre, or bar, and write examples of quasi-courtship behaviour as discussed in this chapter on page 188. List the four phases we described (courtship readiness, preening, positional cues, appeals to invitation) on a sheet of paper, and describe several examples to illustrate each of these phases.

3. Using your Research Navigator, key in one of the following numbers to access an article on intercultural communication and some cultural differences: 3539968; 6084793; 15630796. The class could be divided up into groups with each group assigned one of the numbers. Summarize the article and share your findings with the class.

Weblinks

http://zzyx.ucsc.edu/~archer/intro.html   This site will sharpen your skills in identifying the meaning of non-verbal messages.

www.kwintessential.co.uk/resources/country-profiles.html   This is an excellent site on cross-cultural communication including profiles of countries.

http://anthro.palomar.edu/language/language_6.htm   Communication is far more than spoken or written words. Read the article "Language and Culture: Hidden Aspects of Communication at this site."

www.culture-at-work.com/nvcnegotiation.html   At this site you'll learn about the importance of non-verbal communication when negotiating with others.

Conflict Management Skills

After you study this chapter

you should be able to . . .

1. Define conflict.

2. Compare and contrast three types of interpersonal conflict.

3. Identify commonly held myths about interpersonal conflict.

4. Describe differences between destructive and constructive approaches to managing conflict.

5. List and describe five stages of conflict.

6. Describe five conflict management styles.

7. Identify and describe six win–lose and six win–win negotiation strategies.

8. Identify and use conflict management skills to help manage emotions, information, goals, and problems when attempting to resolve interpersonal differences.

- What Is Conflict?

- Types of Conflict

- Myths about Conflict

- Conflict As a Process

- Conflict Management Styles

- Negotiation Strategies

- Conflict Management Skills

Outside noisy, inside empty.

CHINESE PROVERB

T his house stinks," said Paul, wrinkling up his nose. "It smells like day-old garbage."

"Take it out yourself. It's your job," said Simone, turning her back on him to scrub furiously at an imaginary morsel of food on a frying pan that was already polished clean.

"Hey, hey," said Paul, holding up both hands in front of him, "I wasn't accusing you. I just said it smelled bad in here. Don't be so touchy."

"Oh, no? Well, you're always criticizing me. You think just because you have a big important job that you can come in here and say anything you like. I come home from work feeling tired, too, you know, but you don't do anything to help, not even the things you agree to!" shouted Simone, turning around to confront him with her soapy hands on her hips.

"Well, you're always knocking me for no reason. I'm not putting up with this bad treatment from you anymore," snarled Paul. As he turned on his heel to stalk out of the kitchen, Simone burst into tears.

Does this conflict have a ring of familiarity? Do you know why Paul and Simone reached an impasse in their attempt to communicate? Eventually all relationships experience conflict. Paul and Simone's exchange is complicated, seething with conflicting goals and underlying resentments. How do we avoid the same kind of outcome in our own complicated exchanges?

Conflict management is not a single skill but a set of skills. However, to manage conflict effectively involves more than learning simple techniques.

The best route to success in resolving conflict effectively is to acquire knowledge about what conflict is, what makes it happen, and what we can do about it. We begin by defining conflict, examining some of the myths about it, and focusing on some of its constructive functions. We also discuss the relationship among conflict, power, and conflict management styles.

Next, we discuss how learning about your typical style of managing conflict can give you insight into managing interpersonal differences. Finally, we build on our discussions of listening skills and verbal and non-verbal communication developed in the previous chapters to help you learn to manage the inevitable interpersonal conflicts that arise in the best of relationships.

What Is Conflict?

interpersonal conflict.
Expressed struggle that occurs
when people cannot agree on a
way to meet their needs or
goals.

interdependent. Dependent on
each other; one person's actions
affect the other person.

Simply stated, **interpersonal conflict** is a struggle that occurs when two people cannot agree on a way to meet their needs. When the needs are incompatible, if there are too few resources to satisfy them, or if the individuals opt to compete rather than to cooperate to achieve them, then conflict occurs. The intensity level of a conflict usually relates to the intensity of the unmet needs. People involved in such a conflict are **interdependent**; this means that what one person does or says affects others.[1] Unresolved and poorly managed interpersonal conflict is a significant predictor of an unsatisfactory relationship, and the opposite is also true: partners in relationships with effectively managed conflict report being more satisfied with the relationship.[2]

You typically don't know that someone is upset with you until conflict is expressed by a remark or by non-verbal behaviour such as a glare, steely facial expression, or emotion-laden tone of voice. The intensity level of a conflict (expressed through the intensity of non-verbal expressions of emotion) usually relates to the intensity of the unmet needs or goals. Conflict sometimes escalates into physical abuse. According to recent Canadian statistics, eight percent of women and seven percent of men face some sort of violence in their marriage or common-law relationship.[3] Experts surmise that one reason violence is so prevalent in many relationships is that people don't have the skills to manage conflict and disagreement.[4] The *In Canada* box examines violence in relationships in Canada more closely (and there is more on this area in Chapter 11). One researcher developed the "struggle spectrum," shown in Figure 7.1, to describe conflicts ranging from mild differences to fights.[5] At the bedrock of all conflict are differences—in goals, needs, and experiences.

Figure 7.1
The Struggle Spectrum

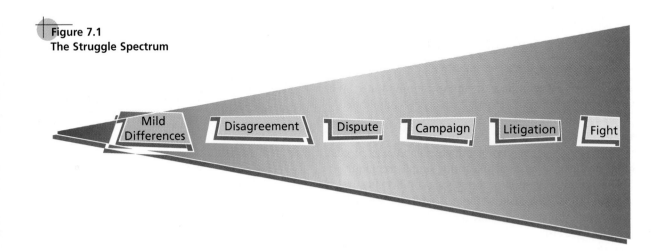

In Canada...

FAMILY VIOLENCE IN CANADA

"Family violence—which includes a range of abusive behaviours that occur within relationships based on kinship, intimacy, dependency or trust—continues to be a disturbingly commonplace occurrence in lives of Canadians through all life stages."[i] While we may think of ourselves as a non-violent society, the family home still represents one of the most violent places in our lives. Conflicts where violence erupts are still occurring in Canada. The most recent report from Statistics Canada, *Family Violence in Canada: A Statistical Profile, 2004*, presents some disturbing statistics.[ii]

- In 2002, females accounted for 85 percent of all victims of spousal abuse reported to police.

- In 2002, girls under the age of 18 represented 79 percent of victims of family-related sexual assaults (as reported to police), with the highest rates being among girls between the ages of 11 and 14.

- Results from parent interviews conducted in the 1998/1999 National Longitudinal Survey of Children and Youth indicate that an estimated eight percent, or one in 12 children, between the ages of four and seven witnessed some type of physical violence in the home.

- Older adults were the least likely of all age groups to be victims of family violence reported to police.

While these previous statistics cover physical and sexual abuse, what about emotional abuse, something that is not likely to come to the attention of the authorities? Emotional abuse includes behaviours like rejecting (such as refusing to acknowledge another person), degrading, terrorizing (such as threatening to hurt a person or stalking), isolating, corrupting and exploiting, and denying emotional responsiveness (such as failing to be responsive to emotional needs). Emotional abuse often accompanies other forms of abuse, but it may also occur on its own. This type of abuse is hard to identify, though there have been some attempts in Canada.[iii] Here are some statistics:

- In 1995, the Canadian Women's Health Test administered at Women's College Hospital in Toronto found that, of 1000 women 15 years of age and over, 36 percent had experienced emotional abuse when growing up, and 39 percent reported experiencing verbal or emotional abuse within the last five years.[iv]

- In a 1993 Canadian study on abuse in university and college dating relationships, 81 percent of male respondents reported they had psychologically abused a female partner.[v]

- The elderly also report incidents of emotional abuse. The 1990 survey on Abuse in the elderly indicated that four percent of seniors residing in private homes experienced abuse and/or neglect.[iii]

Sources: i. Health Canada. *The Family Violence Initiative: Year Five Report*, December 2002, National Clearinghouse on Family Violence, Ottawa. p. ii.
ii. Statistics Canada, Canadian Centre for Justice Statistics. *Family Violence in Canada: A Statistical Profile 2004*, Ottawa: 2004
iii. Health Canada, *Emotional Abuse, The National Clearinghouse on Family Violence*, 1996E. Cat. H 72—22/18 1996E.
iv. Women's College Hospital. *1995 Canadian Women's Health Test*. Toronto, 1995.
v. W.S. DeKeseredy and K. Kelly (1993). *Woman Abuse in University and College Dating Relationships: The Contribution of the Ideology of Familial Patriarchy. The Journal of Human Justice*, 4, 25–52.

Of course, if Wile E. Coyote and Roadrunner ever found a way to resolve their conflicts, we'd stop watching their cartoons. But humans might prefer to find ways to resolve their conflicts.

pseudo-conflict.   Conflict triggered by a lack of understanding and miscommunication.

simple conflict.   Conflict that stems from different ideas, definitions, perceptions, or goals.

ego conflict.   Conflict that is based on personal issues; conflicting partners attack one another's self-esteem.

expressive conflict.   Conflict that focuses on issues about the quality of the relationship and managing interpersonal tension and hostility.

instrumental conflict.   Conflict that centres on achieving a particular goal or task and less on relational issues.

Types of Conflict

At some time or another, many close relationships go through a conflict phase. "We're always fighting," complains a newlywed, but if she were to analyze these fights, she would probably discover that the nature of the fights varied. One research duo found that most conflicts fit into three different categories: (1) **pseudo-conflict**—triggered by a lack of understanding; (2) **simple conflict**—stemming from different ideas, definitions, perceptions, or goals; and (3) **ego conflict**—based on personal differences.[6]

▲●■ Understanding Diversity

GENDER, CULTURE, AND CONFLICT

Research suggests that there are distinctions between feminine and masculine styles of responding to conflict. The feminine style is more likely to focus on relationship issues, whereas the masculine style typically focuses on tasks.[7] Those with the feminine style often interact with others to achieve intimacy and closeness, but those with the masculine style interact to get something done or to accomplish something apart from the relationship. When pursuing a goal, those employing a masculine style are often more aggressive and assertive than those employing a feminine style.[8] The following list summarizes key differences that researchers have observed between feminine and masculine styles of responding to conflict. Note that individuals of either sex may employ some characteristics of both feminine and masculine styles.

Continued

PERCEIVED GENDER DIFFERENCES IN RESPONDING TO CONFLICT[9]

Feminine Styles	Masculine Styles
Are concerned with equity and caring; connect with and feel responsible to others	Concerned with equality of rights and fairness; adhere to abstract principles, rules
Interact to achieve closeness and interdependence	Interact for instrumental purposes; seek autonomy and distance
Attend to interpersonal dynamics to assess relationship's health	Are less aware of interpersonal dynamics
Encourage mutual involvement	Protect self-interest
Attribute crises to problems in the relationship	Attribute crises to problems external to the relationship
Are concerned with the impact of the relationship on personal identity	Are neither self- nor relationship-centred
Often respond to conflict by focusing on the relationship	Often respond to conflict by focusing on rules and being evasive, until a unilateral decision is reached

Although these findings provide a starting point for analyzing our conflicts with members of the opposite sex, we caution against lapsing into "allness" statements such as, "Oh, you're just like all women; that's why you disagree with me," or "You're just like all men; you never want to focus on how I feel." Even thinking in these ways can prevent you from listening to what your partner is saying. Also, although research has identified some gender-based differences in the way we manage conflict, some research studies suggest that the differences can, at times, be quite small. The context for the argument or the specific conflict trigger may be a more important factor than gender in shaping how we respond to and manage interpersonal conflict.[10]

The most recent perspective on analyzing gender differences is called the *partnership perspective*. Rather than viewing gender differences as conflict between people who live on different planets, this perspective suggests that men and women are not locked into particular styles or approaches.[11] The partnership approach emphasizes the importance of keeping channels open and avoiding the tendency to stereotype communication styles by gender.

An individual's culturally learned assumptions influence his or her conflict behaviour. In some cultures, most conflict is **expressive conflict**; it focuses on the quality of relationships, and on managing interpersonal tension and hostility. In other cultures,

instrumental conflict is the norm. It centres less on relationships and more on achieving a specific goal or objective.[12] One researcher noted that for people from low-context cultures (those who derive more meaning from words than from the surrounding context), conflicts are most often instrumental.[13] Most North Americans come from low-context cultures. Many Asian cultures, in contrast, are high-context cultures. They are also collectivist: they value group effort over individual achievement. For people from these cultures, conflicts often centre on expressive, relational concerns. Keeping peace in the group or saving face is often a higher priority than achieving a goal.

Managing culture-based conflict requires a strong other-orientation. One research team has suggested that Anglo-Americans receive little training in how to develop solutions to problems that are acceptable to an entire group.[14] They are often socialized to stick up for their own rights at any cost, and they approach conflict as a win–lose situation. In contrast, people from collectivist cultures approach conflict management situations from a win–win perspective; it is important that both sides save face and avoid ridicule. Such differences in approaches provide a double challenge. In addition to disagreeing over the issue at hand, people from different cultures may also have different strategies for reaching agreement.

Pseudo-Conflict: Misunderstandings

Will: Meet me at the fountain.

Sean: No, that's too far. Meet me by the administration building.

Will: The fountain is closer and more convenient.

Sean: No, it's not.

Will: Yes, it is. It's just off Market Street.

Sean: Oh, you mean the fountain by the administration building.

Will: Sure, that's exactly what I mean.

Sean: Oh, no problem. That's the place I had in mind.

"Pseudo-" means false or fake. Pseudo-conflict occurs when we simply miss the meaning in a message, but unless we clear up the misunderstanding by asking for more information, a real conflict might ensue. Note that in this example, Will offers helpful information ("It's just off Market Street") and Sean checks it with feedback ("Oh, you mean the fountain by the administration building").

How can you avoid pseudo-conflict? A key strategy is to clarify the meaning of words and expressions that you don't understand. Keep the following strategies in mind to minimize misunderstandings before they occur:

- *Check your perceptions:* Ask to clarify what you don't understand; seek to determine whether your interpretation is the same as your partner's.

- *Listen between the lines:* Look for puzzled or quizzical facial expressions of your partner. People may not voice their misunderstanding, but they may express their uncertainty non-verbally.

- *Establish a supportive rather than a defensive climate for conversation:* Avoid evaluating, controlling, using manipulative strategies, being aloof, acting superior, or rigidly asserting that you're always right. These classic behaviours are like pushing the button for increased defensiveness and misunderstanding.

Simple Conflict: Different Stands on the Issues

Simple conflict stems from differences in ideas, definitions, perceptions, or goals. You want to go to Lake Louise for your vacation; your partner wants to go to Quebec City. Your partner wants to fly; you would rather take the train. You understand each other, but you disagree.

A key to unravelling a simple conflict is to keep the conversation focused on the issues at hand so that the expression of differences does not deteriorate into a battle focusing on personalities.

The following exchange between Marc and Nick illustrates a conflict over a simple difference of opinion; notice how both partners stick to the issues and figure out a way to resolve their differences.

Marc: I want to watch *The Simpsons* tonight. It's their Christmas show.

Nick: No way, man. I have to watch a documentary about textiles for my history class. It's an assignment.

Marc: But I've worked all weekend. I'm beat. The last thing I want to watch is some stuffy old documentary on the history of weaving.

Nick: Tell you what. Go ahead and watch *The Simpsons*. I'll video-tape the documentary and watch it later. Deal?

Marc: OK, thanks. And I'll go grill some burgers so we can have supper together first.

This next exchange, between Sue and Nadia, is a bumpier one. What starts as a simple conflict deteriorates into a series of personal attacks.

Nadia: Sue, can I borrow your black skirt? I have a date tonight. It would look great with my new jacket.

Sue: Sorry, Nadia. I'm going to wear it tonight. I've got to give a presentation to the school board about our new volunteer program.

Nadia: In case you don't remember, when you brought it home, you said I could borrow it any time. Besides, you haven't paid back the $20 I loaned you to buy it.

Sue: Yes, but I bought the skirt especially for this occasion.

Nadia: Well, don't ask to borrow anything from me ever again. You're just plain selfish.

Sue: Oh, yeah? Well *you're* the one who hogs all the space in the refrigerator. Talk about selfish. If that's not the pot calling the kettle black!

Nadia: All right, now that we're being honest about who hogs what, *you're* the one who monopolizes the bathroom in the morning.

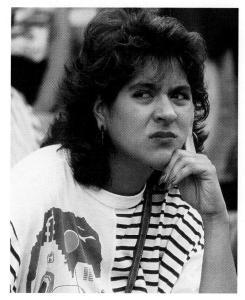

You can avoid pseudo- or false conflict if you ask for clarification, listen between the lines, and work to establish a supportive climate.
(B. Daemmrich/ The Image Works)

So it escalates. The original disagreement about the skirt is forgotten and egos become attacked and bruised.

To keep simple conflict from escalating into personal vendettas, consider the following strategies:

- Clarify your and your partner's understanding of the issues and your partner's understanding of the source of the disagreement.

- Keep the discussion focused on facts and on the issue at hand, rather than drifting back to past battles and unrelated personal grievances.

- Look for more than just the initial solutions that you and your partner bring to the discussion; generate many options.

- *Don't try to tackle too many issues at once.* Perform "issue triage"—identify the important issues and work on those.

- *Find the kernel of truth in what your partner may be saying.* Find agreement where you can.

- *If tempers begin to flare and conflict is spiralling upward, cool off.* Come back to the discussion when you and your partner are fresh.

Ego Conflict: Conflict Gets Personal

As you can see from the preceding example, a personal attack puts your partner on the defensive, and many people behave according to the adage, "The best defence is a good offence." When you launch a personal attack, you are "picking a fight." As Sue and Nadia's exchange illustrates, fights that begin as pseudo- or simple conflicts can easily lapse into more vicious ego conflicts. Here's another example:

Michael: I don't think you should allow students to wear Halloween costumes to school. What can I do with a bunch of monsters and witches in gym class?

Katrina: Well, all the parents are calling me up about it, and the kids are excited.

Michael: Is that how you make decisions? By responding to pressure from parents and kids?

Katrina: You're just disagreeing with me because you wanted to be chair of this committee.

Michael: Not true! I just don't think *you* have the ability to chair it!

Note that as each person in the conflict becomes more defensive about his or her position, the issues become more tangled.

Remember Paul and Simone's argument at the beginning of this chapter? It started with what was probably an offhand remark and escalated into a major argument because both participants began attacking each other and bringing up other sensitive issues instead of focusing on the original comment.

If you find yourself involved in ego conflict, try to refrain from hurling personal attacks and emotional epithets back and forth. Instead, take turns expressing your feelings without interrupting each other, and then take time to cool off. It is difficult to use effective listening skills when your emotions are at a high pitch.

Here are additional strategies to consider when conflict becomes personal:

- *Try to steer the ego conflict back to simple conflict.* Stay focused on issues rather than personalities.

- *Make the issue a problem to be solved rather than a battle to be won.*

- *Write down what you want to say.* It may help you clarify your point, and you and your partner can develop your ideas without interruption. A note of caution: don't put angry personal attacks in writing. Make your written summary rational, logical, and brief rather than emotion-laden.

- *When things get personal, make a vow not to reciprocate.* Use the "I" messages that we talked about in Chapter 5 ("I feel uncomfortable and threatened when we yell at each other.") rather than "you" messages ("You're such a creep. You never listen.") to express how you are feeling.

▶ Recap

TYPES OF CONFLICT

	Pseudo-Conflict	Simple Conflict	Ego Conflict
What It Is	Individuals misunderstand each other.	Individuals disagree over which action to pursue to achieve their goals.	Individuals feel personally attacked.
What to Do	Check your perceptions.	Clarify understanding.	Return to issues rather than personal attacks.
	Listen between the lines; look for non-verbal expressions of puzzlement.	Stay focused on facts and Issues.	Talk about a problem to be solved rather than a fight to be won.
	Be supportive rather than defensive.	Generate many options rather than arguing over one or two options.	Write down rational arguments to support your position.
	Listen actively.	Find the kernel of truth in what your partner is saying; emphasize where you agree.	Use "I" messages rather than "you" messages.

Myths about Conflict

Although not all conflict is destructive to relationships, many cultures have taboos against displaying it in public. The prime experiences in life that shape how we learn to express and manage conflict occur in our families of origin—the families in which we grew up. It's in our families that we learn life lessons about relationships that remain with us throughout our days.[15] According to one researcher, many of us were raised with five myths that contribute to our negative feelings about conflict.[16] As you read the following sections, you may shake your head and say, "That's not where I came from." In some Canadian families, conflict is expressed openly and often. However, even if your experience has been different, reading about these prevailing myths may help you understand your or your partner's emotional responses to conflict.

Myth #1: Conflict Should Always Be Avoided

"If you can't say anything nice, don't say anything at all." Many of us learned early in our lives that conflict is unnatural and that we should eliminate it from our conversations and relationships. Yet evidence suggests that conflict arises in virtually every relationship.[17] Because each of us has a unique perspective on our world, it would be extraordinary for us *always* to see eye to eye with another person. One study found that most romantic couples have some kind of disagreement or conflict, on average, about twice a week. Although such conflicts may not be intense, many differences of opinion punctuate our relationships with people we care about.[18]

Research suggests that contentment in marriage relates not to the amount of conflict but to the way in which partners manage it.[19] Conflict is also a normal and productive part of interaction in group deliberations.[20] It is a myth that we should view conflict as inherently unproductive and something to be avoided. It arises even in the best of relationships.

Myth #2: Conflict Always Occurs Because of Misunderstandings

"You just don't understand what my days are like. I need to go to sleep!" shouts Janice as she scoops up a pillow and blanket and stalks off to the living room. "Oh yeah? Well, you don't understand what will happen if I don't get this budget in!" responds Ron, who is hunched over the desk in their bedroom. It is clear that Ron and Janice are having a conflict. They have identified the cause of their problem as a lack of understanding between them, but in reality, they *do* understand each other. Ron knows that Janice wants to sleep; Janice knows he wants to stay up and work. Their problem is that they disagree about whose goal is more important. This disagreement, not lack of understanding, is the source of the conflict.

Myth #3: Conflict Is Always a Sign of a Poor Interpersonal Relationship

It is an oversimplification to assume that all conflict is rooted in underlying relational problems. Conflict is a normal part of any interpersonal relationship. Although it is true that constant bickering and sniping can be symptomatic of deeper problems, disagreements do not necessarily signal that the relationship is on the rocks. In fact, overly polite, stilted conversation is more likely to signal a problem than are periodic disagreements. The free expression of honest disagreement is a hallmark of a healthy relationship. Assertively expressing honest ideas may mean that a person feels safe and comfortable enough with his or her partner to disagree. As we will discuss later, conflict in interpersonal relationships can play a constructive role in focusing on issues that may need attention. The ebb and flow of interpersonal psychological intimacy and separation inevitably leads to some degree of conflict in any relationship. When conflict happens in your relationships, don't immediately assume that the relationship is doomed.

Myth #4: Conflict Can Always Be Resolved

Consultants, corporate training experts, and self-help book authors often offer advice about how to eliminate conflict so that all will be well and harmony will prevail. Some people claim that with the application of a few skills and how-to techniques, conflicts can disappear, much like a stain from a shirt laundered with the right kind of detergent. This is simply not true. Not all differences can be resolved by listening harder or paraphrasing your partner's message. Some disagreements are so intense and the perceptions so fixed that individuals may have to agree to disagree and live with it.

Myth #5: Conflict Is Always Bad

It's a common fantasy to dream of eliminating all interpersonal conflict from our relationships. It would be bliss, we think, if we could live without disagreement, hassle, haggling, and tension, but conflict is a healthy component of our relationships. In fact, if a relationship is conflict-free, the individuals are probably not being honest with each other. Although it can be destructive, conflict can also help us identify issues that need further discussion and can lead to negotiations that give us fresh insights into the relationship.

> ▶ **Recap**

CONFLICT MYTHS

Myth #1:   Conflict should always be avoided.

Myth #2:   Conflict always occurs because of misunderstanding.

Myth #3:   Conflict is always a sign of a poor interpersonal relationship.

Myth #4:   Conflict can always be resolved.

Myth #5:   Conflict is always bad.

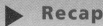

Conflict As a Process

Cathy was reading the Sunday newspaper, enjoying a second cup of coffee, and listening to her favourite classical music station. All seemed well. Suddenly, for no apparent reason, her roommate Kai brusquely stormed into the room and shouted, "I can't stand it anymore! We have to talk about who does what around here." Cathy was completely taken off guard. She had no idea her roommate was upset about the division of household chores. To her, this outburst seemed to come out of the blue; in reality, however, several events had led up to it.

Most relational disagreements have a source, a beginning, a middle, an end, and an aftermath.[21] Let's find out how they function.

Source: Prior Conditions

The first phase in the conflict process is the one that sets the stage for disagreement; it begins when you become aware that there are differences between you and another person. The differences may stem from role expectations, perceptions, goals, or resources. In the previous example, Kai perceived that she and Cathy played different roles in caring for the household.

In interpersonal relationships, *many* potential sources of conflict may be smouldering below the surface. It may take some time before they flare up into overt conflict. Moreover, they may be compounded with other concerns, making them difficult to sort out. However, it may not be just one conversation or issue that triggers conflict; multiple conflict "trip wires" may contribute to a conflict episode.[22]

Beginning: Frustration Awareness

At this stage, at least one of you becomes aware that the differences in the relationship are increasingly problematic. You may begin to engage in self-talk, noting that something is wrong and creating frustration. Perhaps you realize that you won't be able to achieve an important goal or that someone else has resources you need to achieve it. Or you may become aware of differences in perceptions. Kai knew that Cathy's family always used weekends for relaxation. In Kai's family, on the other hand, everyone pitched in on weekends to get household chores done for the week. She may have recognized that difference, even as her frustration level rose.

Becoming aware of differences in perception does not always lead to increased frustration, but when the differences interfere with something you want to accomplish, then your frustration level rises. In Kai's case, she wanted to get the house clean so she could turn her attention to studying for a test she had the next day. Cathy's apparent indifference to helping Kai achieve that goal was a conflict trigger.

Middle: Active Conflict

When you bring your frustration to the attention of others, a conflict becomes an active, *expressed struggle*.[23] If frustrations remain only as thoughts, the conflict is passive, not active. Active conflict does not necessarily mean that the differences are expressed with shouting or emotional intensity. An expression of disagreement may be either verbal or non-verbal. Calmly asking someone to change an attitude or behaviour to help you achieve your goal is a form of active conflict; so is kicking your brother under the table when he starts to reveal your secret to the rest of the family.

Cathy was not aware of the division of labour problem until Kai stormed into the room demanding a renegotiation of roles. Kai had been aware of her frustration for some time yet had not acted on it. Many experts advocate that you do not wait until your frustration level escalates to peak intensity before you approach someone with your conflict. Bottled-up frustration tends to erupt like pop in a bottle that has just been shaken. Intense emotions can add to the difficulty of managing a conflict.

End: Resolution

When you begin to try managing the conflict, it has progressed to the resolution stage. Of course, not all conflicts can be neatly resolved. Couples who divorce, business partners who dissolve their corporation, or roommates who go their separate ways have all found solutions, even though they may not be amicable.

After Kai's outburst, she and Cathy were able to reach a workable compromise about the division of their household labour. Cathy agreed to clean the house every other week; Kai promised not to expect her to do it on weekends.

Aftermath: Follow-Up

After a conflict has been resolved, the follow-up stage involves dealing with hurt feelings or managing simmering grudges, and checking with the other person to confirm that the conflict has not retreated into the frustration awareness stage. As we noted in Chapter 1, interpersonal relationships operate as transactive processes rather than as linear, step-by-step functions. Conflict does progress in stages, but your resolutions can backslide unless you confirm your understanding of the issues with your partner.

The Friday after their discussion, Cathy proudly showed off a spotless apartment to Kai when she came home from class. Kai responded with a grin and a quick hug and privately resolved to get up early on Sunday morning so that she could go out to get Cathy some pastries and the newspaper before she awoke. This kind of mutual thoughtfulness exemplifies a successful follow-up in a conflict.

 Recap

UNDERSTANDING CONFLICT AS A PROCESS

Prior Conditions Stage	The stage is set for conflict because of differences in the individuals' actions or attitudes.
Frustration Awareness Stage	One individual becomes aware that the differences are problematic and becomes frustrated and angry.
Active Conflict Stage	The individuals communicate with each other about the differences; the conflict becomes an expressed struggle.
Resolution Stage	The individuals begin seeking ways to manage the conflict.
Follow-Up Stage	The individuals check with themselves and each other to monitor whether both are satisfied with the resolution.

Understanding the stages of conflict can help you better manage the process. You'll also be in a better position to make the conflict a constructive rather than a destructive experience. Conflict is **constructive** if it helps build new insights and establishes new patterns in a relationship. Airing differences can lead to a more satisfying relationship in the long run. David W. Johnson lists the following as benefits of conflict in interpersonal relationships. Interpersonal conflict:

constructive conflict.
Conflict that helps build new insights and establishes new patterns in a relationship.

- Focuses attention on problems that may have to be solved
- Clarifies what may need to be changed
- Focuses attention on what is important to you and your partner
- Clarifies who you are and what your values are
- Helps you learn more about your partner

By focusing on the problem at hand rather than assuming a defensive attitude, this machinist and his supervisor may reach a constructive solution to their conflict.
(Richard Pasley/ Stock Boston)

- Keeps relationships interesting
- Strengthens relationships by increasing your confidence that you can manage disagreements[24]

Although conflict can be constructive, we don't want to oversell the value or function of conflict in relationships with others. Conflict can also be **destructive**. The hallmark of destructive conflict is a lack of flexibility in responding to others.[25] Conflict can become destructive when people view their differences from a win–lose perspective, rather than looking for solutions that allow both individuals to gain. If the combatants assume that one person will lose, the resulting competitive climate precludes cooperation and flexibility.

One way to minimize destructive conflict cycles is to understand the sequence of conflict-triggering causes so that you can address them at an early stage. It's important to perceive interpersonal conflict not just as something you react to once an issue has surfaced; becoming aware of underlying frustrations before they blossom into active expressions of conflict can help maintain both honesty and trust in a relationship. Also, diagnosing whether the conflict is a misunderstanding, a simple disagreement, or a personal vendetta can give you insight into managing disagreements before they move closer to a fight on the struggle spectrum.

Conflict Management Styles

destructive conflict. Conflict that dismantles relationships without restoring them.

What's your approach to managing interpersonal conflict: fight or flight? Do you tackle conflict head-on or seek ways to remove yourself from it? Most of us do not have a single way of dealing with differences, but we do have a tendency to manage conflict by following patterns that we have used before. The pattern we choose depends on several factors: our personality, the individuals with whom we are in conflict, the time and place of the confrontation, and other situational factors. For example, if your boss gives you an order, you respond differently from the way you would if your partner gives you an order. Virginia Satir author of *Peoplemaking,* a book about family communication, suggests that we learn conflict response patterns early in life.[26]

conflict management styles. The consistent patterns or approaches used to manage disagreements with others.

Several researchers have attempted to identify the patterns or styles of conflict. One of several classifications of conflict is a five-style model based on the work of K. W. Thomas and R. H. Kilmann that includes two primary dimensions: concern for others and concern for self.[27] These two dimensions result in five **conflict management styles**, shown in Figure 7.2. The five styles are: (1) avoidance, (2) accommodation, (3) competition, (4) compromise, and (5) collaboration. Before you read the following sections, try Building Your Skills: Identifying Your Conflict Management Style (pages 227–228), to see what style you typically use in managing conflict.

Avoidance

One approach to managing conflict is to back off and try to sidestep the conflict. Typical responses from someone who uses this style are, "I don't want to talk about it," "It's not my problem," "Don't bother me with that now," or "I'm not interested in that." The **avoidance** style might indicate that a person has low concern for others as well as for himself or herself. This is sometimes called the "lose–lose" approach to conflict. The person using the avoiding conflict style wishes the problem or conflict would go away by itself and appears uninterested in man-

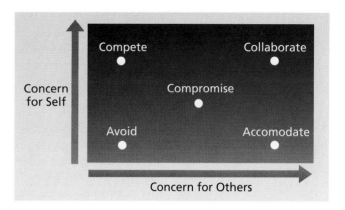

Figure 7.2
Conflict Management Styles
The five conflict manage-
ment styles in relation to
concern for others and
concern for self.

aging the conflict or in meeting the needs of the other person involved in the disagreement. People who avoid conflict may also just not like the hassle of dealing with a difficult, uncomfortable situation. Not dealing directly with conflict may also stem from being unassertive and unable to stand up for one's own rights.

People also avoid conflict sometimes because they don't want to hurt the feelings of others. There may be times when avoiding a major blow-up with someone is a wise strategy, but hoping the conflict will go away on its own is often not the best plan.

Evidence suggests that husbands are more likely to avoid confrontation as a way of managing conflict with their wives. One research team argues that males are likely to avoid conflict because of the way they process information, especially emotions.[28] Avoiding conflict is viewed by husbands as the most comfortable way of managing the uncertainty that is a by-product of conflict. Avoiding becomes a defence mechanism to avoid dissonance that could occur if the conflict were dealt with in a more direct way. In short, husbands may implicitly reason that it's better to keep quiet and avoid conflict than to speak up and try to sort things out; for them, the dissonance that results from speaking up is not worth the effort.

In some respects, avoiding conflict could be perceived as uncooperative. However, although it may not be cooperative, there are some advantages to avoiding conflict. It provides time for each person in the conflict to think about the issues, cool down, and ponder other approaches to dealing with the issues. If the conflict issue really is trivial or silly, it may also be advantageous not to throttle up the tension to make a mountain out of a molehill.

There are also several disadvantages of avoiding conflict. If you avoid the conflict, you may be sending a message that you really don't care about the other person's feelings; you're more concerned about your own needs. Avoiding the conflict may also just make things worse. A conflict that was simply simmering may boil over if it's not tended to. Another disadvantage is that the issue remains unresolved. Like a lump in the throat, the conflict just sits there.

Accommodation

To accommodate is to give in to the demands of others. Someone who accommodates believes it's OK if the other person gets what he or she wants. People may sometimes adopt an **accommodation** style because they fear rejection if they rock

avoidance. Managing conflict by backing off and trying to sidestep it.

accommodation. Managing conflict by giving in to the demands of others.

the boat. They may be seeking approval or trying to avoid threats to their self-worth; to avoid creating a scene, they just do what the other person wants. Or they may be interested in meeting the other person's needs by abandoning their own interests. Sometimes people who accommodate don't seem to get angry or upset; they just do what others want them to do. However, in reality, they also accommodate to serve their own interests—to get people to like them. This conflict management style is sometimes called the "lose–win" approach. If you consistently accommodate, you sacrifice your own needs so that someone else can win the argument.

Using the accommodation style has several advantages. For one thing, it shows that you're reasonable and you want to help. If the issue is a minor or trivial one, you may gain some credibility by just giving in this time. Of course, if you are wrong or have made a mistake, accommodation is an appropriate response.

There are disadvantages to accommodating, just as there are disadvantages to any conflict style. Throughout this book, we've stressed the importance of becoming other-oriented. However, we've also noted that being other-oriented means considering the needs and position of the other person, without necessarily doing what the other person wants. Sometimes a person may accommodate for self-protection rather than because he or she is genuinely interested in others. In the following exchange, note Luke's accommodation response to Martin:

Martin:　Luke, I'm not in agreement with you on the QCN merger. I think the merger should be called off.

Luke:　OK. Whatever you think is best. I just want you to feel good about your decision.

To accommodate can give the accommodator a false sense of security by producing a "pseudo-solution"—one that doesn't really solve anything but just postpones the effort of seeking a solution to the problem. Also, if you consistently accommodate, you may diminish your power to the extent that others take advantage of you; the next time a conflict arises, the expectation may be that you'll give in and the other person will get his or her way again. In addition, if you accommodate too quickly, you short-circuit the possibility of finding a creative solution that is to everyone's liking.

Competition

"You're wrong!" shouts Ed. "Here's how to get our project in on time. We can't waste time in the library. We just have to write up what we have."

"But Ed," notes Derek, "the assignment calls for us to have three library sources."

"No, we don't have time. Just do it," insists Ed.

Ed sees the issue as a competition that he must win.

Each of us has some need to control and also some need to be controlled by others, but people who have a **competition** conflict management style have a win–lose philosophy. They want to win at the expense of the other person, to claim victory over their opponents. They want to control others. They are typically not other-oriented; instead, they are focused on themselves.

People who compete often resort to blaming or seeking a scapegoat, rather than assuming responsibility for a conflict. "I didn't do it," "Don't look at me," and "He made me do it" are typical blaming statements.

If these strategies do not work, people with a competitive style may try threats and warnings. Threats refer to actions that people can actually carry out.[29] Warnings

competition. A conflict management style that stresses winning a conflict at the expense of the other person involved.

are negative prophecies they cannot actually control. The boyfriend who says, "If you don't stop calling me names, I'm going to leave you," has issued a threat; he has the power to leave. If he were to say, "Don't call your parents names or they'll write you out of their will," that would be a warning. In reality, he has no control over his partner's parents.

Obviously, threats are more powerful than warnings in changing behaviour, and then only if the other person would genuinely find the threatened actions punishing or disruptive. If a parent threatens to ground a child, the child will take the threat seriously only if he or she knows the parent will carry it out. If the parent has backed down in the past, the child will probably not pay much attention to the threat.

Is it ever appropriate to compete with others? Yes, if you believe that your position is clearly the best approach and that anything short of achieving your goal would be harmful to you and to others. In an election, someone will win and someone will lose. At the conclusion of a judicial trial, someone typically wins and someone loses, but even hard-fought elections and controversial trials have rules designed to maintain fairness for all involved in the conflict or decision. During often-emotional periods of competition, those involved nonetheless need to maintain an ethical concern for others.

Building Your Skills

IDENTIFYING YOUR CONFLICT MANAGEMENT STYLE

We each learn to manage conflict in different ways. This exercise helps you increase your awareness of your conflict management style.

Complete the following questionnaire, "What Would I Do in a Conflict?" After you've completed and scored the questionnaire, rank-order the five conflict strategies from the one you use most to the one you use least. Your instructor may ask you to discuss your results with another person or with a group of your classmates. Think of examples that illustrate each of the conflict styles.

WHAT WOULD I DO IN A CONFLICT?

1. You and a classmate both want to use the computer at the same time.

   a. I would give up wanting it and give up on the classmate as a friend.
   b. I would try to force the classmate to let me use the computer first.

2. You and a classmate both want the same library book at the same time.

   a. I would give up on wanting it and give up on the classmate as a friend.
   b. I would listen carefully to why my classmate needed the book, and if his reasons were more important than mine, I would let him have it because a good friend is important.

3. You and a classmate both want to use the electric pencil sharpener at the same time.

   a. I would let the classmate go first and give up on her as a friend.
   b. I would ask if we could solve the problem by one person sharpening both pencils so both of us have to wait an equal amount of time.

4. You and a classmate both want to be first in the lunch line.

   a. I would let the classmate go first and give up on him as a friend.
   b. I would compromise by agreeing to alternate who goes first for an equal number of days.

5. You and a classmate both want the same chair at your favourite table in the library.

   a. I would try to force the classmate to let me have the chair, not caring if she is angry or upset with me.
   b. I would listen carefully to why my classmate wants the chair, and if her reasons are more important than mine, I would let her have it because a good friend is important.

Continued

6. You and a classmate are working on a group project. Both of you want to draw the illustrations and neither wants to write the report.

   a. I would try to force the classmate to let me draw the illustrations, not caring if he is angry or upset with me.

   b. I would compromise by agreeing that each of us will draw half of the illustrations and write half of the report.

7. You and a classmate have been playing ball. Neither of you wants to put the equipment away.

   a. I would try to force the classmate to do it, not caring if she is angry or upset with me.

   b. I would ask whether we could solve the problem by putting the equipment away together.

8. You and a classmate are making a video. Both of you want to run the camera, and neither wants to narrate.

   a. I would listen carefully to why my classmate wants to do the filming, and if his reasons are more important than mine, I would let him do it because a good friend is important.

   b. I would ask the classmate to compromise so that each of us films half of the time and each narrates half of the time.

9. You told a classmate a secret, and she told it to several other people.

   a. I would listen carefully to why my classmate told my secret, and if her reasons were more important than mine, I would forgive her because a good friend is important.

   b. I would try to solve the problem by asking my classmate what happened and by working out an agreement about keeping secrets in the future.

10. You and a classmate both believe you did most of the work on a joint report.

   a. I would compromise by agreeing that we both did half.

   b. I would try to solve the problem by reviewing each aspect of the paper and decide who did how much on that aspect.

SCORING PROCEDURE

Circle the letters below that you circled on each question. Then total the number of letters circled in each column.

QUESTION	AVOIDING	COMPETING	ACCOMMODATING	COMPROMISING	COLLABORATING
1.	a	b			
2.	a		b		
3.	a			b	
4.	a				b
5.		a	b		
6.		a		b	
7.		a			b
8.			a	b	
9.			a		b
10.				a	b
Total	____	____	____	____	____

The column with the greatest total indicates your predominant conflict management style. *Remember:* There is no one best style to use all of the time. Although the collaborating or compromising approaches are more likely to result in dialogue, there are times when it may be better to avoid, compete, or accommodate.

Source: David W. Johnson, Reaching Out: Interpersonal Effectiveness and Self-Actualization (Allyn & Bacon, 2000), 253–255. Reprinted/adapted by permission of the publisher.

Compromise

To compromise is to attempt to find a middle ground—a solution that somewhat meets the needs of all concerned. The word *somewhat* is important. Often when people compromise, no one gets precisely what he or she wants; each has to give up a bit of what he or she had hoped to get. When trying to craft a compromise, you're really expecting to lose something and win something simultaneously; you also expect your partner to lose and win. That's why the **compromise** style is called a "lose/win–lose/win" approach to conflict. As shown in Figure 7.2, when you compromise, you have some concern for others as well as some concern for yourself.

Compromise has some advantages. It can be a good thing if a quick resolution to the conflict is needed. To compromise reinforces the notion that all parties involved share in equal power. Compromise can also be useful if what is needed is a temporary solution, and it has the advantage of helping everyone save face because everyone wins at least something.

However, if compromising results in each person giving in but no person feeling pleased with the compromise, then a more collaborative approach to managing the conflict may be appropriate. Compromise can be tempting because it's easy, and while it's true that each party in the conflict may win with a compromise, the flip side is that each party also loses a bit. Finally, to compromise just to make the conflict go away can be another way of avoiding underlying issues that may need to be discussed.

compromise. An attempt to find the middle ground in a conflict.

collaboration. Use of other-oriented strategies to manage a conflict to achieve a positive solution for all involved.

Collaboration

To collaborate is to have a high concern for both yourself and others. People who use a **collaboration** style of conflict management are more likely to view conflict as a set of problems to be solved rather than a game in which one person wins and another loses. Collaboration, which requires other-oriented strategies that foster a win–win climate, is based on the following principles offered by Harvard researchers Roger Fisher and William Ury:[30]

- *Separate the people from the problem.* Leave personal grievances out of the discussion, describing problems without making judgmental or evaluative statements about personalities.

- *Focus on shared interests.* Ask questions such as, "What do we both want?" "What do we both value?" "Where are we already agreeing?" to emphasize common interests, values, and goals.

- *Generate many options to solve the problem.* Use brainstorming and other techniques to generate alternative solutions. (You will learn more about problem-solving techniques later in this chapter).

- *Base decisions on objective criteria.* Establish standards for an acceptable solution to a problem—these standards may involve cost, timing, and other factors. Suppose, for example, that you and your neighbour are discussing possible ways to stop another neighbour's dog from barking all night. You decide on these criteria: the solution must not harm the dog; it must be easy for the owner to implement; the owner must agree to it; it should not cost more than $50; and it must keep the dog from disturbing the sleep of others. Your neighbour suggests, "Maybe the dog can sleep in the owner's garage at night." This solution meets all but one of your criteria, so you call the owner, who agrees to put the dog in the garage by 10:00 p.m. Now everyone wins because the solution meets a sound, well-considered set of objective criteria.

The collaboration conflict management style is best used when those on all sides of the conflict need some new, fresh ideas. Using a collaborative approach also enhances commitment to the resolution of the conflict because all are involved in shaping the outcome. Collaborative approaches to managing conflict build rapport because everyone's concerns are at least noted, if not fully addressed. Finally, collaboration considers feelings and affirms the value of the interpersonal relationship.

It may sound as though collaboration is always the best approach to managing conflict. However, there are times when its disadvantages outweigh the advantages.[31] One of the biggest disadvantages is the time, skill, patience, and energy required to manage conflict collaboratively. If a solution is needed quickly, other approaches such as compromise may be best. Also, some people use the appearance of collaboration as a pretense to compete; a person who is skilled in negotiation and who uses words well can manipulate a collaborative conflict approach to accomplish his or her goals. What may, on the surface, look like collaboration is really competition with a pleasant face and smooth words.

So, which style of managing conflict is best? The short answer to this question is "It depends." It depends on the outcome you seek, the amount of time you have, the quality of the relationship you have with the other people involved, and the amount of perceived power you and others have.[32] Each style has advantages and disadvantages; no style has an inherent advantage all of the time.

The competent, other-oriented communicator consciously decides whether to compete, avoid, compromise, accommodate, or collaborate. Although collaboration seems to be the style preferred by most people, it, too, may not always be appropriate. Research suggests that what most people find most uncomfortable is either: (1) no clear resolution to a conflict, (2) a conflict management process that is poorly managed, or (3) the avoidance of issues that they would like to discuss.[33] *There is no single conflict management style that "works" in all situations.* We do, however, strongly suggest that, when time and other factors permit, a collaborative (win–win) conflict management style is worth exploring.[34] However, because, as the saying goes, "it takes two to tango," it's hard to be collaborative if your partner in the conflict is avoiding or competing. Nonetheless, it's best to be conscious of and competent in the use of strategies and approaches for managing the inevitable disagreements that arise in any interpersonal relationship. The conflict management skills presented at the end of this chapter are anchored in a collaborative approach to managing conflict.

▶ **Recap**

CONFLICT MANAGEMENT STYLES

The person who uses this style...

Avoidance	withdraws from conflict; tries to sidestep confrontation; finds conflict uncomfortable.
	A lose–lose approach to conflict.
Accommodation	easily gives in to the demands of others; typically wants to be liked by others.
	A lose–win approach to conflict.
Competition	dominates the discussion and wants to accomplish the goal even at the expense of others.
	A win–lose approach to conflict.
Compromise	seeks the middle ground; will give up something to get something.
	A lose/win–lose/win approach to conflict.
Collaboration	views conflict as a problem to be solved; negotiates to achieve a positive solution for all involved in the conflict.
	A win–win approach to conflict.

Negotiation Strategies

Negotiation is a communication process in which individuals or groups exchange proposals and interact with each other to create understanding and agreement or to achieve a goal.[35] Negotiation implies that there is a conflict that one or both parties would like to resolve or manage. To agree to negotiate is often the first step toward managing a conflict productively.

Does research offer suggestions for effectively negotiating with others? Yes, but as in many areas of communication research, there is no list of surefire strategies and skills that are guaranteed to be effective in all negotiation situations. Researchers who study how best to negotiate with others have considered two different types of negotiation goals: (1) one of the negotiators wants to achieve his or her goal but is not interested in the other person's achieving his or hers (win–lose), and (2) both negotiators seek the best solution for each person involved in the negotiation (win–win).[36]

negotiation. A communication process in which individuals or groups exchange proposals and interact with each other to create understanding and agreement, or to achieve a goal.

BATNA. The "best alternative to a negotiated agreement": a solution to a conflict that can be achieved without negotiation.

Win–Lose Negotiation Strategies

A win–lose negotiation strategy has many of the characteristics of the competition conflict style. This is not a negotiation style we recommend using as your primary negotiation style. A win–lose posture is typically not other-oriented. Because we acknowledge that there may be situations in which it is appropriate for one person to win and the other person to lose (if, for example, you know the other person is out to destroy you), we describe the win–lose strategies here so that you can recognize these strategies when others employ them when negotiating with you.

- *Win–lose negotiators are typically tough bargainers.* They use a "take it or leave it" approach or say that their offer is only good for a limited time.

- Win–lose negotiators often argue loudly rather than calmly seek consensus.

- *Win–lose negotiators use things the other person values to their own advantage.* They figure out what the other person wants and then skilfully use that to motivate the other person to give in.

- *Win–lose negotiators have other alternatives in mind before starting the negotiation.* Negotiation experts call this the *best alternative to a negotiated agreement,* more commonly known by the acronym **BATNA**.[37] It's a "hip-pocket" way for negotiators to achieve their goal without negotiation.[38]

- *Win–lose negotiators sometimes bluff and mislead their opponent,* although there is research that suggests bluffing can backfire if your negotiation partner calls your bluff.[39]

- *Win–lose negotiators may communicate that they want to reach agreement but may really want to prolong the negotiation* in the hope that the other person will finally just give in.

Win–Win Negotiation Strategies

If your goal is to be collaborative so that all parties involved in the negotiation achieve a benefit, consider the following win–win strategies:

- *Win–win negotiators identify specific, clear, and reasonably high goals for themselves.* International peace negotiator Bill Richardson suggests that making friends, defining your goals, keeping your eyes "on the prize," and shrugging off insults are among the most important elements in any negotiation process.[40]

- *Win–win negotiators are reluctant to lower their goals.* They stand firm while seeking creative ways to achieve what they want.

- *Win–win negotiators know and discuss their priorities.* They make trade-offs on issues of less importance to them.

- Win–win negotiators are good problem solvers.

- *Win–win negotiators know when to hold firm to what is important to them.* They are "selectively contentious," which means they express their passion when the issue or idea under discussion is important to them.[41]

- *Win–win negotiators express a genuine interest in the needs, interests, and goals of the other negotiator* without offering phony support or fake flattery.

 Applying Theory and Research

CULTURAL DIFFERENCES AND PREFERRED CONFLICT MANAGEMENT STYLE

Can cultural differences explain why people have a preference for using a specific conflict management style? That was a question that researchers Deborah Cai and Edward Fink wanted to explore. More specifically, do people from an individualistic culture (people who prefer establishing and maintaining their individual rights) have different preferences for ways of managing conflict than people from a collectivistic culture (where the tendency to work for the good of the group is often stronger than the tendency to achieve individual goals)? The researchers also wanted to know whether there are general trends in preferences for conflict management style.

To address these two issues, the researchers gave people from more than 30 different countries a questionnaire to complete. Some questions were designed to determine whether subjects were from a primarily individualistic or primarily collectivistic culture; other questions assessed subjects' preferred style of managing conflict. The five conflict styles that Cai and Fink defined were similar to the five styles we describe in this chapter: (1) obliging (accommodating), (2) avoiding, (3) domineering (competing), (4) compromising, and (5) integrating (collaborating).

Overall, the researchers found that the integrating (collaborating) style was the most preferred conflict style, regardless of cultural background, followed by obliging (accommodating), compromising, and domineering (competing). People from individualistic cultures preferred the avoiding style more than did people from collectivistic cultures. People from collectivist cultures seemed to prefer compromising and integrating (collaborating) more than did people from individualistic cultures. Another interesting finding was that people from different cultures actually interpreted four of the five conflict styles slightly differently. In other words, people from collectivistic cultures had a different interpretation of what compromising really involved, compared with people from individualistic cultures. Dominating (competing) was the only conflict management style that was interpreted similarly by people in different cultural groups.

APPLYING THE RESEARCH TO YOUR LIFE

What do these results mean to you? Although one survey does not let us draw conclusions that refer to everyone, the results nonetheless suggest some trends.

Continued

- As noted, collaboration (or integration, as it was called in this study) was the most preferred conflict management style, regardless of cultural background. So, if you're uncertain of another person's cultural background, collaboration may be a good "default" approach to managing conflict.
- People from individualistic cultures (such as Canada) are more likely to avoid conflict than are people from collectivistic cultures. Although this is a preference, it doesn't mean that it's always best to avoid conflict; it just means that people from individualistic cultures tend to reach for the avoidance style first. If you're from an individualistic culture, you shouldn't be surprised if others from the same cultural background have a tendency to avoid conflict. Of course, avoidance of conflict does have its advantages, but, as we noted on page 225, it also has disadvantages.
- Because people from collectivistic cultures prefer compromising and integrative collaboration, styles that take time, it may be wise to not rush the conflict management process if you're interacting with someone from a collectivistic culture. In fact, taking your time in managing conflict is probably a good idea no matter whom you're interacting with, unless finding a resolution quickly is important.
- Finally, because someone from a culture other than your own may have a different understanding of what a conflict management style entails, you may think you're being collaborative, but the person from the other culture may not interpret your behaviour as collaborative. The competencies and strategies for enhancing the quality of communication with people from other cultures that will be presented in Chapter 8 are especially useful when managing conflict.

Source: Deborah A. Cai and Edward L. Fink, "Conflict Style Differences Between Individualists and Collectivists," Communication Monographs, 69 (March 2002): 67–87.

Conflict Management Skills

For many people, at the heart of enhancing the quality of interpersonal relationships is learning to manage conflict. Managing conflict, especially emotion-charged ego conflict, is not easy. The more stress and anxiety you feel at any given time, the more likely you are to experience conflict in your relationships with others. When you are under stress, it's more likely that conflict will become personal and degenerate into ego conflict. The opposite is also true: when you're rested and relaxed, you're less likely to experience conflict. However, even while relaxed and with a fully developed set of skills, don't expect to avoid conflict. Conflict happens. The following skills, previewed in our discussion of a collaborative approach to conflict, can help you generate options that promote understanding and provide a framework for collaboration.[42]

Manage Your Emotions

For weeks you have been working on a brochure with a tight deadline. You turned it over to the production department with instructions two weeks ago. Today, you call to check on its progress, and you discover that it is still sitting on the production coordinator's desk. You feel angry and frustrated. How should you respond? You may be tempted to march into her office and scream at her, or to shout at her supervisor.

Try to avoid taking action when you are in such a state. You may regret what you say, and you will probably escalate the conflict.

Often, the first sign that we are in a conflict situation is a feeling of anger, frustration, fear, or even sadness, which sweeps over us like an ocean wave. When we are emotionally charged, we experience physical changes as well. One researcher found that:

> ... our adrenaline flows faster and our strength increases by about 20 percent. The liver, pumping sugar into the bloodstream, demands more oxygen from the heart and lungs. The veins become enlarged and the cortical centers where thinking takes place do not perform nearly as well.... The blood supply to the problem-solving part of the brain is severely decreased because, under stress, a greater portion of blood is diverted to the body's extremities.[43]

Such changes fuel our fight-or-flight responses. If we choose to stay, verbal or physical violence may erupt; if we flee from the conflict, we cannot resolve it. Until we can tone down our emotions (which does not mean eliminating them), we will find it difficult to apply other skills. Let's look at some additional specific strategies that you can draw on when an intense emotional response to conflict clouds your judgment and hampers your decision-making skills.[44]

🌑 Be Aware That You Are Becoming Angry and Emotionally Volatile

One characteristic of people who "lose it" is that they let their emotions get the best of them. Before they know it, they are saying and doing things that they later regret. Unbridled and uncensored emotional outbursts rarely enhance the quality of an interpersonal relationship. An emotional purge may make you feel better, but your partner is likely to reciprocate, which will only escalate the conflict spiral.

Before that happens, become aware of what is happening to you. As we described earlier, your body will start to react to your emotions with an increased heart rate. Be sensitive to what is happening to you physically.

🌑 Seek to Understand Why You Are Angry and Emotional

Understanding what's behind your anger can help you manage it. Realize that it is normal and natural to be angry. It's a feeling everyone experiences. You need not feel guilty about it. Anger is often expressed as a defence when a person feels violated or is fearful of losing something important. Two powerful anger triggers are: (1) feeling that you have not been treated fairly, and (2) feeling entitled to something that you are being denied. Think about the last time you became very angry. Chances are your angry outburst stemmed from a sense that you were not treated fairly or that someone denied you something you were entitled to. Often there is a sense of righteous indignation when you are angry. You are being denied something you feel you should have.

🌑 Make a Conscious Decision about Whether to Express Your Anger

Rather than just letting anger and frustration build and erupt out of control, make a conscious choice about whether you should express your frustration and irritation. We're not denying that there are valid reasons for you to express anger and frustration, or suggesting that you should not express your feelings. Sometimes there is no way to let someone know how important an issue is to you other than by forcefully expressing your irritation or anger. As these lines from William Blake illustrate, sometimes the wisest strategy is to be honest with others and express how you feel.

I was angry with my friend:

I told my wrath, my wrath did end.

I was angry with my foe:

I told it not, my wrath did grow.

If you do decide to express your anger, don't lose control. Be direct and descriptive. The guidelines for listening and responding that we provided in Chapter 4 can serve you well. Keep your anger focused on issues rather than personalities.

Select a Mutually Acceptable Time and Place to Discuss a Conflict

If you are upset, or even tired, you are at risk for an emotion-charged shouting match. If you ambush someone with an angry attack, don't expect him or her to be in a productive frame of mind. Instead, give yourself time to cool off before you try to resolve a conflict. In the case of the lapsed deadline, for example, you could call both the production coordinator and her boss and schedule an appointment to meet with them later in the day. By that time you could gain control of your feelings and also think the issue through. Of course, sometimes issues need to be discussed on the spot; you may not have the luxury to wait. However, whenever it is practical, make sure the other person is ready to receive you and your message.

Plan Your Message

If you are approaching someone to discuss a disagreement, take care to organize your message. Identify your goal and determine what outcome you would like; do not barge in and pour out your emotions.

Breathe

One of the simplest yet most effective ways to avoid overheating is to breathe. As you become aware that your emotions are starting to erupt, take a slow, deep breath. Then breathe again. This can help calm you and manage the physiological changes that adrenaline creates. Deep breathing—the prime strategy women use to manage the pain of childbirth—can be a powerful way to restore calmness to your spirit. Focusing on your breathing is also one of the primary methods of meditation. We're not suggesting that you hyperventilate, but taking deep, slow breaths that not only fill your upper lungs but move your diaphragm is an active strategy to help you regain rational control.

Monitor Non-Verbal Messages

As you learned in Chapter 6, your actions play a key role in establishing the emotional climate in any relationship. Monitoring your non-verbal messages can help to de-escalate an emotion-charged situation. Speaking calmly, using direct eye contact, and maintaining a natural facial expression will signal that you wish to collaborate rather than control. Your non-verbal message should also support your verbal response. If you say you are listening to someone, but you continue to read the paper or work on a report, you are communicating a lack of interest in the speaker and the message.

Avoid Personal Attacks, Name-Calling, and Emotional Overstatement

Using threats and derogatory names can turn a simple conflict into an ego conflict. When people feel attacked, they will respond by protecting themselves. Also, try to avoid exaggerating your emotions. If you say you are irritated or annoyed rather than furious, you can still communicate your feelings, but you will take the sting out of your description. Avoid the bad habit of **gunny-sacking**. This occurs when you dredge up old problems and issues from the past, like pulling them out of an old bag or gunny sack, to use against your partner. Keep your focus on the issues at hand, not on old hurts. Gunny-sacking usually succeeds only in increasing tension, escalating emotions, and reducing listening effectiveness.

gunny-sacking. Dredging up old problems and issues from the past, like pulling them out of an old bag or gunny sack, to use against your partner.

 Becoming Other-Oriented

TIPS FOR MANAGING ANGER

One of the biggest obstacles to being other-oriented during conflict is the anger we often experience when we feel we're not being listened to or our rights are being violated.[45] Anger is an emotional response to fear. Stated another way, anger is an outward response to an inward feeling of fear. Also, fear is often about losing something or not getting something we believe is rightfully ours. We may become angry, for example, if we fear we may lose our job or if we sense a relationship that is important to us may be dissolving or becoming less important to the other person. Anger also occurs when we feel someone is keeping us from what we want and have a right to have, someone is unjustly blaming us for something, or someone is attacking us.

Some people may tell you it is a good idea to express your anger to the person who is making you angry; get your anger out; don't keep it bottled up. There are times when expressing your anger is appropriate. Being assertive in expressing what bothers you is appropriate when the other person is not aware of what is bothering you, but uncensored angry words

can escalate the anger you feel and also increase others' anger.[46] One research team offers these prescriptions for managing your own anger or coping with someone else's anger during conflict.[47]

● *Be determined not to get angry yourself.* If you know you are going to face someone who is likely to tick you off, prepare yourself before you meet with him or her. Assertively express your feelings, but make a promise to yourself not to "lose it" and allow the encounter to degenerate into a shout fest.

● *Get on the same physical level as the other person.* One person should not be standing and the other sitting. Try to face each other eye-to-eye. You can also build rapport by trying to mirror the posture of the other person. We're not suggesting that you mimic your partner (this would probably make him or her more angry), but try to adopt a similar communication position.

● *Be silent.* If you are angry and afraid you might say something you'll regret, just be quiet and listen.

● *Express your concern non-verbally.* Because much of an emotional message is communicated

non-verbally, use your facial expression and eyes to let the other person know you care about him or her. Your communication partner will believe what you do, more than what you say.

● *Make an appropriate empathic statement.* Saying, "I would probably feel angry if I had experienced what you experienced" or "I think I can see why you are so upset" may help. Be careful not to say, "I know just how you feel" or "I know where you're coming from." For many people, those statements can seem patronizing.

● *Remind yourself that you control your own emotions.* Even though others may do and say things that can upset you, you are the only person who can control yourself and your response to others. Try to respond mindfully to others rather than just reacting emotionally to them.

● *Recognize that angry emotional outbursts rarely change someone's mind.* Exploding in an angry tirade may make you feel better for a moment by getting it "off your chest," but it usually does little to advance understanding and manage the issues at hand.

Take Time to Establish Rapport

Evidence suggests that you'll be more successful in managing conflict if you don't immediately dive in and attempt to sort out the issues with your partner.[48]

Taking time to establish a positive emotional climate can pay big dividends; this is especially important if you're not well-acquainted with the person you're having the conflict with. One study compared how effectively conflict was managed in two different groups.[49] In one group, the conflict negotiators spent time face to face, "schmoozing" and getting to know one another before trying to negotiate a solution to a conflict. In the other group, the negotiators exchanged information via e-mail but did not meet face to face. The negotiators who spent time establishing a positive relationship in person were more successful in managing the conflict to everyone's satisfaction. Schmoozing is important in building rapport and establishing a positive communication climate.

What strategies do this mother and daughter seem to have drawn on to manage their conflicts?

Even if you know the other person well, take some time to build rapport. Chatting about such seemingly innocuous topics as the weather or local events can help break the ice and provide a basis for a more positive conversational climate. A positive emotional climate is especially important when trying to sort through vexing, conflict-producing issues.

Several researchers also note how important it is to help the other person in the conflict save face—to help him or her not leave the conversation feeling demoralized and humiliated.

Use Self-Talk

When Tom was chairing the committee meeting, Monique accused him of falsifying the attendance numbers at the last fine arts festival. Instead of lashing back at Monique, he paused, took a slow, deep, yet unnoticed breath and thought, "I'm tired. If I snarl back, all we will do is escalate this issue out of proportion. I'll talk with Monique later after we have both cooled down." Perhaps you think that talking to yourself is an eccentricity. Nothing could be further from the truth. As you saw in Chapter 2, thoughts are directly linked to feelings,[50] and the messages we tell ourselves play a major role in how we feel and respond to others. Ask yourself whether an emotional tirade and an escalating conflict will produce the results you want.

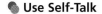

Manage Information

Because uncertainty, misinformation, and misunderstanding are often by-products of conflict and disagreement, skills that promote mutual understanding are an important component of cooperative conflict management. Based on the describing, listening, and responding skills discussed in Chapter 4, the following specific suggestions can help you reduce uncertainty and enhance the quality of communication during conflict.

Clearly Describe the Conflict-Producing Events

Instead of just blurting out your complaints in random order, think of delivering a brief, well-organized mini-speech. When Lise almost had a car accident, she came home and told her husband, "Last week you said you would get the brakes fixed on the car. On Monday, when you still hadn't taken the car in, you said you would do it on Wednesday. Now it's Friday and the brakes are in even worse shape. I had a close call this afternoon when the car almost wouldn't stop. We've got to get those brakes fixed before anyone drives that car again."

"Own" Your Statements by Using Descriptive "I" Language

I feel upset when you post the week's volunteer schedule without first consulting with me," reveals Natasha. Her statement describes her feelings as her own. **"I" language** expresses how a speaker is feeling. The use of the word "I" conveys a willingness to "own" one's feelings and statements about them.

If she had said, "You always prepare a schedule without telling anyone first. All of us who volunteer are mad about that," her statement would have had an accusatory sting. Beginning the statement with "you" sets the listener up for a defensive response. Also, notice that in the second statement, the speaker does not take responsibility for the anger; she suggests that it belongs to other unidentified people as well. If you narrow the issue down to a conflict between you and the other person, you put the conflict into a more manageable framework.

Use Effective Listening Skills

Managing information is a two-way process. Whether you are describing a conflict situation to someone or that individual is bringing a conflict to your attention, good listening skills will be invaluable.

Give your full attention to the speaker and make a conscious point of tuning out your internal messages. Sometimes the best thing to do after describing the conflict-producing events is simply to wait for a response. If you don't stop talking and give the other person a chance to respond, he or she will feel frustrated, the emotional pitch will go up a notch, and it will become more difficult to reach an understanding.

Finally, do not just focus on the facts or details but analyze them so you can understand the major point the speaker is making. Use your understanding of the details to interpret the speaker's major ideas. Remember to stay other-oriented and "seek to understand rather than to be understood."[51]

Check Your Understanding of What Others Say and Do

Respond clearly and appropriately. Your response and that of your conflict partner will confirm that you have understood each other. Checking perceptions is vital when emotions run high.

If you are genuinely unsure about facts, issues, or major ideas addressed during a conflict, ask questions to help you sort through them instead of barging ahead with solutions. Then, summarize your understanding of the information; do not parrot the speaker's words or paraphrase every statement, but check key points to ensure that you have understood the message. Note how Kamal adeptly paraphrases to check his understanding:

Maggie: I don't like the conclusion you've written to the conference report. It does not mention anything about the ideas suggested at the symposium. I think you have also misinterpreted the CEO's key message.

"I" language. Statements that use the word "I" to express how a speaker is feeling.

Kamal: So, if I understand you, Maggie, you're saying the report missed some key information and may also include an inaccurate summary of the CEO's speech.

Maggie: Yes, Kamal. Those are the concerns I have.

Be Empathic

Understand others not only with your head but also with your heart. To truly understand another person, you need to do more than catch the meaning of his or her words; you need to put yourself in the person's place emotionally. Ask yourself these questions: What emotions is the other person feeling? Why is he or she experiencing these emotions? Throughout this book, we have stressed the importance of becoming other-oriented. It's especially important to be other-oriented when you disagree with another person. Trying to understand what's behind your partner's emotions may give you the insight you need to reframe the conflict from your partner's point of view. With this other-oriented perspective, you may see new possibilities for managing the conflict.

How do you become empathic? Use the collection of skills that we've discussed in several previous chapters as well as in this chapter. Here's a brief summary of how to be empathic:

- *Stop:* Stop making your arguments and concentrate on your partner's points. Socially decentre by taking into account the other person's thoughts, feelings, values, culture, and perspective. How is your partner "making sense" out of what has happened to him or her? Don't keep hammering at your own ideas; think about how the other person got to the conclusion he or she has arrived at.

- *Look:* Monitor your partner's emotions by observing his or her non-verbal messages. Look for emotional cues in your partner's face; listen for the tone of voice; observe posture and gestures to gauge the intensity of the feelings being expressed. Mentally summarize what emotions you think your partner is experiencing.

- *Listen:* Concentrate on what the other person is saying. Listen both for the details and for the main points the other person is making. Focus on the overall story he or she is telling. Mentally summarize the key ideas your partner is making.

- *Imagine:* Based on your understanding of what your conflict partner has experienced and is feeling, imagine how you would feel if *you* were in your partner's place. True empathy is feeling what your partner is feeling, or at least trying to imagine as best you can the emotions your partner is experiencing.

- *Question:* If you need more information about what your partner has experienced or if there is something you don't understand, gently ask appropriate questions. Don't blast your partner with accusing or negative questions. Just calmly ask for more background information if you need it.

- *Paraphrase:* To confirm your understanding of your partner's point of view, briefly summarize what you think your partner is thinking or feeling. Statements such as, "You're upset with me because you believe I lied to you," "You're feeling frustrated," or "You're angry with me" are examples of paraphrasing statements.

No checklist of skills will magically melt tensions resulting from long-standing or entrenched conflict, but trying honestly to understand both a person's position and the emotion behind it is a good beginning to developing understanding. Realize that it will be difficult to stop, look, listen, imagine, question, and paraphrase if both you and your partner are emotionally agitated. In fact, it's likely you won't use a rational approach to managing conflict until emotional outbursts and intense feelings are toned down a bit. Unchecked emotions are a formidable barrier to understanding or empathizing with others.

Manage Goals

As we have seen, conflict is goal-driven. Both individuals involved in an interpersonal conflict want something, and for some reason, be it competition, scarce resources, or lack of understanding, the goals appear to be in conflict. To manage conflict, it is important to seek an accurate understanding of these goals and to identify where they overlap.

Identify Your Goal and Your Partner's Goal

After you describe, listen, and respond, your next task should be to identify what you would like to have happen. What is your goal? Most goal statements can be phrased in terms of wants or desires. Consider the following examples:

Problem	Goal
Your boss approaches you and wants you to work overtime; you need to pick up your son from daycare.	You want to leave work on time; your boss wants the work completed ASAP.
Your partner wants to sleep with the window open; you like a warm room and sleep better with the window closed.	You want a good night's rest; your partner wants a good night's rest.
Your six-year-old son wants to go to a swim party where there are no lifeguards.	You want your son to be safe; your son wants to have a good time.

Often in conflicts, you will be faced with balancing the achievement of your goal against the goal of maintaining the relationship that you have with your partner. Eventually, you may decide that the latter goal is more important than the substantive conflict issue.

Research by Charles Pavitt and Bradley Kemp confirms the significant role of relationships in conflict and negotiation situations.[52] If you're negotiating with someone you like, you will expect your negotiation partner to use more supportive approaches to achieve the goal. Conversely, if you're negotiating with someone you don't like, you will expect that person to use more threats and demands and be more obstinate.

Next, it is useful to identify your partner's goal. In each of the problems on page 240 you would need to know what the other person wants so that you can manage the conflict. Use effective describing, listening, and responding skills to determine what each of you wants and to verbalize your goals. Obviously, if you both keep your goals hidden, it will be difficult to manage the conflict.

Identify Where Your Goals and Your Partner's Goals Overlap

Roger Fisher and William Ury stress the importance of focusing on shared interests when seeking to manage differences.[53] Armed with an understanding of what you want and what your partner wants, you can then determine whether the goals overlap. In the conflict over whether the window should be open or closed, the goal of both parties is the same: each wants a good night's sleep. Framing the problem as "how can we achieve our mutual goal," rather than arguing over whether the window should be open or closed, moves the discussion to a more productive level.

If you focus on shared interests (common goals) and develop objective, rather than subjective, criteria for the solution, there is hope for finding a resolution that will satisfy both parties.

Manage the Problem

If you can structure conflicts as problems to be solved (see Table 7.1) on page 242 rather than battles to be won or lost, you are well on your way to seeking strategies to manage the issues that confront you and the other person involved in the conflict. There are many models of problem solving that can be used to arrive at a solution that everyone can live with in all kinds of conflicts. Most models rely on a set of defined steps that help clarify the problem, analyze the problem, generate and evaluate possible solutions, implement the chosen solution, and then evaluate the solution at a given date. These models can be found in business texts and counselling texts and are actively used by many organizations such as the Ontario Provincial Police and many corporations such as IBM Canada. Here, we will focus on a very straightforward model: define the problem, analyze the problem's causes and effects, generate many possible solutions, select a solution that best achieves the goals of the conflicting parties, and then evaluate the solution at a mutually agreed-upon date.

Define the Problem

Most problems boil down to something you want more of or less of. You can think of a problem as a "deviation" from where you would like to be or what you want regarding a specific issue. If you feel you are putting in too many hours at the office, the deviation is the difference between the number of hours you feel you should be working and the number of hours you are actually working.

Table 7.1 Solving Problems: One Method of Organizing Problem-Solving Discussions

1. Define the problem.	What is the issue?
2. Analyze the problem.	What are the causes, symptoms, effects, and obstacles?
3. Determine the goals.	What do you want? What does your partner want? How do the goals overlap?
4. Generate multiple solutions.	List many options rather than debating one or two strategies for achieving the goal.
5. Select the best solution and try it.	Eliminate options that are not mutually agreeable. If possible, take the best ideas from several generated to reach an amicable resolution.
6. Set a time to evaluate the chosen solution.	Periodically, revisit your solution to see if it is appropriate to your current situation.

Make sure that you *define the "real" problem* and not just the symptoms. Cara and Ian have been living together for over a year. Lately, they have been fighting over small issues. They decide to spend some time talking about what is wrong and trying to understand each other. Rather than just dealing with symptoms (Cara complains that Ian snores at night), they keep talking until they get at the "real" or root problem. Cara wants to get married to Ian now. Ian wants to stay with Cara, but he wants to wait until he feels ready for marriage. He also wants to feel financially secure before he marries.

Analyze the Problem

Next, *analyze the problem.* To analyze is to break something down into its components. With the other party, begin by describing the conflict-producing events in chronological order (see page 238). Then, decide what type of conflict it is. If your analysis reveals it as a pseudo-conflict, keep on with the analysis process. Attempt to ferret out the rest of the symptoms, effects, and obstacles; decide whether the conflict stems from several sub-problems or from one major issue. As you proceed, you and the other party may decide that you need more information to help clarify the issues.

After some discussion, Cara and Ian analyze their problem. They realize they come from different family backgrounds and have different expectations about marriage. Cara's parents were high school sweethearts, were married when both were 18, and are still happily married after almost 25 years together. Ian's parents are older; they met after each of them had been divorced, and they married after a long, slow-paced relationship. Cara's and Ian's different frames of reference help explain their feelings about the timing of marriage. Often, it is these different frames of reference, or perceptions of how events should be timed or completed, that can be at the root of interpersonal conflict.

Determine the Goals

The next step in managing the problem is to *determine your goals and your partner's goals* by following the information presented above on managing goals. Generate objective criteria for a solution using the previous guidelines about identifying you and your partner's goals. The more measurable, verifiable, and objective the criteria, the greater the likelihood that both parties will agree when the criteria have been met. Cara and Ian decide that, ultimately, they have the same goal—to get married. The issue boils down to timing. They decide to seek a course of action that will make them both feel secure.

Generate Multiple Solutions

Their next step is to *generate multiple solutions*. Simply understanding the issues and the causes, effects, symptoms, and history of a problem will not enable you to manage a conflict. It takes time and creativity to find mutually satisfactory solutions to most problems. It stands to reason that the more solutions you generate, the greater the probability that you can manage the conflict constructively. One way to generate options is through brainstorming. To use brainstorming, try the following suggestions:

1. Make sure the problem and the goals are clear to both of you.
2. Try to temporarily suspend judgment and evaluation; do not censor your thoughts.
3. Specify a certain time period for brainstorming.
4. Consider having each partner brainstorm ideas separately before a meeting, or write ideas down before verbalizing solutions.
5. Try to develop at least one unique or far-out idea. You can always tame wild ideas later.
6. Piggyback off the ideas of your partner. Encourage your partner to use or modify your ideas.
7. Write down all of the ideas suggested.
8. Review each idea, noting ways to combine, eliminate, or extend them.

If the goal is to find the best way to manage the difficulty, it may take only one good idea to help move the conflict forward to a constructive resolution.

When they brainstorm, Cara and Ian generate the following options: save money for a year and then get married; take turns going to college; take turns working to support the family while the other gets a degree; get married now, get jobs and postpone college; get married now and take out student loans.

Select the Best Solution and Try It

Cara and Ian decide to *select the best solution*. Sometimes, it may take several attempts at defining, analyzing, goal-setting, and generating multiple ideas before a mutually agreeable solution emerges. It is always appropriate to recheck your understanding of the issues and goals. Cara and Ian decide to combine the best of several ideas. They agree to get engaged but not to set a date. Instead, they set a financial goal of $5000 in savings. When they reach that goal, they will set a wedding date. If they are both attending college, they will get part-time jobs so that they have income, and they will also apply for student loans.

If, after repeated attempts, you cannot arrive at a mutually acceptable solution, you may decide to keep trying. Or you may agree to take the issue to an impartial person who can help you identify conflict management strategies and solutions. At work, your immediate superior may be called in to help settle the matter. Or, occasionally, you may agree to disagree and drop it.

The goal of managing conflict is not just to solve a problem but to help manage relational issues with your partner, especially if your partner thinks he or she has "lost" the conflict. When seeking a solution to interpersonal problems, try to find ways for your partner to "win" while you also achieve your goal. Help your partner save face.

The concept of **face**, first introduced in Chapter 2, refers to the self-image or self-respect that you and your partner seek to maintain.[54] Communication researcher Stella Ting-Toomey has conducted studies that emphasize the importance of face-saving or maintaining a positive image, especially in collectivist cultures such as those in Asia, where maintaining face is especially important.[55] How do you help someone save face and avoid embarrassment? Sometimes you can offer genuine forgiveness. Or you can offer explanations that help reframe the differences, perhaps suggesting that it was really just a misunderstanding that led to the disagreement. After a tough-fought hockey game, a victorious, well-mannered coach may say, "They were great opponents. I have much admiration for the way they played." Such face-restoring comments can help mend bruised egos. Such is also the case during interpersonal conflict. Finding ways to be gracious or to allow your partner to save face is an important other-oriented approach to dealing with people.

face. Self-image or self-respect that you and your partner seek to maintain.

● Set a Time to Evaluate the Chosen Solution

To agree to a solution is not enough. Each of the parties must live up to his or her end of the agreement. What if, after a year, Cara and Ian have not saved any money? What might happen if they have to attend different colleges? Once a solution has been agreed on and implemented, many variables can get in the way of the intended goals. Periodic checking, particularly with long-term solutions, is necessary to keep the parties focused and to examine if other problems are creeping into the solution. Cara and Ian may have to go back to any of the previous steps and work through more problems and differences.

Even though we have presented these conflict management steps as prescriptive suggestions, it is important to remember that *conflict rarely follows a linear, step-by-step sequence of events*. These skills are designed to serve as a general framework for collaboratively managing differences, but if your partner does not want to collaborate, your job will be more challenging.

In reality, you don't simply manage your emotions and then move neatly on to developing greater understanding with another person. Sorting out your goals and your partner's goals is not something that you do once and then put behind you. It will take time and patience to balance your goal of maintaining a relationship with your immediate achievement goals. In fact, as you try to manage a conflict, you will more than likely bounce forward and backward from one step to another. This framework gives you an overarching perspective for understanding and actively managing disagreements, but the nature of interpersonal relationships means that you and your partner will respond—sometimes in unpredictable ways—to a variety of cues (psychological, sociological, physical) when communicating. Think of the skills you have learned as options to consider rather than as hard-and-fast rules to follow in every situation.

Summary

Interpersonal conflict is an expressed struggle that occurs when two people cannot agree on a way to meet their needs or goals. At the root of all conflicts are our individual perspectives, needs, and experiences.

Conflict can result from misunderstanding someone (pseudo-conflict), or it can stem from a simple difference of opinion or viewpoint (simple conflict). Ego conflict occurs when personalities clash; the conflict becomes personal and you may feel a need to defend your self-image.

Myths about the conflict management process tell us that conflict should always be avoided; that conflict always occurs because of misunderstandings; that conflict always occurs because of a poor interpersonal relationship; and that conflict can always be resolved. However, conflict in interpersonal relationships is not always destructive. It can actually play a constructive role by identifying areas that need attention and transformation.

Although conflict seems to erupt suddenly, it often originates in events that occur long before the conflict manifests itself. It evolves from these prior conditions into frustration awareness, active conflict, resolution, and follow-up stages. Understanding conflict as a process also involves recognizing how people seek and are given control over others.

People develop patterns or styles of managing conflict. We identified five conflict management styles in this chapter: (1) avoidance, (2) accommodation, (3) competition, (4) compromise, and (5) collaboration. A person using the avoidance style simply seeks to withdraw from conflict. The accommodation style involves easily giving in to the demands of others. To compete is to dominate the discussion in order to achieve the desired goal, typically at the expense of another person's achieving his or her goal. The compromiser seeks a middle ground and is willing to give up something to gain something. Finally, the collaborator views conflict as a problem to be solved and seeks a solution that allows all parties to win.

Closely related to conflict management styles are styles of negotiating disagreements. To negotiate is to exchange proposals and interact with others to create understanding, or agreement, or achieve a goal. We described both win–lose negotiation strategies and win–win strategies.

We concluded the chapter by presenting a summary of conflict management skills. Specifically, we addressed how to manage emotions, manage information, manage goals, and manage the problem. It's usually best to focus on the partner's needs before attempting to resolve the underlying cause of your conflict.

For Discussion and Review

Focus on Critical Thinking

1. Richard has an explosive temper. He consistently receives poor performance evaluations at work because he lashes out at those who disagree with him. What strategies might help him manage his emotional outbursts?

2. Melissa and Antonio always seem to end up making personal attacks and calling each other names when they get into a disagreement. What type of conflict are they experiencing when they do this, and how can they avoid it?

3. Analyze the opening dialogue in this chapter. What are Simone and Paul doing wrong in managing their differences? Are they doing anything right?

4. Log onto your Research Navigator and access article AN13257276, titled "Defence Mechanisms and Self-Reported Violence Toward Partners and

Strangers." This is an interesting study with male college students as subjects with some limitations. Do you think young people are more violent than older people? If so, what strategies would you propose to assist younger people in reducing violence after reading the results of this study?

Focus on Ethics

5. Is it ethical to mask your true emotions to get along with others? Is honesty in a relationship always the best policy? Explain your response.

6. If saving face is important after a conflict, is it ethical to lie in an attempt to make the other person feel better? Explain your answer.

7. Are there situations in which you should *not* assert your point of view? Provide an example to support your answer.

For Your Journal

1. Consider a recent conflict you have had with someone. Determine whether it was a pseudo-, simple, or ego conflict. Describe the strategies you used to manage the conflict. Now that you have read this chapter, discuss the other strategies you could have used to help manage the disagreement.

2. Identify a current or recent conflict you are having or have had with a friend or acquaintance. Use the problem-solving steps presented in this chapter to seek a solution to the problem that is creating the conflict. Define the problem (identify the issues). Analyze the problem (identify the causes, symptoms, effects, and obstacles that keep you from achieving your goal). Determine your goal (identify what you want and what your partner wants). Generate many possible solutions that would solve the problem, and select the one(s) that would permit each person to achieve his or her goal. Finally, select a time when you can review the solution(s) and make any necessary changes.

3. Briefly, describe a conflict during which you did *not* do a good job of managing your emotions, that is, one in which you became angry and upset and lost your cool. Respond to the following questions: Why did you lose control of your emotions? If you could go back in time, what would you do differently to better manage your emotions before and during the conflict? Consider incorporating some of the suggestions discussed in this chapter.

Learning with Others

1. Win As Much As You Can[56]

   This activity is designed to explore the effects of trust and conflict on communication. You will be paired with a partner. There will be four partner teams working in a cluster.

4 Xs: Lose $1 each
3 Xs: Win $1 each
1 Y: Lose $3
2 Xs: Win $2 each
2 Ys: Lose $2 each
1 X: Win $3
3 Ys: Lose $1 each
4 Ys: Win $1 each

Directions: Your instructor will provide detailed instructions for playing this game. For 10 successive rounds, you and your partner will choose either an X or a Y. Your instructor will tell all partner teams to reveal their choices at the same time. Each round's payoff will depend on the decision made by others in your cluster. For example, according to the scoring chart shown above, if all four partner teams mark X for round one of this game, each partner team loses $1. You are to confer with your partner on each round to make a joint decision. Before rounds 5, 8, and 10, your instructor will permit you to confer with the other pairs in your cluster. Keep track of your choices and winnings on the score sheet below. When you finish the game, compare your cluster's results with those of others. Discuss the factors that affected your balances. There are three key rules:

- Do not confer with the other members of your cluster unless you are given specific permission to do so. This applies to non-verbal and verbal communication.

- Each pair must agree on a single choice for each round.

- Make sure that the other members of your cluster do not know your pair's choice until you are instructed to reveal it.

Round	Time Allowed	Confer with	Choice	$ Won	$ Lost	$ Balance	
1	2 min.	partner	_____	_____	_____	_____	
2	1 min.	partner	_____	_____	_____	_____	
3	1 min.	partner	_____	_____	_____	_____	
4	1 min.	partner	_____	_____	_____	_____	
5	3 min.	cluster					Bonus Round:
	1 min.	partner	_____	_____	_____	_____	Pay × 3
6	1 min.	partner	_____	_____	_____	_____	
7	1 min.	partner	_____	_____	_____	_____	
8	3 min.	cluster					
	1 min.	partner	_____	_____	_____	_____	Pay × 5
9	1 min.	partner	_____	_____	_____	_____	
10	3 min.	cluster					
	1 min.	partner	_____	_____	_____	_____	Pay × 10

2. Agree/Disagree Statements about Conflict

Read each statement once and mark whether you agree (A) or disagree (D) with it. Take five or six minutes to do this.

_____ 1. Most people find an argument interesting and exciting.

_____ 2. In most conflicts, someone must win and someone must lose. That's the way conflict is.

_____ 3. The best way to handle a conflict is simply to let everyone cool off.

_____ 4. Most people get upset at a person who disagrees with them.

_____ 5. If people spend enough time together, they will find something to disagree about and will eventually become upset with one another.

_____ 6. Conflicts can be solved if people just take the time to listen to one another.

_____ 7. If you disagree with someone, it is usually better to keep quiet than to express your personal difference of opinion.

_____ 8. To compromise is to take the easy way out of conflict.

_____ 9. Some people produce more conflict and tension than others. These people should be restricted from working with others.

After you have marked the above statements, break up into small groups and try to agree or disagree unanimously with each statement. Especially, try to find reasons for differences of opinion. If your group cannot reach agreement or disagreement, you may change the wording in any statement to promote consensus. Assign one group member to observe your group interactions. After your group has attempted to reach consensus, the observer should report how effectively the group used the guidelines suggested in this chapter.

Weblinks

www.chrc-ccdp.ca   This is the bilingual site for the Canadian Human Rights Commission. It includes the Canadian Human Rights Act, a reference library, recent news releases, and other sources of human rights information.

www.sybilevans.com/quizzes_3.asp   How good are your conflict management skills? Fill out this brief assessment form and find out.

www.newconversations.net   This is the home page of the Cooperative Communication Skills Extended Learning Community. You can access the Journal of Cooperative Communication Skills and information on a wide range of topics including how to encourage dialogue and resolve conflicts.

www.cyberparent.com/talk/negotiations.htm   Visit this site to learn tips and strategies for controlling your emotions during negotiations and when experiencing conflict.

PARTY, © Diana Ong/Superstock

Interpersonal Communication in Relationships

How do we begin relationships, and what are the best strategies for keeping them alive? What makes some relationships last for years and others fall apart? These are just some of the questions we will explore in Part III as we build on our understanding of interpersonal communication skills and principles. Chapter 8 explores the impact that diversity has on communication in relationships. Chapter 9 discusses how we initiate and nurture relationships. Chapter 10 explains the sometimes mysterious experiences of how relationships mature and die and presents strategies for recovery. The final chapter applies interpersonal communication principles and skills to interactions with family, in computer-mediated relationships, and with co-workers.

8

Interpersonal Communication and Cultural Diversity

After you study this chapter

you should be able to ...

1. Define "culture."

2. Identify four values that differentiate cultures.

3. Discuss barriers that inhibit effective intercultural communication.

4. Identify strategies to improve intercultural competence.

● The Nature of Culture

● Barriers to Effective Intercultural Communication

● Improving Intercultural Competence

Every tale can be told in a different way.

GREEK PROVERB

Overheard before class begins: "I've had it with all this cultural diversity stuff. It seems like every textbook in every class is obsessed with it. My history textbook talks about all these obscure people I've never heard of before. In English lit, all we're reading is stuff by people from different cultures. I'm tired of all this politically correct nonsense. I mean, we're all Canadians. Why don't they just teach us what we need to know and cut all this diversity garbage?"

Perhaps you've encountered this kind of "diversity backlash" among some of your classmates. Perhaps you even share this attitude. It may seem unsettling that textbooks are changing, and educators are so concerned with cultural diversity, but these changes are not motivated by an irrational desire to be politically correct. They are taking place because Canada is changing. As the statistics in the Diversity Almanac on page 254 suggest, it is becoming an increasingly culturally diverse country. With this growing diversity, there is also a growing awareness that learning about cultural differences can affect every aspect of our lives in positive ways. You may not plan on travelling the world, but the world is travelling to you. Your boss, teacher, religious leader, best friend, or partner may have grown up with different cultural traditions than your own. Textbooks and courses are reflecting the change, not initiating it.

A goal in our study of interpersonal communication is to learn how we can put aside differences in age, gender, race, or ability that might cause barriers to effective communication.
(Esbin-Anderson/The Image Works)

In Canada...

DIVERSITY ALMANAC

Canada continues to be a cultural mosaic of many races and cultures. The most recent census in 2001 continues to echo the diversity from the 1996 census. Here are a few of its interesting findings:

- As of May 15, 2001, 18.4 percent of the Canadian population were born outside the country.

- Of those who immigrated in the 1990s, 58 percent were born in Asia (including the Middle East), 20 percent in Europe, 11 percent in the Caribbean and Central and South America, 8 percent in Africa, and 3 percent in the United States.

- The People's Republic of China was the leading country of birth among individuals who immigrated to Canada in the 1990s.

- In 2001, 13.4 percent of the pop-

ulation identified themselves as members of visible minorities. Visible minorities are defined by the Employment Equity Act as "persons, other than Aboriginal peoples, who are non-Caucasian in race or non-white in colour."

- The three largest visible minority groups in 2001 were people of Chinese, South Asian, and African ancestry. Together, these three groups accounted for two-thirds of the visible minority population.

- People who identified themselves as Aboriginal in 2001 accounted for 3.3 percent of the nation's total population, up from 2.8 percent in the 1996 census.

- Seventy-three percent of immigrants live in three census metropolitan areas: Toronto, Vancouver, and Montreal.

- Calgary and Ottawa-Hull are emerging as centres of attraction

for new immigrants, accounting for three percent of the labour force, similar to the share of the labour force in Montreal.

- Canada is becoming more multilingual, with more than 100 first languages.

- Chinese is Canada's most common mother tongue after English and French.

- Between 1996 and 2001, language groups from the Middle East and Asia recorded the largest gains.

Sources: i. *Statistics Canada, The Daily, Tuesday, January 21, 2001.*
ii. *Statistics Canada, "The Changing Profile of Canada's Labour Force," 2001 Census: Analysis Series, Feb. 2003, Catalogue no. 96F0030XIE2001009.*
iii. *Statistics Canada, "The Census of Population: Language, Mobility, and Migration," The Daily, Tuesday, December 10, 2002, www.statcan.ca/Daily/English/021210/d021210a.htm*

Throughout this book, we present examples and research conclusions that emphasize how cultural differences affect our interpersonal relationships. In this chapter, we examine in more detail the impact culture has on our lives and suggest some skills for bridging cultural differences in your interpersonal communications and relationships. With these skills, you will be equipped to understand and value the diversity inherent in our population. To live comfortably in the 21st century, we can learn ways to accommodate and understand cultural differences instead of ignoring them, suffering because of them, or wishing that they would disappear.

The Nature of Culture

culture. A learned system of knowledge, behaviour, attitudes, beliefs, values, and norms that is shared by a group of people.

Exactly what is culture? A **culture** is a learned system of knowledge, behaviour, attitudes, beliefs, values, and norms that is shared by a group of people.[1] According to noted anthropologist Edward T. Hall, communication and culture are inseparable. How you interact with others is inextricably linked to how you learned to be a member of your group. Basically, we derive our cultural identity from three factors: elements, values, and contexts.

Sometimes when we speak of a culture, we may be referring to a **co-culture**. A co-culture is a distinct cultural group within a larger culture. Some co-cultures in Canada would include members of minority groups such as black Canadians and Asians. In a large city such as Toronto, many co-cultures live and/or work in specific areas, adding a distinct ethnic flavour to the city. Many communication researchers consider gender one of the most important co-cultures that significantly affects our communication with others. Gays and lesbians constitute another important co-culture in our society. The Amish, Islamic, and Jewish religious groups are examples of important religious co-cultures.

Cultural Elements

Categories of things and ideas that identify the most profound aspects of cultural influence are known as **cultural elements**. According to one research team, cultural elements include the following:

Canada is a multicultural country.
(Kerr/*Toronto Sun*)

- *Material culture:* things and ideas
- *Social institutions:* schools, governments, religious organizations
- *Individuals and the universe:* system of beliefs
- *Aesthetics:* music, theatre, art, dance
- *Language:* verbal and non-verbal communication systems[2]

As we grow, we learn to value these cultural elements. You were not born with a certain taste in music, clothes, and automobiles. Through **enculturation**, the process of communicating a group's culture from generation to generation, you learned what you liked by choosing from among the elements that were available within your culture. Your friends, colleagues, the media, and most importantly, your family, communicate information about these elements and advocate choices for you to make.

co-culture. A culture that exists within a larger cultural context (e.g., the gay and lesbian culture).

cultural elements. Categories of things and ideas that identify the most profound aspects of cultural influence (e.g., schools, governments, music, theatre, language).

enculturation. The process of communicating a group's culture from generation to generation.

Pomp and Circumstance. Which elements of culture are conveyed through Canada's changing of the guard ceremony on Parliament Hill? How do these cultural elements combine to shape the identity of Canadians? (Ottawa Citizen/Chris Mikula)

Building Your Skills

ASSESSING YOUR COMMUNICATION WITH STRANGERS

Your comfort level in communicating with strangers is related to your ability to communicate with people from other cultures. Respond to each statement by indicating the degree to which it is true of your communication with strangers: always false (answer 1), usually false (answer 2), sometimes true and sometimes false (answer 3), usually true (answer 4), or always true (answer 5).

_____ 1. I accept strangers as they are.

_____ 2. I express my feelings when I communicate with strangers.

_____ 3. I avoid negative stereotyping when I communicate with strangers.

_____ 4. I find similarities between myself and strangers when we communicate.

_____ 5. I accommodate my behaviour to strangers when we communicate.

To determine your score, add the numbers you wrote next to each statement. Scores range from 5 to 25. The higher your score, the greater your potential for developing a strong relationship with someone from a different background.

Source: From William B. Gudykunst, Bridging Differences: Effective Intergroup Communication (Newbury Park, Calif.: Sage, 1991), 143.

Understanding Diversity

OUR RANGE OF DIFFERENCES

Cultural diversity includes more than differences in ethnic background or gender. To become other-oriented is to consider a range of differences that affect how we communicate and respond to others. Note the following differences that affect our interactions with others.

AGE

Different generations, because they share different cultural and historical events, often view life differently. If your grandparents or great-grandparents experienced the Great Depression of the 1930s, they may have different attitudes toward savings accounts than you or even your parents. Today's explicit song lyrics may shock older North Americans who grew up with such racy lyrics as "makin' whoopee." The generation gap is real.

LANGUAGE

By far the majority of Canadians outside Quebec claim English as their native tongue, and most Quebeckers claim French as their native tongue. However, a sizable minority of Canadians report a wide range of other languages as their native tongue, and this range reflects the diversity of cultures that are integrally formed by their language. The following is a breakdown of the 20 top minority languages spoken in Canadian homes.

TOP 20 HOME LANGUAGES, CANADA, 2001, EXCLUDING ENGLISH AND FRENCH

1. Italian
2. German
3. Chinese (Cantonese and Mandarin listed separately)
4. Cantonese
5. Punjabi
6. Spanish
7. Portuguese
8. Polish
9. Arabic
10. Tagalog
11. Ukrainian
12. Dutch
13. Vietnamese
14. Greek
15. Mandarin
16. Russian
17. Persian (Farsi)
18. Tamil
19. Korean
20. Urdu

Continued

RELIGION

Religious affiliations and beliefs are another source of diversity. Ways and times of prayer, observed holidays, and attitudes about appropriate attire are just a few of the factors in a person's religious beliefs and traditions that can affect relationships. According to the most recent Canadian census, seven out of every ten Canadians identify themselves as either Catholic or Protestant. In 2001, Roman Catholics were still the largest religious group. However, the number of Canadians who reported their religion as Islam, Hinduism, Sikhism, or Buddhism increased substantially. The number of individuals who identified themselves as Jewish increased slightly. Sixteen percent of the Canadian population reported having no religion.[ii] Diversity in Canada can also be found in the religious and spiritual rituals and ceremonies of the many different Aboriginal groups.

DISABILITY

Although you may not think of the disabled as part of the cultural diversity equation, there is evidence that we unconsciously alter our communication style when we converse with people with disabilities. For example, we make less eye contact with people who are in wheelchairs; we also afford them more personal space when conversing. We often speak more loudly and more slowly to those who are blind. Many people with disabilities find these behaviours insulting.

SOCIAL CLASS

As the Canadian Charter of Rights and Freedoms says, "every individual is equal," but there is dramatic evidence that class differences do exist and affect communication patterns.

Social psychologist Michael Argyle reports that the cues we use to make class distinctions are: (1) way of life, (2) family, (3) job, (4) money, and (5) education. Class differences influence whom we talk with, whether we are likely to invite our neighbours over for coffee, and whom we choose as our friends and lovers. Most of us must make a conscious effort if we want to expand beyond our class boundaries.

GENDER

In this book, we emphasize how gender affects the way we listen, use words, and send and interpret nonverbal messages. Sex differences are biological differences between males and females: only men can impregnate, only women can menstruate, gestate, and lactate. However, gender differences focus on learned behaviour that is culturally associated with being a man or a woman. Gender role definitions are flexible: a man can adopt behaviour that is associated with a female role definition in a given culture and vice versa.

SEXUAL ORIENTATION

During the past decades, gays and lesbians have become more assertive in expressing their rights within society. Many legal battles are being fought by gays and lesbians to obtain the equal rights afforded their heterosexual peers. Their recent victories include the extension of Canadian Pension Plan survivor benefits to same-sex partners and the nationwide legalization of same sex marriage. Being gay has become a source of pride for some, but it is still a social stigma for others. The incidence of suicide among gay teenagers is significantly higher than among non-gay teens.

Although gays and lesbians are gaining legal rights and protections, they are still subject to discriminatory laws and social intolerance. The gay and lesbian community functions as a co-culture or a culture within the larger culture.

RACE

According to the dictionary, race is based on the genetically transmitted physical characteristics of a group of people classified together on the basis of a common history, nationality, or geographical location. Skin colour and other physical characteristics affect our responses and influence the way people of different races interact. Racial prejudice still has a devastating effect on interpersonal communication patterns and relationships.

ETHNICITY

Ethnicity refers to a social classification based on a variety of factors such as nationality, religion, language, or ancestral heritage. Nationality and geographical location are especially important in defining an ethnic group. Those of Irish ancestry are usually referred to as an ethnic group rather than as a race. The same could be said of Britons, Somalis, and Japanese. Ethnicity, like race, fosters common bonds that affect communication patterns. On the positive side, ethnic groups bring vitality and variety to our society. On the negative side, members of these groups may experience persecution or rejection from members of other groups.

Sources: i. *Statistics Canada, 2001 Census, Profile of Language, Mobility and Migration, for Canada, Provinces, Territories, Census Divisions and Census Subdivisions, 95F0488XCB01001, December 10, 2002.*
ii. *Statistics Canada, 2001 Census: Analysis Series Religions in Canada Catalogue no. 96F0030X1E2001015, May 2003*

This girl's clothing and pets reflect the aesthetics and lifestyle of her Inuit culture. (Mike Beedell)

acculturation. The process of acquiring new approaches, beliefs, and values through exposure to other cultures.

cultural values. What a given group of people values or appreciates.

masculine cultural values. Achievement, assertiveness, heroism, and material wealth.

feminine cultural values. Relationships, caring for the less fortunate, and overall quality of life.

Cultures are not static; they change as new information and new influences penetrate their stores of knowledge. We no longer believe that bathing is unhealthy, or that we can safely use makeup made with lead. These changes resulted from scientific discoveries, but other changes take place through **acculturation**; we acquire other approaches, beliefs, and values by coming into contact with other cultures. Today, acupuncture, yoga, tai chi, and karate studios are commonplace in most cities across Canada. Hummus (from the eastern Mediterranean) and basmati rice (from South Asia) are available in every supermarket, and restaurants offer a variety of fare from Mexican to Italian to Thai. In less obvious ways, "new" perspectives from other cultures have also influenced our thoughts, actions, and relationships.

Cultural Values

Identifying what a given group of people values or appreciates can provide insight into the behaviour of an individual raised within that group. Although there are great differences among the world's **cultural values**, one researcher identified four variables for measuring values that are significant in almost every culture.[3] According to Geert Hofstede, each culture places varying degrees of value on masculine and feminine perspectives, avoidance of uncertainty, distribution of power, and individualism (see Table 8.1). Hofstede's research conclusions have been widely summarized to describe differences among these four key cultural values. Although his research has been criticized as being dated (his information is now more than 30 years old) and based primarily on males who worked at IBM (the main source for much of his information), his research remains one of the most comprehensive, data-based studies of understanding cultural values.[4] He surveyed more than 100 000 employees in more than 50 countries; his research effort has yet to be duplicated or surpassed.

Masculine versus Feminine Perspectives

Some cultures emphasize traditional male values, whereas others place greater value on female perspectives. These values are not really about biological sex differences but overarching approaches to interacting with others. People from backgrounds with **masculine cultural values** tend to value more traditional roles for both men and women. Masculine cultures also value achievement, assertiveness, heroism, and material wealth. Research reveals that men tend to approach communication from a content orientation, meaning that they view communication as functioning primarily for information exchange. Men talk when they have something to say. This is also consistent with the tendency for men to base their relationships, especially their male friendships, on sharing activities rather than talking.

Men and women from backgrounds with **feminine cultural values** tend to value such things as caring for the less fortunate, being sensitive toward others, and enhancing the overall quality of life.[5] Women, research suggests, tend to approach communication for the purpose of relating or connecting to others, of extending themselves to other people to know them and be known by them.[6] What women talk about is less important than the fact that they're talking, because talking implies relationship.

Here's a short way of summarizing this difference: *men often communicate to report; women often communicate to establish rapport.*[7] So the point of difference isn't in the way the sexes actually communicate but in the motivations or reasons for communicating. The *how* may not be that different; the *why* may be very different.[8]

Table 8.1   Examples of Countries That Illustrate Four Cultural Values

Cultural Value	Examples of Countries That Scored Higher on This Cultural Value	Examples of Countries That Scored Lower on This Cultural Value
Masculinity: People from countries with higher masculinity scores prefer high achievement, men being in more assertive roles, and more clearly differentiated sex roles than people from countries with lower scores on this cultural dimension.	Japan, Australia, Venezuela, Italy, Switzerland, Mexico, Ireland, Jamaica, Great Britain	Sweden, Norway, Netherlands, Denmark, Yugoslavia, Costa Rica, Finland, Chile, Portugal, Thailand
Uncertainty Avoidance: People from countries with higher uncertainty avoidance scores generally prefer to avoid uncertainty; they like to know what will happen next. People from countries with lower scores are more comfortable with uncertainty.	Greece, Portugal, Guatemala, Uruguay, Belgium, Japan, Yugoslavia, Peru, France	Singapore, Jamaica, Denmark, Sweden, Hong Kong, Ireland, Great Britain, Malaysia, India, Philippines, United States
Power Distribution: People from countries with higher power distribution scores generally prefer greater power differences between people; they are generally more accepting of someone having authority and power than are people from countries with lower scores on this cultural dimension.	Malaysia, Guatemala, Panama, Philippines, Mexico, Venezuela, Arab countries, Ecuador, Indonesia, India	Austria, Israel, Denmark, New Zealand, Ireland, Sweden, Norway, Finland, Switzerland, Great Britain
Individualism: People from countries with higher individualism scores generally prefer individual accomplishment rather than collective or collaborative achievement.	United States, Australia, Great Britain, Canada, Netherlands, New Zealand, Italy, Belgium, Denmark, Sweden, France	Guatemala, Ecuador, Panama, Venezuela, Columbia, Indonesia, Pakistan, Costa Rica, Peru, Taiwan, South Korea

Source: Adapted from Geert Hofstede, Cultures and Organizations: Software of the Mind (London: McGraw-Hill, 1991).

Of course, rarely is a culture on the extreme end of the continuum; many are somewhere in between. For centuries, most countries in Europe, Asia, and the Americas have had masculine cultures. Men and their conquests dominate history books; men have been more prominent in leadership and decision making than women. However, today many of these cultures are moving slowly toward the middle—legal and social rules are encouraging more gender balance and greater equality between masculine and feminine roles.

🌑 Tolerance of Uncertainty versus Avoidance of Uncertainty

Cedric works for the phone company as a customer service representative. He grew up in Jamaica where there is sometimes a higher tolerance for bureaucratic uncertainty than there is in Canada. Jake was raised in Toronto; he expects (sometimes demands) that his problems be solved quickly. Cedric's higher tolerance for uncertainty and Jake's desire for straight, prompt answers to questions created an oil-and-water confrontation. Jake phoned Cedric to complain about the slow response to his request to have a new phone line installed for his fax machine. Cedric tried to be reassuring, but

Jake got the distinct impression that Cedric was not sympathetic and thought that a week's wait for a new line was perfectly reasonable. Jake expected his new line within 24 hours. Both had difficulty tuning in to the cultural difference in their expectations about how quickly a bureaucracy should respond to an individual request.

Some cultures tolerate more ambiguity and uncertainty than others. Those in which people need certainty to feel secure are more likely to have and enforce rigid rules for behaviour and to develop more elaborate codes of conduct. People from cultures with a greater tolerance for uncertainty have more relaxed, informal expectations for others. "Go with the flow" and "It will sort itself out" are phrases that describe their attitudes. One study showed that people from Portugal, Germany, Peru, Belgium, and Japan have high certainty needs, but people from Scandinavian countries tend to tolerate uncertainty.[9]

▶▶▶ Applying Theory and Research

UNCERTAINTY REDUCTION THEORY

Uncertainty reduction theory, developed by Charles Berger and Richard Calabrese, helps explain how we seek to reduce our uncertainty during an initial meeting with strangers or when we find ourselves in a new situation.[10] In some respects, each of us is different from everyone else. The more different we are from others and the less we know about them, the more uncertainty and sometimes anxiety and fear we may have about other people.

Uncertainty reduction theory describes how we strategically interact with others to enhance our understanding of others so that strangers seem less strange to us. The theory predicts that high levels of uncertainty will increase information-seeking behaviour, such as asking questions or doing research about a new place we may be visiting. As we become less uncertain and more certain, we use fewer information-seeking strategies because we have a better understanding of how to predict what will happen to us.[11]

When we are uncertain about someone else, we could use a passive strategy and just observe the person to see if we can learn more about him or her and thus reduce our uncertainty. Another strategy to reduce our uncertainty of others is more active: We could ask others for information about the person who is unfamiliar to us. Or we could use an interactive strategy to try to reduce our uncertainty about someone by asking questions, self-disclosing, and listening for self-disclosures from the other person.

As we noted in Table 8.1, people in some cultures (such as people from Argentina, Chile, and Peru) prefer to avoid uncertainty. They would rather have straight answers and know whom they are talking to; they are uncomfortable with uncertainty. People in other cultures (like Canadians, the British, and Jamaicans) are more comfortable with uncertainty. They feel that eventually things will get sorted out and they can be patient and wait for things to be resolved. Although we caution that these are broad generalizations and are not true in each

situation, we can nonetheless use such generalizations to test our assumptions and help unravel our uncertainty. Geert Hofstede suggests that people who dodge uncertainty by avoiding people who are different from themselves, and who are also more likely to visit places that are in their comfort zone rather than seek new places to visit, operate from the framework that "What is different is dangerous."[12] Hofstede suspects that people in cultures with a low need to avoid uncertainty, people who are more comfortable with uncertainty, would agree with the phrase, "What is different is interesting."

APPLYING THE RESEARCH TO YOUR LIFE

Your comfort level with strangers and people who are different from you may stem from your personal tolerance for uncertainty. If you generally prefer to avoid new places, especially places that are different from your current surroundings, you may also be someone who likes certainty and dislikes uncertainty. If you prefer certainty and you don't prefer ambiguity, you may be more

Continued

likely to use communication strategies to manage the uncertainty, or to avoid situations that create uncertainty. You'll be less likely to strike up a conversation with people who are different from yourself. If you are comfortable with uncertainty, you will not be quite as anxious, nervous, or upset if you don't have all of the answers; you'll likely be more patient finding out information about a stranger. The goal of inviting you to consider your own approach to uncertainty is not to change your tolerance for uncertainty but to help you understand why and how you behave toward others who are different from you.

Consider the following questions to help you apply uncertainty reduction theory to your interactions with others:

1. On a scale of 1 to 10 (with 10 being very comfortable with uncertainty and 1 being very uncomfortable with uncertainty), how would you rate your own level of comfort with uncertainty about others?

2. Do you actively try to reduce your uncertainty level, or do you just live with not knowing information about others, especially others who are different from you?

3. What strategies do you use to learn about others who are different from you? Do you prefer to use passive, active, or interactive strategies to reduce your uncertainty?

4. Do you actively avoid people who are different from you?

5. Would you rather visit new places or return to surroundings that are comfortable and familiar?

Source: C. R. Berger and R. J. Calabrese, "Some Explorations in Initial Interactions and Beyond: Toward a Developmental Theory of Interpersonal Communication," Human Communication Research, 1 (1975): 99–112.

Concentrated versus Decentralized Power

Some cultures value an equal or decentralized distribution of power, whereas others accept a concentration of hierarchical power in a centralized government and other organizations. In the latter, hierarchical bureaucracies are common, and people expect some individuals to have more power than others. Russia, France, and China are all high on the concentrated power scale. Those that often strive for greater equality and distribution of power and control include many (but not all) citizens from Australia, Denmark, New Zealand, and Israel. People from these latter countries tend to minimize differences in power between people.

Individual versus Group Achievement

Kaylie: We've got this group project to do. Let's divvy up the work and then meet back here next week to see what each of us has done.

Ayako: Wait a minute, Kaylie. It might seem to be more efficient to divide up the work into little separate pieces, but in the end, we'll have a better report if each of us works on every section.

Kaylie: Are you kidding? We'll be here all night! Josh, you take the history of the problem. Bert, you look at problem causes and effects. Ayako, why don't you do a literature search on the CD-ROM in the library and start looking up articles.

Ayako: All right, but I still think it would be better to go to the library together. I think we'd have better luck if we worked on each aspect of the problem as a team.

What can be inferred about the use of *cultural context* cues to enhance message and meaning in Canadian Aboriginal culture?
(Royal Canadian Mounted Police)

Kaylie and Ayako clearly have different strategies for working together. Kaylie approaches the project from an individualistic perspective; Ayako prefers a collective or group strategy to achieve the goal. Traditionally, North Americans champion individual accomplishments and achievements. People from Asian backgrounds often value collective or group achievement more highly. One researcher summed up the North American goal system this way:

> Chief among the virtues claimed. . . is self-realization. Each person is viewed as having a unique set of talents and potentials. The translation of these potentials into actuality is concurred the highest purpose to which one can devote one's life.[13]

In a collectivistic culture, conversely, people strive to attain goals for all members of the family, group, or community. In Kenyan tribes, for example:

> . . . nobody is an isolated individual. Rather, his [or her] uniqueness is secondary fact. . . . In this new system group activities are dominant, responsibility is shared and accountability is collective. . . . Because of the emphasis on collectivity, harmony and cooperation among the group tends to be emphasized more than individual function and responsibility.[14]

Individualistic cultures tend to be more loosely knit socially; individuals feel responsible for taking care of themselves and their immediate families.[15] In collectivistic cultures, individuals expect more support from others and more loyalty to and from the community. Because collectivistic cultures place more value on "we" than "I," teamwork approaches usually succeed better in their workplaces. North American businesses, for example, have tried to adopt some of Japan's successful team strategies for achieving high productivity.

cultural context. Information not explicitly communicated through language, such as environmental or non-verbal cues.

high-context cultures. Cultures that derive much information from non-verbal and environmental cues.

low-context cultures. Culture that derive much information from the words of a message and less information from non-verbal and environmental cues.

▶ Recap

CULTURAL VALUES

Masculine versus Feminine	Does the culture place the highest value on assertiveness, heroism, and wealth or on relationships, caring for others, and overall quality of life?
Tolerance of Uncertainty versus Avoidance of Uncertainty	Does the culture have a high tolerance for ambiguity and uncertainty or does it hold more rigid and explicit behavioural expectations?
Concentrated versus Decentralized Power	Does the culture tolerate or accept hierarchical power structures or does it favour a more equal distribution of power?
Individual versus Group Achievement	Does the culture value individual achievement more than collective group accomplishments or vice versa?

Cultural Contexts

As we discussed in Chapter 6, individuals from different cultures use culturally-based contextual cues in varying degrees to enhance messages and meaning and this is called **cultural context**. This led Edward T. Hall to categorize cultures as either high- or low-context.[16] As shown in Figure 8.1, in **high-context cultures**, non-verbal cues are extremely important in interpreting messages. **Low-context cultures** rely more explicitly on language and use fewer contextual cues to send and interpret

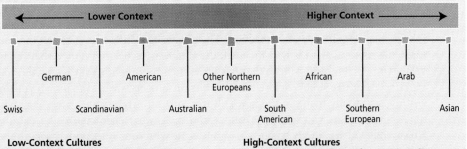

Figure 8.1
High/Low Contexts: Where Different Cultures Fall on the Context Scale

Low-Context Cultures
(Information must be provided explicitly, usually in words.)
• Are less aware of non-verbal cues, environment, and situation
• Lack well-developed networks
• Need detailed background information
• Tend to segment and compartmentalize information
• Control information on a "need to know" basis
• Prefer explicit and careful directions from someone who "knows"
• Consider knowledge a commodity

High-Context Cultures
(Much information drawn from surroundings. Very little must be explicitly transferred.)
• Consider non-verbal cues important
• Let information flow freely
• Rely on physical context for information
• Take environment, situation, gestures, and mood into account
• Maintain extensive information networks

Source: Based on research by Edward T. Hall, *Beyond Culture* (Garden City, NY: Doubleday: 1976) and adapted from Donald W. Klopf, *Intercultural Encounters: The Fundamentals of Intercultural Communication* (Englewood, CO: Morton Publishing, 1998), 33.

information. Individuals from high-context cultures may perceive persons from low-context cultures as less attractive, knowledgeable, and trustworthy because they violate unspoken rules of dress, conduct, and communication. Individuals from low-context cultures often are not skilled in interpreting unspoken, contextual messages.[17]

▶ Recap

THE NATURE OF CULTURE

Cultural Elements	Things and ideas that represent profound aspects of cultural influence, such as art, music, schools, and belief systems.
Cultural Values	What a culture reveres and holds important.
Cultural Contexts	Information not explicitly communicated through language, such as environmental or non-verbal cues. High-context cultures (such as Japanese, Chinese, Korean) derive much information from these cues. Low-context cultures (such as North American, Western European) rely more heavily on words.

Barriers to Effective Intercultural Communication

intercultural communication.
Communication between or among people who have different cultural traditions.

Intercultural communication occurs when individuals or groups from different cultures communicate. The transactional process of listening and responding to people from different cultural backgrounds can be challenging. The greater the difference in culture between two people, the greater the potential for misunderstanding and mistrust.

Misunderstanding and miscommunication occur between people from different cultures because of different coding rules and cultural norms, which play a major role in shaping patterns of interaction. The greater the difference between the cultures, the more likely it is that they will use different verbal and non-verbal codes. When you encounter a culture that has little in common with your own, you may experience **culture shock**, or a sense of confusion, anxiety, stress, and loss. If you are visiting or actually living in the new culture, your uncertainty and stress may take time to subside as you learn the values and codes that characterize the culture. However, if you are simply trying to communicate with someone from a background very different from your own—even on your home turf—you may find the suggestions in this section helpful in closing the communication gap.[18]

The first step to bridging differences between cultures is to find out what hampers effective communication. What keeps us from connecting with people from other cultures? Sometimes it is different meanings created by different languages or by different interpretations of non-verbal messages. Sometimes it is our inability to stop focusing on ourselves and begin focusing on the other. We'll examine some of these barriers first, then discuss strategies and skills for overcoming them.

culture shock. Feeling of stress and anxiety a person experiences when encountering a culture different from his or her own.

Ethnocentrism

Marilyn had always been intrigued by Russia. Her dream was to travel the country by train, spending time in small villages as well as exploring the cultural riches of Moscow, Kiev, and St. Petersburg. Her first day in Russia was a disappointment, however. When she arrived in Moscow, she joined a tour touting the cultural traditions of Russia. When the tour bus stopped at Sparrow Hills, affording them a breathtaking hilltop view of the Moscow skyline, she was perplexed and mildly shocked to see women, dressed in elegant wedding gowns, mounted on horses galloping through the parking lot. Men in suits were cheering them on as a crowd of tipsy revellers set off fireworks and danced wildly to a brass band. "What kind of people are these?" sniffed Marilyn.

"Oh," said the tour guide, "it is our custom to come here to celebrate immediately following the wedding ceremony."

"But in public, with such raucousness?" queried Marilyn.

"It is our tradition," said the guide.

Colourful celebrations like this ritual purification ceremony in Bali can reinforce healthy ethnic pride. When this pride is taken to the extreme through ethnocentric feelings, barriers between groups may result.
(Michael Burgess/Stock Boston)

"What a backwards culture. They're nothing but a bunch of peasants!" pronounced Marilyn, who was used to more refined nuptial celebrations at a country club or an exclusive hotel.

For the rest of the tour, Marilyn judged every Russian behaviour as inferior to those of Westerners. Her first experience coloured her perceptions, and her ethnocentric view served as a barrier to effective communication with the Russian people she met.

Ethnocentrism stems from a conviction that your own cultural traditions and assumptions are superior to those of others. In short, it is the opposite of an other-orientation, which embraces and appreciates the elements that give another culture meaning. This kind of cultural snobbery is one of the fastest ways to create a barrier that inhibits, rather than enhances, communication.

The concept of ethnocentrism is not new. Almost 100 years ago, W. G. Sumner defined it as "the technical name of this view of things in which one's own group is the centre of everything and all others are scaled and rated with reference to it."[19] Many scholars have found that virtually all cultural groups are ethnocentric to some degree.[20] Some even argue that it's not always bad to see one's own cultural group as superior; ethnocentric tendency enhances group pride and patriotism and encourages cultural traditions.[21] A problem occurs, however, when a group views its own preferences as *always* the best way. Extreme ethnocentrism creates a barrier between the group and others.

ethnocentrism. The belief that your cultural traditions and assumptions are superior to others.

Building Your Skills
ASSESSING YOUR ETHNOCENTRISM

The following measure of ethnocentrism was developed by communication researchers James Neuliep and James McCroskey. Answer the following questions honestly. This can be challenging, but remember the goal here is to assess your feelings accurately.

This instrument is composed of 24 statements concerning your feelings about your culture and other cultures. In the space provided to the left of each item, indicate the degree to which the statement applies to you by marking whether you (5) strongly agree, (4) agree, (3) are neutral, (2) disagree, or (1) strongly disagree with the statement. There are no right or wrong answers. Work quickly and record your first response.

_____ 1. Most other cultures are backward compared with my culture.

_____ 2. People in other cultures have a better lifestyle than we do in my culture.

_____ 3. Most people would be happier if they did not live like people do in my culture.

_____ 4. My culture should be the role model for other cultures.

_____ 5. Lifestyles in other cultures are just as valid as those in my culture.

_____ 6. Other cultures should try to be more like my culture.

_____ 7. I'm not interested in the values and customs of other cultures.

_____ 8. It is not wise for other cultures to look up to my culture.

_____ 9. People in my culture could learn a lot from people in other cultures.

_____ 10. Most people from other cultures just don't know what's good for them.

_____ 11. People from my culture act strange and unusual when they go into other cultures.

_____ 12. I have little respect for the values and customs of other cultures.

_____ 13. Most people would be happier if they lived like people in my culture.

_____ 14. People in my culture have just about the best lifestyles of anywhere.

Continued

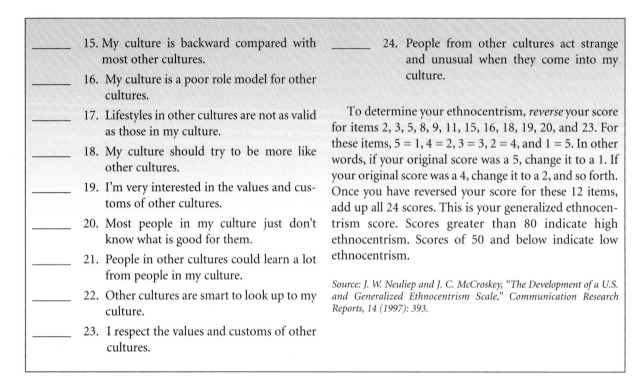

15. My culture is backward compared with most other cultures.

16. My culture is a poor role model for other cultures.

17. Lifestyles in other cultures are not as valid as those in my culture.

18. My culture should try to be more like other cultures.

19. I'm very interested in the values and customs of other cultures.

20. Most people in my culture just don't know what is good for them.

21. People in other cultures could learn a lot from people in my culture.

22. Other cultures are smart to look up to my culture.

23. I respect the values and customs of other cultures.

24. People from other cultures act strange and unusual when they come into my culture.

To determine your ethnocentrism, *reverse* your score for items 2, 3, 5, 8, 9, 11, 15, 16, 18, 19, 20, and 23. For these items, 5 = 1, 4 = 2, 3 = 3, 2 = 4, and 1 = 5. In other words, if your original score was a 5, change it to a 1. If your original score was a 4, change it to a 2, and so forth. Once you have reversed your score for these 12 items, add up all 24 scores. This is your generalized ethnocentrism score. Scores greater than 80 indicate high ethnocentrism. Scores of 50 and below indicate low ethnocentrism.

Source: J. W. Neuliep and J. C. McCroskey, "The Development of a U.S. and Generalized Ethnocentrism Scale," Communication Research Reports, 14 (1997): 393.

Different Communication Codes

You are on your first trip to Calgary. You step off the bus and look around for Stampede Park, and you realize that you have gotten off at the wrong stop. You see a corner grocery store with "Stampede Park" painted on a red sign. So you walk in and ask the man behind the counter, "How do I get to the Calgary Stampede, please?" The man smiles, shrugging his shoulders, but he points to a transit map pasted onto the wall behind the counter.

Today, even when you travel within Canada, you are likely to encounter people who do not speak your language. Obviously, this kind of intercultural difference poses a formidable communication challenge, and even when you do speak the same tongue as another, he or she may come from a place where the words and gestures have different meanings. Your ability to communicate will depend on whether you can understand each other's verbal and non-verbal codes.

In the example above, although the man behind the counter did not understand your exact words, he noted the cut of your clothing, your backpack, and your anxiety. From this, he deduced that you were asking for directions, and you could understand what his gesture toward the transit map meant. Unfortunately, not every communication between the users of two different languages is this successful.

Even when language is translated, there can be missed or mangled meanings. Note the following examples of mistranslated advertisements:

- A General Motors auto ad with "Body by Fisher" became "Corpse by Fisher" in Flemish.

- A Colgate-Palmolive toothpaste named "Cue" was advertised in France before anyone realized that *Cue* also happened to be the name of a widely circulated pornographic book about oral sex.

- Pepsi-Cola's "Come Alive with Pepsi" campaign, when it was translated for the Taiwanese market, conveyed the unsettling news that, "Pepsi brings your ancestors back from the grave."

- Parker Pen could not advertise its famous "Jotter" ballpoint pen in some languages because the translation sounded like "jockstrap" pen.

- One American airline operating in Brazil advertised that it had plush "rendezvous lounges" on its jets, unaware that in Portuguese (the language of Brazil), "rendezvous" implies a special room for making love.[22]

Stereotyping and Prejudice

Europeans dress fashionably.

Asians are good at math.

Canadians are overly apologetic.

These statements are stereotypes. They are all inaccurate. To **stereotype** someone is to push him or her into an inflexible, all-encompassing category. In Chapter 3, we saw how our tendency to simplify sensory stimuli can lead us to adopt stereotypes as we interpret the behaviour of others. When we stereotype, we "print" the same judgment over and over again, failing to consider the uniqueness of individuals, groups, or events. This becomes a barrier to effective intercultural communication. Two anthropologists have suggested that every person is, in some respects: (1) like all other people, (2) like some other people, and (3) like no other people.[23] Our challenge when meeting others is to discover how they are alike and how they are unique.

Can stereotypes play a useful role in interpersonal communication? The answer is a resounding "no" if our labels are inaccurate or if they assume superiority on our part. However, sometimes it may be appropriate to draw on generalizations. If, for example, you are driving lost and alone in a large city at 2:00 in the morning and another car repeatedly taps your rear bumper, it would be prudent to try to drive away as quickly as possible rather than to hop out of your car to make a new acquaintance. You would be wise to prejudge that the other driver might have some malicious intent. In most situations, however, **prejudice**—prejudging someone before you know all of the facts—inhibits effective communication. If you decide that you like or dislike (usually dislike) someone simply because he or she is a member of a certain group or class of people, you will not give yourself a chance to communicate with the person in a meaningful way. Prejudice usually involves negative attitudes toward members of a specific social group or culture.

Certain prejudices are widespread. Although there are more females than males in the world, in many societies, females are prejudged to be less valuable than males. One study found that even when a male and a female hold the same type of job, the male's job is considered more prestigious than the female's.[24] **Discrimination** is often a result of prejudice. When people discriminate, they treat members of groups differently from their own in negative ways. In the past, people of different gender, race, ethnicity, or sexual orientation were often victims of discrimination socially and politically. Today, discrimination of these kinds in hiring and promotion is illegal in Canada, but our social attitudes have not kept pace with the law. Stereotyping and prejudice are still formidable barriers to effective interpersonal communication. While many do not actively engage in discrimination, many people still hold negative attitudes and stereotypes of people different from themselves.

stereotype. To place a person or group of persons into an inflexible, all-encompassing category.

prejudice. Prejudging someone before you know all of the facts or background of that person.

discrimination. Negative behaviours directed toward members of social groups who are the object of prejudice.

In Canada...

MINORITIES IN CANADA: IS DISCRIMINATION STILL A PROBLEM?

A recent report published by Statistics Canada has shed some interesting facts about discrimination in Canada today. The Ethnic Diversity Survey, the first large-scale survey of its kind, was developed by Statistics Canada in partnership with the Department of Canadian Heritage to provide information on the ethnic and cultural backgrounds of people in Canada and how these backgrounds relate to their lives in Canada today. Canada's Aboriginal peoples were not included in the survey as similar information was collected through the 2001 Aboriginal Peoples Survey.

The survey covers many areas of diversity, ranging from reports of ancestries to participation in Canadian society to experiences of discrimination. The area of interest in the context of this chapter is discrimination. However, the entire report is useful to anyone who is interested in Canadian multiculturalism.

The survey asked people how often they felt out of place in Canada because of their ethnicity, culture, race, skin colour, language,

accent, or religion. Most people (78 percent) reported that they never felt uncomfortable. Another 13 percent said they felt uncomfortable or out of place rarely. However, 10 percent indicated that they felt this way most of the time or all of the time because of their ethno-cultural characteristics.

In addition to the above question, respondents were asked whether they had experienced discrimination or been treated unfairly by others in Canada in the five years prior to the survey because of their ethnicity, culture, race, skin colour, language, accent, or religion. The good news: overall, the vast majority (86 percent) of respondents stated that they had never or rarely experienced discrimination. However, seven percent (or 1.6 million) of Canadians said they had sometimes or often experienced discrimination in the past five years because of their ethno-cultural characteristics. Perceived discrimination or unfair treatment varied considerably by minority status. About 20 percent of visible minorities said they had sometimes or often experienced this, with blacks the most likely to report discrimination or unfair treatment. In other words, one in five Canadians who were visible minorities report experiencing discrimination or unfair treatment

because of their racial or ethnic background.

The other question of interest in the survey concerned the location of such unfair treatment or discrimination: on the street; in stores, banks, or restaurants; at work, for instance when applying for a job or promotion; when dealing with the police or courts; or somewhere else. In response, the most common situation where perceived discrimination or unfair treatment had occurred was at work or when applying for a job or promotion. Overall, 880 000 or 56 percent of those who had sometimes or often experienced discrimination or unfair treatment because of their ethno-cultural characteristics said that they had experienced such treatment at work or when applying for work.

FOR DISCUSSION

1. Why do you think such discrimination and unfair treatment is still prevalent, especially for members of visible minorities?

2. Canadian legislation prohibits unfair treatment in the workplace due to racial or ethnic status. How might unfair treatment then still occur?

Source: Statistics Canada, Ethnic Diversity Survey: Portrait of a Multicultural Society Catalogue no. 89-593-XIE, September 2003.

Assuming Similarity

Just as it is inaccurate to assume that all people who belong to another social group or class are worlds apart from you, it is usually erroneous to assume that others act and think as you do. Even if they appear to be like you, all people are not alike. While this statement is not profound, it has profound implications. We often make the mistake of assuming that others value the same things we do, maintaining a self-focused perspective instead of an other-oriented one. As you saw in Chapter 3, focusing on superficial factors, such as appearance, clothing, and even a person's occupation, can lead to false impressions. Instead, we must take the time to explore a person's background and cultural values before we can determine what we really have in common.

Improving Intercultural Competence

The remaining portion of this chapter presents three sets of strategies to help you bridge differences between yourself and people who come from a different cultural background. These three strategy sets—appropriate knowledge, motivation, and skill—are based on our understanding of how to be a competent communicator.[25]

Our suggestion to enhance your understanding or **knowledge** of others is based on the assumption that knowing more about others is important in quality relationships. One of the barriers to effective intercultural communication is having different communication codes. Improving your knowledge of how others communicate can reduce the impact of this barrier. We offer strategies to help you learn more about other cultures by actively pursuing information about others.

A second set of strategies focuses on becoming motivated to improve our intercultural communication knowledge and skills. **Motivation** is an internal state of readiness to respond to something. A competent communicator wants to learn and improve; an incompetent communicator is not motivated to develop new skills. Technically, no one can motivate you to do something; motivation comes from within. However, developing strategies to appreciate others who are different from you may help you appreciate different cultural approaches to communication and relationships. We suggest you endeavour to be more tolerant of uncertainty and to avoid knee-jerk negative evaluations of others.

The final set of strategies—developing **skill** in adapting to others—focuses on specific behaviours that can help overcome the barriers and cultural differences we have discussed. Here, to address the barrier of ethnocentrism, we will identify the advantages of becoming a more flexible communicator. We will also describe the essential competence of becoming other-oriented—focusing on the needs, goals, and values of others instead of only on your own. As we discussed in Chapter 1, becoming other-oriented is critical to the process of relating to others.

knowledge. One of the elements of becoming a competent communicator; information that enhances understanding of others.

motivation. Internal state of readiness to respond to something. An element of interpersonal competence.

skill. Behaviour that improves the effectiveness or quality of communicating with others.

Developing Knowledge: Strategies to Understand Others Who Are Different from Us

Knowledge is power. To increase your knowledge of others who are different from you, we suggest that you actively seek information about others, ask questions and listen to the answers, and establish common ground. Let's discuss these strategies in more detail.

Understanding Diversity

ETHNOCENTRIC THINKING

All good people agree,
And all good people say,
All nice people like Us, are We,
And everyone else is They.

In a few short lines, Rudyard Kipling captured the essence of what sociologists and anthropologists call ethnocentric thinking. Members of all societies tend to believe that "All nice people like Us, are We." They find comfort in the familiar and often denigrate or distrust others. Of course, with training and experience in other climes, they may learn to transcend their provincialism, placing themselves in others' shoes. Or, as Kipling put it,

... if you cross over the sea,
Instead of over the way,
You may end by (think of it!) looking on We
As only a sort of They.

In a real sense, a main lesson of the sociology of intergroup relations is to begin to "cross over the sea," to learn to understand why other people think and act as they do and to be able to empathize with their perspectives.

Source: Adapted from Faun B. Evans, Barbara Gleason, and Mark Wiley, Cultural Tapestry: Readings for a Pluralistic Society (HarperCollins, 1992).

Seek Information about the Culture

Seeking information about a culture or even about a specific communication situation can be a useful strategy to enhance the quality of intercultural communication. Why? Because seeking information helps manage uncertainty and anxiety that we may feel when we interact with people who are different from us.[26] Sometimes we feel uncomfortable in intercultural communication situations because we just don't know how to behave. We aren't sure what our role should be; we can't quite predict what will happen when we communicate with others because we're in a new or strange situation. Actively seeking information about a culture or about people from a culture other than your own can help you manage some of the anxiety and uncertainty you may experience when you communicate in new cultural contexts. Seeking new information can also help counter inaccurate information and prejudice.

world view. Perception shared by a culture or group of people about key beliefs and issues, such as death, the origins of the universe, and the meaning of life, which influences interaction with others.

Every person has a **world view** based on cultural beliefs about the universe and key issues such as death, the origins of the universe, and the meaning of life.[27] According to Carley Dodd, "A culture's world view involves finding out how the culture perceives the role of various forces in explaining why events occur as they do in a social setting."[28] These beliefs shape our thoughts, language, and behaviour. Only through intercultural communication can we hope to understand how each individual views the world. As you speak to a person from another culture, think of yourself as a detective, watching for implied, often unspoken, messages that provide information about the values, norms, roles, and rules of that person's culture.

You can also prepare yourself by studying the culture. If you are going to another country, courses in the history, anthropology, art, or geography of that place can give you a head start on communicating with understanding. One author was invited to a wedding for a Native Canadian friend and part of the ceremony was "smudging." Prior to attending, the author learned about what it was and how it is done (if you do not know, here is a learning opportunity). Learn not only from books, magazines, and the Internet but also from individuals whenever possible.

Intercultural scholar William Gudykunst has discovered some patterns in the way people seek new information to manage the uncertainty they experience when communicating with people from an unfamiliar culture.[29] He's found that people in high-context cultures (who place an emphasis on non-verbal messages) are typically more cautious when communicating in initial conversations than are people from low-context cultures (who emphasize the verbal content of a message). If you're from a low-context culture (such as Canada), you are more likely to pay attention to only the more overt, obvious non-verbal expressions; people from high-context cultures are more likely to focus on more subtle non-verbal cues for their information. Gudykunst has also found that people from high-context cultures are more likely to make assumptions about others than are people from low-context cultures. People from low-context cultures are more likely to use self-disclosure and to be more direct in asking for information to manage uncertainty than are people from high-context cultures.

Even in a high-context culture, no one will fault you for asking directly for help if you show a sincere desire to learn. If you are trying to communicate with someone closer to home who is from a different background, you can study magazines, music, food, and other readily available sources of information about his or her culture. Or exchange visits to one another's homes or hangouts to observe and learn more about the person.

Given the inextricable link between language and culture, the more you learn about another language, the more you will understand the traditions and customs of the culture. Politicians have long known the value of using even a few words of the first languages of their minority constituents. Speaking even a few words can signify your interest in learning about the language and culture of others.

When we speak of culture, we are also referring to co-cultures. As you already know, a co-culture is a cultural group within a larger culture. Learning how men and women, each a separate co-culture, communicate differently can help us improve our communication with the opposite gender. Men, for example, are more likely to develop friendships through participating in common activities with other men (playing on a baseball team, working together).[30] Women are more likely to develop friendships through talking together rather than working together.

Reading books about differences between the way men and women communicate is one strategy to help both sexes improve understanding and develop insight into different approaches to communication. There are many popular books that can help create a dialogue between men and women about communication differences and, thus, promote greater knowledge about how to improve communication.

As you read about other cultures or co-cultures, it is important not to develop rigid categories or stereotypes for the way others may talk or behave. Proclaiming, "Oh, you're just saying that because you're a man" or "You women always say things like that" can increase, rather than decrease, communication barriers. Throughout this book, we will discuss research-based gender differences in the way men and women communicate in order to enhance your understanding and improve communication with members of the opposite sex. However, we don't recommend that you treat men and women as completely separate species from different planets or automatically assume you will immediately misunderstand the opposite sex.

● Ask Questions and Listen Effectively

When you encounter a person from another background, asking questions and then pausing to listen is a simple technique for gathering information and also for confirming the accuracy of your expectations and assumptions. Some cultures, such as the Japanese, have rigid expectations regarding gift giving. It is better to ask what these expectations are than to assume that your good old down-home manners will see you through.

When you ask questions, be prepared to share information about yourself, too. Otherwise, your partner may feel as if you are interrogating him or her as a way to gain power and dominance rather than from a sincere desire to learn about cultural rules and norms.

Communication helps to reduce the uncertainty that is present in any relationship.[31] When you meet people for the first time, you are highly uncertain about who they are and what they like and dislike. When you communicate with someone from another culture, the uncertainty level is particularly high. As you begin to interact, you exchange information that helps you develop greater understanding. If you continue to ask questions, eventually you will feel less uncertain about how the person is likely to behave.

Just asking questions and sharing information about yourself is not sufficient to bridge differences in culture and background. It is equally important to listen to what others share. In Chapter 4, we provided specific strategies for improving your listening skills.

🍵 Develop a "Third Culture"

Several researchers suggest that one of the best ways to enhance understanding when communicating with someone from a different cultural background is to develop a **third culture**. This is created when the communication partners join aspects of separate cultures to create a third, "new" culture that is more comprehensive and inclusive than either of the two separate cultures.[32] The goal of developing a third-culture mentality is to reduce our tendency to approach cultural differences as an "us" versus "them" point of view. Rather than trying to eliminate communication barriers stemming from two different sets of experiences, adopting a third culture framework seeks to create a new understanding of both participants for each other.[33]

Consider the example of Fiona, a businesswoman from Calgary, Alberta and Xiaoxian, a businesswoman from Shanghai, China. In the context of their business relationship, it would be difficult for them to develop a comprehensive understanding of each other's cultural traditions. If, however, they openly acknowledged the most significant of these differences and sought to create a third culture by identifying explicit rules and norms for their interaction, they might be able to develop a more comfortable relationship with each other.

As described by Benjamin Broome, the third culture "is characterized by unique values and norms that may not have existed prior to the dyadic [two-person] relationship."[34] Broome labels the essence of this new relationship **relational empathy**, which permits varying degrees of understanding rather than requiring complete comprehension of another's culture or emotions.

One of the barriers to effective intercultural communication is having different communication codes. In seeking a third culture, you are seeking a way to develop a common code or framework to enhance understanding. Developing such a code that both individuals can understand may include each party's learning the language of the other. It can also include discussing meanings of non-verbal communication so

third culture. Establishing common ground by joining separate cultures to create a third, "new," more comprehensive and inclusive culture.

relational empathy. The essence of the third culture, permitting varying degrees of understanding rather than complete comprehension of another's culture or emotions.

The relationship between this Himalayan Sherpa and Western trekker can be made more comfortable for both of them if they develop a "third culture," different from both of their cultures, with its own rules and expectations.
(David Robbins/Tony Stone Images)

that misunderstandings can be reduced. Further, it involves using the perception check skills we discussed in Chapter 3.

The cultural context includes all of the elements of the culture (learned behaviours and rules or "mental software") that affect the interaction. Do you come from a culture that takes a tea break each afternoon at 4:00? Does your culture value hard work and achievement, or relaxation and enjoyment? Creating a third culture acknowledges the different cultural contexts and interactions participants have experienced and seeks to develop a new context for future interaction.

 Recap

DEVELOP KNOWLEDGE TO ENHANCE UNDERSTANDING

Seek Information about the Culture	Learn about a culture's world view.
Ask Questions and Listen	Reduce uncertainty by asking for clarification and listening to the answer.
Develop a Third Culture	Create common ground.

Developing Motivation: Strategies to Accept Others Who Are Different from Us

To be motivated is to want to do something. To be a competent communicator, the communicator must develop a positive mindset for enhancing his or her ability to relate to others and to also accept others as they are. A key to accepting others is to develop a positive attitude of tolerance and acceptance of those who are different from us. We suggest three strategies to help improve your acceptance and appreciation of others who are different from you: tolerate ambiguity, develop mindfulness, and avoid negative judgments about others.

Building Your Skills

CAN YOU TOLERATE AMBIGUITY?

Respond to each statement with a number from 1 to 5: (1) always false, (2) usually false, (3) sometimes false and sometimes true, (4) usually true, or (5) always true.

_____ 1. I am comfortable in new situations.

_____ 2. I deal with unforeseen problems successfully.

_____ 3. I experience little discomfort in ambiguous situations.

_____ 4. I am relaxed in unfamiliar situations.

_____ 5. I am not frustrated when things do not go the way I expected.

To find your score, add the numbers you wrote next to each statement. Scores range from 5 to 25. The higher your score, the greater your tolerance for ambiguity.

Source: From William B. Gudykunst, Bridging Differences: Effective Intergroup Communication (Newbury Park, Calif.: Sage, 1991), 121.

Tolerate Ambiguity

Communicating with someone from another culture produces uncertainty. It may take time and several exchanges to clarify a message. Be patient and try to expand your capacity to tolerate ambiguity if you are speaking to someone with a markedly different world view.

When Ken and Rita visited Montreal, they asked their hotel concierge to direct them to a church of their faith, and they wound up at one with a predominantly Haitian congregation. They were not prepared for the exuberant chanting and verbal interchanges with the minister during the sermon. They weren't certain whether they should join in or simply sit quietly and observe. Ken whispered to Rita, "I'm not sure what to do. Let's just watch and see what is expected of us." In the end, they chose to sit and clap along with the chanting rather than to become actively involved in the worship. Rita felt uncomfortable and conspicuous, though, and had to fight off the urge to bolt, but after the service, several members of the congregation came up to greet Ken and Rita, invited them to lunch, and expressed great happiness in their visit. "You know," said Rita later in the day, "I'm so grateful that we sat through our discomfort. We might never have met those terrific people. Now I understand why their worship is so noisy—they're just brimming over with joy."

Develop Mindfulness

mindful. To be consciously aware of cultural differences.

"Our life is what our thoughts make it," said Marcus Aurelius in *Meditations*. To be **mindful** of cultural differences is to be consciously aware of them, to acknowledge that there is a connection between thoughts and deeds when you interact with a person from a background different from your own. William Gudykunst suggests that being mindful is one of the best ways to approach any new cultural encounter.[35] Remember that there are and will be cultural differences, and try to keep them in your consciousness. Also, try to consider the other individual's frame of reference or world view and to use his or her cultural priorities and assumptions when you are communicating.[36] Adapt your behaviour to minimize cultural noise and distortion.

If you have seen the movie *My Big Fat Greek Wedding*, you remember that the lead characters in the movie, who decide to get married, are from different cultural traditions. They make a mindful, conscious effort to be aware of their differences yet relate to each other in positive, supportive ways. Not only the married couple, but their parents and family members, eventually develop the skill of being mindful of differences as a way of enhancing the quality of their relationships with one another.

You can become more mindful through self-talk, something we discussed in Chapter 2. Self-talk consists of rational messages to yourself to help you manage your emotions or discomfort with a certain situation. Imagine that you are working on a group project with several of your classmates. One classmate, Suji, was born in Iran. When interacting with you, he consistently gets about 30 cm away, whereas you are more comfortable with 90 to120 cm between you. When Suji encroaches on your space, you could "be mindful" of the difference by mentally noting, "Suji sure likes to get close to people when he talks to them. This might represent a practice in his culture." This self-talk message makes you consciously aware that there may be a difference in your interaction styles. If you still feel uncomfortable, instead of blurting out, "Hey, man, why so close?" you could express your own preferences with an "I" message: "Suji, I'd prefer a bit more space between us when we talk."

Building Your Skills

MEASURING MINDFULNESS

Respond to each statement with a number from 1 to 5: (1) always false, (2) usually false, (3) sometimes false and sometimes true, (4) usually true, or (5) always true.

_____ 1. I pay attention to the situation and context when I communicate.

_____ 2. I can describe others with whom I communicate in great detail.

_____ 3. I seek out new information about the people with whom I communicate.

_____ 4. I try to find rational reasons why others may behave in a way I perceive negatively.

_____ 5. I recognize that the person with whom I am communicating has a different point of view.

To find your score, add the numbers you wrote next to each statement. Scores range from 5 to 25. The higher your score, the more mindful you are when you communicate.

Source: From William B. Gudykunst, Bridging Differences: Effective Intergroup Communication (Newbury Park, Calif.: Sage, 1991), 120.

 # Understanding Diversity

TAO: A UNIVERSAL MORAL CODE

It's clear that there are cultural differences among the world's people and that these differences have existed since there have been people. Anthropologists and communication scholars who study intercultural communication teach us the value of adapting to cultural differences in order to understand others better. However, are there any universal values that are or have been embraced by all humans? The question is not a new one; scholars, theologians, and many others have debated for millennia whether there are any universal underpinnings for all human societies. In Chapter 3, we noted that social psychologists Penelope Brown and Stephen Levinson suggest that

people from all cultures have a universal need to be treated with politeness.[37] Are there other needs and values that all humans share? To uncover such commonalities is to develop a truly human communication theory rather than a theory that applies to a specific cultural context.

C. S. Lewis, a British scholar, author, and educator who taught at both Oxford and Cambridge, argued that there are universal ethical and moral principles that undergird all societies of civilized people, regardless of their religious beliefs, cultural background, or government structure.[38] He suggested that the existence of Natural Laws, or what he called a _Tao_—a universal moral code—informs human ethical decisions. In his book _The Abolition of Man_, Lewis presented eight universal

principles, or laws. He did not claim that all societies have followed these laws—many of them have been clearly violated and continue to be violated today—but he did suggest they provide a bedrock of values against which all societies may be measured. Here are his eight laws:

1. The Law of General Beneficence: Do not murder, be dishonest, or take from others what does not belong to you.

2. The Law of Special Beneficence: Value your family members.

3. Duties to Parents, Elders, and Ancestors: Especially hold your parents, those who are a generation older than you, and your ancestors with special honour and esteem.

4. Duties to Children and Posterity: We have a special obligation to respect the rights of the young and to value those who will come after us.

5. The Law of Justice: Honour the basic human rights of others; each person is of worth.

6. The Law of Good Faith and Veracity: Keep your promises and do not lie.

7. The Law of Mercy: Be compassionate to those less fortunate than you.

8. The Law of Magnanimity: Avoid unnecessary violence against other people.

To support his argument that these are universal values, Lewis offered quotations from several well-known sources, including religious, historical, and political writings, both contemporary and centuries-old. Lewis implied that these eight laws may be viewed as a universal Bill of Rights, and that they constitute an underlying set of principles that either implicitly or explicitly guide all civilized society. Do you agree? Is it useful to search for underlying principles of humanness? Despite cultural differences, are there underlying values or principles that should inform our interactions with others? Is there truly a universal human theory of communication? Or might it do more harm than good to suggest that universal principles underlie what it means to behave and communicate appropriately and effectively?

 ### Avoid Negative Judgments about Another Culture

Canadian tourist on her first visit to France:	"Can you believe it. How repulsive! These people actually eat horse meat and think it's a delicacy."
Black teenager watching his white classmates dance:	"Man, they don't know anything about good music! And those dances are so dumb. I don't call this a party."
Japanese business person visiting Argentina:	"These people are never on time. No wonder they can never catch up to us."
German student, after watching a documentary about life in Japan:	"No wonder they work so hard. They have tiny little houses. I'd work long hours too if I had to live like that."

The kind of ethnocentrism that underlies judgments like these is a communication barrier. It is also an underlying cause of suspicion and mistrust and, in extreme cases, a spark that ignites violence. Instead of making judgments about another culture, try simply to acknowledge differences and to view them as an interesting challenge rather than as an obstacle to be eradicated.

▶ Recap

DEVELOP MOTIVATION TO ACCEPT OTHERS

Tolerate Ambiguity	Take your time and expect some uncertainty.
Develop Mindfulness	Be conscious of cultural differences rather than ignoring the differences.
Avoid Negative Judgments	Resist thinking your culture has all of the answers.

Developing Skills: Strategies to Adapt to Others Who Are Different from Us

To be skilled is to be capable of putting what you know and want to achieve into action. The underlying skill in being interculturally competent is the ability to be flexible, to be other-oriented, and adapt to others.

Develop Flexibility

When you interact with someone from another background, your responding skills are crucial. You can learn only so much from books; you must be willing to learn as you communicate. Every individual is unique, so cultural generalizations that you learn from research may not always apply. It is not accurate to assume, for example, that all French people are preoccupied with food and fashion. Many members of minority groups in Canada find it draining to correct these generalizations in their encounters with others. Pay close attention to the other person's non-verbal cues when you begin conversing; then adjust your communication style and language, if necessary, to put the person at ease. Avoid asking questions or making statements based on generalizations.

Become Other-Oriented

Throughout this book, we have emphasized the importance of becoming other-oriented—focusing on others rather than on yourself—as an important way to enhance your interpersonal competence. We have also discussed the problems ethnocentrism can create when you attempt to communicate with others, especially with those whose culture is different from your own. We now offer two specific ways to increase your other-orientation: social decentring and empathy.

Although our focus in this discussion will be on how to increase other-orientation in intercultural interactions, the principles apply to *all* interpersonal interactions. The major difference between intercultural interactions and those that occur within your own culture is primarily the obviousness of the differences between you and the other person.

Building Your Skills

PREDICTING HOW OTHERS FEEL

Look at the descriptions and rank them from 1 (highest) to 6 (lowest) in order of how readily you could predict each person's reactions on finding out his or her mother or other close relative has just died.

_____ a.   A close friend of yours of the same sex, age, race, and culture.

_____ b.   A 60-year-old male Chinese farmer.

_____ c.   A college student who is 20 years older than you but of the same race, sex, and culture.

_____ d.   A 10-year-old BC girl who is the child of Asian and Hispanic parents.

_____ e.   A college student of a different race from you but the same age, culture, and sex.

_____ f.   A college student of the opposite sex but of the same age, race, and culture as you.

What qualities do you feel provide you with the best information on which to base your judgments? Why? What would you need to know about each person to feel comfortable in making a prediction? How can you get that information?

social decentring. A cognitive process in which we take into account another person's thoughts, feelings, values, background, and perspectives.

1. *Social Decentring.* **Social decentring,** the first strategy, is a *cognitive process* in which we take into account the other person's thoughts, feelings, values, background, and perspectives. This process involves viewing the world from the other person's point of view. The greater the difference between us and the other person, the more difficult it is to accomplish social decentring. In doing the Building Your Skills: Predicting How Others Feel exercise you may find it easier to judge your close friend than any of the other people described.

   The rest of your rankings depend on the various experiences you have had. Your interactions with members of the opposite sex, or with someone from another race, or of a different age are probably the next most frequent, and next highest ranked. Interactions with people from other cultures are probably the most difficult because your experiences in such interactions are often limited. It is easier to socially decentre about someone who is similar in culture and background to you.

   There are three ways to socially decentre or take another's perspective: (1) develop an understanding of others, based on how you have responded when something similar has happened to you, (2) base your understanding of others on the knowledge you have about a specific person, or (3) make generalizations about someone, based on your understanding of how you think most people would feel or behave.[39]

   First, when you draw on your direct experience, you use your past knowledge of what happened to you to help you guess how someone else may feel. To the degree that the other person is similar to you, your reactions and theirs will match. Suppose, for example, you are talking to a student who has just failed a midterm exam in an important course. You have also had this experience. Your reaction was to discount it because you had confidence you could still pull a passing grade. You might use this self-understanding to predict your classmate's reactions. To the degree that you are similar to the classmate, your prediction will be accurate, but suppose your classmate comes from a culture with high expectations for success. Your classmate might feel upset over having dishonoured his or her family by a poor performance. In this situation, understanding your own reaction needs to be tempered by your awareness of how similar or dissimilar the other person is to you. Recognition of differences should lead you to recognize the need to socially decentre in another way.

   The second way we socially decentre—or take the perspective of another—is based on specific knowledge we have of the person with whom we are interacting. Drawing on your memory of how your classmate reacted to a previous failed exam gives you a basis to more accurately predict his or her reaction. Even if you have not observed your classmate's reaction to the same situation, you project how you think he or she would feel based on similar instances. As relationships become more intimate, we gain more information to allow us to more readily socially decentre. Our ability to accurately predict and understand our partners usually increases as relationships become more intimate. In intercultural interactions, the more opportunity you have to interact with the same person and learn more about the person and his or her culture, the more your ability to socially decentre will increase.

   The third way we socially decentre is to apply our understanding of people in general, or of categories of people from whom we have gained some knowledge. Each of us develops implicit personality theories, constructs, and attributions of how people act, as discussed in Chapter 3. You might have a general theory to explain the behaviour of men and another theory for women. You might have general theories about Mexicans, Chinese, Aboriginals, Slovenians, Americans, or black Canadians. As you meet someone who falls into one of your categories, you draw on that conceptualization to socially decentre. The more you can learn about a given culture, the stronger your general theories can be, and the more effectively you can use this method of social decentring. The key, however, is to avoid developing inaccurate, inflexible stereotypes of others and basing your perceptions of others only on those generalizations.

2. *Empathy.* Besides thinking about how another may feel (socially decentring), we can have an emotional reaction to what others do or what they tell us. We feel empathy for another. **Empathy**, a second strategy for becoming other-oriented, is an emotional reaction that is similar to the one being experienced by another person, as compared with social decentring, which is a cognitive reaction. Empathy is feeling what another person feels. Our emotional reaction can be either similar to, or different from, the emotions the other person is experiencing. You might experience mild pity for your classmate who has failed the midterm, in contrast to his or her stronger feelings of anguish and dishonour. On the other hand, you might share his or her same feelings of anguish and dishonour.

empathy. Process of developing an emotional reaction that is similar to the reaction being experienced by another person. Feeling what another person is feeling.

sympathy. To acknowledge that someone may be feeling bad; to be compassionate toward someone.

Some emotional reactions are almost universal and cut across cultural boundaries. You might experience empathy when seeing photos or videos depicting emotional scenes occurring in other countries. Seeing a mother crying while holding her sick or dying child in a refugee camp might move you to cry and feel a deep sense of sadness or loss. You empathize with the woman. You might also experience empathy for your brother, who has just received the devastating news that his best friend has been killed in an automobile accident. You grieve with him. Empathy can enhance interpersonal interactions in a number of ways: it can provide a bond between you and the other person; it is confirming; it is comforting and supportive; it can increase your understanding of others; and it can strengthen the relationship. We can empathize most easily with those who are similar to us, and in situations with which we have had a similar emotional experience.

Grief for the loss of a loved one is a universal emotion that cuts across all cultures.
(David Barnett/Stock Boston)

Developing empathy is different from sympathizing with others. When you offer **sympathy**, you tell others that you are sorry that he or she feels what he or she is feeling. Here are examples and statements of sympathy: "I'm sorry your Uncle Joe died," or "I'm sorry to hear you failed your exam." When you sympathize with others, you acknowledge their feelings, but when you empathize, you experience an emotional reaction that is similar to the other person's; you, too, feel grief or sadness. Recall the strategies for developing empathic listening skills in Chapter 4.

adaptation. Adjusting behaviour in accord with what someone else does. We can adapt based on the individual, the relationship, and the situation.

communication accommodation theory. Theory that suggests all people adapt their behaviour to others' to some extent.

adapt predictively. Modify or change behaviour in anticipation of an event.

adapt reactively. Modify or change behaviour after an event.

Appropriately Adapt Your Communication to Others

The logical extension of being flexible and becoming other-oriented is to adapt your communication to enhance the quality and effectiveness of your interpersonal communication. **Adaptation** means adjusting your behaviour to others to accommodate differences and expectations. Appropriate adaptation occurs in the context of the relationship you have with the other person and what is happening in the communication environment. Adapting to others has its roots in **communication accommodation theory**, which suggests that all people adapt their behaviour to others to some extent. Those who appropriately and sensitively adapt to others are more likely to experience more positive communication.[40]

Adapting to others doesn't mean you only tell others what they want to hear and do what others want you to do. Such placating behaviour is not wise, effective, or ethical. Nor are we suggesting that you adapt your behaviour only so that you can get your way; the goal is effective communication, not manipulation. We are suggesting, however, that you be aware of what your communication partner is doing and saying, especially if there are cultural differences, so that your message is understood and you don't unwittingly offend others. Although it may seem common sense, being sensitive to others and adapting behaviours to others are not as common as you might think.

Sometimes people adapt their behaviour based on what they think someone will like. At other times, they adapt their communication after realizing they have done something wrong. When you modify your behaviour in anticipation of an event, you **adapt predictively**. For example, you might decide to buy a friend flowers to soften the news about breaking a date because you know how much your friend likes flowers. When you modify your behaviour after an event, you **adapt reactively**. For example, you might buy your friend flowers to apologize for a fight.

There are a number of reasons we adapt our communication to the other person. We often adapt our messages in an attempt to make them more understandable. In talking to an individual with limited understanding of English, for instance, you would probably choose simple words and phrases. We also adapt our messages to accomplish our goals more effectively. In our intercultural interactions, we frequently adapt our communication behaviour in response to the feedback or reactions we are receiving. Table 8.2 lists a variety of ways we adapt our verbal messages to others.

Conversation partners also adapt non-verbal cues. For instance, they raise or lower voice volume in response to the volume of a partner, or lean forward toward the partner to match the partner's postural cue.

Adaptation across intercultural contexts is usually more difficult than within one's own culture. Imagine shaking hands with a stranger, and having the stranger hold on to your hand as you continue to talk. In Canada, hand-holding between strangers is a violation of our non-verbal norms, but, in some cultures, maintaining physical contact while talking is expected. Pulling your hand away from this person would be rude. Adapting to these cultural differences means developing that "third" culture that we talked about earlier in the chapter.

Taking an other-oriented approach to communication means considering the thoughts, feelings, background, perspectives, attitudes, and values of your interpersonal partners and adjusting your interaction with them accordingly. Other-orientation leads to more effective interpersonal communication, regardless of whether you are dealing with someone from your family or from another country.

By careful analysis of the factors that affect our communication partners, we can develop understanding and empathy. This understanding and empathy can then help us make the most effective strategic communication choices as we adapt our messages and responses.

Table 8.2   Communication Adaptation Behaviours

Type	Examples
Topical: Choosing a topic or issue to discuss because you know it will interest the other person.	Talking about a mutual friend, talking about a party you both went to, asking if he or she saw a particular play that was in town.
Explanatory/Elaboration: Providing additional information or detail because you recognize that the other person does not know it.	Explaining your mother's eating habits to a new friend, explaining to a neighbour who has squirrel problems how you keep them away from your bean plants.
Withholding Explanation or Information: Not providing explanation because your partner already knows the information; because it might hurt or anger your partner; because of fear of how the other person might misuse it; or to avoid violating a confidentiality.	Not elaborating on the parts of an auto engine when you describe a car problem because you know the listener is knowledgeable about cars; not telling a friend you saw his or her lover with another person because he or she would be hurt; not telling someone about your interest in a mutual friend because you are afraid that person would blab about it to the mutual friend.
Examples/Comparisons/Analogies: Choosing examples that you know your partner will find relevant.	Explaining rollerblading by comparing it to ice skating, something your partner knows how to do.
Personal Referencing: Referring to your partner's specific attitudes, interests, personality, traits, ethnic background, etc.	"I've got something to tell you you'll find funny." "Could you help me balance my cheque book; you're so good at math." "That's a behaviour I'd expect from you, given the way your parents raised you."
Vernacular/Language: Choosing or avoiding certain words because of their potential effect on the receiver. Using words that have a unique meaning for you and your partner. Using words that you think are appropriate to the other person's level of understanding	A wife asking her husband if he was catching flies during a movie, meaning he was asleep with his mouth wide open. A father telling his child that a criminal is someone who does bad things. Two computer jocks talking about "bytes," "ram," and "chips."
Disclosure: Consciously deciding to share information about yourself that the other does not know about you.	Telling your lover about your sexual fantasies. Telling your instructor about family problems.
Immediate Follow-up Questioning: Seeking additional information from the other person about information he or she shares during the interaction.	"So, what was it like growing up in small-town Alberta?"
Delayed Follow-up Questioning: Seeking additional information from the other person about previous information he or she shared.	"Tell me more about your vacation in Toronto." "Where are you going on your date?" "How's your mother doing after her operation yesterday?" "How was your date Saturday night?"
Adapting to Immediate Reaction/Feedback: Modifying your words or behaviour because of your partner's reaction.	If your friend starts to cry when you talk about her mother's death, you might quickly change the topic.

Source: © Mark V. Redmond, 1994. Used by permission.

In an effective interpersonal relationship, your partner is also orienting him- or herself to you. A competent communicator has knowledge of others, is motivated to enhance the quality of communication, and possesses the skill of being other-oriented.

If you learn the skills and principles we have presented here, will it really make a difference in your ability to relate to others? Recent evidence suggests the answer is "yes." A study by Lori Carrell found that students who had been exposed to lessons in empathy linked to a study of interpersonal and intercultural communication improved their ability to empathize with others.[41] There is evidence that, if you master these principles and skills, you will be rewarded with greater insight and ability to relate to others who are different from you.

Becoming Other-Oriented

THE PLATINUM RULE

The ultimate goal of becoming other-oriented goes beyond having sympathy for others. Being other-oriented may even go beyond what is typically labelled as the "Golden Rule": Do to others as you would have them do to you. Or, as stated by the Buddha: Consider others as yourself. In Chapter 2 (page 70), we identified additional interpretations of the same principle from a variety of religious traditions. Communication researcher Milton Bennett calls the ultimate other-oriented principle "the Platinum Rule": *Do to others as they themselves* would like to be treated.[42] Rather than treating people as *you* would like to be treated, interact with others the way you think and

feel *they* would like to be treated. For example, when ordering a pizza for your friends, the golden rule would suggest you order a pizza with toppings you would like; the platinum rule is to order what you think your dining partners would like. Or, if you've decided to buy your friend a book for her birthday, buy a book not because you like it but because you think your friend will like it. According to Bennett, at its essence, empathy is "the imaginative, intellectual and emotional participation in another person's experience."[43] The goal, according to Bennett, is to attempt to think and feel what another person thinks and feels, and then to go beyond trying to feel what the other person feels and take positive action toward others in response to your empathic

feelings.

As you ponder the virtues and challenges of becoming other-oriented, consider the following questions:

1. Is the Platinum Rule always useful, desirable, or even possible? Explain your answer.

2. What are some of the obstacles to applying the Platinum Rule during your everyday interactions with others?

3. How can the Platinum Rule be useful when you are having a disagreement or conflict with another person?

4. Think about a time when you used the Platinum Rule. What was the effect on the person with whom you were communicating?

 Recap

DEVELOP SKILL TO ADAPT TO OTHERS

Develop Flexibility	Learn to "go with the flow."
Become Other-Oriented	Put yourself in the other person's mental and emotional mindset; adapt to others; listen and respond appropriately.
Adapt Your Communication to Others	Adjust your behaviour to others to accommodate differences and expectations.

 Summary

A culture is a system of knowledge that is shared by a large group of people. It includes cultural elements, values, goals, and contexts. Cultural elements are categories of things and ideas that identify key aspects of cultural influence.

Cultural values reflect how individuals regard masculine and feminine behaviours and individual and collective achievements. They also reflect whether individuals can tolerate ambiguity or need a high degree of certainty and whether they believe in concentrated or decentralized power structures. The goals of a culture depend on the way it values individual versus group achievement. In high-context cultures, the meaning of messages depends heavily on non-verbal information; low-context cultures rely more heavily on words than on context for deriving meaning.

Intercultural communication occurs when individuals or groups from different cultures communicate. There are several barriers that inhibit effective intercultural communication. Ethnocentrism is the belief that our own cultural traditions and assumptions are superior to those of others. Differences in language and the way we interpret non-verbal messages also interfere with effective intercultural communication. We stereotype by placing a group or a person into an inflexible, all-encompassing category. A related barrier is prejudice—we often prejudge someone before we know all of the facts. Stereotyping and prejudice can keep us from viewing people as unique individuals and, therefore, hamper effective, honest communication. Finally, assuming that we are similar to others can also be a barrier to intercultural communication. All humans have some similarities, but our cultures have taught us to process the world differently.

Although it is reasonably easy to identify cultural differences, it is more challenging to bridge those differences. To enhance understanding between cultures, we suggest the following: develop knowledge by seeking information about the culture, ask questions and listen effectively, and develop a "third culture." Increase your motivation to appreciate others who are different from you by tolerating ambiguity, developing mindfulness, and avoiding negative judgments about another culture. Finally, enhance your skill by becoming flexible. Be other-oriented by socially decentring and becoming more empathic, and by adapting your verbal and non-verbal behaviour to others.

For Discussion and Review

● Focus on Critical Thinking

1. Christine, a Canadian, has just been accepted as a foreign exchange student in Germany. What are potential cultural barriers that she might face? How should she manage these potential barriers?

2. What's the problem in assuming that other people are like us? How does this assumption create a barrier to effective intercultural communication?

3. If you were to design a lesson plan for elementary school-age students about how to deal with racial and ethnic stereotypes, what would you include?

4. What are appropriate ways to deal with someone who consistently utters racial slurs and demonstrates prejudice toward racial or ethnic groups? Using your research navigator, find one article that suggests some ways to deal with this type of behaviour. Share your article and findings with your class or small group.

● Focus on Ethics

5. Marla is the director of the campus multicultural studies program. She wants to require all students, over the course of their normal four-year program, to take at least four courses that focus on multicultural issues. Is it appropriate to force students to take such a concentration of courses?

6. Should an individual always speak out upon hearing a racist, sexist, or otherwise offensive remark? What if the listener is not a member of the target group? Are there contextual factors to consider before speaking out?

7. Is it ethical or appropriate for someone from one culture to attempt to change the cultural values of someone from a different culture? For example, culture A practises polygamy: one husband can be married to several wives. Culture B practises monogamy: one husband can be married to only one wife. Should a person from culture B attempt to make someone from culture A change his or her ways?

For Your Journal

1. Describe your perceptions of your cultural values, based on the discussion of cultural values beginning on page 258 in this chapter. On a scale of 1 to 10 (where 10 represents the highest value), rate yourself on the value of masculine versus feminine perspective, individual versus group achievement, tolerance of uncertainty versus need for certainty, and centralized versus decentralized power. Provide an example of your reaction to an interpersonal communication encounter to illustrate each of these values.

2. Write a journal entry discussing how you have experienced one of the barriers to effective intercultural communication described in this chapter. Have you been ethnocentric in your thoughts or behaviour or a victim of ethnocentrism? Describe a situation in which communication was difficult because you and your communication partner spoke different languages. Have you been a victim of stereotyping or prejudice? Have you assumed someone was similar to yourself and, later, found that there were more differences than you suspected?

Learning with Others

1. Bring to class a fable, folk tale, or children's story from a culture other than your own. As a group, analyze the cultural values implied by the story or characters in the story.

2. Working with a group of your classmates, develop an ideal culture based on the combined values and elements of people in your group. Develop a name for your culture. Suggest foods, recreational activities, and other leisure pursuits. Compare the culture your group develops with those that other groups in your class develop. How would the communication skills and principles discussed in this chapter help you bridge differences among those cultures?[44]

3. As a group, go on an intercultural scavenger hunt. Your instructor will give you a time limit. Scavenge your campus or classroom area to identify influences of as many different cultures as you can find. For example, you could go to the cafeteria and make a note of ethnic foods that you find. Identify clothing, music, or architecture that is influenced by certain cultures.

4. Log onto your Research Navigator and attempt to find one article about prejudice and discrimination in Canada. Your article should be about recent prejudice or discrimination experienced by a culture or group in Canada. Share your article with the class or another student in small groups or pairs. After sharing your article, discuss why you think prejudice and discrimination are still prevalent in Canada or why there is little of it.

Weblinks

http://strategis.ic.gc.ca/epic/internet/inabc-eac.nsf/en/home   This is the site for Aboriginal Business Canada. There are several links that can be accessed which focus on the development and promotion of Aboriginal business opportunities in Canada.

www.cal.org/pubs/ncrcpubs.html   This site offers a wealth of information for people who teach and learn languages of other cultures.

www.thesurvivorproject.org   This site is maintained by a non-profit organization that promotes understanding and acceptance of human diversity and human rights through education, oral history, and the arts.

http://community-2.webtv.net/SoundBehavior/DIVERSITYFORSOUND   This page highlights excellent links related to multicultural awareness and diversity. It also provides useful resource links for understanding the power of human differences.

Chapter

9

Understanding Interpersonal Relationships

After you study this chapter

you should be able to ...

1. Explain how relationships are systems and processes.

2. Differentiate between relationships of circumstance and relationships of choice.

3. Describe three dimensions of interpersonal relationships.

4. Explain what it means to have an intimate relationship.

5. Describe the elements that contribute to interpersonal attraction.

6. Identify the principles of interpersonal power.

7. Describe the types of power and how to negotiate power in a relationship.

8. Describe two theories that explain how relationships develop.

● An Interpersonal Relationship As a System and a Process

● Relationships of Circumstance and Relationships of Choice

● Intimacy and Attraction in Relationships

● Interpersonal Power in Relationships

● Interpersonal Relationship Development Theories

Pat:	Hi, aren't you in my communication course?
Jinping:	Oh, yeah, I've seen you across the room.
Pat:	What do you think about the course so far?
Jinping:	It's okay, but I feel a little intimidated by some of the class activities.
Pat:	I know what you mean. It gets kind of scary to talk about yourself in front of everyone else.
Jinping:	Yeah. Plus some of the stuff you hear. I was paired up with this one student the other day who started talking about being arrested last year on a drug charge.
Pat:	Really? I bet I know who that is. I don't think you have to worry about it.
Jinping:	Don't mention that I said anything.
Pat:	It's OK. I know that guy, and he just likes to act big.

This interaction between Pat and Jinping illustrates the reciprocal nature of interpersonal communication and interpersonal relationships. As you learned in Chapter 1, interpersonal relationships are connections that we develop with other people as a direct result of our interpersonal communication with them. The character and quality of interpersonal communication is affected, in turn, by the nature of the relationship.

The conversation between Pat and Jinping begins with a casual acknowledgment but quickly proceeds to a higher level of intimacy. Jinping confides in Pat. Pat, an other-oriented listener, offers confirmation and support; this response encourages Jinping to confide even more. In this brief encounter, Pat and Jinping have laid the groundwork for transforming their casual acquaintanceship into a more intimate relationship.

In these last three chapters, we will explore the dynamic link between interpersonal communication and interpersonal relationships. Drawing from the understanding of communication you have acquired from the first eight chapters, you will learn about the nature of relationships, their development from initiation to termination, and the specific communication skills you can apply to maintaining them.

In this chapter, we examine the nature of interpersonal relationships and the principles of how relationships work, building on the descriptions presented in Chapter 1.

An Interpersonal Relationship As a System and a Process

Interpersonal relationships are transactional just like interpersonal communication. This means that each person in a relationship affects the other person. Actually, relationships are affected by a wide range of factors that can best be understood by thinking of a relationship as a system. Systems theory was created originally to explain changes that occur in plant life,[1] but it has also proven valuable in explaining a variety of other phenomena, including interpersonal relationships.

system. A set of interconnected elements in which change in one element affects all the other elements.

A **system** is a set of interconnected elements often described in terms of their relationships as *inputs, throughputs* (or *process*), and *outputs.* The most fundamental notion in systems theory is that a change in any system element affects all the other elements. Relationships can be thought of as a kind of system, which means that a change in one element of the relationship affects the other elements. For example, a change in your best friend's mood or behaviour affects your mood and behaviour as well. The more interdependent we are, the more impact each partner has on the other partner, and the more a change in one affects the other. Married couples can be classified according to how interdependent their relationship is and thus how much they are like a system.

One difficulty in analyzing a relationship as a system is deciding what elements are part of the system; that is, what are the system's boundaries? Is your job, your relationship with your father, your boss's mood, or your communication teacher an element of your relationship with your best friend? Certainly each of these can affect you, and thus can affect your relationship. If your communication instructor acts particularly nasty to you in class one day (this is just hypothetical because we know how great communication instructors are), it might affect how you feel about yourself and influence your interaction with your best friend. For the purposes of this text, you don't need to worry about deciding what is in and what is out of a system; simply recognize that lots of factors affect your relationships, including ones of which you are unaware.

As processes, relationships are constantly changing and evolving. They are always moving to a new level and being redefined. The changes might not be enormous, but because you are part of the relationship system, you change, too. Part of the change stems simply from the fact that relationships are ongoing—they exist over a period of time. Existing over time means that relationships develop a history; they are cumulative. As you interact with a person, you gain a history together that becomes part of the relationship and affects each subsequent interaction. In the movie *As Good as It Gets*, Helen Hunt plays Carol, a waitress who develops a particular impression of and way of interacting with Jack Nicholson's character, Melvin. When Melvin begins to visit Carol and

In an intimate, trusting relationship, we can feel safe in telling our deepest secrets to another person.
(Peter Cade/Tony Stone Images)

help her son, she is confused because she still sees him as a diner customer; their previous interactions are affecting subsequent ones. The accumulation of each succeeding event fosters a romantic relationship.

One last principle of a process is its irreversibility: once something is done, it can't be undone. Melvin's help with her son continues to affect Carol positively, despite his tactless and irritating manner. Consider how your own relationships are ongoing processes, continually building on each interaction.

Relationships of Circumstance and Relationships of Choice

In Chapter 1, an **interpersonal relationship** is defined as an ongoing connection that we make with another person and that we carry in our minds (and, metaphorically, in our hearts) whether the other person is present or not. These ongoing connections can be formed either because of unintentional circumstances or because of intentional choice. **Relationships of circumstance** form not because we choose them but simply because our lives overlap with others' in some way. Relationships with family members, teachers, classmates, and co-workers fall into this category. In contrast, when we seek out and intentionally develop a relationship with someone, it is a **relationship of choice**. These kinds of relationships might include acquaintances, friends, lovers, spouses, or counsellors.

> It is chance that makes brothers but hearts that make friends.
>
> — *von Geibel*

We act and communicate differently in these two types of relationships because the stakes are different. The effect of the same interpersonal communication behaviour on different relationships can be dramatic. If we act in foolish or inappropriate ways, a friend might end the relationship. If we act the same way within the confines of our family, our relatives may not like us much, but we will still remain family.

Of course, these categories are not mutually exclusive. Relationships of circumstance can also be relationships of choice: your brother or sister can also be your best friend. You can break off interacting with family members or quit your job to sever your relationships with fellow employees. In addition, the other individual can define and redefine the relationship. Your boss might fire you, a relative might cut you off, or a lover might desert you.

Intimacy and Attraction in Relationships

One of the most significant aspects of any relationship is its level of intimacy. In everyday usage, the word "intimacy" is often associated with sexual activity; however, interpersonal or psychological intimacy has a broader meaning that applies to non-sexual relationships as well. What qualities (aside from sexual ones) do you associate with relationships that you think of as close or intimate? Here are some qualities that are commonly associated with interpersonal intimacy:

interpersonal relationship. Those connections we make with other people through interpersonal communication.

relationships of circumstance. Interpersonal relationships that exist because of the circumstances in which we are born, circumstances in which we work or study, and so on.

relationship of choice. An interpersonal relationship we choose to initiate, maintain, or terminate.

- Feelings of closeness

- Sharing one's innermost thoughts and feelings

- Mutual appreciation

- Confidence that the partner will provide nurturance and support

- Emotional bonding

- Unconditional support

- Openness and honesty

- Affection and warmth

interpersonal intimacy. The degree to which a person's sense of self is accepted and confirmed by another person in a relationship.

Ultimately, what seems to make relationships the most intimate is our ability to be ourselves with another person, which means being able to be open and feeling accepted and loved. Thus, we define **interpersonal intimacy** as the degree to which each person's sense of self is confirmed and accepted by his or her partner in a relationship. You can measure the intimacy of relationships by the extent to which other people share your image of yourself while expressing positive feelings toward you. In essence, they love you in spite of your flaws and you don't have to hide those flaws from them.

We depend on intimate relationships to provide us with information about ourselves (as exemplified in the Johari window from Chapter 2) and to bolster our self-confidence. The more intimate the relationship, the more we depend on others for acceptance and confirmation of our self-image.[2] During periods when we might not have very intimate relationships, it is sometimes hard to maintain a strong positive self-image. Research confirms that having strong social support networks is related to subjective well-being.[3]

Your self-image can only be confirmed when another person really knows who you are. This is one reason some theorists see self-disclosure as the most significant factor in moving people toward intimate relationships.[4] Chapter 2 discussed how self-disclosure is necessary to develop an intimate relationship. Figure 9.1 orders the labels generally associated with interpersonal relationships according to their relative intimacy.

Going from being strangers to being best friends involves moving through a number of relational stages that are associated with sharing information about ourselves. (Chapter 10 covers more on relationship stages.) Our communication behaviours and strategies are directly linked to the level of relational intimacy—we communicate differently depending on the level of intimacy in a relationship. Interpersonal communication scholars Denise Solomon and Leanne Knobloch hypothesize that in more intimate relationships, people exhibit direct information-seeking behaviour to reduce uncertainties, while those in less intimate relationships exhibit indirect behaviours.[5] For example, if a close friend uncharacteristically began

Figure 9.1
Continuum of Interpersonal Intimacy and Relationships

Non-Intimate   Highly Intimate

Stranger ◄─► Acquaintance ◄─► Casual Friend ◄─► Friend ◄─► Close Friend ◄─► Best Friend/Spouse

binge drinking, you would ask him or her about it. On the other hand, you would be less inclined to ask an acquaintance so directly about his or her drinking. Solomon and Knobloch also speculate that direct information seeking creates greater clarity and understanding, thus increasing the solidarity of intimate relationships.

We communicate our sense of intimacy to others both directly, through our words, and indirectly, through actions. We might tell another person how we feel about him or her and how much we value the relationship. On the other hand, being open and honest by disclosing highly personal information is an indirect way of expressing interpersonal intimacy. We also might use non-verbal cues, such as close physical proximity, eye contact, tone of voice, touch, and time spent interacting.

The process of developing an intimate relationship usually begins and is sustained because of your attraction to another person. Attraction exists whenever you have a positive regard for another person—when you like someone. **Interpersonal attraction** is the degree to which you want to form or maintain an interpersonal relationship. You might find yourself attracted to an acquaintance, which motivates you to increase your interactions, which in turn increases, decreases, or sustains your attraction.

Short-Term Initial Attraction and Long-Term Maintenance Attraction

Interpersonal attraction occurs in the early stages of relational development as short-term initial attraction, and in the later stages of relational development as long-term maintenance attraction. You can understand the difference between the two by looking at your own relationships. Think of the dozens of people whom you initially found attractive but with whom you never developed an intimate relationship. **Short-term initial attraction** is the degree to which we sense a *potential* for developing an interpersonal relationship. For instance, you might find one of your classmates to be physically attractive but never move to introduce yourself. The information you gather in your first interaction with someone can also generate a short-term initial attraction for a relationship, which you may or may not pursue, depending on the circumstances. **Long-term maintenance attraction**, in contrast, sustains relationships like your best friendships. It refers to a level of liking or positive feeling that motivates us to maintain or escalate a relationship. Short-term attraction gives way to long-term attraction as a relationship develops through the stages presented in Chapter 10.

Think about your best friend. How did that relationship start? Perhaps it was because he or she was physically attractive, or perhaps you observed your friend laughing and joking with others and found that quality attractive. Why are you still friends with this person? Rarely (except in some movies or TV shows) do we commit to, and maintain, a long-term intimate relationship such as marriage or an enduring friendship solely because we find another person physically attractive.[6] Perhaps you have discovered that you and your friend have a lot in common or that your personalities are complementary. For instance, your friend's calm, even disposition might balance your fiery temper.

In a study of initial and maintenance attraction, students were asked to think about a person with whom they had a close personal relationship and were given a list of reasons for attraction.[7] One group was asked to identify the reasons for the initial attraction, while another group was asked to explain the current attraction. The number-one reason for initial attraction was the other person's desirable personality, followed by the person's warmth and kindness. The number-one reason for maintenance of attraction was warmth and kindness, followed by desirable personality.

interpersonal attraction. The degree to which you are motivated to form or maintain an interpersonal relationship.

short-term initial attraction. Degree to which you sense a potential for an interpersonal relationship.

long-term maintenance attraction. A liking or positive feeling that motivates you to sustain a relationship.

Elements of Interpersonal Attraction

Why do we feel attracted to some people and not to others? The explanations are complex, but researchers have identified seven elements that influence our feelings of attraction. As you read about them, try to analyze your own feelings about people you find attractive.

🔵 Physical Attraction

physical attraction. The degree to which we find another person's physical self appealing.

The degree to which we find another person's physical self appealing represents our **physical attraction** to him or her. This appeal might be based on body size, height, clothing, hairstyle, makeup, jewellery, vocal qualities, gestures, and so forth. The old adage, "Beauty is in the eye of the beholder," is particularly true in terms of explaining physical attraction. Each culture has its own definition of the physical ideal, which it teaches and perpetuates. In North America, for instance, advertisements and TV programs promote a slender body as the ideal for both males and females. This certainly contributes to our society's fixation on losing weight and staying fit. In some cultures, and at various times throughout history, however, physical attractiveness was synonymous with bulkiness.

Physical attractiveness has been found to be more important for initial attraction than for maintenance attraction.[8] It acts as a convenient filter to reduce relationship possibilities.[9] In general, we tend to seek out individuals who represent the same level of physical attractiveness as ourselves. Suppose you are really into physical conditioning and have a personal philosophy about healthy eating habits, exercise, avoiding drugs, and not smoking. You will probably seek out, and attract, a physically fit person to be your partner. To a certain degree, the physical image a person presents can reflect more substantive qualities. For example, there is a good possibility that a physically fit individual's philosophy about eating and exercise would be similar to yours. This similarity might serve as the basis for a long-term maintenance attraction. As you learned in Chapter 3, we use superficial information to make inferences about personality with varying degrees of accuracy but whether we decide to escalate a relationship depends on what happens in the initial and subsequent interactions.

🔵 Credibility, Competence, and Charisma

Most of us are attracted to individuals who seem competent and credible. We like those who are sure of themselves but not full of themselves. We assume they are competent if they seem skilled, knowledgeable, and experienced. We find people credible if they display a blend of enthusiasm, trustworthiness, competence, and power. Competence, credibility, and, sometimes, physical attractiveness are all important elements in the composite quality we call *charisma*, which inspires strong attraction and allegiance. Political and other types of leaders often depend on their charisma to attract supporters who are motivated to form relationships with them and willing to devote themselves to a chosen cause.

off the mark   by Mark Parisi
w w w . o f f t h e m a r k . c o m

ATLANTIC FEATURE © 1994 MARK PARISI   www.offthemark.com

LIZ AND MONTY TRIED TO HIDE IT FROM THEIR COWORKERS, BUT IT WAS QUITE APPARENT THERE WAS A THING BETWEEN THEM.

Proximity

We are more likely to be attracted to people who are physically close (in **proximity**) to us than to those who are farther away. In this class, you are more likely to form a relationship with classmates sitting on either side of you than with someone seated at the opposite end of the room. This is partly because physical proximity increases communication opportunities. We tend to talk with someone on a casual, offhand basis because he or she is right next to us. We are more likely to talk, and therefore to feel attracted, to neighbours who live right next door than those who live down the block. Any circumstance that increases the possibilities for interacting is also likely to increase attraction.

In impromptu surveys of students in our classes over the years, we have found that a high percentage form close friendships with residence roommates who were randomly assigned. There is a good chance that two individuals will become good friends simply because they share living accommodations. In one study on attraction, a researcher told pairs of people about one another, describing to each the other's dissimilar attitudes on a particular topic.[10] The participants were then asked to rate their attraction to the other person. All of the ratings were low. Then the partners were introduced to one another and allowed to interact. Even when they discussed only the attitude on which they disagreed, they had significantly more attraction for one another. Clearly, the information exchange that communication affords increases our ability to make an informed decision about pursuing a relationship. In addition, in both of these examples, the interaction was between two college students—two individuals who already have a great deal in common. This commonality is the source of the next form of attraction.

Similarity

In general, we are attracted to people whose personalities, values, upbringing, personal experiences, attitudes, and interests bear some **similarity** to ours. We seek them out through shared activities. You may, for example, join a folk dance group because you know the members share a dance interest with you. Within the group, you would be especially attracted to those who have a similar sense of humour, who share the same attitudes on certain issues, or who enjoy some of the same additional activities that you do. As we interact, we discover both similarities and differences between ourselves and others. We assess the relative weight of those similarities and differences and arrive at a level of attraction that may change over time as we continue to discover more information.

In the initial stages of a relationship, we try to emphasize positive information about ourselves to create a positive and attractive image. We reveal those aspects of ourselves that we believe we have in common with the other person, and the other person does the same.[11] Think about your initial interactions with strangers; typically, you spend the first few minutes trying to find topics of mutual interest. You discover that the person is from a place near your hometown, has the same musical tastes, likes the same sports, frequents the same restaurants, has been to your favourite campground, has the same attitude about school, has had the same instructor for history class, and on and on. However, the depth of this information is limited. We save our revelations about important attitudes and issues for a later stage in the relational development process.[12] Attitude similarity is more likely to be a source of long-term maintenance attraction than of short-term initial attraction. Similarity of interests and leisure activities appears more important in same-sex friendships than opposite-sex relationships.[13]

proximity. The quality that promotes attraction because of being physically close to another and, therefore, in a position to communicate easily.

similarity. We are attracted to people whose personalities, values, upbringing, personal experiences, attitudes, and interests are similar to ours.

Complementary Needs

You have heard the adage, "Opposites attract." Although we like people with whom we have much in common, most of us wouldn't find it very exciting to be stuck for the rest of our lives with someone who had identical attitudes, needs, values, and interests. Most of us look instead for someone with **complementary needs**. As we discussed in Chapter 2, Schutz identified three interpersonal needs that motivate us to form and maintain relationships with others: inclusion, control, and affection.[14] *Inclusion* represents the need to include others in your activities, or to be included in theirs. *Control* represents the need to make decisions and take responsibility, or the willingness to accept others' decision making. *Affection* represents the need to be loved and accepted by others, or the willingness to give love and acceptance to others.

If you have a high need to control and make decisions, and little respect for others' decision making, you will be more compatible with someone who does not have similar needs—someone who wants others to make decisions for him or her. In essence, we can view pairs of individuals as a team in which each side complements the other side's weaknesses. If you're not very good at keeping track of your bills and balancing your cheque book, you might pair up with someone who is good at maintaining a budget in order to create a strong personal finance team. In reality, there are no "perfect" matches, only degrees of compatibility relative to needs.

complementary needs. We are attracted to those whose needs complement our own; one person's weakness is the other person's strength.

Building Your Skills

ARE YOUR NEEDS COMPLEMENTARY?

Evaluate your level of interpersonal needs for each of the following by putting your first initial along the rating scale.

1. How much do you like to include others in the activities you do?

   Very little 1———2———3———4———5———6———7———8———9———10 A great deal

2. How much do you like to be included by others when they are involved in activities?

   Very little 1———2———3———4———5———6———7———8———9———10 A great deal

3. How much do you like to take responsibility for decision making?

   Very little 1———2———3———4———5———6———7———8———9———10 A great deal

4. How much do you like to let others make decisions for you?

   Very little 1———2———3———4———5———6———7———8———9———10 A great deal

5. How much do you feel a need to be accepted and loved by others?

   Very little 1———2———3———4———5———6———7———8———9———10 A great deal

6. How much do you feel a need to accept others and to give love to others?

   Very little 1———2———3———4———5———6———7———8———9———10 A great deal

Now think of two close friends. Go back and place their first initials along each rating scale to indicate how much each item applies to them. Or ask your friends to initial the scale for themselves. Compare your ratings with those of your friends. Are there areas where you are similar? Complementary? Are there differences that cause difficulties in the relationship—for example, you both want to make decisions rather than accept others' decisions?

Relationship Potential

We need interpersonal relationships to confirm our self-image. The **predicted outcome value theory (relationship potential)** claims that we assess the potential for any given relationship to meet this relational need and then weigh that assessment against the potential costs.[15] We are attracted to others with whom a relationship may yield a high outcome value (the rewards might exceed the costs). In the romantic comedy *Two Weeks' Notice*, the liberal activist attorney, played by Sandra Bullock, initially thought that working for the capitalist, played by Hugh Grant, would do little to meet the needs of either of them. Over time, the two developed a working relationship that did meet certain needs. At a certain point, they both thought the relationship had gone as far as it could. In the end, however, they discovered that they could have a more intimate relationship with a high outcome value for them both.

Like these film characters, most of us begin predicting outcome values in initial interactions and continually modify our predictions as we learn more and more about the other person. We pursue attractions beyond the initial interaction stage if we think they can yield positive outcomes, and generally we avoid or terminate relationships for which we predict negative outcomes.[16]

predicted outcome value theory (relationship potential). We are most attracted to those relationships that potentially have greater rewards or benefits than costs.

▲●■   Understanding Diversity

DATING CUSTOMS AROUND THE WORLD

The development of relationships varies from culture to culture. The following list describes some dating behaviours from cultures throughout the world.

AFGHANISTAN

Dating is rare because most marriages are arranged by parents, and schools are separate for boys and girls. Opportunities to meet are rare. Girls have a 7:00 p.m. curfew, whereas boys have an 11:00 p.m. curfew.

AUSTRALIA

Most teens go out in large groups and don't pair off until they are 18 or 19 years old. Girls often ask boys out—and pay for the date, too. Couples often go to dinner parties, barbecues, or the beach.

CENTRAL AND SOUTH AMERICA

Dating is not allowed until the age of 15. When of age, most boys and girls date in large groups, going out together to weekend dance parties. When not dancing, teens gather at local clubs to eat and talk.

EUROPE

Dating is usually a group event. In Finland, as many as 30 teens may attend a movie together. Slumber parties are common in Italy and Switzerland, where teens gather for parties at a home and sleep there when the party is over. In Spain,

In Russian small towns, teens often meet in the streets downtown to socialize together. How does this compare with your experiences?

Continued

teens join a *pandilla*, a club or a group of friends with the same interests, such as cycling or hiking. Dating is done one-to-one, and both girls and boys ask each other out and split the cost of the evening's entertainment. In Russia, dates take place at dances or at clubs where teens eat or chat with friends. In small towns, teens meet in the streets downtown or gather around a fountain.

IRAN

It is against the law to date. Teens are separated until they are of marrying age; then their families introduce them to each other and sometimes a courtship follows.

JAPAN AND KOREA

Most high school students don't date or go to parties but spend their time studying instead. Dating begins in college, when only boys do the asking and pay for the dates.

Source: "Dating Customs Around the World." www.factmonster.com/ ipka/A0767654.htm. Infoplease.com, 2003. Pearson Education: www.infoplease.com.

🔴 Reciprocation of Liking

reciprocation of liking. We like people who like us.

We like people who like us. One way to get other people to reciprocate is to show that we like them; we work toward a **reciprocation of liking**. In initial interactions, however, we are often reluctant to let other people know that we are attracted to them. We may hold back from showing our interest because we fear rejection or fear that we may give the other person a certain amount of power over us.

A study conducted by one of the authors and a colleague found that we often underestimate how much a new acquaintance is attracted to us.[17] Pairs of male and female college students interacted for the first time and then indicated their level of attraction for their partner, as well as their perception of how attracted their partner was to them. Most of the students significantly underestimated the amount of attraction the other person felt for them. It is unclear whether we underestimate because we don't have much confidence that others will like us as much as we like them, or because we, as North Americans, in general do not effectively communicate our level of attraction for others. Even in long-term relationships, people sometimes hold back in expressing their continued attraction for their friends or mates. As you interact with new acquaintances, keep in mind that they probably are more attracted to you than you realize, so you might want to adapt your decision making accordingly.

▶ Recap

ELEMENTS OF INTERPERSONAL ATTRACTION

Term	Explanation	Examples
Physical Attraction	The degree to which we find another's physical self appealing.	Elements include body type and size, mannerisms, height, hairstyle, jewellery, facial features, and clothes.
Credibility, Competence, and Charisma	We are attracted to individuals whom we perceive to be enthusiastic, knowledgeable, skilled, and trustworthy.	We find teachers, athletes, and movie and TV stars attractive because we see them as skillful or credible.
Proximity	Physical proximity encourages attraction.	We are more attracted to immediate neighbours than to those who live down the block.
Similarity	We are attracted to those who share similarities with us.	We make friends with people who have personalities, interests, values, beliefs, and attitudes similar to ours.

Continued

Complementary Needs	We seek out people whose needs complement our own.	Those who want control are compatible with those who want to surrender control.
Relationship Potential	We are attracted to those with whom we see the potential for a rewarding relationship.	As Humphrey Bogart said to Claude Rains in the movie *Casablanca*, "You know, Louie, this could be the beginning of a beautiful friendship."
Reciprocation of Liking	We are attracted to those who are attracted to us.	If someone indicates an interest in us, we tend to find him or her attractive.

Interpersonal Power in Relationships

As relationships move toward intimacy, partners often struggle with the question of who makes the decisions or with the problem of one partner's domination over the other. These are issues of power, and they play a significant role in the development, maintenance, and health of a relationship. **Interpersonal power** is the ability to influence another person in the direction you desire—to get another person to do what you want. As relationships develop, interpersonal interactions reflect changes in the interpersonal power between the partners. The ability of partners to reach a mutually acceptable understanding of their interpersonal power is a determining factor in achieving and maintaining intimate relationships.

interpersonal power.   Ability to influence another person in the direction one desires in the context of an interpersonal relationship.

dependent relationship.   A relationship in which one partner has a greater need for the other to meet his or her needs.

Principles of Interpersonal Power

Think about the people with whom you have interpersonal relationships: friends, co-workers, family members, classmates, and teachers. The people in each of these relationships inevitably have some power over you, and you have power over them. Most of us don't like to think that other people have power over us, but interpersonal power is a fundamental element of all our personal relationships. Understanding the following five principles will enable you to more effectively manage power in your day-to-day interactions and ongoing relationships.

1. Power exists in all interactions and all relationships. Influence is one of the defining qualities of interpersonal communication presented in Chapter 1. When you talk, you are attempting to exert power over other people if for no other purpose than to get them to listen to you. Have you ever tried to talk to someone who did not want to listen? This situation can be frustrating because you are exerting power but meeting resistance; the other person's refusal to listen is an exertion of power against you. Most of the time our interactions flow fairly easily as the participants share power, taking turns speaking and listening. By definition, being in a relationship means letting someone have some influence on you.

2. *Power primarily derives from an individual's ability to meet another person's needs within a given relationship.* The degree to which one person can satisfy another person's interpersonal needs (for inclusion, control, and affection) and/or other needs (for food, clothing, safety, sex, money) represents the amount of power that person has. In a **dependent relationship**, one person has a greater need for the partner to satisfy his or her needs. One study of heterosexual romantic

couples found that the partner with less emotional involvement in the relationship had more power, and this was generally the man.[18] Maybe you've wanted to continue a relationship that lost its value for your partner, and as a result of this power imbalance, you agreed to requests that you normally would have rejected. The more we depend on one person to satisfy our needs, the more power that person has over us. On the other hand, the more people who are available to meet our needs, the less power any one individual has.

In the classic movie *Back to the Future*, Marty McFly's dad, George, initially appears powerless against Biff, his supervisor. George lets Biff walk all over him, much to Marty's dismay. Later, George's position changes as he gains confidence and gains power over Biff. Just as George's becoming a successful author makes him no longer dependent on Biff, your ability to satisfy your own needs without reliance on another person reduces the amount of power another person has over you.

3. *Both partners in an ongoing relationship have some degree of power.* In some relationships, it might appear as though one person has all the power and his or her partner is powerless. You might have felt that imbalance in your relationship with your parents as you were growing up. However, children do have power in their relationships with their parents. Parents want their children's love, they want to protect their children, and they want their children to be happy. These parental wants and needs give children some foundation for influencing their parents.

    When two individuals are mutually satisfying each other's needs, they create an **interdependent relationship**; each person in the relationship has a similar amount of power over the other. The more intimate and exclusive a given relationship, the more we turn to that one person to satisfy a broader spectrum of our needs. You've probably had friends reduce their interactions with you when they turned to their romantic partners to fill the needs you once met.

4. *Power is circumstantial.* Because our needs change, so does power. As you were growing up, you were very dependent on your parents and other adults. However, as you grew and developed skills, you no longer needed your parents to meet certain needs, and thus their power diminished. This change isn't always without some tension as parents begin to realize they don't have the degree of control over their children that they used to. One of the authors vividly remembers that sending a young son to his room for "time out" was easy when the son could be carried to his room if he refused to go. However, during the teen years, when the son was as large and strong as his parents, physical power was no longer an option. As you grow even older, your parents might become dependent on you to meet their needs for care. The circumstantiality of power can lead to a feeling of being used when we have been meeting another person's needs, only to have the relationship discarded when those needs no longer exist. For example, you might develop a friendship in which you provide rides to your friend all the time, but once that friend gets her own car, the relationship comes to an end.

5. *Relational development involves a negotiation of each partner's power.* In developing interpersonal relationships, we decide who will have power over us and what type of power they will have. Your relational partners make similar decisions. In Chapter 10, you will read about the tension that is created in deciding to give up some of your autonomy in order to forge a more intimate relationship. Partners often negotiate which individual will have decision making responsibility over which issues. The process often involves tension, conflict, and negotiation. The ability to reach a point at which both partners are content

interdependent relationship. A relationship in which each person has a similar amount of power over the other.

with how power is shared in the relationship is one factor that can affect relational success and satisfaction. Relational stability occurs when partners reach agreement about power in their relationship. In a four-year study of 41 romantic couples, most of whom got married during that time, each couple's reported balance of power remained stable.[19]

An interesting area of research in Canada is relational satisfaction during the retirement years. In a marriage, what happens when one partner retires or when both retire? As employment status changes, power and roles may have to be renegotiated. The *In Canada* feature below explores some of the findings of recent research.

 ## In Canada...

POWER IN RETIREMENT

What if you have been married for many years (this may be a long way off for many of you) and you or your partner retires? How will the retirement affect the relationship? Does it make a difference if the woman retires before the man? Does income have anything to do with marital satisfaction in the retirement years? A recent article in *Canadian Social Trends* attempted to answer some of these questions.

In Canada, there has been an overall decline in the age of retirement since the 1970s, suggesting that retirement is becoming a major issue for many older Canadian couples. Using data from the General Social Surveys of 1995 (approximately 1000 men and 800 women respondents) and 2001 (approximately 2500 men and 2200 women respondents), this article examined older heterosexual couples' (aged 50–74 years) perceptions of their relationships during retirement or the years leading to retirement. This study examined relationship quality that included several scale items including communication (such as frequency of laughing together), conflict (frequency of arguments about chores, etc.), and degree of

happiness with the marriage. Here are a few of the findings:

- Older couples generally report good relationships. On the relationship quality scale—from a value of 9 (lowest) to 35 (highest)—the average score was 30 for both men and women.

- Couples report better relationships when they are both retired. Older couples, where both were looking for work, reported the lowest relationship quality. Women who were still in the workforce while their husbands were retired also reported significantly lower relationship quality. It may be that gender role reversal plays a part, with the husband in the housekeeping role and the wife in the earner and provider role.

- When women contributed more financially than their husbands, women rated their relationships lower, especially in the bracket where the women contributed over 75 percent of the household income. However, while other research has supported this finding, when this study controlled for other factors such as, the labour force factor disappeared.

- On the other hand, in 2001 men who provided less than 50 percent of the household income

rated their relationships higher than men who contributed at least 75 percent. Perhaps men welcome the sharing of breadwinning responsibilities.

- What happens when there are adult children living at home? In both groups, the impact was a negative one. While the children may benefit from living at home, it appears this factor does have a negative impact on the quality of the relationship reported by both husbands and wives.

So how does all this relate to power in relationships? As power is circumstantial, retirement becomes a situation that will likely demand renegotiation of roles and thus power in the relationship. Other factors, too, will change the relationship and affect power as couples get older. Health issues and financial changes will also have an impact on older couples. Thus, effective communication and negotiation skills are not only important at the beginnings of relationships but also are part of satisfying mature relationships as well.

Source: Lee Chalmers and Anne Milan, "Marital Satisfaction During the Retirement Years," Canadian Social Trends, Spring 2005, Statistics Canada-Catalogue No. 11-008.

Types of Power Relationships

complementary relationship.
Relationship in which power is divided unevenly, with one partner dominating and the other person submitting.

symmetric relationships.
Relationship in which both partners attempt to have the same level of power.

competitive symmetric relationship. Relationship in which both partners vie for control or dominance of the other.

submissive symmetric relationship. Relationship in which neither partner wants to take control or make decisions.

parallel relationships.
Relationships in which power shifts back and forth between the partners, depending on the situation.

legitimate power. Power that is based on respect for a person's position.

In the discussion of attraction, you read about complementary needs; for example, one person who likes to make decisions would make a good partner with another person who likes other people to make decisions for him or her. Complementarity also characterizes relationship power. In a **complementary relationship**, one partner usually dominates and the other usually submits. One likes to talk, the other to listen; one likes to lead, the other to follow. You might find such a relationship undesirable for yourself, but for many people, such a relationship works to the satisfaction of both partners.

What happens when both partners want to call the shots and make decisions? In **symmetric relationships**, both partners behave in similar ways.[20] Sometimes both partners want to dominate, and sometimes both want to be submissive. A **competitive symmetric relationship** exists when both partners are vying for control or dominance over the other person. For example, each might try to control which TV program they watch or might insist on participating in every spending decision. Competition in such relationships often increases the amount of conflict and negotiation associated with decision making. In some relationships, neither partner wants to take control or make a decision, and this creates a **submissive symmetric relationship**. The following is an example of submissive symmetry (does it sound familiar to you?):

Bea:　What DVD do you want to rent?

Vic:　Oh, I don't care. You decide.

Bea:　No, you decide. I don't care either.

Most relationships, however, are neither purely complementary nor purely symmetrical; they are parallel. **Parallel relationships** involve a shifting back and forth of the power between the partners, depending on the situation. For example, if Janene knows more about computers than her husband, Justin, then he might defer the decision about which new computer to purchase to her. However, Janene might defer to her husband to plan their upcoming vacation because of his experience planning business trips. Establishing who has power in various situations is a point of contention in developing relationships and takes time for the parties involved to resolve. Power in any relationship changes as individuals change. As Justin gains computer savvy, he might want more say in purchasing a new system. Having knowledge or expertise is one way we hold power over another person.

Who appears to have more power in this interaction? What do you think are the sources of each person's power?

Types of Power

Why does one person in a relationship have more power over the other? There are many explanations; one that works well identifies five sources of power: legitimate (or position) power, referent power, expert power, reward power, and coercive power.[21]

Legitimate power is power that is based on respect for a position that a person holds. Teachers, parents, law officers, store managers, and company presidents all have power because of the position they hold relative to other people. When a police officer tells you to pull off to the side of the road, you respond to this enactment of power by obeying the officer's command.

Referent power is power that comes from our attraction to another person, or the charisma a person possesses. We let people we like influence us. We change our behaviour to meet their demands or desires because we are attracted to them.

Expert power is based on a person's knowledge and experience. We grant power to those who know more than we do or have some expertise we don't possess. This expertise can even include knowledge about how to manage a relationship effectively. We grant power to partners who have more experience in relationships. In many episodes of the *Seinfeld* TV series, the characters deferred to the expertise of their friends when it came to how to handle various relational crises.

Reward power is based on another person's ability to satisfy your needs. There are obvious rewards, such as money and gifts, but most rewards are more interpersonal in nature. Reward power is probably the most common form of power in interpersonal relationships. Withholding rewards is actually a form of punishment, or what is called *coercive power*.

Coercive power involves the use of sanctions or punishment to influence others. Sanctions include holding back or removing rewards. If you have a high need for physical affection, your partner might withhold that affection if you do not comply with a given request. Punishment involves imposing something on another person that he or she does not want.

referent power. Power that results from our attraction to another person, or the charisma a person possesses.

expert power. Power based on a person's knowledge and experience.

reward power. Power based on a person's ability to satisfy our needs.

coercive power. Power based on the use of sanctions or punishments to influence others.

Negotiating Power in Interpersonal Relationships

You decide how much control another person has over you, but the decision is usually the result of weighing the costs of compliance against the costs of non-compliance. Defining who has power can be a source of conflict in interpersonal relationships, potentially bringing about the end of a relationship. When a partner abuses power, ending the relationship may be warranted. Ideally, partners establish a mutually acceptable and rewarding power relationship.

 Applying Theory and Research

POWER IN MARITAL RELATIONSHIPS

Much of the research on the types of power presented so far has been done in the context of organizations; however, Virginia Richmond, James McCroskey, and David Roach examined power in the context of marriage. One hundred and thirty-six married couples voluntarily completed instruments that assessed their marital satisfaction and their perceptions of the types of power used by both partners. When power was used, referent power was used most widely (40 percent of respondents used it themselves; 45 percent of respondents reported their spouse using it), followed by expert power (21 percent of respondents; 28 percent of spouses), reward power (11 percent of respondents; 13 percent of spouses), legitimate power (11 percent of respondents; 12 percent of spouses), and finally, coercive power (6 percent of respondents; 11 percent of spouses).

In examining the impact on relationship satisfaction, the researchers found that use of coercive power related to dissatisfaction in the marriage for both husbands and wives. Further analysis led the researchers to suggest that dissatisfaction (particularly for wives) seemed likely to

Continued

lead to their use of coercion, rather than the use of coercion leading to dissatisfaction. The use of referent power was related to satisfaction (though it did not show as strong a relationship as that between coercive power and satisfaction). The researchers concluded their study by offering the following advice: In attempting to influence your spouse and still maintain your spouse's satisfaction, the best course of action would be to use referent power and avoid using coercive power.

APPLYING THE RESEARCH TO YOUR LIFE

Marital relationships probably differ from other types of relationships in their use of power. Married couples are more likely to have established particular roles, foundations for power, and patterns for decision making. The type of power used in less intimate relationships might be a determining factor in their maintenance or escalation. As the study suggests, the type of power you exert may influence your partner's satisfaction, and the level of satisfaction can affect the type of power used. For each of the relationships listed below, think of a particular person and divide the use of power up among the five types of power to indicate what percentage of the time each type is used (the percentages should total 100).

How do your relationships differ in terms of the types of power you and the other person use to influence each other? What do the differences reveal about power and about your relationships? In what ways have the types of power used changed over the course of the relationships? Answering these questions should help you appreciate the role that power plays in your relationships, whether they are casual relationships or marriage.

Source: Virginia P. Richmond, James C. Mc Croskey, and K. David Roach, "Communication and Decision-Making Styles, Power Base Usage, and Satisfaction in Marital Dyads," Communication Quarterly, 45 (Fall 1997): 410–426.

Type of Power	Example	Relationship with a Friend		Relationship with a Best Friend		Relationship with a Parent/Relative	
		Your Power	Your Friend's Power	Your Power	Your Best Friend's Power	Your Power	Your Parent's Power
Reward	25%	_____	_____	_____	_____	_____	_____
Coercive	10%	_____	_____	_____	_____	_____	_____
Referent	35%	_____	_____	_____	_____	_____	_____
Legitimate	10%	_____	_____	_____	_____	_____	_____
Expert	20%	_____	_____	_____	_____	_____	_____

Assess Needs

The first step to negotiating a satisfactory balance of power is to identify your needs and those of your partner. What are you looking for from your relationships? Remember that needs can include everything from financial rewards to confirmation of your self-concept.

Your assessment should include both needs that are being satisfied and those that are unsatisfied. You friendships could be meeting your interpersonal needs while leaving your desire to start a family unmet. Unmet needs affect both the development of other relationships and the power that other people have over you.

You also should strive to understand the needs of those with whom you have relationships. Identifying your best friends' needs helps you to understand what motivates them as well as appreciate the basis of power that you might have over them. Changes in your friends' needs will also change your ability to influence them. For example, some people have a need to control and dominate other people, and there are others who are perfectly happy to let them do so. If you are not one of those people, then you need to decide whether you wish to develop or maintain a relationship with this type of person.

Assess Need Fulfillment in Relationships

Examine how well a given relationship meets your needs and how well you meet the needs of your relationship partners. The degree to which others satisfy your needs reflects the amount of power those people have. The more needs that are met by one relationship, the more likely you are to sustain that relationship. You might know a person with whom you enjoy jogging (meeting a need for your physical well-being) but with whom you have no other real connection. It would be easier to give up the jogging relationship than to replace a best friend who is meeting many of your needs.

Identify Need-Based Conflicts and Tensions

Examine your interpersonal conflicts for unresolved power issues. For example, in the first year of marriage, couples often argue about balancing job and family, about financial problems (including who spends money and on what), about the frequency of sexual relations, and about the division of household tasks.[22] These problems involve issues of power, control, responsibility, and decision making. Such issues exist in other relationships as well. Examine your relationships for recurring patterns of conflict, and try to determine the role that power is playing. Conflicts can result from unacceptable imbalances of power (feeling that one or the other partner has too much), from equal amounts of power (with each partner attempting to influence the other), or as a reaction to others' attempts to exert control or to dominate.

Directly Discuss Power Issues

Everyday conversation helps engaged and married couples work toward equality of power and task responsibilities and ultimately affects their relational satisfaction.[23] In some instances, your partner might be unaware that he or she is exerting power over you in a manner you dislike. Simply pointing out this problem might be enough to remedy the situation. On the other hand, you might need to adopt a more active conflict management style. For example, describe the power problem without evaluation, describe your feelings about the power situation, solicit information from your partner in an active and open manner, and engage in a cooperative approach to negotiating power.

▶ **Recap**

_____

INTERPERSONAL POWER IN RELATIONSHIPS

Principles of Power
1. Power primarily derives from an individual's ability to meet another person's needs within a given relationship.
2. Both partners in an ongoing relationship have some degree of power.
3. Power exists in all interactions and all relationships.
4. Power is circumstantial.
5. Relational development involves a negotiation of each partner's power.

Continued

Types of Power Relationships

Complementary	One partner dominates and the other submits.
Symmetric	Both partners attempt to have the same level of power.
Competitive Symmetric	Both partners want power and control.
Submissive Symmetric	Neither partner wants power or control.

Types of Power	Basis for Power
Legitimate power	Power based on respect for the position a person holds
Referent power	Power based on attraction to another person or his or her charisma
Expert power	Power based on a person's knowledge or experience
Reward power	Power based on a person's ability to satisfy our needs
Coercive power	Power based on the use of sanctions or punishment to influence others

Negotiating Power in Interpersonal Relationships

1. Assess needs. What needs do you and your partner have?
2. Assess need fulfillment in the relationship. How well is the relationship meeting needs?
3. Identify need-based conflicts and tensions. To what degree is power a factor in relational conflicts?
4. Directly discuss power issues. What issues regarding power need to be discussed?

Interpersonal Relationship Development Theories

While we have discussed what interpersonal attraction is, the elements of attraction, and how power influences relationships, we have not explored why relationships develop and change. In the next chapter, we will look at how relationships escalate and de-escalate, but what motivates us to move into a relationship or to develop a more or less intimate relationship? How do you move from acquaintanceships to being close friends? The earlier description of attraction theories provides a partial answer to this question by offering explanations of what evokes your interest in another person. However, they don't adequately explain why you might stay at one stage, back down from a stage, or move forward to the next. Noted relationship scholar Steve Duck suggests we go through a process of "filtering" in which we develop criteria at each stage of relational development that a potential close friend must pass.[24] In essence, a move toward intimacy from one stage to the next means that a person has passed through another, finer screen filter. These screens represent decision points in which we make some assessment of the relationship and decide how we want to proceed. We can choose either to escalate, maintain, or de-escalate the relationship. Two theories reflect the kind of decision making that might be taking place: social exchange theory and dialectical theory (or dialectics).

Social Exchange Theory

social exchange theory. A theory that claims people make decisions on the basis of assessing and comparing the costs and rewards of a decision.

Social exchange theory is an economic model of human behaviour that has been used to explain how people arrive at decisions in a variety of situations. **Social exchange theory** posits that people seek the greatest amount of reward with the least amount of cost. You've probably been in a difficult relationship where you have asked yourself, "Is this relationship really worth it?" What you are asking is whether the rewards you are gaining from the relationship are worth the trouble or expense necessary to sustain the relationship (the costs). Students frequently tell us about ending long-distance relationships because the expenses (driving time, telephone calls, missing activities where you live, and so on) end up being greater than the rewards of the intermittent contact. Fortunately for some, the rewards associated with long-distance relationships remain greater than the costs, and those relationships continue to prosper.

Relationships can be evaluated in terms of immediate, forecast, and cumulative costs and rewards.[25] **Immediate costs and rewards** occur in a relationship at the present moment in time. You can think about your current relationships and assess their present value. **Forecast costs and rewards** are based on projection or prediction. We make guesses about the potential or future outlook of a relationship (communication scholar Michael Sunnafrank calls this predicted outcome value).[26] When you meet someone and begin to talk, you go through an initial assessment about whether a relationship with this person would be rewarding. You use forecasting to decide whether to remain in existing relationships during troubled times (costs escalate or rewards deteriorate). However, you don't immediately abandon long-term relationships at the first sign of trouble (low immediate rewards or high immediate costs) if you believe that things will improve (forecast rewards).

Another reason people remain in ongoing relationships during periods of low immediate rewards has to do with cumulative rewards and costs. **Cumulative costs and rewards** represent the total rewards and costs accrued during the duration of the relationship. With your finances, when you have greater income than expense, you put your extra money in savings. Analogously, you build up a savings account of the extra relational rewards. You can draw on that savings account during times when the relationship is not paying off well. You hold on to a relationship because you have invested a lot in it and have got a lot out of it. However, just as your savings account can run out of money, so can cumulative rewards be depleted and at that point, you might decide to terminate the relationship.

You can also consider rewards and costs in terms of their magnitude and ratio. Suppose you have two friends, Kelsey and Moira. Kelsey makes you feel good about yourself, is helpful, and is lots of fun (rewards), but she is very needy and demanding (costs). Moira is lots of fun and helpful, but she is also needy. Which friendship would you pursue more? You might be inclined to pursue the relationship with Kelsey because she is helpful, fun, and makes you feel good, whereas Moira is only fun and helpful. The magnitude of the rewards is greater with Kelsey than Moira. However, you might pursue a relationship with Moira because that relationship has a better ratio of rewards to costs (two rewards to one cost compared with Kelsey's three rewards to two costs). You might think that further developing a relationship with Moira could result in increased rewards with the same costs. However, relationships seem to have some point where there is maximum return for the investment; that is, they reach a point where, no matter how much you invest, either the reward does not increase further or the costs increase significantly. Suppose you have a casual friend with whom your only shared interest is movies. Once a week you have a very rewarding visit with this friend talking about the latest releases. You decide to spend more time with this friend (cost) and find awkward dead spots in the conversation because there isn't really anything else of mutual interest to talk about (reward). In terms of your relationship with Moira, this means that having fun with her and getting her help is the only reward you will gain regardless of how much you invest in the relationship.

immediate costs and rewards.
Those costs and rewards that are associated with a relationship at the present moment.

forecast costs and rewards.
The costs and rewards that an individual assumes will occur on the basis of projection and prediction.

cumulative costs and rewards.
The total costs and rewards accrued during the duration of a relationship.

Finding that point where you maximize your rewards while minimizing costs is one challenge of relational development. You've probably been confronted with trying to decide whether to date someone whom you regarded as a friend. Your decision was probably a desire to see if you could increase the amount of reward. You or your partner might have been hesitant to change the relationship for fear that you might lose everything (similar to going bankrupt because of a bad investment). Decisions to spend more time with a given individual are usually attempts to garner more rewards; if we find the costs increase as well, we might reduce the time together.

The example of deciding between time with Kelsey or with Moira reflects how people apply social exchange principles to relational decision making by comparing relationships. We can compare a current relationship to previous relationships, ideal relationships, and potential relationships.[27] We hate to hear someone tell us, "You're just like my previous boyfriend" or "You're different from my last girlfriend; she was wild." Most of us are sensitive enough not to voice such comparisons, but nonetheless, comparing relationships seems to be a natural thing to do. One way to judge the value of a relationship is in terms of how it stacks up against other relationships you have experienced. You might savour a particular friendship because it is more rewarding than any other relationship you have had.

People seem to construct templates in their minds for what relationships should be like. **Expected costs and rewards** represent expectations and ideals about how rewarding a relationship should be relative to its costs. We have a model of the ideal friend, the ideal lover, the ideal co-worker, and so on. We use the expected costs and rewards associated with these ideals to assess current relationships. We might abandon a relationship if we don't think it matches or has the potential to match our ideal. In essence, we set standards or criteria for our relationships by which we assess the desirability of a given relationship. Like Duck's filtering process, ideal images allow you to sort through relationships and focus on those that are closest to or exceed your ideal. The major difficulty associated with such comparisons rests in setting reasonable standards or ideals. For example, some parents adopt a philosophy of never arguing in front of their children. As the children become adults, they may have an expectation that happy marriages are ones that have no conflicts and thus evaluate their own marriages as a failure to reach their ideal. Continual disappointment in the ability to find relationships that measure up to your ideals suggests that you may need to reassess your standards.

Finally, we compare the rewards and costs of our current relationships with those we forecast for other potential relationships. We reduce our time spent with one friend when we believe we can have a more rewarding relationship with another person. Communication researchers Gerald Miller and Malcolm Parks have proposed that we will move quickly to terminate a relationship if it falls below our expectations and we think we have an opportunity to develop a new relationship that has the potential to exceed all of our expectations.[28] We try to spend the most time in those relationships that have the best relative outcomes. All these comparisons work in concert with one another. We compare our current relationships to previous ones, to the ideal, and to potential ones.

A recent research study used social exchange principles to examine whether couples maintained friendships after dissolving their romantic relationship.[29] In this study, couples who continued to provide each other with rewards and/or resources (love, status, services, information, goods, or money) continued to maintain a friendship. Those couples for which there were costs or barriers (lack of support by family or friends for a friendship, involvement in a new romance, or use of neglect to end the romance) had lower-quality friendships.

expected costs and rewards.
The templates we have for how much reward we should get from a given relationship in comparison with its costs.

Dialectical Theory

Three Dialectical Tensions

Researcher Leslie Baxter has identified three dialectical tensions that have been widely used in interpersonal research.[30]

- *Connectedness versus autonomy.* We desire to connect with others and to become interdependent while at the same time we have a desire to remain autonomous and independent. In one study of married couples, these desires to be connected and autonomous were found to be the most frequently occurring of the dialectical tensions.[31]

- *Predictability versus novelty (certainty versus uncertainty).* Knowing what to expect and being able to predict the world around us helps us reduce the tension that occurs from uncertainty. At the same time, we get bored by constant repetition and routine and therefore are attracted to novelty and the unexpected. This might explain why people relish horror movies where the unexpected jumps out at them. Fright becomes joyful because it meets a need for the unexpected.

- *Openness versus closedness.* We wish we could disclose information to others and hear those we are attracted to disclose to us. One ideal we seem to have in relationships is the ability to be totally open with our partner. However, we also value our privacy and feel a desire to hold back information. Research conducted by one of your authors has found that the number one way that people adapt content in interactions is to hold back or modify information.[32] This tension was identified in the study of married couples mentioned earlier as the most important of the three tensions, although it did not occur as often as the other two tensions.[33]

According to the **dialectical theory**, each pair of tensions is present in every relationship, but the impact of each polar force changes as a relationship progresses. Movement in relationships can be seen as a shift that occurs in the relative pull of one tension. For example, when you begin developing a new friendship, one issue you have to address is whether you want to give up some of your autonomy (freedom to do your own things) in order to spend time with this other person (connectedness). Notice how this is similar to social exchange theory in that you weigh costs (giving up autonomy) against rewards (becoming connected).

🔵 Dialectical Tensions and Relational Development

Both forces of autonomy and connectedness can be found even in close relationships.[34] Even though long-married couples have usually settled the issues of interdependence versus independence, dialectical theory asserts (and the research mentioned earlier supports) that tension is still present from these forces. Generally, such tension diminishes as we become more intimate; however, many an engagement has been called off at the last minute because of the inability

> **dialectical theory.** A theory that says relational development occurs in conjunction with various tensions that exist in all relationships, particularly connectedness versus autonomy, predictability versus novelty, and openness versus closedness.

Dialectical theory posits that a tension exists between our desire for predictability and our attraction to the unexpected. (Private Collection / Christian Pierre/Superstock)

of the bride or groom to resolve this tension. This tension represents the challenge faced by individuals forming close relationships who are faced with maintaining their own identities, while at the same time melding their identity with another person.

One study of married couples found that dialectical tensions existed both at the individual level (for example, the wife or the husband trying to decide whether to be open or closed) and at the relational level (partners differing in terms of desires for autonomy, openness, or novelty).[35] In addition, the study found that extreme closeness related to greater autonomy since those couples who share less information may also be likely to share less time together.

Movement in relationships can be seen as moments during the developmental process in which some element of tension has been resolved or overcome.[36] For example, during the initial stages of a relationship you are restrained in your self-disclosures (closeness). As long as you remain closed, the relationship can only progress so far. You are confronted with the question of whether or not you should share information and increase the level of intimacy in the relationship. Thus a tension exists until you make your decision. Once you have decided, some of the tension is relieved. Thus if you decide on more openness, the reduction in tension is accompanied by a change in the relationship.

Both of these theories provide some framework to understand development and changes in relationships. However, these theories do not provide us with all the answers. People become involved in, maintain, and end relationships for a wide variety of reasons. In the next chapter, we will examine relationships more closely, including how they develop, as well as offer skills for starting, maintaining, and ending relationships.

Summary

As a system, an interpersonal relationship is a set of interconnected elements in which a change in one element affects all the others. The ongoing nature of relationships means they are constantly changing. They can be considered relationships of circumstance when they occur because surrounding conditions cause you to interact with someone. In contrast, you create relationships of choice when you intentionally seek to establish a relationship you could otherwise avoid.

Interpersonal intimacy reflects the degree to which interpersonal relationships confirm and show acceptance of the partners' sense of self. Our relationships vary in their level of intimacy, and intimacy affects communication. Interpersonal attraction, the degree to which you want to form or maintain a relationship, is a factor contributing to intimacy.

Before you interact with a stranger or during your first interactions, you might experience short-term initial attraction, but as a relationship develops, you form more long-term maintenance attraction. Elements that influence feelings of attraction include physical appeal, proximity, similarity, complementary needs, relationship potential, reciprocation of liking, as well as credibility, competence, and charisma.

Your ability to influence other people in the direction you desire—interpersonal power—is an important factor in the development and success of relationships. Power derives from individuals' needs, is possessed by both partners, exists in all interactions and relationships, is circumstantial, and is negotiated. The pattern of power in relationships can be complementary (one partner dominates and the other submits), symmetrical (both have the same amount of power, which is competitive when both are strong, or submissive when both are weak), or parallel (changing from situation to situation).

Power is negotiated by first assessing needs, assessing how a relationship meets those needs, identifying how power affects interpersonal conflicts, and finally by directly discussing power issues.

Two theories that explain relationship development are social exchange theory and dialectical theory. Social exchange theory posits that we make decisions about becoming more or less intimate on the basis of the rewards and costs associated with the relationship. This decision is done in concert with forecast and cumulative rewards and costs, as well as in comparison with previous, potential, and ideal relationships. Dialectical theory sees our decisions being based on resolution of competing forces in our lives, particularly connectedness versus autonomy, predictability versus novelty, and openness versus closedness. As these forces are addressed, we move either toward or away from intimacy in our relationships.

For Discussion and Review

🔵 Focus on Critical Thinking

1. Imagine that you wanted to increase an acquaintance's attraction toward you. Formulate strategies to accomplish this using each of the elements that contribute to attraction described in the chapter.
2. Under what circumstances is the exercise of power in a relationship appropriate? Inappropriate?
3. Explain how social exchange theory relates to dialectical theory.
4. Of all the skills for developing interpersonal relationships, which three are the most important? Why? Which three are the least important? Why?

🔵 Focus on Ethics

5. Under what circumstances is it inappropriate for a person to use the power he or she has over another person to satisfy personal goals?
6. Under what conditions is it ethical or unethical to approach (a) a co-worker, (b) a subordinate, or (c) a superior to develop an interpersonal relationship because you feel attracted to him or her?

For Your Journal

1. Monitor a face-to-face, four-minute-long conversation between two or three of your friends. You should play the role of a quiet observer. Write down all of the ways in which your friends attempted to gain or concede power during the interaction. Include examples of the language they used and the non-verbal cues they exchanged.

2. Using one of the theories of relational development, analyze one of your own personal relationships. Does the theory hold true for the relationship or does the theory miss some important aspects? What are the strengths and weaknesses of this theory as it applies to this relationship?

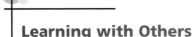

Learning with Others

1. Create two lists of names: people you regard as casual friends and people you regard as close friends. Identify what attracts you to the people on your list. Compare your lists with those of other students. How do your lists fit with the categories for attraction identified in the text? What's different? What's the same?

2. Some people develop relationships of choice with their family members. In groups of five or six, identify someone who has developed such a relationship with (a) a sibling, (b) a parent, and (c) another relative. Discuss why some students have developed friendships with these family members and why other students have not. Explore how these relationships are likely to change over the next 10 to 20 years.

3. In pairs or small groups, log onto Research Navigator. Your task is to find a *research article* that explores a theory about the development of interpersonal relationships. (*Hint:* Journals of social psychology are usually a very good source for this kind of article.) Download the article, answer the following questions, and share your findings with your class.

    a. What theory of interpersonal relationships does this study explore? Is it about a theory of interpersonal attraction or an element of interpersonal attraction?

    b. What is the hypothesis?

    c. Briefly, summarize the methodology.

    d. Was the hypothesis confirmed or disconfirmed? What were the results of this study?

Weblinks

www.afirstlook.com/links.cfm?expand=2   For more information on dialectical theory, check out this site.

www.solvedating.com   Do you believe that people can be "soulmates?" Here's a website devoted to finding your soulmate, including a calculator to determine how many people you have to meet to insure that you find him or her.

www.familydigest.com/stories/marriage_stages.cfm   This site offers a discussion of the relationship stages experienced by couples after getting married.

http://love.ivillage.com   While primarily designed for women, this site will interest men, too. It offers a variety of suggestions, quizzes, and articles related to relationships, dating, and love.

10 Developing, Maintaining, and Ending Interpersonal Relationships

After you study this chapter

you should be able to ...

1. Explain the model of the stages of relational development.

2. Discuss the skills for starting relationships.

3. Identify and describe effective interpersonal communication skills and strategies for escalating and maintaining relationships.

4. Discuss the potential responses to relational problems.

5. Identify some of the causes for relational de-escalation and termination.

6. Describe a model of how relationships end.

7. Discuss strategies for ending relationships.

8. Describe some steps to promote post-dissolution recovery.

● Stages of Interpersonal Relationships

● Skills and Strategies for Developing Interpersonal Relationships

● Skills and Strategies for Initiating and Escalating Relationships

● De-Escalating and Ending Relationships

> *You can't stay in your corner of the forest waiting for others to come to you. You have to go to them sometimes.*
>
> WINNIE THE POOH

Scenario 1: Josh and Nona are strangers standing at a bus stop in Montreal.

Josh: Hi. I noticed your T-shirt says UBC. Are you a student there?

Nona: Oh, no, I picked this up at a T-shirt clearance sale. I just thought it looked cool— I liked the picture of the thunderbird on it. Do you go to UBC?

Josh: My family used to vacation in British Columbia and we've visited the campus.

Nona: Where exactly is it?

Josh: The main campus is in Vancouver. Have you ever been there?

Nona: No, but I've been to Whistler. I went skiing there once with some friends from school.

Scenario 2: Several months later

Nona: Hey Josh, I was thinking that maybe you'd like to go home with me over break and meet my family and friends. How about it?

Josh: Wow. It's really nice that you'd like me to meet your family and all, but I really don't think I'd be very comfortable doing that.

Nona: Oh. OK, I guess. I just wanted them to meet you, but if you don't want to...

Josh: Don't be angry. I just think it's a little early for us to be meeting each other's families. Maybe we can make the trip another time.

Scenario 3: A couple of months later

Josh: Nona, where do you want to go to eat?

Nona: I'm not really up for going out, but you go ahead. I'll see you tomorrow.

Josh: What's wrong?

Nona: I don't know, Josh. I'm just feeling the need to cool things in our relationship right now. I think I just need something different from a relationship.

Josh: Oh. I'm sorry if I haven't been able to give you what you want. I guess I've been feeling a little distant in our relationship too.

Nona: I do like you, Josh, and I really value your friendship. You've really become like a big brother to me.

The three scenarios that start this chapter provide a snapshot of how communication changes as relationships develop. In the first scenario, Josh and Nona are following a getting-acquainted ritual and sharing safe information as they initiate a relationship. The communication in scenario 2 is much more relaxed and personal, reflecting an interaction between two individuals who have got to know each other well. In the final scenario, Josh and Nona discuss a de-escalation of the relationship. These snapshots reflect some of the stages that people experience as their relationships move toward and away from intimacy. While Josh and Nona's relationship is a romantically intimate one, remember that the term *intimacy* is not used in this book to refer to sexual activity but rather to describe any close relationship in which each partner confirms the other's sense of self.

In Chapter 9, we introduced the topics of relationships, why we are attracted to others, intimacy, power, and two theories that explain how relationships develop. This chapter expands your knowledge by beginning with a model and description of the typical stages through which interpersonal relationships progress. We will also explore strategies and skills for developing and maintaining relationships. Finally, we will examine relationship challenges including de-escalating and terminating relationships and how to recover from a relationship loss.

Stages of Interpersonal Relationships

relational development. The process of moving from one stage to another as a relationship moves toward or away from greater intimacy.

turning points. Specific events or interactions associated with positive or negative changes in a relationship.

causal turning points. Events that bring about a change in a relationship.

Although researchers use different terms and different numbers of stages, all agree that **relational development** does proceed in discernible stages. Understanding these stages is important to your studies because interpersonal communication is affected by the stage of the relationship. Individuals in an intimate stage discuss topics and display non-verbal behaviours that do not appear in the early stages of a relationship. We use interpersonal communication to move a relationship forward as we proceed from acquaintances, to friends, to intimates. Outsiders can usually tell what stage a relationship is in by observing the interpersonal communication.

We can think of the stages, from first meeting to intimacy, as the floors in a high-rise. Relational development is an elevator that stops at every floor. As you get to each floor, you might get off and wander around for a while before taking the elevator to the next floor (see Figure 10.1). Each time you get on, you don't know how many floors the elevator will take you up, or how long you will stay at any given floor. In fact, sometimes you will never get back on the elevator, electing instead to stay at a particular stage of relational development, but if you fall head over heels in love, you might want to move quickly from floor to floor toward intimacy. Part of the time you share this elevator with your partner, and the two of you make decisions about how high you will ride the elevator, how long to stay at each floor, and when and whether to ride the elevator down.

Just as there are lights on a panel to let us know the elevator has moved from one floor to another, we have markers that signal a move from one stage to another. These markers are called **turning points**. Turning points are specific events or interactions that are associated with positive or negative changes in a relationship.[1] A first meeting, first date, first kiss, first sex, saying, "I love you" for the first time, meeting a partner's family, going away together somewhere, making up after a conflict, moving in together, providing help in a crisis, or providing a favour or gift might all be turning points that indicate a relationship is moving forward. Two researchers found that, 55 percent of the time, these turning points inspired a discussion about the nature of the relationship.[2] Such discussion helps the partners reach mutual agreement about the nature of the relationship at that time.

Turning points can be divided into two types. **Causal turning points** are events that directly affect the relationship. Finding out that your romantic partner has cheated on you might cause you to terminate the relationship. Because the event causes a change in the relationship, it is a causal turning point. On the other hand,

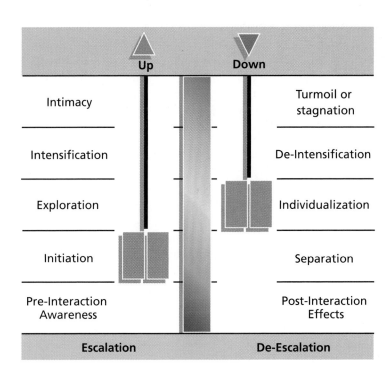

Figure 10.1
Elevator Model of
Relational Stages

receiving and accepting an invitation from a friend to visit his or her family for the first time is a **reflective turning point** because it signals that a change has occurred in the definition of the relationship. The invitation and acceptance don't cause a change but reflect a change in how you and your friend perceive the relationship.

Relational Escalation

Relational escalation is the movement of a relationship toward greater intimacy. This movement usually goes through a series of discernible stages: pre-interaction awareness, initiation, exploration, intensification, and intimacy. Movement from one stage to another represents an increase in the amount of intimacy between two people. Each stage is accompanied by specific communication patterns, turning points, and relational expectations.

reflective turning point. An event that signals a change has occurred in the way a relationship is defined.

relational escalation. The upward movement of a relationship toward intimacy through five stages: pre-interaction awareness, initiation, exploration, intensification, and intimacy.

Pre-Interaction Awareness

As you can see in the model in Figure 10.1, the first floor is the *pre-interaction awareness stage*. At this stage, you might observe someone or even talk with others about him or her without having any direct interaction. Gaining information about others without directly interacting with them is a *passive strategy*.[3] Through your passive observations, you form an initial impression. You might not move beyond the pre-interaction awareness stage if that impression is not favourable or the circumstances aren't right.

Initiation

If you are attracted to the other person and the circumstances are right, you might proceed to the *initiation stage*, one of the first turning points in a relationship. In this stage, the interaction typically is routine; you might each respond to a large number of standard questions during the first four minutes of conversation,[4] sticking to safe and superficial topics, and presenting a "public self" to the other person. Your partner is now riding on the elevator with you, and any decision about whether the elevator should go up, down, or nowhere is a mutual one for the rest of the ride. The relationship could remain at this stage if you don't share any further information about yourselves other than what occurs during the initiation ritual.

Exploration

If you decide to go to the next floor, the *exploration stage*, you will begin to share more in-depth information about yourselves. However, you will have little physical contact, maintain your social distance, and limit the amount of time you spend together. This stage can occur in conjunction with the initiation stage. During this stage, communication becomes easier, and a large amount of low-risk disclosure occurs.

Intensification

If you proceed to the *intensification stage*, you will start to depend on each other for self-confirmation and engage in riskier self-disclosure. You will spend more time together, increase the variety of activities you share, adopt a more personal physical distance, engage in more physical contact, and personalize your language. Also, in this stage, you may often discuss and redefine the relationship, perhaps putting a turning-point label on yourselves such as "going steady," "good buddies," or "best friends." Other turning points associated with this stage include decisions to date each other exclusively, to become roommates, or to spend time with each other's family.

Intimacy

The top floor in the building is the *intimacy stage*. In this stage, the two partners turn to each other for confirmation and acceptance of their self-concept. Their communication is highly personalized and synchronized. They talk about anything and everything. There is a free flow of information and self-disclosure. There is a commitment to maintaining the relationship that might even be formalized through marriage or some other agreement. The partners share an understanding of one another's language and non-verbal cues and have a great deal of physical contact. They use fewer words to communicate effectively, and they have a clearer definition of their roles and of the relationship. Reaching this stage takes time—time to build trust, time to share personal information, time to observe each other in various situations, and time to build a commitment and an emotional bond.

As couples proceed from exploration to intensification, they have more physical contact and begin sharing more activities and confidences. Does it seem as if this couple is heading into the intensification stage?
(Sandra Rice)

Building Your Skills
GRAPHING YOUR RELATIONSHIP CHANGES

Think of an interpersonal relationship that you have had for at least a year. On the graph shown here, plot the development of that relationship from stage to stage, reflecting the relative amount of time you spent in each stage. You can also indicate whether you backed up to a previous stage at any point.

If possible, have your relational partner fill out a similar graph and compare your perceptions of how the relationship has developed. What differences are there, and why?

Classmates might also want to share their graphs with each other to compare how different relationships develop. What can you tell from the graphs about the nature of your classmates' relationships?

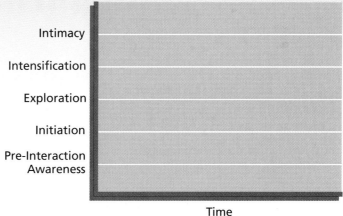

Relational De-Escalation

Relational de-escalation is the movement that occurs when a relationship decreases in intimacy. Our model identifies five stages in this process: turmoil or stagnation, de-intensification, individualization, separation, and post-interaction. These stages can be observed when an intimate relationship becomes less so or comes to an end. The process of ending a relationship is not as simple as going down the same elevator you came up on; it is not a reversal of the relationship formation process. Relational de-escalation can also involve only one or two of the stages. For example, a relationship might move from being one between good friends to a more casual friendship.[5] A **post-intimacy relationship** occurs when partners de-escalate from the intimate stage but still maintain a relationship. A couple might decide they like each other as friends but no longer want a romantic or exclusive relationship; thus, they de-escalate and maintain the relationship at the intensification or exploratory stage.

🌑 Turmoil or Stagnation

In a relational de-escalation, when an intimate relationship is not going well, it usually enters the *turmoil* or *stagnation stage*. Turmoil involves an increase in conflict, as one or both partners tend to find more faults in the other. The definition of the relationship seems to lose its clarity, and mutual acceptance declines. The communication climate is tense and exchanges are difficult.

Stagnation occurs when the relationship loses its vitality and the partners become complacent. Communication and physical contact between the partners decrease; they spend less time together but do not necessarily fight. Partners in a stagnating relationship tend to go through the motions of an intimate relationship without the commitment; they simply follow their established relational routines.

As with the up elevator, individuals can stop at this point on the down elevator and decide to quit descending. The relationship can remain in turmoil or stagnate for a long time, or the individuals can repair, redefine, or revitalize the relationship and return to intimacy.

🌑 De-Intensification

If the turmoil or stagnation continues, however, the individuals might move down to the *de-intensification stage*, decreasing their interactions and their dependence on the other for self-confirmation, and increasing their physical, emotional, and psychological distance. They might discuss the definition of their relationship, question its future, and assess each partner's level of satisfaction or dissatisfaction. The relationship can be repaired and the individuals can move back up to intensification and intimacy, but that is more difficult to accomplish now.

🌑 Individualization

On the next floor down, the *individualization stage*, the partners tend to define their lives more as individuals and less as a couple. Neither views the other as a partner or significant other anymore. Interactions are limited. The perspective changes from "we" and "us" to "you" and "me," and property is defined in terms of "mine" or "yours" rather than "ours." Both partners turn to others for confirmation of their self-concepts.

🌑 Separation

In the *separation stage*, individuals make an intentional decision to eliminate further interpersonal interaction. If they share custody of children, attend mutual family

---

relational de-escalation. The downward movement of a relationship away from intimacy through five stages: turmoil or stagnation, de-intensification, individualization, separation, and post-interaction.

post-intimacy relationship. A formerly intimate relationship that is maintained at a less intimate stage.

gatherings, or work in the same office, the nature of their interactions will change. They will divide property, resources, and friends. Early interactions in this stage are often tense and difficult, especially if the relationship has been intimate. For relationships that never went beyond exploration or intensification, however, the negotiation is often relatively painless.

For former intimates, one of the awkward things about separating is their extensive personal knowledge about one another. Their talk is limited to superficial things, though they still know a lot about each other. This tends to make the interactions fairly uncomfortable. Over time, of course, each partner knows less about who the other person has become. For example, even after spending just a few years away from your high school friends, you might have difficulty interacting with them because the knowledge you both share is out of date.

🔘 Post-Interaction Effects

Although interaction may cease altogether, the effect of the relationship is not over. Our relational stages high-rise is like something out of the *Twilight Zone* TV series: once you enter it, you can never leave it. The bottom floor on the down elevator, where you remain, is the *post-interaction effects stage.* This floor represents the lasting effects the relationship has on your self and, therefore, on your other interactions and relationships. Steve Duck claims that in this final stage of terminating relationships, we engage in "grave-dressing."[6] We create a public statement for people who ask why we broke up and also come to grips with losing the relationship. Sometimes our sense of self gets battered during the final stages of a relationship, and we have to work hard to regain a healthy self-image.

Of course, we are all aware of people who hop on an express elevator to get out of a relationship, bypassing all the normal stages of decline. One study found that of all the various ways to terminate a relationship, abandoned partners most dislike the quick exit without discussion.[7] For the rest of this chapter, we will explore the skills for starting relationships and for escalating and maintaining relationships, and then examine the ending of relationships.

Skills and Strategies for Developing Interpersonal Relationships

So far, this chapter has focused on the nature of relational development. Now, the focus shifts to discussing specific strategies and skills for starting, escalating, and maintaining interpersonal relationships. The lists provided are neither fail-safe nor complete. They are offered primarily to stimulate consideration of your own thoughts and behaviour as you develop new relationships.

When you meet someone that you initially like, how do you go about fostering a relationship? Once you have established a relationship, how do you ensure that it remains healthy and at the level of intimacy with which you are most comfortable? The following three sections provide strategies you can use to address these questions. The first section discusses skills and strategies used primarily in initiating interaction. The next section covers skills and strategies used in both the initial stage and the later stages of relational development. The final section focuses on skills used in either maintaining a relationship or moving it toward more intimacy once it has been established.

We can learn the skills that can help us reduce the interpersonal tensions that most of us feel at the start of a relationship.
(B. Daemmrich/The Image Works)

Skills and Strategies Used Primarily During the Initiation Stage

● Observe and Act on Approachability Cues

Subway riders in large cities learn to avoid eye contact because it is a signal of approachability. Other ways in which we can signal approachability include turning toward another person, smiling, being animated (versus sitting very still), taking an open body posture, winking, and waving. In the absence of these cues, we generally conclude that a person wants to be left alone.

Sometimes circumstances prevent us from exchanging approachability cues. The seating arrangements in your class, for example, might hamper the use of non-verbal cues. So instead, you may try to develop some sensitivity to the way other people respond to your greetings. Saying "Hello" lets people know that you are approachable, and it tests approachability. If the other person responds with a warm smile and a few words, such as "Have you finished today's assignment yet?" then the door might be open for further interaction. However, if the person gives you a silent half smile and hurries on, you can take this as a signal that the door is closed.

● Identify and Use Conversation Starters

Like Nona in the opening scenario of this chapter, we all give off a certain amount of "free" information that others can easily observe. You can use this readily available information to begin conversations and initiate relationships. In the initiation stage of relational development, people generally follow a script that helps both parties reduce their level of anxiety about interacting with a stranger. They also stick to safe topics and disclose only descriptive information about themselves as they begin to build the foundations for a potential relationship.

🔵 Follow Initiation Norms

Many of the early interactions in a relationship are almost ritualistic, or at least scripted. In our culture, when two strangers meet for the first time, they typically follow this pattern of conversation: [8]

Greetings:	Say, "Hello," "Hi," or "How are you?"
Introductions:	Exchange names and pleasantries.
Topic 1:	Discuss the present situation or weather.
Topic 2:	Discuss current or past residences (where they live, hometown, etc.).
Topic 3:	Determine whether they know people in common.
Topic 4:	Discuss their educational backgrounds or occupations.
Topic 5:	Discuss general topics such as TV, movies, music, family, sports, books, and travel.

Discuss Further Meeting (Optional): Say something like, "Let's get together sometime."

Exchange Pleasantries:	Say, "Nice to meet you," "Hope to see you again," and so on.
Close Conversation:	Indicate the intent to end the conversation with such statements as "See you later," "Got to go to class now," or "Give me a call."
Goodbyes:	Make final statements, say "Bye," and move in different directions.

Following the script provides some comfort and security because both partners are able to reduce the level of uncertainty. If you deviate too much from this script, you might undermine your partner's sense of security and discourage him or her from pursuing a relationship. For example, after an initial greeting, how would you react to a stranger who deviated from the script by saying, "Nice to meet you, too. Did you know that television is becoming the vast wasteland of Canadian intellect, draining the very lifeblood of our youth?" Most of us would be a bit leery of jumping directly into a discussion of such an issue with a person we had just met.

As you follow the script, however, you should take advantage of opportunities to expand and develop the conversation in safe ways. Listen for details about the person's background and interests that you can inquire about, and share information about your own interests.

Ask Questions

The very act of asking questions can enhance your partner's attraction toward you.[9] Asking questions shows your interest in the other person in an indirect way and promotes reciprocity of liking. Asking questions can also provide you with information about the other person, helping reduce uncertainty and improving your ability to adapt to your partner. However, accomplishing these benefits requires the ability to ask questions without "interrogating" the other person, to ask open questions that invite elaboration and discussion, and to ask meaningful follow-up, or probing, questions. Starting with impersonal, specific questions, often about the circumstance or surroundings, encourages a response by reducing a person's reluctance to answer; for example (while standing in a movie line), "Have you heard any reviews of this movie?" After the initial question, asking more open and encompassing questions helps to facilitate the conversation: "What did they have to say?" The *Building Your Skills* box lists a number of sample questions.

Building Your Skills

QUESTIONS TO KEEP THE CONVERSATION GOING DURING A DATE

How would you feel if, on a first date, you were asked these questions? Think about other questions that could be asked after you read through this list.

1. Have you ever been here (the restaurant or other setting the two of you are in) before? (Discuss aspects of the facility such as food, amenities, and so forth.)

2. Do you live in (name of town or city)? How long have you lived in the area? How do you like it here? (This can lead into a discussion of area politics and other local issues.)

3. Have you visited the local (park, library, shopping centre)? (Talk about the special attractions of your town.)

4. Did you grow up here? (If the answer is no): Where did you live before this? What was it like there? How does this area compare with that one?

5. Does the rest of your family live nearby? (Parents, grandparents, aunts, uncles?)

6. What do you like most about the area?

7. What kind of movies do you like? What is the worst movie you ever saw? Who is your favourite actor/actress?

8. What is your favourite TV show? What is your least favourite?

9. Did you catch the Academy Awards (or that new show, or the game, etc.) last night?

10. What kind of music do you enjoy? Who is your favourite performer/group/band? Who do you think is the hottest this year? Do you think they still will be next year?

11. What is your favourite type of reading matter? Who is your favourite author? What's the best book you've read recently? Do you subscribe to magazines?

12. Do you belong to any local clubs or organizations?

13. Are you a morning person, or do you find yourself at your peak later in the day?

14. What kind of career are you interested in? What are your career goals?

15. What do you like to do in your spare time (hobbies, interests)?

16. How did you get involved in your hobby? What do you like most about it?

Source: Tim Arends, retrieved and adapted from About.com (December 20, 2000). Used by permission of the author.

Once you've asked an initial question, be flexible and ask follow-up questions related to the answer you get. Be open and provide information about yourself that is relevant to the questions. Usually the other person will also ask you questions. If the other person gives short responses without any reciprocal questions, it may be a signal that he or she is not particularly interested in interacting. If so, you're probably better off not pursuing the interaction any further.

You might ask a question that you believe is safe and appropriate such as, "What does your father do for a living?" to which the stranger gives an unexpected response: "I haven't heard from him since I was five." Unknowingly, you may have evoked uncomfortable feelings and memories. Some questions should obviously be avoided because of their inappropriateness in an initial interaction; however, almost any seemingly simple question can sometimes evoke a negative reaction. Having little information about a stranger on which to base your communication decisions means you need to monitor the interaction carefully. Recognize that the experiences and feelings evoked by your questions differ from person to person. A question that is easy and comfortable for you to answer may not be for others. Be sensitive to how the other person responds to your questions, and be prepared to adapt your comments appropriately. Other-oriented communication skills can help you manage sensitive situations. Put yourself in the other person's shoes. If you hadn't seen your father since you were five, what would you most like your conversation partner to say next?

🌑 Don't Expect Too Much from the Initial Interaction

Initial interactions do not necessarily determine the future of a relationship. In movies, initial interactions between the hero and the heroine are often brusque and unfriendly, but after sharing traumatic experiences, they eventually find love. Although real life does not usually work this way, keep in mind that the scripted nature of an initial interaction limits the opportunity for you and your partner to achieve an in-depth understanding of one another. Relax and arrange another meeting if you feel the spark of attraction. It will probably take a few interactions before you can make a sound cost–benefit analysis of the relationship.

Initiating conversation is only one step in the process of developing an interpersonal relationship. Later in this chapter, we will learn strategies for strengthening relationships with family members, friends, and colleagues.

Skills and Strategies for Initiating and Escalating Relationships

"No kidding! I love chocolate-covered strawberries, too." "It's nice to be able to talk to someone else who's a fan of *The Decorating Challenge*." Statements like these two emphasize commonalities to encourage the listener to like the speaker (this is called "affinity seeking"). We sometimes make these types of statements when we are first getting to know someone, but similar statements are also used when trying to escalate a relationship.

Two of the most important categories of interpersonal relationships that we develop and maintain are friends and lovers. We use these two terms to distinguish relationships that differ in terms of their level of intimacy and sexuality. Both types of relationships are important. Our friendships are one of our most valuable sources of support. In a survey of more than 100 000 men and women, single women rated friends and social life as the most important source of happiness in their lives. Single men rated friends second only to their jobs.[10] Generally, relationships with lovers have both a high degree of intimacy and attachment as well as sexual activity and/or attraction.[11] Also, remember that gay and lesbian relationships reflect intimate romantic relationships with relational dynamics similar to heterosexual relationships, including marriage and child rearing. Trying to increase someone's attraction to us is just one strategy that is common to both the initiation and escalation stages of interpersonal relationships. Other skills and strategies include appropriately self-disclosing, gathering information to reduce uncertainties, monitoring your perceptions, listening actively and responding confirmingly, and socially decentring and adapting. Let's look more closely at each of these ways to initiate and escalate relationships.

Communicate Attraction

When we are attracted to people, we use both indirect and direct strategies to communicate our liking through non-verbal and verbal cues. *Non-verbal immediacy* represents those non-verbal cues we display when we are attracted to someone. For instance, we tend to reduce the physical distance between us; increase our eye contact and use of touch; lean forward; keep an open body orientation; and smile. We also use the courtship readiness behaviours, preening behaviours, positional cues, and appeals to invitation described in Chapter 6.

We also indirectly communicate our attraction verbally. We use informal and personal language, addressing the person by his or her first name and often referring to "you and I," and "we." We ask questions to show interest, probe for details when our partner shares information, listen responsively, and refer to information shared in past interactions. All these behaviours confirm that we value what the other person is saying.

We can also directly communicate our attraction verbally. Most of us don't do this very often, but think about how you feel when a friend tells you that he or she likes you. It raises your self-esteem; you feel valued. You can make others feel that way by communicating your liking for them, although in the early stages of relational development, there are social mores against doing so. We verbally communicate liking in other, more subtle ways as well. We might tell someone that we like a particular trait or ability, such as the way she tells jokes, or the way he handled an irritating customer. Or we might compliment someone's outfit, hairstyle, or jewellery. Each of these messages communicates attraction to the other person and is likely to elicit a positive response from him or her.

affinity-seeking strategies. Ways or methods of getting other people to like you.

We also use **affinity-seeking strategies** to get people to like us. Table 10.1 summarizes strategies identified by the research team of Bell and Daly.[12] Deciding to display non-verbal immediacy cues or to provide verbal self-confirmation are not just ways in which we communicate our attraction to other people, they are also affinity-seeking strategies. Other ways of getting people to like us include establishing mutual trust, being polite, showing concern and caring, and involving people in our activities. Apparently, these strategies do work. Bell and Daly found that individuals who seemed to use many affinity-seeking strategies were perceived as likeable, socially successful, and satisfied with their lives.[13]

Table 10.1 Affinity-Seeking Strategies

	Strategies	Examples
1. Control	Present yourself as in control, independent, free-thinking; show that you have the ability to reward the other person.	• "I'm planning on going to grad school, and after that I'm going to Japan to teach English." • "You can borrow my notes for the class you missed if you'd like.
2. Visibility	Look and dress attractively; present yourself as an interesting, energetic, and enthusiastic person; increase your visibility to the other person.	• "Wow, that was a great show about Chinese acrobats. I do gymnastics, too. Would you like to come watch me next week at our dual meet?"
3. Mutual Trust	Present yourself as honest and reliable; display trustworthy behaviours; show that you trust the other person by self-disclosing.	• "That guy you're having problems with called me and asked about you. I told him I didn't have anything to say." • "I've never told anyone this, but I've always hoped I could find my birth parents."
4. Politeness	Follow appropriate conversational rules; let the other person assume control of the interaction.	• "I'm sorry. I interrupted. I thought you were done. Please, go on." • "No, you're not boring me at all; it's very interesting. Please tell me more about it."
5. Concern and Caring	Show interest in and ask questions about the other person; listen; show support and be sensitive; help the other person accomplish something or feel good about him- or herself.	• "How is your mother doing after her operation?" • "I'd like to help out at the benefit you're chairing this weekend." • "That must have been really hard for you, growing up under those conditions."
6. Other-Involvement	Put a positive spin on activities you share; draw the other person into your activities; display non-verbal immediacy and involvement with the other person.	• "This is a great party, I'm glad you came along." • "A group of us are going to get a midnight snack; how about coming along?"
7. Self-Involvement	Try to arrange for encounters and interactions; engage in behaviours that encourage the other person to form a closer relationship.	• "Oh, hi! I knew your class ended at two, so I thought I'd try to catch you." • "It would really be fun to go camping together this summer; I have this favourite place."
8. Commonalities	Point out similarities between yourself and the other person; try to establish equality (balanced power); present yourself as comfortable and at ease around the other person.	• "I've got that computer game, too. Don't you love the robots?" • "Let's both work on the project together. We're a great team." • "It's so easy to talk to you. I really feel comfortable around you."

Source: Adapted from R. A. Bell and J. A. Daly, "The Affinity Seeking Function of Communications," Communication Monographs, 51 (1984): 91–115.

Building Your Skills

AFFINITY SEEKING OBSERVATION

Put yourself in a place where you can observe strangers interacting, such as a party or a student centre. Without violating anybody's privacy, see if you can observe affinity-seeking behaviours or hear what is being said that communicates attraction between communication partners.

Which of the affinity-seeking strategies seem to be used the most? The least? How do people seem to respond to the affinity-seeking behaviours of their partners?

Be Open and Self-Disclose Appropriately

Disclosing information about yourself allows the other person to make an informed decision about whether to continue the relationship. Remember, both of you need to be in a position to make such a decision. You may have found out what you want to know and decided that you have a lot in common with the other person, but he or she may not have reached that same point. However, be careful not to violate the script or cultural expectations about what is appropriate to disclose in an initial conversation. You have probably had the experience of someone you have just met tell you his or her problems. Such disclosures usually alienate the other, rather than advancing the relationship.

In Chapter 2, we wrote about self-disclosure being a critical element for movement toward intimacy. We cannot form truly intimate relationships without mutual self-disclosure. On the other hand, restricting the amount of self-disclosure is one way to control the development of a relationship. If a relationship is moving too fast, you might choose to reduce how much you are self-disclosing as a way to slow the progression of the relationship. The level of self-disclosure needs to be appropriate to the level of development, and both partners must be sensitive to the timing of the disclosures. Failing to disclose or disclosing the wrong thing at the wrong time can damage a relationship.

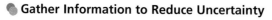

Gather Information to Reduce Uncertainty

uncertainty reduction theory. A theory that claims people seek out information to reduce uncertainty, thus providing control and predictability.

Meeting strangers and starting relationships is rarely easy. We all seem to share a fear of the unknown, which includes interactions with strangers whose behaviour we cannot predict. The research team of Charles Berger, Richard Calabrese, and James Bradac developed a theory to explain relational development.[14] Their **uncertainty reduction theory** is based on one basic assumption: we like to have control and predictability in our lives; therefore, when we are faced with uncertainty, we are driven to gain information to reduce that uncertainty. Reducing uncertainty requires using a number of skills we have already covered but depends primarily on effective perception and active listening. You need to gather as much information as you can about your partner to increase predictability and reduce anxiety.

Usually we reduce uncertainty by gathering either cognitive or behavioural information about others.[15] Cognitive information relates to thoughts, attitudes, and opinions. Behavioural information relates to reactions and remarks in various situations. As you have seen, you gather some of this information during the pre-interaction stage of a relationship through observations and conversations with others who know the person. Later, you can observe the other's behaviours directly in your own interactions with him or her, and also ask direct questions. Usually people gather behavioural information through observation and cognitive information through interactions.

We are particularly motivated to gain information early in a relationship when uncertainty is greatest, and when we are trying to evaluate the relationship's predicted outcome value.[16] We also are likely to seek out information if others behave in an unexpected way.[17] If your close friend who watches *South Park* every night suddenly begins reading during that time slot, you will probably ask why. Whether the friend shares with you what is going on will depend on how comfortable he or she is in revealing information about himself or herself.

 Applying Theory and Research

INITIATION STAGE: MALE-INITIATED VERSUS FEMALE-INITIATED DATE REQUESTS

According to custom in Canada and the United States, men are expected to take the initiative in asking women out (in general). While certain taboos or negative impressions have been associated with women's initiating of dates, more women seem to be taking this initiative. Communication scholars Paul Mongeau, Jerold Hale, Kristin Johnson, and Jacqueline Hillis examined male-initiated versus female-initiated date requests. For one part of their study, they created four written scenarios describing a male asking a female out, a male or a female initiating the date request after hints from the other, and a female asking a male out. Over 400 student participants evaluated the females and

males in these scenarios. In comparison with the woman who waited for the man to ask her out, the woman who directly asked the man out was seen as more active, flexible, truthful, and extroverted, more of a feminist, more socially liberal, and less physically attractive (though no pictures were provided). Female students perceived the female initiator as more likeable and tactful than did the males.

APPLYING THE RESEARCH TO YOUR LIFE

What is your view of a woman who asks a man out for a first date?

To what degree does your view differ if the woman asks the man to (a) go to a movie, (b) come over to her apartment for dinner, or (c) go to a party with her?
(Male students answer these questions:)
Has a woman ever asked you out on a first date?

How was your attitude toward her affected by her request?
(Female students answer these questions:)
Have you ever asked a man out for a first date?
How do you think the man's attitude toward you was affected by your request?
If you haven't initiated a date with a man, how do you think a man would react if you did?

Survey five or six of your male and female friends and collect their answers to the above questions. How similar are their responses? To what degree do males and females agree or disagree?

Source: P. A. Mongeau, J. L. Hale, K. L. Johnson, and J. D. Hillis. "Who's Wooing Whom? An Investigation of Female Initiated Dating," in P. J. Kalbleisch (Ed.), Interpersonal Communication: Evolving Interpersonal Relationships (Hillsdale, NJ: Lawrence Erlbaum, 1993, pp. 51–68).

Monitor Your Perceptions

You need to be aware of your perceptual biases that affect your reactions to your partner. Such biases might inhibit the growth of a relationship because of an inaccurate inference. Effective perception can enhance your ability to understand and adapt to your partner as a relationship escalates. Perception checking helps you reach a more accurate understanding of your partner, and thus provides you with better information about whether to continue the relationship. Directly asking your partner for explanations about things you have perceived can potentially lead to more effective relationship management. For example, suppose you are interacting with a man named Kavi, whom you don't know very well. During the conversation, every time you start to talk about a mutual friend, Sandra, Kavi changes the subject. One interpretation of this observation is that Kavi is rude and impolite, and if you assume this is the case, you might decide to abandon the relationship. Or you might ask Kavi about your perception. The explanation might be that he and Sandra recently had a fight and she prefers not to talk about her. A hasty inference in this case might have precluded the development of a potentially satisfying relationship.

Building Your Skills

ANXIETY LEVEL AND FAMILIARITY

Write down at least 10 different social situations you can recall having been in, such as specific occasions when you attended weddings, funerals, or ball games; went to your grandmother's for dinner; visited a best friend's parents for the first time; or met a new roommate. Next to each one, indicate how nervous you felt in that situation. Use a scale from 1 to 10, with 1 being calm and cool and 10 being highly apprehensive. After you have rated each situation, go back and rate each one on how familiar or unfamiliar the situation was. Again use a scale of 1 to 10, with 1 being very familiar and 10 being very unfamiliar.

According to uncertainty reduction theory, there should be a strong correlation between your level of anxiety and the level of familiarity. Which situations caused the most anxiety? To what degree did your unfamiliarity with the situation affect your level of anxiety? What were you most uncertain about in each situation? In which situations were you most comfortable and why? Did you feel uncomfortable in some circumstances even though the situation was familiar? Why?

🔘 Listen Actively and Respond Confirmingly

Listening skills are also crucial for developing and maintaining relationships. Listening clues you in to others' needs, wants, and values, and it enables you to respond to them in appropriate ways. In the initial stages of a relationship, partners share a great deal of information. The amount of information tapers off in the later stages and as a relationship continues over time. This tapering off creates the illusion that you don't have to listen as much or as well as you did early on, but listening is a way to demonstrate ongoing interest in another person. Even in long-term relationships, you do not know everything your partner has to say. It is still important to stop, look, and listen—to put down the newspaper or turn off the radio when your close friend begins talking to you.

You also need to listen actively and provide confirming responses. In Chapter 4, we discussed the notions of confirming and disconfirming responses. Using confirming responses increases your partner's sense of self-worth and communicates the value you place on him or her. In addition, if you can develop an awareness of the biases that prevent you from responding with empathy, you can deliberately work to overcome them as you ask questions and paraphrase your partner's messages.

🔘 Socially Decentre and Adopt an Other-Oriented Perspective

The skills covered in Chapter 8 for social decentring, empathizing, and adapting to others can enhance the initiation, escalation, and maintenance of relationships.

Social decentring helps you better understand your partner, which provides you with a basis for choosing the most effective strategies for accomplishing your communication goals. We have been discussing the notion of "appropriateness" of your behaviours to the effective advancement and maintenance of your relationships. Determining appropriateness depends on your ability to read the situation and your partner, and then to adapt or choose the best behaviours. Essentially, you can consider either what your partner is thinking now or what he or she will think in response to your actions—put yourself in your partner's shoes. For example, suppose you are on a first date and trying to decide whether to tell your partner about a very intimate relationship you had, which just ended. Put yourself in the other person's shoes. Would you want to hear on a first date about someone's recent breakup? What information do you have about your date that can help you determine your date's reaction? As relationships become more intimate, you receive more and more information that can improve decentring and adaptation.

Well-adjusted couples display support and affection for each other through positive non-verbal cues.
(Comstock Images)

Gaining information about your partners is one way you will be able to make decisions about how to help them in distressing situations. One pair of researchers, Ruth Ann Clark and Jesse Delia, studied how people wanted to be treated by their friends in response to six different distressing situations.[18] Clark and Delia found that there was not a strong desire to talk about the situation and a lot of variation in how people wanted their friends to approach it. When people were distressed, they wanted to be the ones to decide whether to bring up the issue or not. This means that rather than adopting a formulaic approach to distressed friends, you should use your ability to socially decentre and adapt to each one's particular needs. The abilities to provide comfort, social support, and ego support have been found to be associated with being a best friend.[19]

Skills and Strategies Specific to Escalating and Maintaining Relationships

Certain skills and strategies can be used to further escalate a relationship or to keep a relationship at a given stage. These include a willingness to express your emotions, openness to engage in relationship talk, tolerance of your partner's flaws and failures, the ability to manage conflict cooperatively, and finally, skill in gaining compliance. The use of the entire range of skills and strategies covered in these sections can help you develop and maintain strong and satisfying relationships.

Express Emotions

Expressing emotions is a particular form of self-disclosure and is a skill that can be improved, as discussed in several earlier chapters. Many of us are embarrassed about expressing our feelings, yet sharing feelings at the appropriate time during the development of a relationship is one way to continue its escalation. Conversely, sharing the wrong feelings at the wrong time can have a detrimental effect.

There are two ways we share feelings with our partners. The first is to disclose information about our past or current emotional states that does not relate to our partner, such as sadness about the death of a family member or fear about what we will do after we graduate. The second way is to directly express our emotional reactions to our partner, such as feelings of attraction to, love for, or disappointment in our partner. As relationships become more intimate, we have a greater expectation that our partner will disclose emotions openly.

The amount of risk associated with such emotional disclosures varies from person to person. Most of us are comfortable sharing positive emotions such as happiness and joy but are more reserved about sharing negative emotions such as fear or disappointment. We may think expressing negative emotions makes us appear weak or vulnerable. However, in a study of 46 committed romantic couples, researchers found that the number-one problem was the inability to talk about negative feelings.[20] For example, partners often made the following types of observations: "When she gets upset, she stops talking;" "He never lets me know when he's upset with something he doesn't like;" and "He just silently pouts." We generally want to know how our partners in intimate relationships are feeling, even if those feelings are negative.

However, a constant barrage of negative expressions can also alienate a partner. Research has found that marital satisfaction rises with the number of positive feelings the partners disclose, not with the number of negative ones.[21] A balance has to be found that includes expressing both positive and negative emotions at the right time in a constructive and confirming manner.

relationship talk. Talk about the nature, quality, direction, or definition of a relationship.

🔵 Engage in Relationship Talk

Relationship talk is talk about the nature, quality, direction, or definition of a relationship. Relationship talk is generally considered inappropriate in the early stages of a relationship. A relationship might be terminated prematurely if one partner tries to talk about it too early. Willingness to talk about the relationship is one way to implicitly signal your partner about your level of interest and commitment to the relationship. As relationships move toward greater intimacy, however, the amount of direct relationship talk increases. As the relationship escalates, we should be prepared to discuss our thoughts and feelings about it. In more intimate relationships, relationship talk helps the partners resolve differences in their perceptions of the relationship that might be contributing to conflict and dissatisfaction. Unwillingness to talk about the relationship in an intimate relationship can ultimately drive a partner away.

🔵 Be Tolerant and Show Restraint

The most satisfying relationships are those in which both partners refrain from continually disagreeing, criticizing, and making negative comments to each other. Both

individuals learn to accept the other and do not feel compelled to continually point out flaws or failures. One study found that well-adjusted couples focus their complaints on specific behaviours, whereas maladjusted couples complain about one another's personal characteristics. Well-adjusted couples are also kinder, more positive, and have more humour in their interactions. The partners tended to agree with one another's complaints, whereas the partners in maladjusted relationships launched counter-complaints.[22] In addition, happy couples, when compared with unhappy couples, display more affection through positive non-verbal cues, display more supportive behaviours, and make more attempts to avoid conflict.[23]

Maintaining a relationship requires tolerance. You must learn to accept your partner for who he or she is and put up with some things you dislike. When couples lose their tolerance, they begin focusing on and criticizing characteristics that they used to accept. Then the relationship begins to deteriorate.

Manage Conflict Cooperatively

The final skill for developing and maintaining relationships is to be able to manage conflict. Conflicts are inevitable in interpersonal relationships. As relationships develop, the individuals share more personal information and spend more time together, so the likelihood for conflict increases. The key to successful relational development and maintenance is *not* to avoid conflict altogether but rather to manage it effectively. Because effective conflict management is a key to successful relationships, we have devoted an entire chapter to it. Because Chapter 7 discussed in detail the nature, causes, and methods of dealing with interpersonal conflict, we will simply mention at this time that using a cooperative management style can actually transform conflict into an experience that strengthens a relationship. It can clarify the definition of the relationship, increase the exchange of information, and create a cooperative atmosphere for problem solving.

 In Canada...

WHO CHOOSES COMMON-LAW AS A FIRST CONJUGAL RELATIONSHIP?

When looking at the escalation of relationships, many young people choose to live with their lovers rather than to immediately marry them. This type of common-law relationship is on the rise. Set out as follows are some findings from a recent Canadian study of these relationships in Canada.

According to this study, "common-law unions are proliferating rapidly in Canada, and they are the major factor in the diversification of family behaviours." Common-law couples represented one couple in six in 1995. Quebec reported the most common-law unions with one out of every four couples living common-law. In fact, in Quebec, common law is the choice of the majority for their first conjugal union and is entered into earlier than in any other province. By the age of 20, 12 percent of never-married Quebec women had already experienced a common-law union, compared with eight percent of women in other provinces. This study found that Quebec women, whose first language was French, were more likely to choose common-law unions. In fact, in other provinces, an analysis of women who spoke French as their native tongue indicated that "common-law unions are more popular in the French group throughout the country."

Although becoming increasingly popular, common-law relationships are much less stable than traditional marriage relationships. According to this study, 70 percent of common-law unions end in separation within the first five years, with only a minority of them ending in marriage (the estimate was three in

Continued

every ten). This same study also estimated that 50 percent of Canadian women born between 1971 and 1980 will likely enter into a common-law relationship. The makeup of relationships is undergoing many transitions, common-law relationships being one of the many significant changes for Canadian families in the late 20th and early 21st centuries.

Source: From Pierre Turcotte and Alain Belanger, "The Dynamics of Formation and Dissolution of First Common-Law Unions in Canada," Statistics Canada, 1998, 1–26. Adapted from "Moving in Together: The Formation of First Common-Law Unions," found in Canadian Social Trends, Cat. No. 11-008, winter 1997, No. 47.

Seek Compliance

The final skill for escalating and maintaining relationships might seem somewhat contrary to the ones we have been discussing. Strictly speaking, **compliance gaining** involves the use of persuasive strategies to accomplish your personal goals—that is, to get your own way. We are not urging you to force your will on others. We are, however, suggesting that it is sometimes ethical and moral to persuade others to go your way. In an ideal situation, the resulting actions will fulfill both partners' goals.

You need compliance-gaining strategies if you encounter resistance to fulfilling your goal. For example, suppose you want to go out to a movie and you need to borrow money from one of your friends to pay for it. You may simply ask, "Can I borrow 10 dollars so I can go to a movie?" If your friend says, "Sure," the interaction is completed. If your friend says, "No, you haven't paid me back from last time," however, you will probably use some compliance-gaining strategy.

Compliance-gaining strategies are responsive to the ongoing, transactive nature of interpersonal relationships.[24] We plot strategies that develop over a number of interactions and modify them in accordance with others' responses. For example, before you ask to borrow money from your friend, you might first do a few favours for her during the day. Then if your friend says no, you might remind her that she owes you for all you've done for her. If she still says no, you might offer to help her over the weekend with her class project. The type of relationship you have established with the other person will affect your strategy selection. Often we face little resistance to our requests from our partners, so we have no need for any compliance-gaining strategy.

compliance gaining. The use of persuasive strategies to accomplish personal goals.

▶ Recap

SKILLS AND STRATEGIES FOR DEVELOPING INTERPERSONAL RELATIONSHIPS

Skills and Strategies Used Primarily During the Initiation Stage

Observe and Act on Approachability Cues

Identify and Use Conversation Starters

Follow Initiation Norms

Ask Questions

Don't Expect Too Much from the Initial Interaction

Skills and Strategies Used in Both Initiating and Escalating Relationships

Communicate Attraction

Be Open and Self-Disclose Appropriately

Gather Information to Reduce Uncertainty

Monitor Your Perceptions

Continued

Listen Actively and Respond Confirmingly

Socially Decentre and Adopt an Other-Oriented Perspective

Skills and Strategies Specific to Escalating and Maintaining Relationships

Express Emotions

Engage in Relationship Talk

Be Tolerant and Show Restraint

Manage Conflict Cooperatively

Seek Compliance

Becoming Other-Oriented

ADAPTING RELATIONAL STRATEGIES AND SKILLS TO YOUR PARTNER

Besides presenting a model of the stages of relational development, this chapter discusses a variety of skills and strategies you can use to initiate, escalate, and maintain interpersonal relationships. Your decisions about what strategies to implement should be adapted to the anticipated reactions of your partner. In addition, to be effective, you must understand what is appropriate for a given stage of development, and then adapt the strategy or strategies accordingly. Below is a list of some of the skills and strategies covered in this chapter, to which your partner is likely to have some reaction. Think about a friend whom you know fairly well, but who isn't your best friend. Briefly assess how comfortable and skilled you are at using each strategy, what you think your friend's reaction would be to its use, and how you can adapt the strategy to fit the level of intimacy that exists in your relationship.

Skill/Strategy	How would I feel about using this skill/strategy?	How would my friend react/feel if I used this skill/strategy?	How should the skill/strategy be adapted to be appropriate to the relationship stage?
Communicating Attraction			
Being Open and Self-Disclosing			
Listening Actively and Confirmingly			
Expressing Emotions			
Talking About the Relationship			
Being Tolerant and Showing Restraint			
Managing Conflict Cooperatively			

De-Escalating and Ending Relationships

Given the process nature of relationships discussed earlier, you know that relationships are always changing. Sometimes the change is to a less intimate level, and sometimes it's the complete termination of the relationship. Part of effective relationship management involves being sensitive to cues that signal relational problems or change. As "Understanding Diversity: Gender and Ending Relationships" below indicates, women usually sense trouble in a relationship earlier than do men—but what exactly do they sense? Because each stage in a relationship has unique communication qualities, specific verbal and non-verbal cues can tip us off when a relationship begins to de-escalate.[25] There is a decrease in touching and physical contact (including less sexual activity), physical proximity, eye contact, smiling, vocal variety in the voice, and ease of interaction. In addition, there is a decrease in the amount of time spent together, an increase in time between interactions, and more separation of possessions. The interactions become less personal, and so does the language.

 # Understanding Diversity

GENDER AND ENDING RELATIONSHIPS

Men and women differ when it comes to dating and marital breakups. Women tend to be stronger monitors of the relationship, so they usually detect trouble before men do. Women's sensitivity to the health of the relationship may be one factor that makes them more likely to initiate the termination of a relationship as well.[26] However, when some men want out of a relationship, they engage in behaviours that women find totally unacceptable. This allows both partners to feel as if they were the ones who initiated the breakup and therefore lets them "save face."

Relationship-ending problems are sometimes associated with behaviours that appear early in a relationship. Marriages in which the men avoid interaction by stonewalling and responding defensively to complaints are more likely to end in divorce.[27]

In one study of divorce, men tended to see the later part of the process as more difficult, whereas the women said the period before the decision to divorce was more difficult. In addition, two-thirds of the women were likely to discuss marital problems with their children as compared with only one-fourth of the men; and men were twice as likely to say that no one helped them during the worst part of the process.[28]

Couples during de-escalation tend to use fewer intimate terms; they use less present tense and more past tense; they make fewer references to their future in the relationship; they use more qualified language ("maybe," "whatever," "we'll see"); make fewer evaluative statements; and spend less time discussing any given topic. They fight more, and they disclose less. If one person becomes less open about discussing attitudes, feelings, thoughts, and other personal issues, he or she is probably signalling a desire to terminate, or at least redefine, the relationship. Can you pick up the signals of the couple's difficulty reflected in the picture on page 337?

John Gottman, who studied couples for over 20 years, identified four categories of communication behaviour that indicate increasing problems in a marriage.[29] These behaviours undermine effective communication between couples and can lead to the end of the relationship. The first warning sign is criticism of, or attacks on, the other person's personality. The second sign is the display of contempt through insults and psychological abuse. The third sign is defensive behaviour such as denying responsibility, making excuses, whining, and counter-complaining. The final communication behaviour that undermines a marriage is stonewalling, in which the partners withdraw, quit responding to each other, and become minimally engaged in the relationship. Among the four, stonewalling is the single best predictor of divorce. If all four signs are consistently present, there is a 94 percent chance the couple will eventually divorce.[30] Most couples experience some of these behaviours, but happy couples develop effective communication patterns to overcome them.

Responses to Relational Problems

When you pick up signals of relational problems, you have three choices: wait and see what happens; make a decision to end the relationship; or try to repair the relationship. Repairing the relationship involves applying all the maintenance skills we talked about earlier. Some of the strategies for dealing with conflict that you learned in Chapter 7 will also help you. Underlying the success of any repair effort, however, is the degree to which both partners want to keep the relationship going. The nature of the problem, the stage of the relationship, and the commitment and motivation of the partners all affect the success of repair efforts. There is no single quick solution to relational problems because so many factors influence each one. You need to focus on the specific concerns, needs, and issues that underlie the problem, and then use specific strategies to resolve it. Professional counselling might be an important option.

The likelihood of creating a post-intimacy relationship depends on several factors.[31] For gay and lesbian couples, the strongest factors are whether the partners are part of a family-like network with mutual friends, the uniqueness of the relationship, and the degree to which the partners still like each other. For opposite-sex romantic couples, the factors are the degree to which the partners still like each other, how much they hope to renew the romantic relationship, and their expectations or previous experience in maintaining a post-intimacy relationship. Think about your own post-intimate relationships, whether romantic or not. What factors led you to continue contact even though the relationship was no longer intimate? How did you feel about maintaining the non-intimate relationship? How did you feel about those you did not maintain?

What if it is your partner who wants to end the relationship? There is no pat answer for addressing this situation. If a friend stops calling or visiting, should you just assume the relationship is over and leave it alone, or should you call and ask what's up? People lose contact for a myriad of reasons. Sometimes it is beneficial to ask an individual directly if he or she is breaking off the relationship, although such direct requests place your self-concept on the line. How should you react if your friend confirms a desire to end the relationship? If possible, try to have a focused discussion on what has contributed to his or her decision. You might get information you need to repair the relationship. Or you might gain information that will help you in future relationships.

The Decision to End a Relationship

If you do choose to reduce the level of intimacy in the relationship, consider your goals. Do you want to continue the relationship at a less intimate level, or terminate it altogether? Do you care enough about the other person to want to preserve his or her self-esteem? Are you aware of the costs involved in ending the relationship? There is no one correct or best way to end a relationship. Ending relationships is not something you can practise to improve. However, you *can* practise the effective relational management skills such as decentring and empathy, adaptation, and compliance gaining. These skills will also help you in ending relationships.

We rely on our social networks for support and self-confirmation when an intimate relationship comes to an end. Advice about how to handle the loss of a close relationship is plentiful, but basically each person must find a way to compensate for the loss of intimacy and companionship. The loss of an important relationship hurts, but it need not put us out of commission if we make the most of our friends and family.

The de-escalation and termination of a relationship are not inherently bad. Not all relationships are meant to endure. Ending a relationship can be a healthy move if the relationship is harmful, or if it no longer provides confirmation of the self or satisfies interpersonal needs; it also can open the door to new relationships. Sometimes we choose not to end a relationship but rather to de-escalate to a less intimate stage where there is a better balance between benefits and costs.

Breaking up an intimate relationship is hard because of the degree to which we become dependent on the other person to confirm our sense of self. When a relationship ends, we may feel as if we need to redefine who we are. The most satisfying breakups are those that confirm both partners' worth rather than degrade it. "I just can't be what you want me to be," "I'll always love you but...," and "You're a very special person, but I need other things in life" are all examples of statements that do not destroy self-esteem.

The process of ending a relationship is considerably different when only one party wants out of the relationship (unilateral) from when both are agreeable to it (bilateral).[32] In a **bilateral dissolution**, both parties are predisposed to ending the relationship; they simply need to sort out details such as timing, dividing possessions, and defining conditions for the contact after the breakup. In a **unilateral dissolution**, the person who wants to end the relationship must choose a strategy (see pages 341–342) to get his or her partner to agree to the dissolution. Sometimes, however, people simply walk out of a relationship.

How Relationships End

A declining relationship usually follows one of several paths. Sometimes a relationship loses energy and runs down like a dying battery. Instead of a single event that causes the breakup, the relationship **fades away**—the two partners just drift further and further apart. They spend less time together, let more time go by between interactions, and stop disclosing much about themselves. You've probably had a number of friendships that ended this way—perhaps long-distance relationships. Because long-distance relationships require a great deal of effort to maintain, a move away can easily decrease the level of intimacy between two people.

Some relationships end in "sudden death."[33] As the name suggests, **sudden death** moves straight to separation. One partner might move away or die, or, more frequently, a single precipitating event such as infidelity, breaking a confidence, a major conflict, or some other major role violation precipitates the breakup. Sudden death is like taking an express elevator from a top floor to the basement.

Between fading away and sudden death lies incrementalism. **Incrementalism** is the process by which conflicts and problems continue to accumulate in the

bilateral dissolution. Ending a relationship when both parties are agreeable.

unilateral dissolution. Ending a relationship when only one party is agreeable.

fades away. Ending a relationship by slowly drifting apart.

sudden death. Ending a relationship abruptly and without preparation.

incrementalism. Ending a relationship when conflicts and problems finally reach a critical mass.

Which of the three types of relationship termination do you think is evident here: fading away—where the partners drift slowly apart, sudden death—where separation is immediate, or incrementalism—where the conflicts gradually build until they reach the breaking point? (Donna Day/Tony Stone Images)

relationship until they reach a critical mass that leads to the breakup; the relationship becomes intolerable or, from a social exchange perspective, too costly. "I just got to a point where it wasn't worth it anymore" and "It got to the point where all we did was fight all the time" are typical statements about incremental endings.

▲●■   Understanding Diversity

EMPATHY AND SEXUAL ORIENTATION

I once volunteered as a crisis phone counsellor in a large metropolitan area. Counsellors were trained to use effective counselling skills, such as empathy, in relating to the callers' crises. One night, a call came in from a very distressed and depressed man. He had broken up with his homosexual partner, with whom he had had a long-term intimate relationship. At first I was uncomfortable dealing with the situation. Despite extensive training and role-playing, I wondered how I, as a heterosexual male, could empathize or relate to this caller. I continued to ask questions about how he felt, what he saw as his needs, and his perception of the problems. The more we talked, the more empathic I became, because I realized that his description was very familiar. I had been divorced some four years earlier, and this caller's descriptions of his feelings matched the feelings I had experienced during that time. I was able to talk about some of those feelings and this seemed to help him understand his own situation. I realized that though the sex of our partners was different, the overriding issue was the loss of an intimate relationship. I grew a little wiser that night.

— *Mark V. Redmond*

Reasons for De-Escalating and Ending Relationships

The reasons for ending an interpersonal relationship are as varied as relationships themselves. In general, we end relationships when the costs outweigh the rewards. This does not mean that as soon as a relationship becomes difficult we should dump it. Relationships are somewhat like savings accounts. If the relationship is profitable, you deposit your excess rewards into an emotional savings account. Then, at times when the costs exceed the rewards, you draw from your savings account to make up the deficit. In other words, if you have had a strong, satisfying relationship with someone for a long period of time, you will be more inclined to stay in the relationship during rough times. There might be a point, however, at which your savings account will run out, and you will decide to close your account—end the relationship. Of course, if you can foresee that you will reap more benefits in the future, you might decide to keep the account open, even when it is overdrawn. In addition, if you have had even less satisfying relationships in the past, or if your alternatives seem more dismal than your current relationships, you might decide to stick it out.[34] Of course, under those relational circumstances, when attractive alternatives do appear, relationships often suffer a sudden death.

When a relationship comes to an end, we often ask ourselves, "What happened?" "Why did the relationship come to an end?" We engage in this "post-mortem" regardless of whether we or our partner initiated the breakup. If our partner initiated the breakup and did not provide adequate explanations, we are left to wonder and guess about what happened. We may continue behaviours that undermine future relationships because we failed to understand how we contributed to the termination of the present relationship.

According to researcher Michael Cody, students' assessments of what caused their intimate heterosexual relationships to break up can be put into three categories.[35] As Table 10.2 shows, "faults" were cited as the number-one cause. These are personality traits or behaviours in one partner that the other partner dislikes. The number-two cause, "unwillingness to compromise," represents a variety of failings on the part of one or both partners, including failure to put enough effort into the relationship, a decrease in effort, or failure to make concessions for the good of the relationship. The final cause, "feeling constrained," reflects one partner's desire to be free of the commitments and constraints of a relationship. However, a variety of other elements can contribute to the breakup of both romantic and non-romantic relationships, including loss of interest in the other person, desire for independence, and conflicting attitudes about issues affecting the relationship, such as values, sexual conduct, marriage, and infidelity.

Just as there are behavioural rules for making and maintaining friends, there are behaviours that, if you pursue them, will almost certainly cost you a friendship. Listed in order of offensiveness, they are as follows.[36]

1. Acting jealous or being critical of your relationship
2. Discussing with others what your friend said in confidence
3. Not volunteering help in time of need
4. Not trusting or confiding in your friend
5. Criticizing your friend in public
6. Not showing positive regard for your friend
7. Not standing up for your friend in his or her absence
8. Not being tolerant of your friend's other friends
9. Not showing emotional support
10. Nagging your friend

Earlier in this chapter, you read how relationships intensify or sometimes become less intense in predictable stages. Relationship dissolution is also not a single event

Table 10.2   **Reasons Given for Breakups**

Faults

I realized that he/she had too many personality faults.

He/she behaved in ways that embarrassed me.

His/her behaviours were more to blame for the breakup than anything else.

Unwillingness to Compromise

I realized she/he was unwilling to make enough contributions to the relationship.

I felt that he/she no longer behaved toward me as romantically as he/she once did.

I felt that he/she took me for granted.

I felt that he/she wasn't willing to compromise for the good of the relationship.

Feeling Constrained

I felt that the relationship was beginning to constrain me, and I felt a lack of freedom.

Although I still cared for him/her, I wanted to start dating other people.

Although this relationship was a good one, I started to get bored with it.

He/she made too many contributions, and I started to feel suffocated.

Source: Adapted from M. J. Cody, "A Typology of Disengagement Strategies and an Examination of the Role Intimacy and Relational Problems Play in Strategy Selection," Communication Monographs, 49(3), (1982): 162.

but a process. Love relationships usually end more abruptly and with more emotional intensity than friendships do. When one researcher asked individuals to identify why a friendship with a friend of the same sex ended, first on the list was physical separation.[37] Second, respondents reported that new friends replaced old friends as circumstances changed. Third, people often just grow to dislike a characteristic of the friend's behaviour or personality. Finally, one friend's dating activity or romantic relationships can interfere with and contribute to the decay of a friendship. It should come as no surprise that casual friendships are more likely to end than are those between close or intimate friends. Close friendships are better able to withstand change, uncertainty, and separation.

A Model of Ending Relationships

Steve Duck developed a model to show stages in the ending of a relationship.[38] As Figure 10.2 on page 340 shows, first one partner reaches some threshold of dissatisfaction that prompts him or her to consider ending the relationship. Having passed this threshold, the person enters an **intrapsychic phase**, in which he or she privately evaluates the partner's behaviours, often focusing on the reasons in Table 10.2 to justify withdrawing. Social Exchange Theory predicts that in this phase, the person will assess the relationship's costs and rewards and will be inclined to terminate the relationship if he or she finds it no longer "profitable."[39] We might still remain in an unprofitable relationship if there is a reservoir of profits to offset the current costs. However, as with a savings account, there is only so much we can withdraw before we have to close the account or end the relationship. We might also remain in an unprofitable relationship if we predict that the relationship will become profitable again.

intrapsychic phase. The first phase in relationship termination when an individual engages in an internal evaluation of the partner.

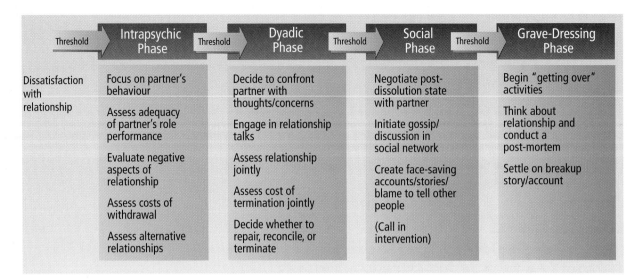

**Figure 10.2
A Model of Ending
Relationships**

Source: S. Duck, "A Typography of
Relationship Disengagement and
Dissolution," from *Personal
Relationships, 4: Dissolving
Relationships,* edited by S. Duck
(Academic Press: London), p. 16.

dyadic phase. The second phase
in relationship termination
when the individual discusses
termination with the partner.

social phase. The third phase in
relationship termination members of the social network
around both parties are
informed of and become
involved in the termination
process.

grave-dressing phase. The final
phase in relationship termination when the partners generate
public explanations and move
past the relationship.

From time to time, we all become frustrated with a relationship—and for some of us, the frustration may become severe enough that we consider terminating but without proceeding further than this phase. However, we might "leak" our thoughts and feelings through our communication, displaying such emotions as hostility, anxiety, stress, or guilt. We might decide to confide in a third party about our dissatisfaction. We might consider various strategies for ending the relationship.

At some point, we might decide to move from our private internal contemplations about the relationship to confronting our partner. This is the **dyadic phase** in the model. If our partner feels challenged and intimidated by our desire to end the relationship, we might have to justify our thoughts and feelings. Our partner might also criticize our behaviour and identify our failings. He or she might raise issues that cause us to re-evaluate the relationship, our partner, and the costs of dissolving the relationship. We might decide instead to work on improving and repairing the relationship.

If we decide to end the relationship, we enter the **social phase** and begin making the information public. Sometimes a person's social network will mobilize to preserve the relationship. Friends might act as mediators, encouraging reconciliation and suggesting ways to repair the relationship. Of course, friends can also reinforce a decision to separate. Rumours and stories about what happened and what is happening can fuel bad feelings and hasten the end of the relationship.

In the **grave-dressing phase**, one or both partners may attempt to "place flowers on the grave" of their relationship to cover up the hurt and pain associated with its death. They need a public story that they can share with others about what happened: "We still love each other; we just decided we needed more in our lives." However, personal accounts of breakups often place blame on the other partner: "I knew he had his faults, but he thought he could change, and he just wasn't able to." During this phase, our friends encourage us to get back into social activities; they might even try to fix us up with dates. Most importantly, we go through an internal stage in which we try to accept the end of the relationship and let go of feelings of guilt, failure, and blame.

Strategies for Ending Relationships

When the vitality in long-term relationships fades away over a period of years, the individuals move slowly through the de-escalation stages before finally going their separate ways. Brand new relationships are far more likely to end abruptly. As you saw in Figure10.1, the farther up the relational high-rise you take the elevator, the longer the ride down.

However, no matter what stage a relationship is in, partners use both direct and indirect strategies when they wish to end it. **Indirect termination strategies** represent attempts to break up a relationship without explicitly stating the desire to do so. **Direct termination strategies** involve explicit statements. The strategy that a person chooses will depend on the level of intimacy in the relationship, the level of desire to help the partner save face, the degree of urgency for terminating the relationship, and the person's interpersonal skills. The Cathy cartoon below illustrates the difficulties we all face in coming up with a unique and non-threatening strategy for ending a relationship.

Indirect Termination Strategies

One researcher identifies three strategies that people use to disengage indirectly: withdrawal, pseudo-de-escalation, and cost escalation. *Withdrawal* involves reducing the amount of contact and interaction without any explanation.[40] This strategy is the most dissatisfying for the other partner.[41] Withdrawal represents an attempt to avoid a confrontational scene and to save face.

In *pseudo-de-escalation,* one partner claims that he or she wants to redefine the relationship at a lower level of intimacy, but in reality, he or she wants to end the relationship. Statements such as, "Let's just be friends" or "I think of you more as a sister" might be sincere, or they might reflect an unspoken desire to disengage completely. When both parties want to end the relationship, they sometimes use mutual pseudo-de-escalation and enter into a false agreement to reduce the level of intimacy as they move to disengagement.

indirect termination strategies. Attempts to break up a relationship without explicitly stating the desire to do so.

direct termination strategies. Explicit statements of a desire to break up a relationship.

Cost escalation is an attempt to increase the costs associated with the relationship to encourage the other person to terminate it. A dissatisfied partner might ask for an inordinate amount of the other person's time, pick fights, criticize the other person, or violate relational rules.

Direct Termination Strategies

The same researcher also identified four direct strategies that we use to terminate relationships: negative identity management, justification, de-escalation, and positive tone.[42] *Negative identity management* is a direct statement of the desire to terminate the relationship. It does not take into account the other's feelings, and it might even include criticisms. "I want out of our relationship," "I just can't stand to be around you anymore," and "I'm no longer happy in this relationship and I want to date other people" reflect negative identity management.

Justification is a clear statement of the desire to end the relationship accompanied by an honest explanation of the reasons. Justification statements may still hurt the other person's feelings: "I've found someone else who I want to spend more time with and who makes me happy," or "I feel as if I've grown a great deal and you haven't." A person who uses justification does not fault the other person, and he or she makes some attempt to protect both parties' sense of self. One researcher found that most people on the receiving end like this strategy best.[43]

De-escalation is an honest statement of a desire to redefine the relationship at a lower level of intimacy or to move toward ending the relationship. One partner might ask for a trial separation so that both people can explore other opportunities and gain a clearer understanding of their needs:[44] "Neither of us seems to be that happy with the relationship right now, so I think we should cool it for a while and see what happens."

Positive tone is the direct strategy that is most sensitive to the other person's sense of self. This strategy can seem almost contradictory because the initiator tries to affirm the other's personal qualities and worth at the same time that he or she calls a halt to the relationship. "I love you; I just can't live with you," "I'm really sorry I've got to break off the relationship," and "You really are a wonderful person; you're just not the one for me" are examples of positive tone statements.

▶ Recap

STRATEGIES FOR ENDING RELATIONSHIPS

	Term	Explanation
How Relationships End	Fading away	The relationship dissolves slowly as intimacy declines.
	Sudden death	The relationship ends abruptly, usually in response to some precipitating event.
	Incrementalism	Relational conflicts and problems accumulate until they become intolerable and the relationship ends.
Indirect Termination Strategies	Withdrawal	One person reduces the amount of contact, without any explanation.
	Pseudo-de-escalation	A desire for less intimacy is claimed when the person really just wants out.
	Cost escalation	One partner increases relational costs to encourage the other to end the relationship.

Continued

Direct Termination Strategies	Negative identity management	A desire to end the relationship is stated directly, without concern for the other person's feelings.
	Justification	A desire to end the relationship is stated directly but with an explanation of the reasons.
	De-escalation	A desire to lower the level of intimacy or move toward termination is stated.
	Positive tone	A desire to end the relationship is stated directly with affirmation of the other person's value.

Building Your Skills

ASSESSING YOUR PAST RELATIONSHIPS

Identify two relationships that you have ended and two relationships that the other person ended. For each relationship, determine which of the indirect or direct strategies were used to end the relationship. What differences were there in how the relationships ended? What effects do you think the choice of strategy had on you and your partner?

Conduct a survey of your friends by asking them these same questions. What conclusions can you draw about how people feel concerning different relationship-termination strategies?

Strategies for Post-Dissolution Recovery

Our identities are often tied to our relationships, and the more intimate the relationship, the more our identity is likely to be threatened if the relationship ends. Letting go of a close relationship is not easy, and the accompanying grief and pain can be debilitating. However, maintaining positive self-esteem and being able to nurture other relationships requires engaging in effective post-dissolution recovery. Relationship researcher Ann Weber created a list of strategies to help address the grief and loss of non-marital breakups.[45] The following strategies are adapted from her list:

1. *Express your emotions.* You need to vent your feelings, if not to your "ex," then to a sympathetic listener, in a journal, or in some other forum. (There are even websites where you can share your story.)
2. *Figure out what happened.* Understanding what occurred in the relationship is one way to get a handle on your current emotions. You need to accept the reasons for the breakup and work toward acceptance.
3. *Realize, don't idealize.* We sometimes view the end of a relationship as the death of a dream. In order to deal with a loss more realistically, Weber suggests mentally reviewing your partner's flaws.
4. *Prepare to feel better.* You might be surprised to find yourself feeling relief and joy. Finding the humour and irony in the breakup can help you cope with the grief. There's a funny side to most situations; we need to be able to joke and laugh about the situation with our friends.
5. *Expect to heal.* Some of the hardest words to accept from others are "It will get better." Although we may not want to believe it, we do recover from injuries, and breakups are a type of injury.

6. *Talk to others.* Isolation is usually not a very healthy way to handle grief. Friends expect to provide comfort by listening to you discuss your feelings. The more open and honest you can be in sharing your thoughts and feelings, the faster you will heal. Don't be afraid to be direct in explaining to friends what you want or need from them; they can't read your mind.

7. *Get some perspective.* This strategy involves a little bit of wallowing in your misery by reading stories, seeing movies, or listening to songs about other people's experiences in breaking up. These can help you put your own situation into perspective. This approach was the focus of an episode of the TV series, *The Gilmore Girls,* in which Lorelai tried to help her stoic daughter, Rory, address a recent breakup by spending a day "wallowing" while watching such movies as *Love Story, The Champ, An Affair to Remember,* and *Old Yeller.*

8. *Be ready for further punishment, or maybe reward.* Weber suggests that once you've gone through the above strategies, it's time to explore potential relationships. Learn from your past experiences, hang onto pleasant memories, and move forward.

Facing the end of a relationship that has meant a great deal to us is one of the more difficult experiences we face in our social lives. The more intimate and involved we become, the more heartbreaking the end. However, as the advice above suggests, there is life after the breakup of a relationship, and it is important to go through a recovery cycle that includes accepting the breakup, accepting the pain, realizing that you still have value and worth, and then moving on. Of course, all of this is easy to say and much more difficult to accomplish—which is one reason we should not isolate ourselves but lean on other interpersonal relationships and family members to help us cope. Regrettably, relationships do come to an end, but just as we develop skills in initiating relationships, we can develop the ability to cope effectively with their termination.

 ## Becoming Other-Oriented

CONSIDERING EMOTIONAL REACTIONS

This chapter has covered various interpersonal situations in which emotion is a key element. Strong emotions are evoked by relational problems and termination. Emotional reactions can't be avoided, but there are various ways of managing the emotions. While each of us responds emotionally in different ways, social decentring and being other-oriented can help us appreciate another person's emotional state. Reflect on each of the following scenarios as you answer the accompanying questions. Compare your responses to those of your classmates or your friends.

• Jane and Jeremy have been dating for two years, and Jane thought that after they graduated from college this spring they would get married. Two months before graduation, Jeremy tells Jane that he isn't ready to settle down and thinks they should break up. What emotions do you think Jane experiences?

• Sierra's best friend since high school, Regina, is a lesbian. Over the years, Sierra has made derogatory remarks about gays and lesbians, so Regina feared revealing her sexual orientation; she always played along whenever the conversation turned to men, dating, or homosexuals. Sierra finds out through some mutual friends about Regina's sexual orientation. What emotions do you think Sierra experiences? What emotions do you think Regina would experience if Sierra confronted her?

Continued

- Jorge waits on tables at a restaurant to help pay for his college education. One night toward the end of a long and demanding shift, he approaches a man and a woman to take their order. The man says, "It's about time you got your f***ing a** over here. You look like a pretty sorry excuse for a waiter. Is there someone else who can wait on us—I don't like people like you serving me my food." What emotions is Jorge likely to experience? (Bonus questions: What might the customer be feeling? Why might he be acting the way he is? What would be the best way for Jorge to respond?)

Summary

Relationships progress through stages, with the movement from one stage to another often signalled by turning points. As relationships escalate, they progress from pre-interaction awareness to initiation, to exploration, to intensification, and finally, to intimacy. Relationships de-escalate as we move to redefine or terminate them, moving from turmoil or stagnation, to de-intensification, to individualization, to separation, and finally, to post-interaction. Even after we end a relationship, its effects remain with us to shape our feelings and responses in other relationships. We use a variety of skills within each relational stage.

A variety of strategies and skills can be applied to the initiation, escalation, and maintenance of interpersonal relationships. Certain skills and strategies are used primarily during the initiation of a relationship, including observing and acting on approachability cues, identifying and using conversation starters, following initiation norms, asking questions, and controlling expectations. Another set of skills and strategies is applicable to both the initiation of a relationship and the escalation of relationships toward greater intimacy. These include communicating attraction, being open and appropriately self-disclosing, reducing uncertainty, monitoring perceptions, listening actively and responding confirmingly, and social decentring and adopting an other-oriented perspective. The remaining skills and strategies covered in this section are used primarily for moving a relationship toward intimacy or for maintaining existing relationships. These include expressing emotions, engaging in talk about the relationship, being tolerant and showing restraint, managing conflict cooperatively, and seeking compliance. All of these skills and strategies can be learned and enhanced to help you more effectively manage your interpersonal relationships.

People can react to relational problems by ignoring them, trying to address and repair them, or choosing to redefine or end the relationship. In a bilateral dissolution, both parties want to end the relationship, whereas in a unilateral dissolution one person wants to end the relationship and the other wants to maintain it. Relationships typically end in one of three ways: by fading away, through sudden death, or incrementally.

In general, relationships seem to end when the costs exceed the rewards over some period of time. Reasons for ending a relationship fall into three categories: faults, unwillingness to compromise, and feelings of constraint.

One model of how relationships end identified four phases: the intrapsychic phase, the dyadic phase, the social phase, and the grave-dressing phase. First, we internally assess the value of the relationship and consider termination; then we discuss it with our partner; we proceed by announcing the termination and interacting with friends and family; and finally, we come to grips with the consequences of separation.

Partners can use direct or indirect strategies to bring a relationship to an end. Indirect strategies to terminate a relationship include withdrawal, pseudo-de-escalation, and cost escalation. Among the direct strategies for ending a relationship are negative identity management, justification, de-escalation, and positive tone. Strategies for post-dissolution recovery include expressing emotions, figuring out what happened, talking to others, and getting a broader perspective.

For Discussion and Review

🔵 Focus on Critical Thinking

1. Of the skills for starting a relationship covered in this chapter, which two are probably the most important and which two are the least important? Why?

2. How do the strategies for escalating and maintaining a relationship relate to the indirect and direct strategies used for terminating a relationship?

3. Trace two close relationships that you have had—one with a friend of the same sex, and one with a friend of the opposite sex—through the applicable stages of relational escalation and de-escalation. What differences and similarities do you find at each stage? How can you explain them?

4. How do you know when it is time to get out of a relationship?

🔵 Focus on Ethics

5. Jack and Jill are in an exclusive romantic relationship, but because they attend different schools, they are living 300 km apart. Things have not been going very smoothly recently, and Jill decided to go out with a guy at school a few times without telling Jack. Is Jill's behaviour ethical?

6. Let's assume that you are very skilled and adept at using strategies for developing interpersonal relationships. How ethical would it be for you to use those skills to satisfy your interpersonal needs in a given relationship, knowing that your partner is less skilled at getting his or her own needs met?

7. You are in a romantic relationship that has become physically intimate. How ethical is it for you to say, "I love you" if you really aren't sure you do? If your partner says, "I love you," should you say it back, even if you don't mean it?

8. Lynn and Mario have had an intimate relationship and have been living together for over a year. The relationship has seemed to be comfortable for both of them. One day, Lynn comes home from work and finds that all of Mario's belongings are gone. A note from Mario says, "I couldn't bring myself to tell you I'm leaving. Sorry. Goodbye." Is Mario's behaviour ethical?

For Your Journal

1. At the end of each day, for three or four days, stop and assess which of the interpersonal communication skills you used the most in your interactions that day. See if there is a consistent pattern in the skills you rely on. What skills do you seem to use the most? What skills do you use the least? How might using other skills affect your interactions and relationships?

2. Think about a close relationship you had and that you ended. What strategy did you use first? How well did this strategy work? What was your partner's

reaction? How did you feel using this strategy? What other strategies were used, if any? What were the reactions to those strategies? If you had it to do over again, what other strategy might you have chosen to use? How do you think your partner would have reacted to that strategy? Why? If you can't think of any relationship that you have ended, use one in which your partner ended the relationship, and adapt the questions accordingly.

Learning with Others

1. In class, form at least five pairs of students. Each pair should choose a particular stage of relational development without telling the rest of the class. Then, each pair should spend two minutes discussing plans for the upcoming weekend in a way that communicates the stage they have chosen. The rest of the class should write down what stage they think each pair is portraying. After all the pairs have finished their dialogues, score each others' responses. Which stage was easiest to portray and identify? Which stage was most difficult? How easy is it to see differences in communication behaviour at various stages?

2. In small groups, brainstorm some of the turning points that each of you has experienced in important relationships. Identify the relational stages that the turning points led to. Which stages crop up most often? Least often? What does the frequency tell you about those stages?

3. Working in groups of four or five students, use your own experiences to develop an answer to the following question: Do the reasons for breaking up a relationship change as the relationship becomes more intimate? To answer this question, start with casual relationships and identify reasons that people end those relationships. Next, talk about friendships and discuss reasons for ending them. And, finally, talk about intimate relationships and the reasons they break up. What are the similarities and differences among these relationships and why they break up?

4. Using Research Navigator, find article AN 12954204. This article is about how advertisers use sexual attraction to sell products. In small groups, review this article. Once this is done, find advertisements that confirm the findings of this study.

Weblinks

www.familydigest.com/stories/marriage_stages.cfm   This site offers a discussion of the relationship stages experienced by couples after getting married.

www.canoe.ca/LifewiseHeartVal00/lies.html   This website has a humorous list of lies men and women tell each other.

http://quiz.ivillage.com/relationships/tests/breaktest.htm   Here's a quick and simple breakup quiz that is supposed to help you decide whether it's time to move on.

http://quiz.ivillage.com/relationships/tests/breakup.htm   Here's a post-breakup quiz for women to find out if you are over the "ex."

http://breakup-songs.com   This site offers a ranking of the top 250 breakup songs, best lyrics from breakup songs, and lists of breakup songs sorted by decade.

11 Interpersonal Relationships at Home, on the Internet, and at Work

After you study this chapter

you should be able to ...

1. Define the term "family" and describe four types of families.

2. Identify and describe ways of improving family communication.

3. Distinguish among the different types of computer-mediated communication.

4. Compare face-to-face communication with computer-mediated communication.

5. Describe principles for using computer-mediated communication to initiate relationships.

6. Describe principles for using computer-mediated communication to maintain existing relationships.

7. Describe the impact of workplace friendships and romances.

8. Describe principles of upward, downward, horizontal, and outward communication.

- Interpersonal Relationships at Home

- Interpersonal Relationships on the Internet

- Interpersonal Relationships at Work

People who have good relationships at home are more effective in the marketplace.

ZIG ZIGLAR

Debbie logs on to her e-mail account and hears the little ring of incoming messages. The first one is from her dad:

It was great seeing you this weekend. Your mom and I always appreciate it anytime you can get home during the semester. As to your changing majors, I want you to know that whatever decision you make is OK with me. Don't worry about having to stay an extra semester to finish up—the world will still be here when you graduate. The communication course you're taking on how to interact with people sounds like a lot of fun—maybe I could take one like it too. Well, I've got to get back to work. Just wanted you to know how nice it was to have you home for a couple of days. Write when you get a chance, Love, Dad.

Debbie clicks on the Reply button and writes her dad a quick response. Next she opens an e-mail from Skyler, one of her co-workers:

Man, you picked a great weekend not to work. Harry went ballistic with all the employees—he yelled his head off, accusing everyone of being lazy and good for nothing before storming out. It was quite the scene. He came back a couple of hours later and apologized, but everyone still felt tense. Be prepared when you come in today. How was your visit with your folks? I haven't seen my family all term. I'm looking forward to break so I can fill up on my mom's baking. See you at work, Sky.

Suddenly a small box appears on the screen with an Instant Message from Maria:

Maria:	What's up girl?
Debbie:	Not much, just got back into town.
Maria:	Whoa, I forgot. You missed a big blowup at work.
Debbie:	Yeh, Skyler e-mailed me about it.
Maria:	Skyler? I didn't know you two were an item—cooooooooooool.
Debbie:	We're just friends, you jerk : -)

Computer-mediated communication is quickly becoming another tool to use in interacting with friends and families. The interactions just described illustrate three specific contexts that are the focus of this chapter: the family, cyberspace, and the workplace. Each of these contexts has unique characteristics and demands that involve particular forms of interpersonal communication. Family relationships and those at work are typically relationships of circumstance—relationships that are created not by choice but because of the situation. In Chapter 9, you read about how these relationships can become relationships of choice when people become friends or develop more intimate relationships with family members or co-workers.

E-mail messages convey information about the nature of the relationships among the correspondents. The opening e-mails show that Debbie has formed friendships with at least two of her co-workers, Maria and Skyler. Debbie's father expresses his feelings about her weekend visit and confirms his support for the decisions she's making. Skyler's e-mail contains information about work, includes personal disclosures, and lets Debbie know he values her friendship. Maria's comments reflect an easy and relaxed interactive style typical of close friends. In each instance, computer-mediated communication supplements face-to-face relationships. It is also possible to develop and maintain relationships over the Internet without ever meeting face to face.

Interpersonal Relationships at Home

Families have changed since your parents were children. In the 1950s, a majority of American and Canadian families were like the Cleavers from the US TV sitcom *Leave It to Beaver*; almost two-thirds consisted of a working father, stay-at-home mother, and at least two biological children. Today, very few families fit that description. Divorce, single-parent families, same-sex couples, mothers with careers outside the home, the longer wait to start families, the move from an agrarian to an industrial society, and increasing mobility all have dramatically altered the very nature of Canadian families and rapidly led to increasingly diverse family structures. For example, common-law unions have tripled from 1981 to 16 percent of all couples in 2001.[1] Of couples whom married in 1996, 37 percent can be expected to divorce.[2] And here is a startling figure for those of you who dream of the idyllic Cleaver family: 70 percent of mothers with pre-school children are employed or actively looking for work, and this jumps to 75 percent for mothers with school-aged children.[3]

While families have changed, so has the communication within the family. The way family members interact with one another has been altered by a variety of social influences. Most research on family communication tends to be descriptive; it describes how different types of families interact. We can offer suggestions on how to improve or enhance communication in families, but *there is no single best way to communicate in families*. Each family faces unique challenges for understanding and improving communication.

Our discussion in this section focuses on the Canadian family. Like many other entities covered in this book, families are dynamic and changing. Because the members of a family get older, roles and relationships change over time. In addition, families add members and lose others. As new children are born, or as a member moves out of the home, the dynamics of the family change. As well, families reflect our increasing cultural diversity, often blending two or more cultures to make their own unique culture. Ultimately, what is true of a family at one moment of time may not hold true later. By now you have already experienced the kinds of change that takes place in families as you have become older and gone from being completely dependent on your parents to becoming more independent. As you get older, you may discover that your relationship with your parents changes still more as you begin providing care for them. As you consider your own family experiences and apply the principles we discuss in this chapter, remember above all to continually monitor your family relationships and adapt accordingly.

Family Defined

You might think that because families are basic to human existence, there's no need for a formal definition of a family—but definitions have been attempted, and there has been considerable controversy as to what constitutes a family. Traditional definitions of a family focus on the roles of husbands, wives, and children who all live together under one roof. Here is one definition written by sociologist George Murdock in 1949:

> The family is a social group characterized by common residence, economic cooperation, and reproduction. It includes adults of both sexes, at least two of whom maintain a socially approved sexual relationship, and one or more children, of one's own or adopted, of the sexually cohabiting adults.[4]

Other definitions of a family de-emphasize the traditional roles of mother, father, and children, placing more emphasis on interpersonal relationships and personal commitment. For example, Statistics Canada defines two different types of families: "Couple families consist of a couple living together, whether married or common law, at the same address and any children living at the same address. A lone-parent family is a family with only one parent, male or female, and with at least one child."[5]

The Vanier Institute of the Family defines family as

> any combination of two or more persons who are bound together over time by ties of mutual consent, birth and/or adoption or placement and who, together, assume responsibilities for variant combinations of some of the following:

- Physical maintenance and care of group members
- Addition of new members through procreation or adoption
- Socialization of children
- Social control of members
- Production, consumption, distribution of goods and services, and
- Affective nurturance—love[6]

So should a homosexual couple be considered a family? The 2001 Canadian census estimated *all couples sharing a household* (married and cohabiting) as same-sex ones at a prevalence of 0.5%.[7] According to one Canadian researcher, Dr. Anne-Marie Ambert, it is likely that this percentage is somewhat higher in reality. She estimates that at least one percent of the homosexual couple population will be seeking marriage and parenthood.[8]

For our purposes in this chapter, we synthesize these various perspectives and include both heterosexual and homosexual couples or families to define the **family** as a self-defined unit made up of any number of persons who live or have lived in relationship with one another over time in a common living space, and who are usually, but not always, united by marriage and kinship.

family. Unit made up of any number of persons who live or have lived in relationship with one another over time in a common living space and who are usually, but not always, united by marriage and kinship.

Family Types

natural family. Mother, father, and their biological children.

blended family. Two adults and their children. Because of divorce, separation, death, or adoption, the children may be the offspring of other parents, or of just one of the adults who is raising them.

single-parent family. One parent and one or more children whom he or she is raising.

extended family. Family unit including relatives such as aunts, uncles, cousins, or grandparents, and/or unrelated persons who are part of a family unit.

family of origin. Family in which a person is raised.

Virginia Satir, a well-known expert in family therapy, has identified four types of families: natural, blended, single-parent, and extended.[9] The traditional family—a mother and father and their biological children—is often considered to be the **natural family**, or nuclear family. However, because changes in culture, values, economics, and other factors have rendered this family type no longer typical, the traditional family is sometimes called an *idealized natural family.*

An increasingly common family type today is the **blended family**. This family type consists of two adults and their children. However, because of divorce, separation, death, or adoption, the children may be the offspring of other biological parents or of just one of the adults who is raising them.

The **single-parent family** is self-explanatory. This type of family has one parent and at least one child. Divorce, unmarried parents, separation, desertion, and death make single-parent families the fastest growing type of family unit in North America today.

The **extended family** typically refers to the relatives—aunts, uncles, cousins, or grandparents—who are part of the family unit. Some extended families also include individuals who are not related by marriage or kinship but are treated like family. These surrogate family members may even be called Mom, Dad, Aunt, or Uncle to honour them as part of the family circle.

In addition to Satir's categories, at least one other can encompass any of her definitions. The family in which you were raised—no matter what type it is—is your **family of origin**. It is in your family of origin that you learned the rules and skills of interpersonal communication and developed your basic assumptions about relationships. You may have had more than one family of origin if you come from a blended family; following divorce, separation, or death of a parent, you may have been reared in more than one family of origin.

Families come in all sizes and forms. A gay or lesbian couple may decide to live together and form a family and raise a child or children. In the 2001 Census, the first to collect information about same-sex couples, approximately 0.5 percent of all couples sharing a household are same-sex ones with 15 percent of lesbian couples having children and three percent of male same-sex couples having children in the family.[10] At the heart of our definition of a family is the concept that it includes people who live in close relationship with one another. A family is a family if the people in it think of themselves as a family.

A Model of Family Interaction

Regardless of the type of family you have, communication plays a major role in determining the quality of family life. As shown in Figure 11.1, one research team found that over 86 percent of the families who reported family difficulty and stress said that communication was the key source of the problem.[11] Virginia Satir thinks good family communication is so important that she calls it "the largest single factor determining the kinds of relationships [we make] with others."[12] Psychologist Howard Markman found that the more positively premarital couples rated their communication with their partner, the more satisfied they were with their marriage relationships more than five and a half years later.[13]

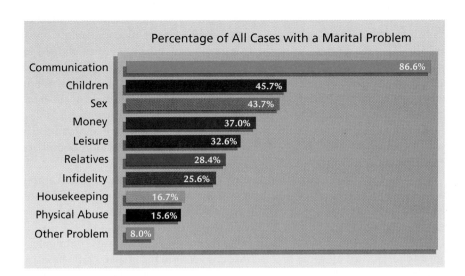

Figure 11.1
Sources of Family Difficulties

Percentage of All Cases with a Marital Problem

Source	Percentage
Communication	86.6%
Children	45.7%
Sex	43.7%
Money	37.0%
Leisure	32.6%
Relatives	28.4%
Infidelity	25.6%
Housekeeping	16.7%
Physical Abuse	15.6%
Other Problem	8.0%

Building Your Skills

IDENTIFYING YOUR FAMILY SYSTEM

Choose the statement from each set of four that best describes the behaviour typical of your family.

LEVEL OF COHESION

1a. There is little closeness in my family. We are all pretty independent of each other. None of us has any really strong feelings of attachment to the family, and once the kids get to move out, there's not much drive to stay connected with the family.

b. There is some closeness in my family and some interdependence, but not much—mainly we each do our own thing. The family usually gets together just for special occasions.

c. My family is connected to each other, but we also have our independence. We get together at times besides just the holidays. There are feelings of loyalty to the family and we are pretty close to each other.

d. My family is very close-knit and tight. We depend a lot on each other. We are always doing things together. There is nothing family members wouldn't do for each other. My family members feel a need for each other.

LEVEL OF ADAPTABILITY

2a. Family members come and go to the dinner table as they see fit. There are few rules about how to behave at the dinner table. My parents don't have a particular role at dinner.

b. There are a few rules that govern dinner table behaviour. My mom and dad are about equal in terms of who says what the kids should do, but the kids get a lot of say in what happens and how things are done. Both parents play a similar role.

c. In my family, usually my mom/dad makes most of the decisions, and my dad/mom goes along with that. The kids get to have some input about what happens. We usually get together for dinner and have a set of rules to follow.

d. Only one parent in my family makes the decisions and the other parent follows along. There are a lot of rules about how the kids should behave. At dinner, there are a number of rules that we follow and roles that we play—who clears the dishes, asking for things, etc.

Look at the family-systems model in Figure 11.2 on page 354 and determine where the statement you chose from the first set fits along the Cohesion continuum; then locate your choice from the second set on the Adaptability continuum. Draw a vertical line down from the point you marked on the Cohesion continuum; draw a horizontal line to the right from the point you marked on the Adaptability continuum. Where the lines intersect gives a rough idea of what your family might be like in terms of its cohesion and adaptability. What communication behaviours might be typical for your family type? How does your family compare with the typical type?

Another team of researchers developed a model called the **Circumplex Model of family interaction** to explain the dynamics of both effective function and dysfunction within family systems.[14] The model's three basic dimensions, as indicated in Figure 11.2 below, are adaptability, cohesion, and communication. Complete the *Building Your Skills* questions about family systems to find out how these dimensions apply to your family. **Adaptability**, which ranges from chaotic to rigid, is the family's ability to modify and respond to changes in its own power structure and roles. For some families, tradition, stability, and historical perspective are important to a sense of comfort and well-being. Other families that are less tradition-bound are better able to adapt to new circumstances.

The term "**cohesion**" refers to the emotional bonding and feelings of togetherness that families experience. Family cohesion ranges from excessively tight, or enmeshed, to disengaged. Because family systems are dynamic, families usually move back and forth along the continuum from disengaged to enmeshed.

The third key element in the model—and the most critical one—is communication. It is not labelled in Figure 11.2 because *everything* in the model is influenced by communication. Through communication, families can adapt to change (or not) and maintain either enmeshed or disengaged relationships or something in-between. Communication determines how cohesive and adaptable families are. Communication keeps the family operating as a system.

The Circumplex Model helps explain relationships among family cohesiveness, adaptability, and communication at different stages of family development. In general, families with balanced levels of cohesion and adaptability function better across the entire family life cycle than do those at the extremes of these dimensions. A balanced family has a moderate amount of cohesion and adaptability—represented by the centre circle on the model. Balanced families can often adapt better to changing

Figure 11.2
A Circumplex Model of Family Systems

Source: Adapted from David H. L. Olson, Candyce S. Russell, and Douglas H. Sprenkle (Eds.), *Circumplex Model: Systemic Assessment and Treatment of Families* (New York: Haworth Press, 1989). Used by permission.

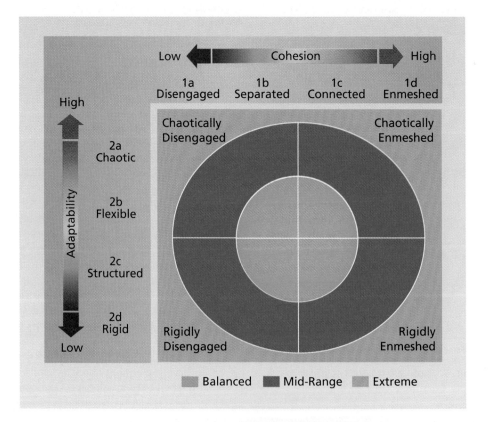

Use what you know about the Circumplex Model and the cues you see in this photo to describe the relationships in this family.

circumstances and manage stressful periods, such as the children's adolescence. Not surprisingly, these balanced families usually have better communication skills.

As we have already emphasized, however, research suggests that *there is no single best way to be a family.* At some stages of family life, the ideal of the balanced family may not apply. Older couples, for example, seem to operate more effectively when there is more rigid structure and a lower level of cohesiveness. Families with young children seem to function well with high levels of both cohesion and adaptability. Only one thing is constant as we go through family life: effective communication skills play an important role in helping families change their levels of cohesiveness or adaptability. These skills include active listening, problem solving, empathy, and being supportive. Dysfunctional families—those that are unable to adapt or alter their levels of cohesion—invariably display poor communication skills. Family members blame others for problems, criticize one another, and listen poorly.

Improving Family Communication

Wouldn't it be fantastic if you could learn special techniques guaranteed to enrich your family life? Alas, there are no surefire prescriptions for transforming your family system into one that a TV sitcom family would envy. Instead, we can pass on some skills and principles that researchers have either observed in healthy families or applied successfully to improve dysfunctional ones.

Building Your Skills

The Circumplex Model Applied to TV and Movie Families

One way to test your understanding of the Circumplex Model of family systems is to see if you can identify families that match the characteristics of family types identified in the model. See if you can think of families portrayed on TV or in the movies that fit each of the four following extreme family types:

Continued

Family Type	TV or Movie Family
Chaotically Disengaged	
Chaotically Enmeshed	
Rigidly Disengaged	
Rigidly Enmeshed	

Is any one of the extreme types portrayed more than others? If so, why do you suppose that type is portrayed more? Which of the types is portrayed the least? Why do you suppose that is? Examine any differences in how you and other students classified the same families. Try to determine why people's views differ.

Virginia Satir found that in healthy families, "the members' sense of self-worth is high; communication is direct, clear, specific, and honest; rules are flexible, humane, and subject to change; and the family's links to society are open and hopeful."[15] In such families, she notes, people listen actively; they look *at* one another, not *through* one another or at the floor; they treat children as people; they touch one another affectionately regardless of age; and they openly discuss disappointments, fears, hurts, angers, and criticism, as well as joys and achievements.[16]

In a recent study, John Caughlin identified 10 factors that were associated with families that had good communication.[17] Those factors, in order of impact, are:

- Openness
- Maintaining structural stability
- Expression of affection
- Emotional/instrumental support
- Mind-reading (knowing what others are thinking and feeling)
- Politeness
- Discipline (clear rules and consequences)
- Humour/sarcasm
- Regular routine interaction
- Avoidance of personal and hurtful topics

After reviewing several research studies, family communication scholars Kathleen Galvin and Bernard Brommel identified eight qualities exhibited by functional families:

- Interactions are patterned and understood.
- There is more compassion and less cruelty.
- Problems are addressed to the person who created them—other family members are not scapegoated.
- There is self-restraint.
- Boundaries about safe territories and roles are clear.
- Life includes joy and humour.
- Misperceptions are minimal.
- Positive interactions outweigh negative ones.[18]

Of the qualities identified in these two studies, how many are present in your family? Which qualities do you think your family could use more of?

Not all of the qualities identified in the above lists specifically involve communication, though all are certainly affected by and affect communication. The following sections explore some of the skills and strategies you can follow to improve your family communication.

◐ Take Time to Talk about Relationships and Feelings

Healthy families talk.[19] The quantity of communication depends on family members' needs, expectations, personalities, careers, and activities. However, the talking extends beyond idle chatter to focus on issues that help the family adapt to change and maintain a sense of cohesiveness.

Often, because of the crush of everyday responsibilities and tasks, family members may lapse into talking only about the task-oriented, mundane aspects of making life work: housecleaning, grocery shopping, errand running, and other uninspiring topics. Healthy families communicate about much more: their relationships, how they are feeling, and how others are feeling. They make time to converse, no matter how busy they are. They have an other-orientation in these conversations, instead of focusing on themselves. In addition, they enjoy each other and don't take themselves too seriously.[20]

◐ Listen Actively and Clarify the Meaning of Messages

Because talking about relationships is important in healthy families, it is not surprising that effective listening is also important. In the often stressful context of family life, good listening skills are essential.

Good listening requires an other-orientation. In Chapter 4, we presented fundamental skills for listening and responding to messages. Family members will communicate with greater accuracy if they learn to stop, look, and listen. *Stop:* minimize mental and outside distractions; don't try to carry on a conversation over a TV blaring, a video game bleeping, or a stereo's distracting rhythmic pulse. *Look:* constantly monitor the rich meaning in non-verbal messages; remember that the face and voice are prime sources for revealing emotional meaning, and that body posture and gestures provide clues about the intensity of an emotion. *Listen:* focus on both details and major ideas. Asking appropriate follow-up questions and reflecting content and feelings are other vital skills for clarifying the meaning of messages. Remember the importance of checking your perceptions of the meaning of non-verbal messages.

◐ Support and Encourage One Another

A smoothly functioning family can be a supportive, encouraging sanctuary from everyday stresses. Through communication, people can let others know that they

THE BUCKETS reprinted by permission of
United Feature Syndicate, Inc.

support and value them. Satir suggests that many, if not most, sources of dysfunction in families are related to feelings of low self-worth.[21] Healthy families take time to nurture one another, express confirming messages, and take a genuine interest in each person's unique contributions to the family. Researchers have found that supportive messages—those that offer praise, approval, help, and affection—can lead to higher self-esteem in children, more conformity to the wishes of the parent, higher moral standards, and less aggressive and anti-social behaviour.[22] Jane Howard, who travelled extensively in search of a "good family," found that "good" families have a sense of valuing and supporting each other.[23]

Wise parents use support and encouragement rather than coercion as a primary strategy for shaping their children's behaviour. The challenge is to find a middle ground that tempers support with appropriate control.

🍂 Use Productive Strategies for Managing Conflict, Stress, and Change

The inability to manage conflict and stress in a family may be a contributing factor to family violence. In 2002, a quarter of all victims of violent crimes were victims of family violence, according to a survey by the Canadian Centre for Justice Statistics. Of these, 62 percent were victims of family violence at the hands of their spouse. Females accounted for 85 percent of this spousal violence.[24] According to a 2002 survey of 94 police departments, children and youth under the age of 18 accounted for 61 percent of victims of sexual assault by other family members and 20 percent of all victims of physical assault by other family members.[25] Abuse and violence are the extreme examples of what happens when people fail to resolve conflicts in a collaborative manner. Husbands and wives must learn to handle conflict in constructive ways and to manage their conflicts with their children similarly.

John Gottman has developed a set of suggestions for handling conflict between couples, some of which apply equally well to parent–child and sibling conflicts.[26] Many of his suggestions reflect recommendations made in Chapter 7 on managing conflict. Gottman suggests picking your battles carefully, scheduling the discussion, employing a structure (build an agenda, persuade and argue, resolve), and moderating your emotions. In dealing with your partner, acknowledge his or her viewpoint before presenting your own, trust your partner, communicate non-defensively, and provide comfort and positive reinforcement. Conflict might be tempered by enhancing the romance and finding enjoyment in the relationship. He further suggests taking stock of the relationship and knowing when to seek help or to end the relationship.

▶▶▶ Applying Theory and Research

FAMILY RITUALS

Family rituals are patterned interactions that take on special meaning or symbolic significance to family members. For instance, your family might have a ritual of gathering on Sunday night to watch TV and eat popcorn, building a backyard hockey rink in mid-winter, or playing Monopoly at the family cottage. Each family establishes its own set of rituals, drawing on the rituals experienced by the parents as children or creating new ones. Blended families present a unique challenge because each of the parents brings his or her own established family rituals to the newly formed family. Rituals can play an important role in establishing a new family identity; however, children in blended families can be frustrated, confused, and angry if rituals they used to follow are abandoned because their new step-parents don't want to follow them.

Continued

Dawn Braithwaite, Leslie Baxter, and Anneliese Harper interviewed 20 step-parents and 33 stepchildren about family rituals that either ended, continued, were adapted, or were created from scratch when the blended family was formed. The researchers found that several children in single-parent situations had special rituals (like talking about their day while fixing dinner with their mom or dad) that were no longer possible when they became part of a blended family. Sometimes the new spouse could not or did not want to continue or participate in the previously established ritual. Also, sometimes the circumstances prevented continuation of the ritual—as when a divorced father moved away and could no longer take his children for weekend outings on his boat. Stepchildren reported more of a sense of loss about ended rituals than did the step-parents.

Some rituals were imported into the blended family unchanged because the ritual previously existed in both families—for example, going to a worship service on Saturday or Sunday. Some rituals were so important that acceptance as a family member required participation: going to Grandma's for Thanksgiving dinner, going out for birthday dinners, and the like. Participation in such rituals was one way a step-parent or child might gain acceptance by the other family members. Sometimes the rituals were adapted to fit the new family circumstances—for instance, continuing to take a summer vacation in July but changing the destination. Several respondents reported that adapting the old rituals was an important part of adjusting to the new family and showed respect for other family members. Again, stepchildren seemed to find this harder to do than the step-parents.

Attempts to impose new rituals often failed because the attempts created conflict and ignored the values of certain family members. New rituals were accepted when all members were involved in their development and when both the old and new family values were recognized and respected.

APPLYING THE RESEARCH TO YOUR LIFE

While you may or may not be from a blended family, you certainly have been exposed to various family rituals. Make a list of your family rituals (remember, these can include simple routines or traditions such as calling home every Sunday night). Which of these rituals is most important to you? Why? How have the rituals changed as you've grown up? What rituals are no longer practised in your family? Why not? What rituals would you like to continue when you start your own family? How will you adapt to the rituals that your spouse may bring into the family? Compare your list with those of other classmates and discuss the similarities and differences.

Source: Dawn O. Braithwaite, Leslie A. Baxter, and Anneliese M. Harper, "The Role of Rituals in the Management of Dialectical Tensions of 'Old' and 'New' in Blended Families," Communication Studies, 49 (Summer 1998): 105–20.

No list of dos and don'ts will help you manage all differences in a family relationship. The suggestions offered here provide only a starting point. As we have emphasized, you will need to adapt these skills and suggestions to the context of your unique family system, but research consistently shows that listening skills and empathy are strong predictors of family satisfaction.

 Recap

HOW TO IMPROVE FAMILY RELATIONSHIPS

Take time to talk about relationships and feelings.
- Be other-oriented in your focus.
- Don't take yourself too seriously.

Listen and clarify the meaning of messages.
- Stop, look, and listen.
- Check your interpretation of messages.

Continued

Support and encourage one another.
- Use confirming messages.
- Be selective in disclosing your feelings.

Use productive strategies for managing conflict, stress, and change.
- Watch for communication warning signs.
- Learn to renegotiate role conflicts.

Interpersonal Relationships on the Internet

Homes and workplaces have been dramatically altered by the introduction of the personal computer and computer-mediated communication. Relationships are no longer only developed face to face, and you are probably forming many relationships over the Internet. **Computer-mediated communication (CMC)** was initially seen as a tool for accessing information, but it has quickly become an integral tool for human interaction. People have moved from using independent computers for word processing to using networked computers that allow them to send and receive messages and documents.

> **computer-mediated communication (CMC).**
> Communication between and among people through the medium of computers (includes e-mail, chat rooms, bulletin boards, and newsgroups).

As the technology has been introduced to the home, more and more families use the Internet to keep in contact. E-mail and instant messaging provide another communication tool for maintaining interpersonal relationships with friends, family members, co-workers, and lovers. With the introduction of chat rooms and discussion groups, you now have the ability to meet strangers and develop new interpersonal relationships. Thus, CMC allows you to meet two interpersonal goals: to make contact with strangers and thus initiate and develop new relationships; and to maintain existing relationships. These two goals affect your Internet interactions differently.

Comparing Face-to-Face and Computer-Mediated Communication

There are advantages and disadvantages to both face-to-face (FtF) communication and computer-mediated communication. In FtF communication, people obtain a lot of information by seeing how other people behave, how they react, and how they look. However, such visual information has a downside when we have biased reactions to what we see (reacting to a person's age, sex, race, or physical size). Such attributes may not be readily apparent in CMC, and we might engage in fruitful and fulfilling chat with someone online whom we might have avoided if we had seen what he or she looked like first. Besides minimizing the use of non-verbal cues, CMC has interesting characteristics related to the importance of the written word, how much time delay there is between the communicators' messages, the occurrence of deception, and ease with which communication partners can simply disappear.

Non-Verbal Cues

CMC is more limited in its use of non-verbal cues than FtF communication, lacking for instance the use of touch and smell and limited in the use of visual and aural cues. Thus, words and graphics become more important in CMC than in FtF because you must rely solely on them to carry non-verbal messages. In FtF communication, you can hear people's voices, see their facial expressions, and watch their body movements. These provide the context by which you attribute meaning to the words they speak. In CMC, such cues are limited or non-existent, which means words are taken at their face value. There are some basic things users do to add emotion to their messages, including CAPITALIZING THE MESSAGE (which is considered "yelling"), making letters **bold,** or using emoticons—keyboard combinations used to represent some emotion—such as =^D (big grin) or >>:-<< (furious), and so on. Despite these efforts, the ability to tease or make sarcastic remarks is limited because there is no tone of voice in the written message, which means the author must usually write out an accompanying interpretation. For example, "Boy, am I insulted by that or what?!!!! (just kidding)."

CMC researchers Lisa Tidwell and Joseph Walther think that the lack of non-verbal communication cues in CMC might be one reason they found that CMC partners use more direct communication strategies like disclosure or asking questions to reduce their uncertainties.[27] In face-to-face interaction, we can tell a person's sex, race, and relative age, which lead to the formation of a certain impression. The lack of non-verbal cues to provide this information necessitates the more direct strategies and open discussions that occur online.

The Role of the Written Word

Besides the restrictions on non-verbal communication, the use of the written word has other impacts on our Internet interactions. One online scholar suggests that a person's typing ability and writing skills affect the quality of any relationship that is developed.[28] The ability to encode thoughts quickly and accurately into written words is not a skill everyone has. Not only do writing skills affect your ability to express yourself and manage the relationship, but they also affect how you are perceived by others. Look at the following two e-mail messages and think about the impressions you form of the two authors.

GigoloMan: "Hey, babe, whad's up? no what im thnking now we shuld do?"

GentleJim: "Hi. Boy, have I been swamped with work lately. How's your day been?"

What's your impression of the two e-mailers? What affected your impression? The first example is filled with grammar and spelling errors that might create a negative impression because the author is not particularly skilled at writing. The second author uses correct grammar and spelling, which is more likely to produce a positive impression. The user name or nickname (also called a "nick" among CMC users) that is listed for each author also affects our impression.[29] "GigoloMan" sends a clear if politically incorrect message to those who see his moniker. The selection of words has a strong impact on the impression others draw about us from the Internet. All the material discussed in Chapter 5 on verbal communication and language is particularly relevant to the Internet, which is heavily word based.

Response Time

It takes longer to formulate a typewritten response than a spoken or non-verbal one. The amount of delay (which is similar to silence in FtF interactions) can have an impact on the interpretation of the message's meaning. In chat sessions, participants expect to see a response to their posting very quickly. This is one reason chat sessions often involve very short and concise messages that can be written and sent rapidly. Most chat sessions involve a rapid succession of short messages that foster a sense of synchronicity and interaction. By the time a long message gets written and sent, it is often no longer germane to the discussion. The exception to this is when people are in private or small-group chat sessions, where they ask questions to which a longer, more developed response is expected.

E-mailing someone allows you time to compose your message and craft it more carefully than you might in a FtF interpersonal interaction. You can take time to consider your message and delete it before sending it if you don't feel you have worded the message the way you want. Even in chat sessions, you might finish typing a line and then decide to delete it and write something else. In face-to-face interactions, people can think about what they want to say, but once the message is spoken, they cannot take it back. As a sender of Internet messages, you have more control over what you say and the impression you create; as the receiver of Internet messages, realize that the other person has had the chance to carefully consider his or her message for its greatest impact on you. Such deliberation is one reason you must be cautious about accepting the validity of Internet messages—deception is relatively easy.

Challenges of Computer-Mediated Communication

The use of CMC as a surrogate for face-to-face encounters creates some unique and intriguing challenges. One overriding rule that you should follow when communicating on the Internet is to follow all the rules you would normally follow in face-to-face interactions.[30] For example, in getting acquainted with someone, don't disclose too much too soon. Be a good "listener" and confirm the statements made by your Internet partners. Be other-oriented by considering how your Internet partners will react to what you have written. What is their context for interpreting your messages? What do they know about you? What do you know about them?

The kind of information you provide and acquire through CMC has a direct impact on impression formation and relational attraction. Even though you are not able to use many of the usual non-verbal cues from which you draw impressions of other people (for example, their physical looks), you still form impressions about those with whom you interact. Prominent Internet researcher Joseph Walther has found that, the more CMC partners interact over the Internet, the more the impressions they develop of each other resemble the impressions formed in face-to-face interactions.[31]

Initially, those in face-to-face interactions are likely to form a more detailed and comprehensive impression than those interacting through CMC; however, the impressions formed in CMC have been found to be stronger or more extreme.[32] This finding may reflect the fact that there are fewer cues in CMC on which to focus; thus, greater emphasis may be placed on those cues, resulting in more stereotyping. This might be one reason that often one of the first questions you're asked when you join a chat room is "A/S/L" for age, sex, and location. This small amount of information serves as the categorical foundation for impressions.

Ease of Deception

The detection of deception in face-to-face encounters is aided by the presence of non-verbal cues. A 50-year-old white male (named Sam) could not claim to be a 20-year-old Chinese female (Samantha) without a major makeover. However, online, this deception is almost as easy as simply typing the words. We say "almost" because you can assess the content of written messages for clues to deceit. Sam writing as Samantha might talk about how much "she" enjoyed watching the Beatles live on the *Ed Sullivan Show* (they appeared in 1964 and 1965) when she was growing up. This should alert you to the fact that Samantha would have to be older than 20, and probably not from China.

One survey of 191 students at one college found that 40 percent had lied on the Internet: 15 percent about their age, eight percent about their weight, six percent about appearance, six percent about marital status, and three percent about what sex they were.[33] College student respondents in one study reported that the most common form of deception detection occurred when someone made an implausible statement or bragged.[34] The criteria for detecting deception apparently changed as the Internet relationship became more intimate. As "friendships" developed over the Internet, to detect deception, the students came to depend on personal knowledge and impressions of their partners acquired over the course of their correspondence.[35] Interestingly, this study also found that those who reported lying most were the ones most likely to suspect other users of lying.[36]

The ease with which someone can create a false persona means that you need to be cautious in forming relationships with Internet strangers.

Ease of Disappearance

Besides the hazards of encountering serious misrepresentation, another pitfall of Internet relationships is that a communication partner can simply disappear or assume another nickname without your ever knowing. Unless the person is using a site-specific user name, such as "flemingc.on.ca" or "swt.edu," which represent college and university locations, you may have no direct knowledge about where the person resides, much less his or her real name. A person's use of a Yahoo, MSN, or Hotmail address means others are virtually in the dark about the person with whom they are interacting. People can simply change their e-mail addresses, and you are totally cut off. Disappearing is more difficult or at least impractical in face-to-face relationships; disappearing from a classmate with whom you've had a relationship would necessitate dropping the course or maybe even dropping out of school. Knowing that you will be continuing to see a person puts different kinds of demands on relationship management and termination than do the demands of the Internet.

Cyber-Bullying

A growing problem is a new form of bullying, called *cyber-bullying*, whereby via the Internet, one person or a group of people target another person and insult, threaten, and bully him or her. This can be done via e-mail, instant messaging, on bulletin boards, or at least in one case in Canada, a website designed for and devoted to bullying a young high school teen. A recent survey found that 14 percent of young Canadian users had been threatened while using instant messaging; 16 per cent admitted they'd posted hateful comments themselves.[37] Bullying in this manner allows the bully to remain anonymous if he or she wishes to remain so. Many hateful and hurtful blows can be delivered via the Internet. To be the receiver of such communication can be damaging to the person, and sending such messages certainly contradicts every goal of interpersonal communication in this text.

Types of Computer-Mediated Communication

E-mail, chat rooms, instant messaging, bulletin boards, listservs, and mailing lists are among the ways we use personal computers to connect with other people. Sometimes we direct our comments to a particular person (e-mail and instant messaging); at other times we simply put our ideas out for anybody to read (bulletin boards, blogs, listservs, and chat rooms). Some forms allow us to have an active conversation with someone (chat rooms and instant messaging), while others allow us to post our ideas for others to read and respond to at a later time (e-mail and bulletin boards). This last distinction refers to *synchronicity*—whether individuals are engaging in an interaction simultaneously or with some period of delay between the message being sent and the message being read. Each form of computer-mediated communication can be used in different ways to establish and maintain interpersonal relationships.

🌑 Synchronous Interaction

In defining interpersonal communication in Chapter 1, we noted that it involves mutual influence, meaning that the participants are influencing each other at the same time. In the cyber world, a **synchronous interaction** involves the active engagement of both participants at the same time. Face-to-face interactions are, by their very nature, synchronous. Only some Internet interactions are synchronous, such as group or private chat sessions.

Chat Rooms   Chat rooms (also referred to as *Internet relay chat,* or *IRC*), where people are actively involved in sending and receiving messages, are more similar to face-to-face interactions than is e-mail. Discussion groups or public chat rooms often involve many people engaged simultaneously in a kind of group discussion. However, one intriguing aspect of public chat rooms is that even though 10 or 12 people might be chatting at one time, the participants often pair up and simply respond to their partner's comments, ignoring the rest. Although this "selective" chatting may at first be confusing, chatters usually develop a knack for being able to discern relevant comments. Typed statements often start with the name of the person for whom the message is intended. Such "interpersonal" dyadic exchanges often draw in the other chat room members because everything that is written is open to public viewing. In this way, it's like sitting in a small group in which you are talking with just one other member, but the other group members can still hear your conversation. Chatters often move to a "private room" where only those who are invited can participate. This allows chatters the privacy to carry on uninterrupted and confidential conversations.

Technology already has been developed that lets users go beyond the limitations of using only written words. Several chat rooms now allow audio links and take on the feeling of a large telephone party line. The introduction of spoken instead of written messages on the Internet adds non-verbal information for listeners. Just like the telephone, audio chat rooms provide information that gives you hints about the person's age, sex, and ethnicity (through accents). In addition, people can use the full range of vocal cues discussed in Chapter 6: pitch, tone, rate, volume, and silence. There are also visual chat rooms and teleconferencing that let you actually see the person with whom you are interacting. The use of video feed on the Internet makes this type of interaction more like face-to-face interactions. Note that the ability to post visual images does not guarantee that people won't post surrogate images rather than actual ones.

Instant Messaging   Instant messaging is similar to interacting in a private chat room. Most Internet providers allow their members to create a "friends and family" list. When any of the "buddies" you've put on your list are logged on to the Internet, you are notified. You can then send them a message and engage them in an "instant" exchange of messages. Instant messaging approximates a personal conversation or a small-group discussion if you are connected with several people at the same time. One disadvantage of instant messaging is that you might be involved in some other activity when someone contacts you. This creates a "listening" problem for you because you might try to continue your other computer activity while still instant-messaging, thus dividing your attention and causing delays or a shortage of confirming responses to your partners. Handling this situation is similar to handling the same dilemma in a face-to-face situation: you either tell your partner you can't talk right now, or you postpone your other activity.

synchronous interaction.
Interaction in which participants are actively engaging at the same time.

Allison Barrows/Universal Press Syndicate.

🌑 Asynchronous Interactions

Most Internet interactions are **asynchronous interactions**, meaning that the participants are not necessarily logged on at the same time but rather send and receive posted messages. Bulletin boards, discussion forums, and e-mail represent asynchronous interactions. They are interactions to the degree that the participants post responses to what they have read. On bulletin boards, a thread about a particular subject can continue for days or weeks.

E-Mail   E-mail is not really a form of interpersonal communication, although it can be used to develop and maintain relationships. The speed with which people can send and receive letters through e-mail makes it seem a lot more interactive than letters sent through the post. One emerging Internet norm is that you are expected to respond as soon as possible to your e-mail; failure to do so sometimes evokes resentment from correspondents.

Bulletin Boards, Mailing Lists, and Listservs   Electronic bulletin boards are similar to traditional bulletin boards: you can post a message electronically that can be read by anyone who happens along, and readers can leave a response. Because the message is essentially displayed in public, you don't know who will read it or respond. Threads develop when an issue evokes a number of postings; the postings resemble a conversation when people read and respond sequentially to each other's messages over a period of time. The anonymity associated with postings, however, sometimes leads to heated exchanges that erupt into "flaming," in which posters attack one another on a personal level (ego conflicts).

Mailing lists and listservs represent a blend of e-mails and bulletin boards; defined and often known lists of individuals receive the same electronic message. The list of recipients can be created by one individual (a mailing list), or interested participants can subscribe to it (a listserv). Instructors who send out class announcements to students by way of the Internet are using a mailing list. Recipients often have the choice of responding only to the originator or to the entire list of readers. Listservs are usually created around some interest or topic, and many have interesting names; for instance, one listserv for communication research is called CRTNET; interpersonal communication instructors can subscribe to a listserv called EMPATHY; and the EPA has a listserv for New England called GREENBYTES-NE. Depending on the size of the list or the number of members on the listserv, you may or may not get to know the members as individuals. The more frequently a specific individual posts messages, the more likely it is that you will form an impression of that person. When the impressions are positive, you may be motivated to exchange personal e-mails and develop more personal relationships.

asynchronous interactions.
Interactions in which participants send and receive messages from each other with delays between reception and response.

Using CMC to Initiate New Relationships

Today, people are forming personal relationships over the Internet. In a study reported in 1996 about discussion groups, over 60 percent of the survey respondents reported forming personal relationships with someone they met on the Internet.[38] Further analyses of these relationships revealed an almost equal number of mixed-sex (55 percent) and same-sex relationships (45 percent), and only eight percent were considered romantic. Over half of the respondents reported communication with their "friend" at least once a week. Interestingly, this study found women were more likely to form personal relationships in these newsgroups than men (72 percent of the female respondents, as compared with 55 percent of the males). In 1999 and 2000, researchers conducted a telephone survey of youth (10- to 17-year-olds) who used the Internet at least once a month and asked about their use of the Internet during the previous year. The results indicated that 55 percent of respondents used CMC with people they hadn't known face-to face; 39 percent had used it more than once with the same person; 25 percent reported forming a casual online friendship, 14 percent had formed a close online friendship; two percent had initiated a romantic relationship; and seven percent reported actually meeting face-to-face with an Internet partner.[39] Most met in chat rooms (59 percent); 30 percent met through instant messaging or e-mail (having made connections on the recommendation of a friend or family member); five percent met in gaming sites; and six percent met in some other way. Most were relationships with someone of the opposite sex. Undoubtedly, the number of young people who establish relationships online has increased since this survey was conducted. A recent Canadian survey found that 99 percent of Canadian students have used the Internet, 48 percent use it for at least an hour a day, and nearly 60 percent use chat rooms and instant messaging.[40] With these statistics, it is likely that more of us will spend more time communicating on the Internet and increasingly likely that you will find yourself in a position of initiating and forming relationships with people you have met through the Internet. In general, the same principles and skills you read about in these last two chapters apply to the Internet. For example, similar strategies are used in the opening and closing of FtF and computer-mediated interactions.[41] However, there are some unique issues you should understand as you enter the world of CMC relationships.

Choose the Right Chat Room

One way we normally make friends is by engaging in activities where we meet people with similar interests. You probably have made friends with people who are members of your religious group, sports team, or math class. One form of attraction discussed in Chapter 9 dealt with being attracted to those who share similar interests. This same form of attraction exists on the Internet and can be used as the basis for starting relationships. Finding people with similar interests on the Internet is relatively easy because chat rooms and listservs are often organized according to topics and interest groups. There are chat rooms or discussion groups for almost every sport, activity, and interest that you can imagine and if there isn't one, you can actually create your own. There are also general social chat rooms that are very unstructured and have the same feeling as visiting a singles bar. Being a regular contributor to the more topically based chat rooms usually provides a safer environment for getting to know other chatters. As chatters share thoughts on the given topic, they often share more and more personal information as well, which allows for the development of online relationships.

Accept the Slower Pace of Relational Development

As mentioned earlier, the development of impressions is slower in CMC than FtF. This means that the process of forming interpersonal relationships is also likely to be slower. The major reason for this difference is that almost all information on the Internet must be put into text, whereas FtF interactions use a variety of non-verbal channels. Early researchers disputed the notion that true interpersonal relationships could be formed online, but subsequent research has found that the kind of effects that occur quickly in FtF interactions also occur on the Internet but just require more time.[42] CMC users can self-disclose honestly and openly with each other, to the point of forming truly intimate relationships. One advantage of the text-only medium is a reduction in our perceptual biases about a person's physical attractiveness.[43] At some point in Internet relationships, the users often provide a physical description of themselves (people seem to want to know the other person's sex, age, and location at the very beginning); eventually they may exchange photographs and even arrange to meet in person.

Apply Strong Verbal Skills

Sending someone a hug and a kiss over the Internet does not provide the same kind of satisfaction as it does in person. Among the conversational skills used in FtF interactions are verbal and non-verbal expressiveness (including being articulate), listening and non-verbal sensitivity, humour, effective question asking, and responsiveness. These skills have their parallels in CMC but, for the most part, are dependent on writing ability. The reliance on verbal strategies is demonstrated by a study that found that e-mail pen pals apparently compensated for the lack of non-verbal feedback by increasing the use of personal questions.[44] Thus, having good question-asking skills would prove advantageous on the Internet.

The most skilled Internet communicators know CMC shorthand, incorporate emoticons and other devices to enhance their text, and adapt to their partners. As a listener/respondent, you can't use eye contact, head nodding, and "uh-huhs" to let the person know you are attentive and interested. You must write responses that show you are listening. This reflects another advantage of the Internet over FtF—you have a record of what was sent by your partner. So instead of not hearing what he or she said because your mind was wandering, you can simply review what was written if you spaced out during a chat session. It's a good idea to hang on to e-mail so you can look through previous correspondence if you are afraid you have forgotten some information your partner shared.

Using Computer-Mediated Communication to Maintain Existing Relationships

A recent study found that the major use of home e-mail was for relationship maintenance.[45] This included using e-mail as a way to keep in touch with family and friends. E-mail is simple, quick, cheap, convenient, efficient, and provides a sense of interaction. For ongoing relationships, e-mail provides a kind of freedom from time zone and schedule conflicts, allowing users to send out messages at their convenience. Survey respondents reported that e-mail made it easier to share ideas, opinions, and information with friends and family all over the world.[46] As of May 2002, the Internet provider America Online (AOL) handled 390 million e-mails and 3.1 billion instant messages daily. A recent Canadian survey found that the average family spends 8.8 hours per week communicating with friends and family on the

computer-supported social networks (CSSN). A virtual community created by the social networking among individuals through CMC.

Internet and 24 percent of the respondents spend over 10 hours engaged in this activity.[47] Multiply this by the number of providers in the United States and Canada and add the growth that is occurring, and we get a glimpse of how important this medium is to interpersonal relationship maintenance. We use e-mail, instant chat, chat rooms, and discussion groups as ways of interacting with our friends and family. The expansion of CMC has begun to produce virtual communities, **computer-supported social networks (CSSNs)**.[48] The development of social networks is enhanced by the ability of users to create buddy lists. These lists result in personal networks of friends with whom you can exchange group-addressed e-mails or create group chat sessions.

For the most part, the rules and principles discussed in the last chapter on how to maintain relationships apply to the use of CMC, as do the other skills we have discussed in the text. The following are some of the ways you can use the Internet to help you maintain and even escalate existing interpersonal relationships.

🔵 Communicate!

The very act of sending regular e-mails or engaging in chat sessions is probably the primary way the Internet helps maintain relationships. Maintaining an active line of communication with people is one of the best ways to preserve the relationship. Interest in the other person and commitment to the relationship is reflected in the very act of communicating. However, the amount of communication that is needed is defined by the people in the relationship. You might have one friend whom you e-mail daily and another whom you e-mail two or three times a year. Are these relationships different? Is one less intimate than the other? The answers are not really cut and dried. You might feel as close to both people, but the daily interactions create a sense of interdependence that is probably not found in the other relationship. Daily interactions mean the two of you are informed about each other's activities and probably providing daily support, confirming each other's value as a person.

Increases or decreases in how much you communicate with someone provide one way to signal your level of interest and commitment to the relationship. A change in the amount of communication represents a turning point in the relationship's development (as discussed in Chapter 10). You establish expectations about how often you e-mail a particular person and deviations from those expectations signal a potential change in the relationship. You might become concerned about the status of a relationship if you have had daily exchanges of e-mails with a friend and then notice that he or she only responds every couple of days. This might prompt you to engage in a direct strategy and inquire about the status of the person and the relationship.

The Internet might actually result in increased communication among friends and lovers who are separated by distance. Information technologist Patricia Wallace speculates that the ease with which people can send each other things like e-mail greeting cards results in increased communication.[49] People are creative in the way they use the Internet to make contact and interact. One of your author's sons still manages to play games over the Internet with a school friend who has moved away. Wallace tells a story in her book, *The Psychology of the Internet*, about a couple who use the Internet to keep in contact when the husband is away on business trips and who link up to play bridge online with other people.[50]

🔵 Use Relational Maintenance Strategies

Keeping in contact with someone is one way to maintain the relationship and show your interest. You can also use a variety of the other strategies discussed in Chapter 10. In your e-mails, you should appropriately disclose information about yourself. Remember that self-disclosure is related to relational development. Don't disclose too much if you are not interested in escalating the relationship; however, not disclosing anything might create stagnation and de-escalation.

Some of these disclosures might include sharing your emotions. Having limited non-verbal cues means that your partner depends on you to verbalize your feelings. You can describe the feelings you have about events in your life and you can also express your feelings toward your partner. Talking about your feelings for your friend and engaging in other relational talk as well is another way to maintain your relationships over the Internet. Relationship talk and expressing feelings are fruitful when done within the norms appropriate to the relational stage. The Internet can seduce you into being too open about your feelings and thoughts about your relationships, as compared with face-to-face discussions. Just as you need to show restraint in face-to-face disclosures, you need to do the same in CMC.

Dependence on verbal messages means that you need to monitor your perceptions to ensure that you have accurately interpreted your partner's messages. Asking for clarification, expressing misunderstanding, or paraphrasing back what you think your partner means are good ways to enhance the accuracy of messages. Such strategies help maintain relationships because they reduce the impact of conflicts and stress associated with misunderstanding. Apply the principles of listening discussed in Chapter 4 to your behaviour during online relational interactions. Empathic listening on the Internet involves writing to let your partners know that you are sensitive to and understand their feelings. You can write back messages that show you are involved and engaged in the discussion of their situation. The use of confirming responses that show you understand their feelings will help maintain a positive relationship.

● Be Other-Oriented and Adapt

The way you write back to your partner depends on your relationship and what you know about your partner. Throughout this text, we have emphasized trying to look at interactions from your partner's perspective—to socially decentre and to empathize. This principle is no less applicable to the maintenance of Internet relationships. As you acquire more and more knowledge about your partner through both your FtF and CMC interactions, apply that knowledge by adapting your communication. If anything, CMC provides you more time to take into consideration what you know about another person and create appropriate messages. As you compose your words on the computer, it is easy to forget that another human being will be reading and interpreting those messages—and not just any anonymous human, but one with whom you have formed a defined relationship, one with whom you share a bond and commitment. Accordingly, compose messages that reflect your understanding and appreciation of that other person.

▶ Recap

USING CMC TO INITIATE AND MAINTAIN RELATIONSHIPS

Initiating Relationships

• Choose the right chat room.	Interact in places where you are likely to find other people who share your interests.
• Accept the slower pace of relational development.	The process of forming trust and getting to know another person online will probably be slower than in FtF relationships.
• Apply strong verbal skills.	CMC favours those who have the ability to express themselves well in a written and graphic mode.

Maintaining Relationships

• Communicate.	The very act of regularly sending messages to another person is one way to help maintain the relationship.

Continued

- Use relational maintenance strategies.

  Appropriate self-disclosing, sharing feelings, and relationship talk are among the strategies that can be used.

- Be other-oriented and adapt.

  Use the knowledge you can acquire about other people through CMC to adapt your communication.

Interpersonal Relationships at Work

While we have discussed informal relationships that we develop with varying degrees of intimacy, up to now we have not focused on the workplace. A large amount of your interaction time is spent at work, at school, and in other more formal organizations. Obviously, communication is important in any organization, but is *interpersonal* communication at work really important? As shown in the *In Canada* box below and on the next page, many organizations seem to think so and put interpersonal communication skills high on the list of workplace skills. Note that skills such as teamwork, joint planning, and making decisions with others all require your ability to communicate effectively at the interpersonal level. More and more, organizations are looking for employees who can effectively relate to other people—bosses, subordinates, peers, and clients. These reflect the four directions of organizational communication: upward (to bosses), downward (to subordinates), horizontal (to peers), and outward (to clients). All the skills you have been studying throughout this text can improve your effectiveness in dealing with organizational relationships.

Interactions in the workplace typically vary according to their degree of task versus social orientation. This variation is the source of both personal satisfaction and conflict. After you graduate, the workplace becomes a major source of interpersonal relationships. You make friends with the people with whom you work. You will socialize both on and off the job with various people from the organization. Conflicts arise when job-related decisions affect personal relationships, and vice versa. As a manager, you might become friends with some of your subordinates, but if the work performance of one of those subordinates falls below a satisfactory level, the friendship could interfere with your ability to address that problem. Many companies used to have policies prohibiting socializing among employees; however, this policy created strong dissatisfaction and discontent. Organizational policies that nurture relationships among employees build camaraderie and a supportive work atmosphere.[51]

 In Canada...

WORKPLACE SKILLS IN A GLOBAL ECONOMY

What soft skills will Canadians need to work in a global economy? In other words, what skills, abilities, and knowledge will employers be seeking as they hire new workers in the next several years? A document developed by the Corporate Council of Education, a program of the National Business and Education Centre of the Conference Board of Canada, outlines the foundation skills for employability. The Corporate Council includes representation from numerous Canadian companies including Air Canada, Bell Canada, General Motors of Canada Limited, IBM Canada, Nortel, Shell Canada Limited, and Xerox Canada Limited, to name a few. The following is a summary of these skills. Note that many of the skills require interpersonal skills and the ability to communicate effectively.

Employability Skills 2000+
The skills you need to enter, stay in, and progress in the world of work—whether you work on your own or as a part of a team. These skills can also be applied and used beyond the workplace in a range of daily activities.

Fundamental Skills The skills needed as a base for further development	Personal Management Skills The personal skills, attitudes, and behaviours that drive one's potential for growth	Teamwork Skills The skills and attributes needed to contribute productively
You will be better prepared to progress in the world of work when you can:	*You will be able to offer yourself greater possibilities for achievement when you can:*	*You will be better prepared to add value to the outcomes of a task, project, or team when you can:*

Communicate
- read and understand information presented in a variety of forms (e.g., words, graphs, charts, diagrams)
- write and speak so others pay attention and understand
- listen and ask questions to understand and appreciate the points of view of others
- share information using a range of information and communications technologies (e.g., voice, e-mail, computers)
- use relevant scientific, technological, and mathematical knowledge and skills to explain or clarify ideas

Manage Information
- locate, gather and organize information using appropriate technology and information systems
- access, analyze, and apply knowledge and skills from various disciplines (e.g., the arts, languages, science, technology, mathematics, social sciences, and the humanities)

Use Numbers
- decide what needs to be measured or calculated
- observe and record data using appropriate methods, tools, and technology
- make estimates and verify calculations

Think and Solve Problems
- assess situations and identify problems
- seek different points of view and evaluate them based on facts
- recognize the human, interpersonal, technical, scientific, and mathematical dimensions of a problem
- identify the root cause of a problem; be creative and innovative in exploring possible solutions
- readily use science, technology, and mathematics as ways to think, gain and share knowledge, solve problems, and make decisions
- evaluate solutions
- make recommendations or decisions, implement solutions, check to see if a solution works, and act on opportunities for improvement

Demonstrate Positive Attitudes and Behaviours
- feel good about yourself and be confident
- deal with people, problems, and situations with honesty, integrity, and personal ethics
- recognize your own and other people's good efforts
- take care of your personal health
- show interest, initiative, and effort

Be Responsible
- set goals and priorities by balancing work and personal life
- plan and manage time, money, and other resources to achieve goals
- assess, weigh, and manage risk
- be accountable for your actions and the actions of your group
- be socially responsible and contribute to your community

Be Adaptable
- work independently or as a part of a team
- carry out multiple tasks or projects
- be innovative and resourceful: identify and suggest alternative ways to achieve goals and get the job done
- be open and respond constructively to change
- learn from your mistakes and accept feedback
- cope with uncertainty

Learn Continuously
- be willing to continuously learn and grow
- assess personal strengths and areas for development
- set your own learning goals
- identify and access learning sources and opportunities
- plan for and achieve your learning goals

Work Safely
- be aware of personal and group health and safety practices and procedures, and act in accordance with these

Work with Others
- understand and work within the dynamics of a group
- ensure that a team's purpose and objectives are clear
- be flexible: respect, be open to and supportive of the thoughts, opinions, and contributions of others in a group
- recognize and respect people's diversity, individual differences, and perspectives
- accept and provide feedback in a constructive and considerate manner
- contribute to a team by sharing information and expertise
- lead or support when appropriate, motivating a group for high performance
- understand the role of conflict in a group to reach solutions
- manage and resolve conflict when appropriate

Participate in Projects and Tasks
- plan, design, or carry out a project or task from start to finish with well-defined objectives and outcomes
- develop a plan, seek feedback, test, revise, and implement
- work to agreed quality standards and specifications
- select and use appropriate tools and technology for a task or project
- adapt to changing requirements and information
- continuously monitor the success of a project or task and identify ways to improve

Source: Employability Skills 2000+ brochure. Ottawa: The Conference Board of Canada, 2000.

Visit the Conference Board of Canada's website at **www.conferenceboard.ca.**

Interpersonal communication skills help us in our interactions with co-workers. Developing satisfying interpersonal relationships in an organization is often a rewarding part of a job. (D. Young-Wolff/PhotoEdit)

Workplace Friendships

Friendships at work are like any other relationships in terms of relational dimensions and development. One study, in which co-workers were extensively interviewed, identified three distinct transitions: acquaintance to friend, friend to close friend, and close friend to "almost best" friend.[52] Interestingly, the researchers found respondents hesitant to refer to a co-worker as "best" friend, opting instead for "best friend at work" or "very close." The initial development of workplace friendships occurred for a variety of reasons, such as proximity, sharing tasks, sharing a similar life event, or perceiving similar interests.[53] As the relationships developed, the changes identified in this study were similar to those typically found in any developing friendship—easier and more flexible communication, increased self-disclosing, more frequent interactions, more socializing, and increased discussion of both work problems and non-work topics.[54]

Workplace friendships might be limited to a particular context: perhaps you have a lunch buddy, or you develop a friendship with someone working on a shared project, in which case the relationship ends when the project is completed. Outside of the workplace, friendships often find us associating with other people who are similar in age, status, and the like; however, workplace friendships often involve people who differ in age or status.[55] For example, you may find yourself becoming friends with a supervisor or subordinate who is considerably older or younger than you. Having a friend of the opposite sex may be more likely at work than it is outside work, where such relationships might be expected to become romantic or might threaten existing intimate relationships. Results of a recent study indicated that men felt that socializing outside the workplace was more important to their friendships with male co-workers than to friendships with female co-workers.[56] In addition, as their workplace relationships became more intimate, same-sex friends continued and expanded their relationships outside the workplace; however, cross-sex relationships continued to be defined specifically as "workplace friendships."

Workplace friendships enhance an organization's communication network by increasing the flow and openness of information. Just as outside friendships provide us with support and resources, so do workplace friendships. Workplace friends are in a position to understand and appreciate our organizational complaints and related frustrations. Friends help friends and, in an organization, that can mean lending a hand, providing information, being an ally, or providing material support.

Workplace Romances

The workplace actually provides an opportune arena for the development of intimate relationships because of the convenience and exposure to a wide pool of potential partners. Many people find their future spouses in the workplace. In a recent survey of managers and executives, 13 percent reported meeting their future spouses at work.[57] Some companies even hire married couples because they see a value in having both partners working for the same company. On the other hand, some companies have policies prohibiting dating a co-worker—but how can a policy prevent people from becoming attracted? In the workplace, you interact with people in a safe and defined context that affords the opportunity to learn about others and share information about yourself. Trust evolves, similarities are discovered, attraction develops, and the interactions move toward more intimacy. In general, dating in the workplace is not particularly problematic when those involved work in different units or when there are no direct job-related power issues.

Dating among members of the same unit can be a problem if it interferes with the ability of the individuals to perform their jobs. If you are involved in such a situation, your interactions with your partner at work need to remain professional. Co-workers sometimes are uncomfortable around romantic partners and may worry about inappropriate sharing of information, unequal work distribution, or other potential problems.

The most significant problems in workplace romances occur when the relationship is between a boss and his or her employee. The employee might feel coerced into the romantic relationship, which constitutes sexual harassment. Even if the superior does not threaten or show favouritism to the subordinate, the subordinate could believe that rejecting the superior's advances would be professionally detrimental. This type of **sexual harassment** is usually referred to as **quid pro quo**, a Latin phrase that basically means "You do something for me and I'll do something for you." A supervisor who says or implies, "Have sex with me or your job will be in jeopardy" or "If you want this promotion, you should have sex with me" is obviously using his or her power as a boss to gain sexual favours in exchange for something the employee wants. At the end of this section is a small unit to help you further understand sexual harassment and other harassment in the workplace.

Upward Communication: Talking with Your Boss

"Please place your suggestions in the suggestion box," announces the boss. The suggestion box is the symbol for **upward communication**. Upward communication involves the flow of communication from subordinates up to superiors. The only person in an organization who does not communicate upward is the boss, president, or chief executive officer (CEO), though even they usually answer to a governing board or to stockholders. Although today's organizational emphasis on quality encourages communication from lower levels to higher levels, effective upward communication is still far from the norm. Many employees fear that their candid comments will not be well received. Others may wonder, "Why bother?" If managers offer no incentive for sharing information up the line, it is unlikely that their subordinates will make the effort. If a supervisor stays holed up in an office away from his or her employees, opportunities for sharing ideas will be limited. Remember the proximity hypothesis described in Chapter 9? People are more likely to talk with those people who are physically close to them.

If there is little upward communication, the organization may be in a precarious situation. Those lower down in the organization are often the ones who make contact with the customer, make the product, or work most closely with the development and delivery of the product or service; they hear feedback about the product's virtues and problems. If supervisors remain unaware of these problems, productivity or quality may suffer. In addition, if employees have no opportunities to share

sexual harassment. Unwanted sexually-oriented behaviour in the workplace that results in discomfort and/or interference with the job.

quid pro quo. Latin phrase that can be used to describe a type of sexual harassment. The phrase roughly means "You do something for me and I'll do something for you."

upward communication. Communication that flows from subordinates to superiors.

problems and complaints with their boss, their frustration level may be dangerously high. Upward communication helps managers to deal quickly with problems and to hear suggestions for improving processes and procedures. One pair of researchers suggests that subordinates can "manage up" by being sensitive to the needs of supervisors.[58] If you know what your boss's most important goals are, along with his or her strengths, weaknesses, and preferred working style, you will be in a good position to establish a more meaningful relationship that will benefit both of you.

This process of managing might be mediated by how influential subordinates perceive their superiors. In 1952, an organizational researcher discovered that subordinates were more satisfied in their jobs when they felt their immediate supervisor had influence on decisions made at higher levels.[59] This is called the Pelz effect, after its discoverer, Donald Pelz. Subsequent research by organizational communication scholar Fred Japlin found that when subordinates perceived their supervisors as supportive, the Pelz effect was particularly strong in creating a sense of openness and satisfaction.[60]

If you are a manager yourself, encourage your subordinates to share both good news and bad. Be visible and cultivate their trust by developing a system that elicits feedback and comments. Use a suggestion box (paper or electronic), informal discussions, or more formal meetings and presentations. Making time for these exchanges will pay off in the long run.

Downward Communication: Talking with Your Subordinates

downward communication.
Communication that flows from superiors to subordinates.

The owner of the local movie theatre tells the manager that she plans on changing the theatre format to specialize in international and independent films. During a weekly meeting, the manager tells the shift supervisors of the impending change. Your supervisor then tells you and the rest of the crew working Friday nights about the new format. This sequence of interactions represents **downward communication**, the flow of information from those higher up in an organization to those of lower rank. It can happen via memo, newsletter, poster, or e-mail—or, of course, face to face. Most downward communication consists of instruction about how to do a job, rationales for doing things, statements about organizational policies and procedures, feedback about job performance, and information that helps develop the mission or vision of the organization.[61]

What is the best way to communicate with employees: in writing or face to face? It depends on the situation. Often the best method is oral, with a written follow-up or e-mail. If you need immediate employee action, face-to-face communication followed by a written reminder is the most effective (sending only a written memo is the least effective).[62] On the other hand, if you are communicating about long-term actions, a written message is the most effective. Certain situations, such as reprimanding an employee or settling a dispute, are best handled in face-to-face interactions rather than through the use of any written messages.[63]

In various situations, the best managers take care to develop and send ethical, other-oriented messages. Then they follow up to ensure that the receiver understood the message and that it achieved its intended effect. Managers need to be especially other-oriented when they are sharing sensitive information or broaching personal topics.

As mentioned earlier, behaviours by supervisors that involve using power against subordinates for sexual favours constitute sexual harassment. However, supervisors also have a responsibility to eliminate a second type of sexual harassment that represents another dark side of interpersonal communication: a **hostile environment**. An employee in a hostile environment feels his or her rights are being violated because of working conditions or offensive behaviour on the part of other workers. Telling lewd or obscene stories or jokes about members of the opposite sex, using degrading terms to describe women or men, or displaying risqué photographs of nude or seminude people can contribute to a hostile working environment. One female firefighter in British Columbia allegedly found pornographic pictures on her bed among many other reported incidents. After many years of harassment, she went public with her complaints.[64] A supervisor who either creates or fails to change work situations that are threatening to a subordinate is a party to sexual harassment. Jokes are not innocent and pictures are not "all in fun" if they make an employee feel degraded. Supervisors must adopt an other-oriented approach with respect to this issue; it is the receiver, not the sender, of the message who determines whether the behaviour is hostile. Wise supervisors do not wait for a problem to occur. They take a proactive approach, offering all workers seminars on how to avoid engaging in sexually offensive behaviour and explicitly discussing what workers should do if they become the victims of sexual harassment.

Horizontal Communication: Talking with Your Colleagues

You poke your head into your co-worker's office and say, "Did you hear about the possible merger between Byteware and Datamass?" Or, while you are tossing a crust in your job at the Pizza Palace, one of your fellow workers asks how much pepperoni to put on a Super Duper Supreme. Both situations illustrate horizontal communication. **Horizontal communication** refers to communication among co-workers at the same level within an organization. In larger organizations, you may talk with other workers in different departments or divisions who perform similar jobs at a similar level; that, too, is horizontal communication. Most often you communicate with your colleagues to coordinate job tasks, share plans and information, solve problems, make sure you understand job procedures, manage conflict, or get a bit of emotional support on the job.[65]

Information travels through a workplace the way gossip travels through "the grapevine." Sometimes errors creep into workplace information that is spread this way. Although grapevine errors can cause problems for an organization, most continue to encourage co-worker communication because it enhances teamwork and allows the work group to develop a certain degree of independence. Some organizations even try to formalize horizontal communication by forming *quality circles,* or groups of employees who meet together on a regular basis. These groups usually talk about such issues as how to improve the quality of services or products, reduce mistakes, lower costs, improve safety, or develop better ways of working together. This active participation in the work process encourages workers to do a better job. Moreover, the training they receive to participate in these groups—in group problem solving, decision-making skills, listening, relating, speaking, and managing conflict—applies to other areas of their work as well.

hostile environment. Type of sexual harassment in which an employee's rights are threatened through offensive working conditions or behaviour on the part of other workers.

horizontal communication. Communication among colleagues or co-workers at the same level within an organization.

Understanding Diversity

AN OFFICE-SPEAK PRIMER

"Dysfunctional communication" typically occurs when men minimize legitimate concerns expressed by women, according to management and organization expert Kathleen Reardon. However, women contribute to this pattern with behaviour that makes them vulnerable, she contends in her book, *They Don't Get It, Do They?*

Consider the following approach taken by Janet, a 40-year-old manager for a food products company, who has learned of an informal meeting that took place without her. She was the only committee member not told about the meeting, where important decisions were made.

Janet: I felt left out of the planning of this project, Fred. The meeting was held without my knowledge.

Fred: Now Janet, let's not make this a personal thing. Frank, Bill, and I happened to run into each other, so we got some work done.

Janet: But I am on the planning team. You could have run it by me.

Fred: You shouldn't waste your energy on this, Janet. It's nothing. Don't feel bad.

Janet: It's happened several times.

Fred: Getting a little paranoid, aren't we?

Janet: I just want to be kept informed.

Fred: OK, Janet. OK. It's no big deal.

Janet erred, according to Reardon, by focusing on her own emotional state rather than the infraction of her colleagues. Reardon contends Janet would have been better off asking herself two questions:

1. What is the problem?

2. What do I want?

By stating the answers to these questions in a simple and direct way, Janet would have been more forceful and received more respect, Reardon said. She believes the following would have been the best approach:

Janet: Fred, no more meetings without me.

If Fred tries to defend his position or suggest she is paranoid, Janet should stop him.

Janet: None of that is relevant, Fred. No personal attacks intended or necessary. I'm on the team. I should be at the meetings. It's simple.

Source: Meg Sullivan, University of Southern California Chronicle, April 17, 1995, vol. 14, no. 28.

Outward Communication: Talking with Your Customers

"Attention, Zellers shoppers: Submarine sandwiches are now on sale for $2 each for the next 15 minutes." This is one kind of communication with customers. However, in addition to just pitching to their customers, today's organizations are also asking customers what they think about the quality of the goods and services the organization produces.

Increasingly, successful organizations are those that are other-oriented; they focus on the needs of those they serve through **outward communication**. They are spending time and money to find out what the *customer* perceives as quality, rather than relying solely on the judgments of their corporate executives. They are also training their staffs to develop more empathy, better listening skills, and more awareness of non-verbal messages from customers.

outward communication.
Communication that flows to those outside an organization (such as customers).

Sexual Harassment

The Canada Labour Code, the Canadian Human Rights Act, the Employment Equity Act, and provincial and territorial human rights codes prohibit all types of harassment including sexual harassment. The Human Rights Code covers the federal public service and federally regulated industries such as banks, communications, and interprovincial transportation. A provincial code, such as that of Ontario, prohibits all types of harassment, and employers are responsible for preventing and discouraging harassment. If an employer fails to do so, the employee may file a complaint with the Ontario Human Rights Commission. Thus, business and industries not covered by the various provincial and federal codes still must provide harassment-free workplaces for all employees. According to Labour Canada, 41 percent of workers covered by major collective agreements have some form of negotiated protection against harassment including sexual harassment.[66]

Division XV.1 of Part III of the Canada Labour Code establishes that all employees have the right to be free of sexual harassment in the workplace and requires employers to take positive action to prevent sexual harassment in the workplace. The Canada Labour Code defines sexual harassment as "any conduct, comment, gesture, or contact of a sexual nature that is likely to cause offence or humiliation to any employee or that might, on reasonable grounds, be perceived by that employee as placing a condition of a sexual nature on employment or on any opportunity for training or promotion."[67] The Supreme Court of Canada defines sexual harassment as unwelcome behaviour of a sexual nature in the workplace that negatively affects the work environment or leads to adverse job-related consequences for the employee.

Sexual harassment can include something as violent as rape or as subtle as making a sexually oriented comment about another person's body or appearance. Decorating the work area with pictures of nude people or displaying pornographic pictures on a computer are examples of more subtle sexual harassment (remember the notion of hostile environment). A Canadian Human Rights Tribunal identified three characteristics of sexual harassment. The first characteristic is that the encounters must be unsolicited and unwelcome to the complainant. An example of this type of behaviour is unwelcome sexual remarks. The second characteristic is that the conduct continues despite the complainant's protests, or if it does stop, there are negative employment consequences. For instance, the comments do not stop or the comments stop and the complainant is denied a promised promotion. Third, any perceived cooperation by the complainant must be due to employment-related threats or promises.[68] However, there is still much "grey area" when interpreting what is considered to be or not to be sexual harassment.

Despite codes, acts, and employer policies, sexual harassment continues to be a serious problem in the workplace. In the past decade, sexual harassment has received increasing attention due to the growing ranks of women in non-traditional work environments. High-profile cases have included alleged cover-ups of harassment in the Canadian military; a murder-suicide at a Sears Canada store in Windsor, Ontario; and women firefighters in British Columbia and increased numbers of men and women reporting sexual harassment. Recent surveys indicate that about half of working women experience some sort of sexual harassment in the workplace. The largest Canadian survey, *The Survey on Sexual Harassment in Public Places and at Work* (SSH-PPW), reported that 56 percent of Canadian working women had experienced sexual harassment in the year prior to the survey.[69] The most common incidents were staring, jokes or comments about women, and jokes about the respondents themselves. While most research is devoted to men harassing women, this does not mean that women do not harass men, or that harassment does not take place between individuals of the same sex. Of interest, a poll conducted in British Columbia indicated that 14 percent of 400 men polled said they had experienced sexual harassment at work.[70] Unfortunately, a recent study by the Centre for Research on Violence against

Women and Children points out that violence and harassment are still grim realities for many women.[71] However, there are some bright lights in some of this gloom. Recent legislation in Quebec is addressing psychological harassment by requiring companies to have clear policies dealing with such harassment, including bullying. More organizations are creating or updating existing policies to protect the rights of all workers. The goal of having such policies and procedures is to create healthy workplaces where employees have high levels of productivity and job satisfaction.

 ## Building Your Skills

AT HOME, ONLINE, AND AT WORK

Throughout this text, we have advocated taking an other-oriented approach to interpersonal communication. There are times when taking an other-oriented perspective or being empathic could be disadvantageous if you ignore your own needs, values, or priorities. Look at the following situations and consider how being other-centred might be counterproductive or lead to poor decisions. How can you be other-centred and still make good decisions in each situation?

- You receive a call from the middle-school principal that your grade 7 son is being suspended for two days for fighting with another student. Because you are other-centred, you understand that your son is very self-conscious about being overweight, and the other kids make fun of him for it. He has been struggling with his studies because he has a hard time concentrating and reading material. He has low self-esteem and does not feel that other kids like him.

- You have developed an online friendship with someone of the opposite sex whom you have never met. You have been exchanging e-mails and instant messaging for over a year and have become very close. You are considering flying out to meet this person. Based on information presented by your friend and your own impressions, you have concluded the following: your cyberpal is very lonely; is an only child whose parents divorced when he or she was 10; was laid off from work two weeks ago; places a lot of importance on the relationship with you; depends on you for confirmation; has lots of self-doubt and appreciates your support and kind words.

- You are a manager and one of your subordinates is increasingly late to work, misses deadlines and appointments, and is turning in poor work. Taking an other-centred approach, you come to realize this employee is facing a divorce, has a child who was recently arrested, and is suffering from panic attacks.

Summary

Interpersonal interactions occur in a variety of contexts. Communication principles and skills can be applied to interpersonal relationships at home, on the Internet, and at work.

A family unit is made up of any number of people who live in relationship with one another over time in a common living space and are usually, but not always, united by marriage or kinship. One model for describing families considers family cohesion and adaptability and the role of communication in affecting family members' roles and relationships. The term "cohesion" refers to the emotional bonding and the feeling of closeness that families experience. The term "family adaptability" refers to the flexibility of family members in responding to changes in family roles, rules, and relationships.

There is no one best way to be a family. However, several skills and strategies can enhance the quality of family life: Take time to talk with other family members about relationship issues; listen to others; support and encourage one another; use productive strategies for managing conflict and stress.

A new context for interpersonal relationships is the Internet. From an interpersonal perspective, you can initiate and develop new relationships totally through computer-mediated communication (CMC) or you can use the Internet as a tool for maintaining existing relationships. CMC includes bulletin boards, e-mail, chat rooms (IRC—Internet relay chat), and instant messaging. Compared with face-to-face (FtF) communication, CMC offers fewer non-verbal cues, more reliance on the written word, variation in terms of being synchronous (interacting at the same time) or asynchronous (interactive but not at the same time), and the ability of posters to be deceptive or even simply disappear.

In initiating new relationships over the Internet, you need to participate in the right kind of chat room, generally one that reflects your interests. Follow the same rules in developing a new relationship over the Internet as you would in person, realizing that the process is generally slower through CMC. People with strong verbal skills have an advantage in using the Internet for initiating and developing interpersonal relationships. Information that would be transmitted in other ways in FtF interactions must be put into written form for Internet interactions. The very act of keeping up with communication through the Internet helps maintain existing relationships. The amount of CMC and changes in the amount provide some indication of a person's interest in and commitment to the relationship. CMC can be used as a tool for implementing the various relational maintenance strategies discussed in Chapter 10. Relationships at work can involve both a task and social dimension. Forming friendships at work is one way people meet social needs and often helps produce a positive work atmosphere. The challenge of workplace interpersonal relationships is maximizing the satisfaction derived from such relationships while minimizing any negative impact on work performance. Workplace romances may present more challenges, especially if the behaviour can be defined in terms of sexual harassment by one of the parties.

In most organizations, communication flows up, down, horizontally, and out to customers. Through upward communication, you can share ideas and strategies for improving the work process; you can also enhance your relationship with your boss. Downward communication involves making contact with those who work for you. Horizontal communication concerns the communication you have with your colleagues on your level throughout the organization; most of the time, however, horizontal communication will occur with those who work in your immediate vicinity. Most organizations are encouraging better communication with customers and clients. Contacting those outside the organization who receive the organization's goods and services is an important way to ensure that what the organization offers is of high quality. Sexual harassment may be a problem in some organizations; legislation and workplace policies and procedures help prevent such harassment.

For Discussion and Review

Focus on Critical Thinking

1. Do you think the institution of the family is deteriorating, or is it just changing? Support your answer.

2. Despite the availability of relatively cheap interactive video setups for Internet use, people don't seem to be turning to them as much as they are to text-only interactions. Why might this be the case? Which would you use if you had a choice of the two? Why?

3. Jerry is president of Northern Technical Computing. He has a sense that his managers are not tapping the wealth of ideas and suggestions that lower-level employees might have for improving productivity. What specific strategies could Jerry implement to improve upward communication?

Focus on Ethics

4. Is it ethical to withhold honest thoughts and feelings from other family members? Should family members always "tell it like it is?" Should parents encourage their children to "tell everything" they know and feel?

5. In chat sessions on the Internet, is it really wrong to present false information about yourself just for fun when you know you will never meet the other people with whom you are interacting? Under what circumstances is describing yourself over the Internet as being of a different sex, age, race, or ethnicity ethical or unethical?

6. Kyle has e-mail at work but not at home. His brother has e-mail at his home. Is it ethical for Kyle to use the computer at work on company time to send and receive e-mail messages from his brother three or four times a week?

For Your Journal

1. Select two TV situation comedies or dramas that revolve around a family. One program could be one that is still broadcast in reruns, such as *Leave It to Beaver, All in the Family,* or *The Brady Bunch,* and the other show could be a more contemporary program. Describe the communication patterns in the TV programs that you observe. Draw on the principles and skills presented in this chapter as you describe the family communication patterns. Discuss which of your TV families seems to do the most effective job of communicating with one another.

2. Log on to a social chat room and then onto a topic-specific chat room. You don't have to post any messages; just be a "lurker" and watch what happens. What do people do to compensate for the lack of non-verbal cues? What do you notice about the messages themselves (for example, how long are they, what is the vocabulary like, how is the grammar, what jargon or slang is used)? How do the two sites compare in terms of language? Focus on a couple of the

posters on each site. What is your impression of these posters on the basis of what you observe?

3. Consider an organization in which you are or were an employee. What was your communication like with your boss? How open was your boss in sharing information with you (downward communication)? How open was your boss to communication from you (upward communication)? How did this flow of information with your boss affect your job satisfaction? How did it affect your job performance? How open was communication with your peers? What kinds of information did you and your peers discuss? How did your communication with your peers affect your satisfaction and performance?

Learning with Others

1. Indicate whether you agree or disagree with the following statements. Then break into small groups and try to get group members to agree or disagree unanimously with each statement. Try to find reasons for differences of opinion. If your group cannot reach agreement or disagreement, you may change the wording in any statement to promote unanimity.

   a. Most family members know how to communicate effectively; they just don't take the time to practise what they know.

   b. Family conflict is a symptom rather than a cause of deteriorating family relationships.

   c. Family conflict is harmful to family harmony, and all conflict should be avoided at all costs.

   d. Most family conflict occurs because we don't understand the other family member; we fail to communicate effectively.

   e. Families function best if there is one central leader of the family.

   f. Ineffective communication is the single most important cause of family conflict, divorce, and family tension.

   g. Non-verbal communication (facial expression, eye contact, tone of voice, posture, and so on) is more important than verbal communication; what you do is more important than what you say.

   h. It is sometimes necessary to ignore the feelings of others to reach a family decision.

   i. The best way to love your marriage partner is to care more for your partner than you care for yourself.

   j. Generally speaking, the quality of family life is deteriorating today.

   k. There is one best approach or set of rules and principles that will ensure an effectively functioning family.

2. Form an Internet study group. Start by finding three or four other students in your class with whom you feel comfortable and confident. Arrange times when you can all log on to the Internet to do instant messaging, send e-mails copied to all the other group members, or create a chat room for your group. Share information with one another about assignments, examinations, or papers for this class. Discuss among yourselves through the Internet what is

expected for the assignments, share any information each of you has that might help the others prepare better, and ask questions to help clarify information. If you are preparing for an exam, each of you might pose practice questions to the others, or each take a turn explaining some concept.

3. Conduct workplace interviews. Divide into teams of two or three people. Each team will interview a business person or supervisor in a non-profit organization such as a hospital or school about the workplace issues covered in this chapter. Ask such questions as these:

- What do you do to enhance upward communication among the people you supervise?
- How do your interpersonal relationships with co-workers affect your job?

    Afterward, discuss your results with other groups and see what general conclusions you can reach.

4. Log on to your research navigator. Use the Link Library and search by subject "Mgt.-HR Management." Look under "S" and click on "Sexual Harassment." From here, several sources are displayed (mostly American content). Find an article or advice about stopping unwanted harassment or policies about sexual harassment. Share your findings.

Weblinks

www.vifamily.ca   This is the site for the Vanier Institute of the Family, an interesting Canadian site that is all about families.

www.emode.com/tests/tvfamily   Although it requires you to register before you can access it, this site has a large number of fun quizzes, including one that tells you what TV family most resembles your own.

www.pewinternet.org/reports/toc.asp?Report=47   Pew Report on the Internet, Community, and Long-Distance Relationships

www.rider.edu/~suler/psycyber/psycyber.html   This site is maintained by a professor at Rider University and has a number of interesting articles on cyber-relationships.

www.workrelationships.com/site/quiz   This quiz should help you to understand behaviours that can create a hostile work environment or that are sexually harassing.

Notes

Chapter 1

1. E. T. Klemmer and F. W. Snyder, "Measurement of Time Spent Communicating," *Journal of Communication,* 20 (June 1972): 142.

2. E. E. Graham and C. K. Shue, "Reflections on the Past, Directions for the Future: A Template for the Study and Instruction of Interpersonal Communication," *Communication Research Reports,* 17 (Fall 2000): 337–48.

3. F. E. X. Dance and C. Larson, *Speech Communication: Concepts and Behavior* (New York: Holt, Rinehart and Winston, 1972).

4. Dance and C. Larson, *Speech Communication.*

5. For an excellent overview of interpersonal communication research, see M. E. Roloff and L. Anastasiou, "Interpersonal Communication Research," in *Communication Yearbook 24* (Mahwah, NJ: Erlbaum, 2000), 51–71.

6. J. T. Masterson, S. A. Beebe, N. H. Watson, *Invitation to Effective Speech Communication* (Glenview, IL: Scott, Foresman, 1989).

7. L. M. Webb and M. E. Thompson-Hayes, "Do Popular Collegiate Textbooks in Interpersonal Communication Reflect a Common Theory Base? A Telling Content Analysis," *Communication Education,* 51 (April 2002): 210–24.

8. M. Buber, *I and Thou* (New York: Scribners, 1958); also see M. Buber, *Between Man and Man* (New York: Macmillan, 1965). For a detailed discussion of perspectives on interpersonal communication and relationship development, see G. H. Stamp, "A Qualitatively Constructed Interpersonal Communication Model: A Grounded Theory Analysis," *Human Communication Research,* 25(4), (June 1999): 531–47; J. P. Dillard, D. H. Solomon, and M. T. Palmer, "Structuring the Concept of Relational Communication," *Communication Monographs,* 66 (March 1999): 49–65.

9. Buber, *I and Thou.*

10. D. Yankelovich, *The Magic of Dialogue: Transforming Conflict into Cooperation* (New York: Simon & Schuster, 1999); for an excellent discussion of dialogue, also see S. W. Littlejohn and K. Domenici, *Engaging Communication in Conflict: Systemic Practice* (Thousand Oaks, CA: Sage, 2001), 25–51.

11. Buber, *I and Thou.*

12. V. Satir, *Peoplemaking* (Palo Alto, CA: Science and Behavior Books, 1972).

13. K. E. Davis and M. Todd, "Assessing Friendship: Prototypes, Paradigm Cases, and Relationship Description," in *Understanding Personal Relationships,* eds. S. W. Duck and D. Perlman (London: Sage, 1985).

14. B. Wellman, "From Social Support to Social Network," in *Social Support: Theory, Research and Applications,* eds. I. G. Sarason and B. R. Sarason (Dordrecht, Netherlands: Nijhoff, 1985).

15. R. Hopper, M. L. Knapp, and L. Scott, "Couples' Personal Idioms: Exploring Intimate Talk," *Journal of Communication,* 31 (1981): 23–33.

16. J. L. Freedman, *Happy People* (New York: Harcourt Brace Jovanovich, 1978).

17. M. Argyle and M. Hendershot, *The Anatomy of Relationships* (London: Penguin Books, 1985), 14.

18. W. M. Kephard, "Some Correlates of Romantic Love," *Journal of Marriage and the Family,* 29 (1967): 470–74.

19. M. Argyle, *The Psychology of Happiness* (London: Routledge, 2001).

20. The Conference Board of Canada, *Employability Skills 2000+,* Ottawa: The Conference Board of Canada, 2000. www.conferenceboard.ca

21. M. Argyle, *The Psychology of Happiness* (London: Routledge, 2001).

22. J. J. Lynch, *The Broken Heart: The Medical Consequences of Loneliness* (New York: Basic Books, 1977).

23. D. P. Phillips, "Deathday and Birthday: An Unexpected Connection," in *Statistics: A Guide to the Unknown,* edited by J. M. Tanur (San Francisco: Holden Day, 1972).

24. Lee Chalmers and Anne Milan, "Marital Satisfaction During the Retirement Years," *Canadian Social Trends,* Spring 2005, Statistics Canada Catalogue No. 11-008.

25. F. Korbin and G. Hendershot, "Do Family Ties Reduce Mortality?: Evidence from the United States 1966–68," *Journal of Marriage and the Family,* 39 (1977): 737–45.

26. Korbin and Hendershot, "Do Family Ties Reduce Mortality?"

27. M. Argyle, *The Psychology of Interpersonal Behaviour* (London: Penguin, 1983).

28. Canadian Mental Health Association, Vancouver, "Understanding Depression" October, 1995.

29. Korbin and Hendershot, "Do Family Ties Reduce Mortality?"

30. For a comprehensive overview of the history of the study of interpersonal communication, see M. L. Knapp, J. A. Daly, K. F. Albada, and G. R. Miller, "Background and Current Trends in the Study of Interpersonal Communication," in *Handbook of Interpersonal Communication,* eds. M. L. Knapp and J. A. Daly (Thousand Oaks, CA: Sage, 2002), 3–20.

31. See V. E. Cronen, W. B. Pearce, and L. M. Harris, "The Coordinated Management of Meaning: A Theory of Communication," in *Human Communication Theory: Comparative Essays,* ed. F. E. X. Dance (New York: Harper & Row, 1982), 61–89.

32. L. C. Tidwell and J. B. Walther, "Computer-Mediated Communication Effects on Disclosure, Impressions, and Interpersonal Evaluations: Getting to Know One Another a Bit at a Time," *Human Communication Research,* 28 (July 2002): 317–48.

33. Survey quoted in Government On-Line, Government of Canada, www.gol-ged.gc.ca/rpt2005/rpt03_e.asp.

34. A. Harmon, "Online Dating Sheds Its Stigma at Losers.com," *The New York Times,* June 29, 2003, p. 1.

35. For an excellent discussion of the effects of computer-mediated communication and interpersonal communication, see J. B. Walther, "Interpersonal Effects in Computer-Mediated Interaction: A Relational Perspective," *Communication Research,* 19 (1992): 52–90; J. B. Walther, "Relational Aspects of Computer-Mediated Communication: Experimental and Longitudinal Observations," *Organization Science,* 6 (1995): 186–203; J. B. Walther, J. F. Anderson, and D. Park, "Interpersonal Effects in Computer-Mediated Interaction: A Meta-Analysis of Social and Anti-Social Communication," *Communication Research,* 21 (1994): 460–87; N. Negroponte, *Being Digital* (New York: Knopf, 1995); J. B. Walther and L. Tidwell, "When Is Mediated Communication Not Interpersonal?" in K. Galvin and P. Cooper, *Making Connections* (Los Angeles, CA: Roxbury Press, 1996); P. Wallace, *The Psychology of the Internet* (Cambridge, England: Cambridge University Press, 1999).

36. J. B. Walther and J. K. Burgoon, "Relational Communication in Computer-Mediated Interaction," *Human Communication Research,* 19 (1992): 50–88.

37. Tidwell and Walther, 2002.

38. L. K. Trevino, R. L. Draft, and R. H. Lengel, "Understanding Managers' Media Choices: A Symbolic Interactionist Perspective," in *Organizations and Communication*

Technology, J. Fulk and C. Steinfield (eds.) (Newbury Park, CA: Sage, 1990), 71–74.

39.   Tidwell and Walther, 2002.

40.   Walther and Tidwell, 1996.

41.   See D. Barnlund, *Interpersonal Communication: Survey and Studies* (Boston: Houghton Mifflin, 1968).

42.   O. Wiio, *Wiio's Laws—and Some Others* (Espoo, Finland: WelinGoos, 1978).

43.   S. B. Shimanoff, *Communication Rules: Theory and Research* (Beverly Hills: Sage, 1980).

44.   M. Argyle, M. Hendershot, and A. Furnham, "The Rules of Social Relationships," *British Journal of Social Psychology,* 24 (1985): 125–39.

45.   T. Watzlawick, J. Bavelas, and D. Jackson, *The Pragmatics of Human Communication* (New York: Norton, 1967).

46.   See J. C. McCroskey and M. [J.] Beatty, "The Communibiological Perspective: Implications for Communication in Instruction," *Communication Education,* 49(1) (January 2000): 1–6; M. J. Beatty and J. C. McCroskey, "Theory, Scientific Evidence, and the Communibiological Paradigm: Reflections on Misguided Criticism," *Communication Education,* 49(1), (January 2000): 36–44. Also see J. C. McCroskey, J. A. Daly, M. M. Martin, and M. J. Beatty (eds.), *Communication and Personality: Trait Perspectives* (Cresskil, NJ: Hampton Press, 1998).

47.   See J. Ayres and T. S. Hopf, "The Long-Term Effect of Visualization in the Classroom: A Brief Research Report," *Communication Education,* 39 (1990): 75–78; and J. Ayres and T. S. Hopf, "Visualization: A Means of Reducing Speech Anxiety," *Communication Education,* 34 (1985): 318–23.

48.   For a discussion of criticism of the communibiological approach, see C. M. Condit, "Culture and Biology in Human Communication: Toward a Multi-Causal Model," *Communication Education,* 49(1), (January 2000): 7–24.

49.   S. R. Wilson and C. M. Sabee, "Explicating Communicative Competence as a Theoretical Term," in *Handbook of Communication and Social Interaction Skills,* eds. J. O. Greene and B. R. Burleson (Mahwah, NJ: Erlbaum, 2003), 3–50.

50.   M. J. Collier, "Researching Cultural Identity: Reconciling Interpretive and Postcolonial Approaches," in *Communication and Identity Across Cultures,* eds. D. Tanno and A. Gonzalez (Thousand Oaks, CA: Sage, 1998), 142. Also see S. DeTurk, "Intercultural Empathy: Myth, Competency, or Possibility for Alliance Building?" *Communication Education,* 50 (October 2001): 374–84.

51.   M. Argyle, *The Psychology of Interpersonal Behaviour* (London: Penguin Books, 1983).

52.   Argyle, *The Psychology of Interpersonal Behaviour.*

53.   M. V. Redmond, "Adaptation in Everyday Interactions," paper presented at the annual meeting of the National Communication Association (November, 1997).

54.   C. H. Adams, "Prosocial Bias in Theories of Interpersonal Communication Competence: Must Good Communication Be Nice?" In *Communication and Community,* eds. G. Shepherd and E. W. Rothenbuhler (Mahwah, NJ: Erlbaum, 2001), 37–52.

55.   M. Argyle is widely acknowledged as the first scholar to suggest a systematic approach to apply learning theory to the development of social skills, including interpersonal communication skills. See: Argyle, *The Psychology of Interpersonal Behaviour.*

Chapter 2

1.   K. Horney, *Neurosis and Human Growth* (New York: W. W. Norton & Co., 1950), 17.

2.   J. M. Jones, S. Bennet, M. P. Olmstead, M. L. Lawson, G. Rodin, "Disordered Eating Attitudes and Behaviours in Teenaged Girls: A School-Based Study," *Canadian Medical Association Journal,* 165(5) (2001): 547–53.

3.   J. T. Masterson, *Speech Communication in Traditional and Contemporary Marriages* (doctoral dissertation, University of Denver, 1977). Also see S. A. Beebe and J. T. Masterson, *Family Talk: Interpersonal Communication in the Family* (New York: Random House, 1986), 91–100.

4.   For an excellent discussion of the role of gender and communication see J. C. Pearson, L. H. Turner, and W. Todd-Mancillas, *Gender and Communication,* 3rd ed. (Dubuque, IA: Wm. C. Brown, Publishers, 1995). Also see D. K. Ivy and P. Backlund, *Exploring Gender Speak* (New York: McGraw-Hill, 1994).

5.   Pearson, Turner, and Todd-Mancillas, *Gender and Communication;* Ivy and Backlund, *Exploring Gender Speak.*

6.   D. G. Ancona, "Groups in Organizations: Extending Laboratory Models," in *Annual Review of Personality and Social Psychology: Group and Intergroup Processes,* ed. C. Hendrick (Beverly Hills: Sage, 1987): 207–31. Also see D. G. Ancona and D. F. Caldwell, "Beyond Task and Maintenance: Defining External Functions in Groups," *Group and Organizational Studies,* 13 (1988): 468–94.

7.   This adaptation of S. L. Bem's work is from R. M. Berko, L. B. Rosenfeld, and L. A. Samovar, *Connecting: A Culture-Sensitive Approach to Interpersonal Communication Competency* (Fort Worth: Harcourt, Brace College Publishers, 1994).

8.   G. H. Mead, *Mind, Self, and Society* (Chicago: University of Chicago Press, 1934).

9.   L. A. Lefton, *Psychology* (Boston: Allyn & Bacon, 2000).

10.   J. C. McCroskey and M. J. Beatty, "The Communibiological Perspective: Implications for Communication Instruc-

tion," *Communication Education,* 49 (January 2000): 1–28.

11.   C. M. Condit, "Culture and Biology in Human Communication: Toward a Multi-Causal Model," *Communication Education,* 49 (January 2000): 7–24.

12.   P. Zimbardo, *Shyness: What It Is, What to Do About It* (Reading, MA: Addison-Wesley, 1977).

13.   S. Booth-Butterfield, "Instructional Interventions for Situational Anxiety and Avoidance," *Communication Education,* 37 (1988): 214–23.

14.   J. C. McCroskey and V. P. Richmond, *Fundamentals of Human Communication: An Interpersonal Perspective* (Prospect Heights, IL: Waveland Press, 1996).

15.   S. Booth-Butterfield, "Instructional Interventions."

16.   Zimbardo, *Shyness.*

17.   E. Berne, *Games People Play* (New York: Grove Press, 1964).

18.   S. Ting Toomey, J. G. Oetzel, and K. Yee-Jung, "Self-Construal Types and Conflict Management Styles," *Communication Reports,* 14 (Summer 2001): 87–104.

19.   Ting Toomey, Oetzel, and Yee-Jung, "Self-Construal Types."

20.   L. Armstrong, *It's Not About the Bike: My Journey Back to Life* (New York: Putnam's, 2000), 146.

21.   Douglas Coupland, "Canada's True Hero," *Maclean's,* July 01, 2004. www.macleans.ca/topstories/canada/article.jsp?content=20040701_83581_83581.

22.   K. Sugarman, "Tennis and Positive Self-Talk," *WorldWide Tennis Ladder* (August 2000): www.sportsladders.com/tennis/tips/artcl-selftalk.asp.

23.   J. Ayres and T. S. Hopf, "The Long-Term Effect of Visualization in the Classroom: A Brief Research Report," *Communication Education,* 39 (1990): 75–78.

24.   F. E. X. Dance and C. Larson, *The Functions of Human Communication* (New York: Holt, Rinehart and Winston, 1976), 141.

25.   M. V. Redmond, "The Functions of Empathy (Decentering) in Human Relations," *Human Relations,* 42 (1993): 593–606. Also see M. V. Redmond, "A Multidimensional Theory and Measure of Social Decentering," *Journal of Research in Personality* (1995).

26.   H. Brody. *The Placebo Response: How You Can Release Your Body's Inner Pharmacy for Better Health* (New York: HarperCollins, 2000). Also see H. Brody, "Tapping the Power of the Placebo," *Newsweek,* August 14, 2000, 68.

27.   A. A. Milne, "Pooh Does a Good Deed," in *Pooh Sleepytime Stories* (New York: Golden Press, 1979), 44.

28.   Summarized by D. E. Hamachek, *Encounters with the Self* (New York: Holt,

Rinehart and Winston, 1982), 3–5, and R. B. Adler and N. Towne (eds.), *Looking Out/Looking In* (Fort Worth, TX: Harcourt, Brace Jovanovich College Publishers, 1993). Also see C. R. Berger, "Self-Conception and Social Information Processing," in *Personality and Interpersonal Communication,* eds. J. C. McCroskey and J. A. Daly (Newbury Park, CA: Sage, 1987), 275–303.

29. A. A. Milne, "Owl Finds a Home," in *Pooh Sleepytime Stories* (New York: Golden Press, 1979), 28.

30. Hamachek, *Encounters with the Self,* and Berger, "Self-Conception and Social Information Processing."

31. W. C. Schutz, *FIRO: A Three-Dimensional Theory of Interpersonal Behavior* (New York: Holt, Rinehart & Winston, 1958).

32. McCroskey and Beatty, "Communibiological Perspective."

33. See J. C. McCroskey and V. P. Richmond, *Fundamentals of Human Communication.*

34. K. Dindia, "Self-Disclosure Research: Knowledge Through Meta-Analysis," in *Interpersonal Communication Research: Advances Through Meta-Analysis,* eds. M. Allen, R. W. Preiss, B. M. Gayle, and N. A. Burrell (Mahwah, NJ: Erlbaum, 2002), 169–85.

35. I. Altman and D. A. Taylor, *Social Penetration: The Development of Interpersonal Relationships* (New York: Holt, Rinehart and Winston, 1973).

36. W. B. Gudykunst and T. Nishida, "Social Penetration in Japanese and American Close Friendships," in *Communication Yearbook 7,* ed. R. N. Bostrom (Beverly Hills, CA: Sage, 1963), 592–611.

37. J. C. Korn, "Friendship Formation and Development in Two Cultures: Universal Constructs in the United States and Korea," in *Interpersonal Communication in Friend and Mate Relationships,* ed. A. M. Nicotera (Albany: State University of New York Press, 1993), 61–78.

38. J. Luft, *Group Process: An Introduction to Group Dynamics* (Palo Alto, CA: Mayfield, 1970).

39. Dindia, "Self-Disclosure Research."

40. Dindia, "Self-Disclosure Research."

41. J. Powell, *Why Am I Afraid to Tell You Who I Am?* (Niles, IL: Argus Communications, 1969), 12.

42. Powell, *Why Am I Afraid to Tell You Who I Am?*

43. L. C. Tidwell and J. B. Walther, "Computer-Mediated Communication Effects on Disclosure, Impressions, and Interpersonal Evaluations: Getting to Know One Another a Bit at a Time," *Human Communication Research,* 28, (July 2002): 317–48.

44. M. Argyle, M. Henderson, and A. Furnham, "The Rules of Social Relationships," *British Journal of Social Psychology,* 24 (1985): 125–39.

45. A. L. Vangelisti, J. P. Caughlin, and L. Timmerman, "Criteria for Revealing Family Secrets," *Communication Monographs,* 68 (March 2001): 1–27.

46. A. P. Bochner, "On the Efficacy of Openness in Close Relationships," in *Communication Yearbook 5,* ed. M. Burgoon (New Brunswick, NJ: Transaction Books, 1982), 109–24.

Chapter 3

1. C. R. Berger, "Self-Conception and Social Information Processing," in *Personality and Interpersonal Communication,* eds. J. C. McCroskey and J. A. Daly (Newbury Park, CA: Sage, 1987), 275–304.

2. P. R. Hinton, *The Psychology of Interpersonal Perception* (New York: Routledge, 1993).

3. D. W. Miller, "Looking Askance at Eyewitness Testimony," *Chronicle of Higher Education,* February 25, 2000: A19–20.

4. P. Watzlawick, J. Bevelas, and D. Jackson, *The Pragmatics of Human Communication* (New York: Norton, 1967).

5. A. L. Sillars, "Attribution and Communication: Are People Naive Scientists or Just Naive?" in *Social Cognition and Communication,* eds. M. E. Roloff, and C. R. Berger (Beverly Hills: Sage, 1982), 73–106.

6. R. D. Laing, H. Phillipson, and A. R. Lee, *Interpersonal Perception* (New York: Springer, 1966).

7. C. R. Berger and J. J. Bradac, *Language and Social Knowledge* (Baltimore: Edward Arnold, 1982).

8. S. Asch, "Forming Impressions of Personality," *Journal of Abnormal and Social Psychology,* 41 (1946): 258–90.

9. D. M. Wegner and R. R. Vallacher, *Implicit Psychology: An Introduction to Social Cognition* (New York: Oxford University Press, 1977).

10. J. S. Bruner and R. Tagiuri, "The Perception of People," in *Handbook of Social Psychology,* ed. G. Lindzey (Cambridge, MA: Addison-Wesley, 1954).

11. A. L. Sillars, "Attributions and Communication in Roommate Conflicts," *Communication Monographs,* 47 (1980): 180–200.

12. D. A. Infante and A. S. Rancer, "Argumentativeness and Verbal Aggressiveness: A Review of Recent Theory and Research," in *Communication Yearbook 19,* ed. B. R. Burleson (Thousand Oaks, CA: Sage, 1996), 319–52.

13. D. Hample, "The Life Space of Personalized Conflicts," in *Communication Yearbook 23,* ed. M. E. Roloff (Thousand Oaks, CA: Sage, 1999), 171–208.

14. F. Heider, *The Psychology of Interpersonal Relations* (New York: Wiley, 1958).

15. G. A. Kelly, *The Psychology of Personal Constructs* (New York: Norton, 1955).

16. A. L. Vangelisti and S. L. Young, "When Words Hurt: The Effects of Perceived Intentionality on Interpersonal Relationships," *Journal of Social and Personal Relationships,* 17 (2000): 393–424.

17. G. W. F. Hegel, *Phenomenology of Mind* (Germany: Wurzburg & Bamburg, 1807).

18. R. Nisbett and L. Ross, *Human Inference: Strategies and Shortcomings of Social Judgment* (Englewood Cliffs, NJ: Prentice-Hall, 1980).

19. Nisbett and Ross, *Human Inference.*

20. E. E. Jones and R. Nisbett, "The Actor and the Observer: Divergent Perceptions of the Causes of Behavior," in E. E. Jones et al., *Attribution: Perceiving the Causes of Behavior* (Morristown, NJ: General Learning Press, 1972), 79–94; D. E. Kanouse and L. R. Hanson, Jr., "Negativity in Evaluations," in E. E. Jones et al., 47–62.

21. F. T. McAndrew, A. Akande, R. Bridgstock, et al., "A Multicultural Study of Stereotyping in English-Speaking Countries," *The Journal of Social Psychology,* 140 (2000): 487–502.

22. Nisbett and Ross, *Human Inference.*

23. Asch, "Forming Impressions of Personality."

24. K. Floyd, "Attributions for Nonverbal Expressions of Liking and Disliking: The Extended Self-Serving Bias," *Western Journal of Communication,* 64 (Fall 2000): 388.

25. Floyd, "Attributions for Nonverbal Expressions of Liking and Disliking."

26. Goffman, *The Presentation of Self in Everyday Life.*

27. Brown and Levinson, *Politeness.*

28. Floyd, "Attributions for Nonverbal Expressions of Liking and Disliking."

29. P. Brown and S. C. Levinson, *Politeness: Some Universals in Language Use* (Cambridge, England: Cambridge University Press, 1987).

30. E. Goffman, *The Presentation of Self in Everyday Life* (New York: Doubleday, 1959).

31. M. V. Redmond, "The Functions of Empathy (Decentering) in Human Relations," *Human Relations,* 42(4), (1993): 593–606.

Chapter 4

1. H. J. M. Nouwen, *Bread for the Journey* (San Francisco: HarperCollins, 1997), entry for March 11.

2. Nouwen, *Bread for the Journey,* March 11.

3. "The Most Valued Workplace Skills," *The Wall Street Journal,* September 9, 2002: 1A.

4. L. Barker et al., "An Investigation of Proportional Time Spent in Various Communication Activities of College Students," *Journal of Applied Communication Research,* 8 (1981): 101–09.

5. K. W. Watson, L. L. Barker, and J. B. Weaver, *The Listener Style Inventory* (New Orleans: SPECTRA, 1995).

6. S. L. Sargent and J. B. Weaver, "Correlates Between Communication Apprehension and Listening Style Preferences," *Communication Research Reports,* 14 (1997): 74–78.

7. M. D. Kirtley and J. M. Honeycutt, "Listening Styles and Their Correspondence with Second Guessing," *Communication Research Reports,* 13 (1996): 174–182.

8. Sargent and Weaver, "Correlates Between Communication Apprehension."

9. W. Winter, A. J. Ferreira, and N. Bowers, "Decision-Making in Married and Unrelated Couples," *Family Process,* 12 (1973): 83–94.

10. O. E. Rankis, "The Effects of Message Structure, Sexual Gender, and Verbal Organizing Ability upon Learning Message Information," Ph.D. dissertation, Ohio University, 1981; C. H. Weaver, *Human Listening: Process and Behavior* (New York: The Bobbs-Merrill Company, 1972); R. D. Halley, "Distractibility of Males and Females in Competing Aural Message Situations: A Research Note," *Human Communication Research,* 2 (1975): 79–82. Our discussion of gender-based differences and listening is also based on a discussion by: S. A. Beebe and J. T. Masterson, *Family Talk: Interpersonal Communication in the Family* (New York: Random House, 1986).

11. This discussion is based on A. Vangelisti, M. Knapp, and J. Daly, "Conversational Narcissism," *Communication Monographs,* 57 (1990): 251–74.

12. J. Thurber, "The Secret Life of Walter Mitty," in *Literature for Composition,* 3rd ed., eds. S. Barnet et al. (Glenview, IL: Scott, Foresman, 1992), 43.

13. R. Montgomery, *Listening Made Easy* (New York: Amacon, 1981).

14. R. G. Owens, "Handling Strong Emotions," in O. Hargie (ed.), *A Handbook of Communication Skills* (London: Croom Helm/New York University Press, 1986).

15. R. G. Nichols, "Factors in Listening Comprehension," *Speech Monographs,* 15 (1948): 154–63; G. M. Goldhaber and C. H. Weaver, "Listener Comprehension of Compressed Speech When the Difficulty, Rate of Presentation, and Sex of the Listener Are Varied," *Speech Monographs,* 35 (1968): 20–25.

16. ABC News, *20/20,* January 12, 1998, featuring the research of communication researcher Kittie Watson.

17. M. V. Redmond, "The Functions of Empathy (Decentering) in Human Relations," *Human Relations,* 42 (1993): 593–606.

18. M. Fitch-Hauser, L. A. Barker, and A. Hughes, "Receiver Apprehension and Listening Comprehension: A Linear or Curvilinear Relationship?" *Southern Communication Journal* (1988): 62–71; P. Schrodt and L. R. Wheeless, "Aggressive Communication and Informational Reception Apprehension: The Influence of Listening Anxiety and Intellectual Inflexibility on Trait Argumentativeness and Verbal Aggressiveness," *Communication Quarterly,* 49 (Winter 2001): 53–69.

19. D. Carnegie, *How to Win Friends and Influence People* (New York: Holiday House, 1937).

20. K. Ruyter and M. G. M. Wetzels, "The Impact of Perceived Listening Behavior in Voice-to-Voice Service Encounters," *Journal of Service Research,* 2 (February 2000): 276–84.

21. J. Harrigan, "Listeners, Body Movements and Speaking Turns," *Communication Research,* 12 (1985): 233–50.

22. S. Strong et al., "Nonverbal Behavior and Perceived Counselor Characteristics," *Journal of Counseling Psychology,* 18 (1971): 554–61.

23. See: R. G. Nichols and L. A. Stevens, "Listening to People," *Harvard Business Review,* 35 (September–October 1957): 85–92.

24. C. W. Ellison and I. J. Fireston, "Development of Interpersonal Trust as a Function of Self-Esteem, Target Status and Target Style," *Journal of Personality and Social Psychology,* 29 (1974): 655–63.

25. D. Goleman, *Emotional Intelligence* (New York: Bantam, 1995).

26. Goleman, *Emotional Intelligence.*

27. O. Hargie, C. Sanders, and D. Dickson, *Social Skills in Interpersonal Communication* (London: Routledge, 1991).

28. J. B. Weaver and M. B. Kirtley, "Listening Styles and Empathy," *The Southern Communication Journal,* 60 (1995): 131–40.

29. J. Gottman and J. DeClaire, *The Relationship Cure* (New York: Crown, 2001), 198–201.

30. O. Hargie, C. Sanders, and D. Dickson, *Social Skills*; R. Boulton, *People Skills* (New York: 1981).

31. E. Sieburg and C. Larson, "Dimensions of Interpersonal Response," paper delivered at the annual conference of the International Communication Association, Phoenix, Arizona, April 1971.

32. S. DeTurk, "Intercultural Empathy: Myth, Competency, or Possibility for Alliance Building?" *Communication Education,* 50 (October 2001): 374–84.

33. Boulton, *People Skills.* We also acknowledge others who have presented excellent applications of listening and responding skills in interpersonal and group contexts: D. A. Romig and L. J. Romig, *Structured Teamwork Guide* (Austin, TX: Performance Resources, 1990); S. Deep and L. Sussman, *Smart Moves* (Reading: MA. Addison-Wesley, 1990); P. R. Scholtes, *The Team Handbook* (Madison, WI: Joiner Associates, 1992); Hargie, Sanders, and Dickson, *Social Skills*; Littlejohn and Domenici, *Engaging Communication in Conflict.*

34. S. Gilbert, "Self-Disclosure, Intimacy, and Communication in Families," *Family Coordinator,* 25 (1976).

Chapter 5

1. B. Spitzberg and J. P. Dillard, "Social Skills and Communication," in *Interpersonal Communication Research: Advances Through Meta-Analysis,* eds. M. Allen, R. W. Preiss, B. M. Gayle, and N. Burrell (Mahwah, NJ: Erlbaum, 2002), 89–107.

2. C. K. Ogden and I. A. Richards, *The Meaning of Meaning* (London: Kegan, Paul Trench, Trubner, 1923).

3. C. F. Hockett. *A Course in Modern Linguistics* (New York: Macmillan, 1958).

4. See G. H. Mead, *Mind, Self and Society* (Chicago: University of Chicago Press, 1934); H. Blumer, *Symbolic Interactionism: Perspective and Method* (Englewood Cliffs, NJ: Prentice Hall, 1969).

5. D. Tannen, *You Just Don't Understand: Women and Men in Conversations* (New York: Morrow, 1990).

6. R. Edwards, "The Effects of Gender, Gender Role, and Values on the Interpretation of Messages," *Journal of Language and Social Psychology,* 17 (1998): 52–71.

7. *The American Heritage Dictionary of the English Language* (Boston: Houghton Mifflin, 1969), 1162.

8. A. Korzybski, *Science and Sanity* (Lancaster, PA: Science Press, 1941).

9. G. Gusdorff, *Speaking* (Evanston, IL: Northwestern University Press, 1965), 9.

10. A. Ellis, *A New Guide to Rational Living* (North Hollywood, CA: Wilshire Books, 1977).

11. C. Peterson, M. E. P. Seligman, and G. E. Vaillant, "Pessimistic Explanatory Style Is a Risk Factor for Physical Illness: A 35-Year Longitudinal Study," *Journal of Personality and Social Psychology,* 55 (1988): 23–27.

12. B. L. Whorf, "Science and Linguistics," in *Language, Thought and Reality,* ed. J. B. Carroll (Cambridge, MA: M.I.T. Press, 1956), 207. This discussion of the Sapir-Whorf hypothesis is based on D. Crystal, *The Cambridge Encyclopedia of Language* (Cambridge, England: Cambridge University Press, 1997).

13. We thank one of our anonymous reviewers for this example.

14. A fascinating article, "The Melting of a Mighty Myth" in *Newsweek* (July 22, 1991) explores the topic of the Inuit people's words for snow.

15. R. L. Howe, *The Miracle of Dialogue* (New York: The Seqbury Press, 1963), 23–24.

16. H. S. O'Donnell, "Sexism in Language," *Elementary English,* 50 (1973): 1067–72, as cited by J. Pearson, L. Turner, and W. Todd-Mancillas, *Gender and Communication* (Dubuque, IA: William C. Brown, 1991), 96.

17. See D. K. Ivy and P. Backlund, *Exploring Gender Speak* (New York: McGraw Hill, 1994).

18. Associated Press. "'Canuck' No Slur, Editor Rehired," *Peterborough Examiner,* Sunday, February 28, 1999, B1.

19. We acknowledge and appreciate D. K. Ivy's contribution to this section on biased language. For an expanded discussion on this topic, see D. K. Ivy and P. Backlund, *Genderspeak* (New York: McGraw-Hill, 2000).

20. J. S. Seiter, J. Larsen, and J. Skinner, "'Handicapped' or 'Handicapable'?: The Effects of Language About Persons with Disabilities on Perceptions of Source Credibility and Persuasiveness," *Communication Reports,* 11(1), (1998): 21–31.

21. D. O. Braithwaite and C. A. Braithwaite, "Understanding Communication of Persons with Disabilities as Cultural Communication," in *Intercultural Communication: A Reader,* 8th ed., eds. L. A. Samovar and R. E. Porter (Belmont, CA: Wadsworth, 1997): 154–64.

22. D. Yankelovich, *The Magic of Dialogue: Transforming Conflict into Cooperation* (New York: Simon & Schuster, 1999).

23. J. R. Gibb, "Defensive Communication," *Journal of Communication,* 11 (1961): 141–48. Also see R. Bolton, *People Skills* (New York: Simon and Schuster, 1979), 14–26.

24. C. Rogers, *On Becoming a Person: A Therapist's View of Psychotherapy* (Boston: Houghton Mifflin, 1961); C. Rogers, *A Way of Being* (Boston: Houghton Mifflin, 1980); C. Rogers, "Comments on the Issue of Equality in Psychotherapy," *Journal of Humanistic Psychology,* 27 (1987): 38–39.

25. B. R. Burleson, "Comforting Messages: Features, Functions, and Outcomes," in *Strategic Interpersonal Communication,* eds. J. A. Daly and J. M. Wiemann (Hillsdale, NJ: Erlbaum, 1994), 135–61.

26. B. M. Gayle and R. W. Preiss, "An Overview of Interactional Processes in Interpersonal Communication," in *Interpersonal Communication Research: Advances Through Meta-Analysis,* eds. M. Allen, R. W. Preiss, B. M. Gayle, and N. Burrell (Mahwah, NJ: Erlbaum, 2002), 213–26.

27. M. Allen, "A Synthesis and Extension of Constructivist Comforting Research," in *Interpersonal Communication Research: Advances Through Meta-Analysis,* eds. M. Allen, R. W. Preiss, B. M. Gayle, and N. Burrell (Mahwah, NJ: Erlbaum, 2002), 237–45.

28. D. J. Dolin and M. Booth-Butterfield, "Reach Out and Touch Someone: Analysis of Nonverbal Comforting Responses," *Communication Quarterly,* 41 (1993): 383–93.

29. A. M. Bippus, "Human Usages in Comforting Episodes: Factors Predicting Outcomes," *Western Journal of Communication,* 54 (Fall 2000): 359–84; A. M. Bippus,

"Recipients' Criteria for Evaluating the Skillfulness of Comforting Communication and the Outcomes of Comforting Interactions," *Communication Monographs,* 68 (September 2001): 301–13.

30. Our prescriptions for assertiveness are based on a discussion by R. Boulton, *People Skills.* Also see J. S. St. Lawrence, "Situational Context: Effects on Perceptions of Assertive and Unassertive Behavior," *Behavior Therapy,* 16 (1985): 51–62; D. Borisoff and D. A. Victor, *Conflict Management: A Communication Skills Approach* (Boston: Allyn & Bacon, 1999).

31. D. Cloven and M. E. Roloff, "The Chilling Effect of Aggressive Potential on the Expression of Complaints in Intimate Relationships," *Communication Monographs,* 60 (1993): 199–219.

Chapter 6

1. A. Mehrabian, *Nonverbal Communication* (Chicago: Aldine-Atherton, 1972), 108.

2. D. Lapakko, "Three Cheers for Language: A Closer Examination of a Widely Cited Study of Nonverbal Communication," *Communication Education,* 46 (1997): 63–67.

3. D. Matsumoto, J. LeRoux, C. Wilson-Cohn, et al., "A New Test to Measure Emotion Recognition Ability: Matsumoto and Ekman's Japanese and Caucasian Brief Affect Recognition Test (JACBART)," *Journal of Nonverbal Behavior,* 24 (Fall 2000): 179–209; J. K. Burgoon and A. E. Bacue, "Nonverbal Communication Skills," in *Handbook of Communication and Social Interaction Skills,* eds. J. O. Greene and B. R. Burleson (Mahwah, NJ: Erlbaum, 2003), 179–219.

4. M. Zuckerman, D. DePaulo, and R. Rosenthal, "Verbal and Nonverbal Communication of Deception," *Advances in Experimental Social Psychology,* 14 (1981): 1–59.

5. P. Ekman and W. V. Friesen, "The Repertoire of Nonverbal Behavior: Categories, Origins, Usage and Coding," *Semiotica,* 1 (1969): 49–98.

6. E. Hess, *The Tell-Tale Eye* (New York: Van Nostrand Reinhold Company, 1975).

7. P. Ekman, "Communication Through Nonverbal Behavior: A Source of Information About an Interpersonal Relationship," in *Affect Cognition and Personality,* eds. S. S. Tomkins and C. E. Izard (New York: Springer, 1965).

8. J. K. Burgoon, L. A. Stern, and L. Dillman, *Interpersonal Adaptation: Dyadic Interaction Patterns* (Cambridge, England: Cambridge University Press, 1995).

9. A. S. E. Hubbard, "Interpersonal Coordination in Interactions: Evaluations and Social Skills," *Communication Research Reports,* 17 (Winter 2000): 95–104.

10. R. L. Birdwhistell, *Kinesics and Context* (Philadelphia: University of Pennsylvania Press, 1970).

11. N. Zunnin and M. Zunnin, *Contact: The First Four Minutes* (New York: Signet, 1976).

12. J. H. Bert and K. Piner, "Social Relationships and the Lack of Social Relations," in *Personal Relationships and Social Support,* eds. S. W. Duck with R. C. Silver (London: Sage, 1989).

13. S. M. Jones and L. K. Guerrero, "The Effects of Nonverbal Immediacy and Verbal Person Centeredness in the Emotional Support Process," *Human Communication Research,* 27 (October 2001): 567–96.

14. A. F. Koerner and M. A. Fitzpatrick, "Nonverbal Communication and Marital Adjustment and Satisfaction: The Role of Decoding Relationship Relevant and Relationship Irrelevant Affect," *Communication Monographs,* 69 (March 2002): 33–51.

15. Burgoon and Bacue, "Nonverbal Communication Skills."

16. B. M. DePaulo and H. S. Friedman, "Nonverbal Communication," in *The Handbook of Social Psychology,* eds. D. T. Gilbert, S. T. Fiske, and G. Lindzey (New York: McGraw-Hill, 1998).

17. Argyle, *Bodily Communication.*

18. W. G. Woodal and J. K. Burgoon, "The Effects of Nonverbal Synchrony on Message Comprehension and Persuasiveness," *Journal of Nonverbal Behavior,* 5 (1981): 207–23.

19. Argyle, *Bodily Communication.*

20. N. Blurton-Jones and G. M. Leach, "Behavior of Children and Their Mothers at Separation and Parting," in *Ethological Studies of Child Behavior,* ed. N. Blurton-Jones (Cambridge: Cambridge University Press 1972).

21. P. Ekman and W. V. Friesen, "Constants Across Cultures in the Face and Emotion," *Journal of Personality and Social Psychology,* 17 (1971): 124–29; Argyle, *Bodily Communication,* 157; I. Eibl-Eibesfeldt, "Similarities and Differences Between Cultures in Expressive Movements," in *Nonverbal Communication,* ed. R. A. Hinde (Cambridge, England: Royal Society & Cambridge University Press, 1972); P. Collett, "History and Study of Expressive Action," in *Historical Social Psychology,* eds. K. Gergen and M. Gergen (Hillsdale, NJ: Erlbaum 1984); E. T. Hall, *The Silent Language* (Garden City, NY: Doubleday, 1959); R. Shuter, "Gaze Behavior in Interracial and Intraracial Interaction," *International and Intercultural Communication Annual,* 5 (1979): 48–55; R. Shuter, "Proxemics and Tactility in Latin America," *Journal of Communication,* 26 (1976): 46–52; E. T. Hall, *The Hidden Dimension* (New York: Doubleday, 1966). For an excellent discussion of world view and the implications for intercultural communication, see C. H. Dodd, *Dynamics of Intercultural Communication* (Dubuque, IA: Brown & Benchmark, 1995); G. W. Beattie, *Talk: An Analysis of*

Speech and Non-Verbal Behavior in Conversation (Milton Keynes: Open University Press, 1983); O. Hargie, C. Sanders, and D. Dickson, *Social Skills in Interpersonal Communication* (London: Routledge, 1994); O. Hargie (ed.), *The Handbook of Communication Skills* (London: Routledge, 1997).

22.   This example originally appeared in Collett, "History and Study of Expressive Action."

23.   Birdwhistell, *Kinesics and Context.*

24.   A. E. Scheflen, "Quasi-Courtship Behavior in Psychotherapy," *Psychiatry,* 28 (1965): 245–57.

25.   M. Moore, *Journal of Ethology and Sociology* (summer 1994); also see D. Knox and K. Wilson, "Dating Behaviors of University Students," *Family Relations,* 30 (1981): 255–58.

26.   M. Reece and R. Whitman, "Expressive Movements, Warmth, and Verbal Reinforcement," *Journal of Abnormal and Social Psychology,* 64 (1962): 234–36.

27.   A. Mehrabian, *Silent Messages* (Belmont, CA: Wadsworth Publishing Company, 1972), 108.

28.   P. Ekman and W. V. Friesen, "The Repertoire of Nonverbal Behavior: Categories, Origins, Usage and Coding," *Semiotica,* 1 (1969): 49–98.

29.   A. T. Dittman, "The Body Movement–Speech Rhythm Relationship as a Cue to Speech Encoding," in *Studies in Dyadic Communication,* eds. A. W. Siegman and B. Pope (New York: Pergamon, 1972).

30.   A. A. Cohen and R. P. Harrison, "Intentionality in the Use of Hand Illustrators in Face-to-Face Communication Situations," *Journal of Personality and Social Psychology,* 28 (1973): 276–79.

31.   C. Darwin, *Expression of Emotions in Man and Animals* (Chicago: University of Chicago Press, 1965). Originally published 1872.

32.   A. Mehrabian and M. Williams, "Nonverbal Concomitants of Perceived and Intended Persuasiveness," *Journal of Personality and Social Psychology,* 13 (1969): 37–58.

33.   M. Argyle, F. Alkema, and R. Gilmour, "The Communication of Friendly and Hostile Attitudes by Verbal and Nonverbal Signals," *European Journal of Social Psychology,* 1 (1972): 385–402.

34.   D. Morris, *People Watching* (London: Vantage Press, 2002), 104.

35.   A. Kendon, "Some Functions of Gaze-Direction in Social Interaction," *Acta Psychologica,* 26 (1967): 22–63.

36.   S. W. Duck, *Understanding Relationships* (New York: The Guilford Press, 1991), 54.

37.   M. Knapp and J. A. Hall, *Nonverbal Communication in Human Interaction* (New York: Holt, Rinehart and Winston, 1978), 313.

38.   P. Ekman, W. V. Friesen, and S. S. Tomkins, "Facial Affect Scoring Technique: A First Validity Study," *Semiotica,* 3 (1971): 37–58; P. Ekman and W. V. Friesen, *Unmasking the Face* (Englewood Cliffs, NJ: Prentice-Hall, 1975).

39.   A. Mehrabian, "Significance of Posture and Position in the Communication of Attitude and Status Relationships," *Psychological Bulletin,* 71 (1969): 363.

40.   Ekman and Friesen, *Unmasking the Face;* Ekman, Friesen, and Tomkins, "Facial Affect Scoring Technique."

41.   Ekman and Friesen, *Unmasking the Face;* Ekman, Friesen, and Tomkins, "Facial Affect Scoring Technique."

42.   R. Buck, R. E. Miller, and C. F. William, "Sex, Personality, and Physiological Variables in the Communication of Affect Via Facial Expression," *Journal of Personality and Social Psychology,* 30 (1974): 587–96.

43.   Ekman and Friesen, *Unmasking the Face.*

44.   Ekman and Friesen, *Unmasking the Face.*

45.   G. J. McHugo, "Emotional Reactions to a Political Leader's Expressive Displays," *Journal of Personality and Social Psychology,* 49 (1985); 513–29.

46.   D. LaPlante and N. Ambady, "Multiple Messages: Facial Recognition Advantage for Compound Expressions," *Journal of Nonverbal Behavior,* 24 (Fall 2000): 211–25.

47.   J. Elliott, "If You're Happy and You Know It, You're a Buddhist," *The Sunday Times* [London], May 25, 2003: 1.14.

48.   "The Crying-Baby Translator," *The New York Times Magazine,* December 15, 2002: 78.

49.   J. R. Davitz, *The Communication of Emotional Meaning* (New York: McGraw-Hill, 1964).

50.   Davitz, *The Communication of Emotional Meaning.*

51.   K. K. Sereno and G. J. Hawkins, "The Effect of Variations in Speakers' Nonfluency upon Audience Ratings of Attitude Toward the Speech Topic and Speakers' Credibility," *Speech Monographs* 34 (1967): 58–74; G. R. Miller and M. A. Hewgill, "The Effect of Variations in Nonfluency on Audience Ratings of Source Credibility," *Quarterly Journal of Speech,* 50 (1964): 36–44; Mehrabian and Williams, "Nonverbal Concomitants of Perceived and Intended Persuasiveness."

52.   R. L. Street, R. M. Brady, and W. B. Putman, "The Influence of Speech Rate Stereotypes and Rate Similarity on Listeners' Evaluations of Speakers," *Journal of Language and Social Psychology,* 2 (1983): 37–56.

53.   T. Bruneau, "Communicative Silences: Forms and Functions," *Journal of Communication,* 23 (1973): 17–46.

54.   S. J. Baker, "The Theory of Silence," *Journal of General Psychology,* 53 (1955): 145–67.

55.   E. T. Hall, *The Hidden Dimension* (Garden City, NY: Doubleday and Company, 1966).

56.   R. Sommer, "Studies in Personal Space," *Sociometry,* 22 (1959): 247–60.

57.   Sommer, "Studies in Personal Space."

58.   See B. Stenzor, "The Spatial Factor in Face-to-Face Discussion Groups," *Journal of Abnormal and Social Psychology,* 45 (1950): 552–55.

59.   A. Montague, *Touching: The Human Significance of the Skin* (New York: Harper and Row, 1978).

60.   Montague, *Touching.*

61.   N. M. Henley, *Body Politics: Power, Sex, and Nonverbal Communication* (Englewood Cliffs, NJ: Prentice-Hall, 1977).

62.   J. Kelly, "Dress as Non-Verbal Communication," paper presented to the annual conference of the American Association for Public Opinion Research, May 1969.

63.   K. J. Narduzzi and T. Jackson, "Sociotropy-Dependency and Autonomy as Predictors of Eating Disturbance Among Canadian Female College Students," *The Journal of Genetic Psychology,* 163(4), 389-401.

64.   J. C. Valentine, V. Blankenship, H. Cooper, and E. S. Sullins, "Interpersonal Expectancy Effects and the Preference for Consistency," *Representative Research in Social Psychology,* 25 (2001): 26–33.

65.   J. Lefkowitz, R. Blake, and J. Mouton, "Status Factors in Pedestrian Violation of Traffic Signals," *Journal of Abnormal and Social Psychology,* 51 (1955): 704–06.

66.   J. T. Molloy, *Dress for Success* (New York: Warner Books, 1975); J. T. Molloy, *The Woman's Dress for Success Book* (Chicago: Follett, 1977).

67.   Mehrabian, *Nonverbal Communication.*

68.   L. Hinkle, "Nonverbal Immediacy Communication Behaviors and Liking in Marital Relationships," *Communication Research Reports,* 16(1), (1999): 81–90.

69.   J. K. Burgoon and B. A. Le Poire, "Nonverbal Cues and Interpersonal Judgments: Participant and Observer Perceptions of Intimacy, Dominance, Composure, and Formality," *Communication Monographs,* 66 (1999): 105–24.

70.   Jones and Guerrero, "The Effects of Nonverbal Immediacy;" also see D. J. Dolin and M. Booth-Butterfield, "Reach Out and Touch Someone: Analysis of Nonverbal Comforting Responses," *Communication Quarterly,* 41 (1993): 383–93.

71.   Argyle, *Bodily Communication.*

72.   K. J. Tusing and J. P. Dillard, "The Sounds of Dominance: Vocal Precursors of Perceived Dominance During Interpersonal

Influence," *Human Communication Research,* 26 (January 2000): 148–71.

73. Mehrabian, *Nonverbal Communication.*

74. Argyle, *Bodily Communication.*

75. For an excellent review of gender and nonverbal cues see J. Pearson, L. Turner, and W. Todd-Mancillas, *Gender and Communication* (Dubuque, IA: William C. Brown, 1991); D. Ivy and P. Backlund, *Exploring Gender Speak: Personal Effectiveness in Gender Communication* (New York: McGraw-Hill, 1994).

76. Burgoon, Stern, and Dillman, *Interpersonal Adaptation.*

77. B. A. Le Poire and S. M. Yoshimura, "The Effects of Expectancies and Actual Communication on Nonverbal Adaptation and Communication Outcomes: A Test of Interaction Adaptation Theory," *Communication Monographs,* 66 (1999): 1–30.

78. Burgoon and Bacue, "Nonverbal Communication Skills."

79. See Birdwhistell, *Kinesics and Context.*

80. E. Hatfield, J. T. Cacioppo, and R. L. Rapson, *Emotional Contagion* (New York: Cambridge University Press, 1994).

81. Hubbard, "Interpersonal Coordination in Interactions."

Chapter 7

1. Our definition of conflict is adapted from W. Wilmot and J. Hocker, *Interpersonal Conflict* (New York: McGraw-Hill, 2000).

2. D. Cramer, "Relationship Satisfaction and Conflict Style in Romantic Relationships," *Journal of Psychology,* 134 (2000): 337–41.

3. Statistics Canada, Canadian Centre for Justice Statistics. Family Violence in Canada: A Statistical Profile 2004, Ottawa: 2004

4. D. J. Canary, W. R. Cupach, and R. T. Serpe, "A Competence-Based Approach to Examining Interpersonal Conflict: Test of a Longitudinal Model," *Communication Research,* 29 (February 2001): 79–104.

5. J. W. Keltner, *Mediation: Toward a Civilized System of Dispute Resolution* (Annandale VA: Speech Communication Association, 1987); also see Wilmot and Hocker, *Interpersonal Conflict.*

6. G. R. Miller and M. Steinberg, *Between People: A New Analysis of Interpersonal Communication* (Chicago: Science Research Associates, 1975), 264.

7. C. M. Hoppe, "Interpersonal Aggression as a Function of Subject's Sex Role Identification, Opponent's Sex, and Degree of Provocation," *Journal of Personality,* 47 (1979): 317–29.

8. W. Wilmot and J. Hocker, *Interpersonal Conflict* (New York: McGraw-Hill, 2000); also see S. W. Littlejohn and K. Domenici, *Engaging Communication in*

Conflict: Systemic Practice (Thousand Oaks, CA: Sage, 2001).

9. J. M. Olsen, *The Process of Social Organization* (New York: Holt, Rinehart and Winston, 1978).

10. B. M. Gayle, R. W. Preiss, and M. Allen, "A Meta-Analytic Interpretation of Intimate and Nonintimate Interpersonal Conflict," in *Interpersonal Communication Research: Advances Through Meta-Analysis,* eds. M. Allen, R. W. Preiss, B. M. Gayle, and N. Burrell (Mahwah, NJ: Erlbaum, 2002), 345–70.

11. Olsen, *The Process of Social Organization.*

12. S. Ting-Toomey, "A Face Negotiation Theory," in *Theories in Intercultural Communication,* eds. Y. Kim and W. Gudykunst (Newbury Park, CA: Sage, 1988).

13. Ting-Toomey, "A Face Negotiation Theory."

14. Wilmot and Hocker, *Interpersonal Conflict,* 15–16.

15. R. Dumlao and R. A. Botta, "Family Communication Patterns and the Conflict Styles Young Adults Use with Their Fathers," *Communication Quarterly,* 48 (Spring 2000): 174–89. Also see W. Aquilino, "From Adolescent to Young Adult: A Prospective Study of Parent–Child Relations During the Transition to Adulthood," *Journal of Marriage and the Family,* 59 (1997): 670–86.

16. R. J. Doolittle, *Orientations of Communication and Conflict* (Chicago: Science Research Associates, 1976), 7–9.

17. D. Canary, W. Cupach, and S. Messman, *Relationship Conflict* (Thousand Oaks, CA: Sage, 1995); J. Gottman, *What Predicts Divorce? The Relationship Between Marital Process and Marital Outcomes* (Hillsdale, NJ: Erlbaum, 1994).

18. S. A. Lloyd, "Conflict in Premarital Relationships: Differential Perceptions of Males and Females," *Family Relations,* 36 (1987): 290–94.

19. E. H. Mudd, H. E. Mitchell, and J. W. Bullard, "Areas of Marital Conflict in Successfully Functioning and Unsuccessfully Functioning Families," *Journal of Health and Human Behavior,* 3 (1962): 88–93; N. R. Vines, "Adult Unfolding and Marital Conflict," *Journal of Marital and Family Therapy,* 5 (1979): 5–14.

20. B. A. Fisher, "Decision Emergence: Phases in Group Decision-Making," *Speech Monographs,* 37 (1970): 60.

21. A. C. Filley, *Interpersonal Conflict Resolution* (Glenview, IL: Scott, Foresman, 1975); R. H. Turner, "Conflict and Harmony," *Family Interaction* (New York: John Wiley and Sons, 1970); K. Galvin and B. J. Brommel, *Family Communication: Cohesion and Change* (New York: HarperCollins, 1991).

22. L. N. Olson and T. D. Golish, "Topics of Conflict and Patterns of Aggression in

Romantic Relationships," *Southern Communication Journal,* 67 (Winter 2002): 180–200.

23. J. Hocker and W. Wilmot, *Interpersonal Conflict,* (New York: McGraw Hill, 2001) 10.

24. Adapted from D. W. Johnson. *Reaching Out: Interpersonal Effectiveness and Self-Actualization* (Boston: Allyn & Bacon, 2000), 314.

25. M. Deutsch, *The Resolution of Conflict* (New Haven, CT: Yale University Press, 1973).

26. V. Satir, *Peoplemaking* (Palo Alto: Science and Behavior Books, 1972).

27. R. Kilmann and K. Thomas, "Interpersonal Conflict-Handling Behavior as Reflections of Jungian Personality Dimensions," *Psychological Reports,* 37 (1975): 971–80.

28. A. Buysse. A. De Clercq, L. Verhofstadt, et al., "Dealing with Relational Conflict: A Picture in Milliseconds," *Journal of Social and Personal Relationships,* 17 (2000): 574–79.

29. J. T. Tedeschi, "Threats and Promises," in *The Structure of Conflict,* ed. R. Swingle (New York: Academic Press, 1970).

30. R. Fisher and W. Ury, *Getting to Yes: Negotiating Agreement Without Giving In* (Boston: Houghton Mifflin, 1988). Also see D. Yankelovich, *The Magic of Dialogue: Transforming Conflict into Cooperation* (New York: Simon & Schuster, 1999).

31. Our discussion of the advantages and disadvantages of using different conflict management styles is based on material in Wilmot and Hocker, *Interpersonal Conflict.*

32. L. Powell and M. Hickson, "Power Imbalance and Anticipation of Conflict Resolution: Positive and Negative Attributes of Perceptual Recall," *Communication Research Reports,* 17 (Spring 2000): 181–90.

33. D. Cramer, "Linking Conflict Management Behaviors and Relational Satisfaction: The Intervening Role of Conflict Outcome Satisfaction," *Journal of Social and Personal Relationships,* 19 (2000): 425–32.

34. D. A. Cai and E. L. Fink, "Conflict Style Differences Between Individualists and Collectivists," *Communication Monographs,* 69 (March 2002): 67–87.

35. M. E. Roloff, L. L. Putnam, and L. Anastasiou, "Negotiation Skills," in *Handbook of Communication and Social Interaction Skills,* eds. J. O. Greene and B. R. Burleson (Mahwah, NJ: Erlbaum, 2003), 801–33.

36. This section on negotiation, including each of the suggested win–lose and win–win strategies, is adapted from Roloff, Putnam, and Anastasiou, "Negotiation Skills."

37. R. Fisher and W. L. Ury, *Getting to Yes: Negotiating Agreement Without Giving In* (Boston: Houghton Mifflin, 1981).

38. Fisher and Ury, *Getting to Yes.*

39. Roloff, Putnam, and Anastasiou, "Negotiation Skills."

40. D. Wallis, "Negotiator at Large," *The New York Times Magazine,* January 26, 2003, 13.

41. Roloff, Putnam, and Anastasiou, "Negotiation Skills."

42. Our discussion of conflict management skills is based on several excellent discussions of conflict management prescriptions. We acknowledge Fisher and Ury, *Getting to Yes*; R. Boulton, *People Skills* (New York: Simon & Schuster, 1979); D. A. Romig and L. J. Romig, *Structured Teamwork® Guide* (Austin, TX: Performance Resources, 1990); O. Hargie, C. Saunders, and D. Dickson, *Social Skills in Interpersonal Communication* (London: Routledge, 1994); S. Deep and L. Sussman, *Smart Moves* (Reading, MA: Addison-Wesley, 1990); Wilmot and Hocker, *Interpersonal Conflict*; M. D. Davis, E. L. Eshelman, and M. McKay, *The Relaxation and Stress Reduction Workbook* (Oakland, CA: New Harbinger Publications, 1982); W. A. Donohue and R. Kolt, *Managing Interpersonal Conflict* (Newbury Park: CA: Sage, 1992); O. Hargie (ed.), *The Handbook of Communication Skills* (London: Routledge, 1997); Littlejohn and Domenici, *Engaging Communication in Conflict;* and M. W. Isenhart and M. Spangle, *Collaborative Approaches to Resolving Conflict* (Thousand Oaks, CA: Sage, 2000).

43. Boulton, *People Skills,* 217.

44. For additional strategies on managing emotion, see J. Gottman, *Why Marriages Succeed and Fail: And How You Can Make Yours Last* (New York: Simon & Schuster, 1994); J. Gottman, *The Seven Principles for Making Marriage Work* (New York: Crown, 1999). Also see D. W. Johnson, *Reaching Out.*

45. A. Ellis, *A New Guide to Rational Living* (North Hollywood, CA: Wilshire Books, 1977).

46. Fisher and Ury, *Getting to Yes*; Boulton, *People Skills*; Romig and Romig, *Structured Teamwork® Guide*; T. Gordon, *Leader Effectiveness Training* (L.E.T.)*: The No-Lose Way to Release the Productive Potential of People* (New York: Wyden Books, 1977).

47. S. Deep and L. Susman, *Smart Moves* (New York: Addison-Wesley, 1990).

48. J. Gottman, *What Predicts Divorce? The Relationship Between Marital Process and Marital Outcomes* (Hillsdale, NJ: Erlbaum, 1994).

49. M. Morris, J. Nadler, T. Kurtzberg, and L. Thompson, "Schmooze or Lose: Social Friction and Lubrication in E-Mail Negotiations," *Group Dynamics: Theory, Research and Practice,* 6 (2002): 89–100.

50. A. Ellis, *A New Guide to Rational Living* (North Hollywood, CA: Wilshire Books, 1977).

51. S. R. Covey, *The Seven Habits of Highly Effective People* (New York: Simon and Schuster, 1989), 235.

52. C. Pavitt and B. Kemp, "Contextual and Relational Factors in Interpersonal Negotiation Strategy Choice," *Communication Quarterly, 47*(2), (1999): 133–50.

53. Fisher and Ury, *Getting to Yes.*

54. E. Goffman, *Interaction Rituals: Essays on Face-to-Face Interaction* (Garden City, NY: Doubleday, 1967).

55. S. Ting-Toomey, "Face and Facework: An Introduction," in S. Ting-Toomey (ed.), *The Challenge of Facework* (Albany, NY: SUNY Press, 1994), 1–14; S. Ting-Toomey, "Managing Intercultural Conflicts Effectively," in *Intercultural Communication: A Reader,* eds. L. A. Samovar and R. E. Porter (Belmont, CA: Wadsworth, 1994), 360–72. Also see S. Ting-Toomey and L. Chung, "Cross-Cultural Interpersonal Communication: Theoretical Trends and Research Directions," in *Communication in Personal Relationships Across Cultures,* eds. W. B. Gudykunst, S. Ting-Toomey, and T. Nishida (Thousand Oaks, CA: Sage, 1996), 237–61; M. W. Isenhart and M. Spangle, *Collaborative Approaches to Resolving Conflict,* 19–20.

56. J. W. Pfeiffer and J. E. Jones (eds.) *A Handbook of Structured Experiences for Human Relations Training* (La Jolla, CA: University Associates, 1974), Vol. 2, 62–76.

Chapter 8

1. A. G. Smith (ed.), *Communication and Culture* (New York: Holt, Rinehart and Winston, 1966).

2. P. Cateora and J. Hess, *International Marketing* (Homewood, IL: Irwin, 1979), 89; as discussed by L. A. Samovar and R. E. Porter, *Communication Between Cultures* (Belmont, CA: Wadsworth, 1991), 52.

3. G. Hofstede, *Culture's Consequences: International Differences in Work-Related Values* (Beverly Hills, CA: Sage, 1980).

4. For an extensive summary and critique of Hofstede's research, see M. W. Lustig and J. Koester, *Intercultural Competence,* 111.

5. G. Hofstede, *Culture's Consequences*; also see G. Hofstede, "Cultural Dimensions in Management and Planning," *Asia Pacific Journal of Management* (January 1984): 81–98.

6. For an extensive review of communication gender differences see L. H. Turner, K. Dindia, and J. C. Pearson, "An Investigation of Female/Male Verbal Behaviors in Same-Sex and Mixed-Sex Conversations," *Communication Reports,* 8 (summer 1995): 86–96.

7. An excellent analysis and application of gender communication research has been compiled by A. Cornyn-Selby, "Are You from Another Planet or What?" presented at the Joint Service Family Readiness Matters Conference, July 14, 1999, Phoenix, Arizona.

8. See D. K. Ivy and P. Backlund, *Exploring GenderSpeak: Personal Effectiveness in Gender Communication* (New York: McGraw-Hill, 2000).

9. G. Hofstede, "Cultural Dimensions in Management and Planning," *Asia Pacific Journal of Management* (January 1984): 81–98.

10. C. R. Berger and R. J. Calabrese, "Some Exploration in Initial Interactions and Beyond: Toward a Developmental Theory of Interpersonal Communication," *Human Communication Research,* 1(1975): 99–112.

11. For an excellent comprehensive discussion of uncertainty reduction theory, see R. West and L. H. Turner, *Introducing Communication Theory: Analysis and Application* (Mountain View, CA: 2000), 132-46.

12. G. Hofstede, *Cultures and Organizations: Software of the Mind* (London: McGraw-Hill, 1997).

13. Hofstede, *Culture's Consequences.*

14. W. B. Gudykunst, *Bridging Differences: Effective Intergroup Communication* (Newbury Park, CA: Sage, 1991), 45.

15. Gudykunst, *Bridging Differences.*

16. E. T. Hall, *Beyond Culture* (Garden City, NY: Doubleday, 1976).

17 . Samovar and Porter, *Communication Between Cultures,* 234.

18. M. V. Redmond and J. M. Bunyi, "The Relationship of Intercultural Communication Competence with Stress and the Handling of Stress as Reported by International Students," *International Journal of Intercultural Relations,* 17 (1993): 235–54; R. Brislen, *Cross-Cultural Encounters: Face-to-Face Interaction* (New York: Pergamon Press, 1981).

19. W. G. Sumner, *Folkways* (Boston: Ginn, 1906), as cited by James W. Neuliep, *Intercultural Communication: A Contextual Approach* (Boston: Houghton Mifflin, 2000), 160.

20. M. W. Lustig and J. Koester, *Intercultural Competence: Interpersonal Communication Across Cultures,* (Boston: Allyn and Bacon, 2003)

21. J. W. Neuliep and J. C. McCroskey, "The Development of a U.S. and Generalized Ethnocentrism Scale," *Communication Research Reports,* 14 (1997): 385–398.

22. R. E. Axtell, *Do's and Taboos of Hosting International Visitors* (New York: John Wiley and Sons, 1989), 118.

23. J. S. Caputo, H. C. Hazel, and C. McMahon, *Interpersonal Communication* (Boston: Allyn and Bacon, 1994), 304.

24. S. Kamekar, M. B. Kolsawalla, and T. Mazareth, "Occupational Prestige as a Function of Occupant's Gender," *Journal of Applied Social Psychology,* 19 (1988): 681–88.

25. B. H. Spitzberg and W. R. Cupach, "Interpersonal Skills, " in *Handbook of Interpersonal Communication,* ed. M. L. Knapp and J. A. Daly (Thousand Oaks, CA: Sage, 2002): 564-611.

26. S. A. Myers and R. L. Knox, "The Relationship Between College Student Information Seeking Behaviors and Perceived Instructor Verbal Responses," *Communication Education,* 50 (2001): 343–56; J. R. Baldwin and S. K. Hunt, "Information-Seeking Behavior in Intercultural and Intergroup Communication," *Human Communication Research,* 28 (April 2002): 272–86.

27. For an excellent discussion of world view and the implications for intercultural communication see C. H. Dodd, *Dynamics of Intercultural Communication* (Dubuque, IA: Brown and Benchmark, 1995).

28. Dodd, *Dynamics of Intercultural Communication,* 75.

29. W. B. Gudykunst, "Similarities and Differences in Perceptions of Initial Intracultural and Intercultural Encounters," *Southern Speech Communication Journal,* 49 (1983): 49–65; W. B. Gudykunst, "Theorizing in Intercultural Communication: An Introduction." In *Intercultural Communication Theory: Current Perspectives,* edited by W. B. Gudykunst (Beverly Hills, CA: Sage, 1983), 13–20; W. B. Gudykunst, "A Model of Uncertainty Reduction in Intercultural Encounters," *Journal of Language and Social Psychology,* 4 (1985): 79–97; W. B. Gudykunst, E. Chua, and A. Gray, "Cultural Dissimilarities and Uncertainty Reduction Processes," in *Communication Yearbook 10,* ed. M. L. McLaughlin (Beverly Hills, CA: Sage, 1987), 456–69; W. B. Gudykunst and T. Nishida, "Individual and Cultural Influences on Uncertainty Reduction," *Communication Monographs,* 51 (1984): 23–36; W. B. Gudykunst and Y. Kim, *Communicating with Strangers: An Approach to Intercultural Communication* (New York: McGraw-Hill, 1997); W. B. Gudykunst, S.-M. Yang, and T. Nishida, "Cultural Differences in Self-Consciousness and Self-Monitoring," *Communication Monographs,* 14 (1987): 7–14; Baldwin and Hunt, "Information-Seeking Behavior."

30. Julia T. Wood, *Communication Mosaics: A New Introduction to the Field of Communication* (Belmont, CA: Wadsworth, 1997), 207; C. C. Innman, "Men's Friendships: Closeness in the Doing," in Julia T. Wood, (ed.), *Gendered Relationships* (Mountain View CA: Mayfield), 95–110.

31. C. R. Berger and R. J. Calabrese, "Some Explorations in Initial Interactions and Beyond," *Human Communication Research,* 1 (1975): 99–125.

32. Benjamin J. Broome, "Building Shared Meaning: Implications of a Relational Approach to Empathy for Teaching Intercultural Communication," *Communication Education,* 40 (1991): 235–49.

33. F. L. Casmir and N. C. Asuucion-Lande. "Intercultural Communication Revisited: Conceptualization, Paradigm Building, and Methodological Approaches," in J. A. Anderson (ed.), *Communication Yearbook,* 12 (Newbury Park, CA: Sage, 1989): 278–309.

34. Broome, "Building Shared Meaning."

35. W. B. Gudykunst and Y. Kim, *Communicating with Strangers* (New York: Random House, 1984); Gudykunst, *Bridging Differences.*

36. L. B. Szalay and G. H. Fisher, "Communication Overseas," in *Toward Internationalism: Readings in Cross-Cultural Communication,* eds. E. C. Smith and L. F. Luce (Rowley, MA: Newbury House Publishers, 1979).

37. P. Brown and S. Levinson, *Politeness: Some Universals in Language Usage* (Cambridge, England: Cambridge University Press, 1987).

38. C. S. Lewis, *The Abolition of Man* (New York: Macmillan Publishing Company, 1947).

39. M. V Redmond, "The Functions of Empathy (Recentering) in Human Relations," *Human Relations,* 42 (1993): 593–606. Also see M. V. Redmond, "A Multidimensional Theory and Measure of Social Decentering," *Journal of Research in Personality* (1995); for an excellent discussion of the role of emotions in establishing empathy see Daniel Goleman, *Emotional Intelligence* (New York: Bantam, 1995).

40. See H. Giles, A. Mulack, J. J. Bradac, and P. Johnson, "Speech Accommodation Theory: The First Decade and Beyond," in *Communication Yearbook,* ed. M. L. McLaughlin, Vol. 10 (Newbury Park, CA: Sage, 1987), 13–48. For an excellent summary and application of accommodation theory, see R. West and L. H. Turner, *Introducing Communication Theory: Analysis and Application* (Mountain View, CA: Mayfield, 2000).

41. Lori J. Carrell, "Diversity in the Communication Curriculum: Impact on Student Empathy," *Communication Education,* 46 (1997): 234–44.

42. M. J. Bennett, "Overcoming the Golden Rule: Sympathy and Empathy," in *Communication Yearbook 3,* ed. D. Nimmo (Beverly Hills, CA: Sage, 1979), 407–22.

43. Bennett, "Overcoming the Golden Rule."

44. Adapted from Samovar and Porter, *Communication Between Cultures.*

Chapter 9

1. L. von Bertalanffy, "Der Organismus als Physikalisches System Betrachtet," *Die Naturwissenschaften,* 28 (1940): 521–31.

2. F. E. Millar and L. E. Rogers, "A Relational Approach to Interpersonal Communication," in *Explorations in Interpersonal Communication,* ed. G. R. Miller (Newbury Park, CA: Sage, 1976), 87–103.

3. K. Chow, "Social Support and Subjective Well-Being Among Hong Kong Chinese Young Adults," *Journal of Genetic Psychology,* 160 (September 1999): 319–316.

4. I. Altman and D. Taylor, *Social Penetration: The Development of Interpersonal*

Relationships (New York: Holt, Rinehart, and Winston, 1973).

5. L. K. Knobloch and D. H. Solomon, "Information Seeking Beyond Initial Interaction: Negotiating Relational Uncertainty Within Close Relationships," *Human Communication Research,* 28 (April 2002): 243–57.

6. W. Stoebe, "Self Esteem and Interpersonal Attraction," in *Theory and Practice in Interpersonal Attraction,* ed. S. Duck (London: Academic Press, 1977).

7. S. Sprecher, "Insiders' Perspectives on Reasons for Attraction to a Close Other," *Social Psychology Quarterly,* 61 (1998): 287–300.

8. Sprecher, "Insiders' Perspectives."

9. S. W. Duck, *Personal Relationships and Personal Constructs: A Study of Friendship Formation* (New York: John Wiley and Sons, 1973).

10. M. Sunnafrank, "A Communication-Based Perspective on Attitude Similarity and Interpersonal Attraction in Early Acquaintance," *Communication Monographs,* 51 (1984): 372–80.

11. M. Sunnafrank, "Interpersonal Attraction and Attitude Similarity: A Communication-Based Assessment," in *Communication Yearbook* 14, ed. J. A. Anderson (Newbury Park, CA: Sage, 1991), 451–83.

12. Sunnafrank, "Interpersonal Attraction and Attitude Similarity."

13. Sprecher, "Insiders' Perspectives."

14. W. Schutz, *Interpersonal Underworld* (Palo Alto, CA: Science and Behavior Books, 1966).

15. M. Sunnafrank, "Predicted Outcome Value During Initial Interactions: A Reformulation of Uncertainty Reduction Theory," *Human Communication Research,* 13 (1986): 3–33.

16. Sunnafrank, "Predicted Outcome Value During Initial Interactions."

17. M. V. Redmond and D. A. Vrchota, "The Effects of Varying Lengths of Initial Interaction on Attraction and Uncertainty Reduction," paper presented at the annual meeting of the Speech Communication Association.

18. S. Sprecher and D. Felmlee, "The Balance of Power in Romantic Heterosexual Couples over Time in 'His' and 'Her' Perspectives," *Sex Roles,* 37 (1997): 361–79.

19. Sprecher and Felmlee, "The Balance of Power in Romantic Heterosexual Couples."

20. F. E. Millar and L. E. Rogers, "Relational Dimensions of Interpersonal Dynamics," in *Interpersonal Processes: New Directions in Communication Research,* ed. M. E. Roloff and G. R. Miller (Newbury Park, CA: Sage, 1987), 117–39.

21. J. R. P. French and B. H. Raven, "The Bases of Social Power," in *Group Dynamics,*

ed. J. D. Cartwright and A. Zander (Evanston, IL: Row, Peterson, 1962), 607–22.

22. M. G. Lawler and G. S. Risch, "Time, Sex and Money: The First Five Years of Marriage," *America,* 184 (2001): 16–20.

23. M. Honeycutt and J. M. Wiemann, "Analysis of Functions of Talk and Reports of Imagined Interactions (IIs) During Engagement and Marriage," *Human Communication Research,* 25 (1999): 399–419.

24. S. Duck, "Interpersonal Communication in Developing Relationships," in *Explorations in Interpersonal Communication,* ed. G. R. Miller (Newbury Park, CA: Sage, 1976), 127–47.

25. I. Altman and D. A. Taylor, *Social Penetration: The Development of Interpersonal Relationships* (New York: Holt, Rinehart and Winston, 1973).

26. Sunnafrank, "Predicted Outcome Value During Initial Interaction."

27. J. W. Thibaut and H. H. Kelley, *The Social Psychology of Groups* (New York: Wiley, 1959).

28. G. R. Miller and M. R. Parks, "Communicating in Dissolving Relationships," in *Personal Relationships 4: Dissolving Personal Relationships,* ed. S. W. Duck (London: Academic Press, 1982), 127–54.

29. A. L. Busboom, D. M. Collins, M. D. Givertz, and L. A. Levin, "Can We Still Be Friends? Resources and Barriers to Friendship Quality After Romantic Relationship Dissolution," *Personal Relationships,* 9 (2002): 215–23.

30. L. A. Baxter, "Dialectical Contradictions in Relationship Development," in *Handbook of Personal Relationships,* ed. S. W. Duck (Chichester, England: Wiley, 1988), 257–73; L. A. Baxter and B. M. Montomery, "Rethinking Communication in Personal Relationships from a Dialectical Perspective," in *Handbook of Personal Relationships,* 2nd ed., ed. S. W. Duck (Chichester, England: Wiley, 1997), 325–49.

31. D. R. Pawlowski, "Dialectical Tensions in Marital Partners' Accounts of Their Relationships," *Communication Quarterly,* 46 (1998): 396–416.

32. M. V. Redmond, "Content Adaptation in Everyday Interactions," paper presented at the annual meeting of the National Communication Association, Chicago, 1997.

33. Pawlowski, "Dialectical Tensions."

34. L. A. Baxter, "Interpersonal Communication as Dialogue: A Response to the 'Social Approaches' Forum," *Communication Theory,* 2 (1992): 330–38.

35. A. Hoppe-Nagao and S. Ting-Toomey, "Relational Dialectics and Management Strategies in Marital Couples," *Southern Communication Journal,* 67 (Winter 2002): 142–59.

36. Baxter, "Interpersonal Communication as Dialogue."

Chapter 10

1. L. A. Baxter and C. Bullis, "Turning Points in Developing Romantic Relationships," *Communication Research,* 12 (1986): 469–93.

2. Baxter and Bullis, "Turning Points."

3. C. R. Berger and J. J. Bradac, *Language and Social Knowledge: Uncertainty in Interpersonal Relations* (Baltimore: Edward Arnold, 1982).

4. W. Douglas, "Question Asking in Same and Opposite Sex Initial Interactions: The Effects of Anticipated Future Interaction," *Human Communication Research,* 14 (1987): 230–45.

5. S. W. Duck, "A Topography of Relationship Disengagement and Dissolution," in *Personal Relationships 4: Dissolving Relationships,* ed. S. W. Duck (New York: Academic Press, 1982).

6. Duck, "A Topography of Relationship Disengagement and Dissolution."

7. D. DeStephen, "Integrating Relational Termination into a General Model of Communication Competence," paper presented at the annual meeting of the Speech Communication Association, 1985.

8. Adapted from K. Kellerman et al., "The Conversation MOP: Scenes in the Stream of Discourse," *Discourse Processes,* 12 (1989): 27–61.

9. A. E. Lindsey and W. R. Zahaki, "Perceptions of Men and Women Departing from Conversational Sex Role Stereotypes During Initial Interaction," in *Sex Differences and Similarities in Communication,* eds. D. J. Canary and K. Dindia (Mahwah, NJ: Erlbaum, 1998): 393–412.

10. For an excellent review of the nature of friendship, see M. Argyle, *The Psychology of Interpersonal Behavior* (London: Penguin, 1983).

11. A. M. Nicotera, "The Importance of Communication in Interpersonal Relationships," in *Interpersonal Communication in Friend and Mate Relationships,* ed. A. M. Nicotera and Associates (Albany: State University of New York Press, 1993), 3–12.

12. R. A. Bell and J. A. Daly, "The Affinity Seeking Function of Communication," *Communication Monographs,* 51 (1984): 91–115.

13. Bell and Daly, "The Affinity Seeking Function of Communication."

14. C. R. Berger and R. J. Calabrese, "Some Explorations in Initial Interaction and Beyond: Toward a Developmental Theory of Interpersonal Communication," *Human Communication Research,* 1, (1975): 99–112; C. R. Berger and J. J. Bradac, *Language and Social Knowledge: Uncertainty in Interpersonal Relations* (Baltimore: Edward Arnold, 1982).

15. Berger and Bradac, *Language and Social Knowledge.*

16. Sunnafrank, "Predicted Outcome Value During Initial Interactions"; and "Interpersonal Attraction and Attitude Similarity," in *Communication Yearbook 14,* ed. J. A. Anderson (Newbury Park, CA: Sage, 1991), 451–83.

17. Berger and Bradac, *Language and Social Knowledge.*

18. R. A. Clark and J. G. Delia, "Individuals' Preferences for Friends' Approaches to Providing Support in Distressing Situations," *Communication Reports,* 10 (1997): 115–21.

19. S. A. Westmyer and S. A. Myers, "Communication Skills and Social Support Messages Across Friendship Levels," *Communication Research Reports,* 13 (1996): 191–97.

20. A. L. Vangelisti, "Communication Problems in Committed Relationships: An Attributional Analysis," in *Attributions, Accounts, and Close Relationships,* eds. J. H. Harvey, T. L. Orbuch, and A. L. Weber, (New York: Springer Verlag, 1992), 144–64.

21. G. Levinger and D. J. Senn, "Disclosure of Feelings in Marriage," *Merrill-Palmer Quarterly* 12, (1967): 237–49; A. Bochner, "On the Efficacy of Openness in Close Relationships," in *Communication Yearbook 5,* ed. M. Burgoon (New Brunswick, NJ: Transaction Books, 1982), 109–24.

22. J. K. Alberts, "An Analysis of Couples' Conversational Complaints," *Communication Monographs,* 55 (1988): 184–97.

23. M. A. Fitzpatrick and D. M. Badzinski, "All in the Family: Interpersonal Communication in Kin Relationships," in *Handbook of Interpersonal Communication,* eds. M. L. Knapp and G. R. Miller (Beverly Hills: Sage Publications, 1985), 687–736.

24. G. R. Miller and F. Boster, "Persuasion in Personal Relationship," in *A Handbook of Personal Relationships,* ed. S. Duck (New York: Wiley, 1988): 275–88; M. G. Garko, "Perspectives and Conceptualizations of Compliance and Compliance Gaining," *Communication Quarterly,* 38(2) (1990): 138–157.

25. G. R. Miller and M. R. Parks, "Communication in Dissolving Relationships," in *Personal Relationships 4: Dissolving Personal Relationships,* ed. S. W. Duck (London: Academic Press, 1982), 127–54.

26. S. W. Duck, *Understanding Relationships* (New York: Guilford Press, 1991).

27. J. M. Gottman and S. Carrere, "Why Can't Men and Women Get Along? Developmental Roots and Marital Inequities," in *Communication and Relational Maintenance,* eds. D. J. Canary and L. Stafford (San Diego: Academic Press, 1991): 203–229.

28. G. O. Hagestad and M. A. Smyer, "Dissolving Long-Term Relationships: Patterns of Divorcing in Middle Age," in Duck, *Personal Relationships,* Vol. 4: *Dissolving Personal Relationships,* ed. S. Duck (London: Academic Press, 1982), 155–88.

29. J. Gottman with N. Silver, *Why Marriages Succeed or Fail* (New York: Simon and Schuster, 1994).

30. Gottman and Silver, *Why Marriages Succeed or Fail.*

31. P. J. Lannutti and K. A. Cameron, "Beyond the Breakup: Heterosexual and Homosexual Post-Dissolution Relationships," *Communication Quarterly,* 50 (Spring 2002): 153–70.

32. G. R. Miller and M. R. Parks, "Communication in Dissolving Relationships," in *Personal Relationships,* Vol. 4: *Dissolving Personal Relationships,* ed. S. W. Duck (London: Academic Press, 1982), 127–54.

33. Duck, "A Topography of Relationship Disengagement and Dissolution."

34. Miller and Parks, "Communication in Dissolving Relationships."

35. M. J. Cody, "A Typology of Disengagement Strategies and an Examination of the Role Intimacy, Reactions to Inequity and Relational Problems Play in Strategy Selection," *Communication Monographs,* 49(3), (1982): 148–70.

36. M. Argyle and M. Henderson, *The Anatomy of Relationships* (New York: Guilford Press, 1991).

37. Duck, *Understanding Relationships.*

38. Duck, "A Typography."

39. Miller and Parks, "Communication in Dissolving Relationships."

40. L. A. Baxter, "Accomplishing Relationship Disengagement," in *Understanding Personal Relationships: An Interdisciplinary Approach,* eds. S. Duck and D. Perlman (Beverly Hills: Sage, 1984): 243–65.

41. D. DeStephen, "Integrating Relational Termination into a General Model of Communication Competence," paper presented at the annual meeting of the Speech Communication Association.

42. Baxter, "Accomplishing Relationship Disengagement."

43. DeStephen, "Integrating Relational Termination into a General Model of Communication Competence."

44. Cody, "A Typology of Disengagement Strategies."

45. A. Weber, "Loving, Leaving, and Letting Go: Coping with Nonmarital Breakups," in *The Dark Side of Close Relationships,* eds. B. H. Spitzberg and W. R. Cupach (Mahwah, NJ: Erlbaum, 1998), 267–306.

Chapter 11

1. Statistics Canada, "Update on Families," *Canadian Social Trends,* Summer 2003, 11.

2. Vanier Institute of the Family, *Profiling Canada's Families II,* online: Vanier Institute of the Family, www.vifamily.ca.

3. *Profiling Canada's Families II.*

4. G. P. Murdock, *Social Structure* (New York: Free Press, 1965). Originally published in 1949.

5. Statistics Canada, Family Income, The Daily, Friday, May 20, 2005, www.statcan.ca/Daily/English/050520/d050520c.htm.

6. Vanier Institute of the Family, www.vifamily.ca/about/about.html.

7. Statistics Canada, *2001 Census*: Marital status, common-law status, families, dwellings and households, *The Daily*, October 22, 2002.

8. Dr. A.-M. Ambert, "Same-Sex Couples and Same-Sex-Parent Families: Relationships, Parenting, and Issues of Marriage," The Vanier Institute of the Family Virtual Library, 2005, www.vifamily.ca/library/cft/samesex_05.html.

9. V. Satir, *Peoplemaking* (Palo Alto, CA: Science and Behavior Books, 1972).

10. Ambert, Same-Sex Couples and Same-Sex-Parent Families.

11. D. E. Beck and M. A. Jones, *Progress on Family Problems: A Nationwide Study of Clients' and Counselors' Views on Family Agency Services* (New York: Family Service Association of America, 1973).

12. Satir, *Peoplemaking.*

13. H. J. Markman, "Prediction of Mental Distress: A 5-Year Follow-Up," *Journal of Consulting and Clinical Psychology,* 49, (1981): 760–62.

14. D. H. L. Olson, H. L. McCubbin, H. L. Barnes, et al., *Families: What Makes Them Work* (Beverly Hills, CA: Sage, 1983).

15. V. Satir, *The New Peoplemaking* (Mountain View, CA: Science and Behavior Books, 1988), 4.

16. Satir, *Peoplemaking,* 13–14.

17. J. P. Caughlin, "Family Communication Standards: What Counts as Excellent Family Communication and How Are Such Standards Associated with Family Satisfaction?" *Human Communication Research,* 29 (January 2003): 5–40.

18. K. M. Galvin and B. J. Brommel, *Family Communication: Cohesion and Change,* 5th ed. (New York: Longman, 2000).

19. J. Stachowiak, "Functional and Dysfunctional Families," in *Helping Families to Change,* eds. V. Satir, J. Stachowiak, and H. A. Taschman (New York: Jason Aronson, 1975).

20. A. Bockner and E. Eisenberg, "Family Process: Systems in Perspectives," in *Handbook of Communication Science,* eds. C. Berger and S. Chaffee (Beverly Hills: Sage, 1987).

21. Satir, *The New Peoplemaking.*

22. P. Noller and M. A. Fitzpatrick, *Communication in Family Relationships*

(Englewood Cliff, NJ: Prentice Hall, 1993), 202.

23. J. Howard, *Families* (New York: Simon & Schuster, 1978), 286–91.

24. Canadian Centre for Justice Statistics, *Family Violence in Canada: A Statistical Profile 2004.* Statistics Canada: Ottawa, Catalogue no. 85-224-XIE.

25. Canadian Centre for Justice Statistics, *Family Violence in Canada.*

26. J. Gottman with N. Silver, *Why Marriages Succeed or Fail* (New York: Simon and Schuster, 1994).

27. L. C. Tidwell and J. B. Walther, "Computer-Mediated Communication Effects on Disclosure, Impressions, and Interpersonal Evaluations, *Human Communication Research,* 28 (July 2002): 317–48.

28. J. Shuler, "E-Mail Communication and Relationships," in *The Psychology of Cyberspace,* www.rider.edu/users/suler/psycyber/psycyber.html (August 1998).

29. P. Wallace, *The Psychology of the Internet* (New York: Cambridge University Press, 1999).

30. N. L. Buerkel-Rothfuss, "Rule-Breaking in Cyberspace Relationships: Netiquette Vs. Interpersonal Competence," paper presented at the annual meeting of the National Communication Association, Chicago (November, 1999).

31. J. B. Walther, "Impression Formation in Computer-Mediated Interaction," *Western Journal of Communication,* 57 (1993): 381–98.

32. J. T. Hancock and P. J. Dunham, "Impression Formation in Computer-Mediated Communication Revisited," *Communication Research,* 28 (June 2001): 325–47.

33. D. Knox, V. Daniels, L. Sturdivant, and M. E. Zusman, "College Student Use of the Internet for Mate Selection," *College Student Journal,* 35 (March 2001): 158.

34. K. M. Cornetto, "Suspicion in Cyberspace: Deception and Detection in the Context of Internet Relay Chat Rooms," paper presented at the annual meeting of the National Communication Association, Chicago, November 1999.

35. Cornetto, "Suspicion in Cyberspace."

36. Cornetto, "Suspicion in Cyberspace."

37. Joan Leishman, "Cyber-bullying," aired October 10, 2002, updated March 2005 CBC News Online, www.cbc.ca/news/background/bullying/cyber_bullying.html.

38. M. R. Parks and K. Floyd, "Making Friends in Cyberspace," *Journal of Communication,* 46 (1996): 80–97.

39. J. Wolak, K. J. Mitchell, and D. Finkelhor, "Close Online Relationships in a National Sample of Adolescents," *Adolescence,* 37 (Fall 2002): 441–55.

40. Joan Leishman, "Cyber-bullying."

41. E. S. Rintel and J. Pittam, "Strangers in a Strange Land: Interaction Management on Internet Relay Chat," *Human Communication Research,* 23 (1997): 477–506.

42. J. B. Walther, J. F. Anderson, and D. W. Park, "Interpersonal Effects in Computer-Mediated Interaction: A Meta-Analysis of Social and Antisocial Communication," *Communication Research,* 21 (1994): 460–87.

43. Walther et al., "Interpersonal Effects."

44. L. Pratt, R. L. Wiseman, M. J. Cody, and P. F. Wendt, "Interrogative Strategies and Information Exchange in Computer-Mediated Communication," *Communication Quarterly,* 47 (1999): 46–66.

45. L. Stafford, S. L. Kline, and J. Dimmick, "Home E-Mail: Relational Maintenance and Gratification Opportunities," *Journal of Broadcasting & Electronic Media,* 43 (1999): 659–69.

46. Stafford et al., "Home E-Mail."

47. RBC Financial Group, "Canadian Families and the Internet", Ipsos Reid Survey, October 2001.

48. B. Wellman, J. Salaff, D. Dimitrova, L. Garton, M. Gulia, and C. Haythornthwaite, "Computer Networks as Social Networks: Collaborative Work, Telework, and Virtual Community," *Annual Review of Sociology,* 22 (1996): 213–38.

49. Wallace, *The Psychology of the Internet.*

50. Wallace, *The Psychology of the Internet.*

51. See reviews in C. Conrad, *Strategic Organizational Communication: Toward the Twenty-First Century,* 3rd ed. (Fort Worth, TX: Harcourt Brace, 1994); and T. D. Daniels, B. K. Spicer, and M. J. Papa, *Perspectives on Organizational Communication*, 4th ed. (Dubuque, IA: Brown and Benchmark, 1997).

52. P. M. Sias and D. J. Cahill, "From Coworkers to Friends: The Development of Peer Friendships in the Workplace," *Western Journal of Communication,* 62 (1998): 273–99.

53. Sias and Cahill, "From Coworkers to Friends."

54. Sias and Cahill, "From Coworkers to Friends."

55. E. M. Berman, J. P. West, and M. N. Richter, Jr., "Workplace Relations: Friendship Patterns and Consequences (According to Managers)," *Public Administration Review,* 62 (2002): 217–30.

56. P. Sias, G. Smith, and T. Avdeyeva, "Sex and Sex-Composition Differences and Similarities in Peer Workplace Friendship Development," *Communication Studies,* 54 (Fall 2003): 322–40.

57. American Management Association, "Workplace Dating" [AMA online news release], February, 2003. Retrieved July, 2004, from: www.amanet.org/press/amanews/workplace_dating.htm

58. J. Gabarro and J. Kotter, "Managing Your Boss," *Harvard Business Review,* 58 (1980): 92–100.

59. F. Japlin, "Superior's Upward Influence, Satisfaction, and Openness in Superior-Subordinate Communication: A Reexamination of the 'Pelz Effect,'" *Human Communication Research,* 6 (1980): 210–20.

60. Japlin, "Superior's Upward Influence."

61. D. Katz and R. Kahn, *The Social Psychology of Organizations* (New York: Wiley, 1966).

62. D. A. Level, Jr. "Communication Effectiveness: Methods and Situation," *Journal of Business Communication,* 10 (Fall 1972): 19–25.

63. Level, "Communication Effectiveness: Methods and Situation."

64. Newswire, "Female Firefighters Fight More than Fires," *The Lethbridge Herald,* 09/04/2004, p. 5.

65. R. W. Pace and D. F. Faules, *Organizational Communication* (Englewood Cliffs, NJ: Prentice Hall, 1994).

66. "Sexual Harassment Clauses," *Worklife Report,* 8(3), 4–7.

67. Human Resources Development Canada, *Information on Labour Standards,* 12, *Sexual Harassment.* Available: http://info.load-otea.hrdc-drhc.ca/publications/labour_standards/ harassment.shtml.

68. H. F. Schwind, H. Das, W. Werther, and K. Davis, *Canadian Human Resource Management,* 4th ed. (Toronto: McGraw-Hill Ryerson Canada, 1995).

69. Diane Crocker and Valery Kalemba, "The Incidence and Impact of Women's Experiences of Sexual Harassment in Canadian Workplaces," *Canadian Review of Sociology & Anthropology,* 36(49), (November 1999), 541–59.

70. M. Jimenez, "Sexual Harassment at Work Prevalent in B.C., Poll Shows," *Vancouver Sun,* May 4, 1998, A1, A2.

71. Colin Perkel, "Violence and Harassment in Ontario Workplaces Still Common, Study Shows," *The Chronicle-Journal,* October 7, 2004.

Index

Note: Entries for tables, figures, and notes are followed by "*t*," "*f*," and "*n*," respectively.